Palgrave Studies in American Economic History

**Series Editor**
Barbara Alexander
Department of Economics
Babson College
Babson Park, MA, USA

Since the social upheavals of the 1960s and 1970s and the free-market resurgence of the 1980s, American society has been enmeshed in a continuing process of profound change. Economic change has been oriented around the regulation of business, the information and telecommunication revolutions, and widening roles played by women and minority groups. Authors in the innovation area will assess how America arrived at its current position of technological dominance that is nonetheless under pressure from institutions that arguably are not well-configured for the future. Regulatory and legal historians will evaluate the reasons for concurrent regulatory breakdown and overreach in industries ranging from finance and health care to energy and land use. Finally, researchers working at the intersection of society and economic history will explore continuing struggles around issues of gender, ethnicity, and family structure, and the distribution of income, wealth, and political power. The series will address topics of interest to scholars, undergraduate and graduate students, and general readers drawn to the interplay of economics and cultural issues. Series contributors will be economics and business historians, or economists working with historians.

More information about this series at
http://www.palgrave.com/gp/series/14650

Aaron Gurwitz

# Atlantic Metropolis

## An Economic History of New York City

palgrave
macmillan

Aaron Gurwitz
New York, NY, USA

Palgrave Studies in American Economic History
ISBN 978-3-030-13351-1 ISBN 978-3-030-13352-8 (eBook)
https://doi.org/10.1007/978-3-030-13352-8



This Palgrave Macmillan imprint is published by the registered company Springer Nature Switzerland AG
The registered company address is: Gewerbestrasse 11, 6330 Cham, Switzerland

*This book is dedicated to*
*My Grandparents,*
*Harry Gurwitz*
*Ida Gurwitz,*
*Samuel Shapanka, and*
*Sarah Forman Shapanka*

*And my Parents,*
*Reuben Gurwitz and*
*Beatrice Shapanka Gurwitz,*
*who all chose New York.*

# Acknowledgements

Numerous friends, relatives, and colleagues have, over many years and mostly unknowingly, helped make *Atlantic Metropolis* possible by adding to my understanding how and why New York City came to be the place in which I love to live and in which my family has prospered. Three individuals, in particular, are entitled to a large share of any credit that accrues to this book.

First, I want to thank Barbara Alexander, the series editor of the *Palgrave Studies in American Economic History*, for recognizing the potential in my initial proposal and, especially, for her astute recommendations as to how that overly ambitious and somewhat unfocused concept could be reshaped into a realistic and more interesting project plan. Dr. Alexander's suggestions for changes to draft manuscripts improved the final product, especially by directing my attention toward the human beings who populate economic categories.

Two members of my immediate family also helped make this book better than it might have been. My wife, Dr. Susan Abramowitz, deserves a great deal of credit for tolerating my obsession with this project over the course of many years of what was supposed to be a fun and relaxing retirement. That the obsession did not become compulsive is largely due to her emotional guidance. She also applied her own scholarly skills to draft chapters, much to the benefit of this final product.

Our Daughter, Dr. Beatrice Gurwitz, a real historian, also read, commented on, and improved early drafts. She was particularly helpful in making sure readers would be able to follow clear paths through some particularly convoluted lines of analysis.

The remaining errors and infelicities are my own.

# Contents

# List of Figures

# List of Tables

# Prologue

## This Story Is Personal

All of the people who have ever lived in New York City were there because of a decision they or someone else made to locate in this place rather than somewhere else. The economic history of New York City is the story of how millions of such decisions made over a period of some 400 years collectively produced one of the twenty-first century's very few truly global cities.

Over the course of the last 120 of those years, my own family's decisions have been part of that story.

Ida Gurwitz was the only one of my grandparents I knew. She was born in Chernobyl, Ukraine, during the 1880s and, as a young woman, made her way to Kiev, where she owned and operated a successful dress-making shop. In 1906, two years after her husband, my grandfather, also a Chernobylyer, had migrated to New York to establish himself, Grandma embarked on a transatlantic liner sailing to Montreal. The details are vague, but evidently settlement in Canada was a possibility. Family legend has it, however, that Ida took umbrage at the attitude of the Canadian immigration official and decided that her destination would be New York, where some cousins were already living. When she became pregnant with my Father, she decided to return to the Ukraine by herself to give birth. As her husband was, by then, prospering in a small way as a retailer, she returned to New York two years later with my toddler father in tow. The next time she left the immediate vicinity of New York City was 68 years later when she flew to Washington, DC, to attend my wedding. My grandparents, after trying their luck and, in fact, finding some in Kiev, decided to locate in New York City because my shopkeeper grandfather and my seamstress Grandmother were both able to make what they considered a decent living there. The fact that people they knew were already in New York made the decision easier. But there was a random element. If the Canadian immigration official had been more polite or my Grandmother's temper less volatile, perhaps some other grandson of Ida's would be writing an economic history of Montreal.

My father served as an Army Air Force radio electronics instructor at a base near St. Louis, MO, during World War II. One of his buddies, who had also grown up in the retail business, haled from Des Moines, Iowa. Again, the details are vague but, there was some serious discussion of setting up a business in the Midwest. But Ida, by then a widow, was unlikely to leave New York and my mother's two brothers, each with their own New York connections, were also eager to start a retail business and wanted my more experienced father to join them. So Des Moines was off the table. The best retail opportunities in the New York region at the time were in the suburbs, so a candy-stationary store in Hempstead eventually evolved into a luncheonette in Roslyn Heights, both on Long Island. It must have been a reasonably successful business; it supported three growing families and several employees and eventually paid for a large proportion of eight college educations. How would Des Moines have worked out? We'll never know. Their web of connections kept my parents in the New York region.

Most of my life has been spent in metropolitan New York City, but between 1969 and 1982, I lived in a variety of other places: Seoul, South Korea, northern California, Michigan, and, finally, Washington, DC. At the end of that period, I was happily ensconced at the Rand Corporation doing contract research work mostly for the

U.S. government mostly about urban economies and urban education. But my part of Rand's business entered into a temporary lull, which left me the spare time to act on my observation that professionals in the financial services industry were doing much the same thing that I was—crunching numbers, writing reports, and briefing other professionals—but getting paid high multiples of what I was. There were only a few places in the world where someone with my particular skill set could easily be matched with such lucrative work: London, perhaps Tokyo, possibly Chicago, and, of course, New York City. It turned out that my path of least resistance from Rand to an investment house ran through a two-year stint as manager of the regional economics group at the Federal Reserve Bank of New York. From there my career led through a succession of four firms in the booming late twentieth-century investment banking industry. My wife was also able to land good jobs as a social scientist in New York's healthcare sector. So, like my grandparents, the opportunity to earn good real wages drew our family to this City. But, as with them, there was certainly a random element to our decision to move to New York. Suppose the flow of contracts to Rand hadn't slowed and I'd stayed too busy to look for something else. Or suppose the financial services industry hadn't been in the early stages of what turned out to be a research-fueled, multi-decade boom. Or supposed the New York Fed hadn't been looking for someone to manage their regional economics group at just the right time.

My two children's long-term location has yet to be determined. One of them and his spouse are living, working, and studying in New York. The other and her husband are starting their working lives in Washington, DC. Where they all wind up will depend on the vagaries of various national and global job markets, but the New York City metropolitan area is one of a small number of plausible outcomes.

Over the past 120 years and over four generations members of my family decided to live substantial parts of their lives in or around New York City, sometimes but not always with the principal aim of earning a higher real wage than was available elsewhere. Any of those decisions might easily have gone some other way. Or perhaps not all that easily. Starting several hundred years ago a very large number of individuals and families have faced this same decision and reached the same conclusion we did. Why? Many more, of course, have chosen to live elsewhere. Why? These are essentially the questions this book aims to answer.

## History, Economics, and Economic History

This is a history book; it aims to explain how and why the material conditions of life in the lower Hudson Valley changed over decades and centuries. As such, this work builds on two bodies of literature: New York City and Atlantic history. Rigorous scholarly study of the history of the New York City dates back to the mid-nineteenth century. Anyone, including myself, seeking to understand New York's political, social, cultural, or economic history finds no lack of ably curated primary and deep, extensive, and diverse secondary source material. The production of this literature is at present a flourishing enterprise to which I hope to make a contribution.

The aim of this work is to answer a specific question: How and why is New York different from other large cities in the United States and elsewhere in the world? One obvious difference is the fact that New York is much more populous than any other U.S. city, and understanding when and why this particular location rose to the apex of the North American hierarchical system of cities is an important part of the analytical agenda. But there are other less obvious differences to be explained. Why, for example, did New York become the principal national center for the manufacture of clothing but not of shoes? Or why did unemployment rise more slowly than in other large cities during the onset of the Great Depression and then fall much more slowly as the national economy began to recover. Or why did New York City's population decline by less in percentage terms than that of other large northeastern cities between 1950 and 1980 and then rise to a new all-time high by 2000 while the likes of Philadelphia and Chicago remained well below their previous peaks?

Because the focus is on what makes this City different from other U.S. metropolitan centers, less attention will be devoted to aspects of New York's history that, interesting as they may be, are similar in their causes and impacts to what occurred elsewhere. Accordingly, for example, sad as it is to forego tales of Boss William Marcy Tweed, I will not delve in any depth into the topic of government corruption.

More often than not the answer to the question what makes New York different is discovered by reference to the second body of historical literature on which this book is based and to which I hope to contribute, namely Atlantic history. "Atlantic history, as John Elliot elegantly puts it, involves the study of 'the creation, destruction, and re-creation of communities as a result of movement, across and around the Atlantic basin, of people, commodities, cultural practices, and values'" (Green & Morgan, 2009, p. Loc. 55/5100). Atlantic history has its critics as a methodology, but, if it makes sense anywhere, it is as a framework for understanding New York's history, especially its economic history.

This is also a work of economics. The starting point from which I try to understand what happened—why, for example, New York's seventeenth-century population was more ethnically diverse than New England's or why antebellum German immigrants were more likely to move inland immediately upon arrival in New York than were Irish immigrants—will be to try to understand the phenomenon under investigation as the result of individuals' rational decision-making in the context of the contemporary market prices and institutional arrangements. Not everything that happened in New York City can be best explained by applying an economic model. But many historical changes that are very hard to understand otherwise do become clearly explicable when subject to this kind of analysis.

This book, however, is not meant to be read only or even primarily by professional economists. Any economic model that's brought to bear will be accompanied by a brief, and I hope, clear and correct explanation of the underlying concepts.

Economic history is a specialization within the general field of economics. In recent years, it has come to be defined in the minds of traditional historians and of some of its own practitioners as the use of economic models and econometric techniques to shed light on history or the use of historical data to test economic hypotheses. To be sure, empirical testing of hypotheses is very much a part of what economic historians do. And, to be sure, whenever explanations for historical events presented in this book can be tested against or fleshed-out with quantitative information, they will be. What really defines economic history, however, is not the use of statistics but, rather, the presupposition that economic outcomes are "path dependent"; that is, that "history matters."

Paul David defines "path dependent social dynamics" as "systems of human social interaction, whose motions remain under the influence of conditions that are themselves the contingent legacies of events and actions played out within each system's history….Although economic agents' behaviors may be the deliberate resultants of rational calculation on current prevailing circumstances, the particularities of that decision context itself may well be consequences of the contingent chain of events to which … remote critical events had given rise….The drama of an historical narrative becomes more acute when the presence of just such a critical juncture, 'a forking of the road' has been identified in the flow of events….Consequently, the quintessential and most persuasive form for an 'historical' economic history narrative rightly involves those circumstances in which alternative local states of the world are plausible as well as merely conceivable" (David, 2007, p. 3).

Consideration of my family's successive decisions to move to or stay in New York City may help make this abstraction more concrete. Each of us opted for New York because it was the best of the alternatives we considered at the time. But one of the chains of events that made New York the best place for my family and so many others to live and work in 1906, 1945, and 1982 began, by my reckoning, between 1815 and 1820 when a die was cast that destined New York to become North America's predominant port of entry for people and goods. Was New York's eventual position at the apex of the North American system of cities "contingent"? Are alternative states of the world "plausible as well as merely conceivable"? That New York is, by far, the largest city in the United States is not the only historical fact that will be subject to this kind of path-dependence inquiry. Could there, for example, have been a plausible chain of events that led to the New York region, rather than the North Shore of Boston, becoming the main U.S. center for shoe manufacturing? Is it plausible that Silicon Valley could have emerged on the banks of the Raritan River in Middlesex County, New Jersey, rather than along San Francisquito Creek in Santa Clara County, California? One of the things that makes this book a work of historical economics is the search for these "forks in the road" that *happened* to make New York what it was and what it is.

In this context, it is surprising the relatively few economic historians have looked closely at the processes of urbanization. There are exceptions, of course, most notably William Cronon; his economic history of Chicago and its vast hinterland, *Nature's Metropolis: Chicago and the Great West* (Cronon, 1994), has served as a model for my work as reflected in this book's title. But there should be much more than there is because so much about cities—their geographic locations, their internal spatial structure, the shape of their skylines, the adequacy of their sewer systems, the events commemorated by their monuments, and so on, is fraught with path dependencies. It is, for example, plausible and not just conceivable that New York could have become the nation's largest City but *not* the location of its dominant capital markets? Despite this and despite the fact that the percentage of the U.S. population living in places with populations greater than 100,000 rose from 0% in 1790 to 50% in 1920, *The Cambridge Economic History of the United States* volume on the long nineteenth century does not include a chapter on urbanization (U.S. Census Bureau, 1976, pp. 11, 12). Nor does Albert Fishlow's chapter on transportation in that volume include urbanization as one of the consequences of the build-out of the canal, riverboat, and railroad networks (Fishlow, 2000). As a work of economic history, therefore, this volume aims to help augment the intellectual synapses that link economic history and urban studies.

## Chronology

This book is divided into four parts, which correspond to successive chronological epochs. Each of these parts begins with an introductory chapter that sketches the broad, fundamental changes in the material conditions of life in the lower Hudson Valley that took place during the period. Each introduction is followed by individual chapters most of which focus on ways in which developments in the Atlantic world economy influenced what happened in New York during the period. The first part begins about one-thousand years ago and ends in 1815. It incorporates consideration of the "pre-contact" societies on the east and west shores of the Atlantic Ocean, the Dutch and British colonial periods, and the early years of the American republic. The second period, the "displaced nineteenth century," extends from the end of the War of 1812 to the passage of the Immigration Act of 1924. The third section, the "Short Twentieth Century," begins in 1924 and ends with the aftermath of the City's mid-1970s financial crisis. The final epoch, the "Post Crisis Recovery," begins in 1979 and is cut off, arbitrarily, around 2008.

The reasons for these demarcations should become apparent as the narrative progresses but a few words on the subject are appropriate in the Introduction. Most, if not all, of the economic changes that took place in New Amsterdam and New York during its first two centuries were driven directly or indirectly by a nearly constant state of armed conflict around the North Atlantic region: three Anglo-Dutch wars during the seventeenth century, four French and Indian Wars, to give them the collective name used in U.S. history, the American Revolution (1775–1782), the Napoleonic wars from 1799 to 1815, and the continuous capture, forced migration, and enslavement of millions of Africans. The ups and downs of the economic activities for which the lower Hudson Valley were particularly suited during this whole period were driven, in large part, by the exigencies and vicissitudes of these conflicts.

The period from 1815 until 1914 was the era of *Pax Britaninca*. These hundred years of peace—albeit only on the surface, especially toward the end of the period, and, albeit, punctuated dramatically from a U.S. perspective by the Civil War—allowed the first phase of economic globalization to emerge and flourish. As the premier port of the country that prospered the most under this geopolitical regime, much of what happened in New York was a manifestation of movement of goods, money, and people across and around the Atlantic Ocean.

Although the era of *Pax Britaninca* did end abruptly in August 1914, the pre-war environment of international economic, financial, and demographic integration died a lingering death. The conflict set off by the assassination of the Austrian Grand Duke was, after all, a *world* war.

And while the financing of the British and French war efforts did accelerate a reversal of what had been westward trans-Atlantic capital flows, the money continued to move around in huge volumes both during and after the fighting.

The one trans-Atlantic movement did that come to a nearly complete halt in the immediate aftermath of World War I, the flow of immigrants from Europe to the United States, had exerted a particularly powerful influence over the political, the cultural, and, most definitely, the economic character of New York City. The appropriate end point for this epoch of the City's history is, therefore, 1924, when Congress passed the Johnson-Reed Act, the culmination of a series of new laws that limited total immigration to about one-tenth of what it had been at its peak early in the twentieth century.

Over the 55 years after 1924, the blockage of what had been the previous principal source of new New Yorkers and the eventual collapse of transatlantic trade and capital flows along with a combination of purely domestic economic and social trends led to a relative and then an absolute contraction of New York's economy. At an accelerating pace, a syndrome of urban pathologies became increasingly acute and culminated in what some thought was a mortal crisis by the mid-1970s. Other large U.S. cities suffered similar maladies, but New York's "urban problems" were exacerbated international influences in ways that other cities' were not.

After 1979 the situation began, at first imperceptibly but gradually more obviously, to improve. Trends in several indicators of economic conditions began either to deteriorate much more slowly or to show absolute improvement. By 2012 total private sector employment in New York City reached an all-time high exceeding the previous record set in 1969. This final period, the post-crisis recovery, appears at this writing still to be underway.

The organization of the four main parts of this book follows this sequence of epochs. Individual chapters within each part are not necessarily ordered chronologically but will focus on specific aspects of how New York's position within the North Atlantic economy affected this City's attractiveness as a place to live and work for people like my family and me.

## References

Cronon, W. (1994). *Nature's Metropolis: Chicago and the Great West*. New York: W. W. Norton.

David, P. A. (2007). Path Dependence—A Foundational Concept for Historical Social Science. *Cliometrica—The Journal of Historical Economics and Econometric History, 1*(2), 3.

Fishlow, A. (2000). Internal Transportation in the Nineteenth and Early Twentieth Centuries. In S. Engerman & R. E. Gallman (Eds.), *The Cambridge Economic History of the United States, Volume II, The Long Nineteenth Century* (pp. 543–642). Cambridge: Cambridge University Press.

Green, J. P., & Morgan, P. D. (2009). *Atlantic History: A Critical Appraisal*. Oxford: Oxford University Press.

U.S. Census Bureau. (1976). *The Statistical History of the United States from Colonial Times to the Present*. New York: Basic Books.

# Part I

## Introduction 1600–1815: From Pre-Contact to the Treaty of Vienna

The first two-hundred years of New York's economic history can be usefully understood as a tale of two commodities: beaver pelts and sugar.

Immediately upon the first contact between the indigenous peoples of the Hudson Valley and Europeans in 1609, the two groups began exchanging commodities. The newcomers to the area probably already knew that the natives could provide effectively unlimited quantities of beaver pelts, which were highly valued on the far side of the Atlantic Ocean. And Europeans could offer in exchange goods made of metal and glass that enhanced the locals' quality of life substantially. Both peoples were already quite familiar with trade as a potentially mutually beneficial form of social interaction. Of course, not all of the interactions between first peoples and the newcomers benefited both groups. There were occasional bloody conflicts, which the Europeans, with their superior military technology usually won. More devastating to the Native Americans were the imported communicable diseases, which came close to wiping out native populations.

The profitability of buying beaver pelts in North American and selling them in Amsterdam provided the economic incentive, which, along with geopolitical considerations, motivated the Dutch in 1624 to establish New Netherlands as a permanent settlement centered in the Hudson Valley with its capital, New Amsterdam, on Manhattan Island. So much so that to this day a beaver appears on the corporate seal of the City of New York. Native Americans accommodated the newcomers' presence because of the benefits they realized on the same transactions.

Chapter 1, therefore, centers on the North American market for beaver pelts: the identities and situations of the sellers and buyers, the sources of demand and supply, the venues for and structures of transactions, the ancillary activities that developed to sustain the trade, its profitability, and that it was the New Netherlands' principal economic *raison d'etre*.

The Dutch were, however, motivated to establish a permanent presence in the Middle Atlantic region of North America at least as much, and probably more so, by geopolitical considerations as by business interests. And it was geopolitical priorities that motivated the Netherlands to cede the territory to an English Proprietor, James, Duke of York, in 1664.

During the 150 years after the British gained suzerainty over New York City, the Atlantic world was the theater of nearly continuous warfare, mostly between the English and the French leading varying groups of allies. Military conflict, however, did not prevent the massive increase in cane sugar production in the Caribbean basin. Expansion of sugar cultivation, refining, and trading increased demand for plantation laborers, food to feed them, specialized capital goods, ships, and commercial services. Because the indigenous populations had been decimated by disease and harsh treatment, production of all of these and of other colonial exports such as tobacco necessitated the "peopling" of the Americas. Most of those who arrived in the Caribbean and the South Atlantic coast were forced from their homes in Africa by slave traders. A large majority of migrants to the British Middle Atlantic and New England colonies were induced to move voluntarily by ideological or economic incentives.

Chapter 2 begins with an explanation of how the Caribbean sugar industry developed and of its importance to the Atlantic economy as a whole. This is followed by a discussion of the ways in which this industry's growth, the concurrent imperial warfare, and local public policies influenced the patterns of population growth in the British North

American colonies. The initial perspective encompasses the development of the Middle Atlantic and New England regions and their principal port cities, Philadelphia, Boston, and New York. Then the focus narrows onto New York and an analysis of why this City grew relatively slowly before about 1763 and why immigration accelerated thereafter. The chapter concludes with a review of the economic and political influences that positioned New York City as the central metropolis of a region extending from the headwaters of the Mohawk and Hudson Rivers to Montauk Point on Long Island and from New Haven, Connecticut, to the Raritan River valley in New Jersey.

In 1800, New York was one of three roughly equal-sized port cities serving as central places in the region comprised by the nine northern U.S. states. One important economic function of each of these cities was the provision of mercantile services—transportation of goods and people, trade-goods dealing and brokerage, wholesale and retail sales, commercial jurisprudence, business journalism, etc. Chapter 3, therefore, deals in some detail with the ways in which commerce was conducted in the Atlantic world from the late seventeenth to early nineteenth century. One aim of this analysis is to identify ways in which New York as a commercial center differed from the other two important ports so as to set the stage for understanding how and why this City became *the* North American metropolis during the next phase of its history. Chapter 3 begins with an analysis of how eighteenth-century merchants used social networks to help mitigate some of the risks of doing business across a turbulent ocean in an age of sail and in a world lacking institutions of credit intermediation. This section explores the hypothesis that, as the nexus of more ocean-spanning national, ethnic and religious social networks than either Boston or Philadelphia, New York had a comparative advantage as an entrepot that would stand it in good stead in the future. The final section of Chapter 3 and of Part I deals with local and imperial public policy as it affected commerce with the goal of identifying ways, if any, in which governments influenced the development of the three ports.

# 1

# Beverstad

In and around the Hudson River Valley during the second quarter of the seventeenth century, early modern European and late woodlands Native American peoples met and interacted with each other. Although communicable diseases carried by the Europeans would eventually lead to the decimation of Native American populations and although some interactions were brutally violent, for the most part the early engagement was mutually beneficial.

At the time and to us in retrospect, the differences between these cultures were more apparent than their similarities, and historians have generally emphasized their mutual strangeness. One, in particular, of these differences commands the attention of an economist. Northwestern Europe was one of the most densely occupied and intensively exploited land areas on the planet. By contrast, among similarly fertile and climatically benign regions, northeastern North America was surely one of, if not *the,* least densely occupied and least intensively exploited. And the contrast became starker during the seventeenth century as Native American populations collapsed.

The differences were very important, but the two cultures were similar enough to make it possible for them to engage in mutually beneficial



A. Gurwitz, *Atlantic Metropolis*, Palgrave Studies in American Economic History,
https://doi.org/10.1007/978-3-030-13352-8_1

exchanges beginning immediately after contact. For one thing, both Western Europe and northeastern North America were themselves home to arrays of diverse, independent societies, speaking different languages, dealing with different environmental and economic challenges, worshiping different gods in different ways, exerting and acquiescing to different forms of political authority, sometimes living peacefully and doing business side by side, and sometimes fighting wars. In this regard, both cultures differed from the geographically extensive and politically unified societies of, for example, China or Peru. So, at first contact, both sides had some experience in dealing with the "other" and, at least potentially, benefitting from such interactions. Second, by the year 1600 societies on both sides of the North Atlantic had developed stable, productive systems of agriculture capable of producing more than minimal subsistence requirements in the average crop year. Finally, both societies had at least some familiarity with the practice of trade: in consumer staples with near neighbors and in exotic, luxury, or prestige goods across longer distances.

Although people of European descent would eventually come to dominate life in the region, the changes that took place during the first post-contact decades reflected European and Native American influences in roughly equal degrees. In this regard, the immediate post-contact period in the Hudson Valley appears to have differed from contemporary experiences in the Chesapeake tidelands or on the shores of Massachusetts Bay, where the emerging American societies reflected much less indigenous influence.

## Two Late Woodlands Cultures

### Commonalities

Archaeologists characterize the pre-contact Native American way of life in the area that became New York as "late woodlands culture."

The indigenous peoples made their living by hunting, fishing, gathering, and cultivating crops. Animal husbandry was not practiced. They lived in structures framed by tree branches and covered with bark.

Settlement populations ranged from single-family units to several thousand individuals living in multifamily dwellings. A dense, extensive network of trails and streams and ingeniously designed canoes facilitated transportation and communication (Bailyn, 2012).

Men specialized in hunting, sometimes migrating seasonally from settlements to distant hunting grounds. Women tended highly productive, mixed gardens of the "three sisters" crops of corn (maize), beans, and squash or pumpkins. Cultivating these three crops on the same plot of ground was efficient, the beans helped maintain soil fertility by fixing nitrogen, the corn stalks provided a framework on which the bean vines could climb, and the broad-leaved squash plants inhibited weed growth. The combination of crops also provided a balanced mix of carbohydrates, protein, and vitamins (Hart, 2008).

After a few years or, at most, a few decades, as soil became depleted, as garbage accumulated, and as pests multiplied, settlements were abandoned and reestablished at some distance away through a slash-and-burn process (Richter, 1992; Starna, 2009). As a consequence of this quasi-sedentary and quasi-nomadic way of life, late Woodland Native Americans' understanding of the relationship between specific social units—individuals, families, kinship groups, or settlements—and specific plots of land seemed vague and ambiguous to Europeans. But, while ownership demarcations were not explicit, communities seeking new settlement sites probably had a clear idea of where they could settle without being challenged and where they could not (Starna, 2009, p. 78).

As expected, given the low population density and the fecundity of the environment, the pre-contact Native American subsistence system was highly land-intensive. While three sisters horticulture was demanding of human labor during each growing season, frequent resettlement meant that over time each social group needed a great deal of land to make a living. And hunting is a relatively land-intensive source of animal protein.

Pre-contact Native Americans engaged in short- and long-distance trade. As with most of what we know of pre-contact Native American life, the source of the information we have about late Woodland's trade comes from archaeological excavations. Consequently, we know much more about durable items that were traded than about food or clothing. There is apparently no convincing evidence of pre-contact trade in perishable goods among the Native American peoples in the area that became New Netherland, although we do know that similarly situated groups elsewhere in northeastern North America did engage in such exchanges, and swaps of European goods for Indian-grown food became routine almost immediately after contact (Romney, 2014). By contrast, there is a great deal of evidence that Native Americans exchanged durable goods over long distances. Archaeologists have found copper, probably sourced from around Lake Superior, in waste middens and graves near the East Coast, and excavations of pre-contact settlements in the Midwest frequently turn up seashells and seashell products. The spatial distribution of these and other trade goods in excavations points to two patterns of long-distance trading activity: broad-based trade and focused trade. Appearance of a trade good in a wide range of sites with the frequency of items' appearance diminishing with distance from the source is consistent with the "broad-based" or "down-the-line" pattern in which a single item might have changed hands several times before reaching the site where archaeologists find it. Appearance of a specific trade good at a single location or a small number of locations distant from its point of origin reflects focused trade. As such items frequently appear in "special" situations such as high-status grave sites, it appears that Native American traders traveled long distances to obtain or deliver highly valued items (Stewart, 1989).

At least some transactions were evidently not executed on an explicit "*quid pro quo*" basis. In addition to providing what economists refer to as "gains from trade," exchange may also have been perceived as a way of maintaining social connections between neighboring groups. In any case, actual exchanges were frequently expected to be preceded by mutual "gift" giving and feasting. Such activities have modern equivalents as when salesmen entertain clients at high-priced restaurants. In any case, Europeans were quick to accommodate these indigenous customs. These practices do, however, make it difficult to determine the "all-in" prices—including the value of "gifts" and entertainment expense—of say, a canoe-load of Beaver pelts or the island of Manhattan (Rich, 1960).

## Distinctions

The Native American societies in the area that became New Netherland spoke many different languages, each of which belonged to one of two linguistic lineages: the Iroquoian and the Algonquian.

During the late Woodlands period, groups of Iroquoian speakers ranged from the Mohawk River Valley northward to Labrador, southward to the Appalachian foothills of what is now North Carolina, and westward to Lake Huron.[1] Settlements of the five (later six) Iroquoian groups that were members of the Haudenosaunee or Iroquois Confederation ranged from the Mohawk River Valley and across the Finger Lakes region and southern tier of what is now New York State. The Five Nations' homeland was particularly well situated geographically with respect to the main pre- and post-contact trade routes; it incorporated watersheds and canoe-navigable streams leading to the Hudson Valley to the east, the Susquehanna River Valley leading and the Chesapeake Bay to the south, the Allegheny River tributaries leading to the Ohio Valley to the west, and the Great Lakes to the north.

Iroquoian speakers had introduced three sisters horticulture to this region sometime between 800 and 1200 C.E. (Crawford, 1996; Snow, 1995), and these crops provided a large part of their diet, supplemented by venison and other animal protein obtained by men in winter hunting expeditions. They lived in multifamily dwellings—Haudenosaunee means "People of the Long House"—clustered in towns with populations as large as 2,000. As with other late Woodlands settlements, the residents of these towns relocated their dwellings and their surrounding gardens periodically.

The Iroquois Confederation was organized to maintain the peace among its five constituent communities. Leaders would meet periodically near modern Syracuse, New York, to renew ties by exchanging gifts, discussing issues, and feasting. Member groups were not, however, compelled to follow common policies with respect to relations with outsiders.

---

[1]Unless otherwise indicated the source of the material in this discussion of Iroquoian culture is (Richter, 1992).

Among many of their neighbors, the confederation members had a fiercely war-like reputation. Conflicts arose between the Five Nations and other Iroquoian speakers, the Hurons to the north and the Susquehannocks to the south. The objective of many of these wars was to take captives, some of whom would be tortured and killed but many of whom would be adopted into families, designated as replacements for dead relatives, and integrated into the community. Thus, Iroquois's pre-contact geopolitical strategy, like their agricultural practices, may have been a consequence of the scarcity of labor relative to land.

Although they shared the late Woodlands way of life, the cultures of the Algonquian-speaking peoples who lived along the Hudson Valley and on Long Island were different from the Iroquois's in several respects. Likely as a consequence of the greater emphasis on hunting, fishing, and foraging relative to agriculture, Algonquian speakers' settlements were smaller and shorter-lived than Iroquois towns (Gehring, 1992). Although there was no Hudson Valley or Long Island equivalent of the formal Iroquois Confederation, Algonquian speakers were likely able to rely on kinship ties to maintain cohesion among neighboring communities (Romney, 2014). Finally, and of considerable importance to early European settlers, the region's Algonquian peoples did have a tradition of short-distance trade in staples.

The Algonquian-speaking Mahicans were the dominant community in the area around the current city of Albany, New York. They did cultivate crops, but apparently sourced a larger proportion of their diet from hunting, gathering, and fishing than did the Iroquois. The peoples of the lower Hudson and upper Delaware Valleys and Long Island have come in the historical literature to be referred to as Munsees, a reference to the family of Algonquian languages they spoke. In the southernmost part of the region around Long Island, sound archaeological evidence suggests modest pre-contact farming and much greater reliance on shellfish gathering (Ceci, Locational Analysis of Historic Algonquin Sites in Coastal New York: A Preliminary Study, 1980b) for food or trade.

## Early Modern Europe

The "early modern" period of European history spans the years between 1500 and 1800. As the aim of this chapter is to explain the development of New Amsterdam which ceased to exist as a political jurisdiction after 1664, our focus now will be on the first 150 years of the era. Developments at both the bottom and the top of Europe's stratified early modern society affected what happened in the Hudson Valley during the early post-contact period in important ways. In broad terms, this period was *not* a good time for most Europeans who made their living by supplying labor, although Dutch workers may have been an exception to this generalization. In contrast, people at the top end of the wealth distribution—the Dutch at least as much as everyone else—were able to benefit disproportionately from a complex of social, technological, and intellectual changes that began or accelerated during this period. The lives of all Europeans were, however, disrupted and, all too frequently, ended by a more or less continuous state of warfare on their continent and across the wider Atlantic world. In this respect, too, the Dutch were no exception.

### Labor and Land

In 1798, Thomas Malthus, in *An Essay on the Principle of Population*, posited a tendency for human populations to increase when living standards were higher than subsistence levels. When typical families were living below subsistence, population would tend to decline as mortality increased and fertility decreased. In a period of stable agricultural and transportation technology, a region's capacity for per capita food production is limited by the amount of land available for cultivation. So, once all arable land is cultivated, the marginal product of labor is very small and real wages decline toward the subsistence level. Malthus believed, in other words, that the natural or equilibrium state of human society was for a large proportion of the population to live at the margin between subsistence and starvation. It was predictions like these that earned economics its designation as the dismal science. Fortunately,

Malthus's hypothesis has not been confirmed by subsequent events. During the early seventeenth century, however, much of Europe's population was very much living in a Malthusian world.

Scarcity of arable land had not been a problem in the immediate wake of the Black Death of 1348–1350, which, by the best estimates, reduced Europe's population by between 20 and 30%, or for the 100 years thereafter, when the plague, now endemic, kept population growth close to zero (Rich & Wilson, 2008). In the year 1300, Europe's population may have been about 94 million people, many of whom were living on the margin of subsistence. It did not reach that level again until sometime in the mid-1500s. Economic historians have pieced together evidence that is generally consistent with the Malthusian prediction that real wages were high in the post-plague years, when populations were below the levels the European continent could sustain at subsistence wages. Further, a range of evidence supports the conclusion that food prices rose relative to wages over the hundred years after the mid-sixteenth century, likely reflecting a combination of near fully exploited arable land, stable farming technology (Malanima, 2009), the worst of what may have been a "Little Ice Age" that lasted from about 1550 to 1850, and sixteenth-century population growth. Thus, real wages probably decreased during the first 150 years of the early modern period. Robert C. Allen estimates, for example, that real wages declined by an average of 16% across 14 European cities between 1500 and 1600 and by another 8% over the subsequent fifty years (Allen, 2001).

As the price of food rose and as land became the scarce factor of production, the incomes of landowners increased relative to what workers were earning. And, to the extent that owners of wealth could shift capital between agriculture and manufacturing or trade, leading to an equalization of returns across all activities, the equilibrium real return on capital in general would also have a tendency to rise relative to wages. In other words, under reasonable assumptions, a rising population in the context of more or less fixed agricultural technology and land area would likely lead to an increase in the share of total national income accruing to owners of wealth. That, indeed, appears to have happened (O'Rourke & Williamson, 2002; Van Zanden, 1995).

## Transformations

Although they played out slowly over the course of decades, many of the changes taking place in Europe between the late fifteenth and early seventeenth century deserve to be called revolutionary, at least relative to the pace of economic change during the medieval period.

At the beginning of the period, European seafaring technology had not advanced much from what it had been when the Roman Empire fell, and the maritime movement of goods was largely confined to the Mediterranean Sea. By the year 1700, after 250 years of innovations in shipbuilding technology, numerous geographic "discoveries," the accumulation of oceanographic knowledge, and a lot of learning by doing transoceanic shipping had become routine as had trade across Northern European waters.

Maritime advances, cultural changes such as the Protestant reformation, and the rise to political power of commercial interests in Northwestern Europe combined to shift Europe's economic center of gravity away from the Mediterranean toward the North Sea, the Atlantic Ocean, and the Baltic (Acemoglu, 2005; Rapp, 1975).

These transformations were not painless. At least two major European states were at war with each other in most years from the beginning of the revolt of the Protestant Netherlands against its Roman Catholic rulers in 1566 until 1815, when the Napoleonic Wars ended and ushering in a century of Pax Britannica.

Despite this ongoing geopolitical turmoil and despite the fact that enemies' merchant shipping was very much military fair game, world trade grew more rapidly than other measures of economic activity. Over the course of the sixteenth and seventeenth centuries, the population of Western Europe increased by about 40%; over roughly the same period the carrying capacity of the world's, mostly Western European, merchant fleet more than quadrupled (Maddison, 2001). As one would expect, given the concurrent trends in the income distribution, the expansion of early modern trade volumes was fastest for what were "high end" consumer goods: spices, fine fabrics, tobacco, sugar, and, importantly for the New Netherland story, furs and fur products.[2]

## Dutch Exceptionalism[3]

### Under and Over the Water

Every country is exceptional in its patriots' eyes, but, objectively, some are more so than others. The Netherlands has, objectively, always been an unusual place, starting from the fact that the country's very name describes its most salient geological characteristic. Most of the country's land area comprises the deltas of three European river systems, the Meuse, the Rhine, and the Scheldt. As such, its highest elevation is only a bit more than 1,000 feet and, at present, one-third of the country lies below sea level at high tide. Thus, the Netherlands is a "high maintenance" region for agriculture. The well-drained "highland" soil is not fertile, and the rich potential of the lowlands can only be realized after costly drainage and desalinization.

In the early Modern European context, however, Dutch geography also offered some distinct advantages. First, the impact of the little ice age may have been less malign in the Netherlands than elsewhere in Europe and, indeed, the climatic changes may have had a net positive effect on the country's economy. For one thing, flooding became less frequent when the little ice age lowered sea levels. Also, the important Dutch fishing industry's annual catch was enhanced when herring populations shifted southward from Scandinavian waters. So, the Netherlands' farm and fisheries productivity may have been relatively high when the rest of Europe

---

[2]O'Rourke & Williamson (1999) highlight the concentration of early modern intercontinental trading growth in spices, tobacco, and sugar and the relationship between seventeenth-century trade expansion and the growth of "surplus income." Unfortunately, they do not discuss the market for furs and fur products, which provides a counterexample to some of the points they made.

[3]Except When Otherwise Noted, the Material in This Section Summarizes Material in (de Vries & van der Woude, 1997).

was experiencing a period of dearth. Second, the country's low-lying bogs provided an easily accessible source of peat, an important fossil fuel during the early modern period. Third, the local effort required to drain lowlands, maintain dykes, and allocate reclaimed land, fostered a culture of locally directed, decentralized collective action. Finally, and most importantly for purposes of understanding New Amsterdam, the network of rivers, channels, and canals positioned Dutch towns as the most convenient transshipment points for goods moving between the North and Baltic Sea regions, on the one hand, and two of Northern Europe's most active late-medieval concentrations of economic activity—Flanders, especially, Antwerp, and the Rhine Valley—on the other. Because agriculture was so hard, because the needed fuel for manufacturing activities was relatively cheap, and because the Netherlands enjoyed a comparative advantage as a provider of transportation and fisheries services, the early modern Dutch economy was considerably more urban than the rest of Europe's. But because the inland water transportation network was so dense and because localities knew how to organize themselves, Dutch urbanization was characterized by many small and mid-sized cities and towns rather than only a few big civil and clerical administrative centers.

These unique attributes combined to place the Netherlands in the vanguard of several of the transformations that expanded investment and consumption opportunities for European elites during the late sixteenth and early seventeenth centuries. Limited opportunities in agriculture had two consequences. First, employers in other businesses—fisheries, merchant marine, shipbuilding, and other manufacturing—benefited from an elastic labor supply. In particular, because the seasonalities of the herring fishery and the Baltic grain trade were complementary and because the human and physical capital needed in the two activities were somewhat similar, the maritime workforce could be employed particularly efficiently. Second, because the return on investments in land was limited, wealthy Dutch men and women learned to deploy liquid assets in a diversified way. Jan de Vries and Ad van der Woude offer an interesting example illustrating the multifaceted, opportunistic business practices of early modern Dutch merchant networks, a theme that will be important in New York's economic history until well into the nineteenth century.

> …[T]he Delft merchant Claes Adriaensz van Adrichem…took over his father's grain trade – principally concerned with grain produced in the [Delft] region – in the 1560s. He invested surplus fund in real property, short-term government bonds (*losrenten*), life annuities (*liffrenten*), and short-term loans to farmers (*schulden van coren*). He also began investing in the fishery of Delfshaven, buying shares in herring busses. This became his entry route to the Baltic trade, for the new herring busses were capable of adaptation for use as merchant vessels in the off-season. By 1569 we know he was shipping salt and herring to Danzig and returning with grain. To be more accurate, Claes Adriaensz invested in partnerships that financed ships for these purposes. For instance, in 1579 he owned shares in six separate ships, all of which sailed to the Baltic. In 1583…[h]e owned 1/8th of four ships, 1/10th of one, and ½ of yet another. The other owners of shares were the shipmasters, relatives, and a circle of non-relatives whose names appear with regularity in the partnerships…This risk-reducing strategy substituted for maritime insurance, which long remained unusual in this trade. (de Vries & van der Woude, 1997, pp. 361–362)

Supported by local demand from merchants and the availability of labor and capital, the Dutch shipbuilding industry became the largest in Europe and a source of export earnings by the mid-seventeenth century. The Netherlands' contribution to maritime technology, the *fluitschip* (flyship), was designed solely for the purpose of facilitating long-distance bulk trade, and, as noted, the herring fleet could be put to multiple purposes.

In this context, it is not surprising that by the early seventeenth century the Dutch republic had become Europe's principle shipbuilding and trading nation and Amsterdam, the continent's principal entrepôt.

## The Business of Geopolitics

Intercontinental trading, in particular, also served Dutch geopolitical purposes. Disrupting Iberian commerce by expanding the Netherlands global trading activities and by encouraging lucrative privateering became a potent weapon in the protestant, pro-business United

Provinces' war for independence from the Roman Catholic, statist Hapsburg rulers of Spain. To pursue these objectives, the Dutch government turned to a policy instrument that was considered best practice among Northwestern European governments at the time: for-profit, public-benefit, limited liability companies.

The structure was first adopted by the Dutch with the aim of disrupting Portugal's trade with Asia. By the end of the sixteenth century, the magnitude of the monopoly profits the Portuguese and their European distributors were earning on the East India spice trade was apparent to Dutch merchants seeking further diversification. Initial efforts to penetrate the market met with mixed results but with enough success to motivate private partnerships to outfit trading expeditions. By 1602, however, policymakers in The Hague concluded that an East Indies trading monopoly might be able to earn shareholders a competitive return *and* subsidize the pursuit of Dutch political interests in the region. Thus, the charter granted by the States General to the United East India Company (*Verenigde Oostindische Compagnie* or "VOC") authorized engagement in commercial, political, and military activities.

It took almost 20 years for the VOC to identify a business model that could deliver both profitability and strategic impact and almost another ten years to put the system in place. Two decades of trial and error included repeated efforts, none of them successful, to find a shorter, faster, and, therefore, cheaper northeast or Northwest Passage to Asian markets. On one such attempt in 1609, Henry Hudson, an Englishman in the employ of the VOC, sailed up the river that bears his name as far north as it was navigable before abandoning his hope that the route would lead to the Pacific Ocean.

What eventually worked for the VOC was a combination of monopolies on important channels of intra-Asian carrying trade and the export of spices and textiles to Europe. Profits earned, for example, on the exchange of Chinese porcelains for Japanese silver could more than meet the VOC's operating costs in Asia and offset some of the expenses of equipping the annual trading fleet from Europe. Establishing the Asian monopolies required a combination of focused local strategic leadership in Batavia (Jakarta), aggressive competition in some markets, military conquest in other places, and astute diplomacy. Luck also played a role, as when the Dutch were in the right place at the right time when Japan's government decided to expel all foreigners except the VOC factors at a Nagasaki trading post.

During the 1620s, therefore, the VOC was beginning to demonstrate that outsourcing some sovereign powers to a for-profit company could be good public policy. So, when the 12-year truce between the United Provinces and the Hapsburgs ended in 1621 and the war of independence resumed, establishing a West India Company (*Verenigde West Indische Coimpagnie*, or "WIC") must have seemed like the obvious thing to do. From a legal perspective, the Dutch colony of New Netherland was an instrumentality of the WIC.

## Expensive Labor

The WIC, however, was never able to reproduce the financial success of the VOC, due in some part to the unique condition of the Dutch labor market. The VOC had been able to operate without a large resident European labor force in densely populated Asia. That was not the case in the Americas. Recruiting such a labor force might not necessarily have been a problem. Recall that the Early Modern period was, in most of Western Europe for most working people, a time of declining real wages and, likely, stagnant or deteriorating standards of living. In parts of Europe where population had returned to pre-plague "capacity" levels, where farming was the only game in town, and where agricultural technology was stagnant, it was very much an employers' market for unskilled labor.

This was not the case, however, in the prosperous parts of the United Provinces over the last quarter of the sixteenth and first half of the seventeenth centuries. Booming textile and ship manufacturing, multi-seasonal seafaring, dealing in the burgeoning luxury goods markets, high value-added farming, and rural and urban infrastructure development combined to boost the demand for workers of all skill levels faster than the labor force was expanding. De Vries and van der Woude summarize the combined impact as follows:

> [N]atural increase, immigration, urbanization, and the increase in the length of the work year combined to generate a phenomenal 3 percent per annum growth of Holland's effective nonagricultural labor supply over the half century 1570–1620. In a period when much less rapid rates of population growth sent real wages plummeting all over Europe, the demand for labor in Holland grew even faster, causing nominal wages repeatedly to be increased, so that they outstripped price increases to secure real wages for unskilled laborers 62 percent higher in 1615-19 than in 1575-9... (de Vries & van der Woude, 1997, pp. 671–672)

Real wage growth in Amsterdam and in nearby Antwerp brought the local standard of living substantially above levels in the rest of Europe. Economic historian Robert C. Allen has assembled comparable data on welfare ratios for skilled and unskilled construction workers in 15 European cities from the late middle ages until World War I. The welfare ratio is defined as the ratio of the workers' average annual income divided by the cost of maintaining a poverty-level standard of living. For building craftsmen, the skilled workers during the 1600–1649 period, the ratios were 1.93 and 2.27 in Amsterdam and Antwerp, respectively. These were the two highest ratios in the sample for the period; both were more than one standard deviation above the 15-city average. For unskilled construction laborers, the Amsterdam and Antwerp ratios were 1.34 and 1.36, respectively, for the same period. These were, again, the two highest in the sample and nearly two standard deviations above the average (Allen, 2001).

Among European workers, therefore, Dutch men and women would likely have been the least motivated to abandon their home country to populate a start-up colonial venture in a distant wilderness.

## New Netherland

From beginning to end, the Dutch colony in North America had a specific, explicit economic *raison d'être*: the fur trade. In this regard, it differed from the two early English settlements on the continent. The Chesapeake colonies were initially speculative; there *had* to be some way to make money in North America. Only after almost two decades of considerable hardship and poverty did the settlers in Virginia and Maryland determine that tobacco could be their cash crop. It also took almost 20 years before New England's combination of farming, fisheries, and trade was able to come close to balancing payments in and out of the colonies without relying on the capital accompanying ideologically motivated migrants (Bailyn, 2012).

To be sure, New Netherland's sponsors had multiple motives for establishing a presence in the midst of Virginia, New England, and New France. For one thing, the "middle Atlantic" coast of North America lies along the maritime path of least resistance from the Caribbean to Europe. Having a base of operations in this region, therefore, was a strategic imperative for would-be marauders of shipping routes from the Spanish Main (Van der Donck, 1993). Further, in both legal and practical terms, secure possession of colonial territory required some permanent settlement. Nor were those who thought about the matter satisfied with sole reliance on a single export; over the course of its existence, policymakers and investors in both old and New Amsterdam sought ways to diversify the colony's economic base (Bachman, 1969). It is, however, impossible to understand why anyone chose to migrate to this region during the middle of the seventeenth century or what happened once they got there without reference to the international market for furs, in general, and for beaver pelts, in particular.

## The Beaver Pelt Market

### Demand

Furs and fur products were among the luxury goods in increasing demand by the beneficiaries of rising returns on capital. Specifically, a high-quality, extremely broad-brimmed and high-crowned hat was an essential article of attire for well-turned-out seventeenth-century gentlemen. Such hats were made of felt, a fabric produced by compressing heated fibers. With the technology available in the seventeenth century, beaver fur fibers produced the softest, supplest felt. In general, the thicker the fur the better for the felter's purposes. So skins of animals taken in winter were preferred to summer pelts, and the farther north the animal's habitat, the better.

A beaver pelt, however, is not useful to a felt-maker without further processing. For one thing, beaver coats consist of two types of fiber: a coarse outer layer and a dense, soft inner layer of fur, the input to the felting process. In addition, the dead animal's skin itself is insufficiently supple. During the early seventeenth century, outer hair-free, softened pelts could be obtained from one of two sources: from Russian craftsmen who applied a proprietary technique to process raw fur or as second-hand garments from Native Americans. Such second-hand garments were referred to as "coat" and commanded a premium price in the market. So, the most valuable North American pelts were "coats" made from the pelts of animals captured in the north.

Demand for beaver pelts in the early seventeenth century was derived from the demand for prestigious hats. As upper-bracket incomes continued to rise, we would expect that demand for luxury goods such as really big hats to rise disproportionately. But since there were other luxuries rich early moderns could buy and since other, pelt-saving dimensions of hat design could substitute for sheer size, we would expect that demand for pelts in Amsterdam, Paris, or London would be fairly price inelastic at any point in time (Kemp, 1998). In other words, large increases in supply would likely be followed by large decreases in price.

## Supply

During the late sixteenth century, Western Europe's principal source of beaver pelts was Russia, which, until the founding of St. Petersburg in 1703, was accessed via the White Sea port of Archangel. As with much of the trade with Eastern Europe, this market was dominated by Dutch merchants (de Vries & van der Woude, 1997, p. 377). By the early seventeenth century, however, it seems that beaver stocks from this source had been at least somewhat depleted (Crean, 1962).

North America's potential as a source of furs was apparent to the earliest explorers and to the first routine European visitors to the continent's northeastern coastline, the fisherman who arrived seasonally beginning in the early sixteenth century to exploit the Grand Banks (Davis, 1974). Likewise, Native Americans learned quite quickly that animal skins were among the items in exchange for which Europeans would provide valuable goods. Thus, when the French explorer Jacques Cartier visited the St. Lawrence river valley in 1534 he found that the indigenous people made "signs to us that they had come to barter with us; and held up some furs of small value…and they made signs to us that they would return on the morrow with more furs" (Morrison, 1984). By the early seventeenth century, fur trading in the St. Lawrence valley had evolved from a sideline for fisherman to a routine activity conducted at establishments that were occupied seasonally by independent French entrepreneurs for this purpose. And the pelt supply channel had evolved into the down-the-line pattern of trade that was a part of Woodlands Indians' cultural repertoire (Rich, 1960, p. 38).

This business was evidently lucrative enough for the French crown to anticipate that the fur trade could generate sufficient profits to cover its own costs and subsidize the establishment of a French settlement in what became Lower Canada, support missionaries, and pay a return to the royal treasury (Davis, 1974, pp. 170–171).

Thus, by the time Henry Hudson and his crew first encountered the inhabitants of the river valley that would later bear his name the North American fur trade had been underway, albeit at a modest level, for almost 100 years. Hudson would not, therefore, have been surprised when some of the Native Americans who greeted him arrived bearing furs for exchange. Contemporary accounts of the first encounters, however, seem to indicate that first Native Americans to approach the Halve Maen (Half Moon) with furs to trade did not appear until the ship had sailed about 150 miles up what they called the North River. The Indians they had encountered before that point had brought food and tobacco, presumably in the expectation of exchange, and were wearing animal skin clothing, but either had no fur pelts on hand to offer or were unaware of the European demand for these items. The Half Moon entered Lower New York Bay on September 2, 1609. It was not until September 19 that Robert Juet, a ship's officer, recorded in his log of the journey, that "The people of the Countries came flocking aboord, and brought us Grapes and Pompions, which wee bought for trifles. And many brought us Bevers skinnes, and Otters skinnes, which we bought for Beades, Knives, and Hatchets" (Juet, 1909). It may have been that the hinterland of the French fur-trading operations extended no farther south than present-day Albany or that the residents of the lower Hudson Valley played a different role in the regional trading economy that had evolved over the previous 100 years. Whatever the case, the spatial pattern first recorded by Juet persisted through the history of New Netherland: European traders sourced furs from Native American suppliers in the vicinity of Fort Orange, present-day Albany, while indigenous residents of the lower Hudson Valley, New York Bay, and Long Island played an integral but different and indirect role in the fur trade.

In the first years after the Half Moon's voyage, most of the furs on offer in the Hudson Valley were probably simply redirected away from the St. Lawrence market, i.e., the animals were likely either trapped locally or obtained via down-the-line transactions with the intention of exchanging the pelts for European goods. But local sources alone could not provide adequate supplies over the long run to sustain robust activity in New Netherland. For one thing, the local habitat may have become depleted.[4] For another, furs sourced farther north, in the Quebec market's hinterland, were more plentiful and of higher quality.

The flow of product within North America was seasonal. Winter, when coats were fullest and when capturing beavers was easiest, was the hunting season. Fresh pelts and second-hand coats were carried to one of a few market towns after the spring thaw. The official Albany fur market, for example, was active between May 1 and November 1.

Overall, North America's beavers remained numerous enough, European "Indian trade" goods remained attractive enough to Native

---

[4]There are of course no studies of beaver populations around the lower Hudson Valley in the seventeenth century. Evidence for a tendency toward depletion comes from the policies adopted by the Hudson Bay Company, a monopsonist in the market for pelts in Northern Ontario and Quebec, starting in the eighteenth century, that capped the number of furs purchased in certain places, in certain years, or at certain times of year (McManus, 1972, pp. 45–46). Exactly when beaver became scarce in the Iroquois territory is subject to dispute (Norton, 1974).

Americans, and the cost of delivering pelts from north country ponds to a port of embarkation proved low enough so that, as long as high-quality beaver felt hats remained fashionable, the price at which supply was equal to demand was sufficient to motivate Indian hunters, New Netherlands middlemen, and trans-Atlantic traders to remain engaged in the pelt market.

## Market Mechanisms: The Economics of Wampum

The fur trade operated as a barter system; the Indians exchanged pelts for goods they valued at least as much as the time spent acquiring and processing pelts. Indians valued European manufactured goods such as iron products, decorative or prestige goods such as glass beads, a coarse woolen cloth called duffel, and, eventually, firearms and liquor. Europeans bought skins as long as the European price of the pelts was greater than the sum of the cost of the trade goods, round-trip transportation, and a return on invested capital at the rate available for other, equally risky activities. Initially, absent a common, agreed-upon measure of value or a standard-package of European goods, each exchange had to be negotiated individually. Such bespoke transactions would have been inefficient, especially in the hectic atmosphere of the annual Fort Orange trading season. How, for example, was a Mohawk trader with a bundle of pelts to sell to decide which of two different combinations of metal pots, glass beads, yards of duffel, and shots of rum on offer from two different Dutch buyers was worth more? How did the buyers know whether they were over-paying?

Very quickly, therefore, market participants came to accept a few common measures of value or, in jargon, "numeraire" commodities. One such item was a repurposed Native American cultural artifact: uniformly shaped and sized cylindrical white and purple (or black) seashell beads, usually strung together into single or multiple strands. The Dutch called this commodity *sewant*. New Netherland and New England Indians all used the Algonquin word, wampum. Prior to its use in the fur trade, wampum was not thought of as a measure of value or as a currency. Instead, it served a number of decorative, symbolic, ceremonial, and spiritual functions in Native American cultures. It was, however, one of the few products of native manufacture that Indians would accept in exchange for furs. Wampum had a number of characteristics that made it suitable as a measure of value and medium of exchange. It was valued in and of itself in that it had well-defined prestige uses for some important market participants, particularly the Iroquois (Ceci, 1982), in much the same way as precious metals did in the Old World. It was easily transported, it could be divided into small units, its quality was easily ascertained, and it was fully fungible in that, for example, any white bead of standard quality was worth exactly as much as any other white bead (Ceci, 1980a). By some point in the early seventeenth century, therefore, our hypothetical Mohawk seller and Dutch buyer could know the price, in white or purple beads, of an iron pot, a yard of duffel, or standard-quality beaver pelt and could, therefore, compare different exchange packages. Further, the Dutch buyer would know the current exchange rate between *sewant* and guilders, and, to have any chance of surviving in the business, at least a rough idea of the guilder price of pelts in Amsterdam.

Thus wampum became, in effect and for a while, a currency in the fur trade; New Netherlands Director General Peter Stuyvesant (1647–1664) and his Council were probably correct when they informed the Amsterdam chamber of the WIC that "… no beavers can be obtained from the *wilden* [Indians] for just trade goods without *zewant*" (Jacobs, 2009). Further, because the fur trade was New Netherland's raison d'être and because, as will be discussed in more detail in the next chapter, North American colonies in general and New Netherland/New York, in particular, suffered from a chronic insufficiency of precious metal-based currencies, wampum was officially designated as legal tender in the colony, along with beaver pelts and Dutch guilders.

Wampum was a measure of value and a medium of exchange in New England during much of the seventeenth century and in New Netherland/New York, apparently well into the eighteenth century (Peña, 2001), but it was not a stable measure of value. The value of wampum relative to other commodities declined on average over the course of the colonial period, and wampum, as a currency, depreciated relative to Dutch guilders and British pounds. The reason was that the cost of producing new beads was low relative to the wampum value of other commodities, including beaver pelts. Further, wampum was durable; the quantity in circulation only increased. A Native American craftsperson could produce approximately 42 highly durable white beads per day. In 1634, the same 42 white beads could purchase a single beaver pelt. Given how labor-intensive and seasonal beaver hunting was, killing, processing, and transporting a single beaver probably required more than one day of Native American labor time, essentially the sole input to both production processes. So, in 1634, at least, it was profitable to purchase trade goods and exchange them with Native Americans for wampum, which could then be used to purchase furs. The cost of production was reduced further in New England but not in New Netherland by coercing Indians to produce wampum.

While there are no continuous price series for the key components of this trade there is enough evidence to demonstrate the continuous decline in the relative value of wampum. Some of the data points mentioned in the literature are listed in Table 1.1. As the Table indicates, if we take "a few years later" to mean 1663, over the life the Dutch colony wampum depreciated against guilders at an average annual rate of 7.4%. This depreciation was apparently entirely the result of a decline in the value of wampum rather than a general appreciation of the guilder or a downward trend in pelt prices. Between 1626 and 1641, the wampum price of pelts increased at an average annual rate of 7.6%, almost the same as the trend depreciation of wampum versus the guilder. And the guilder price of beavers was volatile but basically trendless over the course of New Netherland's history.

Historians have used the term "inflation" to describe the decline in the relative value of wampum (Ceci, 1980a; Jacobs, 2009). For a twenty-first century reader, this characterization is more confusing than useful because it problematizes the phenomenon in a way that may not have been troublesome to New Netherlanders. Wampum was a currency in the Colony, but it was not *the* currency. Within the colony, the price of any given item or the terms of any given contract might have been quoted in any one of three currencies: wampum, beaver pelts, and silver-based guilders. To make matters even more confusing, all three currencies were denominated in units called "guilders" and "stivers"

**Table 1.1** Wampum prices of beaver pelts, wampum-guilder exchange rates, and guilder prices of beaver pelts (Ceci, 1980a; Jacobs, 2009)

| Year | White beads per guilder |
|---|---|
| 1626 | 29 |
| 1634 | 42 |
| 1641 | 100 |
| 1658 | 160 |
| "A few years later" | 400 |
| | *White beads per beaver pelt* |
| 1626 | 144 |
| 1628 | 252 |
| 1634 | 504 |
| 1632–1636 | 1,080–1,440 |
| 1641 | 2,160 |
| | *Guilders per beaver pelt* |
| 1628 | 5 |
| 1634 | 12 |
| 1656 | 6 |
| 1657 | 8–10 |
| 1662 | 7 |
| 1663 | 6 |

(20 stivers = 1 guilder). So, in 1641, for example, five wampum beads were equal in value to one silver stiver. Thus, at that time, 100 beads (5 × 20) would have constituted a wampum guilder, and the price of a beaver pelt would have been 21.6 wampum guilders. In official Dutch silver guilders, however, the price of a pelt was never higher than 12. These complications need not have been problematic if the relative prices of beads, pelt, and silver were stable or if rates of change in relative value were more or less steady and more or less fully anticipated. If, however, large numbers of people were frequently surprised by unanticipated changes in prices, agreeing, for example, to accept a fixed weekly wampum salary for a prolonged period could be risky for a worker who paid rent in silver guilders. Such a worker would, of course, prefer to be paid in silver-based currency, but since the latter was scarce in the colony, the employer might be unwilling to enter into such a contract or would agree to pay hard currency only at a much lower salary in terms of current purchasing power. New Netherlanders entered into such contracts, and as unanticipated changes in exchange rates occurred, there

were some losers and some winners. As always, the losers' complaints are much more likely to turn up in the historical record than evidence of the winners' self-satisfaction.

The colony's leaders recognized that the risk associated with three forms of legal tender subject to exchange rate volatility was an impediment to the expansion of economic activity, and on at least two occasions, Peter Stuyvesant petitioned the WIC to ship quantities of silver currency New Amsterdam. The request was rejected. Nor was the colony permitted to follow the lead of New England in minting its own currency (Ceci, 1980a). So New Netherland's monetary problem was not "inflation," per se, but the risk associated with multiple make-shift commodity currencies and, at its base, too little of the most stable currency on hand to support the volume of economic activity that was taking place.

### Market Structure

By the second decade of the seventeenth century, all of the pieces needed for a market to develop were in place: willing buyers, willing sellers, and a market mechanism whereby mutually advantageous transactions could be executed with reasonable efficiency, albeit not without risk. The market's supply chain ran from the beaver ponds around the Great Lakes through Indian country to one of several market centers to the holds of European merchants for transatlantic shipment. Much about the histories of New Netherland, New France, Iroquoia, and, to a lesser extent, New England turns on the determination of which Native Americans would source the furs, which market center would capture the bulk of the North American pelt trade, and which merchants' ships would carry the product to Europe.

## Which Indians' Territories?

Beaver did and still do inhabit the homeland of the Iroquois Confederacy, and during the initial phases of trading activity, Five Nations' hunters probably did kill a large proportion of what they sold. Apparently, too, from an early date Mohawks, the members of the

Haudenosaunee confederation who had the easiest access to the Hudson and St. Lawrence River valleys, where the European buyers congregated, served as middlemen in addition to hunting on their own. But it was not a foregone conclusion that the supply side of the New Netherlands fur trade would come to be dominated by Mohawks acting as middlemen for furs originating over an area extending throughout the Great Lakes basin and northward toward Hudson Bay.

Before the Dutch established themselves on the Hudson River Indians wishing to exchange furs for European manufactured goods had little choice other than to bring their pelts to the St. Lawrence Valley or to sell them to middlemen who would bring them there. When the Dutch first arrived nearby Native American communities involved in the trade could reduce transportation costs by redirecting the pelts they had hunted themselves or had sourced from other Native American groups through down-the-line trading to the new trading post. There were two Indian communities that lived near modern Albany: the Iroquoian Mohawks and the Algonquian Mahicans. Both had evidently been involved in the early fur trade and both had trading and ethnic connections with the St. Lawrence region. The Mahicans lived closest to Fort Orange and the Dutch initially established friendly relations and began trading with that group. The militarily more aggressive Mohawks, probably seeing the Mahican-Fort Orange connection as a threat to their own activity as middlemen, fought and won a war with the Algonquian group. In the aftermath of the conflict, in which the Dutch garrison at Fort Orange had sided with the Mahicans, the WIC's New Netherlands commander, Pieter Minuit, traveled upriver from New Amsterdam to negotiate an agreement that gave the Mohawks preferred access to the local fur market.

The Mohawks remained the dominant supplier of pelts to New Netherland and New York for as long as the Fort Orange/Albany fur trade remained active. Neither the Mohawks, however, nor their Five Nations' confederates were able to dominate the main channel of fur supply from the area north of Lakes Ontario and Erie. The transport-cost minimizing channel for furs originating in this region and headed toward Europe would be down the St. Lawrence River. The area was inhabited by the Iroquoian-speaking Hurons and a number of

Algonquian communities. In addition to sourcing their own pelts, the Hurons had acted as middlemen between other northern Indian groups and the French downstream buyers. Military conflict between the Haudenosaunee and the Hurons had been endemic for a long period, but in the 1640s the war turned brutal. The Hurons lost and essentially disappear from history. It is hard to conclude that the intensified conflict was motivated by anything other than the goal of gaining access to the northern region's furs. Despite their victory, the Iroquois were unable to supplant the Huron-St. Lawrence flow of furs with an Iroquois-Hudson channel. Other northern Native American groups took over the Huron's role along the geographic path of least resistance between the beaver ponds and Europe (Norton, 1974, pp. 9–11).

The Iroquois were eventually able to deflect a large proportion of the flow of northern pelts through their territory to Fort Orange and Albany. As the next section shows, however, their ability to do so probably reflected the advantages offered by New Netherlands and New York as a place to sell furs more than the Five Nations' military might or diplomatic skill.

## Which Market Centers?

The fur trade was evidently promising enough for three Northern European powers to vie for market share aggressively over the course of the seventeenth and eighteenth centuries. On one level, the competition played out among fur-trading hubs of the European establishments in the region: New France, initially at Quebec and later at Montreal, New Netherland at Fort Orange, and New England at modern Hartford, Connecticut. The last of these flourished briefly but faded quickly as it became apparent that the Connecticut River Valley was too distant from the principle supplies (Davis, 1974, p. 170). Competition between Montreal and Albany continued until well into the eighteenth century. European traders in these two centers vied to attract Native American hunters and middlemen to their markets. They competed not only in terms of price—what value of products would be offered per pelt—but also with respect to the varieties of products on offer.

Historian E. E. Rich, for example, points out that after taking over New Netherland the British, as an exception to their mercantilist policies, allowed Dutch traders in Albany to continue purchasing their trade goods in Amsterdam because that was what Native American suppliers expected (Rich, 1960, p. 50). Later, during the eighteenth century, after the sugar industry took off (see next chapter) Albany was advantaged in being able to offer rum, which the Native Americans preferred to the more expensive brandy on offer at Montreal (Norton, 1974). And Albany's closer geographic and political proximity to wampum sources gave it a continuing advantage vis-à-vis Canadian market centers.

New Netherlands' and New France's political leadership did what they could, sometimes successfully, sometimes less so, to maintain cordial relations with the Native American peoples involved in the fur trade. Under normal circumstances, diplomatic interactions conformed to Native American norms and included periodic multi-day councils that were attended by top men on each side and were invariably accompanied by gift giving and feasting. Indians expected their counterparties to vie with each other in the lavishness of their entertainments. But because the various Indian groups were in competition and, frequently, in conflict among themselves over access to pelts and markets, French and Dutch diplomats found it challenging to strike the right balance in their relationships with the Native Americans.

Mistakes were made and one of the earliest of these mistakes may have had a long-lasting effect on the development of New Netherland and New Amsterdam. In 1628, Daniel van Krieckenbeeck, the Dutch leader of the Fort Orange settlement and trading post, sided with his near neighbors, the apparently well-connected Mahicans, against the Mohawks in a war being fought over shares of the fur supplies and access to the trading post at Fort Orange. This mistake cost Krieckenbeeck and three other Dutchmen their lives. It also led to the decision by the WIC representatives in New Netherland to abandon the peripheral settlements on the Delaware and Connecticut Rivers, to concentrate the colonial population on Manhattan, and to reduce the WIC presence at Fort Orange to a trading post and military encampment staffed by 16 individuals (Bailyn, 2012, p. 227). We'll never know whether, absent this incident, the Dutch would have maintained settlements bordering more closely on New England and Virginia or whether this would have changed the way in which European colonialism in North America developed. But WIC leadership did not conclude that concentrating New Netherlands' population on Manhattan was the right policy until efforts to establish Fort Orange as a major fur-trading hub went temporarily and tragically awry.

## Which European Merchants?

The question of which Europeans would be entitled to participate as principals in the New Netherland fur trade was fought out in Amsterdam, The Hague, and the Hudson Valley over the thirty years following the Half Moon's voyage. The specific questions in this regard were whether the colony's fur market would be competitive or monopolized and, if the latter, who would be granted the monopoly?

Some economic activities are "natural monopolies." These usually involve a production process characterized by substantially increasing returns to scale, so that whichever producer becomes the biggest first can earn profits while charging prices below competitors' cost of production, thereby driving all other suppliers out of the market. The North American fur trade was not a natural monopoly. Bigger was not necessarily better in the process of buying furs from Indians within the vast, sparsely settled northeastern quadrant of North America and shipping them to Europe via any reliable departing ship that was available. Quite the contrary, in fact; as it turned out the fur trade in New Netherland was something of a "natural competitive market." If there were to be a monopoly in the fur trade, the market structure would have to have been imposed and enforced by the Dutch authorities. So, this aspect of the development of the market, like the question of which market centers and which Indians' territories, was at least as much a political story as an economic one.

When reports of Hudson's voyage reached Amsterdam merchants seeking ways to further diversify their sources of income immediately began forming partnerships to finance fur-trading expeditions to the Hudson Valley. Records of the earliest post-1609 voyages to the area are vague—a trading vessel that *may* have visited the region sailed from Amsterdam as early as 1610—because throughout the early modern period ship captains and supercargoes were granted a great deal of discretion with respect to where to go and what to buy and sell. By 1614, enough Amsterdam merchants had visited the Hudson Valley—sometimes arriving at the same time and bidding up prices for a limited spot supply—to conclude that trying to compete with the French might not be worth the cost without some more permanent establishment on the ground and an enforceable limitation on competition. Accordingly, a group of traders applied to the Dutch government for a monopoly charter. This was granted to the New Netherland Company (NNC) on October 11, 1614, for four voyages to be conducted within three years (Bachman, 1969, pp. 4, 10).

Granting such a temporary monopoly or patent was astute public policy. First, there should have been a presumption that establishing a reliable trading presence in the hinterland of a profitable French operation might be costly and risky, so a trial run by a non-governmental group willing to finance the effort made sense. Second, a direct, plentiful source of pelts would complement the existing Dutch felting industry. But, third, a *permanent* monopoly would likely eventually restrict supply and raise the price of skins to Amsterdam felters. In any case, the charter was not expanded to include the Delaware River Valley when application to that effect was made and was not renewed when it expired in 1618.

The NNC established a trading station on a Hudson River Island near today's Albany and, possibly, some other semi-permanent outposts. Company buyers ventured throughout the territory around the Hudson, Delaware, and Housatonic Rivers in search of Native Americans who had or could obtain and would be willing to trade furs. This activity must have been reasonably profitable because some of the participants in the NNC continued their activities in the region after the company's charter expired and until the trade was taken over by a new monopoly, the WIC (Bachman, 1969, pp. 14–15).

In its enabling legislation the Dutch government, apparently hoping to reproduce the success of the VOC, granted the WIC monopoly rights over most trading activity among the Netherlands, West Africa, and the Americas. With respect to the North American fur trade this meant that, while any individual Dutchmen could buy furs from Indians or other Europeans, the final sale of each pelt within the colony had to be to the WIC at a price determined by the Company. And only the WIC could execute the initial sale of North American pelts in the Netherlands. Thus, the Company was a monopsonist (sole buyer) in New Netherland and, with respect to pelts sourced in the Dutch North American colony, and a monopolist (sole seller) in the home country.

## The WIC's Search for a Business Model

Between the end of a 12-year truce in 1621 and the end of Dutch-Iberian hostilities in 1648, the WIC tried to reproduce the success of the VOC. Despite occasional "wins" it never developed a business model that delivered the hoped-for combination of reliable profits or long-lasting geopolitical success.

In broad terms, a modified version of the VOC strategy made sense, *ex ante*. The centerpiece would be Brazil, where the Dutch would displace the Portuguese, as they had in Asia, and sugar production would play the same role as pepper did in Indonesia. Enslaved workers for labor-intensive sugar plantations would be obtained in Africa in exchange for European manufactured goods. And an array of lightly garrisoned stations around the Atlantic rim could serve three purposes. First, through them the WIC could source and export a range of products such as tobacco, timber, dyes, salt, and salted fish, etc. The WIC would sell these products as a monopolist in the Netherlands and in Dutch colonies and as a cost-advantaged competitor elsewhere. Second, the trading stations could serve as a base for privateering operations against Hapsburg interests. Finally, they could serve as entrepôts for the type of intra-regional carry trade that played such an important role in the Dutch homeland economy and in the East Indies. Together these activities looked to stand a decent chance of meeting their own costs and, given the WIC's monopoly power, generating enough surplus to pay a VOC-like dividend.

On a conceptual level, New Amsterdam fit neatly into this strategy. As a trading station (or "factory") it could source furs. Its excellent harbor, adjacent to the main North Atlantic trade routes and well supplied with timber for ship repair, was an ideal haven for Dutch privateers. It was also well positioned to develop an active carrying trade among New England, New France, Virginia, and the West Indies. Further, New Netherlands, with its fertile soil and benign climate could serve as a breadbasket, either for the homeland or for the WIC's sugar colonies. And a resident population of farmers would solidify, and, if necessary, defend the Netherlands's disputed claims on the territory. Finally, to the diversification-sensitive Dutch merchant class, New Netherland, with its northerly location relatively close to the Dutch homeland and wide range of productive potential, would have seemed like a good, if speculative, addition to the WIC's portfolio of colonies. And, indeed, the colony delivered on many of these promises, but not in ways that contributed substantially to the WIC's or the Netherlands's success.

The WIC's attempt to become "VOC-west" was a fundamentally flawed strategy because the Americas differed from Asia in one crucial way. China, Japan, India, and Java were densely populated and, in many respects, richer than Europe. America was not and was becoming even less so as the native population died out. So, in Asia the VOC could rely on local populations to work on plantations, supply garrisons with provisions, and support a lucrative local carrying trading. The WIC could not. While some of these elements of the VOC strategy became viable in the Americas once Caribbean sugar planters had kidnapped their labor force from Africa and become wealthy consumers in their own right, these developments did not come to fruition until late in the seventeenth century, by which time New Netherland had become New York.

All of the uses to which New Netherland could be put required at least some local labor force with adequate skills in terms of level and variety. Fur traders had to be supplied and provisioned. A base of privateering or carry trade operations required ship repairmen and chandlers. The production of staples required farmers. But inducing workers to migrate from Europe to and stay in North America, where, for example, of the 2000 people who had migrated from England to Virginia in the nine years after 1607, only 351 were still alive and there in 1616, was difficult to say the least (Bailyn, 2012, p. 69). Recruitment of appropriately skilled European labor was a challenge for all colonial powers but was particularly challenging for the Dutch because, as discussed above, early in the seventeenth century real wages in the Netherlands were substantially higher than elsewhere in Europe. And to most of those adventurous Dutchmen willing to try their luck in foreign lands, a job with the VOC or, if with the WIC, in Brazil probably looked more promising.

For these reasons, a debate within the WIC leadership as to how much and how to populate New Netherlands led to a series of fits and starts of development for the first 20 years of the colony's existence. The parties to the disagreement were two factions within the WIC's Amsterdam branch ("Chamber"). Supporters of what historian Oliver Rink calls the "Company view" thought of New Netherland as a trading post or "factory," much like the many lightly garrisoned establishments the VOC maintained in Asia. Advocates of the "patroons' view" envisioned a semi-feudal economy populated by European tenant farmers and supplying grain and other staples to local fur traders and ships chandlers, to the homeland, to the sugar plantations in Brazil and the Caribbean, and more generally around the Atlantic basin (Rink, 1986).

The arguments on both sides of the debate within the WIC leadership turned out to be wrong at the time they were put forward. Even a minimally garrisoned trading post needed provisions, which, absent a local population of farmers, would have to be shipped from Europe or purchased from the Natives. Either way would have been expensive. Buying from the Indians incurred an opportunity cost; trade goods would have to be diverted from the purchase of furs to the acquisition of corn, beans, and preserved meat or fish. Relying on provisions shipped from Europe was expensive per calorie and risky, given the infrequency of transatlantic sailings in the early seventeenth century, the hazards of those voyages, and the consequences to the garrison of a missed shipment.

Kiliaen van Rensselaer, the principal leader of the patroons' faction, framed the argument against the minimal-population model as follows:

> ...[I]t will be found, no matter how economically it may be managed, that the ship which must go with merchandise from the Fatherland and return ... the garrison and fort at the Manhattans, the garrison and fort at Fort Orange, the yachts and sloops for trade on the South [Delaware] River and the northern regions, besides the sloops plying between, counting all expenses of building, arming, equipping, keeping up, manning and victualing, will cost so [much] that the aforesaid 60,000 or 70,000 guilders [annual revenue from the sale of furs], which are the utmost to be expected thence, will come far short by many thousands. (Bachman, 1969)

Historian Van Cleaf Bachman assembled information from a wide range of sources to test van Rensselaer's assertions and found that it was probably close to correct. For example, the WIC reported receipts of 725,117 guilders on the sale of furs over the 11-year period from 1624–1635, or an average of 66,000 guilders per year. The cost of trade goods to exchange for furs may have totaled about 30,000 guilders. Insurance for round-trip transatlantic shipments might have equaled about six percent of the value of the goods or about 5,760 guilders. And, on the assumption that 75 men would be sufficient to garrison the two forts, the overhead items listed by van Rensselaer probably totaled close to 32,000 guilders. Total costs by this reckoning come to 67,760 guilders and, on the assumption that 66,000 annual revenue was sustainable, the average annual loss to the WIC on the garrison strategy would be 1,760 guilders. Not exactly van Rensselaer's "many thousands," but a loss. To be sure, even a minimal Dutch presence in North America might convey strategic advantages, but the WIC's goal was to generate both geopolitical benefits *and* cash-on-cash profits (Bachman, 1969, pp. 126–128).

## The Peopling Problem

Van Rensselaer and the rest of the patroons' faction may have been right about the Company view being wrong. But their alternative, developing relatively populous agricultural settlements, was not successful either. Their proposal to the WIC, which was similar in many ways to a policy the Company had already enacted for the settlement of Guyana, was that Dutch entrepreneurs be allowed to purchase large tracts of land in New Netherland from the Indians, recruit tenants, and pay to transport them, their provisions, livestock, and the implements required to establish a settlement. In addition to the sale of the products of their "patroonships" the settlements' founders would be allowed to profit from trading goods other than furs along the Atlantic coast of North America.

Advocates of the Company view argued against any proposal that would increase the European population of New Netherland. Their concern was that, given difficulty of enforcing the WIC's fur-trading monopoly in a vast territory and unorganized market, more people meant more "smuggling" of furs, more competition, and lower profits for the Company. In fact, there is circumstantial evidence that, for some of the would-be patroons, their faction's proposal was a subterfuge to provide cover for extensive fur-trading activity. Van Cleaf Bachman, who has examined all the available evidence, concludes, however, that, while profiting on the fur trade may have been one of the patroons' motives, their advocacy of settlement was fundamentally sincere (Bachman, 1969, pp. 109–119).

In any case, the patroons' view won the political day, and in 1629, the WIC adopted the "freedoms and exemptions for the patroons, masters or private persons who will plant any colonies in and send cattle to New Netherland" (Bachman, 1969, p. 108).

Upon adoption of the "freedoms and exemptions," four individuals or groups initiated efforts to establish patroonships at locations ranging from Delaware Bay at the colony's southern extreme to the vicinity of modern Albany in the north. Of the four, only the northernmost settlement, Rensselaerswyck, survived for any appreciable length of time. The details of each failure and the one success differ, but they all faced the same fundamental problem. Recruiting tenants proved very difficult. It was hard to induce Dutch men and women to migrate when good-paying jobs were to be had at home. To staff his patroonships, for example, Kiliaen van Rensselaer had to pay nominal salaries an average of 25% higher than homeland levels (Rink, 1986, p. 153). Even that wage premium, however, was not enough to induce voluntary migration given the high cost of imported goods in New Netherland. Van Rensselaer himself estimated the cost of shipping provisions to his Patroonship to be roughly 50% of the original purchase price in Amsterdam. As late as the 1660s, the price of shoes at the WIC store in New Amsterdam was 140% above the wholesale price in the Netherlands (Rink, 1986, pp. 209–210).

Even after employees had been brought to New Netherland, keeping them on the farm was hard, even before their contract terms had expired. The Europeans who did wind up in the colony, especially during the first two decades of settlement, were, almost by definition, a relatively footloose lot; of the immigrants to Rensselaerswyck between 1630 and 1644 for whom identifying information is available, more than 80% were single men, mostly in their early 20s or late teens (Rink, 1981). Alternative locations and alternative occupations, very much including the local fur trade, beckoned. The patroons may, in fact, have faced the same challenge the anti-settlement faction had feared; a larger population meant more competition for furs. In the 1650s, after the WIC had relinquished its fur trade monopoly, profits were likely squeezed by increased competition, "[A] moderately successful trader in a single season could earn twelve times the annual wages of a local farmer" (Bailyn, 2012, p. 251).

The evidence we have is consistent with the view that in its early years New Netherland employers could not offer high enough real wages to attract large numbers of Dutch immigrants. Population grew very slowly before the 1640s. Although New Netherland did not remain an isolated lightly garrisoned trading post, Kiliaen van Rensselaer's vision of thriving farming estates producing staples for export and, at most, only peripherally involved in the fur trade, also failed to materialize.

The question of which merchants would participate in the New Netherland fur trade legally as principals was finally resolved in 1639. Under political pressure from the Republic's central government, which was concerned about the colony's slow pace of population growth, and from influential shareholders, who saw an independent business opportunity, the WIC relinquished its monopsony and monopoly on the fur trade. Thenceforth, anyone who wanted to could export pelts, provided that they shipped their merchandise through New Amsterdam and paid the WIC a fee.

## Equilibrium Market Structure

The market structure that developed after 1639 was apparently highly competitive within New Netherland while the transatlantic trade between New and Old Amsterdam was concentrated in the hands of four large trading firms.

Within the colony, many buyers transacted directly with many sellers and competition was evidently fierce. Dutch authorities enacted regulations designed to limit transactions to certain places at certain times under certain terms. Purchases from Mohawk traders were supposed to take place within the boundaries of Fort Orange and the adjacent town of Beverwijck during the official trading season, and exchange of liquor or firearms for pelts was forbidden. But violations of these regulations were apparently routine, suggesting that too many small, individual transactions were taking place for effective policing (Jacobs, 2009, pp. 113–117).

Once a beaver skin was held by a European it might change hands within the colony many times; pelts were, after all, a form of legal tender. Eventually, however, most furs made their way to New Amsterdam, designated as New Netherland's sole official export port. Holders of pelts who wished to exchange their holdings for bulk quantities of imported goods had little choice but to deal with a local representative of one of a few large Amsterdam-based merchant firms. Four homeland-based firms, in particular, accounted for most of the direct trade between New and old Amsterdam: the Verbrugges, the de Wolffs, the Rensselaers, and Gillis van Hoornbeeck and Associates. Over the last fifteen years of the New Netherland's existence, these firms organized regular voyages between old and New Amsterdam, generally in partnership with other, smaller trading firms or with one another. All four either had or tried to develop New Netherland-based businesses other than the fur trade. For three of these firms—the ones that survived the longest—the New Netherland trade was one of several, diverse trading activities in which they were actively engaged.

The four-firm concentration ratio—measured by the percentage of direct sailings from the Netherlands to New Amsterdam organized by one of these firms—ranged between 50% in normal years to 90% in wartime when higher maritime insurance rates raised the fixed costs of voyages. And although not all of the cargo carried on these voyages was owned by one of the four principals, the organizers of voyages probably exercised some influence over the business practices of their junior partners. Such a high degree of concentration along with the fact that the leading firms were frequently partners in individual voyages may have offered opportunities for oligopolistic collusion in setting purchase prices for pelts in New Amsterdam and sales prices in the homeland. Further, the small number of firms involved and the fact that these companies interacted intensively across a wide range of activities would have made it easier to prevent cheating on any explicit or implicit collusive pricing arrangement.

We have only circumstantial evidence that such collusion took place. Namely, the returns on this business must have been very high, even considering the risks. Financing for Dutch intercontinental trade during most of the seventeenth century took the form of bottomry bonds: advances made by investors to organizers of a trading voyage secured by the "bottom" of the ship. That is, if the borrower did not pay off the loan principal and interest as stipulated in the bond, the lenders could seize the ship and the cargo. Under these terms, the lenders bore the bulk of the risk that the ship would sink or be captured. Bottomry bonds were an expensive source of capital. The annualized interest rate on bottomry bonds on voyages between Amsterdam and New Netherland ranged from a low of 19.5% to a high of 39.0% between 1651 and 1664. Revenues on trading activity that could cover these capital costs and still leave enough profit to encourage additional voyages and allow the owners of three of the four trading firms to accumulate substantial wealth must have been very high. This does not prove that the Dutch transatlantic fur trade was operated by a cartel, but the evidence is certainly suggestive of collusion (Rink, 1986, pp. 172–209).

Historian Oliver Rink has suggested that the concentration of New Netherland's transatlantic trading activity in a single export commodity and in the hands of Amsterdam-owned and operated firms impeded the economic development of the Dutch colony relative to what occurred in New England over the same period. New England's Atlantic basin trade was fostered by locally owned firms tapping into a diverse range of exports, and the capital generated by this activity stayed and was reinvested in the colonial economy (Rink, 1986, pp. 211–213). This may be true. But the highly competitive New Netherlands pelt industry created opportunities for a large number of small entrepreneurs, many of whom engaged in other activities to "top-off" their profits from fur trading. And because wages in the Dutch homeland were relatively high, many of the immigrants attracted to New Netherland after 1639 had migrated from other parts of the Atlantic world. Thus, while it is plausible that financial capital failed to accumulate as quickly in New Netherland as it did in New England, the Dutch colony seems to have attracted a uniquely diverse stock of entrepreneurial human capital.

## The Population: Who Came? Who Didn't? Why?

The WIC's initial New Netherland business plan was foiled by the difficulty of simultaneously enforcing the fur trade monopoly and recruiting even a minimal viable population. After the WIC relinquished its monopoly and opened the fur trade to free competition, population growth began to accelerate. The fact that more immigrants started arriving in increasing numbers after the adoption of a free fur trade policy does not, of course, necessarily mean that the latter caused the former. That, however, seems to be the explicit or implicit assumption of many of the historians who have examined the period.[5]

An analytical case for such a cause and effect relationship might be framed as follows. Population growth accelerated because of either

a. "Pull" toward New Netherland: an increase in the demand for labor within the colony as manifest by improvement in real wages (i.e., the

[5]Russell Shorto expresses the cause and effect view as follows: "In 1640 the company gave up its monopoly on trade in the region, which had kept the place from developing in any areas except piracy and smuggling…The effect was electric. Small scale entrepreneurs in Amsterdam who were willing to brave the hazards of the ocean voyage now had, in Manhattan, a hub to exploit – a base around which the circle of Atlantic trade could turn" (Shorto, 2004).

achievable standard of living) in the colony relative to what could be realized elsewhere or

b. "Push" away from Europe or elsewhere in the Atlantic world: an increase in the supply of labor to the colony because the achievable quality of life elsewhere had deteriorated.

Of course, we don't have the good observations of real wages for this period, so the plausibility of the case must rest on other evidence.

## The Pull: Why the Fur Trade Mattered Most

Given the high cost of enforcement, a monopolized Hudson Valley fur trade could not generate sufficient profits to subsidize WIC activities elsewhere. Nevertheless, net earnings on this activity, even in a competitive market, were evidently sufficient to induce independent entrepreneurs to locate in New Netherland, to buy and sell pelts as principals, to provide goods and services to those who were directly involved in the trade, or to engage in other activities that were complementary to the main activity. Thus, while the post-1640 new New Netherlanders may have come from a wide variety of places to engage in a wide range of occupations, in most cases, they came for one basic reason: to benefit, directly or indirectly, from the fur trade.[6]

In fact, though, only a small minority of New Netherlanders were directly engaged in the fur trade, or any other long-distance trading activity, as their principal occupation. And to the limited extent that we know immigrants' motivations it does not appear that many of these individuals arrived with the explicit intention of participating directly in this business. To be sure, representatives dispatched to New Amsterdam to serve as factors for large homeland merchant companies must have anticipated that much of their stock in trade would consist of beaver pelts. But most immigrants probably expected that they would continue

[6]The main exceptions to this generalization were the English settlers on eastern Long Island, whose economic lives were more closely integrated into New England's markets than New Netherland's.

to pursue the same occupations they had in their homelands. Of those who arrived between 1654 and 1664 for whom such information is available, for example, the vast majority was farmers, craftsmen, or laborers and many of the rest were soldiers (Cohen, 1981). What, then, does it mean to assert, as Bernard Bailyn does, that "it was the fur trade that mattered most…" (Bailyn, 2012, p. 251)?

To clarify the role of the fur trade in the development of New Netherland (and early New York) it will be helpful to introduce a concept that will be referred to frequently in subsequent chapters: base-multiplier analysis. Workers and entrepreneurs in any geographic region are engaged in some combination of two types of economic activity. Some workers produce goods and services that are sold to residents of other places. These "exports" bring in income and are referred to as the region's economic base.

Producing goods for export requires inputs: raw materials, capital goods, and, importantly, labor. Some of the physical inputs may be produced locally and some may be imported from elsewhere. We generally assume, especially for the historical period in question, that all of the workers have to be hired locally. The workers who specialize in producing exports need food, shelter, and clothing. Some of what they buy comes from elsewhere, but some of it is supplied locally. Workers who produce these locally consumed goods, who themselves also need such commodities, are engaged in "non-base" economic activities. If sales of the region's exports increase, the number of base industry workers will rise and the demand for locally produced inputs will grow as will the number of workers engaged in non-base activities. So, we can expect that an increase in base industry employment of, say, 10 new jobs, might be followed by an increase in total employment—including both those producing goods for export and for local consumption—of substantially more than 10 jobs. The ratio of the increase in total employment to an increase in base industry employment is referred to as the region's export or base multiplier.

Export multipliers differ across regions. In general, the larger the population of a region the higher the multiplier because, with more workers available, a larger proportion of the goods people need or want can be produced locally at efficient scale. Also, the more remote the region is from alternative sources of goods in demand, the more expensive it will be to import goods and the larger the proportion of local needs likely to be filled locally (Mullilgan & Fik, 1994). The tendency of multipliers to rise as population grows—i.e., the tendency of growth to be self-reinforcing—will become increasingly important when examining the New York City economy in the nineteenth century and thereafter. For New Netherland, however, the high cost of transporting goods from production centers in Europe was likely a more important determinant of the export multiplier. For every New Netherlander who was actively and exclusively engaged in the fur trade, the colony needed a large number of local farmers, shoemakers, carpenters, beer brewers, coopers, and so on relative to the requirements of a similarly sized town in the homeland. In other words, although we don't have anything like the data we would need to estimate the export base multiplier for the New Netherland fur trade, it must have been quite high.

A "pull-side" explanation for the acceleration of New Netherland's growth that began in the 1640s should, therefore, include answers to two questions: What were the colony's exports or base activities and what might have caused employment in those industries to increase starting in the 1640s? Even a modest increase in the number of full-time equivalent workers directly engaged in export activities could have led to much more substantial growth in total population, given this isolated region's likely high export base multiplier.

New Netherland did export a few things other than furs, including timber, tobacco, and maritime transportation services. The Netherlands was home to a large shipbuilding industry at the time although the country was largely treeless. New Netherland was, by contrast, densely forested and felled timber was a by-product of the expansion of farmland. But the Baltic region and especially Norway, where the Dutch merchants were actively engaged, was a closer source of this heavy, bulky commodity. So timber and lumber were exported, but the growth was ancillary to the main reason ships were coming to New Netherland, namely, to deliver European-made goods and pick up furs (Bachman, 1969, pp. 91–92; de Vries & van der Woude, 1997, pp. 423–429).

Tobacco cultivation likely made more of a contribution to the colony's growth than lumber. Over the life of the colony ships sailing from

New Amsterdam carried increasing volumes of tobacco. Initially, much of this cargo was grown in the Chesapeake colonies and was transshipped through New Amsterdam to England or the Dutch homeland. The growth of this carry trade was stimulated by the English Civil War (1642–1651), which disrupted British commercial activity for its duration (Jacobs, 2009, p. 125). Attempts to develop a commercially viable tobacco-growing industry in New Netherland were initially stymied by the short growing season in much of the colony and the labor-intensity of the production process. Eventually, efforts met with modest success, but New Netherland-grown tobacco never played an important role in the European market. Jaap Jacobs presents evidence suggesting that in 1663 exports of New Netherland-grown tobacco probably didn't amount to more than about one-twelfth of Virginia product marketed in Amsterdam, where leaves from the Dutch colony would probably have accounted for a larger market share than elsewhere in Europe (Jacobs, 2009, p. 90). In the context of the Atlantic economy, therefore, New Netherland was a minor exporter of tobacco to Europe; it was, with Montreal, one of the two major suppliers of peltry. It seems unlikely, therefore, that Europeans would migrate to New Netherland with the intention of making a living by cultivating tobacco.

New Netherlanders tried to develop other export industries. They experimented with crops such as indigo, talked about using native grapes to make wine (Van der Donck, 1993) and launched salt refining and potash production enterprises (Rink, 1981, pp. 179, 186–194). None of these ventures went anywhere. Producing food for export to Brazil and other plantation economies was part of Kiliaen van Rensselaer's plan for his patroonship. In this he was prescient if premature; as will become clear in the next chapter, food production for the Caribbean sugar islands did become an important part of New York's eighteenth-century economic base. But the Dutch lost control of Brazil before the Rensselaers and other landowners could solve their labor supply problems (Rink, 1986, p. 150).

An economic region can also "export" services by, for example, serving as a base of operations of a carrying trade. This activity, in fact, was a key component of the United Provinces' economic base, and by the 1640s New Netherlands-based merchants had begun commissioning ships to buy, sell, and carry goods between various points around the Atlantic littoral, including the North American English colonies and England itself. As with van Rensselaer's plan to sell grain to sugar planters, this carrying trade would become one of New York's economic mainstays from the eighteenth century onward. But the English Parliament's adoption of the first of the Navigation Acts in 1651 achieved its purpose of shifting much of this trading and shipping activity out of Dutch and into English hands (Jacobs, 2009, pp. 141–142). Finally, there may have been some discussion of establishing New Amsterdam as a transshipment point for the North American coastal slave trade (Rink, 1986, p. 169).

In sum, there does not seem to have been any export activity other than the fur trade, with the possible minor exception of tobacco cultivation, that might have played an important role in attracting substantial numbers of European immigrants.

The capital of New Netherlands was named after Holland's metropolis. A more descriptive name would have been Beverstad or Beavertown.

## The Push

Changes taking place elsewhere in the Atlantic world could have enhanced New Netherland's relative attractiveness to potential migrants even absent any new "pull" from the colony itself. Economic growth across Western Europe, including the Netherlands, was slower after 1620 than it had been before and some areas of the Continent experienced absolute declines. The 30 Years' War (1618–1648) devastated large parts of central Europe and the physical destruction and associated religious persecutions drove large populations out of their homelands to seek new places to live. During the "Golden Age" of Dutch economic growth, which Jan de Vries and Ad van der Woude date from the mid-1580s until the mid-1660s, many of these refugees found their way to the Netherlands. But Dutch growth rates probably peaked before the 1620s, and de Vries and van der Woude also point out that by the second quarter of the seventeenth century "[o]nly the Western Hemisphere seemed to hold a promise of new markets." In short, continued growth of Dutch trade now required, more than ever before, direct confrontations with rivals for enlarged shares of existing markets. Jan de Vries and Ad van der Woude put it this way: "The Republic's economy was now swimming against the stream and would, by the 1650s, provoke the active resistance of powerful rivals" (de Vries & van der Woude, 1997, p. 672). So, by the early 1640s refugees from the war-torn regions of Central Europe may have faced a cooler welcome in the United Provinces, and Dutch merchants may have welcomed the opportunity to add the North American fur trade to their portfolios of business ventures.

The WIC's loss of Brazil in the years leading up to 1654 also pushed some migrants toward New Netherland. The lives of many of the seventeenth-century migrants were punctuated by repeated moves from one location to another around the Atlantic shores. Many individuals' itineraries included periods of time in Brazil. When one very important destination was effectively eliminated from many migrants' choice set, a larger proportion of this itinerant population would spend some time in New Netherland or settle there permanently.

As important as these changes may have been in raising the relative attractiveness of New Netherland to potential migrants, they don't help explain the timing of the post-1640 acceleration in the colony's population growth. The 30 Years War was closer to its end than its beginning in 1640. The deceleration of Dutch economic growth, which eventually allowed England to supersede the Netherlands as Europe's dominant economic power, was gradual and the pace of trading capital accumulation, urbanization, and land reclamation remained robust through the first half of the seventeenth century and beyond (de Vries & van der Woude, 1997, pp. 672–673). And the tide of geopolitical events did not turn decisively against the Dutch until after the 1640s.

By process of elimination, therefore, it seems that the opening of the fur trade to competition was, indeed, the initial impetus for the acceleration of New Netherland's population growth after 1640. Over the subsequent two and one-half decades, however, as the number of individuals engaged in the fur trade stabilized, other influences, such as the expansion of tobacco cultivation, the deceleration of economic growth in the Dutch homeland, and the WIC's loss of Brazil may have pulled or pushed increasing numbers of immigrants in New Netherland's direction.

## Demographic Diversity

In some respects, New Netherland's settlement pattern paralleled that of the English colonies in North America in that it took a decade or more before population growth began to accelerate. English deaths in Virginia came close to outnumbering new arrivals for the first dozen years or so after the colony's founding in 1607; only after experimentation had identified a high-quality strain of tobacco that could thrive in the mid-Atlantic climate did it become worthwhile for entrepreneurs to put up the £20 per-person transportation and start-up cost for large numbers of new settlers (Bailyn, 2012, pp. 79, 93). Thus, the Chesapeake colonies population growth was stimulated by the demand "pull" of tobacco cultivation. New England's "great migration" of the 1630s by contrast, was driven more by the "push" of a deteriorating quality of life in England for Puritan religious dissidents, compounded in East Anglia and the West Country, the origin of many migrants, by crop failures and a secular decline of the local textile industry (Bailyn, 2012, pp. 365–378).

The experience of the Dutch colony did, however, differ from that of the English settlements in a way that seemed no more than a curiosity at the time but exerted a profound influence on the economic development of New York in the eighteenth century and thereafter. The vast majority of seventeenth-century settlers in Virginia, Maryland, and New England were British. In New Netherland, at least a large minority and, in some parts of the colony, a majority of the migrants were not Dutchmen.

Historians of the Netherlands and New Netherland have consistently remarked on the number of foreign-born residents in both places compared with other locations in Europe or North America. In his study of the early years of European settlement in Virginia, New England, and New Netherlands, for example, Bernard Bailyn points out that 40% of the people who registered for marriage in old Amsterdam in the early seventeenth century were foreign-born. He goes on to observe that, in contrast to the peopling of the English North American colonies, population growth in New Netherland "was not an organized migration …

but an almost untraceable drift into the colony of a miscellany of people from outside the Netherlands: Huguenots, directly or indirectly from France; Germans; Walloons; Swedes and Finns; and refugees from Brazil and the Dutch colonies in the Caribbean" (Bailyn, 2012, pp. 192, 243).

No doubt the oft-cited Dutch religious tolerance played a role in attracting some immigrants, although the influential role of the established Dutch Reformed Church probably also helped attract Calvinist refugees from other parts of Europe.

The condition of the Dutch labor market through the middle of the seventeenth century probably influenced both the "don't ask don't tell" attitude toward Christian denominations and the willingness of refugees and voluntary migrants to choose the United Provinces or its colonies as their destinations. Foreign workers, including many non-Calvinists, may have been glad to migrate to a high-wage area, and local employers may have been happy to hire them, presumably at a modest discount to the going rate for native-born Dutchmen. In a high-wage region, religious prejudice could be expensive, so tolerance may have paid. Although several historians of the period have mentioned that tolerance was "good business," there is apparently very little direct evidence to support this hypothesis. Policies regarding religion, most of which were adopted and administered on the local level, were hotly contested, and the advocates of tolerance seem not to have framed their arguments in economic terms. But the fact that the pro-tolerance forces were generally aligned with the business-oriented civil authorities in opposition to the Calvinist clergy provides circumstantial evidence for an economic motive (Pettegree, 1996, pp. 182–198).

The situation in New Netherlands was similar to that in the homeland. Here, however, the local civil authority, the Director General in the person of Peter Stuyvesant, sided with the local clergy in efforts to restrict the activities of minority religions. The pro-tolerance role was played, at a distance, by the Amsterdam chamber of the WIC. In the North American colony freedom of conscience, if not explicit freedom of public worship, won the day and all immigrants were accepted, even Quakers and Jews. For this colony, operated as it was in the interest in a for-profit business, struggling to attract even the minimally required workforce, and bordering obsessively sectarian New England, tolerance was the best policy. Indeed, a frequently cited statement by the WIC directors made this conclusion explicit. Regarding the arrival of a small group of Quakers, after making clear their wish that these "sectarians" stay away from the colony, the bottom-line statement of policy was that "we doubt very much, whether we can proceed against them rigorously without diminishing the population and stopping immigration, which must be favored at so tender a stage of the country's existence" (Jacobs, 1998). Finally, for potential migrants motivated to leave Europe, rumors of a 25% nominal premium to high Dutch wages must have looked particularly attractive.

Thus, among the migrants van Rensselaer dispatched to populate his patroonship during the 1630–1644 period, all of whom were recruited within the United Provinces, more than 20% of the individuals for whom information is available were born outside of the Netherlands (Rink, 1981, Table 1, pp. 19, 26). Likewise, of the migrants who sailed directly from the Netherlands to New Netherland between 1657 and 1664 for whom explicit national origin information is available, a bit more than 20% were registered as foreigners (Rink, 1981, Table 4, pp. 36–37).

This likely represents an underestimate of the proportion of non-Dutch immigrants to the colony during this period, perhaps a substantial underestimate. Unambiguous information on national origin was available for only 64% of the 1,079 passengers for whom data were tabulated, and all of the enumerated individuals embarked in the Netherlands itself. Many immigrants, presumably including a higher proportion of non-Dutch, may have arrived in New Netherland on voyages that originated elsewhere. Many of the life histories of New Netherland residents from all points of origin involved repeated relocations around the Atlantic region. Peter Stuyvesant served the WIC on the islands Fernando de Noronha off the coast of Brazil and Curaçao before assuming office as Director General of New Netherland (Jacobs, 2009, p. 44). Janneken Jans van Leeuwarden was living with her shoemaker husband, who may have been of German or Scandinavian origin,[7] in Recife in 1640s, returned to the Netherlands in 1650, joined her husband in New Netherland in 1655, returned to Amsterdam in 1658, and then sailed back to New Netherland the next year (Romney, 2014, pp. Loc. 2014–2064). The 23 Jews who arrived in New Amsterdam from Recife in 1654 arrived aboard a French ship. By way of contrast, the largest number of recorded foreigners on any of the 31 voyages tabulated by Rink was 22 (Jacobs, 2009, p. 98; Rink, 1981, Table 4, pp. 36–37). And likely none of the New Netherlanders of African origin, who may have constituted about four percent of the colony's 1655 population, arrived directly from the United Provinces (Bailyn, 2012, p. 258). Finally, the record of direct Netherlands-New Netherland voyages does not count the many New Englanders who settled on Long Island and in the lower Hudson Valley.

It would be difficult, therefore, to argue against Oliver Rink's assertion that "studies based on a thorough reading of genealogical material suggest that the proportion of foreigners in New Netherland was much larger [than 20 percent], constituting perhaps as much as 50 percent of the colony's population" (Rink, 1986, p. 155).

## The Market for Land or What Did $24 Signify?

Possibly the most widely known "fact" about the economic history of New York City is that Manhattan Island was purchased from the Indians for "trinkets" worth twenty-four dollars, that this was a ridiculously low price, and that the sophisticated Dutch buyers took advantage of the sellers' naiveté. Possibly the second most widely known fact is that the details of this legend have been thoroughly debunked. The value of the goods exchanged for the real estate was, at that time and place, substantially more than $24, and most likely neither party understood what was happening to be a "purchase" in the European sense of complete alienation with the expectation that the seller would shortly

[7] His name was Reinholt Reinholts.

vacate the premises. Indeed, in one version of the story the group of Indians involved in the deal had no particular connection with the Island but were visiting from elsewhere. So, it isn't entirely clear which, if either, of the two parties to the transaction was being naïve. Even though no one believes the legend any more, an examination of what did and didn't take place in 1626 is worthwhile for the light it sheds on the ways in which Europeans became landowners in New Netherland.

No deed of sale for this transaction has survived, although, as most land-related transactions between the Dutch and the Native Americans were memorialized in writing, some document was probably drawn up and signed or marked by both parties. In seventeenth-century North America, this process of land acquisition—parcel-by-parcel transactions executed in writing between Native American community leaders and individual European natural or legal persons—was unique to the Middle Atlantic and New England charter colonies. Around the Chesapeake and in New France colonial leaders representing the homeland sovereign negotiated sales or cessions of large blocks of property which the colonial proprietor would then sell or distribute to individual Europeans (Grumet, 2011). The Indians' "sale" of Manhattan was one of a large number of such transactions that continued into the eighteenth century.

Absent a deed or other legal document, evidence that the sale took place and of the purchase price is drawn primarily from a November 1626 report of news about the colony sent from the WIC to the Dutch government (Burrows, 1999). To have meaning to the report's author and recipients, the 60-guilder consideration reported by the WIC probably would have represented the free on-board Amsterdam value of the goods exchanged for the Island. If so, the goods would have been much more valuable in North America than they were in Amsterdam due to the cost of transatlantic shipping and their scarcity value in early seventeenth-century North America. Indeed, the economic motive for establishing New Netherland was that European goods were much more valuable in North America than at home while beaver pelts were much more valuable in Amsterdam than at Fort Orange. In equilibrium, the difference between the price of trade goods in New and Old Amsterdam would have been equal to the all-in, risk-adjusted transportation cost.

But at this early stage of the trade relationship price differentials would probably have been much wider than their equilibrium values.

The $24 figure was first put forward by the premier nineteenth-century historian of New York City, E. B. O'Callaghan, and represents the U.S. dollar value of 60 Dutch guilders at exchange rates current in 1846.[8] The written record is silent on exactly what European goods were exchanged in the transaction, although the package was probably similar to the collection of items paid for Staten Island at about the same time: axes, hoes, needles, awls, scissors, knives, and kettles (Burrows, 1999, p. 19). These were valuable capital goods in the context of time and place and hardly "trinkets."

At some point during New Netherland's first two decades, the Dutch and the Indians came to realize that the land purchases and sales they had been executing had different meanings to the two sides of the transactions. Lawyer-investor-politician Adriaen van der Donck, writing during the 1640s, knew that to Native Americans proprietorship did not automatically convey the right to restrict access to the property. He wrote that "wind, stream, bush, field, sea, beach, and riverside are open and free to every nation with which the Indians are not embroiled in open conflict" (Shorto, 2004, p. 125). In this context, the sellers of land may have understood the transaction to be a diplomatic engagement and the resulting document and exchange of gifts to be analogous to a treaty testifying to the fact that the parties were not engaged in "open conflict." If so, the Native Americans may have understood that they were acknowledging the Dutch right to access and use the land but not to exclude the sellers from access and usufruct. Further, the ceremony affirming the state of peace between the Native American community that "sold" some of their land and the Dutch who "bought" it was not necessarily a one-time event. Peaceful relations required periodic renewal invariably accompanied by feasting and gift giving. Finally, since transactions were affirmations of friendly relations, there was no reason why access and use of any given territory could not be granted to more than one party.

[8]Since the seventeenth century guilder was stably pegged at 10.4 grams of silver, at year-end 2013 prices 60 1626 guilders would be worth about $430 (Kugler, 2013).

The Indian sachems didn't leave any first-person written records indicating whether or when they came to understand the Dutch point of view: that the deed of sale transferred the right, which would probably be exercised immediately after purchase, to restrict access to and use of a precisely demarcated parcel of land. But they did figure this out eventually. By the 1650s at the latest sachems were able to exploit conflicts among European settlers over land titles to maintain access and usufruct and/or receive additional payments. Historian Robert Grumet, who has delved extensively into colonial era deeds and court documents, relates several illustrative incidents.

> One of the longest-lasting land disputes in Munsee country occurred at Matinecock in the present-day Long Island towns of Hempstead, Huntington, and Oyster Bay. Much of this dispute centered on contested meanings of deed provisions...Dutch officials ... tended to take more nuanced views of such ambiguities than [the English] local townsfolk did. They could afford to see these deeds as preliminary agreements requiring future negotiation of the finer details ... Hempstead settlers in particular chose to regard their 1643 deed as a final sale. They did not feel that it was their job to keep paying off Indians to maintain peace...They only wanted them gone as soon as possible.
>
> The Indians, however, refused to go. Frustrated townsfolk dispatched a delegation to meet with Stuyvesant at Fort Amsterdam on August 23, 1647, seeking to get the Dutch to drive the Indians out.... Neither Stuyvesant nor ... the West India Company directors were inclined to indulge them at the expense of one of the colony's more dependable Indian allies.
>
> Massapequa and Matinecock sachems managed to sow further dissension among their English neighbors by subsequently selling adjoining, unclearly bounded tracts to rival townfolk. Arguments over [these] ... sales would embroil settlers for decades.

Sachems were able to further exploit these situations by providing corroborative testimony to the side of the dispute that treated them and their people the best.

The ambiguity regarding what exactly happened when land was sold seems to have been resolved fairly frequently in the Indian's favor.

And, as a result, colonists often had to "purchase" the same property more than once before secure European-style title could be established. This does not seem to have happened in the case of Manhattan Island, but Staten Island was apparently bought three times from three different groups of Indians and under the auspices of two different European governments. And even the final transaction "did not, however, put a complete end to Indian occupation."

Further, the fact that all sales were not necessarily final sheds some light on the issue of naiveté. To be sure, 60 seventeenth-century guilders, the equivalent of about 624 grams of silver, does seem like a very low price to pay for a future global city. More to the point, "[a] number of sources show that Indians in Munsee country soon learned that the prices they received for their land rarely matched what settlers were charged for the same parcel…." And in the dense, interlocking networks of a society where, as Penn wrote …, "wealth circulateth like the blood, information of such critical importance to so many people almost surely traveled fast and far" (Grumet, 2011, pp. 77–84).

Would a substantial price differential between European-European and Indian-European transactions necessarily indicate that the Native Americans were, as Grumet puts it "compelled to accept unequal exchanges?" In other words, should the law of one price have applied in this situation?

The economic "law" of one price states that identical, easily transportable goods should sell at the same price at any location or under any circumstances. If the prices of identical goods in different places or under different circumstances differ substantially, then an arbitrageur could buy the commodity in question where it was cheaper, sell it where it was more expensive, and earn a risk-free profit. The opportunity to make such "free money" would draw in a large number of potential arbitrageurs, and their added demand at the cheaper location and additional supply at the more expensive place would quickly bring the two markets into alignment.

Whether the law of one price should apply to this situation depends on whether European-European transactions were, except for price, identical to Indian-European transactions. This, in turn, depends on how often sales of land by Indians to Europeans resulted in unambiguous transfer of free and clear title to the property in a way that could not be legally challenged; the presumption being that all European-European transactions were legally sound. If the vast majority of Indian land sales were of this nature, then any price differential that continued over the long-term would be evidence of "unequal exchange." If, however, there was a high likelihood than any given Indian-European transaction would result in a legally or politically shaky claim, then the two types of land sales were not the same commodity. Purchase from a European got you clear title; purchase from an Indian may have gotten you no more than your day in a court where legal precedents *and* political considerations both carried weight.

Obviously, we don't have the kind of data we need to test the hypothesis that exchange was unequal in this respect. Circumstantial evidence, however, suggests that very little arbitrage was taking place. For one thing, Europeans do not seem to have been systematically buying parcels from Indians and then quickly selling them to other Europeans. In fact, some evidence suggests that attempts to "broker" New Netherland land were money-losers. As late as 1652, well after population growth had begun to accelerate, Cornelis van Werckhoven purchased land in Flatbush (in modern Brooklyn) with the intention of establishing a patroonship. As a patroon van Werckhoven would have gone on to lease the land to tenants, which, if profitable, would have constituted an instance of the arbitrage described above. Evidently, the Indian "owners" of this parcel had already contracted to sell the property to the WIC but not yet received full payment. The colony's governor at the time, Peter Stuyvesant, objected to Van Werckhoven's offer both because he believed the price was too high and because he didn't want to acquiesce in voiding a partly paid contract. In the event, Van Werckhoven, like all of the other would-be patroons other than Van Rensselaer, was unable to attract enough settlers to make the land purchase worthwhile.

Further, it is not as if there was any "rush" to buy Indian land. Grumet reports that the "amount of lost land came to a bit more than 10 percent of the total ancestral Munsee estate." The fact that much of this 10% was some of the best-located parts of the territory may have been balanced by the Indians' continuing ability to make use of the property after the sale transaction took place.

The original inhabitants of the region that became Greater New York were, of course, eventually completely displaced by Europeans and Africans. Many of the Munsee-speakers who survived repeated epidemics pioneered a pattern followed by subsequent generations of Americans of all origins; they moved westward. At new locations in the Ohio River Valley and the Great Lakes basin, they gradually assimilated into other Native American communities and eventually into the broad North American cultural amalgam.

Their departure from their ancestral homelands and abandonment of their traditional way of life was probably not entirely voluntary, and, no doubt, many Indian land-sale transactions were coerced or otherwise disadvantageous to the seller. But buyers, too, were often taken in and subsequently found themselves on the losing side of title disputes and/or paying more than once for the same parcel. There simply isn't enough evidence to support the assertion that the law of one price should have applied in this market or that, in general, Indian land sales during the Dutchcolony represented "unequal exchanges."

## The New Amsterdam Economy at the End of the Dutch Rule

By the end of the Dutch period, the population of New Netherland was somewhere between 5,000 and 9000 Europeans and Africans. In this regard, the colony lagged far behind New England and the Chesapeake colonies, with estimated 1660 populations of 33,000 and 38,000, respectively (U.S. Bureau of the Census, 1976). New Amsterdam's population may have been around 2500 and it may have been about half the size of Boston at the time. This population was likely typical of many Dutch small ports specializing in a niche economic activity, in this town's case the fur trade (Jacobs, 2009, p. 32; Rink, 1986, p. 158).

Despite this relatively unimpressive early record, the colony was well positioned to prosper in the context of the late seventeenth-century Atlantic economy. First, the Beverwyck-New Amsterdam, now Albany-New York City route had established itself as one of the only two channels for North American fur exports, still very much a viable economic base. That position was secure, given the relationship Dutch merchants had established with the Iroquois Confederation and, especially, with the Mohawks who maintained tight control on much of the flow of north country pelts to market. Second, New Netherlands farmers had succeeded in cultivating tobacco in industrial quantities. Third, transplanted New Englanders had brought with them their home region's diversified agricultural staples and fisheries economy, which thrived on Long Island. Fourth, the competitive but lucrative trading patterns of the fur market had nurtured numerous small and mid-sized, full- and part-time, female and male merchants with clear eyes for the main chance. Finally, while the colony's population may have been smaller than that of either the New England or the Chesapeake colonies, it was much more diverse with regard to national origin, language, and religion. As such, from its beginning, New York City formed a nexus of an unusually large number of affinity groups, and, with that, access to dense webs of personal contacts in Europe, Africa, and elsewhere in the Americas.

This combination of a reliable base industry, a productive agricultural sector, a scrappy trading community, and numerous intersecting networks of contacts around the Atlantic rim would stand New York in good stead for the next 150 years.

## References

Acemoglu, D. S. (2005). The Rise of Europe: Atlantic Trade, Institutional Change, and Economic Growth. *The American Economic Review, 95*(3), 546–579.

Allen, R. C. (2001). The Great Divergence in European Wages and Prices from the Middle Ages to the First World War. *Explorations in Economic History, 38*, 426.

Bachman, V. C. (1969). *Peltries or Plantations: The Economic Policies of the Dutch West India Company in New Netherland, 1623–1639*. Baltimore: The Johns Hopkins Press.

Bailyn, B. (2012). *The Barbarous Years: The Conflict of Civilizations: 1600–1675*. New York: Alfred A. Knopf.

Burrows, E. G. (1999). *Gotham: A History of New York City to 1898*. New York: Oxford University Press.

Ceci, L. (1980a). The First Fiscal Crisis in New York. *Economic Development and Cultural Change, 28*(4), 839–847.

Ceci, L. (1980b). *Locational Analysis of Historic Algonquin Sites in Coastal New York: A Preliminary Study* (Research Report 19). Proceedings of the Conference on Northeastern Archaeology, Anthropology Research Report Series. https://scholarworks.umass.edu/cgi/viewcontent.cgi?article=1006&context=anthro_res_rpt19nce.

Ceci, L. (1982). The Value of Wampum Among the New York Iroquois: A Case Study in Artifact Analysis. *Journal of Anthropological Research, 38*(1), 97–107.

Cohen, D. S. (1981). How Dutch Were the Dutch of New Netherland. *New York History, 62*(1), 47.

Crawford, G. W. (1996). Migration in Prehistory: Princess Point and the Northern Iroquoian Case: Comments. *American Antiquity, 61*(4), 782–790.

Crean, J. F. (1962). Hats and the Fur Trade. *The Canadian Journal of Economics and Political Science, 28*(3), 376.

Davis, K. G. (1974). *The North Atlantic World in the Seventeenth Century*. St. Paul: University of Minnesota Press.

de Vries, J., & van der Woude, A. (1997). *The First Modern Economy: Success, Failure, and Perseverance of the Dutch Economy, 1500–1815*. Cambridge: Cambridge University Press.

Gehring, C. T. (1992). Dutch and Indians in the Hudson Valley: The Early Period. *Hudson River Valley Review,* 9–25. http://www.hudsonrivervalley.org/review/pdfs/hvrr_9pt2_gehringandstarna.pdf.

Grumet, R. S. (2011). *First Manhattans: A Brief History of the Indians of Greater New York* (63rd ed.). Norman: University of Oklahoma Press.

Hart, J. P. (2008). Evolving the Three Sisters: The Changing Histories of Maize, Bean, and Squash in New York and the Greater Northeast. *Current Northeast Paleoethnobotany, II*, 87–88.

Jacobs, J. (1998). Between Repression and Approval: Connivance and Tolerance in the Dutch Republic and in New Netherland. *de Halve Maen, 71*(3), 57.

Jacobs, J. (2009). *The Colony of New Netherland: A Dutch Settlement in Seventeenth-Century America*. Ithaca: Cornell University Press.

Juet, R. (1909). The Third Voyage of Master Henry Hudson. In J. Franklin (Ed.), *Narratives of New Netherland, 1609–1664* (p. 14). New York: Scribner, Electronic Reproduction by General Books, 2009.

Kemp, S. (1998). Perceiving Luxury and Necessity. *Journal of Economic Psychology, 19*(6), 591–606.

Kugler, P. (2013). *The Changing Regime of the Pound/Guilder Exchange Rate 1600–1912.* Mimeo. Basel: University of Basel.

Maddison, A. (2001). *The World Economy: A Millennial Perspective.* Paris: Development Studies Center of the Organization for Economic Co-operation and Development.

Malanima, P. (2009). *Pre-modern European Economy: One Thousand Years (10th–19th Centuries).* Leiden: Brill.

McManus, J. C. (1972). An Economic Analysis of Indian Behavior in the North American Fur Trade. *The Journal of Economic History, 32*(1), 36–53.

Morrison, K. M. (1984). *The Embattled Northeast: The Elusive Ideal of Alliance in Abenaki-Euramerican Relations.* Berkeley: University of California Press.

Mullilgan, G. E., & Fik, T. J. (1994). Úsing Dummy Variables to Estimate Economic Base Multipliers. *Land Economics, 46*(3), 368–377.

Norton, T. E. (1974). *The Fur Trade in Colonial New York, 1686–1776.* Madison: University of Wisconsin Press.

O'Rourke, K. H., & Williamson, J. G. (1999). *Globalization and History: The Evolution of the Nineteenth-Century Atlantic Economy.* Cambridge, MA: MIT University Press.

O'Rourke, K. H., & Williamson, J. G. (2002). After Columbus: Explaining Europe's Overseas Trade Boom, 1500–1800. *The Journal of Economic History, 62*(2), 452–453.

Peña, E. S. (2001). The Role of Wampum Production at the Albany Almshouse. *International Journal of Historical Archaeology, 5*(2), 155–174.

Pettegree, A. (1996). The Politics of Toleration in the Free Netherlands, 1572–1620. In O. P. Grell & B. Scribner (Eds.), *Tolerance and Intolerance in the European Reformation* (pp. 182–198). Cambridge: Cambridge University Press.

Rapp, R. T. (1975). The Unmaking of the Mediterranean Trade Hegemony: International Trade Rivalry and the Commercial Revolution. *The Journal of Economic History, 35*(3), 499–525.

Rich, E. (1960, February). Trade Habits and Economic Motivation Among the Indians of North America. *The Canadian Journal of Economics and Political Science, 26*(1), 50.

Rich, E., & Wilson, C. (2008). *The Cambridge Economic History of Europe, Vol 5, The Economic Organization of Early Modern Europe* (Vol. 5). Cambridge: Cambridge University Press.
Richter, D. K. (1992). *The Ordeal of the Longhouse*. Chapel Hill: University of North Carolina Press.
Rink, O. (1981). The People of New Netherland: Notes on Non-English Immigration to New York in the Seventeenth Century. *New York History, 62*(1), 15, 18.
Rink, O. A. (1986). *Holland on the Hudson: An Economic and Social History of Dutch New York*. Ithaca: Cornell University Press.
Romney, S. S. (2014). *New Netherland Connections: Intimate Networks and Atlantic Ties in Seventeenth-Century America*. Chapel Hill: University of North Carolina Press.
Shorto, R. (2004). *The Island at the Center of the World: The Epic Story of Dutch Manhattan and the Forgotten Colony That Shaped America*. New York: Doubleday.
Snow, D. R. (1995). Migration in Prehistory: The Northern Iroquoian Case. *American Antiquity, 60*(1), 59–79.
Starna, W. A. (2009). American Indian Villages to Dutch Farms: The Settling of Settled Lands in the Hudson Valley. In R. Panetta, *Dutch New York: The Roots of Hudson Valley Culture* (p. 74). New York: Fordham University Press.
Stewart, R. M. (1989). Trade and Exchange in Middle Atlantic Region Prehistory. *Archaeology of Eastern North America, 17*(Fall), 47–78.
U.S. Bureau of the Census. (1976). *The Statistical History of the United States From Colonial Times to the Present* (p. 1061). New York: Basic Books.
Van der Donck, A. (1993). *A Dialogue Between a Netherland Patriot and a New Netherlander, on the Advantages of the County* (J. Johnson, Trans.). Ithaca, NY: Cornell University Library Digital Edition.
Van Zanden, J. L. (1995). Tracing the Beginning of the Kuznets Curve: Western Europe During the Early Modern Period. *The Economic History Review, New Series, 48*(4), 643–664.

# 2

# An Island in the Center of Its Hinterland

Over the course of the century and a half after 1664, when the English took control of New Netherlands, New York became a city of some consequence in the North Atlantic economy. At the beginning of 1664, New Amsterdam was small town supporting the North American fur-trading operations of the Dutch West India Company with a population of, perhaps, 2,500. In 1800, New York was very much a city, with a diverse manufacturing and service economy and a population of about 66,000.[1] It was the most populous municipality in North America at the time and, a bit larger than Bristol and a bit smaller than Glasgow, the seventh largest city in the English-speaking world (Jacobs, *The Colony of New Netherland: A Dutch Settlement in Seventeenth-Century America*, 2009, p. 32; New York State, Department of Economic Development, State Data Center, 2018; Schofield, 1994).

Throughout most of this period and in many respects—in its population, the range and organization of its economic activities, its governance, and its social and cultural life—New York was very similar to two other North American urban ports: Boston and Philadelphia

[1] 1800 U.S. Census, population of New York and Kings Counties.



A. Gurwitz, *Atlantic Metropolis*, Palgrave Studies in American Economic History,
https://doi.org/10.1007/978-3-030-13352-8_2

(Bridenbaugh, 1938, 1955). To be sure, there were differences among the three, and some of these differences would eventually contribute to New York taking its place at the apex of the United States system of cities. But while it was part of the British Empire, and during the early years of the Republic, New York City's economic development traced a very similar path to that of the other North American ports. All three grew rapidly through the eighteenth century, boosted by the expansion of West Indian sugar production; all three served as the principal "central places" of their economic hinterlands, and all three functioned as entrepôts within the burgeoning Atlantic trading economy. Although at points in time one of the three was more populous than the other two—first Boston, then Philadelphia, and, by the beginning of the nineteenth century, New York—during this period, none of them superseded the other two as *the* national urban center the ways London did in Britain or Amsterdam did in the Netherlands at the time or New York would eventually in the United States.

## Sugar and the Atlantic Economy

The transition from Dutch to English political control over the Hudson Valley was one early episode in a fundamental transformation of the Atlantic political economy. During the first half of the seventeenth century, the Atlantic Ocean was a theater of the nearly constant European religious conflict: the Dutch War of Independence, the Thirty Years War, and the English Civil War. Economic activity in the Caribbean and on the East Coast of North America during this period consisted largely of a series of speculative ventures. Sponsors hoped that these beachheads would enhance a combatant's strategic position and/or generate profits that could help pay the costs of waging war.

Over the decades after the mid-seventeenth century, when the religious wars ended, however, some of these early start-ups began to succeed. Most importantly, production of sugar by enslaved Africans on large factory farms on Caribbean islands became spectacularly successful. In the Chesapeake region of North America cultivation and of tobacco by a combination of free and forced labor also expanded rapidly. The extraction or cultivation and processing of other commodities—preserved fish, beaver pelts, indigo, mahogany, etc.—was also successful, although it is unlikely that the sourcing of these would have motivated the "peopling" of North America and the Caribbean to the same extent as the two boom crops.

The increasing supply of sugar products and high-grade tobacco met the expanding European bourgeois demand for luxuries. The rapid growth of these markets necessitated much more extensive movement of people and commodities between various Atlantic ports: slaves from Africa and settlers from Europe to the Americas, trade goods to exchange for the slaves, rice, wheat, corn, and fish to feed the slaves, salt to preserve the fish, manufactured capital goods to support farming and sugar refining, manufactured consumer goods for the growing American populations, and, of course, the sugar, tobacco, and other colonial exports themselves. Thus, after 1650, a process began that over the subsequent 100 years would lead to the development of a robust Atlantic trading economy.

This process was frequently accompanied by armed conflict among England, France, the Netherlands, Spain, and Portugal. But, whereas during the earlier period much economic activity in North America was, in part, at least, a tactic in an ideological conflict, by the late seventeenth and early eighteenth centuries, imperial economic aggrandizement became a fundamental goal of public policy and, frequently, a war aim. England—after 1707, the UK—won more of these wars than it lost so that by the late eighteenth century it was appropriate to describe the North Atlantic trading activity as the British Empire of Goods.

The transformation of the Atlantic economy drove the concurrent development of British North America and of its urban centers. Although one can discern some pre-1664 developments that presaged subsequent changes, in 1650 New York was still little more than one of the handful of European speculative ventures along the North American coast. Through most of the eighteenth century, by contrast, New York City's principal export base was, like Boston's and Philadelphia's, as a producer of diversified commercial services—shipping, factoring, brokerage, dealing, wholesale distribution, specialty retailing, credit intermediation, and information processing—all related directly to the movement of goods around the Atlantic region and most related indirectly to the production of sugar and tobacco.

Ports have two broad economic functions. First, they serve their hinterlands as a transshipment point for locally produced exports and for imports to be sold to local consumers. Second, they can serve as an entrepôt: a transshipment point for goods originating elsewhere and destined to find a final buyer outside the port's hinterland. For example, some bolts of Irish linen might arrive in New York and then, as part of an original plan or because no local buyer could be found, be reloaded for shipment to, say, Jamaica. Most ports provide a mix of both of these functions, but it is unlikely that a vibrant entrepôt could develop absent a reliably high volume of shipping traffic bringing goods from producers or to final buyers located in the port city itself or its hinterland. So, the initial concern of this chapter is to understand how the post-1650 takeoff of the Atlantic economy affected New York City's eighteenth-century economic backcountry: northeastern New Jersey, western Long Island, southwestern New England, and the Hudson-Mohawk watershed.

## Economic Takeoff

During the 1950s, economist Walter Rostow characterized economic development leading to self-sustained growth in per capita production as occurring in three sequential stages:

> [a] long period (up to a century or, conceivably, more) when the preconditions for take-off are established; the take-off itself, defined within two or three decades; and a long period when growth becomes normal and relatively automatic. (Rostow, 1956, p. 29)

He went on to identify three related individually necessary and collectively sufficient conditions for a successful takeoff:

a. a rise in the rate of productive investment from (say) 5% or less to over 10% of national income….;

b. the development of one or more substantial manufacturing sectors, with a high rate of growth;
c. the existence or quick emergence of a political, social and institutional framework which exploits the impulses to expansion in the modern sector and the potential external economy effects of the take-off and gives to growth an on-going character (Rostow, 1956, p. 32).

Finally, Rostow associates takeoff with the growth of "leading sectors" of the economy. Newfound profitability of one or more *primary growth sectors* creates the initial impetus for acceleration. Growth of the primary sector, in turn, necessitates the expansion of several *supplementary growth sectors*, "where rapid advance occurs in direct response to – or as a requirement of – advance in the primary growth sector" (Rostow, 1956, p. 43). The broad changes in the economy brought about by the rapid expansion of the primary and supplementary sectors stimulate activity in *derived growth sectors* which prosper in the new environment of rising per capita incomes.

The changes that took place around the Atlantic world during the 150 years after 1650 conform quite neatly with Rostow's paradigm. The "preconditions" were the previous 150 years of European economic experimentation on the American continents. The Caribbean sugar industry was the primary growth sector, expansion of which increased demand for the products of supplementary growth sectors, the slave market in West Africa and food staples and naval stores produced in North America. The growth of sugar production also stimulated the development a wide range of mercantile service activities, the derived growth sectors. As was the case in Boston and Philadelphia, New York City's hinterland produced food staples for export to the Caribbean, and New York City's merchant community seized the opportunities created by the expansion of the volume of Atlantic basin trade.

## The Preconditions

The Atlantic economy could not have taken off unless Europeans had frequented, lived, and tried to make money in the Americas for long enough to discover what this New World was and was not good for.

Nor could the takeoff have occurred absent means to buy slaves in West Africa and convey them to labor camps in the Americas.

Europeans experienced a series of disappointments during the early post-contact decades. North America, it turned out was not a good place to produce silk or wine. The land mass was too impenetrable to serve as a way station for trade with Asia. Commercial quantities of precious metals were, at this point, only found in South America and Mexico. A century of half of exploration and experimentation did reveal, however, that with the right combinations of factors of production in place the Americas could produce commercially worthwhile quantities of fish, furs, wood and wood products, tobacco, and sugar.

Provision of one of those factors of production, labor, was, however, problematic. Wars of conquest and, especially, infectious diseases had decimated the indigenous populations. And too few Europeans were willing to migrate to America to undertake onerous labor under harsh conditions. So, the institutions and mechanisms for capturing Africans as slaves and transporting them to the Americas that had developed beginning early in the sixteenth century were preconditions for the development of the American economies during the seventeenth, eighteenth, and early nineteenth centuries.

## The Primary and Supplementary Growth Sectors

People traveled to and settled in North America and the Caribbean to make a living sourcing all of these goods, but it was sugar that provided the impetus for the Atlantic takeoff. As such, this commodity exerted a powerful, if indirect, influence on New York City's economic history. By rights, a sugar cane plant may deserve depiction on the City's corporate seal as much as the beavers and barrels of flour that do appear.

Fishing, fur trading, and forestry were moneymakers but could not have served as the primary sector for an American growth take off because none of these activities required a large, non-indigenous, year-round workforce. Indeed, as the Dutch West India Company and English fishing interests discovered, a large resident population of Europeans could increase the costs of doing business, make it harder for a would-be monopolist to restrict potential competitors' entry, or both (Davis, 1974, pp. 162–163, 172). Until the markets for tobacco and sugar began to expand rapidly, therefore, population growth in North America and the Caribbean was very slow.

Tobacco cultivation and processing, however successful an industry it may have been, was also an unlikely primary takeoff sector. Starting in the third decade of the seventeenth-century land area devoted to tobacco cultivation expanded rapidly throughout the English and Dutch North American settlements, albeit, except in the Chesapeake region, mostly as a sideline. Over the 80 years after 1620, the volume of English imports of this product, largely from Virginia and Maryland, increased by at least 430-fold or at an average compound annual rate of 7.9% (Davis, 1974, p. 146). The rapid growth of the market, however, did not require large increments of labor or capital inputs. Once tree cover is removed by girdling so that sunlight can reach the plants, it is easy to bring in a marketable crop of tobacco quickly for a few years. Warehouses must be constructed where the harvested leaves can be dried and packed for shipping, but these can be minimal structures. Tobacco does deplete the soil quickly and a workforce must be fed and housed, so maintaining and expanding production requires ever increasing increments of land area under cultivation. But suitable space for expansion of both the cash crop and of food for local consumption was readily available on the sparsely populated North American continent, especially so after indigenous populations were decimated. The labor requirements of tobacco cultivation were modest relative to what sugar planters needed. And, given conditions in the early seventeenth-century British labor market, the temperate climate of the Chesapeake region, and the opportunities available to indentured servants at the end of their contract period, it was possible to attract free labor for this work. But some forced migration via the slave trade was also evidently required, albeit in nowhere near the numbers needed in the Caribbean. Only 5.6% of the slaves brought from Africa to the Western Hemisphere between 1651 and 1750 arrived in the British mainland North American colonies (Eltis, 2001). In sum, the marginal cost of production was low and, as planters accumulated experience, was probably declining. So, supply continued to increase rapidly even as the price of the product declined by 85% between 1630 and 1645 and continued generally downward thereafter (Davis, 1974, p. 151). In the context of Rostow's framework, therefore, Tobacco cultivation, by itself, did not stimulate the expansion of enough activity in "supplementary growth" activities to generate sustained, broad-based development.

The first commercial production of sugar on a Caribbean island was on Barbados in the late 1630s. The remarkable, widely publicized success of this experiment inspired imitators on other islands. Eventually, sugar production came to account for the lion's share of Atlantic trade and of population growth in the Americas; from 1660 through the colonial period, the value of British imports of sugar exceeded the combined value of all other colonial imports (Mintz, 1985, p. 44).

Sugar is not easy to produce at maximum efficiency using seventeenth-century technology. Fields need to be cleared completely. Cane is ready for processing about 18 months after planting, but only certain times of year are optimal for harvesting and processing. For this reason, scheduling seasonal work in the fields can be a complex process. Cane cutting is difficult and exhausting work. To prevent spoilage, the cane must go through the initial phase of processing—pressing in a mill and boiling in a sugar house to concentrate the juice—immediately post-harvest. All of this requires large inputs of gang labor organized under harsh conditions and intense time pressure. And then the semi-processed product—molasses or muscovado (brown) sugar—must be packed and stored for shipment. A second processing stage, refinement into white sugar or distillation into rum, which took place closer to the point of final consumption in Europe or North America, were also technologically complex industrial processes.

Sugar cultivation and production were surely one of the seventeenth century's most capital-intensive industries. A would-be sugar planter had to acquire control over a substantial area of land; because of the long growing period, the difficulty of coordinating planting, harvest, and initial refining, and the importance of proximity of mill and boiling house to the fields, small-scale production was not successful. Further, a large part of the cost of plantation labor was paid to slave traders before production could begin. Finally, the mill and sugar boiling facilities, some of the most extensive and elaborate industrial equipment in use during the early modern period, needed to be imported. All in all, the fixed costs of establishing an efficient Caribbean sugar plantation during the seventeenth century ran into the thousands of pounds at a time when a "middling" urban lifestyle might have been sustained on about 100 pounds per year (Emsley, Hitchcock, & Shoemaker, 2018; Mintz, 1985, p. 49).

Demand was growing quickly enough to generate competitive returns on investments of this magnitude. But, much more than fish, furs, or tobacco, the build-out of the sugar industry as a primary growth sector required large quantities of a wide range of inputs produced by secondary growth sectors. Such secondary sectors included both "backward" and "forward" linkages. The former are industries that produce inputs to the primary sector. The latter use the primary sector's product as an input and are required to make the primary output profitably marketable. The sugar industry's backward linkages included, first and foremost, the slave trade, and producers and processors of food to feed slaves and their drivers. Most food was imported so as to keep as much of the limited Caribbean land as possible in sugar production. Backward linkages also included, the slave market, suppliers of milling and boiling equipment and fuel for the fires, a large merchant fleet to transport slaves, food, the final product, and the myriad of other commodities necessary to make life on a Caribbean plantation at least tolerable for owners and free workers. Finally, the industry could not have developed absent a flow of mercantile services to organize and finance the transport of all of these goods. The forward linkages included the sugar refining and rum distilling industries.

## Derived Growth Sectors

Unlike fish, furs, or even tobacco, the expansion of the sugar industry did require the establishment of a substantial, permanent population in the Americas. In the Caribbean itself, residents included the field workers, mostly slaves, the skilled laborers, some slave and some free or indentured, to operate the mills and boiling houses, plantation managers, some non-absentee plantation owners, and small port-town populations to process, physically and financially, the flow of goods on and off the islands. North America needed farmers and fishermen to produce wheat, corn, rice, preserved meat, and salt cod for the Caribbean populations, middlemen to process, physically and financially, the exports produced locally, and merchants to import and distribute imports to meet the needs of the resident population. As the North American resident, populations grew the variety of goods and services that could be produced locally at efficient scale increased. So, over the course of the eighteenth century, each increment of increased sugar production led to increasingly larger impacts on the aggregate size and diversity North American economic activity.

## The New York Hinterland's Slow Start

One of Kiliaen van Rensselaer's hopes for his Hudson River patroonship was that it would produce food for export to the Dutch sugar plantations in Brazil. This expectation was prescient but about a century premature and somewhat misdirected geographically. Not until well into the eighteenth century were British North American colonies exporting substantial amounts of fish, meat, and flour and bread. And these goods were shipped, not to Brazil, which had returned to Iberian control, but mostly to the British, Dutch, French, and Danish colonies in the West Indies.

The demand for these food exports created an opportunity for farmers and fishermen, and their service providers to make a good living in North America. This potential for higher real incomes, in turn, in combination with labor market trends in Britain, boosted immigration rates. Before the 1760s, however, relatively few of these immigrants chose to settle in the Province of New York. Thereafter, just as emigration from Great Britain began to accelerate rapidly, New York became a very popular destination. The province's slow start and the timing of the turnaround in its popularity attracted attention from contemporaries and from historians of the period. It turns out that there are several plausible explanations.

## Farmland and Farmers

Economic historians have assembled data on *legal* exports by commodity type and colonial region for the years between 1768 and 1772. Essentially, all of the 13 colonies' fish and fish products exports were shipped by New Englanders from a Massachusetts port (Boston, Marblehead, or Salem). New England was also the source of three-quarters of the colonies' 1770 exports of livestock and meat. These products, along with a small volume of grain and grain products, accounted for 80% of New England's exports.

Delaware, New Jersey, New York, and Pennsylvania, the "middle colonies," together accounted for 53% of the 13 colonies exports of grain and grain products, and this category accounted for 72% of the Middle Atlantic region's exports. Almost all of this volume would have been shipped from either Philadelphia or New York. Since most colonists were engaged in farming, the relative magnitude of export activity at the two ports would have been roughly proportional to their respective hinterlands' populations. At about 200,000, the population of New York City and its hinterland in 1760 was about 40% smaller than Philadelphia's 280,000, and in a primarily agricultural economy like that of eighteenth-century North America that would have resulted in less exports and a less active port[2] (Carter, 2006; McCusker & Menard, 1985).

One reason why New York's hinterland was so much smaller than Philadelphia's is geographic and would be obvious to anyone who has travelled through the respective river valleys in which the two Cities are located, the Hudson and the Delaware. The former, which constituted a large part of New York City's hinterland in the eighteenth century, is, for most of its length, very narrow and hemmed in on both sides by steep, wide highlands. Philadelphia's Delaware Valley is broad, flat,

---

[2]By 1760, New York City's economic hinterland included the Hudson Valley, the lower Mohawk River valley, and most of Long Island, northeastern New Jersey and southwestern Connecticut. Assume, therefore, that the population the City's hinterland included all New Yorkers plus half of New Jersey's and one-quarter of Connecticut's populations. Philadelphia's hinterland at the time encompassed all of Pennsylvania's population, the other half of New Jersey's, all of Delaware's, and, perhaps, 10% of Maryland's.

and fertile in most places. To be sure, there is plenty of good farmland in New York's vicinity, in northern New Jersey, on Long Island. And, as will become apparent, the Mohawk Valley, Finger Lakes basin, and the Great Lakes littoral had huge economic potential. But in the seventeenth and eighteenth centuries, Philadelphia was at the staple port of a much more extensive potential "bread basket" than was New York.

Further, New York's geographic position on the front line of the Anglo-French wars that continued, on and off, between 1688 and 1763 discouraged settlement in the province. For one thing, settlers, who might have been attracted to the Mohawk valley by its agricultural potential and access to markets, must have been put off by memories of the 1690 French and Indian attack on Schenectady, a British settlement in that region, that left scores dead and captured. Southeastern Pennsylvania, the area that was being settled through most of the early eighteenth century, was farther from the fighting. Second, because each colony was responsible for financing its own defense, New York's provincial taxes were apparently more burdensome than other colonies' (Kammen, 1975). High exactions, in money or in militia duty, would have discouraged new settlement in New York and may have induced some of the residents, even of places like New York City or Long Island, both remote from the fighting, to move elsewhere.

## To the Manor Borne?

The Province's land tenure system may also have slowed settlement. Proprietors of the Britain's middle colonies, where slave labor played a smaller role than in the south, could choose between two broad strategies to meet the fundamental challenge of inducing European migrants to settle as farmers in a wilderness. One way of peopling a colony, the "headright" system, was to develop a society of yeoman farmers by offering individual migrants subsidized access to land of their own. The second way was to grant large blocks of land to entrepreneurs who would then be expected to populate their "manors" or "patents" with tenant farmers. New England's and Pennsylvania's authorities adopted the headright strategy. The Chesapeake colonies generally adopted the latter approach. Although there were many family-owned farms in New York, especially on Long Island, the Province's early British governors opted to award large grants of Hudson Valley land to individual entrepreneurs. Numerous, political jurisdictions, and city streets around New York State bear the names of these manor lords' families: the Philipses, the Livingstons, the van Cortlandts, the DeLancys, and the Rensselaers.

Initially, at least, the headright strategy seemed to be a much more successful way of peopling a colony than the manor lord approach. All else held equal, most early modern Englishmen would have preferred to develop their own property than to lease and pay rent on someone else's and, thus, might opt to settle in Pennsylvania or New Hampshire rather than New York. Further, a yeoman farmer had no choice but to clear and begin cultivating his land immediately in order to support his family and pay his taxes. The manor lords had other sources of income; many of the initial grantees were merchants who viewed their agricultural ventures as diversifying sidelines, not as a primary source of livelihood. So, these large landholders could, within limits, afford to delay paying the fixed costs of bringing tenants from Europe and starting up their farms until conditions in the Atlantic grain market warranted doing so.

The manorial system may have slowed but did not completely stymie population growth and economic development in New York City's Hudson Valley hinterland. For one thing, migrants with enough money to pay for their own passage but not enough to buy livestock and other capital goods and feed themselves while waiting for the first crop to come in would have had no choice but to sign on as a tenant or a laborer on a manor. In addition, postponing development was not costless for manor lords. The province levied a quitrent—essentially an annual property tax levied by the provincial proprietor—at a non-trivial 1.25–2.5% of the early eighteenth-century purchase price of farmland in the lower Hudson Valley.

It is impossible to estimate the relative impacts of these Provincial characteristics—geography, geopolitics, and land tenure policy—on the pace of New York's population growth during the seven decades of British rule. But contemporary observers and historians of the period have assigned the manorial system a great deal of the blame for the Provinces relatively sluggish advancement. In 1716, for example, General Robert Hunter, then serving as New York's Governor, reported to the Lords of Trade, the British governmental body overseeing the colonies that: "It is apparent that extravagant tracts of land being held by single persons unimproved is the true cause that this Province does not increase in numbers of inhabitants in proportion to some of the neighboring ones" (Kim, 1978, p. 237). Two hundred years later historian Frederick Jackson Turner echoed General Hunter's assertion: "The most important aspect of the history of the movement into the frontier of New York at this period, therefore, was the evidence which it afforded that in the competition for settlement between colonies possessing a vast area of vacant land, those which imposed feudal tenures and undemocratic restraints, and which exploited settlers, were certain to lose. The manorial practice gave a bad name to New York as a region for settlement, which not even the actual opportunities in certain parts of the colony could counteract" (Turner, 1920).

One particular incident illustrates the view that New York's land tenure policies were a serious impediment to rapid population growth. In 1709, the British government dispatched a group of 3000 German Protestant refugees to New York. The idea was that they would be resettled in the Hudson or Mohawk valleys where they would produce maritime stores for the Royal Navy. When they arrived in the colony, the Provincial government apparently was not sure what to do with them. After a long wait in tents on Governor's Island, the group was sent to the Livingston Manor in Albany County, where they did set to work on their assignment. Dissatisfied with their serf-like status, the group migrated to a then-remote region west of the Hudson. When title to their new homes was invalidated the group subsequently responded favorably to a generous offer from the Pennsylvania government to resettle in that territory. There is some evidence that this episode left New York with a tarnished reputation relative to that of Pennsylvania among the numerous subsequent German immigrants (Proper, 1900, p. 37).

More recent scholarship, however, has called the assessment that the "manorial" system was an important impediment to New York's growth into question on several grounds. First, widespread tenantry was not confined to New York and the other "manorial" colonies: A large proportion of the adult populations of the "headright" colonies were also either tenants or laborers on others' property. In 1760, for example, about 45% of the married couples and single men of Chester County, Pennsylvania, an agricultural region near Philadelphia, were landless (Henretta, 1978). So, the difference between land tenure experiences of New Yorkers and Pennsylvanians may have been less dramatic than Hunter and Turner claimed.

Second, working as a tenant on a manor did not necessarily lead to a "dead-end" career path. The manorial system that evolved in New York was far from "feudal." Most importantly, tenants owned the "improvements" on the property they farmed. Thus, at the termination of a lease, if rents had been paid in full, the manor lord would owe the tenant the difference between the value of cleared and uncleared land and of buildings, orchards, and other capital assets on the property. Also, leases on manorial land, terms on which ranged from one year to perpetuity, were treated as liquid assets within the colonial economy and were apparently actively purchased and sold, sometimes by nonresident speculators or arbitrageurs. Farming for some years as a tenant, accumulating equity in improvements, liquidating these assets, and redeploying the capital into an independent farm was apparently a feasible economic life cycle pattern for many colonials in New York and elsewhere.

Third, the rapid expansion of the Province's population after the 1763 British victory in Canada supports the alternative view that New York's position on the front line of the French and Indian Wars had been impeding population growth. By the 1770s, New York was attracting more British farming families as immigrants than any other colony and substantially more than its rival Middle Atlantic province, Pennsylvania. These immigrants were settling as tenants on manors north of Albany or West of the Hudson that had previously been exposed to military incursions.

Fourth, post-1763 British emigrants who cited the "tyranny of landlords" as a reason for leaving their homeland were evidently quite willing to settle in New York. Migration to New York's frontier was part of a larger mid-century movement of population from the British Isles to North America. When emigration to North America began to accelerate after 1760 concerns arose among some British landowners and government officials about a possible depletion of population in parts of the

Kingdom. As part of an effort to assess the magnitude of this problem, port officials were instructed to record information about passengers embarking in England and Scotland and bound for the American colonies. Data were assembled between 1773 and 1775 and consolidated in London. Although the information is incomplete—many emigrants may have escaped official notice and reporting practices were not uniform—historian Bernard Bailyn makes a strong case that these data paint a true-to-life portrait of British emigration and American immigration during the period (Bailyn, 1988).

Of the total 9,364 individuals recorded in Bailyn's database, about 20% intended to settle in New York. About 25% of the migrants recorded in the Register were headed to Maryland, the only more popular destination than New York. But this differential probably understates New York's relative attractiveness. As part of his assessment of the quality of the data Bailyn points out that "…[c]omparisons of the Register lists with the notices of ship arrivals in Maryland newspapers and with Maryland customs records shows, for example, an underregistration at the British exit ports of 17% for ships and 12% for people… Similar evidence for New York shows an even higher rate of omission: 33 percent of all vessels and at least 39 percent of all travelers that arrived in New York City were missed by customs officials when they left Britain …" (Bailyn, 1988, p. Loc. 2256/13769). Further, compared with most other colonies' experience during this period, New York's immigrants were more likely to be complete farming families. Of the migrants headed for one of the 13 colonies for whom information on previous occupation is available, 17% reported that they had been farmers. For New York, the figure was 31%; only North Carolina's percentage, at 39%, was higher (Bailyn, 1988, p. Loc. 4146/13769).

Finally, despite the fact that many of them worked as manorial tenants, it does not appear that New Yorkers were on average worse-off in terms of living standards than other North Americans during the eighteenth century. There is, in fact, some evidence that the average New Yorker's standard of living was relatively high. There are no contemporary statistics on real incomes in different colonies. It is reasonable to assume, however, that under eighteenth-century conditions differences in the standard of living would be reflected in how well children were fed. If so, we can measure real income differences by comparing the stature of adults who grew up in different regions. In a careful statistical analysis of data on the stature of French and Indian (1756–1763) and Revolutionary (1775–1783) war recruits into the American army economic historians Kenneth Sokoloff and Georgia Villaflor found that, all else, including occupation and birthplace, held equal, recruits who grew up in New York, were on average, three-quarters of an inch taller than New Englanders and Pennsylvanians and about the same height as Southerners (Sokoloff & Villaflor, 1982). Based on this evidence, it would be hard to conclude that living standards in New York were lower than in other colonies during the second quarter of the eighteenth century.

This post-1760 acceleration notwithstanding, by 1775, at about 277,000, the population of New York City's hinterland was still only two-thirds' the size of Philadelphia's 411,000 (Carter, 2006). And the difference between the two cities' populations closely reflected the relative size of their hinterlands. New York City's 1775 population of perhaps about 25,000 accounted for about 9% of the city plus hinterland total. The equivalent figure for Philadelphia's 35,000 population was also close to 9% (Rosenwaike, 1972; U.S. Census Bureau, 2018).

## A Central Place

Since the earliest Dutch settlement there had been farms in the colony. Initially, the economic role of agriculture was to produce food for local consumption; fur traders and local service-providers needed to eat while waiting for Indians to show up with pelts, and the colony's proprietors judged that local production was more cost-effective than imports. By the early eighteenth century, however, food and food products had become the Province's principal export industry.

Economic geographers have theorized about how towns—places, where dispersed farm families can travel to exchange their food surplus for goods and services they can't produce on their own—emerge in the midst of agricultural regions. "Central place theory" describes the process by which hierarchies of villages, small towns, big towns, and cities form within in such geographic regions. The smallest of these towns, the local market centers serving, perhaps, a few dozen farm families are the most numerous central places. Residents of the smallest towns and their surrounding farms, in turn, travel to larger towns to acquire goods and services that cannot be produced efficiently on a small scale. These large towns will also serve as local market centers for the farmers in their immediate vicinity. Residents of the large towns will travel to cities to acquire goods and services that can only be produced efficiently at very large scale. There will be fewer large towns than small towns and fewer cities than large towns. In most regions, one "metropolis," the only center for production of goods and services characterized by the most powerful economies of scale.

Further, to minimize aggregate transportation costs, central places tend to be centrally located. The abstract models that describe the process of hierarchy formation envision a region in which individual farm households are dispersed uniformly across a "flat, featureless plain extending indefinitely in all directions." In this abstract world, the smallest towns are located at the geometric center of a group of farms; each of the larger towns is centralized within their hinterlands of smaller towns, and the metropolis is at the geometric center of its surrounding big towns.

The economic geography of colonial North America appears to have developed in just this way (Lemon, 1967). Of course, the East Coast of North America is not a flat, featureless plain. Towns tended to be located in the most accessible places, at the confluences of navigable streams or at sheltered harbors. In each region—New England, the Hudson Valley, the Delaware Valley, the Chesapeake Bay—relatively numerous villages and small towns served as market centers, where farmers brought their crops for milling and marketing and where small-scale craftsmen, such as blacksmiths, offered their services. The small-town blacksmith looking to replace a damaged forge, a prosperous farmer seeking a fine piece of dinnerware, or a property owner suing an encroaching neighbor would travel to a larger town. The large-town shopkeeper looking to stock up for the fall season might travel to the regional metropolis where a number of wholesalers might be offering what was needed at competitive prices.

New York City was the metropolis for its hinterland. A list of the occupations of the 203 apprentices whose indentures were filed with the City between 1718 and 1727 (Table 2.1) gives some indication of the range of goods and services available in this high-order central place. Several of the occupations on the list—shipwright, mariner, sailmaker, the large number of coopers—reflect the City's role as a port. And more than a few of the bakers may have been producing hardtack for seafarers. Other occupations—blacksmith, shoemaker, and carpenter, for example—would have been found in much smaller towns throughout the colony, although some of those who plied these trades in the City might have been more specialized. One would have encountered "merchants," a term that encompassed shopkeepers in eighteenth-century America, in all but the smallest towns. It is unlikely, however, that one would find glovers, resident limners, periwigmakers, felt makers, highly specialized woodworkers, goldsmiths, hatters, printers, saddlers, silversmiths, tobacconists, or braziers outside of the largest city in a region. These top-level, market demand-oriented occupations account for 20% of the registered apprenticeship indentures. New York City was clearly the metropolis of the region. But why?

## How "Central" Was New York City

Central place theory describes how market forces lead to the development of hierarchies of small towns, large towns, cities, and a metropolis in a geographic region. The theory also implies that the metropolis will be located at the geographic "center" of the region, if we define "center" as the location that minimizes aggregate transportation costs for those who need to travel from their residences to the metropolis. The theory is, however, silent as to what constitutes an economic region in this context. To say that the region is the area for which the metropolis is the premier central place is circular. No doubt, New York City was the metropolis for its hinterland as we've defined it. But did the Hudson and Mohawk Valleys, Long Island, northeastern New Jersey and southwestern Connecticut have anything in common other than that their metropolis was New York City? Why, for example, didn't most of Long

**Table 2.1** Occupations of apprenticeships registered in the city of New York, 1718–1727 (Kammen, 1975, pp. 182–183)

| Occupation | Number |
|---|---|
| Cordwainer (shoemaker) | 38 |
| Joiner (specialty carpenter) | 13 |
| Shipwright | 12 |
| Cooper (barrel-maker) | 10 |
| Barber and wigmaker | 9 |
| Blacksmith | 8 |
| Glover | 8 |
| Mariner | 6 |
| Baker | 6 |
| Felt maker | 6 |
| Turner (lathe operator) | 5 |
| Merchant | 5 |
| Carpenter | 4 |
| Tailor | 4 |
| Goldsmith | 4 |
| Hatter | 3 |
| Weaver | 3 |
| Printer | 3 |
| Tanner and Currier (leathergoods finisher) | 2 |
| Limner (portrait painter) | 2 |
| Butchers | 2 |
| Periwigmakers (powdered wigmaker) | 2 |
| Saddler | 2 |
| Gunsmith | 2 |
| Sailmaker | 2 |
| Silversmith | 2 |
| Pulley maker | 2 |
| Reaper | 1 |
| Painter | 1 |
| Leather dresser | 1 |
| "Inginnear" | 1 |
| Boatman | 1 |
| Tabacconist | 1 |
| Brazier (brass-worker) | 1 |
| Currier | 1 |
| General service | 30 |

Island remain part of Boston's hinterland given higher cost of moving goods and people overland than by water during the eighteenth century? Or why didn't people living in northeastern New Jersey look to

Philadelphia as the place to buy their periwigs, leaving New York City to serve as nothing higher order than their local big town? Was New York City's metropolitan role inevitable or was it contingent?

In retrospect, it looks inevitable: fully pre-determined by geography and market forces. From its origin as a fur-trading factory through the colonial period, the colony's economic base involved the export of commodities, and New York's harbor is easily accessible, well-sheltered, deep, and usually ice-free. Further, because the Hudson "River" is a tidal estuary, two-way flows facilitate both up- and down-stream transportation between the port and much of its hinterland. It was likely, therefore, that New York would have been a cost-effective location for ocean-going vessels to load and unload cargoes. By itself, however, the quality of the harbor did not determine the location of a regional central place during this period. Philadelphia's harbor is far inferior to New York's; approaches to the former are shallower and more treacherous, the Delaware River flows in only one direction, quite powerfully at times and places, and freezes much more frequently in the wintertime than the salty Hudson. But Philadelphia was the metropolis for its region and substantially more populous than New York City for most of the eighteenth century.

Further, New York's position as an important North American port was successfully challenged by Boston during the first decade of the eighteenth century. At that time, just as the sugar boom and associated demand for grain products was expanding rapidly, New York's most productive agricultural region may have been Long Island. The eastern towns on the Island had been settled by New Englanders, who's geographic, cultural, and economic ties were closer with Boston than New York City. Further, Boston-based merchants were evidently aggressive in efforts to expand their share of Atlantic trade. So, as Michael Kammen reports:

> In 1696, forty square-rigged vessels, sixty-two sloops, and as many boats were entered at the New York customhouse. In 1700 [Governor] Bellomont reported that forty-three topsail vessels and eighty-one sloops belonged to the port of New York. Eight years later [Governor] Cornbury found only twenty-eight of both. What could possibly have caused such a dramatic decline? Wartime losses, in part; but principally the Boston

> carriers had simply driven New York's merchant marine from their own port. New Englanders offered lower rates and thereby dominated New York commerce between 1702 and 1709…Exports from the port of New York in 1706 had fallen to one-sixth of what they were in 1700. The value of imports from London was only 40 percent of what it had been in 1700. (Kammen, 1975, pp. 151–152)

Bostonians were eventually thwarted in their efforts to corner New York's Atlantic maritime services market, and Long Island farmers eventually shipped most of the exports through New York City. Surely market forces played some role in preserving New York's metropolitan status. As Long Island, agriculture reached its maximum capacity increments of production increasingly came from northeastern New Jersey and the Hudson Valley. Boston was not the transport cost-minimizing staple port for these farmers.

## The Political Economy of Centrality

On several occasions in its early history, however, New York's position in the North American hierarchy of central places was boosted, not by decentralized market forces, but by decisions of its governing authorities. Some of these decisions may simply have validated outcomes that were market-driven. But some of them reflected considerations other than profit maximization or transportation-cost minimization.

The earliest example is the decision by the Dutch West India Company to concentrate settlement in the southern end of the Hudson Valley. Dutch territorial ambitions in North America covered the entire area between the English settlements around the Chesapeake in the south and New England in the north, and, evidently, the initial plan was to establish four colonies: one near the confluence of the Mohawk and Hudson rivers and three more at the mouths of the Delaware, Hudson, and Connecticut Rivers. Second thoughts concerning the vulnerability of tiny isolated settlements led to the subsequent decision to concentrate the population in one place, and Manhattan was centrally located (Rink, O. A., *Holland on the Hudson: An Economic and*

*Social History of Dutch New York*, 1986). There would have been a lot to be said in favor of Fort Orange (Albany) as the optimal central location; it was best positioned to tap into the flow of beaver pelts. The fact that the upper Hudson River wasn't accessible during the winter would not have been a problem because that was the season when beaver were being hunted. Pelts were brought to market in the spring, when ocean-going vessels could sail that far north. Shipping directly and only from Fort Orange might have helped keep the Hudson Valley beaver trade tightly controlled by the WIC and reduced some of the smuggling of pelts that ate into the company's profits. But, after four WIC employees, including Dutch commander at Fort Orange, were killed in a war among local Indians, Peter Minuit, the WIC commander in New Netherland, appeased the victorious Mohawks by relocating the settlers to Manhattan and leaving only an lightly staffed, unthreatening trading post in place (Rink, 2009). One can question Minuit's judgment in this regard. The right business decision may have been to give the Mohawks more generous gifts to get them to accept a more populous settlement at Fort Orange and station no more than a small military force on Manhattan, as was being done at the mouths of the Delaware and Connecticut River.

The decision to concentrate New Netherland's population so far from the source of furs had adverse consequences for the WIC and for New Netherlands' trading economy. It was evidently too tempting for fur vessels to sail directly to Fort Orange, perhaps buying furs along the way from itinerant traders or Hudson Valley patroons, and, thereby, dodging the WIC's charges. To limit this form of smuggling in 1633, local commander Wouter van Twiller granted New Amsterdam as the status of "staple port" of New Netherland. "By virtue of this concession vessels carrying merchandise up or down the river had to stop at New Amsterdam and pay duties whether they discharged their cargoes there or not" (Shepherd, 1917). The requirement that all ships sailing to or from the Hudson Valley stop at New Amsterdam gave local merchants an advantage over other locations in the region, they got the first look at goods coming in and a last chance to top-off a cargo of exports. The purpose of these regulations, which were tightened over the course of

Dutch rule, was to make sure that the WIC was able to capture its share of economic activity in New Netherland, the extra transportation cost imposed by the added stop notwithstanding.

New Amsterdam's position as the region's principal central place was further supported by the location of the WIC's North American headquarters; it was where most of the colony's governmental and appellate legal proceedings took place. During the Duke of York's proprietorship, Manhattan remained the locus of most administrative activities. High-level public administration, on the one hand, and mercantile activities, on the other, can be complementary; they reinforce each other within the economy of a regional metropolis. More trading takes place where associated administrative procedures are easy to execute, and the more trade the more administrators are needed. In particular, given the importance of trade documentation during the mercantilist era, it was probably much easier to do legal business in places where the relevant public records were maintained. New Yorkers' adverse reaction when the colony's erstwhile Proprietor, reigning as King James II, acted to consolidate the administration of his northern North American colonies in Boston can be taken as evidence of this complementarity. Part of the consolidation process involved moving New York's official records to Boston. In his discussion of this episode, historian Michael Kammen quotes testimony of Francis Nicholson, a career colonial official of the era: "how fatall it hath been to this city and the Province of New York for to be annexed to that of Boston, which if it had continued would have occasioned the total ruin of the Inhabitants of said Province" (Kammen, 1975, p. 120). One can speculate, therefore, that administrative consolidation might have reinforced Boston's market dominance, which was particularly evident during the first decade of the eighteenth century, so that the northern metropolis might have emerged from the colonial period as the "London" of the North American urban hierarchy. We cannot know whether this "alternative history" is plausible, but the reassertion of New York's status as a separate province after William and Mary replaced James II on the British throne in 1688, may be one of the ways in which "history matters" with regard to economic geography.

A final British government action may have reinforced New York's position as a top-level central place. On several occasions during the colonial period, particularly during wartime, British officials found it advisable to establish scheduled mail packet service between the colonies and the mother country. New York was invariably selected as the service's Western terminus. This may reflect the City's central location between the two other urban centers or its position nearest the front lines of the Anglo-French conflicts (Jones, 2007).

New York municipal government consistently and the Provincial Assembly sporadically adopted policies aimed at raising the City's position within the regional urban hierarchy. Between 1680 and 1694, for example, City millers were granted a monopoly on flour production within the Colony (Kammen, 1975, p. 387). The ostensible purpose of the 1680 Bolting Act was to assure a reputation for quality for New York's main export on international markets. Because, however, the milling of flour is a "weight losing" production process—milled flour is easier to transport than un-milled grain—the cost-minimizing location for an early modern (water) mill would have been along the adequate stream closest to the wheat field. Thus, limiting "bolting" to New York City may have been an expensive way, in terms of social cost, of assuring product quality. Indeed, rural interests eventually won the day in the Provincial Assembly and the City lost its milling monopoly. But new requirements for inspection and labeling of flour and other food exports probably helped assure that flour milled elsewhere in the Province would continue to be transported for export through New York City (Harrington, 1935; Kim, 1978).

In addition, during the second decade of the eighteenth century, perhaps in response to Boston's expanding market share, New York authorities imposed a series of provincial taxes on imports and on shipping activity. The principal purpose of these imposts was to raise revenue, but it is hard to explain some of the provisions as anything other than measures to protect the New York City-based maritime services industry. In 1713, the Provincial Assembly enacted an additional tariff on European goods, rum, and wine that had been transshipped through other colonies. Additional duties imposed after 1715—five percent on English products imported through Boston and three shillings per ton on

Massachusetts vessels importing goods directly from the West Indies—provide the clearest evidence that the New York legislatures were concerned about competition with New England shippers. These tax rates were high relative to the value of the goods involved; Michael Kammen cites evidence that "[w]ine, distilled liquor, and cocoa were to cost twice as much when coming from Boston as when shipped directly from the place of origin." A 1714 appeal to the New York Assembly provides evidence that, by discouraging visits to New York by New England shippers, the Province's protectionist policies also affected the market for exports. Residents of eastern Long Island reportedly complained that they were unable to access the Boston market where wheat was selling for 5 s. 6 d. per bushel compared to the going price of 3 s. 4 d. in New York City (Kammen, 1975, p. 164).

Most early-modern national systems of cities are characterized by a single central place at the pinnacle of the urban hierarchy, which is much larger than the second biggest city. This was certainly the case in eighteenth-century Great Britain, where, at 675,000, London's 1750 population was almost 12 times larger than second-place Edinburgh's, and France, where Paris was five times larger than Lyon. This pattern was not universal. In pre-unification, eighteenth-century Germany, for example, Berlin was only about 25% larger than Hamburg. During the eighteenth century, the geographic region that would become the United States resembled Germany in this respect. In 1720, first place Boston was 20% larger than second-largest Philadelphia. In 1760, the latter had risen to number one but was only about one third larger than second-place New York City. Further, while the economic linkages among these cities were numerous, by the mid-eighteenth-century transactions appear to have been generally balanced in terms of sales and purchases. Philadelphians sold wheat to New Yorkers and bought hats from them. Bostonians bought wheat from and sold fish to New Yorkers (Haggerty, 2006; Kammen, 1975, p. 166). So, although at any point in time one or another of these cities was larger than the other two and although at one point Boston may have had a chance to rise to the pinnacle of a North American system of cities, until the second decade of the nineteenth century each played a nearly identical role as the metropolis of its geographic region and as an integral port within the Atlantic trading economy.

These three cities were similar in many ways, but they were not identical. And one of the ways in which New York differed from the other two would stand its economy in very good stead through the early decades of the displaced nineteenth century.

## References

Bailyn, B. (1988). *Voyagers to the West: A Passage in the Peopling of America on the Eve of the Revolution*. New York: Vintage Books.

Bridenbaugh, C. (1938). *Cities in the Wilderness: The First Century of Urban Life in America, 1625–1742*. New York: Ronald Press Company.

Bridenbaugh, C. (1955). *Cities in Revolt: Urban Life in America, 1743–1776*. New York: Knopf.

Carter, S. B. (2006). *Table Eg1-59: Population, by Race and by Colony or Locality: 1610–1780*. Retrieved from Historical Statistics of the United States Millennial Edition Online http://hsus.cambridge.org/SeriesEg1-193.

Davis, K. G. (1974). *The North Atlantic World in the Seventeenth Century*. St. Paul: University of Minnesota Press.

Eltis, D. (2001). The Volume and Structure of the Transatlantic Slave Trade: A Reassessment. *William and Mary Quarterly, Second Series, LVIII*(1), 17–46.

Emsley, C., Hitchcock, T., & Shoemaker, R. (2018). *London History—Currency Coinage and the Cost of Living*. Retrieved from Old Bailey Proceedings Online https://www.oldbaileyonline.org/static/Coinage.jsp#costofliving.

Haggerty, S. (2006). *The British Atlantic Trading Community, 1760–1781: Men, Women, and the Distribution of Goods*. Leiden: Brill.

Harrington, V. D. (1935). *The New York Merchant on the Eve of the Revolution*. New York: Columbia University Press.

Henretta, J. A. (1978). Families and Farms: Mentalité in Pre-industrial America. *William and Mary Quarterly, 35*(1), 7–8.

Jacobs, J. (2009). *The Colony of New Netherland: A Dutch Settlement in Seventeenth-Century America*. Ithaca: Cornell University Press.

Jones, J. H. (2007, January). *Falmouth Packets*. Retrieved from TPO & Seapost Society http://www.tpo-seapost.org.uk/tpo2/spfalmouthpkt.html.

Kammen, M. (1975). *Colonial New York: A History*. Oxford: Oxford University Press.

Kim, S. B. (1978). *Landlord and Tenant in Colonial New York: Manorial Society, 1664–1775*. Raleigh: University of North Carolina Press.

Lemon, J. T. (1967). Urbanization and the Development of Eighteenth Century Southeastern Pennsylvania and Adjacent Delaware. *The William and Mary Quarterly, Third Series, 24*(4), 501–542.

McCusker, J. J., & Menard, R. R. (1985). *The Economy of British America, 1607–1789*. Raleigh: The University of North Carolina Press.

Mintz, S. W. (1985). *Sweetness and Power: The Place of Sugar in Modern History*. New York: Penguin.

New York State, Department of Economic Development, State Data Center. (2018). *Population of New York State by County: 1790 to 1990*. Retrieved from http://ocgov.net/sites/default/files/planning/PlanPages/censustables/nyshist17902000.pdf.

Proper, E. E. (1900). *Colonial Immigration Laws, A Study of the Regulation of Immigration by the English Colonies in America* (p. 37). Dissertation, Columbia University, New York.

Rink, O. A. (1986). *Holland on the Hudson: An Economic and Social History of Dutch New York*. Ithaca: Cornell University Press.

Rink, O. A. (2009). Seafarers and Businessmen: The Growth of Dutch Commerce in the Lower Hudson River Valley. In R. Panetta (Ed.), *Dutch New York: The Roots of Hudson Valley Culture* (p. 21). New York: Fordham University Press.

Rosenwaike, I. (1972). *Population History of New York City*. Syracuse, NY: Syracuse University Press.

Rostow, W. W. (1956). The Take-Off into Self-Sustained Growth. *The Economic Journal, 66*(261), 29.

Schofield, R. (1994). British Population Change, 1700–1871. In R. Roderick Floud & D. N. McCloskey (Eds.), *The Economic History of Britain Since 1700: 1700–1860* (p. 88). Cambridge: Cambridge University Press.

Shepherd, W. R. (1917). *The Story of New Amsterdam*. New York: The Holland Society of New York.

Sokoloff, K. L., & Villaflor, G. C. (1982). The Early Achievement of Modern Stature in America. *Social Science History, 6*(4), 453–481.

Turner, F. J. (1920). *The Frontier in American History* (pp. 82–83). New York: Henry Holt.

U.S. Census Bureau. (2018). *Population in the Colonial and Continental Periods*. Retrieved from https://www2.census.gov/prod2/decennial/documents/00165897ch01.pdf.

# 3
# Port and Entrepôt

New York's role as the principal transshipment point for its own and its hinterland's international trade was integral to its function as the region's top-order central place through the eighteenth and early nineteenth centuries. New York City was where consignments of furs, food, wood products, and iron ingots produced in the backcountry were consolidated, insured, documented, and loaded onto seaworthy and adequately manned vessels. It was also where imports destined for purchase by City and hinterland residents were unloaded, inspected, taxed, and dispatched on their way down the regional supply chain.

The goods shipped through New York were not, however, limited to exports produced in or around the City or imports destined for final sale to regional residents. Some proportion of the port's traffic involved the re-export of commodities brought to New York from elsewhere.

Some of this re-export activity was ancillary to the basic businesses of shipping locally produced goods out and unloading imports to resell to regional retailers. A New York shipowner with a large vessel ready to sail but unable to find sufficient locally milled flour to fill his hold might, for example, choose to top off the cargo with additional flour ordered from Pennsylvania or with salt cod brought in from New England.



A. Gurwitz, *Atlantic Metropolis*, Palgrave Studies in American Economic History,
https://doi.org/10.1007/978-3-030-13352-8_3

Or a dry goods importer, finding that she had ordered more whale oil candles than the local market could absorb but hearing that prices were very high in South Carolina, might ship her excess inventory to an associate in Charleston on the next southbound vessel. Some goods, however, were imported with the intention of re-exporting them. An opportunistic New York merchant might order a large shipment of porcelain, only a small proportion of which could be sold locally, in the expectation of reloading the bulk of the goods onto the next ship bound for, say, Jamaica. Taken together, a collection of maritime trade-related activities—including both regional port and entrepôt functions—was New York City's base industry during the British colonial era and the first 40 years after American Independence. Further, evidence presented in this section suggests that New York may have had a comparative advantage as an entrepot relative to the other North American ports.

## The Risks

It was possible to make a fortune trading goods around the Atlantic in the eighteenth century, but, as is usually the case with fortunes, it wasn't easy. Consider the risks surrounding a hypothetical purchase of assorted manufactured goods from a Bristol merchant by a New York City importer. The first set of risks related to the slow and uncertain movement of information and goods. The New York buyer would have had to decide to place the order at least five or six weeks before this information would be received by a correspondent in Bristol. And it would be at least another six weeks and probably much more before the ordered goods arrived in New York. Even if the goods survived the nautical hazards of the North Atlantic—storms, doldrums, pirates, and privateers—and arrived in a reasonably timely manner and in reasonably good shape, market conditions in New York for the commodities in question could have changed radically over this four-, five-, or six-month period. Another ship with a similar cargo might, for example, have docked the previous week and glutted the market.

Eighteenth-century traders also necessarily incurred credit risk. In North America throughout the early modern period, cash in the form of gold and silver coins was always scarce relative to the volume of transactions taking place. The New Yorker would, therefore, likely have had to purchase the goods on credit, with the Bristol-based seller assuming the risk of non-payment and the importer risking default, bankruptcy, and/or debtors' prison. In order to pay when the bill came due, the buyer would have had to sell the goods in a timely manner. But again, since cash was scarce, the New York merchant might have had to accept commodities—barrels of flour, say—in exchange for the British manufactured goods. In order, therefore, to pay the Bristol exporter, who, under normal circumstances, would have had little interest in receiving flour, the New York importer might have had to sell the flour in, say, Jamaica. Even if the demand in the Caribbean was solid, successful execution of the flour sale would have been subject to the risks of another sea voyage. The buyers in Jamaica were also unlikely to have cash on hand to pay for the flour.

More often it would be the case that a London-based merchant would owe Caribbean planters money as payment for earlier shipments of sugar, and the New York merchant might receive "Bills of Exchange" as payment for the goods shipped to Jamaica. Each of these Bills would have been a written order to a named London merchant, who purportedly owed a named Jamaica planter money, authorizing payment of a stated amount of money on or after a specific date. The New Yorker might then arrange to ship Bills of Exchange received as payment for the flour back to Bristol, again facing maritime hazards. If all went well, the Bristol merchant would accept this form of payment for the original shipment of goods to New York, present the Bills to the obligated sugar importer in London, and receive cash. While all these sea voyages were taking place, however, the Bristol exporter might, for example, have learned that the London-based sugar importer had gone bankrupt. Or the London merchant might claim that the Jamaica planter had already been paid and refuse to honor the Bill.

As illustrated by this hypothetical example of a chain of transactions, the risks faced by eighteenth-century traders fall into three categories: maritime risks, including weather, piracy, and privateering, market risk, and credit risk.

The structure of the mercantile service industry that evolved during the early modern era was the set of business practices that, despite these risks, enabled enough traders to operate profitably enough for the market to thrive and for the North American economy to grow. Atlantic traders, acting individually, in groups, or as a community, adopted two broad strategies to reduce or manage the risks inherent in the situation: diversification and selectivity.

## Spreading the Risks

Diversification worked because, while each individual transaction involved substantial risk, the average trading venture made money. While any given ship might be wrecked at sea, the average oceanic voyage arrived at its destination safe and sound and in a reasonably timely manner. Although there were occasional gluts of specific products in specific markets, the prices of British manufactured goods delivered to North America, for example, usually fluctuated in a narrow and at least somewhat predictable range. And while counterparty bankruptcies and frauds occurred occasionally to disastrous effect, the average borrower met his or her obligations in a timely manner. The trick was to avoid, at all cost, situations in which losses following a hurricane, forced sales of imported goods into a saturated market, or a single obligor's default could deplete a merchant's net worth.

Eighteenth-century merchants used both individual business strategies and institutional mechanisms to reduce the risk that the failure of any single venture might lead to ruin. The individual strategies, then as now, involved spreading business investments across a wide range of activities. Ideally, the success or failure of individual ventures within a merchant's portfolio would be mutually uncorrelated. So, for example, sending many small shipments of flour from New York to Jamaica in a season might reduce the risk of a single ship sinking but would not help much if the Caribbean grain market turned out to be glutted that year. By contrast, when a war seemed imminent, simultaneous investments in vulnerable but potentially unusually lucrative wartime normal trading voyages *and* in outfitting a vessel as a privateer could have made a lot of sense.

Merchants used both approaches: spreading investments across a wide range of similar individual ventures and seeking to combine uncorrelated activities.

One method of diversification was through the ownership and utilization of ships. Vessels were usually owned or chartered by ad hoc syndicates rather than by single persons or firms, and individual merchants or firms might participate in more than one such syndicate simultaneously. Similarly, cargoes were frequently collections of shipments by numbers of different merchants, only some of whom would have been members of the ownership syndicate. The example of the *Adriana*, which sailed from Liverpool to Philadelphia in 1790, may be illustrative, if a bit extreme. "There were a total of nineteen 'agents' or exporters listed on the Liverpool side, and a total of fifty-seven in Philadelphia" (Haggerty, 2006).

The large number of shipments to Philadelphia via the *Adriana*, many of them presumably quite small, may reflect another way in which eighteenth-century American merchants diversified their risk; they were less likely to specialize in trading a single category of goods than their European contemporaries. Although some New York traders, especially those who, like ironmongers or tobacconists, were engaged in manufacturing as artisan-retailers, did specialize in a narrow category of goods, most apparently maintained quite eclectic inventories. Virginia Harrington, whose 1935 publication *The New York Merchant on the Eve of the Revolution* remains an essential source in this field, cites the examples of "William Gilland, who kept an 'Earthen and Glassware Shop' in Broad Street, and also had for sale 'linen and cotton checks, striped cotton Hollands, Indian gartering, buckles, gunlocks, coffee and wines [,]'" and of "Hugh Wallace …[who]… advertised constantly 'Choice Madeira, Sherry, Lisbon and some excellent Old Mountain Wine; and has just imported a Cargo of Jamaica Rum, Sugar and Molasses which he will sell cheap.' To this, however, he added in another notice 'Oranges and Lemmons, Sallad Oil, Capers and Anchovies, Gold and Silver Lace, Men's shoes and pumps, Boots and Spatterdashes, Silk Handkerchiefs, Scots Carpets, Men's and Women's Gloves, Irish Linens and sundry European goods'" (Harrington, 1935, pp. 62–63).

Although some merchants apparently did specialize in trade between two markets—the UK and New York, for example—others diversified their risk by sending goods to and receiving them from places all around the Atlantic world. Historian Sheryllynne Haggerty cites the example of Philadelphia-based Andrew Clow, "a tradesman from Manchester [who] set up his own 'house' in Philadelphia. .... Clow used his knowledge of the textile trade in order to buy the correct quality and quantity of goods. He quickly built up a business importing manufactured goods from Britain and wines from Portugal and Madeira, exporting flour, wheat, and other goods from Philadelphia back to Britain and all around the Atlantic. He had dealings with Nova Scotia, New York, Charleston, Jamaica, Cadiz and all around Britain" (Haggerty, 2006, p. 235). Even specialists evidently had at least some dealings with other markets. James Beekman was a New York-based dry goods importer. Although 80% of his business correspondence was with the UK, he also communicated with individuals and firms in Amsterdam, Madeira, Londonderry, Barbados, Lisbon, Quebec, South Carolina, St. Kitts, and Curacao (White, 1956).

Finally, merchants diversified their risks by making investments outside of their own trading business. Then as now real estate was a favored diversifying asset class; Atlantic trading was the principal occupation of most proprietors of New York manors and patents (Kim, 1978). Commercial and mortgage lending to other business people—another use of merchant's surplus funds—may not have reduced risk exposure to the general condition of the Atlantic economy but did provide some diversification across enterprises. Similarly, participation in maritime insurance syndicates spread investors' risk across the overall trading economy and provided a way for shipowners and shippers to protect themselves against the hazards of the sea. Investments in manufacturing enterprises were less common during this period than they would become in the subsequent century, but there were some important ones. Sugar refining and rum distilling were integral to the overall workings of the Atlantic economy, and these became important industries in all three northern port cities, including New York. And North America had a comparative advantage in iron smelting because the ore and wood fuel were plentiful (Harrington, 1935, pp. 145–150).

## Selecting Ventures and Counterparties: Information Asymmetries and Business Networks

Access to reliable information is a necessary condition for business success. Before the development of steam-powered transport and electrical telecommunication technology, information—about the price of muscovado sugar in Amsterdam, about crop conditions in Pennsylvania's wheat belt, about James Beekman's credit history, etc.—moved very slowly. And once information arrived at a location, absent a robust business press and given the advantages of "insider" exclusivity, it was not necessarily widely disseminated. Most communication took place in private, either by word of mouth or by personal correspondence. Under such circumstances, the party on one side of a proposed transaction would have good reason to suspect that his or her counterparty was privy to undisclosed material information. Such suspicions can be an impediment to potentially profitable transactions.

In an influential 1970 article entitled "The Market for 'Lemons': Quality Uncertainty and the Market Mechanism," George Akerlof initiated a fruitful line of research that investigates how it can be difficult for markets to function effectively when one of the counterparties to a potential transaction has much more information about the situation than the other (Akerlof, 1970). Akerlof illustrated such situations with reference to a privately used car transaction. The seller knows whether the vehicle is a "lemon." The buyer knows (a) that the car might have some hidden problem, (b) that the seller knows whether it does or not, and (c) that, if the car is a lemon, the seller has no incentive to disclose that fact.

Such informational asymmetries can lead to market failures. Under the circumstances, even if there is a price that would satisfy two fully informed parties, buyer and seller may not be able to discover what that price is, and, if so, the mutually beneficial transaction would not take place. In the United States, the used car market has evolved in a way that mitigates this problem; automotive dealers, who stand behind the quality of the products they sell either implicitly or by contract, now execute most "pre-owned" car sales and purchases (CNW Research, 2013).

Eighteenth-century Atlantic traders also developed business practices and institutions that overcame the impediment of mistrust in the presence of informational asymmetries.

Much early modern maritime trading was not conducted in an impersonal or "atomistic" market; most of the surviving records analyzed by historians communicate information related to transactions between buyers and sellers or lenders and borrowers who knew each other personally and/or had done business previously. Of the approximately 1,100 business letters exchanged by New York dry goods importer James Beekman with 75 different correspondents between 1750 and 1776, the five most frequent counterparties account for almost 60% of the total. Beekman corresponded every year between 1753 and 1776 with his two most frequent counterparty firms, Peach and Pierce of Bristol and Samuel and Thomas Fludyer of London (White, 1956). Repeated, mostly profitable transactions between the same persons or firms increased the parties' confidence that future business would also be successful on average. Instead of engaging in mostly impersonal transactions, therefore, eighteenth-century merchants did repeated business with individuals or firms with whom they had established relationships. In other words, most merchants operated within a *network* of individuals or firms.

Some of these networks were formed through a process of doing repeated business with a single distant counterparty. But many of the early modern mercantile networks that operated across the Atlantic world had their basis in non-economic social relationships. Members of kinship, neighborhood, ethnic, or religious groups could apply peer pressure to enforce norms of fair dealing. Family ties offered two additional advantages. First, they expanded the volume of collateral that could be reliably pledged, either explicitly or implicitly, to secure loans (Mathias, 2000, Morgan, 2000). Second, under the British legal system of the time, it was easier for a businesswoman to conduct her affairs under the aegis of a family network than on a stand-alone basis (Zabin, 2009).

Four ethno-religious networks, in particular, played an important role in facilitating early modern British Atlantic trade: Dutch, Huguenot, Jewish, and Quaker. By the late seventeenth century, all four groups had established trading networks that spanned the Atlantic world. Of the merchants active in trade between Amsterdam and London between 1701 and 1710, for example, about 30% were English, 13% were Dutch, 29% were Huguenot, 21% were Jewish, and 8% were German (Ormrod, 1993).

Even after the Netherlands relinquished their sovereign presence in North America and despite the restrictions imposed by Parliament on continental Europeans' direct trade with British colonies, Dutch merchants remained very active in both the transatlantic and intra-American carrying trades. Some of this activity involved Dutch financing of British merchants' ventures and some involved routine violation of the Navigation Acts by Dutch, British, or American smugglers. It may be indicative of the Dutch role in the Atlantic trade that at times during the latter half of the eighteenth century the entrepôt at Oranjestad on the tiny Netherlands-owned Caribbean island of St. Eustatius was the busiest port of the Atlantic world (Gilmore, 2013).

Huguenots began fleeing France in large numbers after 1685, when Louis XIV's government outlawed public Protestant worship by revoking the 1598 Edict of Nantes. They migrated to Protestant principalities in Germany, to Holland, to Great Britain, and to America. Relative to the French population as a whole and even relative to the pre-revocation Protestant population, the refugees were disproportionately bourgeois, and by the mid-eighteenth century, important Huguenot merchant communities had been established in cities around the Atlantic world and were doing international business with each other. Thus, an Atlantic Huguenot trading network was active during the late seventeenth and early eighteenth centuries. It isn't clear, however, how tightly knit this network was. Since Huguenot refugees tended to assimilate rapidly, these networks lost their ethno-religious character quickly as the eighteenth century progressed. Nevertheless, the "protestant international" business networks forged during the early years of the Huguenot exile may have persisted (Butler, 1983).

The simultaneous dispersal of Jewish refugees expelled from the Iberian Peninsula and the rapid expansion of trading activity during the early modern era gave rise to an international community of "Port Jews" around the Atlantic world. "Far-flung Sephardic Jewish families … were well-positioned to participate in the world-wide maritime commercial circuits. The Sephardim had a particularly broad reach. As crypto-Jews or as Jews … they were present in all the Atlantic empires, from the early Spanish and Portuguese through the Dutch, French, and British. With their familial and commercial networks cutting across imperial lines, they provide an excellent example for the comparative history of different empires, as well as the intersections between them" (Dubin, 2006).

Quaker merchants could be found in all of the major ports of the British Atlantic world. Some of the greatest trading houses of London were run by Quakers. And, perhaps because meetings could impose discipline on their members, Quakers gravitated toward co-religionists as business counterparties (Tolles, 1948).

Interpersonal ties within the Quaker and Jewish networks were strengthened by the fact that, because these groups tended to be endogamous, individuals were frequently linked by a combination of commercial, ethno-religious, and familial relationships.

Kinship and ethno-religious networks served an important role in overcoming the obstacles to trade presented by informational asymmetries. But it is also important to recognize that these networks were not hermetic. Quakers did a lot of business with other Quakers, and Jews with other Jews. But both groups also did repeated business with others, as, for example, New York's James Beekman, a descendant of a Dutch immigrant to New Amsterdam, corresponded with Moses Franks, scion of a leading New York Jewish family, who had moved to London (White, 1956, pp. 582–597). And Philadelphia Quakers did business with New York Anglican Caleb Heathcote and Boston Huguenot Andrew Faneuil (Tolles, 1948, p. 91). In this way, the early modern Atlantic port cities served as venues where linkages across networks could be formed.

Further, in contrast to the dense linkages among individuals with business, familial, and ethno-religious ties, these solely commercial connections may have served as what network theorists refer to a "weak ties." One conclusion of network theory is that information diffuses particularly effectively within communities characterized by a collection of tightly linked networks that are connected with one another by weak ties that act as "bridges" for information. The general idea is that all the members of tightly connected groups know the same things and share the same areas of ignorance. Links between these informationally homogenous communities allow intelligence that has been thoroughly vetted within one tightly knit network to be transmitted to other such groups, thereby improving the overall level of knowledge within, in this case, a trading community (Goyal, 2007; Granoveter, 1973). If so, an important function of port cities like New York, Philadelphia, or Bristol was to serve as a nexus of trading networks. And it seems reasonable to conclude that the more tightly knit networks that are represented in a city, the greater the value of knowledge exchange across networks, the lower the barriers to transactions presented by informational asymmetries, and the greater the volume of mutually profitable trading that can take place, all else held equal.

In this regard, New York City may have been particularly well positioned among colonial ports to serve as a clearinghouse—a place where transactions could be based on reliable information about markets for a diverse array of goods in a wide range of locations—and, therefore, as an entrepôt. The City's reputation for ethnic and religious diversity was probably well deserved and was reflected in the demographics of the City's merchant community. Philadelphia's trading economy was dominated by the tightly knit network of Quaker grandees and Boston's by English immigrants. By contrast, New York's market does not seem to have been dominated by any one ethnic or religious group. Descendants of New Netherland's original settlers retained links with Dutch business associates and family members in Holland and around the Atlantic world over multiple generations. New York was one of the principal destinations of the first Huguenot immigrants to America. By the end of the seventeenth-century Flushing, New York was home to a Friends meeting, which was described as "large" by a visiting Quaker missionary and which counted a number of merchants among its members. And the City's Jewish community was the oldest and probably the largest in North America (Goodfriend, 1992).

Of course, we don't have the data we would need to conduct a rigorous test of the hypothesis that entrepot activities played a disproportionately large role in the business of New York's port relative to Boston or Philadelphia during the colonial period. Such information as we do have, however, is at least consistent with that circumstance.

Table 3.1 presents data on the number and tonnage of vessels outbound from the three ports at points in time during the third quarter of the eighteenth century.[1] In aggregate terms, the New York port was the smallest of the three. These official statistics, of course, reflect only legal trading activity, and we know that New Yorkers were actively engaged in illegal activity. If New Yorkers were less concerned with legalities than Philadelphians or Bostonians, the statistics in Table 3.1 may not reflect the true rankings. There are some reasons to think that such may have been the case earlier in the eighteenth century (see below). After 1763, however, British enforcement of its trade laws became stringent, so the figures in the table may be a reasonably fair indicator of the relative volumes of port traffic.

The table also indicates that, throughout the period, the average registered vessel sailing from New York was smaller than the ships leaving Boston and Philadelphia. This would be consistent with a port that was proportionately less engaged in the conveyance of bulk commodities such as grain or naval stores to regional distribution hubs such as Liverpool or Kingston. The smaller vessels that brought down the New York average tonnage may have been and more involved in the opportunistic shipment of higher-value items to specific points of final sale such as, say, Nevis.

The most definitive conclusion must be that New York, as a nexus of various trans-Atlantic social networks, was well positioned to compete for entrepôt business activities by the mid-eighteenth century and that this activity played a very important absolute role in New York City's economy during the colonial period. There is also some circumstantial evidence that supports the assertion that entrepot activity played a disproportionately large role in New York relative to the other North American port cities.

[1] Statistics regarding inbound traffic are, unsurprisingly, about the same.

**Table 3.1** Outbound shipping from North American ports (U.S. Census Bureau, 1976, pp. 1,180, 1,181)

| Port | New York | | | Boston | | | Philadelphia | | |
|---|---|---|---|---|---|---|---|---|---|
| Year | Number | Tonnage | Average tonnage | Number | Tonnage | Average tonnage | Number | Tonnage | Average tonnage |
| 1754 | 322 | 13,322 | 41 | 447 | 26,669 | 60 | | | |
| 1768 | 483 | 23,566 | 49 | | | | 641 | 36,944 | 58 |
| 1772 | 700 | 28,574 | 41 | 845 | 42,506 | 50 | 759 | 44,822 | 59 |

## Public Policy: Helpful vs. Unhelpful, Effective vs. Ineffective

Faced with the challenges of earning a profit in the Atlantic empire of goods, individual traders and merchant communities had by the beginning of the nineteenth century developed a reasonably successful business model. It involved numerous, opportunistic transactions executed repeatedly with a circumscribed group of counterparties involving a wide variety of goods in a diverse range of geographic markets. Where and when possible, traders purchased maritime insurance to protect their ventures against the hazards of the sea. And, while the typical merchant household probably allocated the bulk of their capital and working hours to trading activity, they were also careful to diversify risk by investing in other activities such as frontier real estate, manufacturing, and insurance syndicates.

While this Atlantic mercantile system as it functioned in Philadelphia, Boston, and New York was, in most ways, a world created by merchants themselves interacting in a market, its evolution over the course of the early modern period was also influenced by the economic policies of the British imperial government, by the colonial provincial governments and their state successors, and by the government of the United States.

Three areas of government policy affected the conduct of the Atlantic trading business in the eighteenth century: geopolitical policy, trade policy, and monetary policy. At some times, some of the specific government actions may have helped some North American traders overcome some of the obstacles to profitable business. At other times, government policies may have created additional impediments to the development of the mercantile economy. Some of these encouragements and impediments had powerful effects; the impacts of others were minimal. This section aims to sort out the direction (helpful or harmful) and the impact magnitude (effective or ineffective) of eighteenth-century government policy as it affected the New York City trading economy.

## Geopolitics

Continuous competition for national aggrandizement among European powers erupted in six major wars during the course of the long eighteenth century (Table 3.2). As noted previously, New York's position before 1763 on the North American front line of this conflict may have

**Table 3.2** Atlantic Theater Wars of the long eighteenth century

| American War | European War | Begin | End | Britain's Allies | Britain's Enemies |
|---|---|---|---|---|---|
| King William's War | Nine Years' War<br>War of the Grand Alliance<br>War of the League of Augsburg | 1688 | 1697 | Netherlands<br>Holy Roman Empire<br>Spain<br>Sweden | France |
| Queen Anne's War | War of the Spanish Succession | 1701 | 1714 | Austria<br>Netherlands<br>Holy Roman Empire<br>Prussia<br>Portugal | France<br>Spain<br>Bavaria |
| King George's War | War of the Austrian Succession | 1740 | 1748 | Hapsburg Monarchy<br>Netherlands<br>Sardinia<br>Russia | France<br>Prussia<br>Spain<br>Bavaria<br>Sicily and Naples<br>Sweden |
| French and Indian War | Seven Years' War | 1754 | 1763 | Prussia<br>Portugal | France<br>Austria<br>Spain<br>Russia<br>Sweden |
| American Revolution | | 1775 | 1783 | | United States<br>France<br>Netherlands<br>Spain |
| French Revolution/Napoleonic Wars | | 1793 | 1815 | Various | France<br>various |

seriously impeded settlement of the City's hinterland during the first half of the eighteenth century leaving local merchants with less flour to export than their Philadelphia contemporaries. Except for a few frightening incursions on the northern frontier, however, not much actual fighting took place in New York or on its borders. It wasn't until the French and Indian War that massed armed forces were stationed in and around New York. Not until then, therefore, were New York merchants able to profit on large military supply contracts.

Before the French and Indian War and especially during King George's War, the principle way in which North American merchants were able earn war profits was to invest in privateering ventures. Not only could successful privateering be very profitable, but participation in this activity was a diversifying investment for a merchant facing higher maritime insurance costs. Peacetime insurance premiums on one-way voyages between New York and the Caribbean ranged between four and four and a half percent of the value covered; during the French and Indian War, the rate rose as high as 20% (Harrington, 1935, pp. 155–156). Privateering provided a way for a merchant to profit from a situation that may have been reducing risk-adjusted returns on routine business.

New York and Newport, R.I., merchants grasped this opportunity particularly readily. During King George's War, New York accounted for an estimated 28% of British colonial privateering prizes, and Newport, a much smaller city, for 23%. By contrast, Boston and Philadelphia merchants claimed 7 and 8% of prizes, respectively, and all of the ports of the British West Indies combined, 18%. Why were New York and Newport merchants disproportionally engaged in this activity? Historian Carl Swanson has suggested several possible reasons. Because New York's and Newport's hinterlands were relatively small, these cities' merchants may have been more attuned to non-routine business opportunities. Also, Philadelphia's pacifist Quaker merchants may have avoided privateering, which sometimes required violent engagement with prizes. Further, Massachusetts was more actively engaged militarily than New York or Rhode Island in campaigns during King William's, Queen Anne's, and King George's Wars and may not have had the manpower to spare for privateering (Swanson, 1985).

Carl Swanson also pointed out that the ability to dispose of captured goods expeditiously was a necessary condition for profitable privateering. Here, too, New York-based merchants may have had an advantage. Except for the legalities, the process of disposing of pirates' booty was similar to what privateers needed to do, and the historical literature suggests that New York was particularly active as a buccaneers' port of call in the years around the turn of the eighteenth century. Benjamin Fletcher, who served as governor from 1692 until 1697, was notoriously pirate-friendly, as were many of the City's leading merchant families of the time. While Fletcher's immediate successor, the Earl of Bellomont, aggressively aimed to suppress illegal activity, New York remained pirates' "favorite American port" (Nash, 1986) One reason both pirates and privateers may have favored New York, in addition to the occasionally willful blindness of those charged with enforcing the law, was that local merchants may have been particularly knowledgeable about where around the Atlantic world the broadest array of commodities was most likely to find a buyer. Historian Serena Zabin provides an illustration of the take from a successful privateering voyage.

> A typical issue [of the *New York Weekly Journal*] from May 1740 … [reported that] 'the same Day Captain Bayard in the Sloop *Ranger* also came into this Harbour.' The description…culminated with the highlights of Bayard's catch, *many* of which were objects of Catholic ritual…
>
> The rest of the cargo was made accessible to the public through an advertisement of [New York merchant] Guilian Verplank. He offered for sale 'the following Prize Goods just imported by Capt. *Sam Bayard*; Eleven Pipes of Brandy; Two Ditto Wine, Havanna Hides, Tanned Leather, Snuff in small Baggs, Ditto superfine in Canisters, Gum Elemmi, Muscovado Sugar, Powder Sugar, Campech Logwood and Sundry other. (Zabin, 2009, pp. 111–112)

Whether it was because pirates had helped create an entrepôt, because local merchants could not rely solely on the hinterland economy to sustain profitable businesses, because New York was the nexus of the full array of tightly linked Atlantic trading networks, or for some other reason, the City was able to capture a much larger share of privateering profits than its two more populous competitors. In 1740, for example, New York's Admiralty Court condemned 213 privateering prizes worth a total of £450,000; this at a time when the colony's recorded trade with Great Britain was averaging around £120,000 annually (Brock, 1975; Nash, 1986, p. 109).

Although privateering probably added more to New York merchants' collective net worth, the military supply contacts associated with the French and Indian War were not trivial. At least that was Benjamin Franklin's assessment when he observed that, "…New York is growing immensely rich, by Money brought in from all Quarters for the Pay and Subsistence of the Troops." From 1754 to 1756, approximately £475,000 in specie or cash-equivalents flowed into New York for these purposes (Brock, 1975, p. 350).

Trading with the enemy was illegal during the colonial wars and suppression of trade with the prosperous French Islands in the Caribbean might have reduced merchants' profits, but correspondence and court records indicate that a great deal of such illegal activity took place. New Yorkers were apparently happy to let New Englanders do the fighting during Queen Anne's and King George's Wars while the lucrative trade between Albany and French Montreal continued. And smuggling Haitian sugar into North America or Europe, which was already prohibited under the Molasses Act since 1733, continued, now illegal on two counts, during the French and Indian War (Matson, 2002, pp. 213–214).

Philadelphians were evidently as engaged as New Yorkers in trading with the enemy during the French and Indian War. Because of the two islands' geographic proximity and because the authorities in Kingston were lax in enforcement, many voyages between North America and the French colony Saint-Domingue (Haiti) involved stops in Jamaica. When, in February 1760, British naval forces brought 18 North American ships into Kingston on charges of trading with the enemy, 10 were from Philadelphia, five from New York, and three from Newport, Rhode Island. Boston's absence from this list is apparently representative; that City seems to have been less involved in this form of war profiteering than the other two major North American ports (Tolles, 1948, p. 87; Truxes, 2008, pp. 79–96).

Thus, the New York merchant community had four "good" Anglo-French colonial wars. The assessment might have been different, of course, if the British had not, in the end, been successful in these engagements. Profits earned as a result of these wars, however, probably added substantially to the collective net worth of the North American merchant community. And the preponderance of evidence suggests that a greater proportion of New York's aggregate wealth was derived, directly or indirectly, from war profits than that of Boston or Philadelphia.

The experience of the subsequent two conflicts of the era was different. The American Revolution devastated New York, physically and economically. The City was occupied by the British for the duration, much of the population fled, and much of the City burned down. While there was money to be made supplying British troops from local sources, much external trade with the hinterland and the other 12 colonies was cut off.

During the early years of the Napoleonic Wars, New York merchants were, like their contemporaries in Philadelphia, and, especially, Boston, able to take advantage of American neutrality by trading with both sides of the conflict. But sustaining neutrality became increasingly difficult, and, after 1807, when the Jefferson administration imposed a complete export embargo and all of the port cities entered into a depression that did not end until 1815. This later episode will be discussed much more extensively in the next chapter.

## "Mercantilism"

Eighteenth-century British government's "mercantilist" trade policy has had an unsavory reputation among economists; the profession's founding text, Adam Smith's *The Wealth of Nations*, is, after all, an anti-mercantilist polemic. It is far from obvious, however, that the British Empire, collectively or its components individually, would have been noticeably wealthier as of, say, 1750, if freer trade policies had prevailed through the early modern period.

The general aim of mercantilist policy was to encourage British subjects' international trading activity in a way that maximized the home country and the Empire's current account surplus: that is, the amount by which the combined value of exports *plus* "invisible" earnings on shipping and other trade-related services together exceeded the value of imports. In their final form, the mercantilist Navigation Acts stipulated that (i) all goods moving between places in the Empire be carried in ships owned by British subjects, (ii) certain "enumerated" items[2] produced within the Empire could only be shipped directly to Great Britain or to its colonies, not to the European continent, and (iii) all goods imported into colonies originating anywhere outside the Empire had to be transshipped through Great Britain. In addition, the Molasses Act of 1733 imposed a prohibitive duty on sugar products from outside the Empire imported into North America.

As with most economic legislation, each of the provisions of the Navigation Acts created some winners and some losers, and political interest groups throughout the British Empire were well aware of the stakes involved. Were North American merchants, in general, or New York merchants, in particular, net winners or losers under these laws? On the positive side, as intended, restricting intra-Empire shipping to vessels owned and manned by British subjects eliminated the Dutch competition from some proportion of the carry trade among the numerous and increasingly populous British Atlantic possessions (McCusker & Menard, 1985, pp. 46–50). New York and other British colonial merchants could only have benefited from this provision. As written, however, the Navigation Acts prohibited the potentially lucrative shipment of enumerated goods, including many of the most profitable colonial products, directly from the Americas to much of Continental Europe. While the principal effect of this aspect of mercantilism was to reduce the net revenues received by producers of tobacco, sugar, and other enumerated commodities, it could also have imposed a cost on law-abiding North American merchants in terms of missed

[2]The list of enumerated goods eventually came to include sugar, tobacco, cotton, indigo, rice, molasses, naval stores, furs, and iron.

opportunities to sell goods directly to continental Europeans at a higher price than what British Empire buyers were paying.

The Molasses Act might have been the most damaging to North American merchants. Because sugar was cheaper and manufactured imports more expensive on the French and Dutch Islands than on Jamaica or Barbados, this last major piece of mercantilist legislation would, if strictly enforced, have ended a highly profitable line of business. The North American colonies' London agents and propagandists in London were vociferous in their opposition to this legislation, but the British West Indian plantation interest was more politically influential.

As it happened, however, when it came to enforcement of the Navigation Acts, it was much easier to prevent Dutch traders from trafficking in British ports than it was to stop North American merchants carrying enumerated cargoes from bypassing Great Britain on their way to Continental markets or to determine whether barrels of molasses unloaded in New York had been refined from Jamaican or Haitian cane. It seems likely, therefore, that the provisions of the Navigation Acts that would have benefited New York merchants were more strictly enforced than those that imposed impediments to profitability. This does not mean that all of the benefits of lax enforcement accrued to North American traders. Public officials, through bribes and other considerations, may have captured a substantial proportion of the gains from laxity. Further, enforcement of all of the Navigation Acts became more stringent as the eighteenth century progressed. As Robert Paul Thomas concluded regarding the aggregate net impact of the Navigation Acts on the welfare of Britain's North American colonies as a whole, the impact of mercantilism on the well-being of New York's eighteenth-century trading economy, in particular, whether for better or worse, was probably relatively small (Thomas, 1965).

A comparison of commercial activity before and after the American Revolution might have served as something of a controlled experiment to determine the effects of the Navigation Acts. Unfortunately, we have no direct way of assessing the results of that experiment; no one was collecting reliable North American trade data during the period between 1775 and 1790. Nevertheless, it would *not* have been surprising for

New York's postwar recovery to have been sluggish. Not only did the British government impose restrictions aimed at excluding U.S. products from British possessions in the Caribbean, but the French and the Dutch discontinued the mercantile leniencies allowed their erstwhile wartime ally. Despite these obstacles, the City's population, which had halved during the occupation, returned to pre-war levels within two years after the British evacuation on November 25, 1783. The rising population included some returning New Yorkers and some newcomers, including "[a] procession of merchants…from New England." Finally, as soon after the British evacuation as ice in the harbor would allow what the contemporary press referred to as "so many large ships" began to sail out from New York (Burrows & Wallace 1999, pp. 265–276). This circumstantial evidence indicating that economic conditions in the City returned to something close to what had been the pre-war norm fairly quickly is consistent with the conclusion that mercantilist restrictions on free trade and free traders had, at most, a modest impact on the trajectory of New York City's economy during the long eighteenth century.

## Monetary Policy Avant la Lettre[3]

The final way in which governments sometimes facilitated and sometimes impeded trading activity was through the eighteenth-century equivalent of monetary policy. The British American monetary system emerged from colonial governments' struggle to deal with two problems: (i) how to finance government military operations in an emergency, and (ii) how to make sure that a scarcity of currency or its functional equivalents did not seriously impede economic activity.

To finance routine operations, colonial governments sold land and levied taxes: property taxes, or "quitrents," and duties on exports and imports. But wars, while frequent, were not routine. In the absence of banks or government bond markets, raising money quickly to pay soldiers and defense contractors wasn't easy. To satisfy the troops' and

[3]Unless otherwise indicated, the material in This Section Is Drawn from (Brock, 1975).

contractors' demand for compensation that could be spent immediately, colonial legislatures authorized the issuance of "Bills of Credit," which were paid out by governments in lieu of gold or silver coins.

Although the specific terms of these Bills varied from colony to colony and evolved over time, many of them shared the following characteristics. First, in order to induce soldiers and contractors to accept this form of payment, the Bills were declared by law to be legal tender. Tradespeople and creditors could not refuse to accept them as payment and they could be used to pay taxes at their full face value. Second, in order to maintain confidence in this medium of exchange, legislatures usually specified a source of revenue that would be used to exchange outstanding bills for specie before a specified date.

The immediate purpose of the first Bills of Credit emissions, starting with Massachusetts's 1690 issue, was to deal with a fiscal crisis. But colonial legislatures and colonial business people soon realized that, as a widely accepted medium of exchange within the local economy, Bills of Credit could also mitigate another problem, the insufficient supply of money. Although such concepts as national income and money supply had yet to be articulated, business people and policymakers seem to have had clear and reasonably correct ideas about how the availability of media of exchange could influence aggregate prosperity and its distribution among social groups. A scarcity of currency and its equivalents relative to the potential volume of mutually beneficial transactions could stymie economic activity. As noted previously, during the early modern period, only gold and silver coins minted by governments, "specie," were universally accepted as payment for goods and services in the Atlantic economy. The scarcity of this universal currency necessitated the routine use of credit. Physical evidence of credit obligations in the form of Bills of Exchange, issued by businesses, could be used as currency-equivalents to make some payments. But while Bills of Exchange, mostly evidencing payment obligations of British merchants to Americans, could be an adequate medium for clearing routine Atlantic trade or substantial payments between American merchants, they were inconvenient vehicles for smaller, purely local transactions. Bills of Credit emitted by colonial governments, if widely accepted and of reasonably stable market value, it was quickly realized, could serve this purpose.

Policymakers and businesspeople also understood that creation of currency-equivalents could have adverse consequences. The main concern was that if the outstanding volume of Bills grew much faster than the potential volume of substantive transactions in the economy, the market value of this form of currency would decline. Uncertainty about the future purchasing power of the local currency would, in turn, raise the risk of doing business in the colony and might impede the growth of the market. Creditors, in general, and British exporters, in particular, were, of course, worried about being repaid in depreciated colonial currency. These were not just theoretical concerns; over the first half of the eighteenth century, the local currency of Massachusetts depreciated by an average of 4% per year relative to British sterling; the worst one-year decline was 19% between 1733 and 1734.

The conflict between colonial governments and British merchants played out in controversies between American legislatures and the imperial government over the size, frequency, and offering terms of Bill emissions. The British government frequently exercised its prerogative to veto specific issues, favored rapid redemption of new offerings, opposed legal tender provisions, and sought to impose "suspension" clauses, which required explicit assent from London before emission legislation went into effect. In the political battles waged over this issue, transatlantic traders on both sides of the ocean were arrayed on one side; colonial consumers and agricultural interests, on the other. Colonial governors were frequently caught in the middle. Individual colonies' monetary history was driven in large part by the local balance of power among these two interests. Eventually, however, the London-based merchants opposing Bill emissions gained the political upper hand.

New York's legislature authorized its share of Bills, usually but not invariably related to the colony's preparation for or waging of war. As Fig. 3.1 indicates, Bill issues were retired fairly quickly after they were issued. The total volume of bills outstanding in 1748, at the end of King George's War, was about the same as what had been issued in the previous two years and was well below the cumulative issuance up to that point. Probably as a result of the policy of redeeming issues quickly New York's Bills, like Pennsylvania's, did not depreciate anywhere near as much as those of Massachusetts and South Carolina.

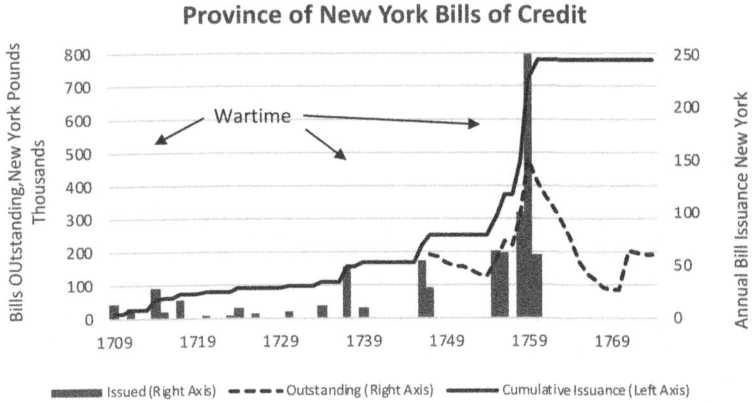


**Fig. 3.1** Issuance of bills of credit by the province of New York (Brock, 1975)

What accounts for the differences in these colonies' monetary policies? One likely reason is that New York, unlike Massachusetts, did not participate in large-scale offensive military operations prior to the French and Indian War. It may also be that the creditor class had greater political influence in the Middle Atlantic colonies than in New England. In any case, the disruptions attendant on currency instability and its subsequent suppression never jeopardized New York's (or Philadelphia's) economic development. On the other hand, although it would be impossible to test the hypothesis empirically, an endemic scarcity of currency would likely have raised the costs and risks of doing business and, thereby, impeded economic development.

The concern about colonial monetary independence reflected the experience of South Carolina and the New England colonies. The large volumes issued and the recurrent practice of postponing scheduled redemptions of outstanding Bills led to rapid depreciation of these colonies' currencies during the first half of the eighteenth century (Fig. 3.2). Although Massachusetts, after experiencing hyperinflation during 1730s and 1740s, moved independently in 1750 to return to a specie-only monetary system, in 1751 Parliament imposed strict controls on the New England colonies' Bill emissions and the Board of Trade, the British government body that supervised colonial affairs, began scrutinizing of

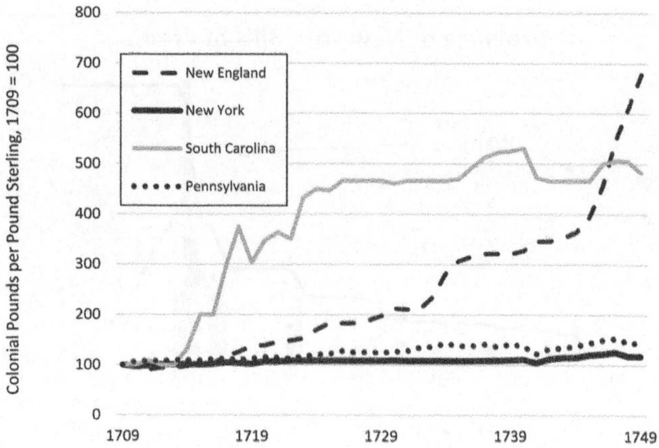


**Fig. 3.2** Depreciation of colonial currencies relative to sterling, 1709–1749 (*Source* Carter, 2006)

other colonies' monetary management. Particular attention was paid to make sure that Bills were only issued to deal with bona fide fiscal emergencies and that outstanding issues were redeemed as scheduled. Finally, in the Currency Act of 1764, Parliament effectively eliminated Bill emission as a tool of colonial economic policy; any new Bill issues would be null and void, and all outstanding issues had to be redeemed on schedule. The result was to reduce the volume of Bills outstanding steadily after the end of the French and Indian Wars. The consequent contraction of the colonial money supply and resulting deflationary pressure must have exacerbated the postwar economic downturn. Although the strict limitations imposed in 1764 were later relaxed, the loss of control over this tool of economic policy added to the array of grievances that eventually led to the American Revolution.

## Early Republican Financial Policy

The new Republic's economic policymakers, unlike their British predecessors, did not assign a particularly high priority to maximizing international trading activity or the nation's current account surplus.

Instead, their attention was absorbed by two financial issues. First, they faced the challenge of tying up the loose ends left by the makeshift ways in which the Continental Congress and the States had financed the Revolutionary War effort so as to leave the new nation with a functional financial system. Second, they had to respond to the business people, some of whom also served as public officials, who were petitioning state legislatures for limited-liability banking charters. Their solutions to the first challenge—redemption of the wartime "continental" currency, assumption of state Revolutionary War debts, chartering a central bank, and the assignment to the Federal government of sole responsibility for minting coins—tended to concentrate financial power in the national capital. New York City was the seat of the central government from 1785 until 1790. Over the subsequent decades, as the new financial system was being put in place, Philadelphia was the nation's political capital, its largest city, and its principal financial center. Thus, the new central bank was headquartered there.

But, whether intentionally or not, the new financial system that began to emerge at the time also reserved an important role for decentralized, market-driven financial institutions: state-chartered, privately owned banking corporations. In subsequent chapters, it will become clear how this aspect of the new nation's financial system would eventually work in New York City's distinct favor (Brock, 1975).

## Colonial Era Public Policy: An Assessment

By the eve of the Napoleonic Wars, Philadelphia, New York, and Boston, which had been small towns a century earlier, had become mercantile centers of some importance within the North Atlantic economy. Whatever their faults, British and colonial government policy had not prevented this quantitative expansion and qualitative transformation. Was policy on balance helpful or harmful? Did it, on balance, help one of these cities more than the others? Even in the absence of the data we would need to try to answer this question statistically, we can reach some judgment on the matter by observing how American merchants of the time responded to the possibility that their connection to the British

Empire might be severed. It may be telling that 55% of the merchant members of the New York Chamber of Commerce alive in 1775 sided against independence, while only 25% supported the revolutionaries (Harrington, 1935, p. 349). Further, loyalist sentiment was evidently more prevalent among New York traders than among their contemporaries in Boston or Philadelphia. This preponderance may reflect aspects of New York's political culture and the great merchants' fear of "leveling" tendencies among the City's artisans. But it may also reflect the City's merchants' belief that they had gained more than they lost through their association with the British Empire (Nash, 1986).

## Conclusion

As the Napoleonic Wars, the American War of 1812, and "early modern" era ended in 1815, New York was, by a small margin, the largest city in North America. At that point, however, no city in the United States could have been called *the* national metropolis. That was about to start changing.

## References

Akerlof, G. A. (1970). The Market for 'Lemons': Quality Uncertainty and the Market Mechanism. *The Quarterly Journal of Economics, 84*(3), 488–500.

Brock, L. V. (1975). *The Currency of the American Colonies, 1700–1764: A Study in Colonial Finance and Imperial Relations, Arno Press, 1975, 74 (N).* New York: Arno Press.

Burrows, E. G., & Wallace, M. (1999). *Gotham: A History of New York City to 1898* (p. 1252). Oxford: Oxford University Press.

Butler, J. (1983). *The Huguenots in America: A Refugee People in New World Society*. Cambridge: Harvard University Press.

Carter, S. B. (2006). *Table Aa22035*. Retrieved from Historical Statistics of the United States Millennial Edition Online http://projects.ilt.columbia.edu/seneca/svcurric/images/byward2_early.html.

CNW Research. (2013). *Will Surge in Private Party Used Vehicle Sales Affect Fleets*. Retrieved from Automotive Digest http://automotivedigest.com/2013/06/will-surge-in-private-party-used-vehicle-sales-affect-fleets/.

Dubin, L. (2006). Introduction: Port Jews in the Atlantic World Jewish History. *Jewish History, 20,* 119–120.

Gilmore, R. G. (2013). St. Eustatius: The Nexus for Colonial Caribbean Capitalism. In D. Comer (Ed.), *The Archaeology of Interdependence: European Involvement in the Development of a Sovereign United States* (p. 44). New York: Springer.

Goodfriend, J. D. (1992). *Before the Melting Pot: Society and Culture in Colonial New York City, 1664–1730*. Princeton: Princeton University Press.

Goyal, S. (2007). *Connections: An Introduction to the Economics of Networks*. Princeton: Princeton University Press.

Granoveter, M. S. (1973). The Strength of Weak Ties. *American Journal of Sociology, 78*(6), 1360–1380.

Haggerty, S. (2006). *The British Atlantic Trading Community, 1760–1781: Men, Women, and the Distribution of Goods*. Leiden: Brill.

Harrington, V. D. (1935). *The New York Merchant on the Eve of the Revolution*. New York: Columbia University Press.

Kim, S. B. (1978). *Landlord and Tenant in Colonial New York: Manorial Society, 1664–1775*. Raleigh: University of North Carolina Press.

Mathias, P. (2000). Risk, Credit and Kinship in Early Modern Enterprise, Camb. In J. J. McCusker & K. Morgan (Eds.), *The Early Modern Atlantic Economy* (pp. 15–62). Cambridge: Cambridge University Press.

Matson, C. (2002). *Merchants and Empire: Trading in Colonial New York*. Baltimore: Johns Hopkins University Press.

McCusker, J. J., & Menard, R. R. (1985). *The Economy of British America, 1607–1789*. Raleigh: The University of North Carolina Press.

Morgan, K. (2000). Business Networks in the British Export Trade to North America, 1750–1800. In J. J. McCusker & K. Morgan (Eds.), *The Early Modern Atlantic Economy* (pp. 16–62). Cambridge: Cambridge University Press.

Nash, G. B. (1986). *The Urban Crucible: The Northern Seaports and the Origins of the American Revolution* (pp. 40–42). Cambridge: Harvard University Press.

Ormrod, D. (1993). The Atlantic Economy and the 'Protestant Capitalist International', 1651–1775. *Historical Research, 66*(160), 201.

Swanson, C. E. (1985, July). American Privateering and Imperial Warfare, 1739–1748. *The William and Mary Quarterly, Third Series, 42*(3), 357–382.
Thomas, R. P. (1965). A Quantitative Approach to the Study of the Effects of British Imperial Policy upon Colonia Welfare: Some Preliminary Findings. *The Journal of Economic History, 25*(4), 615–638.
Tolles, F. B. (1948). *Meeting House and Counting House: The Quaker Merchants of Colonial Philadelphia, 1682–1763*. Chapel Hill: University of North Carolina Press.
Truxes, T. M. (2008). *Defying Empire: Trading with the Enemy in Colonial New York*. New Haven: Yale University Press.
U.S. Census Bureau. (1976). *The Statistical History of the United States from Colonial Times to the Present.* New York: Basic Books.
White, P. L. (1956). *The Beekman Mercantile Papers, 1746–1799* (Vol. II). New York: The New York Historical Society.
Zabin, S. R. (2009). *Dangerous Economies: Status and Commerce in Imperial New York*. Philadelphia: University of Pennsylvania Press.

# Part II

## Introduction 1815–1924: The Displaced Nineteenth Century

In 1815 at the end of the Napoleonic Wars, the United States was an almost entirely rural nation with a few small cities serving as central places for their agricultural hinterlands. By the 1920s, about half of the nation's population lived in places defined as "urban" by the Census Bureau. The pace of this transition accelerated markedly after about 1840. From 1800 to the present New York has been the largest U.S. city, initially by a small margin. Since about 1850, however, New York has consistently been about twice as populous as the country's second largest urban center.

From 1815 to 1924, New York was distinguished from other cities not just by its size but also by the consistent prominence of four industries—wholesaling, clothing manufacturing, financial services, and printing and publishing—in the City's mix of economic activities, and by its particular attraction as a place to live for European immigrants. I refer to this period as New York's "displaced nineteenth century" because it lasted about 100 years and because throughout this period the City's growth was, in very large part determined by the ways in which the United States engaged with the rest of the Atlantic world. In particular, the end point of the period, 1924 is the year in which the United States became much less welcoming to immigrants from abroad than it had been before.

Chapters 4–11, therefore, aim to explain (i) why the process of urbanization accelerated when it did, (ii) how and why New York became the nation's largest city, (iii) when, why, and how City's particular economic specialty industries gravitated to this location, and (iv) what about New York made it relatively more attractive as a place to live and work for immigrants from abroad than for native-born Americans.

## Chapters 4–9: Antebellum Ascent

Chapter 4 begins by framing an economic model of the urbanization process. This conceptual framework, referred to as "the new economic geography," aims to identify the determinants of *when* cities will coalesce and of the size distribution of urban places in a country or region. The conditions identified by the model as being conducive to the formation of cities include declining transportation costs, rising demand for goods produced under increasing returns to scale, and a preference for variety in the commodities and services households buy. The second part of the chapter shows that these conditions came into much greater effect in the United States during the years between 1815 and about 1850 than they had been before. The chapter concludes with a theoretical consideration of *where* on the map urbanization is likely to take place.

After the fact, it seems to have been inevitable that New York would rise to its position as the largest U.S. city once the pace of urbanization had accelerated, given its deep, easily accessible, and generally ice-free harbor and its central position between population centers in New England and the Chesapeake Bay area. In the context of the inevitability paradigm, if there was a "critical juncture" along the New York's path to dominance, it would have been the construction of the Erie Canal, presumably because it directed Midwestern agricultural exports through New York's port. Chapter 5 presents the case for the view that, from the perspective of the early 1830s, New York's rise was not inevitable and that alternative U.S. urban hierarchies with some other city, most likely Philadelphia or Baltimore, at its pinnacle were, in fact, plausible.

The view that New York's premier rank was inevitable correctly emphasizes New York's position as the North America's busiest port, and, accordingly, the chapter explains how New York initially came to supersede its northeastern rivals, Philadelphia and Boston, and how it maintained that dominant position over time. This discussion also aims to make clear why a new era in New York City's economic history began when the Napoleonic Wars, including America's War of 1812, ended in 1815.

The global context for New York's rise to prominence was the structure of international trade during the first half of the nineteenth century. Chapter 5, therefore, also highlights the particular importance of one group of commodities, raw cotton, and cotton textile products, to the Atlantic economy as a whole and to New York's.

There is no doubt that the Erie Canal played an important role in New York City's rise to ascendancy. Chapter 5 argues, however, that providing a low-friction linkage between the eastern seaboard and the rapidly growing Midwestern states was *not* the principle way in which the completion of the canal in 1825 stimulated the City's growth through the 1830s and 1840s. The part of the Midwest that was growing most rapidly by far at that time was the Ohio River valley, and the Canal did not ease New York's access to that region. Instead, the staged construction of the canal opened the New York State counties along the Mohawk and Genesee Rivers and the Ontario and Erie lakeshores to economic development, so that by boosting the growth the City's hinterland, the Canal accelerated the City's expansion.

Chapter 5 concludes with discussions of whether two other cities, Philadelphia and Baltimore, both of which were situated much closer to the Ohio River Valley and to the cotton-growing South, could have gained cost-effective access to those sources of trade goods and, thereby, have beaten out New York during the crucial decades when the U.S. system of cities was coming into place. Such access would have to have been via a railroad connection, and, so, an assessment of its plausibility must be based on an understanding of the state of the art of locomotive technology during the 1830s and 1840s. The requisite engine power required to haul freight cars across the Appalachian Mountain passes was not available in 1830 but it was before 1850. For the business and political leaders of Philadelphia and/or Baltimore, making a commitment to long-line railroad construction early in this twenty-year period would have been incredibly audacious, but not much more so, perhaps, than planning to construct a 363-mile canal with 83 locks and 18 aqueducts was in 1817.

Chapter 6 turns to an exploration of New York's antebellum manufacturing sector, its aggregate size and its industrial composition. One principle predictions of models of urban economic geography is that the proportion of the population engaged in "footloose" manufacturing activities, that is, those industries that are not geographically tethered to the source of their raw materials or to the locations of their customers, will increase with city size. Analysis of 1860 census manufacturing employment data demonstrates that this was very much the case in the United States on the eve of the Civil War. It is not surprising, therefore, that New York City was an important mid-nineteenth-century manufacturing center.

The proportion of the population working in manufacturing industries in New York was among the highest across U.S. cities. Contrary to what a naive application of an abstract economic model might have led us to expect, however, the concentration of manufacturing employment was not *the* highest among large U.S. cities. Metropolitan Boston, for example, with only about three-quarters of metropolitan New York's population, had a larger manufacturing workforce. Thus, New York's manufacturing sector was "unsurprisingly large" but, from a purely theoretical perspective, anomalously small.

Chapter 6 explores this juxtaposition along several routes. First, a series of brief case studies of individual urban industries makes the case that what developed rapidly in urban America during the antebellum period was not generic "manufacturing" activity but, rather, a number of specific industries, each with its own unique geographic imperatives. Some of these industries were highly concentrated in the lower Hudson Valley, while others that one might have expected would have been New York specialties had, in fact, gravitated to either Philadelphia or Boston. New York's specialty industries, which collectively accounted for about 40% of the region's total manufacturing employment, shared some common attributes. With a single exception, they were all industries, such as stone carving or coal gas production, that fed into the City's rapid absolute population growth at the time or were, like publishing or men's clothing, directly or indirectly associated with New York's position as the Nation's principle conduit for imports. The development of the other footloose specialty industries in New York and elsewhere was based on the contingency of which region's residents happened to succeed in the business soonest. Thus, this first avenue of exploration leads to the plausible but unsatisfying conclusion that total manufacturing employment in New York in 1860 was somewhat smaller than one might have expected because, for example, metropolitan Boston's late eighteenth-century entrepreneurial shoemakers were luckier than New York's.

A second, more theoretically satisfying possibility is that the robust growth of cities in upstate New York, especially in the economically dynamic region bordering the Erie Canal, met some of the "hinterland" demand for manufactured goods. Philadelphia and Boston, the central places of less populous and less urbanized regions, may have met more of their respective backcountry's needs.

One other possible explanation for the aggregate size of New York's manufacturing sector on the eve of the Civil War is that the local service industries' demand for labor in an approximately "right sized" city may have "crowded out" manufacturing. The subsequent chapters explore this possibility by explaining why the population of the largest city in the United States as of 1860 could not have been much more or less than what New York's was, about one million.[1]

The City's population during the antebellum decades was determined by three types of decisions made by millions of individuals and households around the North Atlantic world. These were

1. Trans-Atlantic migration decisions by Europeans as to whether to leave their homelands and move to North America,
2. Trans-Appalachian decisions by immigrants from abroad and by native-born residents of the New England and the Middle Atlantic states as to whether to move to the American Midwest, and
3. Decisions by those who chose to stay in the Northeastern United States to live in New York City rather than elsewhere.

[1]In 1860, the combined populations of New York and Kings counties were 1.09 million.

Of course, the third decision is the principle concern of this book and constitutes the subject matter of Chapter 8. Chapter 7 sets the stage for that analysis by, first, pointing out that antebellum New York had a terrible reputation as a place for working-class families to live. This introductory chapter then sets out the motives for the mass migrations across the Atlantic Ocean and the Appalachian Mountains. A considerable body of evidence assembled and analyzed by economic historians over the past twenty years supports the belief that large numbers of Europeans moved to the United States and both immigrants and native-born Americans moved west because real wages were higher and workers' standard of living was better at the destinations than at the origins of these migrations.

Evidence that this straightforward consideration motivated the first two decisions makes it harder to understand why so many people chose to live in New York City. Chapter 8 begins by presenting evidence that real wages were *lower* and important aspects of the standard of living were *worse* in New York City than in other places in the United States. Although on-point quantitative information is very limited, there is a considerable body of indirect and circumstantial evidence that the cheapest available housing in New York City would have been substantially more expensive and of lower quality than elsewhere in the United States by the end of the antebellum decades. Demand for low-quality housing would have been expanding massively in a City where the population was growing rapidly and where a very large proportion of the newcomers were impoverished European immigrants. While plenty of new homes were being built, almost all of the new construction was of relatively expensive single-family row-houses located far beyond easy walking distance from most working-class jobs. New Yorkers seeking "affordable" housing had, therefore, to make due with subdivided, formerly single-family homes situated on very expensive land near southern Manhattan's central business district.

Evidence that real wages were, in fact, lower in New York than elsewhere raises the obvious question of why its population was growing fast enough to bring the City to the pinnacle of the U.S. urban hierarchy. One goal of the second part of Chapter 8, therefore, is to explain why individuals and households, who could have chosen to live elsewhere, were attracted to New York notwithstanding the relatively low real wages on offer.

A complete account of antebellum New Yorkers' motives for their location decisions must also establish and account for the fact that the City was more attractive as a place to live and work for immigrants than for native-born Americans. The proportion of immigrants in New York's population was among the very highest across all U.S. counties on the eve of the Civil War. Further, based on a statistical regularity called "Zipf's law" that describes the distribution of city sizes, New York's population was approximately "right sized," given the overall level of development and urbanization in the United States at the time. The combination of these observations suggests that foreign-born newcomers to New York replaced or displaced some number of native-born Americans who might otherwise have been attracted to the City.

One reason New York was more attractive—or less unattractive—to immigrants than to the native born is that a relatively large proportion of the former belonged to demographic groups for whom the quality housing was not particularly important. Young, single men, for example, would have needed little more than a border's bed by way of residence, and many young Irish immigrant women found housing as well as employment as live-in servants.

The availability in New York of job opportunities for all family members, including pre-teenage children and stay-at-home mothers, may have been especially important to newcomers to the United States who were trying to establish themselves in a new country. Finally, there is evidence that robust social networks that enable newcomers to navigate the labor markets can be especially important to immigrants.

If the City was, in fact, right sized, then robust service sector demand for labor might very well have constrained the growth of local manufacturing industries. Accordingly, Chapter 9 traces the development of the U.S. financial services industry through the displaced nineteenth century as it affected the size and structure of New York City's economy. This industry was very highly concentrated in New York City, was an important local employer in and of itself, and influenced the broader development of the City's economy. The general aim of the chapter is to assess whether the high local concentration of financial services employment was simply an inevitable by-product of New York's position as the nation's largest city. In other words, is a counterfactual outcome in which banking and capital markets employment was distributed more evenly across cities nationwide with only a modestly greater concentration in New York plausible?

The first topic covered in the chapter is New York's unique role in the organization of the nation's monetary and banking system. Between 1836 and 1863, there was no centralized governance of the nation's money supply; each individual bank created its own currency in the form of banknotes, which were primarily used for local transactions. During this period, anyone in a business involving interregional or international trade had to have access to funds on deposit in the place where the most such transactions were effectuated. The effect was that banks from around the nation, in order to facilitate their customers interregional and international transactions, arranged on have funds on deposit in New York City. The Civil War era banking legislation codified and reinforced New York's status as the preferred location for interbank deposits under a new federal regulatory regime.

Banks located elsewhere may have kept even more money in New York than was needed to meet customer transactional needs for two reasons. First, competition among the City's banks kept the interest rates paid on these deposits at levels out-of-town banks considered attractive. Second, out-of-town bankers may have taken comfort from the New York banks' track record of acting in concert to head-off some incipient financial crises. Except at times when this fail-safe mechanism broke down, therefore, a combination of operational imperatives, the competitive organization of the local banking market, preferential regulatory treatment, and at least some assurance of stability drew a disproportionately large share of the nation's total money supply to New York banks from about 1840 until the eve of World War I.

The second part of Chapter 9 focuses on what the New York institutions did with their interbank liabilities, and the impact this had on the development of the U.S. financial system and of the City's economy. A substantial proportion of these funds were deployed as "call" or margin loans to participants in financial markets. Such lending was the ideal way to earn competitive interest rates on interbank funds. And the ready availability of financing for stock and bond holdings contributed to the development of deep, liquid securities markets in the

United States and tethered this activity to the location where the call loans were on offer.

The chapter concludes by tracing a counterfactual trajectory for the development of the U.S. monetary and financial system through the nineteenth century. The premise is that a plausible political compromise might have allowed the Bank of the United States to survive. If it had, a more decentralized financial system might have developed in the United States, in which regional banks played a much larger role in the nation's money and capital markets.

## Chapters 10 and 11: Global Heyday

The pace at which goods, money, and people moved around the Atlantic world, which had begun to pick-up after 1815, accelerated markedly between the end of the U.S. Civil War and the onset of World War I. This was also the period of New York City's most dramatic growth, both absolute and relative to the United States as a whole. Chapters 10 and 11 trace the connections between these two historical developments.

The first of these two chapters begins by asking why Chicago, which was geographically much closer to the U.S. population center and to the bulk ofits economic activity, did not overtake New York as the nation's largest City. The outcome of the two cities' rivalry is all the more surprising in light of evidence that real wages paid to working-class Chicagoans were noticeably higher than in New York. The general answer to this question is that New York was better positioned than any other U.S. city to make the most of accelerating globalization.

Chapter 10 considers the impact of increasing trade in goods through New York's port and of trans-Atlantic financial flows intermediated through the City's financial services firms. Rising trade volumes more than made up for the gradual decrease in New York's share of total U.S. trade, and employment directly and indirectly related to port activity increased substantially. At the same time, a mutually reinforcing beneficial relationship developed between trans-Atlantic investment flows and

America's New York-based securities markets. In describing, the evolution of this interaction Chapter 10 adds the international dimension to the previous chapter's account of how New York's financial services industry rose to national dominance.

Chapter 10 concludes with the observation that, as substantially as port and financial services activity may have been increasing, the expansion of these sectors alone, even taking into account the indirect impacts of their growth, cannot explain more than a small proportion of the rise in New York City's population between 1870 and 1910. The task of Chapter 11, therefore, is to identify the large, labor-intensive sectors that generated demand for many tens of thousands of workers and the identities and motives of the population groups that moved to New York City to fill that demand.

The two industries were construction and women's wear. And the two population groups were Southern Italians and East European Jews.

Between 1890 and 1920, the population of New York City's five boroughs grew by more than three million, the largest increase, by far, for any thirty-year period. Accommodating this many new New Yorkers required an unprecedented amount of housing and infrastructure construction, especially so because forging transportation connections across a tidelands archipelago was more complex than extending pavement into prairieland or building elevated rail lines. An elastic supply of diversely skilled construction workers was a necessary condition for New York City's growth.

Just when the demand for this type of labor was increasing rapidly in New York the preconditions for mass migration—rapid population growth and disruptive economic change—came into place in the southern *compartimenti* of the Kingdom of Italy. This cohort of emigrants were mostly male rural laborers who expected to return to their homelands or migrate elsewhere when they'd earned what they deemed to be enough money or when work opportunities at their first destination dried up. These workers were drawn to New York by the opportunity to earn much higher wages than were available at home or in alternative destinations and by the emergence locally of a labor market institution that was indigenous to southern Italy. *Padrones* were labor market brokers who earned the fees they charged by reducing newcomers' periods of unemployment and by facilitating workforce recruitment among Italian immigrants.

The industrial production of men's clothing became a New York City specialty during the antebellum decades. Production of women's clothing, by contrast, was, for the most part, an artisanal activity well into the second half of the nineteenth century. By the eve of World War I, however, rising incomes, increased female labor force participation, and a taste for simpler styling had provided the impetus for the industrialization of women's wear manufacturing. The industry that developed was characterized by volatile demand fluctuations and a combination of intense competition and cooperation within an eco-system of numerous, tiny, highly specialized businesses. Successful engagement in this business by bosses and workers required access to a continuous flow of reliable information about, for example, style changes, market conditions, which firms were hiring workers with which skills, who was offering commercial credit on attractive terms, and so on. The women's garment industry, like its men's wear predecessor, functioned best when embedded within a dense array of social networks.

The background, motives, and social institutions of the East European Jewish immigrant communities fit the requirements of the garment industry as if by design. Many of these newcomers had been seamstresses or tailors in the old country. Another substantial segment of this population had owned and operated small businesses in the homelands. And diaspora Jewish populations routinely establish communal organizations that, among other functions, serve as business information clearinghouses. Further, Jewish newcomers were more likely than other groups to plan on staying in America indefinitely and to migrate as family units. The rapidly expanding garment industry, which sought skills many of these immigrants already possessed, employed large numbers of both men and women and offered opportunities for career advancement, met these immigrants' needs.

As of the late nineteenth century from a purely domestic perspective, Chicago would have appeared likely to become North America's largest city. But New York, with its international connections—its port, its investment bankers, and its immigrant communities—maintained its top position in the U.S. urban hierarchy in a globalizing world.

# 4

# Catastrophic Agglomeration

"Catastrophe theory" develops "methods used to study and classify the ways in which a system can undergo sudden large changes in behavior as one or more of the variables that control it are changed continuously" (Britanica Encyclopedia on Line, 2018). Economists use the term "agglomeration" to denote the process by which large numbers of households and businesses choose to locate close to one another. Thus, "catastrophic agglomeration" refers to a sudden acceleration in the emergence and growth of cities. Over the past twenty-five years a body of scholarly literature, referred to as the new economic geography ("NEG"), has developed ideas about how, why, when, and where catastrophic agglomeration takes place. The applicability of this set of ideas to all economies at all stages of development is open to question, but the body of analysis does a good job of explaining the acceleration of North American urbanization during the second-quarter of the nineteenth century.[1]

[1]The material in the following section characterizes the models and discussions which were first presented in Krugman (1991) and received their most complete expression in Fujita, Krugman, and Venables (1999). The term "catastrophic agglomeration" appeared in Neary (2001). The discussion also bears in mind some of the critiques of the NEG approach drawn, for example, from Davis and Weinstein (1998) and Davis (1998).



A. Gurwitz, *Atlantic Metropolis*, Palgrave Studies in American Economic History,
https://doi.org/10.1007/978-3-030-13352-8_4

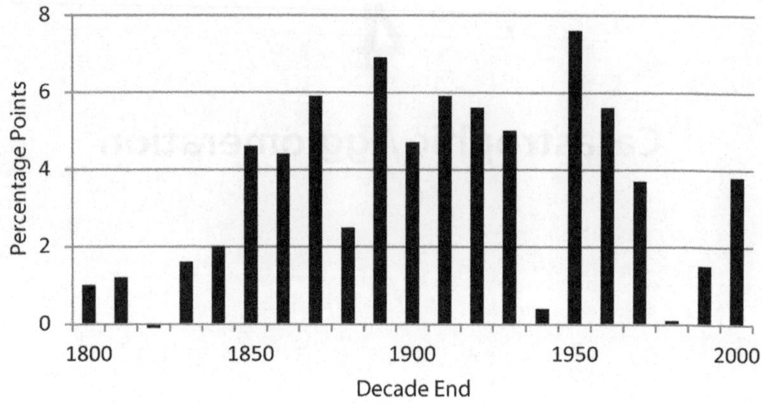


**Fig. 4.1** 10-year changes in the "Urban" percentage of U.S. population (Carter, 1976)

In 1790, only 5% of the new nation's population lived in places categorized as "urban" in that year's census, some of which were not much larger than a village. The 1920 census found that a bit more than half of the population was urban. This transition from an almost entirely rural society to a predominantly urban one did not occur at a steady rate. As Fig. 4.1 indicates during the 1810s, 1870s, 1930s, and 1970s, Americans tended, as it were, to stay down on the farm. The figure also indicates that the pace of urbanization accelerated markedly in the decades after 1840. Further, this process of agglomeration was not simply one in which the previously existing, roughly equal-sized small cities all became bigger at the same rate. Rather, growth of the largest cities accounted for a substantial proportion of the increase in the urban percentage. Thus, the period also saw the development of a hierarchy of central places with New York City at its pinnacle (Fig. 4.2). There is no precise definition of how large or how sudden a change counts as a "catastrophe," but it is apparent that something about the process of city growth in the United States was very different after about 1840 than it had been before. The NEG points us in the direction of some reasons why, when, and where this happened.

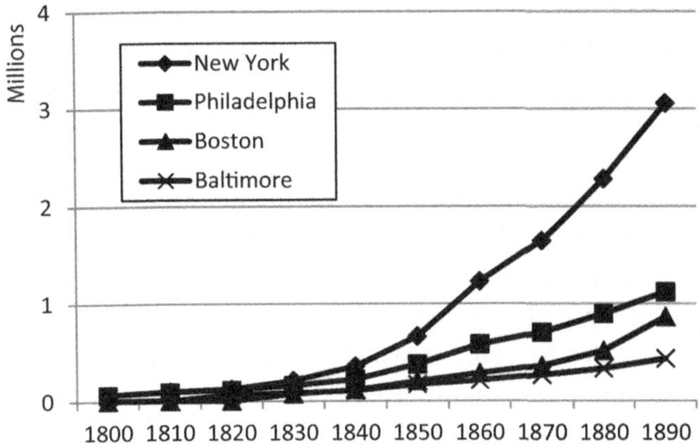


**Fig. 4.2** Populations of four urbanized areas (Carter, 1976)

## The Centripetal Tip

If families and businesses are free to decide where to locate, then whether economic activity agglomerates in cities or is spread out more or less evenly across a broad area depends on the balance between the centrifugal (dispersing) and centripetal (centralizing) forces that influence location decisions.

We can characterize the spatial distribution of economic activity in most of the Northern United States circa 1830 in a stylized way as a population consisting in large part of mostly, but not entirely self-sufficient farmers spread across a very broad area. Under such circumstances, the principle centrifugal influence will be transportation cost. Small towns populated by small-scale craftspeople who produced the few manufactured goods a farm family could not provide for themselves were also spread out broadly across the landscape because that pattern minimized the transportation cost incurred by evenly spaced consumers in acquiring the things they could not make for themselves.

Basic NEG models posit two centripetal forces: Economies of scale in manufacturing and households' preference for variety in the consumer goods they can buy. Specifically, the models assume that, at any given level of technological development, firms' production cost per unit of any particular manufactured good decreases as output increases up to some cost-minimizing production volume.[2] Further, different manufacturers produce differentiated products within a single category of goods. For example, one seamstress might specialize in sewing inexpensive, durable workday dresses for farm women while another might be known for producing more delicate, eye-catching garments to wear in church on Sundays. Either type of seamstress would need some minimum level of sales to make it worth her while to develop the requisite skills, set up shop, and maintain a stock of the appropriate fabrics and notions. It is easy to imagine that the volume of dressmaking business in a rural central place would be too small to support more than one seamstress. If so, the women of any given town and its hinterland might have to make do without either durable work clothes or, more likely, stylish dresses for special occasions.

As long as transportation costs are high enough and farm families' demand for manufactured goods is too small to support efficient production of a variety of goods at scale, agglomeration will be minimal and large cities will not form. As transportation costs decline, and/or as families come to spend a larger proportion of their income on manufactured goods produced by others, and/or as consumers' tastes become more diverse, centripetal forces gradually become more powerful relative to the centrifugal. Transportation costs may decline and the demand for manufactured goods may expand in both quantity and variety for a long time without any noticeable change taking place in the size of cities. Eventually, however, these gradual quantitative changes may reach a tipping point at which the formation of a large city becomes possible. Again, nothing may happen for a while. But once the conditions are ripe, if and when one of the scattered small towns

[2]The production of some services is also characterized by economies of scale, and this consideration became an important determinant of which activities concentrated in New York during the twentieth century. Early in the nineteenth century, however, economies of scale primarily affected the location of manufacturing.

happens by chance to become a little bigger than the others, a self-reinforcing process of agglomeration will begin.

Because the slightly larger town's home market is now bigger, its manufacturers will be able to produce at slightly larger scale and, therefore, at lower cost. If, as we assume, these local firms aim to maximize profits, they will seek ways to use their newfound cost advantage to expand their sales. They will be able to do so because, with transportation costs and per-unit production costs now lower and with farm families' demand for diverse manufactured goods growing, firms can increase their profits by shipping their products over a wider area while still charging less than local small-town, small-scale competitors. The larger population of the slightly bigger town may also be able to support firms producing a wider variety of consumer goods at efficient scale. The expanding manufacturing firms in the slightly larger town will be able to attract workers without raising wages appreciably because transportation costs for food products have declined and because the efficiently sized, diverse local manufacturers now offer a wider variety of attractively priced consumer goods to local residents. The growing local population allows more firms, producing more varieties to operate at efficient scale and the town, now even bigger, will be able to expand the hinterland in which it sells its manufactured products even further. In this way, the growth process becomes continually self-reinforcing, and the town quickly becomes a city. The city's population and the extent of its market reach will expand up to the point that transportation costs to the edge of the hinterland raise the prices of the city's products up the level where small-town, small-scale production is still competitive.

The agglomeration story might end here in a geographic region that was only large enough to support one city populated by efficiently sized firms. In more populous regions, however, the process of city formation might occur in several, widely separated places simultaneously. Further, if the cost-minimizing production volume and/or per-unit transportation cost differ across varieties of manufactured goods, a hierarchy of city sizes may evolve. The goods characterized by the most powerful returns to scale or the lowest transportation costs would only be produced in the biggest city. Other products, for which the cost-minimizing production volume is smaller and/or transportation costs are higher, will be produced in the metropolis *and* in smaller cities situated within their own, less-extensive hinterlands. Thus, in a large region a decline of transportation costs and increase in the share of families' income spent on manufactured goods may lead to the formation of a hierarchy of cities.

## System Control Variables: 1825–1850

### Transportation Cost

It is not an overstatement to characterize the nineteenth century's changes in transportation technology and infrastructure as revolutionary. In 1810, overland transportation of goods on one of the 4,684 miles of improved turnpikes would have been by horse-, mule-, or ox-drawn wagon at an approximate cost of 30 cents per ton-mile. By 1900, shipping a ton of freight over one of the nation's 260,000 miles of railroad track averaged less than three-quarters of a cent per mile. This "revolution" was closely associated with the development of railroad technology and the build-out of a dense and extensive rail network, most of which occurred after the civil war; 86% of the track mileage in operation in 1900 had been added after 1865 (Carter, 1976, pp. 728–729; Fishlow, 2000). That said, the second-quarter of the nineteenth century did benefit from a large reduction in transportation costs, especially within the northeastern states.

The next chapter will devote attention to one aspect of the transportation revolution's early decades: the canal craze. At this point, it will suffice to point out three salient facts about the canal network, most of which was put in place between 1825 and 1850. First, shipping by canal was cheap and getting cheaper; freight rates for canal shipments had declined from around five cents per ton in 1817 to 1.8 cents in 1840 and less than a penny a decade later. Second, by 1860 the system was quite extensive with a total of about 4,500 miles in operation, more than half of which was located in the Middle Atlantic states of Delaware, Maryland, New Jersey, New York, and Pennsylvania (Segal, 1972).

Finally, the freight rates and mileage alone understate the extent to which canal development improved the overall American transportation system. The function of canals was not to carry goods from the point of production all the way to the final consumer's doorstep. Rather, by their nature, canals broke transportation bottlenecks by linking bodies of water which were already established as thoroughfares of commerce.

Over the course of the second-quarter of the nineteenth century, steamboats carried a rapidly increasing proportion of traffic on those commercial thoroughfares. Again, the impact on freight costs was dramatic. In 1804, prior to the introduction of steam technology in the United States, the cost of shipping a ton of goods one mile upstream averaged eight cents. By 1825, the cost had fallen to a penny. And travel time between New York City and Albany via the Hudson River had fallen from four-and-a-half, days in 1800 to about a day and a half by 1830 (Carter, 1976, Table Df17-21; Paullin & Wright, 1932).

The cost of transoceanic and coastal transportation also decreased substantially during the first half of the nineteenth century. Between the five-year periods ending in 1825 and 1850, an index of average maritime freight rates computed by economic historian C. Douglass North declined by about 45%[3] (North, 1968).

The cost of long-distance travel by road was prohibitive for everything except the lightest or highest-priority goods. Over shorter distances, however, improved roads could reduce relevant transportation costs and thereby expanded a city's potential hinterland. A "rage" for turnpike construction, especially in New England and the Middle Atlantic states, played out during the first-quarter of the nineteenth century and left a trail of financial failures in its wake. Nevertheless, by 1830 northeastern travelers and shippers could have moved over nearly 12,000 miles of improved turnpikes. At 0.30 and 0.17 turnpike

[3]Subsequent research by C. Knick Harley found that the dramatic decline in freight rates reflected in North's index may have been driven primarily by improved efficiency in the shipment of cotton and, therefore, may have only affected the coastal and transoceanic trade of the United States. Large decreases in the cost of shipping other goods on other global routes had to await the widespread use of steam technology and metal hulls during the second half of the nineteenth century. Since, as the next chapter will demonstrate, cotton played a particularly important role in New York City's commercial economy, North's findings are more relevant here (Harley, 1988).

miles per square mile of land area, respectively, the density of improved roadways was particularly high in Connecticut and Rhode Island, both of which had strong economic ties to New York City (Fishlow, 2000, p. 549; Taylor, 1951, pp. 24–26; U.S. Census Bureau, 2018).

## Industrial Production

Although we don't have direct statistical information on typical household budgets for this period, the proportion of the average American family's income spent on manufactured goods must have grown rapidly during the second-quarter of the nineteenth century because the quantity of product sold expanded much faster than household incomes. Despite the stimulus to domestic manufacturing provided by pre-war and wartime embargoes and blockades, U.S. industrial production expanded slowly during the first-quarter of the nineteenth century. Thereafter, manufacturing experienced the kind of take-off described by Walter Rostow; industrial production increased much more rapidly than household incomes. Between 1830 and 1850, U.S. per capita industrial production increased by 87% or by more than three percent at an average annual rate. And even as the domestic industrial production grew, imports were also increasing; the per capita nominal value of manufactured imports grew by almost 50% between 1830 and 1850. Over the same period of time United States, real per capita gross domestic product may have increased by around 20% and real wages paid to manufacture workers in the Brandywine region of northern Delaware and southeastern Pennsylvania grew by 18% (Adams, 1982, p. 904; Carter, 1976, Table Ee446-457; Davis, 2004, p. 1189; Johnston & Williamson, 2018).

## Population Size and Diversity

Whether catastrophic agglomeration leads to the growth of a single large city or a system of cities depends in part on the size of the region's population, the larger the population the more cities that can emerge.

So, it is worth noting in this context that the first half of the nineteenth century witnessed the fastest rate of population growth in U.S. history.

The NEG attributes potential importance to households' preference for a diverse array of consumer goods. The basic NEG models build on the simplifying assumption that all households are identical in all respects and that each assigns the same value to the variety of choices available. Thus, for example, a population of identical beer drinkers might be happier if they can enjoy a pale ale one evening, a lager the next, and a hearty stout the next. Such fickle beer drinkers will be able to achieve a higher level of utility if they live in a city with three specialty breweries than they could in a town with just one supplier. It is also possible, however, to think of otherwise similar households differing in the type of consumer goods they prefer. One household may prefer ale, another, lager, and a third, stout. A populous city would be attractive to all types of beer drinker, while a smaller, one-brewery town might only be an attractive place to live for one type. Cities able to offer the broadest variety of consumer goods have to potential to attract residents—i.e., potential willing workers—of all types. And the greater the number of different types of consumer that live in a region, the higher the likelihood that agglomeration, once underway, will become self-reinforcing.[4]

There was good reason to choose beer as the exemplar of a differentiated consumer product. Aggregate consumer preferences with respect to this beverage became more diverse toward the end of the nineteenth century's second-quarter when the first wave of mass migration began to hit U.S. shores. The causes and effects of transatlantic migration will be treated in more detail when our focus shifts to the New York labor market. At this point, it will suffice to point out that the new immigrants were not only more numerous than their predecessors, but also more ethnically diverse. Great Britain was recorded as the origin of more than a quarter of the roughly 100,000 1820s immigrants but only about

[4]In terms of the basic identical-households NEG model as presented by Fujita, Krugman, and Venables, the assertion here is that an increase in the number of different types of consumers would have the same impact on the likelihood of agglomeration as a decrease in the elasticity of substitution across products in the universal utility function.

16% percent of the 1.4 million who arrived during the 1840s. A large proportion of the latter decade's immigrants were German, with a taste for lagers and Sunday excursions to beer gardens but little if any liking for the English porters and ales served over a saloon counter. And the increasingly numerous Irish immigrants would probably have opted for stouts sooner than either the German or British varieties (Baron, 1962, pp. 175–184; Carter, 1976).

## Agglomeration, but Where?

This chapter aimed to explain why and when catastrophic agglomeration occurred in the United States guided by the framework of the NEG. Put simply: By the second-quarter of the nineteenth-century transportation costs had fallen by enough, manufactured products had come to account for a large enough proportion of household spending, population had expanded enough, and, perhaps, too, consumer tastes had diversified enough for a hierarchy of cities to emerge with one metropolis at its pinnacle. The NEG framework has less to say about where exactly within geographic region cities will form. The basic notion is that when the time is ripe for catastrophic agglomeration, whichever of the small, roughly equal-sized central places happens by chance to be a little bigger than the others will become the metropolis through a process of self-reinforcing growth. The observation that large cities tend to be located along navigable rivers or at maritime ports is not inconsistent with the NEG understanding of the process of urbanization. These tend to be the places where transportation costs to and from all other locations are, on average, lowest. But there were many such places in the United States at the beginning of the nineteenth century, and four of these locations—Baltimore, Boston, New York, and Philadelphia—were the sites of roughly equal-sized, economically very similar, small cities. Within the context of the NEG, therefore, New York City became the metropolis because it just happened to be, by a modest but sufficient margin, the largest of the four at the time in the 1820s or 1830s when transportation costs, industrial production, and population happen to have reached the point where city growth was ready to accelerate.

There is another, more traditional school of thought about the location of cities that emphasizes the numerous natural differences among geographic locations and looks to the comparative advantages conveyed by these differences as places to locate. From this perspective, for example, New York's direct access to the Atlantic through the Narrows conveys advantages relative to, for example, Baltimore's route to the open sea around the southern end of the Delmarva Peninsula. This intuitively satisfying approach has much to be said for it as reason for New York's premier position in the North American urban hierarchy; the City's geographic advantages relative to its competitors include the fact that, as an estuary, the Hudson flows in two directions over the course of a day and the deep, well-sheltered, generally ice-free, and easily accessible harbor. In retrospect, given that we know which city was the "winner," these advantages make New York's ascendance seem inevitable. But other places have advantages, too. Although Baltimore was farther from the Atlantic as a ship sails, in the early nineteenth century its location roughly 200 miles closer to the rapidly growing Ohio Valley and to the booming, cotton-exporting south might arguably have outweighed the superiority of New York's harbor. Like the NEG, the comparative-advantage approach helps us ponder but does not answer the question: "Why here and not elsewhere?"

One final way in which the location of cities might be determined is also worth considering. Sometimes the site of a city is determined by political decisions. The most obvious example in U.S. history is Washington, DC. No doubt either Alexandria, Virginia, or Georgetown, Maryland, or both, situated as they were at the head of the Potomac River tidewater, would have grown substantially during the nineteenth century. But it is unlikely that this would have been the site today of the nation's seventh-largest metropolitan area absent the political compromise that moved the U.S. capital to the Maryland-Virginia border.

What combination of natural advantages, political decisions, and randomness brought New York City to the pinnacle of the U.S. urban hierarchy? Were alternative outcomes "plausible as well as merely conceivable"? The next chapter explores these questions.

## References

Adams, D. R. (1982). The Standard of Living During American Industrialization: Evidence from the Brandywine Region, 1800–1860. *The Journal of Economic History, 42*(4), 903–917.

Baron, S. (1962). *Brewed in America: A History of Beer and Ale in the United States*. Boston: Little Brown.

Britannica Encyclopedia on Line. (2018). *Catastrophe Theory*. Retrieved from http://www.britannica.com/EBchecked/topic/99235/catastrophe-theory.

Carter, S. B. (1976). *Historical Statistics of the United States Millennial Edition Online*. Cambridge: Cambridge University Press.

Davis, D. R. (1998). The Home Market, Trade and Industrial Structure. *American Economic Review, 88*(5), 1264–1276.

Davis, D. R., & Weinstein, D. E. (1998, November). *Market Access, Economic Geography and Comparative Advantage: An Empirical Assessment* (National Bureau of Economic Research Working Paper No. 6787).

Davis, J. H. (2004). An Annual Index of U.S. Industrial Production, 1790–1915. *The Quarterly Journal of Economics, 119*(4), 1177–1215.

Fishlow, A. (2000). Internal Transportation in the Nineteenth and Early Twentieth Centuries. In S. Engerman & R. E. Gallman (Eds.), *The Cambridge Economic History of the United States, Volume II, The Long Nineteenth Century* (pp. 543–642). Cambridge: Cambridge University Press.

Fujita, M., Krugman, P., & Venables, A. (1999). *The Spatial Economy: Cities, Regions, and International Trade*. Cambridge: MIT Press.

Johnston, L., & Williamson, S. H. (2018). *What Was the U.S. GDP Then?* Retrieved from MeasuringWorth.com https://www.measuringworth.com/datasets.html.

Neary, J. P. (2001). Of Hype and Hyperbolas: Introducing the New Economic Geography. *Journal of Economic Literature*, 536–561.

North, D. C. (1968). Sources of Productivity Change in Ocean Shipping, 1600–1850. *Journal of Political Economy, 76*(5), 953–970.

Paullin, C. O., & Wright, J. K. (1932). *Rates of Travel from New York City, 1857*. Retrieved from Atlas of the Historical Geography of the United States http://dsl.richmond.edu/historicalatlas/138/c/.

Segal, H. H. (1972). Cycles of Canal Construction. In C. Goodrich (Ed.), *Canals in American Economic Development* (pp. 211–213). Port Washington, NY: Kennikat Press.

Taylor, G. R. (1951). *The Transportation Revolution: 1815–1860*. New York: Rinehart & Co., Inc.

U.S. Census Bureau. (2018). *State Area Measurements and Internal Point Coordinates*. Retrieved from Geography https://www.census.gov/geo/reference/state-area.html.

# 5

# A Port in Time

New York City happened to be somewhat larger than other North American central places on the eve of catastrophic agglomeration for two main reasons. First, in 1815 New York became the principal port of entry for foreign goods coming into the United States. Developments over the subsequent decade solidified the City's international trade ranking and extended New York's dominance to the domestic coastal trade. Second, during the early decades of the nineteenth-century New York City's immediate economic hinterland grew more rapidly than those of the other contenders for the role of national metropolis, Philadelphia, and Baltimore. A third reason is also worth considering. The relative rapidity of New York's growth during the crucial period may also reflect the failure of these two other cities' political and business leadership to exploit their own potential advantages effectively.

## Cotton Was the New Sugar

In 1815, the series of wars that had embroiled varying combinations of the major Western European powers since the late sixteenth century came to an end, and the world entered what would turn out to be a



A. Gurwitz, *Atlantic Metropolis*, Palgrave Studies in American Economic History,
https://doi.org/10.1007/978-3-030-13352-8_5

100-year period of relative calm under the aegis of the British Empire. The wars themselves and the mercantilist policies that were both a cause and effect of the conflicts had slowed the expansion of world trade through much of the long eighteenth century. Conflicts in which privateering served as a belligerent tactic raised the cost of moving goods around the Atlantic world as shippers paid higher insurance rates. And embargoes and blockades restricted the flow of goods.

During the military conflict, the prices of imports in most countries were, on average, higher relative to domestic goods prices than had been the case before 1793 or would be the case after 1814.[1] This suggests that war suppressed trade so that, had the world been at peace during the interval, international commerce would have grown faster and by more than it did. If so, the end of the wars should have been followed by a rapid expansion of trade and economic integration, especially so because the wars' biggest winner, the UK, was a "nation of shopkeepers." That, in fact, is what happened. The nineteenth century witnessed large increases in trade volumes and decreases in international price differentials for traded commodities (Jacks, 2005). Rising commodity trade volume is the primary focus at this point, but it is worth noting that other aspects of this first great wave of economic globalization, such as mass transatlantic migration and international capital flows, also played major roles in New York City's economic history and will command attention in subsequent chapters.

At the same time, as international trade was increasing and, perhaps in part, *because* international trade was increasing, the changes in manufacturing operations referred to as the industrial revolution began to accelerate, especially in the northern counties of England where the

---

[1]The decrease in trade was reflected both in decreases in the volume of legally imported commodities and, more tellingly, in large increases in the prices of imported goods relative to domestically produced products in both belligerent and neutral countries around the Atlantic world. Kevin O'Rourke found, for example, that "the increase in the relative price of importables was particularly pronounced during the blockade years [1807–1814], with increases of more than 100%, or even 200%, being common." O'Rourke points out the decreases in reported (i.e., legal) trade volumes does not necessarily reflect a decline in trading activity because the volume of goods smuggled cannot be observed directly. If that volume had been large, however, it would have offset any effect of trade restrictions on the relative prices of imports (O'Rourke, 2006).

first innovations had been introduced in the mid-eighteenth century. By the best available estimates, British industrial production grew at an average annual rate of 3.1% between 1815 and 1840, almost twice as fast as the previous 45 years' 1.6% pace. Britain's industrial production also grew faster than its economy as a whole; on average, manufacturing generated about 21% of British GDP between 1760 and 1810 and about 34% during the subsequent four decades. The postwar expansion of the British manufacturing sector—or at least that part of it involved in international markets—was concentrated in a small number of industries, of which textile production was by far the most important. Between 1844 and 1846, textiles accounted for 69% of total British exports and 78% of manufactured exports. Cotton textiles' rapid rise to prominence among British export industries was particularly dramatic. During the mid-1780s, a relatively peaceful interval between the American and French revolutions, cotton goods accounted for 6% of British exports compared to 40% for woolens and other textile products. By the mid-1840s, cottons' share was 44% and other textiles' was 25% (Stokey, 2001).

Cotton production and processing can usefully be viewed as the leading industry of the nineteenth-century "take off" of the North Atlantic industrial and trading economy in much the same way as sugar influenced the eighteenth-century expansion of the British Empire of goods. There are numerous similarities. Both raw cotton and sugar cane were (semi-)tropical products of American plantations; both were cultivated by gangs and slave labor; both were processed by means of what were at the time cutting-edge industrial technologies; and both served as the principal raw material inputs to very rapidly expanding industries. The parallels go further. As with sugar during the eighteenth century, the Middle Atlantic region of the United States was not directly engaged in the production of raw cotton or, at least in comparison with England, in textile manufacturing, the "primary growth sector" of the nineteenth-century takeoff. Instead, the growth of the New York City, Philadelphia, and Baltimore and their hinterlands was driven primarily by the expansion of such "secondary growth sectors" as food production for slaves and textile workers, shipbuilding, and mercantile services to manage the burgeoning flow of raw and manufactured commodities.

There were also, of course, important differences between the eighteenth- and nineteenth-centuries' takeoffs. For one thing, the Middle Atlantic colonies' engagement in the sugar industry was as an integral part of the British Empire. While Parliament's mercantilist policies had imposed some impediments on colonists' trading activities, North Americans were free to ship their flour to the Caribbean, bring Jamaican and Barbadian molasses and muscovado to old or New England, and to carry manufactured goods from England to anywhere within the Empire. During the early years of the nineteenth-century takeoff, Americans were excluded from many of these lucrative trading channels. In particular, the Corn Laws, enacted by Parliament in 1815 to protect British agricultural interests, imposed prohibitive taxes on the import of grains and grain products to the UK, except in years when home-grown supplies were deemed inadequate. Until these laws were gradually relaxed and ultimately repealed in the 1840s, U.S. grain exporters were effectively barred from their largest potential market.

Second, the United States loomed much larger as a potential importer and exporter during the nineteenth century than the North American colonies had during the earlier period. The first decades of the nineteenth century were a period of rapid growth in the United States in almost every dimension. Between 1800 and 1840 total population more than tripled, total land area organized as states doubled, and industrial production increased 600%. Expansion took place everywhere but was most dramatic in the west; in 1810, three percent of the nation's population lived in trans-Appalachia; and in 1840, the figure was about 25%. These changes must have been noticeable in a global context. In 1750, the total population of the colonies may have been about one-sixth of Great Britain's; by 1830, the U.S. population was about half as large as its former mother country's (Census, 1976).

Third, while sugar cane was not grown in large quantities in North America, over the course of the first half of the nineteenth century the United States became the dominant producer and exporter of cotton. U.S. raw cotton exports increased more than 40-fold. Production expanded rapidly as lands in the South Central region were brought under cultivation, as the slave population that almost tripled in size, as better strains of cotton plants came into use, and as slave-owners developed new ways to enforce greater field-worker productivity. Between 1820 and 1860, the weight of cotton the average slave could pick in a day increases 2.3-fold, and by the early 1840s, the US share of worldwide raw cotton production peaked at close to 90% (Baptist, 2014, p. 128; Irwin, 2003).

Finally, over the course of the postwar decades the process of moving commodities around the Atlantic world became more systematic, more efficient, and cheaper. This evolution was not primarily driven by technological change in the shipping industry, at least not until the 1840s when the steam-powered trans-Atlantic ships began coming into service. Instead, the earlier changes mostly involved the ways in which trade was organized and financed. As the nineteenth-century progressed shipping, schedules became more regularized, downtime in port decreased, and the flow of goods gravitated more and more to the most efficient channels. This contributed to the decline in transoceanic and coastal freight rates discussed in the previous chapter. On the financial side, banknotes began to replace the more variegated Bills of Exchange as the principal vehicle for the international and domestic movement of cash and credit.

New York's port rose to dominance and New York's hinterland grew particularly rapidly because more of these global and domestic trends worked—or were made to work—in the City's favor than was the case for the other potential North American metropolises.

## The Rise of New York Port

As Fig. 5.1 illustrates, on the eve of the War of 1812 imports to New England and Middle Atlantic states were roughly evenly divided among the ports of New York, Pennsylvania, and Massachusetts. In the years after the war ended, New York's share of imports, as measured by customs revenue collections, consistently exceeded the combined value of goods flowing in via the other two states. This sudden rise to dominance reflects five developments: (i) the decision by British exporters to direct the bulk of their first peacetime deliveries to New York, (ii) New York State's enactment of legislation that encouraged auction activity, (iii) the inauguration of scheduled "packet" shipping service between

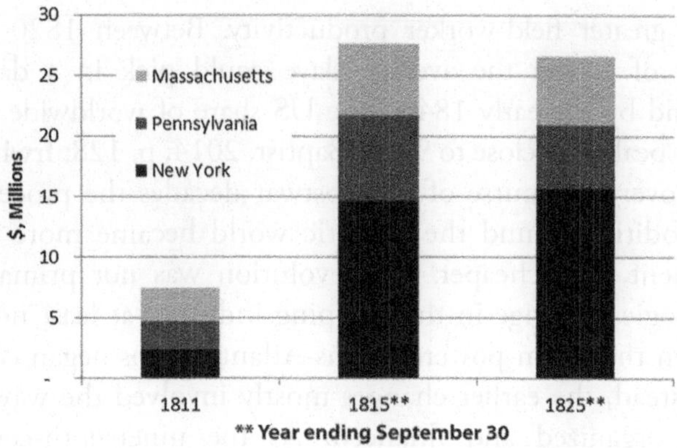


**Fig. 5.1** Customs collections by state (Albion, The Rise of New York Port, 1815–1860, 1939, pp. 12–13)

Great Britain and North America with, for several crucial initial years, New York City as its sole western terminus, (iv) the relatively rapid growth of New York's hinterland, and (v) the emergence of an Atlantic region "cotton triangle" with New York as one of its vertices.

## War and Peace

Most Americans, if they were touched at all by the French Revolutionary and Napoleonic Wars or War of 1812, experienced these conflicts as a series of booms and busts in international trade (Fig. 5.2). At first, as each European combatant barred enemy flagships from its own and its allies' ports and dispatched privateers to prey on enemy merchant shipping, Americans, as sea-faring neutrals, were able to capture a large portion of the global carry trade (Fichter, 2010, pp. Chapter 4, passim). In addition, wartime disruptions of normal economic activity boosted European demand for American products.

As the wars continued, however, both the French and the British adopted strategies aimed at restricting or disrupting neutral trading with their respective enemies. And, faced with manpower shortages, the British Navy began "impressing" alleged British subjects working as crew on American merchant vessels. Between 1807 and 1812, as

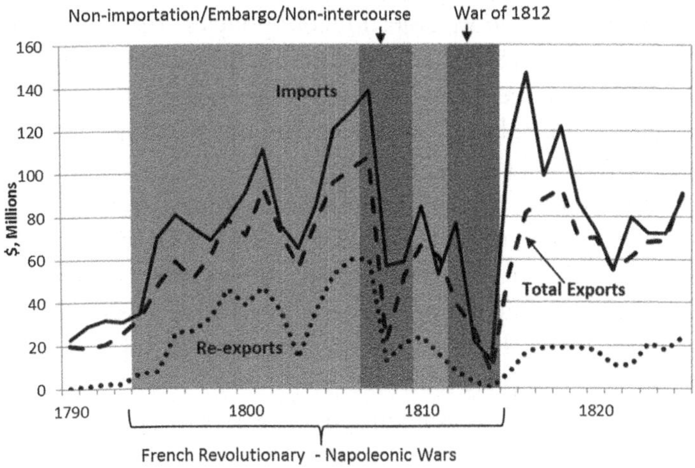


**Fig. 5.2** U.S. International Trade (Census, 1976)

European combatants interfered with some 900 American ships (Hickey, 2012), and these occasionally violent confrontations at sea between American and, most frequently, British vessels threatened to lead to outright warfare between the UK and United States. To pressure the British and French to leave U.S. shipping alone by means short of war the Jefferson administration and its supporters in Congress enacted a series of laws restricting international commerce. The aim of the Non-Importation Act of 1806, which prohibited a long list of specific British products from entering the United States on pain of confiscation, was to punish the UK by denying its manufacturers access to their largest export market. The draconian Embargo Act of 1807 forbade U.S.-registered ships from leaving port for other countries (Stuart, 1984) regardless of their destination. Foreign-flag carriers were permitted entry and unlading, provided they weren't carrying prohibited goods of British origin. In 1809, Congress replaced the Embargo Act with the Non-Intercourse Act, which permitted U.S. ships to sail for ports outside of the British and French Empires. Although enforcement of these laws was somewhat confused and uneven, they did have the effect of reducing legal trading activity. And, despite a high volume of smuggling, the U.S. trading restrictions may have induced the British government to moderate some of its most objectionable policies. In the end, however, the Jefferson (1801–1809) and Madison (1809–1817) administrations failed in their objective of maintaining peace and on June 18, 1812 the United States declared war on Great Britain (Heaton, 1941; Hickey, 2012, pp. Loc. 601–1187/12784).

Both combatants' arsenals included economic weapons. The U.S. enacted laws against trading with the enemy, and Britain blockaded U.S. ports to cut off all international and coastal commerce. So, as Fig. 5.2 indicates, while the pre-war trading restrictions may have ended the (legal aspects of the) "neutral" trading boom, war brought (legal) trading to a near complete halt.

The Jefferson-Madison foreign policy was extremely unpopular in New York and elsewhere in the northeastern part of the United States. Compared with other declarations of war in U.S. history, the 1812 vote in Congress was very close, partisan, and sectional. The northeastern states, where maritime commerce was an economic mainstay, strenuously opposed the Non-Importation, Embargo, and Non-Intercourse Acts. And a majority of congressmen from states north of Pennsylvania, including many members of the administration's own Democratic-Republican Party, voted against going to war. Opposition in New York, both to economic warfare before 1812 and the military conflict that ensued, was so impassioned that the President's principal opponent in his closely fought wartime campaign for reelection was sometime New York City Mayor and New York State Governor DeWitt Clinton, nominally a member of the President's Democratic-Republican Party and nephew of Madison's first Vice President (Cernog, 1996).

New England, where the Federalists, a fading political party elsewhere, still had considerable influence, was even more anti-embargo and anti-war than New York. Opposition there was so virulent that in late 1814, representatives of the New England states convened at Hartford with secession from the United States on the agenda. New England's opposition to the Jefferson-Madison pre-war policies and to the war itself was expressed in actions as well as words. Throughout the period of trade disruption, New Englanders continued to transact business with the British Empire, in large part through Quebec, Nova Scotia, and New Brunswick. The UK government was apparently well aware of New England's dissent and attempted to exploit it by helping the region's smugglers evade American interdiction and the British blockade (Heaton, 1941, p. 189; Hickey, 1981; Stuart, 1984).

British exporters, who had been barred from their U.S. market much of the time since 1807, were, of course, avidly awaiting the end of hostilities and would have learned about the Treaty of Ghent before Americans got the same information. In any case, a flood of imports entered the United States immediately after the war ended. Goods, some of which had been stockpiled in Bermuda and Halifax, Nova Scotia, were shipped before orders could be received, so the British exporters had to guess where would be the best place to direct their first shipments.

New York City would have been the obvious best first destination. The New England ports were closest to Great Britain and Halifax. But the high incidence of wartime smuggling may have taken the edge off of New Englanders' hunger for British goods. The next closest major port to the Maritime Provinces and Great Britain was New York, and this City may also have had a reputation as an entrepôt where anything could be sold at a price. Whatever the exporters' reasoning, the result is clear; New York's share of three-state total customs collections, which had been 32% in 1811, was 53% in the twelve months ending in September 1815.

The more important question is why trade flows did not return to their pre-war channels quickly after inventories had been dumped and pent-up demand slaked. Why, at 59%, was New York's share of three-state total customs collections even higher in 1825 than it had been in the first postwar year?

## Orders vs. Auctions

War, peace, and the associated trade booms and busts affected not only the volume of goods traded but also engendered changes in the organization of the mercantile services industry. During most of the eighteenth century, North American merchants mediated most routine imports. Trading firms owned and operated by permanent residents of North American port cities would place orders with British and other

European manufacturers or dealers for varieties and quantities of goods based on locally sourced information regarding demand. Merchants occasionally made mistakes by ordering too much of a commodity, and sometimes goods would arrive by surprise, as when a privateer brought a rich prize into port. In such cases, absent better means of price discovery, goods might be consigned to one of the small number of auction houses operating in North American port cities. But most goods at most times were brought into the country and dispatched down the local supply chain in response to information about local demand conditions. One anonymous contemporary source indicates that some 90% of pre-war imports into New York City fulfilled specific orders (Anonymous, 1828, Reprint 2017, p. 7).[2]

The policies and wars that disrupted routine international and domestic commodity flows, however, also blocked the flow of information on which American importers had relied. The most reliable information about local demand would have been generated by recent transactions. So, after many months with no imported muslins to sell, for example, a New York City wholesaler finally in a position to acquire goods might have little idea of how much pent-up demand there was in the Hudson Valley, how high a price the first few shipments might command, or how much more to order from Liverpool. At such times, when proprietary information was scarce, an auction, where the bidding would, in principle, reflect all of the information available in New York City regarding nationwide demand, would be the best way for an importer to discover the goods' value.

Other changes were taking place during the postwar period that also increased the popularity of auctions among both sellers and buyers. For one thing, the supply of and demand for imports remained erratic for several years after 1815. The initial flood of British goods evidently swamped the domestic market and prices collapsed in 1816 (Anonymous, 1828, Reprint 2017, p. 7). Then postwar financial instability climaxed in a severe downturn in 1819 followed by a slow recovery through the 1820s, (Sellers, 1991, p. 137 ff.) and macroeconomic volatility reduced the reliability of current market information.

[2]The source is an anti-auction polemic and may not be reliable.

Changes were also taking place in the way international trade was financed. In the eighteenth century, British exporters sold goods to American merchants on credit, and this conveyed an advantage for repeat customers with established reputations for reliability. As the U.S. economy grew and matured, American banks became an important source of credit for importers. The development of local sources of funds, which enabled U.S. buyers to pay for British goods when purchased, was timely as credit conditions were tight in postwar Britain (Cohen, 1971). The availability of local credit sources also made buying at auctions, which generally required either immediate or very briefly deferred payment terms, easier than it had been relative to relying on British vendor financing of purchases on order.

Finally, postwar British textile manufacturers may have faced something of a buyers' market. As raw cotton production expanded, as factories became larger, and as the volume of capital invested in the textile industry increased, continuous operations, regardless of short-term demand fluctuations, may have become imperative. Thus, British manufacturers may have felt increasingly compelled to continue producing goods and shipping them to the United States even in the absence of orders. Accordingly, the manufacturers' involvement in the American market became more proactive, and British firms began stationing representatives in American port cities. These agents' roles were to gather and communicate information about local demand trends *and* to manage the disposal at the highest possible price of goods already produced and shipped, willy-nilly, to the United States. For this purpose, too, auctions would have been a preferred distribution vehicle (Mokyr, 1977).

At its peak in 1827, half of the imports entering the U.S. through New York—that is, about 25% of total U.S. imports—were sold at auction. As the postwar decades progressed, as international commodity flows stabilized at higher levels or accelerated steadily, and as macroeconomic conditions stabilized the popularity of auction sales as a price-discovery mechanism dissipated; during the 1830s, the percentage of U.S. imports sold at auction in New York City fluctuated between 8% and 20% (Cohen, 1971, p. 496). But the period when the proportion of U.S. imports sold through auctions peaked and New York emerged as the best place to execute such transactions coincided with the crucial decades when internal transportation costs were starting to decline more rapidly and when cities' destinies within the North American urban hierarchy were being determined.

New York City was the best place in the United States to execute auction sales during this crucial period in some part because of a somewhat serendipitous, perfectly timed, and remarkably well-conceived tax law adopted by the State Legislature in 1817.[3]

The positive impact of this legislation on New York City's auction market was serendipitous because the Legislature's aim in 1817 had little to do with auctions per se but was mainly intended to raise revenues to help finance building the Erie Canal, construction of which was authorized in that year. The financing of the Erie Canal construction will be discussed below. At this point, it will suffice to state that proceeds from a revised State tax on auction sales was one of the revenue sources dedicated to this purpose.

The timing was perfect because the law was enacted just when the initial dumping of British wartime inventories had largely run its course and trade patterns might have been expected to return to the pre-war norm with imports arriving in approximately equal volumes in New York, Boston, Philadelphia, and Baltimore. One important reason why this did not happen was that the late 1810s was also a time when British exporters and American importers, adjusting simultaneously to rising supplies and macroeconomic volatility, were most inclined to opt for auction sales.

Finally, the particular structure of auction taxation—advocated and, perhaps, drafted by Abraham Thompson, the lobbyist dispatched to Albany by the New York City auction industry—turns out to have been effective public policy. The Legislature was looking for revenues, and, at any given tax rate, the level of proceeds from this tax would depend on the volume of goods auctioned in New York City. Further, a rising volume of auctions at a particular location can become a self-reinforcing process. Potential buyers will be attracted to a city's auction houses if they believe that large volume of goods will be available for purchase at

[3]The material in this and the following four paragraphs synthesizes material in (Albion, 1939; Cohen, 1971).

potentially attractive prices. And potential sellers will be attracted by the expectation of finding a large number of bidders. But both buyers and sellers would be put off by high tax rates. In 1814, the Legislature had reduced auction tax rates and the 1817 law retained these lower rates with only small modifications.

But the new law also had the effect of changing the incentives facing sellers at auctions with regard to setting their reservation prices for goods. The reservation price is the minimum price at which the seller is willing to let go of his or her goods. To guarantee that the winning bid won't be below the minimum, the seller simply bids at the auction at the reservation price. If no potential buyer bids more than that price, the seller retains the goods. Prior to 1817, the New York auction tax was, in effect, only imposed if the goods changed hands. The new law expanded the tax base to include winning bids by sellers. This new tax structure imposed a cost on sellers equal to a percentage of their own bid. Economists Richard Engelbrecht-Wiggans and Tomas Nonnenmacher have shown that this expansion of the auction tax base would, under reasonable assumptions, have had the effect of reducing reservation prices.[4] Lower reservation prices, in turn, increased the chances of any given buyer getting what he or she considered a bargain. This would have had the effect of making New York a more attractive auction venue for potential buyers. And the prospect of finding more potential bidders may have more than offset any negative impact of the new tax structure on sellers' willingness to offer their goods in New York City (Albion, 1939; Cohen, 1971).

The specific structure of the tax law enacted in 1817 pretty clearly did no harm to New York's reputation as good place to dispose of unordered goods. It is less clear that the legislation, in and of itself, played an independent role in developing and maintaining the vibrancy of New York City as a venue for auction activity. Indeed, the causality may have run in the opposite direction. During the early nineteenth

[4]If there is no tax on goods that do not change hands, then, if the highest outsider bid is lower than the reservation price, the seller keeps the goods and incurs no cost. If there is a tax in such cases, the seller keeps the goods but incurs an out-of-pocket cost equal to a percentage of the reservation price. The change in the tax regime increases the cost to the seller of holding out for a high price and creates an incentive to set a lower reservation price (Engelbrecht-Wiggans & Nonnenmacher, 1999).

century, auctions and auctioneers were unpopular in many quarters. In particular, merchant firms, which had made a good living prior to the embargo and the war by ordering imports from Britain and selling them in North America, found themselves cut out of the postwar flow of goods by direct auction sales from British manufacturers to American distributors. Opponents seeking legislation to restrict the use of this method of sales accused auctioneers and U.S.-based British manufacturers' agents of, among other things, misrepresenting the quality of goods and of deceiving customs authorities about shipments' values. The passage of pro-auction legislation in New York in 1817 and the failure of other port cities' state legislatures to do likewise may reflect differences in the balance of power in New York, Massachusetts, Pennsylvania, and Maryland between advocates of the old and new ways of doing business in the Atlantic trading economy. And, if, in fact, New York had been more of an entrepôt than Boston, Philadelphia, or Baltimore during the eighteenth century, it would not have been surprising if New York's auctioneers were more influential in public affairs than their counterparts were in the other cities.

Whatever the causes, by the late 1810s the New York City auction market was, by far, the most active in the United States. Thus, a British or French exporter shipping goods to the United States in the absence of a specific order but in hopes of getting off a timely sale at the best possible price would have had good reason to choose New York as the port of entry. And, for this reason, among others, New York's port would have been the obvious choice as the western terminus for any regularly scheduled transatlantic "packet" shipping service.

## The Packets[5]

The terms "packet" and "liner" refer to one of a number of maritime vessels operated under unified management that traverse between two ports on a regular schedule. The British government inaugurated

[5]Unless otherwise noted, the material in this section is drawn from (Albion, Square-Riggers on Schedule: The New York Sailing Packets to England, France, and the Cotton Ports, 1938).

the first transatlantic packet service in 1755 to carry mail between the mother country and its North American colonies. New York City was chosen as the terminus of this service, presumably because of its central location among the most active colonial transatlantic correspondents. Until January 1818, however, commercial maritime activity was carried on entirely by either transient vessels or regular traders. The former did not follow regular routes, but travelled from port to port depending on where lucrative cargoes could be obtained or disposed of. Regular traders shuttled back and forth between two ports but did not keep to a schedule. Instead, they sailed whenever their holds were sufficiently full.

The transition from regular trading operations to a packet service did not require any technological innovation; the same types of vessels were used for both purposes. Instead, the key innovations introduced by the New York-based Black Ball Line, the first commercial transatlantic packet operation, involved business organization. For one thing, operating a packet line required a larger capital investment than owners or lessors of regular traders had needed. Given the duration of early nineteenth century, transatlantic voyages assuring the Black Ball Lines' monthly departures from Liverpool and New York required a line of at least four vessels in constant operation. This differed from previous practice whereby individual vessels were usually owned or leased by transitory syndicates. Further, operating costs, including ship maintenance, would have been high for packet services because the ships had to sail throughout the year, including the winter months when seas were stormy, wear on tear on vessels was particular punishing, and eastbound cargoes were harder to find. By contrast, regular traders tended to remain in port between November and February.

The five New Yorkers—all of them Quakers with Yorkshire connections and involved in the cotton and/or textile trade–who founded what came to be called the Black Ball Line were making the bet that the attraction of reliable departure on a date certain for time-sensitive customers would generate enough business to more than offset the cost of the roughly $100,000 initial capital investment for ship acquisition and the higher annual expenses incurred by year-round operations. Definite and frequent year-round departure dates and relatively reliable arrival dates would have appealed most to transatlantic cabin passengers, business correspondents, payers and receivers of specie, and British manufacturers seeking quick sales of continuous, rapidly increasing product volumes. During the late 1810s and early 1820s, eastbound shippers of Middle Atlantic products—mostly time *in*sensitive and/or low-value-per-bulk items such as apples, wood ash, and flax seed—would have generated some revenues, but would have had little reason to prefer a packet to a regular trader. Further, while packets might have been able to capture a large share of or charge a premium for transatlantic cabin passenger, specie transfers, and mail, the net revenues generated by these activities would have been small relative to the total packet service capital and operating costs. Thus, what would make or break the packet business would be British exporters' preference for reliable, timely, year-round deliveries to a U.S. port where a wide range of manufactured goods, many shipped in advance of orders, could be sold at the highest possible price. In 1818, and especially during the volatile recession years of 1819 to 1821, that port would have been New York.

The cargoes of the inaugural packet voyages illustrate both the relatively low value of the eastbound commodity cargo and the importance of New York's active auction market in attracting time-sensitive, high-value commodity shipments to this port. The *James Monroe*, which departed from New York on January 5, 1818, carried eight cabin passengers, mail, 1148 barrels of apples, 860 barrels of flour, 200 barrels of wood ash, 71 bales of cotton, 14 bales of wool, and a range of miscellaneous items including cranberries and turpentine. The inclusion of flour on *James Monroe's* manifest is noteworthy. The British Corn Law, which restricted imports of grain and grain products, was very much on the books but was in temporary abeyance; in 1835, for example, no significant quantity of flour was shipped from New York to Liverpool (Albion, 1938, pp. 307–308).

Passengers, six in cabins and seven in steerage, also sailed on the Black Ball Line's inaugural westbound voyage. Information about the westbound cargo, however, is limited to the types of containers and their consignees; we know little about what the contents were other than that there was some quantity of coal on board. The customs manifest lists 1,330 separate items. Of these 402 "bales" and 247 "trunks" would likely have contained textiles of one variety or another. Almost a quarter of the total packaged cargo (321 of 1,330 packages) was consigned to one or another of the Black Ball Line's owners, all of whom, as noted, were textile importers. Most of the remaining 1,006 packages "were addressed to 76 different firms or individuals. The largest of these shipments, almost rivalling those of the [packets'] … owners, were consigned to the auctioneers, one of whom received 42 trunks, 20 cases and 1 bale; another, 49 trunks, 2 cases and 2 bales (Albion, 1938, pp. 36–37)."

We have no direct information on the return earned by the owners of the Black Ball Line in the early years of its operation. Indirect evidence suggests that the results might have been at least somewhat disappointing. For one thing, starting in 1819, the Black Ball Line's second year of operation, the United States entered what would become a severe economic downturn; between 1818 and 1821, U.S. merchandise imports declined by 55%, from $122 million to $55 million. Further, although the barriers to entry into the packet business would not have appeared particularly formidable to potential competitors since many New York importers already had interests in small fleets of cargo ships in service as regular traders, the initial four-ship Black Ball Line had no competition until 1822.

The Black Ball Line's business results during the downturn must, however, have been promising enough to attract competitors as soon as trade began to recover in 1822, when service commenced on two additional lines on the New York-Liverpool route and one to run between New York and Le Havre. By 1825, 16 New York-based vessels were offering scheduled service to Liverpool, 12 to Le Havre, and 4 to London. This would have translated into four monthly departures from New York to the Mersey, three to the Seine, and one to the Thames. The Cope Line, a packet service between Philadelphia and Liverpool, also began operations in 1822. This was the only long-lived transatlantic packet service between North America and Europe with a western terminus other than New York. Sailing lines established to run between Europe and either Boston or Baltimore did not survive more than a few years.

The number and size of packets sailing between New York and Europe continued to grow throughout the first half of the nineteenth century. By 1850, total ocean-going vessels on these services had reached 52, offering thrice weekly scheduled sailings. And the size of the largest sailing packet in service had increased fourfold. Between the 1820s and the 1850s, however, the packet line business model changed substantially. As transoceanic steamers came into service starting in the 1840s, these faster, more reliable vessels captured most of the high-margin, time-sensitive traffic. In response, sailing packets moved to accommodate immigrants' booming demand for steerage passage to America. At the same time, however, the expanding cotton market provided New York packet operators with a steady and reasonably lucrative eastbound cargo.

## The Cotton Triangle

Robert Albion, whose 1930s-vintage books are still the standard source of information and insight into this period of the City's maritime history, saw New York's role in the Atlantic cotton trade as, in some way, an "abnormal arrangement."

> The close relations between New York and … [the southern] … cotton ports resulted from the creation of the 'cotton triangle' – one of the most impudent acts in American commercial history. The New Yorkers dragged the trade between the South and Europe two hundred miles out of its normal course in order that they might exact their lucrative toll from it and secure eastbound cargoes for their ocean packets….
>
> There was no logical need for such service from New York …. [N]o natural reason existed for such service for the Southern exports and imports. Charleston or Savannah or Mobile or New Orleans could perfectly well have established direct shuttle trade themselves with Liverpool and Havre. (Albion, 1938, pp. 50–51)

From the perspective of the early-twenty-first century, however, indirect flows of goods and passengers between nodes of a transportation network do not seem at all unnatural. The rapid transformation of the domestic U.S. air travel network from a "point-to-point" to a "hub-and-spokes" structure after route choice was deregulated in 1978 demonstrates that, under some configurations of transportation costs and traffic densities, the former can be the "unnatural" situation.

With respect to the cotton trade, however, the story is more complicated than the "point-to-point" vs. "hub-and-spokes" dichotomy suggests. The shipping network that brought cotton from southern ports to the textile mills in Europe and New England and carried manufactured goods back to the south had a hybrid structure. It combined some direct voyages between, for example, New Orleans and Le Havre and some transits between Europe and the south by way of a northeastern US port, usually New York. Southern plantation owners and factors were aware, albeit in only a general way and with a time lag, of price differentials, net of shipping costs, for various grades of raw cotton among New Orleans, New York, and Liverpool and would decide where to direct their shipments accordingly (Woodman, 1968).

During the early postwar decades, a not-insignificant minority of cotton exporters decided to ship their goods to northern cities, mostly to New York. In 1822, cotton accounted for some 40% of exports from the Port of New York by value and other southern products, such as tobacco and naval stores, for another 15%. Of the 204,000 bales of cotton shipped from New Orleans in 1825, half went directly to Great Britain, one-quarter to New York, 16% to France, 3% to Boston, and 1% to Philadelphia (Albion, 1939, pp. 100–101). Return voyages of ships bringing cotton to New York would have carried manufactured goods, both imports and domestic products, to southern consumers.

What incentive did Southerners have to direct some of the Europe-bound cotton to and purchase some of their European imports from New York-based middlemen? Nineteenth-century observers asked themselves the same question. Like Robert Albion antebellum advocates of cotton-growing interests wondered about—and objected to—New York's and other northern cities' involvement in what looked like essentially a two-way trade between European manufacturers and southern plantation owners (Woodman, 1968, pp. Chapter 12, passim). Unambiguous transportation cost advantages alone could not have been the deciding influence because both point-to-point and hub-and-spokes shipping networks operated simultaneously throughout the period. Instead, the explanation of New York City's role in what was called its "southern trade" is more likely to be discovered by examining the markets for transatlantic maritime services and for cotton.

## Maritime Services

By committing to a strict schedule, packet line operators incurred the risk of having to sail with their cargo holds mostly empty. The "profit center" that motivated them to take this risk was the large and growing New York-bound flow of "fine freight." Lucrative, locally produced eastbound cargoes were, as noted, much harder to procure. Packet line operators seeking to cover as much as possible of the fixed costs of their eastbound voyages would, therefore, have had an incentive to adopt a strategic pricing policy.

Detailed information on antebellum ocean freight rates is scarce. What we do have, however, indicates that New York-based shippers did have room to maneuver with respect to pricing and used it. During the mid-1830s, the freight rate for shipments of cotton from New Orleans to Liverpool averaged about 1.3 US cents per pound of cotton or $5.85 for the average 450-pound bale. The freight rate on the same bale shipped from New York to Liverpool would have been about $4. During the same period, shipping rates from New Orleans to New York fluctuated seasonally between an annual peak of about $3 per bale to a low of about $1. If so, over the course of a year the all-in cost of a cotton shipment from New Orleans to Liverpool via New York might have fluctuated within a $5 to $7 range, plus some transshipment costs. Further, Albion states that "…westbound freight from Europe….was generally carried at a fixed rate, normally $10 a ton, but the New York rates on cotton, flour, naval stores and other eastbound cargoes sometimes varied from week to week and it was necessary to keep up to the minute on these fluctuations[6]" (Albion, 1938, p. 73). So the shipping cost differential between the direct route from New Orleans to Liverpool and a journey with a stopover in New York was on average, small, and it fluctuated frequently, presumably as shipping companies responded to short-term shifts in the supply of and demand for cargo space.

[6]Between 1810 and 1840, producers gradually shifted from shipping bags of ginned cotton to standard sized, compressed bales weighing an average of 450 pounds (Bennett, 1962). Sterling rates on New York and New Orleans to Liverpool shipments are from (Taylor, 1951, pp. 147–148). Calculations assume a $4.85/£1 exchange rate. New Orleans to New York rates from (Albion, 1938, p. 111).

Now consider a packet line operator facing an imminent scheduled departure from New York to Liverpool but with a nearly empty hold or a low-value cargo, presumably a fairly common combination of circumstances. Any additional revenues that could be earned on this voyage would be welcome, and offering a discount on the most plentiful eastbound cargo would be an attractive strategy. Thus, assuming that transshipment costs were not too high, given even a modest discount on the New York-to-Liverpool leg, the all-in price of a two-stage voyage between the cotton-growing south and the European manufacturing centers could be lower than a point-to-point transit. Since the main motive for offering such discounts would have been the exigencies of a scheduled packet service and since New York had, by far, the most packet lines in operation, New York would have been the best place to look for bargain rates on transatlantic shipping.

Presumably, too, southern plantation owners and cotton factors would be aware that such discount freight rates might be available from New York. A cotton seller who anticipated a near-term decline in raw cotton prices in European markets and wanted to get product to Liverpool as quickly as possible would look for the fastest, most direct shipment mechanism. But a seller who was in less of a hurry to liquidate the crop, perhaps because of an anticipated future price rise, might happily ship the commodity to New York in the first instance in the expectation of either being able to sell the cotton advantageously there or to catch a bargain-basement cost of shipping to Europe.

In these ways, the structure of the transatlantic maritime services market would have evolved after 1815 as a hybrid point-to-point and hub-and-spokes structure, which is exactly what seems to have happened.

## Cotton and Credit

The cotton market boomed during the first half of the nineteenth century. Between 1800 and 1850, U.S. production of this crop grew at an average compound annual rate of 7.0%, not a lot slower than, for example, the 7.9% annual rate by which the number of smartphones in use in the United States grew between 2000 and 2014. Expanding production at this pace required large amounts of capital to acquire and clear land, to build infrastructure, and buy slaves. Further, production growth was volatile on a year-to-year basis; during the first half of the nineteenth century, production declined by 10% or more from the previous year's level in 1823, 1827, 1838, 1840, 1843, and 1845. So, plantation owners, cotton factors, and southern merchants had to maintain sufficient reserves or untapped sources of credit to survive through the occasional bad years (Census, 1976, pp. Table Da775–765; International Telecommunications Union, 2018).

As profitable as cotton production was, up-and-running plantations themselves could not generate sufficient surplus to finance both a comfortable life for their owners and to exploit available opportunities for profitable expansion. As a result, the South Atlantic and southwestern states were capital-importing regions throughout the antebellum period. So, however, was the United States as a whole; much of the capital required to finance the rapid expansion of cotton cultivation—and canal and railroad construction, and the settlement of the Midwest, and the building of rapidly growing cities—had to come from somewhere else, namely Europe. Thus, aggregate net liabilities owed by Americans to foreigners increased 2.7-fold between 1815 and 1850 (Census, 1976, p. Table E22).

Much more will be said in subsequent chapters about New Yorkers' and New York institutions' role in mediating nineteenth-century financial flows. At this point, the immediate task is to understand why and how the circuitous route by which European, mostly British, capital found its way into the hands of southern plantation owners ran through New York.

Long-term loans secured by land, equipment, or slaves were not available to planters during most of the antebellum period. Lenders were, however, willing to advance farmers cash or goods on the security of current-year crops in transit to market or in the ground. In particular, cotton factors, southern port-city merchants, and rural store owners were willing to provide goods on credit, with payment due, either in cash or in kind, when the current-year crop was sold. Southern banks were also involved in these intra-year credit arrangements; they were willing to provide funds to the factors, merchants, and store owners by discounting plantation owners' IOUs. If, as evidently frequently happened, at the end of the year an otherwise solvent planter's earnings on the sale of his crops was insufficient to pay off all the money he owed, the creditor would usually be willing to accommodate a reliable customer by rolling the unpaid portion of a loan over and securing eventual repayment with the proceeds of the subsequent year's crop sales. In this way, plantation owners came to accumulate long-term liabilities by rolling over short-term obligations, always backed by the next year's crop. This form of credit enabled planters to devote money that would otherwise be used to pay current-year expenses to clearing more land and buying more slaves.

But the cotton factors and others who delivered goods to plantation owners on nominally short-term credit had to buy their stock in trade from someone. And few of these business people had accumulated sufficient surplus capital to be able to pay for goods on delivery; they, too, had to buy on credit to be paid off when the crop was eventually sold and the plantation owners repaid their annual borrowing. And so on up the supply chain. Since many of the commodities that southern retailers delivered to plantation owners were imports, the ultimate source of some part of the credit that financed the expansion of cotton production were European, mostly British, exporters. By allowing American importers to maintain debit balances in Liverpool and London, British exporters enabled wholesalers to provide extended payment terms to retailers and retailers to provide credit to plantation owners. Alternatively, British exporters might finance purchases by accepting as payment U.S. banknotes borrowed by U.S. importers or by buying U.S. bank stocks. So, the circuitous route by which British capital found its way into the hands of southern plantation owners ran through the mechanisms by which Americans paid for British imports.

Since New York was, by far, North America's most important import depot, some of the credit, commodities, and cash that flowed between British exporters to American plantation owners passed through the warehouses and/or ledgers of the City's banks and merchant houses. In particular, southern retailers incurred liabilities due to New York importers. Some of these obligations would be paid in cash after crops were sold, but frequently these debts were paid in kind by the transfer of cotton from the possession of, say, a Mobile, Alabama factor to that of a New York merchant house. Sometimes this transfer would take the form of physical delivery of the cotton to a New York warehouse. Sometimes, and more often as the antebellum period progressed, it would involve a paper transaction with the physical commodity remaining in place wherever it happened to be.

Exports of cotton through the Port of New York accounted for a much smaller proportion of New York port's activities by the end of the antebellum period; in 1860, 90% of U.S. cotton exports were shipped directly from New Orleans, Mobile, Savannah, or Charleston. Even at that point, however, perhaps a quarter of imports purchased by southern consumers had been transshipped in a northern port.[7] By that time, however, New York-based shippers had found other sufficiently lucrative eastbound cargoes. In 1860, about one-third of total U.S. exports other than gold and silver coins, but only 6.5% of the cotton was shipped from New York (Albion, 1939, p. 400). During the 1830s, on the eve of catastrophic agglomeration, however, economic activity in New York and, therefore, the City's position in the U.S. urban hierarchy were boosted by its position at a vertex of the Atlantic cotton triangle.

## The Canal and the Hinterland

The population for which New York City served as the regional metropolis expanded rapidly over the decades during which the stage was being set for catastrophic agglomeration; New York State's share of total U.S. population rose from 11% in 1800 to its all-time high of

[7]Assume that regions' share of aggregate import demand was roughly proportionate to their share of total free population. In 1860, the free population of New Orleans's hinterland, by a broad definition (Louisiana, Mississippi, Alabama, Arkansas, Texas, and half of Tennessee), was about 2.5 million or about 9% of the U.S. total. At the same time, 6.3% of total U.S. imports entered through the Port of New Orleans. So it might be reasonable to surmise that perhaps 30% of the imports purchased by Southerners would have entered through some other port, most likely New York. This rough estimate, however, may be on the high side. Economic historian Douglas C. North points out that quasi-subsistence farmers constituted a particularly large proportion of the southern population. If so, the region's demand for imports would have been less than proportional to its share of the nation's non-slave population (Albion, 1939, p. 401; Census, 1976; North, 1966).

15% in 1830. By 1840, New York City's hinterland population of 3.6 million was more twice as large as that of Boston's and four times the size of Philadelphia's.[8] The impetus for this growth derived in large part from the construction of the Erie Canal. The western New York counties with access to either the Canal or the Great Lakes,[9] home to 7% of the New York's population in 1800, accounted for 32% of the State's population growth over the subsequent four decades. Much has been written about the origins, execution, and effects of this infrastructure project from political, geographic, financial, managerial, and engineering perspectives. In the current context, however, the focus is on the canal's impact while it was being constructed and during the first few years after its completion in 1825 on its immediate vicinity in New York State and on its regional metropolis.

One aspect of the Canal's pre-history that has gotten relatively little attention should be of considerable interest for anyone in search of what economic historian Paul David refers to as "critical junctures" leading to a "contingent chain of events" (David, 2007). Achieving political consensus in support of this technologically and financially unprecedented construction project was difficult within a single jurisdiction. The involvement of multiple political entities would probably have made it impossible. The political impediments that, for decades, stymied the completion of the Baltimore and Ohio Railroad, which had to cross the territories of Maryland, and Virginia or Pennsylvania to connect the Chesapeake Bay with the Ohio River (see below),

[8]Hinterlands were defined as follows:

> Philadelphia: All of the Pennsylvania and New Jersey counties on the Delaware and Schuylkill Rivers and the entire State of Delaware. At this time, the counties bordering on the Susquehanna River and its tributaries would have been in easier communication with Baltimore than with Philadelphia.
> New York: The entire States of New York and Vermont, the New Jersey Counties that were not included in Philadelphia's hinterland, all of Connecticut other than Tolland and Windham Counties, and Berkshire, Franklin, Hampden, and Hampshire Counties, MA.
> Boston: The entire states of New Hampshire, Maine, and Rhode Island, Massachusetts except for Berkshire, Franklin, Hampden, and Hampshire Counties, and Tolland and Windham, Counties, CT.

[9]Cayuga, Chautauqua, Erie Genesee, Jefferson, Livingston, Monroe, Niagara, Onondaga, Ontario, Orleans, Oswego, Seneca, and Wayne counties.

demonstrate just how important it was that the entire length of the Erie Canal was within a single jurisdiction. Until sometime in the 1790s, however, it was far from obvious that the western border of New York State extended all the way to Lake Erie.

Before 1800, the area west of the headwaters of the Susquehanna, Delaware, and Mohawk Rivers was populated almost solely and sparsely by Native Americans. Colonial era maps of the Province of New York depicted vague and inconsistent western boundaries somewhere in the vicinity of the northern tributaries of either the Delaware or the Susquehanna Rivers. The Iroquois Confederation, the Commonwealth of Massachusetts, the State of Connecticut, the Federal Government, and the State of New York all claimed sovereignty over the territory to the west of this vague boundary. New York's legal case was probably the weakest. The Iroquois clearly owned the land under common law; they had inhabited and farmed the region for at least five centuries. The New England colonies could point to their original royal charters, which pre-dated the creation of the Province of New York and granted them territory extending to the Pacific Ocean. The Federal government's claim was based on the Treaty of Paris and the Articles of Confederation, which granted Congress jurisdiction over all the territory ceded by Britain to the United States that was not part of a state. But the New England states had little hope of establishing effective governance at such a distance from Boston and Hartford and across the territory of another State. The Federal government was preoccupied with other matters. The Iroquois, for their part, were unable to mount a unified political effort to assert their rights. New York State was nearby and its leader, Governor George Clinton, was determined to achieve sovereignty over the disputed region and had the political skills to make it happen. The historical record is unclear as to when, exactly, and how New York State established its jurisdiction on the shores of Lake Erie, but maps drawn in the mid-1790s depict the borders that are familiar to us now (Rumsey, 2018; Taylor, 2006).

Given the universal and correct consensus that the construction of the Canal was instrumental to the subsequent "contingent chain of events" and given how difficult it would have been to build it across state borders, George Clinton's *fait accompli*, whenever and however he made it happen, deserves designation as a "critical juncture" in the economic history of New York State and New York City.

While there is agreement that the Canal made a huge contribution to New York State and City's economic development, the nature of its impact changed over time. By the end of the antebellum period, the Canal had positioned Buffalo and New York City as the principle transshipment points for goods moving between the Midwestern states of Ohio, Indiana, Illinois, Michigan, and Wisconsin and global markets; in 1860, 30 million bushels of grain arrived in Buffalo and 48% of U.S. grain exports were shipped from New York. Our interest at this point, however, is in the Canal's impact during the decades before the 1840s, and as Fig. 5.3 indicates, shipments of Midwestern grain through New York did not begin to accelerate until after 1846, when Parliament repealed the British Corn Laws. Instead, during the pre-agglomeration decades the impact of the Canal was to open the western part of New York State to settlement. The project was deemed a success well before Midwestern grain began flowing through Buffalo; in 1837, the year the Canal commissioners were able to report that all of the debt incurred for construction had been paid in full, intrastate shipments still accounted for 82% of total eastbound and 56% of westbound tonnage (Albion, 1939, p. 411; Bernstein, 2005).

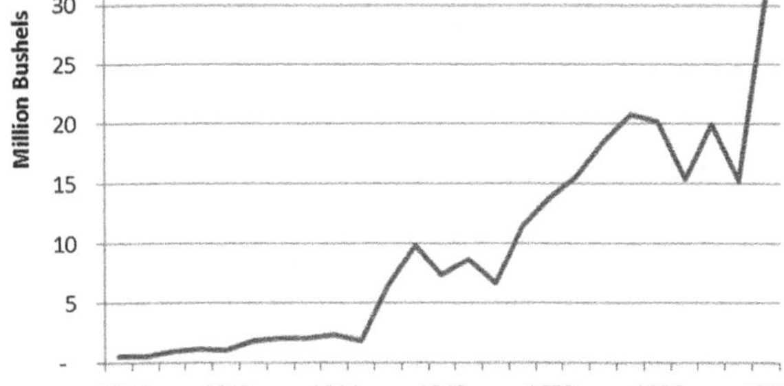


**Fig. 5.3** Receipts of Flour and Grain at Buffalo from the West, 1836–1860 (North, 1966, p. 253)

What's more, the population and freight traffic figures may understate the effect the Canal had on the level of activity in the State as a whole and the City, because the economy that developed in the directly affected counties during the period before 1840 was apparently quite dynamic. In a study of the geographic distribution of inventive activity during this period, economic historian Kenneth Sokoloff hypothesized that access to markets was a necessary condition for technological advances, and, indeed, he found that the per capita number of patents issued by the U.S. government to residents of a county tended to be high in many but not all places with access to navigable waterways. Sokoloff's statistical analysis identified the Erie Canal counties as one of the regions where innovated activity was particularly intense between 1830 and 1836 (Sokoloff, 1988).

The Canal counties also scored high on another index of development: urbanization. In 1840, there were 22 cities in the United States with populations greater than 10,000. Three of them, Albany, Rochester, and Buffalo, were located along the Erie Canal. So at a time when the Canal region was home to about 5% of the nation's population, it accounted for 14% of "large" cities.

New York State's investment in strategic transportation infrastructure was a striking success both financially and with respect to its impact on the overall economy of the State and its largest city. This leaves open the question of whether other parts of the country could have matched New York in this regard and thereby have stimulated the growth of some other city's hinterland during the years before the 1840s. If they could have but did not, then the juxtaposition of New York State's success and other places' failures deserves designation as a critical juncture in the City's economic history. If, however, it would have been practically impossible for other states to reproduce the Empire State's achievement, then we would have to consider New York City's stature as the largest urban place in 1840 and, therefore, its subsequent emergence as North America's continental metropolis as inevitable once the Erie Canal was completed.

## Was There Any Plausible Competition?

An active imagination could conger many counterfactual urban histories of varying degrees of plausibility. One, in particular, seems worth exploring. The idea of driving a low-friction transportation corridor (i.e., water or rail) through the Appalachian Mountain Range had been on national policymakers' and property speculators' agenda since before independence. The most notable of the active advocates in both the political and financial categories was George Washington, who devoted part of his energies between the end of the Revolutionary War and his election to the Presidency promoting an ultimately unsuccessful plan to extend the navigability of the Potomac River westward (Bernstein, 2005, pp. Chapter 3, passim).

Linking the East Coast with the "West" was, of course, one of the stated goals of the Erie Canal project. In the context of the early nineteenth century, however, the American "West" meant the Ohio River Valley, while the Erie Canal provided access to the then much less developed Great Lakes basin. In 1830, the population of the Ohio Valley states was 2,423,007 or 19% of the U.S. total. At the time, however, only seven percent of Ohio's population lived in counties bordering Lake Erie, Illinois and Indiana had yet to organize their Lake counties, and Michigan and Wisconsin were six and 18 years away from statehood, respectively. Only in subsequent decades did economic activity around the Great Lakes begin to expand rapidly. And it was not until 1833 that a canal linking the Ohio River with Lake Erie was completed. The population of Cuyahoga County, Ohio, (Cleveland), for example, more than doubled between 1830 and 1840, but this doubling only brought the total to 26,506, about half the size of Hamilton County (Cincinnati) at the time.[10] Even in the latter year, tonnage of vessels employed on western rivers was still 2.4 times larger than that of lake shipping (North, 1966, p. 252). There may, therefore, have been an opportunity for an Atlantic coast city to boost its growth substantially

[10]The "Ohio Valley" was defined as the States of Ohio, Indiana, Illinois, and Kentucky and the Pennsylvania and Virginia counties along the Ohio and Allegheny Rivers.

during the 1830s or 1840s by establishing efficient transport access to the Ohio Valley. Further, if such a transportation corridor also opened the territory through which it ran to more rapid population growth, the city occupying this position might very well have given New York a run for its money during the crucial period.

Two of the nation's five largest cities as of 1830 stood little chance of succeeding in this goal. Boston was too far from the Ohio Valley; indeed, its leaders had to exert some effort to avoid becoming an urban backwater. And New Orleans was too distant from the 41% of 1830 U.S. population living in the Middle Atlantic and New England states to serve as the continental metropolis. Thought leaders in two geographically well-situated States, Pennsylvania and Maryland, however, recognized this potential and spent serious money on three infrastructure projects aimed at linking their tidelands with the Ohio River: the Chesapeake and Ohio ("C&O") Canal, and the Baltimore and Ohio (B&O) Railroad, and Pennsylvania Main Line of Public Works. The latter was a combination of canals, railroad lines, and a funicular connecting Philadelphia to Pittsburgh.

We know the outcomes. The C&O Canal never extended beyond Cumberland, Maryland, at the eastern base of the Appalachian range. The Pennsylvania Main Line reached Pittsburg in 1834, and the B&O Railroad became a profitable operation even before reaching the Ohio River at Wheeling, Virginia in 1852. But none of these investments succeeded in boosting their sponsor-cities' growth by enough or soon enough to challenge New York. Did these initiatives fail in their purpose because the project was technologically unfeasible at the time or because the execution was flawed?

The search for answer to this question must begin with an appreciation of just how audacious the Erie Canal project was. To be sure, the basic technology of building a canal with locks had been known for centuries, and steam operated pumps were already in widespread use by 1817 in a variety of milieus. Nevertheless, when plans were being made for what was projected to be a 364 mile-long Erie route the longest canal in operation in the United States as the 28-mile Middlesex Canal connecting Boston with the Merrimack River, which was a financial failure. The elaborate and successful canal systems that had been constructed in

Britain and France ran through much more densely settled territory than upstate New York was in early nineteenth century. Further, unlike the British and French Canals, the Erie was certain to freeze and be closed to traffic for months at a time each winter. Finally, the $6 million projected cost of construction, which amounted to one-third the total capitalization of banks and insurance companies in New York, would have to be raised by issuing bonds backed by the full faith and credit of the State (Bernstein, 2005, Loc. 1830, 2624, 2639/7128). As daunting as the Erie Canal project's physical challenges may have been, at least they weren't unprecedented in kind; not compared with what faced the Philadelphians and Baltimoreans. The distances involved were roughly the same: 364, 350, and 386 miles for the Erie Canal, the Pennsylvania Main Line, and the B&O Railroad, respectively. But the highest elevation on the Canal route was 566 ft. while the Pennsylvania Main Line had to traverse a pass about 2,200 feet above sea level and the B&O route to Wheeling involved an ascent of about 2,600 ft. Raising canal boats by that amount through a system of locks was not feasible.

The alternative low-friction technology was rail transport powered by horses, stationary steam engines, or steam locomotives. The decade of the 1830s was a period of rapid improvement in railroad technology. By the end of 1841, for example, the locomotive-powered Western Railroad in Massachusetts had been completed, linking Worcester, which had been connection to Boston by rail in 1835, with the Erie Canal terminus near Albany, New York. The highest elevation on this line was 1,457 feet at Washington Summit in the Berkshire Hills (Stover, 1961). The full length of the Boston to Albany route was 200 miles. Thus, while this project was somewhat less challenging than what Pennsylvania and Maryland faced, its success suggests that by some point in the late 1830s or early 1840s, it could have been technologically feasible, albeit extremely ambitious, to complete locomotive-powered railroads linking Philadelphia with Pittsburgh or Baltimore with Wheeling.[11]

---

[11]This conclusion contradicts the assertion by Albert Fishlow, who, in a discussion of the Pennsylvania Main Line, asserts that "Choice of a railroad technology would not have been a successful strategy. Costs at that date were still prohibitive" (Fishlow, 2000). It does not appear

But to finish a project by that point it would have been necessary to break ground in the early 1830s. To have opted for rail locomotive technology, which was beyond the technological frontier at that point, would have required an immense leap of faith.[12]

Pennsylvania and Philadelphia were quite capable of executing ambitious infrastructure projects. Private investors with state assistance were able to open a toll roll linking Harrisburg with Pittsburgh across the Appalachians by 1818. And Philadelphia succeeded in installing a state-of-the-art municipal water supply system some 30 years before New York City (Committee to Review the New York City Watershed Management Strategy, 2000). Faced with the challenge to their City's stature posed by New York's Erie advantage, Philadelphia business leaders felt compelled to start building their own low-friction trans-Appalachian facility shortly after the Canal was completed in 1825. A vociferous, well-informed group of railroad advocates backed by deeply researched policy papers tried to make the case for the emerging technology. It was potentially much faster than canal transport and could operate year round. But the few such facilities operating in England as of the mid-1820s were small and highly specialized. Locomotive technology, for example, was still experimental, and much rail transport was still horse-drawn. The argument that the technology could only and almost certainly would improve quickly failed to win the day, and, as a canal-only solution was not feasible, the State opted to construct a hybrid system of canals and railroads, powered over its highest elevation by a stationary steam engine pulling rail cars up a steep inclined plane. Because of its multimodal design transport between Philadelphia and Pittsburgh on the Main Line required numerous transshipments, and because the project cost about twice as much to build as the

---

that cost differential was the main consideration pushing the Pennsylvanians toward the multimodal solution, and it seems unlikely that laying rail lines around the State could have been more expensive all-in than digging channels and constructing locks and aqueducts *and* laying rails over much of the distance. What stymied the all-rail alternative was a combination of technological risk-aversion and panic over the Erie Canal's success (Rubin, 1961).

[12]Unless otherwise noted, material in this and the subsequent few paragraphs is drawn from (Rubin, 1961).

Erie Canal, tolls set at levels commensurate with debt service were too high to be competitive. Although the Main Line and its feeder canals and rail lines do seem to have made important contributions to Pennsylvania's economic development, especially in the coal fields and for Pittsburgh's emerging iron industry, the facility was never a financial success. In any event, it failed to provide Philadelphia with the holy grail of cost-effective access to the Ohio Valley. Worse, legislative concerns about maintaining toll revenues on the Main Line impeded progress on railroad development even after it became obvious that the latter technology was far superior.

Support for the Chesapeake and Ohio canal project in Baltimore was tempered by the fact that the principal eastern terminus would be near Washington, DC.[13] And, given the rapid pace of progress in railroading, only two years after Pennsylvania chose to build the Main Line, Baltimore's many railroad supporters could point to additional evidence emerging from Britain of the new technology's potential. Accordingly, on February 19, 1827 a committee of influential Baltimore businessmen resolved that "...these roads are far better adapted to our situation and circumstances than a Canal across the Mountains would be: ... [We] therefore recommend that measures be taken to construct a double Rail Road between the City of Baltimore and some suitable point on the Ohio River" (Stover, 1995, p. 70). The committee's petition to the Maryland Legislature for a corporate charter authorizing $5 million capitalization was approved quickly and the initial public stock offering was successful.

The C&O Canal project also had political support, especially from Virginia and the Federal government. As it happened, ground was broken for both projects on July 4, 1828. In contrast to the Erie Canal, which was completed in about seven years, it was not until 1852 that the B&O line reached Wheeling, Virginia (now West Virginia) on the Ohio River. The impediments to more rapid progress were mostly political. The routes of both the rail line and the canal ran through the

[13]Unless otherwise indicated, material in this and the following paragraph is drawn from (Stover, 1995).

narrow Potomac Valley, where in some places there was not enough room for both. Disputes between the two competitors occasionally halted construction and required route and design compromises that raised costs. By the time, the line had reached Harpers Ferry, Virginia, in late 1834—60 miles from Baltimore as the crow flies—the railroad, having run through its original capitalization and operating at a loss, was nearly bankrupt. Infusions of funds borrowed by the State of Maryland allowed construction of the segment between Harpers Ferry, VA, to Cumberland, MD, at the eastern foot of the Appalachians to begin in 1839. This project was completed late in 1842. From there, the line would run through Virginia, and further progress required an act of that State's Legislature, which was not forthcoming in a satisfactory form until March of 1847. During the same period, the Pennsylvania Legislature, influenced by Philadelphia interests, blocked plans for a B&O branch line to Pittsburgh. Construction on the difficult Cumberland to Wheeling leg did not begin until 1849, after the costly resolution of another time-consuming dispute with the C&O Canal company.

Because of technological risk-aversion in one case and intermodal and interstate rivalry in the other, neither of the cities that might have established commercially viable transportation linkages between the Middle Atlantic tidewater and the Ohio River valley managed to do so before 1852. By that point, the period of rapid North American urbanization, centered on New York City, was well underway. The fact that by 1852, New York City already had two rail connections to the, by then, rapidly growing Great Lakes region is emblematic of the City's premier status by that time.

Could either Baltimore or Philadelphia have challenged New York's modest edge as the largest U.S. city by driving a state-of-the-art railroad corridor to Wheeling or Pittsburgh by the early 1840s?

Pennsylvania appears to have had the better chance. The "Keystone State" had the advantage of being the only jurisdiction to encompass within its territory both the Atlantic tidelands and the Ohio River. It could, had it chosen to do so, have chartered and subsidized construction of a monopoly rail line and eliminated any legal impediments to completion. Maryland did not enjoy this advantage, and the B&O

Railroad's progress was impeded by a competing project and by the Virginia and Pennsylvania Legislatures' reluctance to support a neighboring state's economic development. Even if a more realistic assessment of the feasibility of a canal linking the Chesapeake Bay and the Ohio River had prevailed, so that the competition over the Potomac Valley right of way might not have materialized, interstate competition would still have been an impediment. In the 1820s, the first instance of interstate collaboration in infrastructure development and operation, the Port Authority of New York and New Jersey, was some 100 years in the future.

It would have been asking a lot of Pennsylvania's mid-1820s leaders to have been bold enough to opt for an all-rail line, given the primitive, experimental state of the technology at that time. There was, however, also a body of opinion in the State arguing that a multimodal system would not be cost-effective and making the case for a few years' delay to allow the new technology to develop (Rubin, 1961, pp. 47–48). Indeed, Massachusetts, which faced only slightly less-daunting physical challenges, did opt to postpone the decision for a few years, but was able to complete a locomotive-driven line from Boston to Albany by 1841. In the end, the post-Erie panic and incipient "canal craze" carried the day. It does seem plausible, however, that what turned out to have been the right position might have prevailed, and Philadelphia, at that time still the nation's financial capital and a rising manufacturing center, might have been a serious contender for the status of continental metropolis during the 1840s.

## Conclusion

In retrospect, the timing was perfect. During the first 25 years of *Pax Britannica*, international trade was expanding rapidly in the North Atlantic region, the second industrial revolution was underway, and internal transportation costs in the United States were beginning to decline. Taken together, these trends set the stage for a period of rapid urbanization and the emergence of a distinct hierarchy of cities in North America.

Simultaneously, New York City's population was growing noticeably faster than that of other geographically well-positioned northeastern U.S. cities. Job creation in New York was relatively robust during the period because the City had established its position as the, by far, leading U.S. port, especially for imports. New York achieved this position through a combination of luck, timely, serendipitous public policy support for the auction industry and as the home of the Black Ball Line's founders. The latter, happily, had enough capital and nerve to survive the sharp contraction of trade between 1819 and 1822. The audacious construction of the Erie Canal provided a second boost. As each segment of the project was completed, a new, fertile region of New York City's hinterland gained access to national and global markets and attracted rapid, commercially oriented settlement. The regional economy that emerged along the Canal was particularly dynamic, as reflected in the volume of patents registered by residents and by the degree of urbanization.

Was New York's position as the first among more or less equal northeastern cities circa 1840 inevitable? Possibly so, but there is at least one plausible scenario by which Philadelphia, or possibly Baltimore, might have wound up almost as populous as New York on the eve of catastrophic agglomeration, had either city been able to drive an efficient transportation facility through to the Ohio Valley. If the leaders of Pennsylvania had had the foresight and nerve as of the early 1830s to cut their losses on the multimodal Main Line and to make a huge bet on the rapidly emerging locomotive-powered railroad technology, the two largest Middle Atlantic cities might have been much closer rivals during the 1840s. Maryland's leaders, who did believe in railroads at an early date, would have to have had, in addition, Virginia's opinion leaders on board to achieve the same result.

Leaving it to the reader to decide whether or not any of the counterfactual pre-1840 urban histories is plausible, we can now proceed to the subsequent years of New York City's economic history. From this point on, this will be the story of North America's sole continental metropolis.

## References

Albion, R. G. (1938). *Square-Riggers on Schedule: The New York Sailing Packets to England, France, and the Cotton Ports*. Princeton: Princeton University Press.

Albion, R. G. (1939). *The Rise of New York Port (1815–1860)*. New York: Scribner's.

Anonymous. (1828, Reprint 2017). *Remarks Upon the Auction Systems, as Practised in New-York: To Which Are Added Numerous Facts in Illustration.* New Delhi: Reink Books.

Baptist, E. E. (2014). *The Half Has Never Been Told: Slavery and the Making of American Capitalism*. New York: Basic Books.

Bennett, C. A. (1962). Cotton Ginning Systems in the United States and Auxilliary Developments. *Cotton Ginners Journal and the Cotton Gin and Oil Mill Press*. Mimeo.

Bernstein, P. L. (2005). *Wedding of the Waters: The Erie Canal and the Making of a Great Nation*. New York: W. W. Norton.

Census, U. B. (1976). *The Statistical History of the United States from Colonial Times to the Present*. New York: Basic Books.

Cernog, E. (1996). *The Birth of Empire: DeWitt Clinton and the American Experience*. Oxford: Oxford University Press.

Cohen, I. (1971). The Auction System in the Port of New York, 1817–1837. *The Business History Review, 45*(4), 491–492.

Committee to Review the New York City Watershed Management Strategy. (2000). *Watershed Management for Potable Water Supply: Assessing the New York City Strategy.* Washington, DC: National Academy Press.

David, P. A. (2007). Path Dependence—A Foundational Concept for Historical Social Science. *Cliometrica—The Journal of Historical Economics and Econometric History, 1*(2), 3.

Engelbrecht-Wiggans, R., & Nonnenmacher, T. (1999). The Theoretical Baiss for 19th-Century Changes to the Port of New York Imported Goods Auction. *Explorations in Economic History, 36*, 232–245.

Fichter, J. R. (2010). *So Great a Profit: How the East Indies Trade Transformed Anglo-American Capitalism*. Cambridge: Harvard University Press.

Fishlow, A. (2000). Internal Transportation in the Nineteenth and Early Twentieth Centuries. In S. Engerman & R. E. Gallman (Eds.), *The Cambridge Economic History of the United States, Volume II, The Long Nineteenth Century* (pp. 543–642). Cambridge: Cambridge University Press.

Heaton, H. (1941). Non-importation, 1806–1812. *Journal of Economic History, 12,* 178–198.

Hickey, D. (1981). American Trade Restrictions During the War of 1812. *The Journal of American History, 68*(3), 528–529.

Hickey, D. R. (2012). *The War of 1812: A Forgotten Conflict*. Champagne: University of Illinois Press.

International Telecommunications Union. (2018, June 5). *Statistics*. Retrieved from Committed to Connecting the World: International Telegraphic Union (ITU) http://www.itu.int/en/ITU-D/Statistics/Pages/stat/default.aspx.

Irwin, D. A. (2003). The Optimal Tax on Antebellum US Cotton Exports. *Journal of International Economics, 60,* 277.

Jacks, D. S. (2005). Intra- and International Commodity Market Integration in the Atlantic Economy, 1800–1913. *Explorations in Economic History, 42,* 381–413.

Mokyr, J. (1977). Demand vs. Supply in the Industrial Revolution. *Journal of Economic History, 37*(4), 981–1008.

North, D. C. (1966). *The Economic Growth of the United States, 1790–1860*. New York: W. W. Norton.

O'Rourke, K. H. (2006). The Worldwide Economic Impact of the French Revolution and Napoleonic Wars, 1793–1815. *Journal of Global History, 1,* 123–149.

Rubin, J. (1961). Canal or Railroad? Imitation and Innovation in the Response to the Erie Canal in Philadelphia, Baltimore, and Boston. *Transactions of the American Philosophical Society, New Series, 51*(7), 48–57.

Rumsey, D. (2018, June 6). *Pennsylvania, Nova Jersey et Nova York*. Retrieved from David Rumsey Map Collection, Cartography Associates https://www.davidrumsey.com/luna/servlet/detail/RUMSEY~8~1~283018~90055432:45-Pensylvania,-Nova-Jersey-et-Nov?sort=Pub_List_No_InitialSort%2CPub_Date%2CPub_List_No%2CSeries_No&qvq=w4s:/where%2F-New%2BYork%2Fwhen%2F1748;sort:Pub_List_No_InitialSort%2CPub_D.

Sellers, C. (1991). *The Market Revolution: Jacksonian America, 1815–1846* (pp. 137 ff.). Oxford: Oxford University Press.

Sokoloff, K. L. (1988). *Inventive Activity in Early Industrial America: Evidence from Patent Records, 1790–1846* (NBER Working Paper #2707). National Bureau of Economic Research.

Stokey, N. L. (2001). A Quantitative Model of the British Industrial Revolution, 1780–1850. *Carnegie-Rochester Conference Series on Public Policy, 55*(1), 55–109.

Stover, J. F. (1961). *American Railroads*. Chicago: University of Chicago Press.

Stover, J. F. (1995). *History of the Baltimore and Ohio Railroad*. Lafayette, IN: Purdue University Press.

Stuart, R. C. (1984). Special Interests and National Authority in Foreign Policy: American-British Provincial Links During the Embargo and the War of 1812. *Diplomatic History, 8*(4), 311–328.

Taylor, A. (2006). *The Divided Ground: Indians, Settlers, and the Northern Borderland of the American Revolution*. New York: Alfred A. Knopf.

Taylor, G. R. (1951). *The Transportation Revolution: 1815–1860*. New York: Rinehart & Co., Inc.

Woodman, H. D. (1968). *King Cotton and His Retainers: Financing and Marketing the Cotton Crop of the South, 1800–1925*. Lexington: University of Kentucky Press.

# 6

# Manufacturing Employment at Mid-Century

## Unsurprisingly Large

The 1850 census enumerated 23.1 million residents of the 31 states and deemed 943,305 persons, or 4.1% of the total population, to be employed by manufacturing establishments. In that year, New York City's manufacturing workforce numbered 80,302, or 15.6% of its 515,547 population. Thus, the percentage of New Yorkers engaged in manufacturing was 3.8 times the national average (=15.6% ÷ 4.1%). This statistic, the employment concentration ratio,[1] will prove useful in this and subsequent chapters.

Of the 1,606 counties in the United States at the time, New York's 3.8 manufacturing employment concentration ratio ranked 30th, and at 5.5 and 5.0, respectively, the City's two metropolitan neighbors, Essex and Passaic Counties, New Jersey, ranked 15th and 17th. For the

[1]The employment concentration ratio for an industry in a location is generally defined as the percentage of local employment in that industry divided by the percentage of total national employment in the same industry. Occasionally, as in this instance, because some data required for the standard definition are not available, the industrial employment percentages will be calculated with respect to the total population of the locality and the nation.


A. Gurwitz, *Atlantic Metropolis*, Palgrave Studies in American Economic History,
https://doi.org/10.1007/978-3-030-13352-8_6

New York metropolitan area as a whole,[2] the concentration ratio was 3.5. Other large cities and metropolitan areas were also important industrial centers; the manufacturing employment concentration ratios for metropolitan Philadelphia and Boston were 3.0 and 4.9, respectively.

That a large proportion of mid-nineteenth-century manufacturing activity took place in and around large cities would not surprise economic geographers.

When thinking about the location of industrial activity, we can distinguish between two types of industries: (i) transportation cost-sensitive and (ii) "footloose." For the former, an important raw material may be much more expensive to transport than the final product; such "weight losing" industrial processes will gravitate to places that are close to the input source. Or the final product might be harder to move long distances than the inputs; for such "weight gaining" manufacturing locations close to the point of final sale are advantageous. For footloose industries, our primary interest here, transportation costs of inputs and products are about equal and/or quite small for both.

In the context of the new economic geography ("NEG") introduced in Chapter 3, the fundamental forces driving the formation of cities are economies of scale in weight-gaining and footloose industries, decreases in transportation costs in general, and the satisfaction consumers derive

---

[2]The geographic foci of this chapter are the three large northeastern metropolitan regions of the antebellum United States, New York, Philadelphia, and Boston, each consisting of a central county and its surrounding, industrialized counties. This regional perspective is appropriate because some important industries were attracted to the vicinity of large urban markets but needed either waterpower or more space than they could afford in the central city. Many firms in such industries located in what are now "suburban" counties (Stott, 1989).

The three metropolitan regions are defined as follows.

New York: New York and Kings Counties, NY, and Hudson, Essex, and Passaic Counties, NJ.

Philadelphia: Bucks, Chester, Delaware, and Philadelphia Counties, PA, and Camden County, NJ.

Boston: Essex, Norfolk, Plymouth, Middlesex, and Suffolk Counties, MA.

The source for all of the data in this chapter is the 1850 Census (U.S. Department of the Interior, 1990). In general reference to 1850 data is most appropriate for the purposes of this chapter because that year was exactly at mid-century and was tabulated before Americans began to adjust their commercial relationships in anticipation of possible Civil War. Because county-level employment data for specific industries are more reliable and more readily accessible for 1860, however, some of the discussion refers to conditions in that census year.

from the availability of a diverse array of attractively priced products. Although product diversity and economies of scale characterize many service industries, the NEG paradigm seems most applicable to manufacturing, particularly during the nineteenth century. The opportunity to produce goods at cost-minimizing scale attracts manufacturers to larger local markets and enables them to compete for labor by offering relatively high wages. Urban pay rates need not, however, be much higher than what's on offer elsewhere because potential migrants view the wide variety of consumer goods and services available in more populous places as attractive. Thus, a modest wage premium and other big-city attractions further increase the local population and instigate another phase of self-reinforcing growth. As manufacturing activity, which had previously been dispersed more or less evenly across the landscape, concentrates in a few locations, a growing proportion of the economy's total manufacturing employment becomes concentrated in large towns and cities. And because the growth process driven by manufacturing agglomeration is self-reinforcing, the larger the city the greater the local concentration of manufacturing activity.

Practitioners of an older tradition of economic geography have also developed useful insights into how locating near other firms in the same and related businesses—that is, "agglomerating" in cities—could convey advantages to individual manufacturers and their employees relative to operating in more isolated locations. As early as 1890 Alfred Marshall, one of the founders of what has come to be called neoclassical economics, identified three such "agglomeration externalities," and the process of formalizing and elaborating on Marshall's intuitions continues. Marshallian economic geography can be summarized as follows (Duranton & Puga, 2003):

- Labor market interactions: In a large city, where many firms hire similarly skilled workers, any individual employer will have an easier time replacing a key employee who leaves. Likewise, it will be easier for a skilled worker who is dissatisfied with his or her current employer to find a new position. Thus, both firms and workers are attracted to cities.

- Linkages between intermediate and final goods: Economies of scale can reduce the cost of manufactured inputs to subsequent processes (e.g., printing presses as an input to the publishing industry). In such cases, all else held equal, intermediate-goods producers would find it advantageous to locate near where the final product is manufactured, and vice versa.
- Knowledge spillovers: When a large number of producers in the same industry locate near each other "[t]he mysteries of the trade become no mysteries; but are as it were in the air, and children learn many of them unconsciously. Good work is rightly appreciated, inventions and improvements in machinery, in processes and the general organization of the business have their merits promptly discussed: if one man starts a new idea, it is taken up by others and combined with suggestions of their own; and thus it becomes the source of further new ideas" (Marshall, 1895).

Thus, in the context of both the old economic geography and NEG we expect that the manufacturing employment concentration ratio would increase with population across geographic regions. To see that this expectation was realized on average in the middle of the nineteenth century, consider Fig. 6.1, in which each point represents the natural logarithms of population and the manufacturing employment concentration ratio for each county with at least one person reported as employed in such an establishment in the 1850 census.[3] The line through the points represents the estimated average relationship across counties between (log) populations and (log) concentration ratios. The shaded area around the line denotes the approximate range of relationships between the two variables that can be considered statistically close to the average.[4]

[3]The statistical relationship is more apparent graphically using logarithms rather than the underlying numbers. The relationship between the logarithms also reflects the tendency for county manufacturing concentration ratios to rise faster than linearly as population increases.

[4]The estimated regression equation is

$$\begin{aligned}\text{Log(Concentration Ratio)} &= -5.39 + 0.43\,\text{Log(Population)}\\ &\quad\ (0.30)\quad\ (0.03)\end{aligned}$$

$$R\text{-squared} = 0.12$$

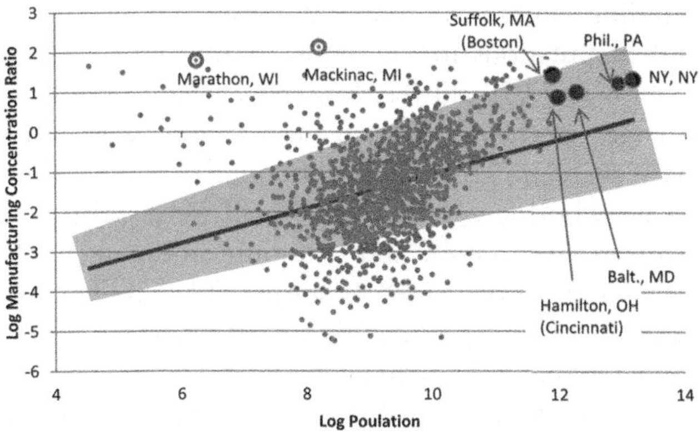


**Fig. 6.1** County populations and manufacturing employment concentration ratios, 1850 (U.S. Department of the Interior, 1990)

The chart illustrates several points. First, the line through the middle of the cluster of points represents the average relationship between the two variables, and its rising slope indicates that, as expected, the percentage of the population engaged in manufacturing is higher in more populous counties.

Second, the wide range of values over which points are scattered reflects the fact that the tendency of manufacturing activity to agglomerate in populous places by itself explains no more than a modest proportion of the variation in manufacturing concentration ratios across counties. Unless, as is unlikely, manufacturing activity is distributed randomly across the landscape, some other county characteristic(s) in addition to population must play some role. For example, the high concentration ratios for the two less-populous counties identified in the chart reflect the impact of a weight-losing manufacturing process, turning timber into lumber; 38% of the combined 1850 manufacturing workforce of Wisconsin and Michigan was engaged in processing

Standard errors in parentheses. The shaded area on the chart is the approximate range of one standard error.

their surrounding white pine forests (Cronon, 1991). Or some of the counties with populations in the 3,000–20,000 range (log population between about 8 and 10) and very low concentration ratios may be geographically large, sparsely populated jurisdictions where any manufacturing activity, such as a gristmill or cotton gin, serving local residents is located in a neighboring county. Nor should we dismiss the possibility that, given the transportation and communications technology of the times, census enumerators in 1850 simply failed to find some blacksmiths' and cobblers' shops in recently settled regions.

Third, some highly mechanized, labor-intensive antebellum industries, such as textile manufacturing, depended on waterpower. Accordingly, many of the populous places with unusually high concentration ratios are "metropolitan" counties such as Middlesex, MA, and Passaic, NJ, with access to waterpower and situated near large northeastern cities.

Finally, the concentrations of manufacturing activity in the country's most populous counties, including New York, are close to what one would expect based solely on their populations.[5] That is, the points representing New York, Philadelphia, Baltimore, and Cincinnati all lie within the shaded area that is statistically "close" to the average relationship between log population and log concentration ratio.

[5]The regression residuals for New York, Philadelphia, Baltimore, Hamilton, OH, (Cincinnati) counties illustrated in Fig. 5.1 are all positive, albeit within one standard error. More tellingly, perhaps, *all* of these observations are above the fitted line and there are no very large counties below the line. An alternative statistical specification, which included a log population squared term, did, indeed, have a better fit.

$$\text{Log(Concentration Ratio)} = \underset{(1.30)}{15.75} - \underset{(0.28)}{4.28}\,\text{Log(Population)} + \underset{(0.016)}{0.26}\,\text{Log(Population)}^2$$

$$\text{R-squared} = 0.27$$

Under this specification, the residuals for New York, Philadelphia, and Baltimore are negative but, again, by less than a standard error.

## Surprisingly Small

From another perspective, however, the aggregate size of metropolitan New York's manufacturing sector appears surprisingly small, at least relative to Philadelphia's and, especially, Boston's. As noted in the previous chapter, on the eve of catastrophic agglomeration in 1840 the population of New York City's immediate hinterland was much larger than Philadelphia's or Boston's. Given that a substantial proportion of the demand for any city's manufacturing output is generated within its immediate surroundings, as a first approximation the relative size of a metropolitan region's manufacturing workforce should reflect the size of its broader regional population. Further, for manufactured goods and services subject to the most powerful economies of scale and/or the lowest transportation cost, the relevant "hinterland" of the top-ranked city in an urban hierarchy encompasses the whole country. Thus, antebellum New York City supplied some of the goods and services it produced to buyers in the southern and western states. If anything, therefore, the relative size of New York's manufacturing sector should have been even larger than what we would have expected based solely on the population of its geographic region.

Neither of these expectations was realized. By 1850, New York's hinterland was five times larger than Philadelphia's and still twice the size of Boston's, and the City had firmly secured its position at the pinnacle of the U.S. urban hierarchy. Nevertheless, at 94,479 and 113,571, respectively, metropolitan Philadelphia's and Boston's 1850 manufacturing workforces were only somewhat smaller and slightly larger than New York's 110,029.[6]

Further, we expect that the larger the city the larger the number of different industries operating within its metropolitan area. That is, the top-ranked places within the urban hierarchy should contain all of the types of manufacturing found in smaller towns (except for industries

[6]The data in this and subsequent paragraphs are drawn from (U.S. Department of the Interior, 1865). Caution is necessary when attempting to draw conclusions from this source about county-level characteristics of specific manufacturing sectors because enumerators' definitions of industries apparently varied from place to place.

operating weight-losing production processes that need to locate near sources of raw materials) *plus* those industries characterized by the greatest economies of scale and lowest transportation costs. The highly ranked cities supply these goods to very broad regions at prices that cannot be matched by local producers or manufacturers located in smaller cities. Thus, top-ranked New York City should have been home to a broader array of industries than second-ranked Philadelphia. This expectation notwithstanding, of the 631 separate manufacturing industries identified by census enumerators in the United States in 1860, 299 were represented by establishments in Philadelphia and 258 in New York.

These observations invite our attention back to the fact, as reflected in the wide scatter of points in Fig. 6.1, that in 1850 county population alone explained no more than 30% of the variation in manufacturing employment concentration ratios across counties. Other county characteristics or pure chance accounted for the rest. Identifying the relevant characteristics that distinguish New York from Philadelphia or Boston as a manufacturing center or concluding that random events determined observed outcomes requires a more detailed look at the nature of each metropolitan area's manufacturing base.

## Antebellum Manufacturing in New York, Philadelphia, and Boston

In the context of the NEG, American cities grew rapidly between 1840 and 1860 largely because big-city manufacturers, by supplying populous urban markets and able to ship goods over long distances at lower cost, were increasingly able to exploit potential economies of scale. The relatively large size of metropolitan industrial firms in terms of annual sales, number of workers, and total capital investment (Table 6.1, columns 1, 2, and 3) is consistent with this expectation.

Metropolitan economies of scale were not, however, apparently achieved on average through relatively heavy investment in plant and equipment; metropolitan manufacturing in New York, in particular, was less capital-intensive than the national average (Table 6.1, column 4).

**Table 6.1** Aggregate characteristics of regional manufacturing industries, 1860 (U.S. Department of the Interior, 1865)

| Region | Establishment average | | | (4) Capital invested per worker |
|---|---|---|---|---|
| | (1) Annual sales | (2) Workers | (3) Capital invested | |
| U.S.A. | $13,215 | 9 | $7,191 | $770 |
| NY County | 36,553 | 21 | 13,991 | 679 |
| NY Metro | 35,349 | 20 | 14,205 | 707 |
| Philadelphia Co. | 21,591 | 16 | 11,642 | 741 |
| Philadelphia Metro | 18,908 | 14 | 10,525 | 766 |
| Suffolk Co., MA (Boston) | 35,887 | 18 | 13,836 | 761 |
| Boston Metro | 34,541 | 29 | 16,449 | 562 |

Instead, urban manufacturers, with some exceptions, were able to reduce cost as their markets expanded through division of labor. Complex manufacturing processes, such as turning bolts of fabric into men's coats, were broken down into a number of specific tasks that could be performed by individual workers. Productivity improved and costs were reduced as, say, buttonhole stitchers became more and more adept at finishing their task quickly and as managers became better at moving goods efficiently through the piecework production process. Much of this piecework was performed by outworkers at home or in small garret shops, frequently through subcontractors. This form of industrial organization was particularly suited to densely populated places, where it was easy to move goods between outworkers' homes or small shops and a manufacturer's principal place of business. Also, this system maximized the productivity of real estate, a particularly expensive input to any urban manufacturing process, by putting single spaces to use as both residence and workshop.

One final observation suggested by Table 6.1 is that, in comparison with the nation as a whole and with respect to these broad aggregate characteristics, New York's manufacturing sector was not markedly different from those of Philadelphia and Boston.

These three metropolitan economies did, however, differ widely with respect to the industrial composition of their manufacturing sectors.

**Table 6.2** 1860 metropolitan employment concentration ratios for important urban manufacturing industries (U.S. Department of the Interior, 1990)

| Industry | NY metro total empl. | Concentration ratio | | |
|---|---|---|---|---|
| | | NY | Phil. | Boston |
| Clothing, men's | 30,216 | 2.70 | 1.76 | 0.43 |
| Boots and shoes | 5,999 | 0.50 | 0.24 | 4.22 |
| Printing and publishing | 5,739 | 2.91 | 1.44 | 0.81 |
| Hats & caps | 4,425 | 3.83 | 0.92 | 0.70 |
| Clothing, ladies' | 2,595 | 4.63 | 1.13 | 0.71 |
| Marble and stonework | 2,323 | 1.55 | 0.60 | 0.05 |
| Jewelry | 2,094 | 3.61 | 1.13 | 0.33 |
| Ship & boat building | 1,818 | 2.01 | 0.60 | 1.20 |
| Bread and crackers | 1,598 | 2.51 | 1.67 | 0.64 |
| Carpets | 1,185 | 1.82 | 3.99 | 1.55 |
| Cigars | 1,181 | 1.52 | 2.20 | 0.33 |
| Gas | 1,163 | 2.08 | 1.69 | 0.65 |
| Glass | 459 | 0.52 | 1.76 | 0.00 |
| Hosiery | 170 | 0.19 | 3.31 | 0.27 |
| Fisheries | 167 | 0.06 | 0.09 | 1.71 |
| Cotton goods | 164 | 0.01 | 1.61 | 1.55 |
| Nails, cut, wrought, and spikes | 26 | 0.04 | 0.19 | 2.17 |

Highlighted entries indicate which city or metropolitan area had the highest employment concentration in an industry

Table 6.2 presents the metropolitan employment concentration ratios[7] for the seventeen industries that met the following two criteria in 1860: They were of national importance, as indicated by total nationwide employment of 5,000 or more, and they were predominantly "urban" or "metropolitan," as indicated by a concentration ratio of at least 1.5 in at least one of the three metropolitan regions.

The list is sorted by total New York metropolitan employment.

With very few exceptions, each of these important urban industries is highly concentrated in one and only one of the three metropolitan regions. In many cases, in fact, an industry that is highly concentrated in one area is markedly underrepresented in the other two regions'

[7]Note that these concentrations ratios reflect industry-specific employment as a percentage of the total *manufacturing* workforce rather than as a percentage of total population as in previous applications of this statistic in this chapter.

workforces. For example, the percentage of metropolitan Philadelphia's working in the "hosiery" industry was more than three times greater than the national average, while unusually small proportions of Boston's and New York's metropolitan workforces were engaged in this activity. This pattern suggests that an assessment of why certain specific industries tended in agglomerate in one of these places rather the others could provide clues for understanding the relative aggregate sizes of the three regions' manufacturing workforces. Thus, Table 6.2 sets the agenda for a series of case studies of specific industries with the aim of understanding why some did and some did not locate disproportionally in New York.

## Transportation Cost-Sensitive Industries

The regional concentrations of two of the industries listed in Table 6.2—fisheries and glass production—reflect physical geographic advantages of the metropolitan areas in which they were located. Both of these industries involved "weight-losing" production processes, that is, important input(s) were, in effect, more expensive to transport than the final product. The optimal location for these industries, therefore, was as close as possible to the source of supply.

The fisheries industry is not usually thought of as a manufacturing sector. In New England, however, preserved fish had always been an important export. Thus, the concentration of this industry in the Boston metropolitan area and its near absence in New York and Philadelphia can be viewed as an example of a "weight-losing" manufacturing process; indeed, in the nineteenth century it was impossible to ship fresh fish over any considerable distance. So, this industry located in the city closest to the Grand Banks fisheries.

The main inputs to glass production are silica and heating fuel in the form of either wood or coal. Southern New Jersey had been a prime source of both of these resources, and a large proportion of metropolitan Philadelphia's activity in this industry in 1860 took place in Camden County, NJ. After local wood supplies were depleted and once trans-Appalachian transportation costs had declined sufficiently, western Pennsylvania emerged as the greatest U.S. concentration of glass production. In 1860, the Philadelphia region was still an important center of glassmaking, but well past its peak; in 1840, New Jersey accounted for 31% of total U.S. glass production and by 1860 the percentage had declined to 14% (Davis, 1949, pp. 42, 73).

## Urban Growth Industries: Stonework and Gas

Between 1830 and 1860, the total population of the New York urbanized area increased by 562,243, which was almost two-times the growth of Philadelphia's and Boston's populations *combined.* In percentage terms, New York's population almost tripled while Philadelphia's and Boston's "just" doubled. Now, it stands to reason that the faster a region's population is growing in percentage terms, the higher will be the proportion of the regional workforce engaged in the activities that facilitate expansion. The most obvious example of such activity would have been the construction industry, but this was not treated as a manufacturing sector in the 1860 census. Among the sectors highlighted in Table 6.2 two, in particular, are local-growth oriented, the marble and stonework industry and the gas industry.

Although some of its product may have been shipped elsewhere, the marble and stonework industry can serve as a reasonable proxy for local construction in general, and New York's relatively rapid absolute and proportionate population growth during the last antebellum decades seems to be sufficient to explain this industry's 1.55 concentration ratio. The very low ratios for this industry in Philadelphia and, especially, Boston, both of which did, after all, double in size over the period, are harder to explain. It may have been that New York builders were more inclined than Philadelphians or Bostonians to use stone in construction rather than wood, perhaps because of the number of high-quality stone quarries in the former's hinterland (Greeley, 1872) and perhaps because New York experienced devastating fires in during the second quarter of the nineteenth century while the other two cities did not.

The functions of the second urban growth industry during the nineteenth century were to manufacture hydrocarboniferous gas for interior- or street-lighting by heating wood or coal in an enclosed retort and to build and maintain the requisite infrastructure of storage tanks and pipelines. Before the development of long-distance gas pipelines, all of these activities took place near the end users, i.e., within cities, and the process of urban growth required the expansion of production facilities and the distribution network.

Initiating gas lighting service required governmental acquiescence. During the early nineteenth century, establishing a limited liability corporation, something of a necessity for a venture involving a capital-intensive cutting-edge technology for producing a highly flammable product, required a specific act of a legislature. And installing gas mains under city streets and switching from oil-lamp to gas street-lighting could not proceed without local government approval. Proposals to install gas facilities met with opposition from purveyors of whale oil and other competing products. And, once gas was available, consumers had to be persuaded to install the required newfangled piping and lamps in their businesses and homes. New York's government and consumers seem to have adopted the new lighting technology more willingly than residents of some other cities.

The Gas Light Company of Baltimore, the first such enterprise in the United States, began service in 1816, seven years before the second, the New York Gas Light Company, began offering the same product and service. As late as 1836, however, the Baltimore Company had installed only two miles of gas mains, while as early as 1824 New York had six miles. The first Boston gas company, the third such operation in the country, was established in 1828, while Philadelphia was relatively slow to adopt the new technology. That City's first gas company was not chartered until 1836. Further, Philadelphia was served by a single gas company, which was eventually taken over by the local government. In New York, by contrast, by the early 1860s four companies operated simultaneously within separate assigned territories. Although there was no direct competition among these entities, customers of, say, the New York Gas Light Company operating in lower Manhattan would have been aware of the prices charged by the Metropolitan Gas Light Company in midtown. Because the companies operated under the supervision of the City government, consumers were able to influence the price and quality of the service on offer. The result was downward pressure on prices and consequent expansion of service. Even so, the profitability of the New York-based gas companies remained high (Stotz, 1938, pp. 20–66, 92–97).

## Port-Related, Directly and Indirectly

New York differed from the other two cities as a manufacturing center—and, indeed, as a financial center and a wholesaling center—principally because it was, by far, the busiest port in the United States, especially for imports. In 1860, New York accounted for 60.3% of total national imports, compared to 7.5% for Philadelphia and 15.7% for all the Massachusetts ports combined. Some of the linkages between port functions and manufacturing activity are direct and obvious; others are less obvious and/or indirect but still very important.

### Bread and Crackers

The connection between the bakeries and the port, for example, is not intuitively obvious. Commercial bread baking was a quintessentially urban industry in the nineteenth century; most country people would have made their own bread. Thus, the concentration ratios for this industry in New York, Philadelphia, and Suffolk, MA (Boston) counties were 2.45, 1.83, and 1.88, respectively. To some extent, the relatively high number for New York in 1860 may reflect the fact that this was the most "urban" of the three places. But part of the high concentration of this industry in New York along with the fact that New York was the only place where census marshals designated the product as "Bread and Crackers" rather than as simply "Bread" reflect the fact that a relatively large proportion of the output of the region's commercial bakers were producing long shelf-life product for sea voyages.

By contrast, the connection between port activity and the shipbuilding industries may be less obvious than it seems. The concentration of shipbuilding in New York does not reflect any particular locational advantage with respect to either the availability of heavy raw materials or the market for the final product. The heaviest inputs to antebellum sailing shipbuilding were certain narrowly defined types of lumber. These either did not grow in New York's nearby hinterland or had been largely depleted by the 1850s. Northern New England was much better situated in this regard than New York. Nor was it costly to transport a sailing ship built elsewhere on the coastline to a buyer in New York City. For both of these reasons, Maine's share of U.S. shipbuilding by tonnage exceeded New York State's in every year but one between 1833 and 1860.[8]

The key linkage between port activity and shipbuilding ran through the repair activities related to the City's role as the American terminus of the packet lines. Maintaining a profitable regular schedule of frequent departures of sailing vessels imposed two requirements on packet operators; (i) they had to operate all year, even through the harsh, damaging North Atlantic winter conditions and (ii) they had to limit time in port. So, the full range of ship repair services had to be located at the terminal port. Because repairing vessels and building new ones require the same facilities, such as dry docks, and worker skills and because ship repair activity tends to be seasonal, it makes sense for the same firms to do both and, therefore, for an important port city also to be an important shipbuilding center.

New York was also the central place and principal transshipment point for its hinterland. Even in the early 1850s, railroads had not yet replaced steamboats as the transportation mode of choice between New York City and upstate New York, New England, and coastal New Jersey. Further, because metropolitan New York City was, in large part, an archipelago, ferries were the main means by which goods and people moved around the region. As it was risky to deliver steamboats designed for river or bay service to destinations across open seas, these vessels tended to be built along the waterways on which they were to be used. Accordingly, throughout the period between 1833 and 1860 New York was second only to Pittsburgh among U.S. cities in the production of steamers.

---

[8]Except when otherwise indicated the material in this section on shipbuilding is taken from Albion (1939).

The final stimulus to the development of this industry was the decision of the U.S. Navy to locate one of its most important shipbuilding and repair yards in Brooklyn.

At 1818, the number of New Yorkers directly engaged in ship and boatbuilding was not huge; the industry accounted for only 1.4% of the metropolitan area's total manufacturing workforce. The importance of shipbuilding to the local economy becomes more apparent, however, if we include employment in separately tabulated sectors that provided inputs to the final construction and outfitting of a vessel. Table 6.3 identifies several likely candidates for inclusion on a list of shipbuilding-related sectors. Some of these sectors only produce inputs to shipbuilding; others would have supplied other industries or final consumers as well. On reasonable conservative assumptions, New York metropolitan area manufacturing employment related directly or indirectly to shipbuilding rises to a respectable 4.6%.[9]

Although New York remained the nation's premier port well into the twentieth century, the 1850s marked the high point of New York's role as a major shipbuilding center. The total tonnage of vessels built in New York State before the Civil War peaked in 1854, and the State's share of total US-manufactured tonnage topped out at 26% in 1851. New York's decline as a shipbuilding center coincided with the shift in demand on the main North Atlantic commercial routes away from wooden sailing vessels to steam-powered, screw-driven, iron- or steel-hulled ships. The process of manufacturing a sailing ship was similar in many ways to constructing a building and did not require much more space than a typical urban construction site. The newer, much larger,

[9]This estimate is based on the assumption that each for each industry listed in Table 6.3, that the amount by which the industry's concentration ratio in New York exceeds that of the higher ratio of Philadelphia's and Boston's represents the proportion of industry employment in New York connected with the shipbuilding industry. For example, the concentration ratio for the steam engine industry was 1.34 in New York and 0.76 in Philadelphia. This industry accounted for 2.76% of total U.S. employment. The percentage of total metropolitan manufacturing workforce employed in this industry, therefore, was 3.71% in New York and 2.1% in Philadelphia. If New York's percentage had been the same as Philadelphia's, there would have been 2,690 individuals employed in the industry instead of 4,753. I assume that the difference between these two numbers, or 2,063, to be the number of New York steam engine makers supplying the steamboat building industry.

**Table 6.3** 1860 employment and employment concentration in shipbuilding-related industries

| Industry | NY metro total empl. | % US workforce | % NY workforce | Metropolitan employment concentration ratio | | |
|---|---|---|---|---|---|---|
| | | | | NY | Phil. | Bos. |
| Steam engine & related machinery | 4,753 | 2.76 | 3.71 | 1.34 | 0.76 | 0.46 |
| Cordage | 872 | 0.27 | 0.68 | 2.57 | 0.47 | 0.19 |
| Carpentering | 1,944 | 0.23 | 1.52 | 6.62 | 3.70 | 1.44 |
| Brass founding, &c. | 355 | 0.11 | 0.28 | 2.44 | 1.75 | 1.00 |
| Sails | 160 | 0.05 | 0.12 | 2.55 | 0.82 | 1.37 |
| Coppersmithing | 183 | 0.04 | 0.14 | 3.97 | 0.95 | 0.74 |
| Rigging | 145 | 0.02 | 0.11 | 5.05 | 0.84 | 1.19 |

and much more complex vessels, by contrast, were built most efficiently in huge shipyards close to the sources of heavy inputs. Space was expensive in New York, and iron and steel mills were far way. Further, the ocean steamers were less subject to routine damage than the older sailing ships, so the linkage between repair and new construction was looser during the second half of the nineteenth century than it had been earlier.

These shifts notwithstanding, metropolitan New York remained an important shipbuilding center well into the twentieth century, supported by such repair services as were needed at a major port and by continuing activity at the Brooklyn Navy Yard.

## Printing and Publishing

Four characteristics of antebellum publishing activity influenced New York's role in this large, dynamic urban industry: (i) rapid, accelerating growth in both the number and variety of publications, (ii) increasing geographic centralization of production and marketing, (iii) intense competition among publishers, and (iv) the importance of foreign-origin content. The last of these considerations determined that the nation's premier port of entry would also become an important center for printing and publishing.

The decades after 1830 were boom times for the American book, newspaper, and magazine businesses. The average number of titles published in the United States annually rose from about 100 during the 1830s to 1,350 in on the eve of the Civil War; two-fifths of this increase took place after 1853 (Tebbel, 1972, p. 222). The number of daily newspapers in existence grew from 42 in 1820 to 254 in 1850, with more than half of that increase coming in the last decade of the period (Lee, 1937, p. 717). And the number of magazines grew from about 100 in 1825 to about 600 in 1850. Even this growth may understate the dynamism of the mid-century magazine business; by one estimate, the roughly 600 magazines being published in 1850 were the survivors of between 4,000 and 5,000 start-ups initiated during the preceding quarter century (Tebbel & Zuckerman, 1991, p. 11).

This expansion was driven by the growth of the literate population and by a series of important advances in printing technology. The latter involved mechanization and the use of steam power in all of the processes involved in producing a book, newspaper, or magazine from type-founding and paper making to paper cutting and binding. There are no broad measures of total improvement in productivity, but the increase in impressions per hour produced by the most advanced available presses from about 800 in 1810 to 15,000 by 1865 may be indicative (Tebbel, 1972, pp. 258–259).

Economies of scale became more important in the printing industry as the shift from hand presses to a fully mechanized production process raised the fixed cost of setting up a state-of-the-art printing operation. At the same time, transportation costs were starting to decline and average transportation speeds to increase. The combination of more powerful scale economics and lower transportation costs led to a centralization of production in large cities. Accordingly, the percentage of American-authored fiction published outside of Boston, Philadelphia, or New York declined from about 50% during the first decade of the century to only eight percent by 1840 (Tebbel, 1972, p. 206). Further, as the number of titles expanded so did the volume of information about which books were available. Publishers needed some way to communicate what they had for sale to readers and shopkeepers around the country. As in other industries specialized wholesaling institutions and firms developed to communicate information and to execute transactions. In the book publishing industry, this involved book fairs, specialized book jobbers and auctioneers, and trade publications including consolidated catalogs of multiple publishers' offerings. It was natural that these distribution-related activities would take place near where the greatest number of books was published. So this segment of the industry, too, concentrated in New York City (Tebbel, 1972, pp. 229–238).

Despite the increase in start-up costs associated with more and more expensive capital equipment, it was evidently still easy enough to get into the publishing business so that the industry was highly competitive. Much of the competition in the book publishing sector involved which house would be first to print and distribute copies of the latest offerings of popular English authors, some of whose works sold more briskly in the more populous and more literate United States than in their home country (Liebowitz, 2015, p. 12). As international copyright protection did not come into effect until late in the second half of the nineteenth century, the first U.S. firm to its hands on a copy of the latest potential best seller would likely be the first to publish and to get a U.S. edition onto store shelves. At least one well-known author, Anthony Trollope, is on record as referring to this practice as "piracy in spirit, though it may not be so by law" (Smith, 2001, p. 485). Thus, not for the first or last time in its history, a form of piracy played an important role in New York City's economic development. Indeed, the antebellum book publishing history had something of a swashbuckling character. Those who were successful in the competition "learned to estimate publication schedules in hours instead of days or weeks and could make a quick profit simply by getting out a first edition of a new English novel a few hours earlier than their rivals. Some had agents in England who hovered like vultures over the bookstalls, or the printers whenever that was possible, to get sheets or books which would be shipped on the fastest ship available. In New York or Philadelphia, the copy would be rushed from the dock or, in some cases from a fast packet which had met the incoming boat offshore, to a publisher's composing room, where the speediest compositors would be employed and the presses would run day and night until the book was ready to be rushed to the stores, or sold on the street like fish. Some ingenious and enterprising publishers even had type set aboard ships while they were making the passage to America" (Tebbel, 1972, p. 208).

Access to information from abroad also played a role in the periodicals segments of the publishing industry. A large part of the content of newspapers around the country consisted of news and other material copied from big-city papers or provided by press syndicates or wire services such as the Associated Press (established in New York in 1846). So, the metropolitan content-providers that could be relied on to provide the most up-to-date, hardest-to-obtain foreign news could expect to enroll the most out-of-town subscribers.

The same ships that brought foreign physical commodities to the United States also carried information. Because New York City was the principal U.S. port of entry for goods, it was also the chief conduit through which written matter and word-of-mouth news from Europe entered North America and from which foreign-sourced media content was transmitted elsewhere on the continent.

Further, the distribution channels for up-to-date foreign news between New York and the rest of the country, which also conveyed domestic news, opinion pieces, *belles lettres*, etc., created operating habits and connections that survived the continent-wide build-out of the telegraph wire network and the advent of transatlantic cables. Editors of local papers with nationwide influence, in the mold of James Gordon Bennett of the *Herald* or Horace Greeley of the *Tribune*, remained highly influential, guaranteeing that a disproportionate share of the nation's media content would originate in or be transmitted through New York (Tebbel, 1963, pp. 93–124).

As with shipbuilding, the number of people enumerated as directly employed in printing and publishing understates the importance of this industry in the New York economy. An additional 3,900 New Yorkers were employed in industries directly related to printing and publishing, and in all of these sectors the region's concentration ratio was very high (Table 6.4), although in some cases metropolitan Philadelphia's was higher, albeit with a smaller absolute number of workers. Printing press manufacturing, in particular, provides a dramatic example of how an

**Table 6.4** 1860 employment and employment concentration printing and publishing-related industries (U.S. Department of the Interior, 1865)

| Industry | NY metro total empl. | % US workforce | % NY workforce | Metropolitan employment concentration ratio | | |
|---|---|---|---|---|---|---|
| | | | | NY | Phil. | Bos. |
| Bookbinding and blank books | 1,014 | 0.36 | 0.79 | 2.17 | 4.78 | 0.98 |
| Type founding | 410 | 0.08 | 0.32 | 3.79 | 2.67 | 1.48 |
| Lithography | 321 | 0.06 | 0.25 | 4.18 | 5.46 | 0.30 |
| Printing, presses | 515 | 0.05 | 0.40 | 7.46 | 0.76 | 1.41 |
| Stereotyping and electro-typing | 162 | 0.02 | 0.13 | 5.44 | 5.04 | 0.00 |

intermediate input industry can become highly concentrated geographically, especially when its production is characterized by important economies of scale. Metropolitan New York accounted for fully 73% of total U.S. employment in this industry.

## Ready-Made Clothing

The men's clothing industry was by far the largest manufacturing sector in New York in 1860; it accounted for almost a quarter of all manufacturing jobs in the metropolitan region. No doubt some of this business still took the traditional form of custom tailoring for individual local residents, but the disproportionate concentration of this industry in New York reflects the importance to the local economy of ready-made clothing produced for export from the region. The concentration ratio for the Ladies Clothing industry was even higher, but the absolute size of this sector was much smaller because American women did not begin buying ready-made garments in large quantities until the end of the nineteenth century. Industrial-scale production of ladies' garments in 1860 was limited to a few fashion items, such as hoopskirts, that could not be produced efficiently at home or in small craftswomen's shops[10] (Mendeslsohn, 2015).

One reason the Men's Clothing industry was able to transition from a custom- to a ready-made standard relatively quickly may have been that pre-sewn, standard-sized shirts, trousers, and coats were being produced and sold in North American cities by the end of the eighteenth century. "Slops" was a term used to describe relatively inexpensive, ready-made men's garments sold to individuals who either could not afford custom-tailored clothes or were in transit and could not wait for a bespoke garment to be completed. Many of the latter would have been sailors. At the end of the eighteenth century, slops were sold in specialty shops, most of which located near dockyards. Sometimes slops were manufactured in or near the shop where they were sold, but frequently these garments were assembled at home or in separate business establishments by "outworkers" from pieces cut from a pattern at a central location. Thus, the basic structure of the mid-century men's ready-made garment industry—the use of patterns, centralized cutting, and assembly and finishing by outworkers—was well established on a small, specialized scale before this business "took off" after 1830 (Putnam, 2015).

Four catalysts combined to transform the slops niche into New York's largest manufacturing industry during the nineteenth century's second quarter. First, the supply of the raw materials for garment production, fabric of various descriptions and qualities, was growing rapidly and unit prices were declining. Second, it was becoming easier to recruit an appropriately skilled workforce to execute the labor-intensive task of turning fabric into finished garments. Third, the development of new patented systems of drafting standard-sized men's garment patterns enabled ready-made manufacturers to deliver stylish, well-fitting products requiring minimal customization. Finally, it was becoming easier to distribute ready-made clothing over long distances

[10] The statistics for the ladies clothing industry probably do not include small custom dressmaking businesses, which would have been enumerated in the "millinery goods" sector. At the time the latter term referred to more than hat-making and included custom-made dresses and a variety of accessories. New York's 7.27 concentration ratio in the millinery industry may, however, have presaged the future importance of the ladies' garment industry in the City's industrial economy.

as transportation costs declined and as commercial networks developed linking northeastern urban manufacturers and distributors nationwide. Late in the antebellum period a fourth development, the invention and adoption of sewing machines, enhanced productivity in the garment industry and accelerated the growth of the ready-made market, but the transition was well underway before machines replaced hand sewing (Zakin, 2003).

All three large northeastern cities were well positioned with respect to the preconditions for the industrial production of ready-made clothing. Slops shops did business in all three cities, all three were important ports, the populations of all three were growing rapidly, and manufacturers and jobbers in all three cities were in touch with networks of wholesalers and rural shopkeepers. New York did, however, have an edge in most respects, and all of the City's advantages can be traced directly or indirectly to the City's role as the premier U.S. port.

New Yorkers may have had more collective experience in producing ready-made clothing as of 1830 than residents of other cities. Although the slops shops' clientele included local laborers, a large proportion of their customers were sailors. It would, therefore, have been likely that New York, as the busiest port by far after 1815, would have been home to many more such establishments than other cities. If so, proportionally more New Yorkers than Philadelphians or Bostonians would have had some knowledge of how ready-made men's clothing could be produced and marketed.

New York manufacturers would have had more ready access to the right raw materials for the production of quality menswear. At the time, a large proportion of the British textiles arriving in the United States, like all other imports, were channeled through the Port of New York for reasons discussed in Chapter 4. Access to imported textiles was particularly important as the ready-made clothing business moved up-market from slops toward gentlemen's attire because, unlike cotton goods, higher-quality woolens do not seem to have been produced domestically in industrial quantities.

The New York labor force was larger and expanding faster than Boston's or Philadelphia's. The next chapter will explore New York's antebellum labor market and its interaction with the region's largest manufacturing industry in more depth. At this point, it will suffice to point out that the City's labor force served as a comparative advantage for New York vis-à-vis Philadelphia and Boston with respect to labor-intensive manufacturing activities. At least part of this advantage derived from the City's position as the nation's principle port of entry for immigrants.

Because New York was the marketing hub for U.S. imports, local wholesalers had the most extensive out-of-town contacts. Finally, while manufacturers and jobbers in all three of these cities were linked to nationwide distribution networks, New York's marketing connections with its own, larger hinterland, with the cotton-growing South, with regions bordering the Great Lakes, and after 1850, with California were particularly extensive.

As with the other important urban industries, employment in the men's clothing industry understates the full impact of this activity on the regional economy. In particular to the 30,216 employees directly engaged in the production of men's garments we should add some large proportion of the 666 New Yorkers engaged in sewing machine manufacture (regional concentration ratio, 2.98). This industry was of modest quantitative importance as an employer but given that a sewing machine was about as complex a mechanical technology as the antebellum period produced, the industrial linkages and worker skills that would have developed around this activity may have influenced the region's subsequent industrial progress.

## Other Fashion Industries

Fashions in the United States closely followed European trends until well into the twentieth century. Therefore, categories of goods for which the *au courant* commanded a premium price were most advantageously produced near places at which up-to-date news about fashion changes was most readily available and from which information about fashion trends was communicated. In the antebellum period that would have been New York. Such goods would very much have included menswear (Zakin, 2003, pp. 185–211), but because of this industry's size it was discussed separately. Other "fashion-sensitive" industries included ladies' garments, jewelry, silk fringes and trimmings, millinery, and millinery goods. The term "millinery" has come to refer to the manufacture of hats, but the narrative accompanying the published 1860 Census of Manufactures defined it in this way: "Milliners' work includes the making of bonnets, caps, scarfs, and all outward attire worn by females except the gown. It is supposed to demand a higher exercise of skill and taste than that of dress-making" (U.S. Department of the Interior, 1865, p. lxxxvi). The "millinery goods industry" produced intermediate goods, such as artificial flowers, that were incorporated into final fashionable products. Total New York metropolitan employment in these combined industries was 6,396 and the metropolitan concentration ratio for the combined sector was 4.22. To be sure, not all of the products of these businesses were the height of fashion, but the New York branch of these industries may have been particularly attuned to the latest trends. New York State accounted for 30.3% of total national production of ladies' cloaks and dresses while New York City and Brooklyn alone accounted for 46% of domestic production of hoopskirts, a fashion item of the time *par excellence.*

## Early Adopters' Advantage

Most of New York's antebellum specialties among important urban manufacturing sectors were concentrated there either because they were a by-product of the City's rapid population growth or because they benefitted directly or indirectly from proximity to the port. All but one of the other industries on Table 6.2 were more heavily concentrated in either Philadelphia or Boston. The only exception was the manufacture of men's headwear, which will be discussed briefly below.

What many of Philadelphia's and Boston's manufacturing specialties have in common is that local entrepreneurs began to expand each of these lines of business in one or both of those cities very early during the process of industrialization or even before that process began. It is difficult to characterize the initial matching of entrepreneurs with industries and cities in these cases as anything other than serendipitous.

Once an industry happened to get started in a particular city sooner than elsewhere it seems that the third of Alfred Marshall's three benefits of industrial agglomeration—namely, the notion that "[t]he mysteries of the trade become no mysteries; but are as it were in the air"—conveyed an advantage to local practitioners that led to self-reinforcing growth of the particular line of business in a particular locality.

## Cotton Goods

In 1860, at more than $93 billion, the total capital invested in the manufacture of "cotton goods" was greater than that of any other manufacturing sector. This was ten percent more than the next most highly capitalized industry, flour and meal milling. In that last antebellum year, one in four female industrial workers was employed in this industry.

Cotton goods manufacturing was highly concentrated in New England, notwithstanding the somewhat higher concentration statistic for metropolitan Philadelphia in Table 6.2. The six New England states accounted for 45% of cotton goods production compared to the region's 10% of U.S. population and 15% of total enumerated manufacturing employment. Now, this part of the country had no obvious unique natural advantages as a location for textile manufacturing. New England was farther from the cotton-growing regions than the more populous Middle Atlantic States. The region's geography was conducive to generating waterpower, but so were the inland regions of the states to New England's south. To be sure, New Englanders did produce many more offspring than the poor local soils could support as farmers, but there were outlets other than nearby factory towns for the excess local population including migration westward. Nor did the Middle Atlantic States' industries have much apparent problem recruiting workforces for even more labor-intensive activities than textile production.[11]

[11]The cotton goods industry employed about the same number of people as the men's clothing industry, while capital invested per worker in the former was $810 compared to $237 in the latter (U.S. Department of the Interior, 1990).

Industrial textile production seems to have prospered in this region because a few well-placed New Englanders were more successful in appropriating the machinery and know-how developed in England during the second half of the eighteenth century, despite British prohibitions on both the export the new textile manufacturing technologies and the emigration of skilled craftspeople. During the early 1790s, several groups of entrepreneurs in the Middle Atlantic and New England regions, often with the encouragement of state or Federal government officials, tried to establish water-powered cotton thread factories, using the technology developed by Richard Arkwright twenty years earlier, by encouraging the immigration to the United States of British subjects with the requisite knowledge and skills. None of these early attempts were successful enough to serve as a model for similar enterprises until Moses Brown, a Rhode Island entrepreneur, came into contact with Samuel Slater, a British immigrant residing in New York, who had an extensive, practical understanding of the requisite technology and manufacturing processes. Brown and Slater's operation in Pawtucket, RI, was very successful, as was the independent firm subsequently established by Slater and his in-laws, also in Pawtucket. "These two small establishments .... were, directly or indirectly, the sources whence the workmen who erected cotton spinning mills in different parts of the country prior to 1810 drew their knowledge of the business" (Ben-Atar, 1995; U.S. Department of the Interior, 1865, p. xvi). By 1810, during the pre-war domestic manufacturing boom, the U.S. Secretary of the Treasury reported that there were 87 cotton mills in operation or under construction in the United States, 57 of which were in New England. Initially, the thread produced in the mills using the Arkwright technology was woven into fabric on handlooms. Given the density of local supply of thread and of textile-related mechanical expertise, though, it is not surprising that the first industrial power looms in the United States were installed in Massachusetts and that the nation's largest complex of textile mills was developed in and around Lowell in that State.

New England was not the only place in the United States where water-powered spinning mills were established in the 1790s. Famously, with the encouragement of U.S. Treasury Secretary Alexander Hamilton, the Society for the Encouragement of Useful Manufactures (SEUM) established a spinning mill on the falls of the Passaic River in Patterson, New Jersey, in 1791. Operations were established there, and Patterson did eventually become a specialty textile center of some importance, but financial setbacks in the early years apparently discouraged emulation of the undertaking by entrepreneurs in the New York region.

## Footwear

At 123,000, more Americans were engaged in the production of boots and shoes than in any other manufacturing industry in 1860. The footwear industry was even more concentrated in New England than cotton goods manufacturing; almost 60% boots and shoes by value was produced in Massachusetts and vicinity. Essex County, situated on the North Shore of Massachusetts Bay, alone accounted for 16% of total U.S. production. As with the textile industry, this region had no obvious natural comparative advantage with respect to the transformation of animal hides on the hoof into shoes and boots on consumers' feet. If anything, in fact, the New York region was better situated than New England as a locus for this activity during most of the antebellum period. The input that went into the production of shoes at the time that was, in effect, the most expensive to transport was hemlock bark, an extract of which was used in the preferred leather tanning technology. The material was not particularly heavy, but the active chemical agent in the bark deteriorated quickly after harvest. As it happened, the period from about 1820 until the local hemlock stands was depleted by the late 1840s, just when the U.S. shoe industry was undergoing its transformation from a custom-made to a ready-to-wear organization, the most productive source of tanning bark on the East Coast was in the Catskill highlands west of the Hudson River. Consequently, Green County, New York, just south of Albany was a major leather tanning center (Bruegel, 2002, pp. 81–83). So, to the extent that the cost of transporting either inputs or the final product determined the location of this manufacturing activity, the Hudson Valley would have been a likely locus of concentration. In fact, however, transportation costs were not an important determinant of the location of the footwear industry in the United States (Hoover, 1937, p. 263). Shoe and boot manufacturing was footloose.

To be sure, as was the case with the textile industry, New England's "excess" rural population and the large number of sailors' and fishermen's wives who were available to staff the labor-intensive process of shoe assembly as outworkers may have conveyed some advantage. But shoe production was harder to "deskill" than, say, textile manufacturing or men's clothing assembly. The availability of labor with the ability to deal with such uneven material as individual pieces of shoe leather drove the location of this activity through most of the nineteenth century. And because learning by doing and face-to-face training was the most effective way of developing the requisite skills, regions with the longest history of commercial-scale shoe production would have been home to the largest appropriate labor force.

Shoemakers able to meet such local needs as were not met by family manufacture were among the earliest residents of many of the British North American colonies. Why it started where and when it did is unclear, but the earliest record of colonial North American production of footwear for shipment beyond a local community dates from 1650 when shoemakers in Lynn in Essex County, MA, began manufacturing women's shoes for delivery to Boston in advance of orders. Lynn's record of "firsts" continued through the eighteenth century. "The earliest improvements in the domestic manufacture of shoes were made about the year 1750 by John Adam Dagyr … who settled in Lynn where the business was as yet quite limited, only three persons … [employed] journeymen. He possessed superior skill in making ladies' shoes, and by his instructions the native workmen … were soon able to make shoes nearly equal to those imported. The business in Lynn was thenceforward … chiefly confined to the manufacture of women's shoes. In 1764 the London Chronicle stated that women's shoes were made in Lynn, 'exceeding in strength and beauty any that were imported from London.' … No inconsiderable part of the boots and shoes worn in the country at the date of the Revolution was of domestic manufacture, chiefly the production of Massachusetts, which supplied many for the army during the [Revolutionary] war. The heavy importations which followed the peace nearly prostrated the infant industry, which, however, so far revived in Lynn that 100,000 pairs were exported from the town in 1788. In 1795 Lynn employed 200 master workmen and 600 journeymen and apprentices in the shoe business and sent 300,000 pairs of shoes chiefly to southern markets" (U.S. Department of the Interior, 1865, p. lxix).

The evidence we have, sparse though it is, suggests that the concentration of skilled workers and commercially oriented, innovative professionals that developed, apparently serendipitously, in New England and especially around the City of Lynn during the second half of the eighteenth century, was sufficiently attractive to shoe manufacturers to offset the cost of transporting tanned leather to the Massachusetts Bay area and of shipping the finished product along somewhat longer routes to the south and Midwest.

## Specialty Textiles: Hosiery & Carpets

Two specialty textile industries were highly concentrated in metropolitan Philadelphia in 1860 for similar reasons. In both of these cases, craftspeople in and around Philadelphia were engaged in commercial production of these goods very early in the nineteenth century, well before these activities got underway elsewhere. Some writers attribute this early regional specialization to the prevalence of the requisite skills among the German-speaking immigrants to southeastern Pennsylvania in the eighteenth century (U.S. Department of the Interior, 1865, p. lxix).

At the time the term "hosiery" referred to, not only socks and stockings, but a wide range of knitted fabric products including gloves, underwear, shawls, comforters, etc. During the first half of the nineteenth century, knitwear was produced in the United States in three ways: within households using knitting needles by family members for their own use, commercially on handlooms or "knitting frames" by craftspeople working in "manufactories"[12] or at home, and in factories on water-powered

[12] Sean Wilentz defines a manufactory as "oversized workshops that gathered between five and ten skilled workers with a few boys and women to produce, by hand, large lots of light consumer goods" (Wilentz, 2004, p. 31).

knitting looms. The earliest mention of the use of knitting frames in the North American colonies dates from 1723 and refers to a craftsman in Chester County, Pennsylvania, near Philadelphia. In 1810, the (rudimentary) Census enumerated a total of 148 "stocking looms" in operation in manufacturing establishments nationwide, 136 in Pennsylvania and 12 in Maryland. This early start in industrial hosiery production by craftspeople need not necessarily have conveyed an advantage to the Philadelphia region as a location for this activity at the end of the antebellum period if power looms operated by unskilled personnel had come into widespread use by that time. But, perhaps because the knitting process produced a wide variety of final products power-driven technology was slower to take hold in the hosiery industry than, say, the cotton goods industry, which manufactured large quantities of a uniform intermediate product. Whatever the reason, the 1860 high employment concentration ratio of the hosiery industry in metropolitan Philadelphia probably represents the operations of large number of craftspeople working on handlooms individually at home or in manufactories.

As with knitting, early nineteenth-century production of fabric floor coverings in North America was, for the most part, a household activity; there is limited evidence of specialized craftspeople producing rugs for sale. The Philadelphia area was, however, an exception to this generalization. "As early as 1811, there were said to be 4,000 handlooms in operation in Philadelphia upon fabrics of various sorts; and, while it is impossible to estimate … the number engaged upon carpets, possibly … 'a goodly proportion' were thus employed." The commercial production of rugs and carpets on handlooms by individual craftspeople or in small manufactories continued well into the era when carpet factories had come to dominate this industry elsewhere in the country. Nor was the Philadelphia region a laggard when it came to the introduction of factory production. The earliest reference to factory production of floor coverings in the United States dates from 1810 and refers to an establishment in Philadelphia. And evidence suggests that the first use of the superior Jacquard carpet weaving technology in the United States took place in 1825 in a Philadelphia area mill (Cole & Williamson, 1941, pp. 8, 12, 26).

There is no clear evidence of how the Philadelphia region's early start in commercial manufacture of these specialty textiles by skilled craftspeople led to the region's high concentration ratio in 1860 when production had largely shifted to factories (carpets) or was moving in that direction (knitwear). We can speculate that the distribution network for knitwear and carpets that Philadelphia producers and jobbers developed in the early years of the nineteenth century continued to convey an advantage to the region's larger scale manufacturers through the 1850s. Some support for a regional marketing advantage can be found in the claim by a chronicler of antebellum Philadelphia manufacturing that "[t]he term 'Germantown Woolen Goods,' is now as familiar to most dealers as Nottingham Hosiery; while the quality of the American product is far superior to that of the foreign" (Freedley, 1859, p. 241).

## Nails

The New England region offered no obvious natural advantage to manufacturers of fabricated metal products during the antebellum period; the relatively heavy raw materials, for example, were produced elsewhere, and demand for building materials was growing more rapidly in regions much closer to input supplies. Nevertheless, production of a wide variety of hardware was highly concentrated in this region, especially in Massachusetts. First-mover advantage seems to be the most likely explanation for this continuing specialization. In the case of nails, the main center of manufacture was in Plymouth County, south of Boston, "where machinery for cutting nails was introduced as early as 1786" (U.S. Department of the Interior, 1865, p. cxcv).

## Cigars

Until well into the nineteenth century most tobacco users in North America and elsewhere preferred pipes and snuff to cigars. Philadelphia was one of several important North American centers of tobacco product manufactures by the end of the eighteenth century. For some reason, Philadelphia craftspeople shifted to cigar production relatively quickly when demand for the product began to expand. Pennsylvania was the only state mentioned as manufacturing cigars in the 1810 census, which reported that of a total of twenty-nine million cigars produced in the United States, twenty-seven million were produced in Pennsylvania. An early start does *not*, however, seem to have conveyed any long-term advantage in the case of this industry either in terms of technological advances in production or of broad, well-articulated distribution networks. By the eve of the Civil *War*, metropolitan New York was close to the Philadelphia region with respect to cigar industry employment concentration ratio. Further, although New York's cigar industry workforce was almost 25% smaller than Philadelphia's, the value the product produced by the former was slightly greater. As cigar production was a small-shop craft industry everywhere until the 1870s, it is unlikely that this reflected any productivity differential. Rather, the greater value of the New York product may reflect local manufacturers' easier access to the higher-quality cigar wrapper leaves imported from the Caribbean through the Port of New York or grown in the nearby Connecticut River Valley (Baer, 2008, pp. 31, 37–38, 41; Prus, 1990; U.S. Department of the Interior, 1865).

## Hats and Caps

As noted previously men's headwear manufacturing was the only important urban industry that was both (a) concentrated in metropolitan New York and (b) neither an enabler of rapid urban growth nor connected to the port. Although the evidence is sparse and tenuous, this too may be an instance of serendipitous first-mover advantage.

Commercial hat production began throughout North America during the colonial era and was evidently so successful that Parliament enacted restrictions on exports. Newark, New Jersey, and New York City were evidently two of many places where this activity took place, but hat production does not appear to have been particularly concentrated in this region prior to the 1830s. During that decade a number of mechanized techniques for the production hat bodies were patented in Britain and the United States and the subsequent industrial changes seem to have worked in the New York region's favor. The most important technological advance evidently occurred in 1846. The 1860 census reported that, by this method, four workers could "complete in a day 400 to 450 hat bodies, all alike in weight, shape, and thickness, and better made than they were by the old process, by which one man could make only four or five a day. The cost of labor for forming and sizing hat bodies has been reduced in proportion from 56 cents to 6 and 10 cents. Nearly all the hat bodies are now made by this mode, either by Messrs Burr & Co., in New York, or by their agents and licensees throughout the country…From January 1, 1846, when this machinery went into operation, to December 31, 1859, the number of hat bodies made under this patent by Messrs. Burr & Co., and by others, at Milburn and Newark, New Jersey, was 41,431,693….[A further] improvement for making hat bodies was patented [in 1860] by Seth Boyden, of Newark, New Jersey, which we believe is used in one or more of the large establishments in that place." The 1860 census reported that New York and New Jersey produced close to 60% of U.S. hat and cap output by value and 73% of all hat bodies (U.S. Department of the Interior, 1865, pp. cixi–cixii).

## Persistence of the Patterns

It takes discipline to describe the changes that took place in the United States between the Civil War and the end of the displaced nineteenth century without using exclamation points. From 1860 to 1910, total population almost tripled; manufacturing employment increased almost sixfold; and urban population rose almost sevenfold. The last pre-World War I census reported that close to 250,000 people were working in industries that had not existed before the Civil War. As population spread across the continent Chicago overtook Philadelphia as the nation's second largest city and St. Louis rose to fourth place. Despite these huge quantitative changes, important qualitative characteristics of the manufacturing activity in the Nation's largest cities were unchanged. Table 6.5 presents information similar[13] to what appears in Table 6.2 but drawn from the later census year. Again, the listed industries are "important" in the context of the times (total national employment greater than 40,000) and "urban" (a concentration ratio of 1.5 or greater for at one of the five largest urban places). Again, the industries are listed in descending order of total employment in New York City.

The table indicates that, in both 1859 and 1909, as the various schools of economic geography lead us to expect, employment agglomerated in large cities. In the latter year, contrary to what theory might lead us to expect and, again, as in 1859, New York's manufacturing employment concentration ratio was not the highest among the largest cities. In fact, it was the lowest.

In both years, each of these large cities tended to specialize in certain industries. In most cases in both years individual industrial concentration ratios in one or two of these five cities were substantially higher than in the other three or four. And, again, for some of these industrial specialties one of these cities had a distinct geographic advantage, other than its sheer population size, that explained why a particular industry located there. Chicago, for example, was the best Midwestern physical location for a transshipment point among multiple rail and steamboat lines and, therefore, also as the natural home of the meat

[13]Information from 1909 provides the best representation of the industrial and geographic structure of the U.S. economy at the end of the "displaced nineteenth century" because this was the last census of manufacturing undertaken during the 1815–1924 period before wartime mobilization. Reproducing statistics equivalent to those presented in Table 6.2 was not possible because the data on individual industries were reported on the county level for the 1860 census and on cities with populations over 50,000 in 1910. This makes it impossible to present information for identically defined metropolitan areas for the two census years. Further, between 1860 and 1910 Chicago and St. Louis rose to the near the top of the U.S. urban hierarchy and the boundaries of the City of New York were expanded to encompass The Bronx, Kings, Queens, and Richmond Counties. The New York, Philadelphia, and Boston "metropolitan areas" in Table 6.4 consist of the respective central cities and all other cities with 1910 populations greater than 50,000 that lie within a one-hour drive of the central city in 2015. There were no such cities near Chicago and St. Louis at the time. Data for the New York metropolitan area include statistics for Yonkers, NY, and Bayonne, Elizabeth, Hoboken, Jersey City, Newark, Passaic, and Patterson, NJ. Data for Camden and Trenton, NJ, were consolidated with Philadelphia. And metropolitan Boston included Brockton, Cambridge, Lawrence, Lowell, Lynn, Somerville, and Worcester, MA.

**Table 6.5** 1909/10 manufacturing employment concentration ratios for important urban industries (U.S. Department of Commerce and Labor)

| | NYC employment | Employment concentration ratios | | | | |
|---|---|---|---|---|---|---|
| | | Metro. New York | Chicago | Metro. Philadelphia | St. Louis | Metro. Boston |
| Total manufacturing[c] | 878,670 | 1.81 | 1.96 | **2.30** | 1.83 | 2.28 |
| Clothing, women's | 110,567 | **5.52** | 0.80 | 2.01 | 1.13 | 0.91 |
| Clothing, men's, including shirts | 77,543 | 2.68 | **3.04** | 1.21 | 1.42 | 0.61 |
| Printing and publishing | 74,118 | 1.77 | **1.85** | 1.28 | 1.53 | 1.27 |
| Millinery and lace goods | 24,712 | **4.85** | | 1.57 | 1.04 | 1.13 |
| Bread and other bakery products | 20,404 | 1.47 | 1.32 | 1.23 | **1.69** | 1.22 |
| Copper, tin and sheet-iron products | 11,399 | 1.49 | 1.14 | 0.92 | **1.85** | 0.86 |
| Musical instruments, pianos and organs and materials | 9,305 | 1.94 | **2.97** | 0.28 | | 2.06 |
| Boots and shoes, including cut stock and findings | 9,177 | 0.44 | 0.33 | 0.46 | 4.42 | **5.69** |
| Silk and silk goods, including throwsters | 8,887 | **2.53** | | 0.73 | | |
| Furnishing goods, men's | 8,051 | **1.60** | 1.11 | | | |
| Boxes, fancy and paper | 8,018 | 1.86 | **1.97** | 1.94 | **1.46** | 1.15 |
| Leather goods | 7,672 | 1.88 | 1.28 | 1.11 | **2.03** | 0.50 |
| Confectionery | 7,641 | 1.35 | 1.52 | 1.49 | 1.94 | **3.05** |
| Furniture and refrigerators | 6,878 | 0.46 | 1.66 | 0.68 | **1.69** | 0.30 |
| Liquors, malt | 6,878 | 1.13 | 1.11 | 0.79 | **5.91** | 0.61 |
| Hosiery and knit goods | 6,082 | 0.69 | 0.13 | **2.88** | | 0.17 |
| Patent medicines and compounds and druggists' preparations | 5,450 | 1.24 | 1.58 | 1.78 | **2.90** | 1.05 |
| Slaughtering and meat packing | 4,863 | 0.52 | **5.37** | 0.33 | 1.22 | 0.81 |

(continued)

Table 6.5 (continued)

| | NYC employment | Employment concentration ratios | | | | |
|---|---|---|---|---|---|---|
| | | Metro. New York | Chicago | Metro. Philadelphia | St. Louis | Metro. Boston |
| Shipbuilding, including boat building | 4,328 | 0.84 | 0.15 | **1.88** | | |
| **Dying and finishing textiles** | 3,198 | 1.30 | | **1.94** | | |
| Carriages and wagons and materials | 2,379 | 0.30 | 0.59 | 0.42 | **2.21** | 0.26 |
| Stoves and furnaces, including gas and oil stoves | 1,342 | 0.27 | 0.63 | 0.53 | **3.50** | |
| **Pottery, terra-cotta, and fire-clay products** | 647 | 0.09 | | 2.26 | **2.70** | |
| **Leather, tanned, curried and finished** | 533 | 0.64 | 0.91 | **2.59** | 0.27 | 0.52 |
| Woolen, worsted, and felt goods and wool hats | 468 | 0.38 | | **2.79** | | 4.44 |
| Cotton goods, including cotton small wares | 428 | 0.05 | | 0.62 | | **1.50** |

[a]The total manufacturing concentration ratio is the proportion of local population engaged in manufacturing divided the proportion of national population engaged in manufacturing. The industrial concentration ratios measure the relative proportions of total local and national manufacturing employment engaged in each particular industry (Highlighted entries indicate which city or metropolitan area had the highest employment concentration in an industry)

packing industry. But, as in the earlier year, for many of these urban industrial specialties—malt liquor production in St. Louis, for example—there was no particular physical geographic advantage. New York, Philadelphia, and Boston maintained some but not all of the industrial specialties they had developed before the Civil War through at least the pre-World War I period. Boston retained its leading role in shoes and cotton goods, and Philadelphia in specialty textiles. The largest bulk of activity in the other important urban industries had shifted away from their antebellum homes by 1909. For reasons discussed previously, shipbuilding was no longer concentrated in New York City. And, as industrial production of men's clothing shifted away from outwork and small shops into large factories, New York's comparative advantage in this segment of the clothing industry diminished. More generally, as overland transportation and communication costs continued their decline, the advantages conveyed to New York manufacturers by the City's position as the nation's premier import port seem to have diminished.

One category of rapidly growing industries did, however, became even more concentrated in New York, namely the fashion industries. Boosted by social changes—increased female labor-force participation and a shift in taste toward structurally simpler garments—that fostered a shift from bespoke to ready-made garments and the continuing importance of small shops in the organization of the industry, total metropolitan New York women's clothing employment increased 43-fold between 1859 and 1909 and its concentration ratio rose from 4.63 to 5.52. More broadly, *all* four of the industries for which New York's concentration ratio was highest among the five urban areas were fashion-related. Presumably New York's continuing position as the nation's media hub and, therefore, the point from which fashion trends were first noted, acted on by flexible cadres of manufacturers, and communicated nationwide supported the City's expanding role as *the* singular national center of women's clothing and accessories and men's furnishings. The causes and effects of the growth of the "fashion" or "ladies' garment" industry over the five post-Civil War decades and of its concentration in and singular importance to New York City will be examined in detail in Chapter 11.

So, while two Midwestern Cities took their places near the top of the nation's urban hierarchy and while the development of some industries did lead to new geographic concentrations, the basic forces that emerged during the second quarter of the nineteenth century and determined the locations of important footloose industries appear to have remained the same at least through the eve of World War I. Throughout the displaced nineteenth century population size alone did not determine the relative size of a region's manufacturing sector. Indeed, by 1910 metropolitan New York's manufacturing employment concentration ratio was the smallest among the augmented list of nation's largest cities. Throughout the period, these cities tended to specialize in certain industries. A few of these specializations reflected location close to "heavy" inputs, but most did not. For many industries being the geographic "first-mover" with a new production or marketing technique conveyed a persistent advantage. Finally, although the influence of New York's port on the region's manufacturing activities appears to have diminished, being the entry and dissemination point for information, especially about fashion changes, continued to influence the City's manufacturing specialties. In the most general sense, therefore, the story of antebellum urban manufacturing geography is the whole displaced nineteenth-century story.

## Composition and Size

The series of brief case studies presented in this chapter suggests two very different antebellum paths toward industrial development taken by New York, on the one hand, and by Philadelphia and Boston, on the other. All three cities, of course, served as the central places for their respective hinterlands; all three were home to goodly numbers of furniture makers, jewelers, machinists, milliners, etc. In some important, urban industries, however, one or more of these three cities—usually only one—appears to have served a national, continental, or hemispheric market. Seventeen important urban industries are listed in Table 6.2, and for nine of these sectors metropolitan New York's concentration ratio was higher—usually substantially higher—than that of the other two cities. Eight of these nine New York specialty industries were either benefitting from New York's extremely rapid antebellum population growth or were concentrated in New York because it was, by far, the nation's most important port. Together these eight industries along with their closely linked sectors (sewing machine manufacturing, typefounding, etc.) accounted for about 44% of total metropolitan industrial employment. Of the eight other industries listed in Table 6.2, fisheries and glassmaking, were concentrated close to the source of raw materials that were costly to transport. The evidence we have suggests that the other six industries were concentrated where they were because either New Englanders or Philadelphians got a head start in these businesses either with respect to technological advances in production or the development of specialized distribution networks.

This is not to say that New York had no physical geographic or first-mover advantages. The Hudson estuary's oyster beds deserved their national fame and, once the rail network was in place, enjoyed national distribution. Also, sugar refining was a weight-losing process for which most of the main input was imported from abroad through New York and was highly concentrated in the region (1860 concentration ratio, 5.26). A possible influence of a regional first-start in the Hat and Cap industry was discussed above. And New York continued to benefit from its seventeenth-century head start in the fur industry through the antebellum period (1860 concentration ratio, 6.33) to the present.

Nevertheless, with respect to the urban industries of national importance, New York does seem to have been something of a one-trick pony; the City's position as the nation's leading port apparently determined not only its trajectory as a commercial center, but also the industrial composition of its manufacturing base. By contrast, for footloose industries characterized by important economies of scale in production or distribution and few or no international linkages it does appear that "history mattered." Potential economies of scale and/or Marshallian benefits of agglomeration drew these industries to metropolitan areas but not necessarily to *the* largest local market in *the* most densely populated region. The location of any particular footloose, domestically oriented industry—carpets in Philadelphia or shoes in Boston, for example—seems to have been determined by, in Paul David's words, a "contingent chain of events to which … remote critical events had given rise."

This observation leaves unanswered the question with which this chapter opened: Why was New York's aggregate manufacturing workforce "surprisingly small." That is, as, by far, the largest City with, by far, the most populous adjacent hinterland and the most extensive nationwide network of commercial relations, why was metropolitan New York's total manufacturing sector smaller than Boston's and only modestly larger than Philadelphia's in 1860? Why didn't New York achieve first-mover advantage in more urban industries of national importance than just hat-making. Why, for example, didn't New York's large local market for fabrics, its extensive distribution capabilities, its importance as a port of call for the raw cotton trade, and its early start in industrial spinning in Patterson draw more than a minuscule proportion of the nation's cotton goods manufacturing to its vicinity? Or why didn't New York's proximity to the Catskill hemlock forests give the region more of a leg up in shoe and boot production? Or why didn't more of Philadelphia's carpet weaving craftspeople pick up their looms and migrate to what must have been a much larger market for their wares? Surely it wasn't because New York's businesspeople were less aggressive or creative than Boston's or Philadelphia's.

Three possible answers to such questions suggest themselves. One is suggested by the NEG. The large population of New York's adjacent hinterland might have "cut two ways" with respect to the size of the metropolitan region's manufacturing sector. Specifically, an extension of the basic NEG model demonstrates how, once a system of cities is formed, as population continues to grow some of the peripheral population agglomerations will eventually be able to achieve economies of scale in the production of goods that had previously been confined to the largest city. As noted several times previously, New York's upstate hinterland was very populous, economically dynamic, and relatively highly urbanized. So, it may be that manufacturing establishments in, say, Rochester, New York were able achieve sufficient economies of scale to take business away from New York City firms while businesses in, say, Worcester, Massachusetts, or Wilmington, Delaware could not compete with producers in Boston or Philadelphia. Table 6.6 presents

**Table 6.6** Number of industries tabulated in the 1860 census of manufacturers for in hinterland urban places (U.S. Department of the Interior, 1865)

| County | City | Number of industries | County population |
|---|---|---|---|
| New York Co., NY | NYC | 258 | 813,669 |
| Albany Co., NY | Albany | 124 | 113,917 |
| Erie Co., NY | Buffalo | 118 | 141,971 |
| Monroe Co., NY | Rochester | 119 | 100,648 |
| Onondaga Co., NY | Syracuse | 73 | 90,686 |
| Rensselaer Co., NY | Troy | 97 | 86,328 |
| Philadelphia Co, PA | Philadelphia | 299 | 565,529 |
| Berks Co., PA | Reading | 55 | 93,818 |
| Lancaster Co., PA | Lancaster | 78 | 116,314 |
| New Castle Co., DE | Wilmington | 78 | 54,797 |
| Suffolk Co., MA | Boston | 174 | 192,700 |
| Hampden Co., MA | Springfield | 74 | 57,366 |
| Hillsboro Co., NH | Manchester | 107 | 62,140 |
| Penobscot, Co., ME | Bangor | 58 | 72,731 |

*Note* These are all the counties (a) containing an urban place with population greater than 15,000 and (b) situated within the adjacent hinterlands of New York, Philadelphia, and Boston as defined in Chapter 5 but (c) not part of one of the three metropolitan areas as defined in this chapter

some evidence that is consistent with this explanation for the surprisingly small size of New York's manufacturing sector. The smaller cities located within New York's adjacent hinterland (but not in the local metropolitan area) were home to a much broader array of different manufacturing industries than the smaller urban places that would have looked to Philadelphia or Boston as their regional metropolis.

The other two explanations for why New York's manufacturing sector was "surprisingly small" require a more extensive examination. One is that at mid-century New York City was about as large as the contemporary technology of things like multifamily housing, intra-urban transportation, and public health could sustain without jeopardizing the quality of life residents could achieve. Another, related hypothesis is that New York's entrepreneurs and young working people had many more opportunities to pursue non-manufacturing career paths, such as commerce and banking, than their contemporaries in other cities. The next several chapters will explore both of these possibilities.

## References


Albion, R. G. (1939). *The Rise of New York Port (1815–1860)*. New York: Scribner's.

Baer, W. N. (2008). *The Economic Development of the Cigar Industry in the United States*. Mansfield Center, CT: Martino Publishing.

Ben-Atar, D. (1995). Alexander Hamilton's Alternative: Technology Piracy and the Report on Manufactures. *The William and Mary Quarterly, Third Series, 52*(3), 390–391.

Bruegel, M. (2002). *Farm, Shop, Landing: The Rise of a Market Society in the Hudson Valley, 1780–1860*. Durham, NC: Duke University Press.

Cole, A. H., & Williamson, H. F. (1941). *The American Carpet Manufacture: A History and Analysis*. Cambridge, MA: Harvard University Press.

Cronon, W. (1991). *Nature's Metropolis: Chicago and the Great West*. New York: W. W. Norton.

Davis, P. (1949). *The Development of the American Glass Industry* (pp. 42, 73). Cambridge: Harvard University Press.

Duranton, G., & Puga, D. (2003). *Micro-foundations of Urban Agglomeration Economies* (NBER Working Paper 9931).

Freedley, E. T. (1859). *Philadelphia and Its Manufactures: A Hand-Book Exhibiting the Development, Variety, and Statistics of the Manufacturing Industry of Philadelphia in 1857*. Philadelphia: Edward Young.

Greeley, H. E. (1872). *The Great Industries of the United States—Being an Historical Summary of the Origin, Growth, and Perfection of the Chief Industrial Arts of This Country—Quarries*. Retrieved from Stone Quarries and Beyond http://quarriesandbeyond.org/articles_and_books/great_industries.html.

Hoover, E. M. (1937). *Location Theory and the Shoe and Leather Industries*. Cambridge, MA: Harvard University Press.

Lee, A. M. (1937). *The Daily Newspaper in America: The Evolution of a Social Instrument*. New York: Macmillan.

Liebowitz, S. (2015, August). *Paradise Lost: The Payment of British Authors in 19th Century America*. Retrieved from http://papers.ssrn.com/sol3/papers.cfm?abstract_id=2676048.

Marshall, A. (1895). *Principles of Economics* (Vol. 1, 3rd ed.). New York: Macmillan.

Mendeslsohn, A. D. (2015). *The Rag Race: How Jews Sewed Their Way to Success in America and the British Empire*. New York: New York University Press.

Prus, M. J. (1990). Mechanisation and the Gender-Based Division of Labour in the US Cigar Industry. *Cambridge Journal of Economics, 14*, 63–79.
Putnam, T. R. (2015). Joseph Long's Slops: Ready-Made Clothing in Early America. *Winterthur Portfolio, 49*(2 and 3), 63–91.
Smith, W. E. (2001). Anthony Trollope in America: A Brief Survey of His Publishing History. *The Princeton University Library Chronicle, 62*(3), 479–500. Retrieved from Princeton. https://www.jstor.org/stable/pdf/10.25290/prinunivlibrchro.62.3.0479.pdf?refreqid=excelsior%3A9ff77e87fa95eef-5c4f731f41f079ff9.
Stott, R. (1989). Hinterland Development and Differences in Work Setting: The New York Region, 1820–1870. In W. Pencak & C. Wright (Eds.), *New York and the Rise of Capitalism: Economic Development and Social and Political History of an American State, 1780–1870*. New York: The New York Historical Society.
Stotz, L. (1938). *History of the Gas Industry*. New York: Stettiner Brothers.
Tebbel, J. (1963). *The Compact History of the American Newspaper*. Portland, OR: Hawthorn Books.
Tebbel, J. (1972). *A History of Book Publishing in the United States, Volume I: The Creation of an Industry, 1630–1865*. Ann Arbor: R. R. Bowker.
Tebbel, J., & Zuckerman, M. E. (1991). *The Magazine in America, 1741–1990*. Oxford: Oxford University Press.
U.S. Department of the Interior. (1865). *Manufactures of the United States in 1860; Compiled from the Original Returns of the Eighth Census*. Washington, DC: Government Printing Office.
U.S. Department of the Interior. (1990). *Abstract of the Statistics of Manufactures according to the Returns of the Seventh Census*. New York: Norman Ross Publishing.
Wilentz, S. (2004). *Chants Democratic: New York City and the Rise of the American Working Class, 1788–1850*. Oxford: Oxford University Press.
Zakin, M. (2003). *Ready-Made Democracy: A History of Men's Dress in the American Republic, 1760–1860*. Chicago: University of Chicago Press.

# 7

# Huddled Masses of Rational Optimizers

This chapter and the next aim to solve a puzzle. Much of what's been written about the condition of the working class in antebellum New York City, by journalists at the time and in retrospect by historians, describes a scene of dismal workshops, slums, and degradation. Some of the language is downright histrionic. In 1849, a *New York Tribune* commentator described the Five Points slum neighborhood that encompassed much of the City's Sixth Ward as "the great central ulcer of wretchedness—the very rotting Skeleton of Civilization, whence emanates an inexhaustible pestilence that spreads its poisonous influence through every vein and artery of the whole social system, and supplies every heart-throb of metropolitan life with a pulse of despair."[1] More judiciously, economic historian Robert William Fogel described the situation between 1848 and 1855 of the largely urban "native-born craftsmen, tradesmen, and petty merchants" as "one of the most severe and protracted economic and social catastrophes of American history" (Fogel, 1989, pp. 354–355).

[1] Quoted in (Ambinder, 2001).



A. Gurwitz, *Atlantic Metropolis*, Palgrave Studies in American Economic History,
https://doi.org/10.1007/978-3-030-13352-8_7

But if conditions for urban workers were all that bad, why, one wonders, did New York City's population grow by 157% between 1840 and 1860? (Carter, 2006). And why would the population of the City's Sixth Ward, already very crowded and run down in the 1840s, grow by 55% over the subsequent two decades? Since natural increase—births minus deaths of the City's 1840 residents—could not have generated such rapid population growth, large numbers of people must have migrated to New York during the period.

From the broadest perspective, there are two possible reasons why migrants would have wanted to move to or stay in a "wretched" place under "catastrophic" circumstances. One is that conditions were even worse elsewhere. The other is that the situation of workers in American cities, in general, and in New York, in particular, was not as bad as it appeared from the outside at the time or in retrospect. In either case, the key to solving this puzzle is the evidence we have about why individuals and families chose to remain in or migrate to New York City during the antebellum decades.

The size of New York's population and labor force as of the eve of the Civil War was determined by three categories of decisions made by millions of individuals and families around the North Atlantic region during the previous several decades. These were (i) millions of Europeans' decision to migrate to the United States, (ii) the decisions of millions of these immigrants and of native-born residents of the northeastern states to move westward, and (iii) the decisions of those who chose to remain in the northeast to live and work in New York City rather than elsewhere in the region. This chapter will deal with the transatlantic and trans-Appalachian decisions. Chapter 8 will substantiate the "wretchedness" of New York's working-class residences and explain why so many people decided to settle in the City, the exorbitant cost of terrible housing notwithstanding.

## The Transatlantic Decision

During the antebellum decades, immigration was at an historical peak relative to total U.S. population growth and a very large proportion of the newcomers were of prime working age. Immigration—predominantly during this period, from Ireland, Germany, and Great Britain—involved two decisions. One, whether to leave one's home country and resettle in the United States, was made in Europe and brought most emigrants to New York City as their port of entry. The second choice, where in North America to settle initially, may have been made before departure from Europe but was often decided upon or shortly after arrival at an East Coast port of entry.

Irish, German, and British working people chose to migrate to the United States between 1840 and 1860 because demographic, economic, and political changes taking place during this period in their home countries disadvantaged them, because they were aware that they stood a good chance of raising their standard of living if they moved to America, and because the all-in cost of moving and settling across the Atlantic was affordable. In other words, in effect they understood themselves to be trying to make the most of their situation in a labor market that encompassed their current locations, other places in Western Europe, and the parts of the United States where jobs were to be had.

Young adults are the likeliest people to migrate. A large population in this age group has, therefore, been a necessary condition for mass migration, and Ireland, Britain, and Germany all experienced periods of particularly rapid population growth in the decades leading up to the 1840s. At an estimated average annual rate of 1.3% between 1750 and 1845, Ireland's population growth rate was particularly rapid by European standards of the time. But at 1.0% and 0.8%, respectively, England's and Scotland's population growth rates far outpaced France's 0.4% over the same period. Pre-1800 demographic data for Germany are scarce, but the population of the territory that became the German Empire in 1871 apparently grew at an average annual rate of more than 1% in the years after the end of the Napoleonic Wars (Ó Gráda, 1989, p. 6; Pierenkemper & Tilly, 2004, p. 88).

Job creation in these countries during the second quarter of the nineteenth century did not keep pace with labor-force growth. Early in the century, most of the population was rural, and, as commercial agriculture displaced family subsistence farming, actively aided and abetted by the UK and Prussian government policies, the demand for labor in the countryside declined. In 1816, for example, 18.5 million Prussians or

80% of total population lived in rural areas; in 1858, the rural population had declined to 16.1 million and accounted for 45% of a much larger total (Pierenkemper & Tilly, 2004, p. 46). In the three southern provinces of Ireland in 1841, there were between two and three agricultural workers per farm (Cohen, 2009, p. Loc. 1352/6887). In Ohio, by contrast, there were about 2.3 farms for every farm laborer (Engerman & Goldin, 1991, p. Table 1). Further, as factories displaced labor-intensive craft production (Cohen, 2009, p. Loc. 1368/6887), British, Irish, and German young people, who might in the past have sought an apprenticeship in a nearby town, had to look for something else to do for a living and someplace else to do it.

Many of those displaced by agricultural commercialization and industrialization migrated to the nearby, rapidly growing towns and cities to take the new factory jobs. Britons would have had an easier time than the Germans or Irish finding better prospects in their home country. Industrialization was proceeding apace in northern England and the Scottish lowlands, and the British economy was growing robustly. By one estimate, British per capita real GDP increased by almost one-third between 1830 and 1850, while the same period may have been one of relative economic stagnation in Germany (Cohen, 2009). Population pressures and limited economic prospects had led large numbers of Irish to leave their homeland for Britain or North America before 1846. Then the situation became desperate as successive potato crop failures starting that year led to excess mortality of, perhaps, one million people in a country with a pre-famine population of 8.5 million and, of course, devastated the economy as a whole (Ó Gráda, 1989, p. 41).

The imbalance between the growth of the working-age population—the supply of labor—and the pace of job creation in Europe should have put downward pressure on wages, both absolutely and relative to regions of the world where the rates of demographic and economic expansion were more advantageously matched from the workers' point of view. The relevant variable is "real wages," the nominal dollar, pound, or thaler amount paid to, say, a journeyman carpenter per unit of time, adjusted to reflect differences across space and over time in the cost of purchasing a defined bundle of goods and services. We never observe real wages directly. Instead, we must combine information about nominal wages and consumer goods prices to deduce estimates of the purchasing power of employee compensation. Until recently, it was impossible to test the hypothesis that demographic pressures suppressed real wages in Europe during antebellum decades with any empirical precision. Over the past twenty years, however, a community of economic historians has assembled enough information about nominal wages and prices to construct comparable real wage time series for a number of countries. The time period covered differs by country, and data are more plentiful and reliable for the late nineteenth century than for the antebellum period. Nevertheless, the work of Robert Margo with respect to the United States and Jeffrey Williamson and his collaborators regarding international comparisons shed considerable light on how the purchasing power of antebellum Atlantic region workers incomes differed across space and time.

Thus, we can be reasonably confident that even for British workers, the best-off Europeans on average, it would have required a great deal of luck to reach a better standard of living over time at home than what they could reasonably expect to achieve in the United States. Although by one estimate 1850 real GDP per capita was 40% larger in the UK than in the United States[2] (Maddison, 2001, p. 185), the purchasing power of the average worker's wages was substantially higher in the U.S. through most of the nineteenth century. As Table 7.1 indicates, real wages—i.e., nominal money wages paid per day, week, or month adjusted in light of international differences in the price of a standard package of consumer goods—for unskilled urban workers were upwards of 50% higher in the United States than in Great Britain through most of the antebellum years. The American advantage was even more pronounced in comparison with Ireland and Germany. The statistics for France, a country that sent relatively few migrants to America, illustrate that a large real wage differential was insufficient, by itself, to stimulate mass migration. Although rural life in France may have had attractions that are hard to measure, it does appears that the combined effects of

[2]Other estimates of real GDP per capita for 1840 indicate that the levels for the U.S. and UK may have been much closer with the United States slightly ahead (Prados de la Escosura, 2000).

**Table 7.1** U.S. real wages of urban unskilled workers in the United States as a percentage of European levels, decade averages (Williamson, 1995)

| Decade | Great Britain | Ireland | Germany | France |
|---|---|---|---|---|
| 1830s | 148% | 247% | | 201% |
| 1840s | 169 | 283 | | 243 |
| 1850s | 170 | 236 | 199% | 236 |

the "push" of demographic pressure and the "pull" of higher American real wages were what motivated the mass of antebellum migrants.

Higher real wage rates do not by themselves indicate that American workers achieved a higher standard of living than Europeans. It may have been that Americans were unemployed for longer periods on average than Europeans and that the apparently higher wage rates did no more than compensate workers for the periods of involuntary idleness. Indeed, much antebellum economic activity in U.S. cities was highly seasonal (Engerman & Goldin, 1991, p. 1; Stott, 1990, p. 22). The evidence we have, however, indicates that American workers were, in fact, able to live better than even their English peers during the antebellum years. Food, unsurprisingly, was much cheaper in land-abundant North America. The average nineteenth-century New York City worker's household spent less than half of their income on food; the equivalent figure in London was more than two-thirds. And apparently, Americans got more for their money. New York workers' families may have consumed a *minimum* of 2.8 pounds of "butcher's meat" per person per week on average in 1851, a pound more than what an equivalent London household would have been able to consume around mid-century (Stott, 1990, p. 177). New York households did spend a larger proportion of their income on rent than Londoners and, the preponderance of evidence, discussed in detail below, suggests that the New Yorkers got less for the money they spent on housing. Nevertheless, it does seem likely that food would have been much cheaper than in Europe not just in New York, but throughout the United States. And there is no obvious reason to expect that rent per square foot of housing was systematically higher nationwide in the U.S. than in Britain. If anything, because land, construction materials, and fuel for home heating were also relatively cheap in the United States, it seems likely that Americans, on average, would have gotten more for the money they spent on shelter.

As noted, conditions in Great Britain were notably better than in Germany; all estimates agree that real GDP per capita within Germany's pre-World War I borders was at least one-third lower than in the UK in 1850 (Prados de la Escosura, 2000, p. 24). And conditions in Ireland were worse still, especially after the onset of the potato famine.

Not only did the average worker's family in the United States live better than they could in Ireland, Germany, or Britain, but the average immigrant could anticipate enjoying the American lifestyle within a reasonable amount of time after arrival. Specifically, by 1860 on average, the immigrants included in a sample assembled by economic historian Joseph P. Ferris of males who had disembarked in New York during the 1840s had either held their own in the occupational hierarchy or advanced to skilled-labor or white-collar employment. On arrival, 27% of immigrants who reported an occupation could have been described as white collar or skilled workers and 51% identified themselves as unskilled. By 1860, the proportion of the workers in the sample identified as white collar or skilled in that year's census had risen to 48% and the proportion categorized as unskilled had fallen to 37% (Ferrie, 1997, p. 78). Further, on average immigrants in Ferris's sample reported owning $408 worth of personal assets and $926 in real estate in 1860, suggesting that they had been earning more than what was required for subsistence.

These transatlantic differences in workers' standard of living and of the opportunities open to immigrants would have been well-known in Europe. Large numbers of letters home from family members or acquaintances already in America containing a great deal of such information began arriving shortly after the pace of immigration began to accelerate. Between 1833 and 1835, the Liverpool post office processed more than 700,000 letters addressed to Ireland that had arrived on ships from New York. Such letters, some of which were published in newspapers, along with the numerous how-to guides and accounts of American travel available in Europe during the antebellum years, provided potential emigrants with a great deal of information (Cohen, 2009, p. Loc.

1607/6887) and, no doubt, a lot of misinformation, about conditions in the United States.

Finally, the all-in cost of transatlantic migration declined over the course of the antebellum years and the resources available to potential migrants increased. As the packet lines captured the bulk of the cabin passenger traffic and high-value westbound freight, the unscheduled regular traders competed to fill their lower decks with steerage passengers. As a consequence, average transatlantic fares declined from between seven and twelve pounds during the late 1810s to between three and five pounds after the early 1830s (Cohen, 2009, p. Loc. 1573/6887).

Other migration costs also declined. Transportation from emigrants' homes to their port of embarkation and from New York to other North American destinations declined in tandem with the general decrease in overland and inland waterway transportation costs. And the opportunity cost of remaining unemployed for the many months between departure from home and the first U.S. wage payment declined as public and private immigrant job placement institutions evolved. By the late 1840s, employers seeking skilled factory hands or laborers for interior railroad and canal construction projects were stationing recruiters in New York. Further, once the number of arrivals reached the critical mass required to support an immigrant press, "help wanted" advertisements in these newspapers helped match employers seeking specific skills and immigrants in possession of the sought-after capabilities (Ferrie, 1997, p. 53). Transatlantic shipping companies, labor contractors, port-city innkeepers, and local authorities in underpopulated regions of North America all engaged or encouraged agents in Europe to facilitate the process of migration (Cohen, 2009, pp. Loc. 1506, 1573/6887).

Remittances from family members already established in the United States, along with smaller aggregate amounts provided by philanthropists, landlords, or governments striving to reduce poor-relief expenses, also enhanced the affordability of emigration for many at the lowest end of the wealth distribution. We do not know the aggregate amount of such assistance, but an illustrative calculation demonstrates that its order of magnitude made it quite important. In 1846, for example, the total amount transferred to Ireland, the destination of about 50%

of total remittances, was about $1 million or about £207,000. If all of this money had been used to purchase transatlantic steerage tickets at £4 apiece, remittances would have paid for about 52,000 fares. That would have been more than total Irish immigration to the United States in 1846 and about one-third of the combined 1846 and 1847 total (Cohen, 2009, p. Loc. 1602/6887) (U.S. Treasury, Bureau of Statistics, 1889, pp. 8–33).

Viewing the puzzle, this chapter aims to solve in the context of transatlantic migration provides a simple solution. The City's population grew rapidly during the antebellum period because New York workers' standard of living, as catastrophically wretched as it may have appeared to domestic, middle-class observers, was markedly better than what immigrants could expect in Europe. This would be the conclusion of the discussion were it not for the fact that European immigrants could expect to earn even higher real wages than in New York by moving elsewhere in the United States immediately upon or shortly after their arrival.

## The Trans-Appalachian Decision

Over the three antebellum decades, the U.S. population moved westward more quickly than during any other thirty-year period of U.S. history. Over the 200 years between the 1800 and the 2000 censuses, the population center of the United States shifted west-southwestward an average of 36 miles per decade; between 1830 and 1860, the average decadal shift was 61 miles, more than during any other 30-year period[3] (Blue MM, 2007; U.S. Census Bureau, 2018). Economic opportunities—to obtain cheap fertile land and to ship Midwestern grain and meat products or Gulf-states cotton to the North American East Coast or to Europe with increasing efficiency—drew would-be farm or plantation owners across the Appalachian mountain chain. Other migrants joined them to provide goods and services to burgeoning local populations.

---

[3]The population center is the point on the map of the United States such that half of the country's population will be on each side of a straight line drawn through that point in any direction.

**Table 7.2** U.S. real wages of workers in the Midwest as a percentage of Northeastern levels (Margo, 2000, p. 104)

| Occupation category | 1821–1830 | 1831–1840 | 1841–1850 | 1851–1860 |
|---|---|---|---|---|
| Common laborers | 132% | 136% | 115% | 116% |
| Artisans | 176 | 159 | 136 | 130 |
| Clerks | 175 | 143 | 157 | 131 |

Much of the migration from the South Atlantic region to the South Central states was involuntary; slaves were transported or force marched to places where they could generate higher returns for their masters (Baptist, 2014, pp. 1–38). The incentive to move from the U.S. Northeast or directly from Europe to the Ohio Valley and Great Lakes basin, however, was reflected in the higher real wages free migrants could earn on average in the Midwest than they could on the East Coast early in the antebellum period.

The work of economic historian Robert Margo provides clear evidence that this was the case. Margo assembled and analyzed extensive, reliable data about antebellum wage rates across the United States over the antebellum period by mining the information contained in the payroll records of U.S. Army posts across the country and in the manuscripts of the 1850 and 1860 censuses. He combined this information on the (nominal) dollar wages of various categories of workers with data on regional price differences to calculate estimates of real wages across time and locations. The information in Table 7.2, which is derived from statistics reported by Margo indicates that real wages were much higher in the Midwest than in the Northeast early in the second quarter of the nineteenth century; for artisans and "white collar" clerks, the Midwest advantage over the U.S. East Coast was about the same as the United States advantage over Britain at the same time (Table 7.1). Over the course of the antebellum decades, however, the trans-Appalachian differential diminished substantially, as wages grew more slowly in the Midwest than in the Northeast (Table 7.3). No such consistent "convergence" trend is apparent in the antebellum transatlantic comparisons shown in Table 7.1.

As the first wave of mass migration crested in the late 1840s and the early 1850s, therefore, European workers in large numbers were

**Table 7.3** Average annual growth rates of real wages, 1821–1860 (Margo, 2000, p. 51)

| Region | Common laborer | Artisan | White collar |
|---|---|---|---|
| Northeast | 1.28 | 1.18 | 1.57 |
| Midwest | 0.71 | −0.07 | 0.87 |
| South Atlantic | 0.97 | 0.24 | 1.12 |
| South Central | 0.85 | 0.66 | 1.44 |

choosing to move from one distinct segment of the transatlantic labor market to another. Wages in Europe were still much lower than what workers could expect to earn in the United States. Within the northern United States—and for a variety of reasons most immigrants settled in the north—native-born and immigrant workers were deciding where to settle among locations within a pair of regional labor markets that, while well on their way toward integration, were still distinct. Real wages in the Midwest were still higher than in the Northeast, albeit much less so than they had been twenty years earlier. Whether it made sense for a common laborer or an artisan to incur the cost of moving from, say, New England to Illinois, was a much closer call than whether to move from, say, County Cork to Boston. Fares charged for the two journeys were approximately the same by the late 1840s, when the largest numbers of antebellum immigrants arrived (Ferrie, 1997, p. 57), but, by the best available estimates, real wage differentials between Europe and the United States were at that point much greater than between the Midwest and the Northeast.

Many of these "second decisions" took place in New York City. An initial emigration decision, based on transatlantic real wage differentials, brought Europeans to the United States, and a large majority of them disembarked in New York. A second decision as to whether to stay in the immediate vicinity of their port of entry or to move on elsewhere would have been made in light of information available about labor market conditions within North America. Some immigrants had made both decisions before leaving Europe and took pre-arranged jobs in New York or some other planned destination immediately upon arrival. Others decided whether to stay or move on shortly after arrival, perhaps in light of information provided by inland employers' recruiters or one of several public and private placement agencies. Still others settled and worked in New York for a time and then moved elsewhere. And others settled in the New York area and stayed. At the same time, native-born New York residents and potential domestic migrants to the City were considering a similar range of locational options.

## References

Ambinder, T. (2001). *Five Points: The 19th-Century New York City Neighborhood that Invented Tap Dance, Stole Elections, and Became the World's Most Notorious Slum*. New York: Free Press.

Baptist, E. E. (2014). *The Half Has Never Been Told: Slavery and the Making of American Capitalism*. New York: Basic Books.

Blue MM. (2007, January 6). *Excel Formula to Calculate Distance Between 2 Latitude, Longitude Points*. Retrieved from http://bluemm.blogspot.com/2007/01/excel-formula-to-calculate-distance.html.

Carter, S. B. (2006). *Table Aa22035*. Retrieved from Historical Statistics of the United States Millennial Edition Online http://projects.ilt.columbia.edu/seneca/svcurric/images/byward2_early.html.

Cohen, R. L. (2009). *Mass Migration Under Sail: European Immigration to the Antebellum United States*. Cambridge: Cambridge University Press.

Engerman, S., & Goldin, C. (1991). *Seasonality in Nineteenth Century Labor Markets* (Working Paper No. 20: NBER Working Papers Series on Historical Factors in Long Run Growth).

Ferrie, J. P. (1997). The Entry into the U.S. Labor Market of Antebellu European Immigrants, 1840–1860. *Explorations in Economic History, 34*, 295–330.

Fogel, R. W. (1989). *Without Consent or Contract: The Rise and Fall of American Slavery*. New York: W. W. Norton.

Maddison, A. (2001). *The World Economy: A Millennial Perspective*. Paris: Organization for Economic Co-operation and Development.

Margo, R. A. (2000). New Estimates of Nominal and Real Wages for the Antebellum Period. In R. A. Margo (Ed.), *Wages and Labor Markets in the United States* (pp. 1820–1860). Chicago: University of Chicago Press.

Ó Gráda, C. (1989). *The Great Irish Famine*. Cambridge: Cambridge University Press.

Pierenkemper, T., & Tilly, R. (2004). *The German Economy during the Nineteenth Century, Berghahn Books, 2004*. New York: Berghahn Books.

Prados de la Escosura, L. (2000). International Comparisons of Real Product, 1830–1990: An Alternative Data Set. *Explorations in Economic History, 37*, 1–41.

Stott, R. B. (1990). *Workers in the Metropolis: Class, Ethnicity, and Youth in Antebellum New York City*. Ithaca: Cornell University Press.

U.S. Census Bureau. (2018, April 24). *Annual Estimates of the Resident Population: April 1, 2010 to July 1, 2016—United States—Metropolitan and Micropolitan Statistical Area; and for Puerto Rico More Information 2016 Population Estimates*. Retrieved from American FactFinder https://factfinder.census.gov/faces/tableservices/jsf/pages/productview.xhtml?src=bkmk.

U.S. Treasury, Bureau of Statistics. (1889). *Tables Showing the Arrivals of Alien Passengers and Immigrants in the United States from 1820–1888*. Washington, DC: U.S. Government Printing Office.

Williamson, J. G. (1995). The Evolution of Global Labor Markets since 1830: Background Evidence and Hypotheses. *Explorations in Economic History, 32*, 141–196.

# 8

# The Attractions of the Slums

## The New York City Decision

Were individuals' decisions to move to or stay in New York determined by the same kind of real wage comparisons that drove transatlantic and trans-Appalachian migrations? Probably not. A considerable volume of evidence indicates that during the decades of catastrophic agglomeration, when the City's population was growing very rapidly, real wages in New York were substantially *lower* than in most other places in the northern United States. In other words, the dismal characterizations of antebellum working-class life in New York City seem to have had a correlate in relative real wage rates, albeit one we cannot measure precisely given available evidence. If so, why did enough working people decide to stay in or move to New York to bring the urban area's population to above one million by the eve of the Civil War?

As noted previously, real wages are never observed directly, they must be inferred by combining information about differences in nominal wages—the number of dollars paid a worker per period of time—with information about differences in the cost of living, that is, in the prices of goods and services worker households buy. When deriving



A. Gurwitz, *Atlantic Metropolis*, Palgrave Studies in American Economic History,
https://doi.org/10.1007/978-3-030-13352-8_8

his estimates for the interregional and intertemporal differences in real wages presented in Tables 7.2 and 7.3, Robert Margo combined information on nominal wages from War Department records with information on selected commodity prices, which were regularly reported in local newspaper in cities around the U.S. The available price data covered wholesale food prices extensively, but information about other things worker households buy is sparse. Margo argued, however, that, because food constituted a large proportion of the average household's budget and because the costs of other goods and services, such as transportation or rent costs, are incorporated into wholesale food prices, the available data are sufficient for the purpose of calculating trends over time in average real wages across broad geographic regions.

## Housing Prices and Real Wages

That may be so, but consumers' cost of living in individual cities can vary substantially from regional averages because of differences in the second largest component of consumer expenditures, shelter. And there are good reasons to suspect that, during the later antebellum years, the cost of housing of any given quality, especially for the lowest-quality housing, would have been substantially higher in New York than in the Midwest or in other large northeastern cities. The component of the overall cost of shelter that varies the most across locations is the price of the land. Urban land prices, in turn, reflect the city's total population—the larger the higher—and the property's location within the city. The closer an acre of land is to the city's greatest concentration of employment, its "central business district", the higher its price, all else held equal.

Between 1840 and 1860, Manhattan's population grew by a bit more than 500,000 or by a bit less than 100%. This alone would have raised land prices across the City. Further, because transit fares on horse-drawn multi-passenger vehicles were high relative to workers' incomes and because working hours were long, most unskilled laborers and artisans sought housing within walking distance of their workplaces in lower Manhattan. Thus, the value of locations close to the City center would have risen particularly quickly as population grew. Eventually, the impact of high demand for affordable housing in the parts of the city where land was most expensive would be mitigated to some degree by the development of purpose-built working-class housing in the form of multistory, multifamily tenements. But this process was just getting started late in the antebellum period. Instead, rapidly rising numbers of workers' households were accommodated in the City's densely populated lower wards through a process of "filtering" whereby older single-family town houses were subdivided into multiple units, some of them in basements and some in sub-basement cellars, each accommodating a household and, frequently, one or more borders as well. As these buildings, referred to derisively as "rookeries," would have been past their prime and would not have been designed with subdivision in mind, the apartments would have provided minimal floor space per resident. And because the land on which these dwellings were built was very valuable, tenants would likely have been paying a lot for what they got. Thus, the cost of the cheapest available housing was probably rising more quickly in New York than elsewhere because the City's population was growing by more than other cities' and because progress toward cheap intra-urban transportation was no faster here than elsewhere.

Testing this hypothesis by comparing the prices of housing of a particular quality across space and time would be challenging, even if masses of relevant data were available. The problem, familiar to anyone who has done any house hunting, is that shelter is not a homogeneous good but one of the most variegated commodities households consume. Individual nineteenth-century residences differed in location within the city, square footage, construction quality, heating costs, number of rooms with and without ventilation, neighborhood amenities and disamenities, distance to an outhouse, distance to the nearest public pump, that pump's water quality, and so on, and on. So even if we had good data on average rents paid by workers in different locations, it would not be clear whether the higher housing costs in one place relative to another reflected higher average housing quality or a higher price for the same quality. Ideally, we would like to be able to compare across locations and over time the monthly rental for, say, a 300 square foot, three-room apartment in a 50-year-old subdivided former single-family dwelling containing a total of six such units, heated by a new-model cast-iron stove, with easy access to a shared outhouse, a quarter of a mile from the central business district (CBD), etc.

Robert Margo recognizes the importance of getting a handle on quality-adjusted housing price differences for his efforts to estimate antebellum real wage trends across time and space and he is well aware of the analytical difficulties involved. He has confronted the challenge as effectively as possible, given the available data, and, happily for the purpose of this book, his analysis focused on New York City (Margo, 1996). Margo assembled data on antebellum housing rents in New York City from information listed in newspaper advertisements of homes, apartments, and rooms for rent. These advertisements included information on such characteristics of the particular property such as location, the number of rooms, whether the property had a yard, a bath, a kitchen, and storage space, and whether the unit was part of a multifamily building. Information about the advertised rental and the characteristics of units over a period of years enabled Margo to calculate an index of New York City housing prices for the period between 1831 and 1860.

Margo found that the time trend in "quality-adjusted" rents in New York City generally followed national business cycles (Fig. 8.1). Over the 1831–1860 period as whole rents on "constant-quality" units rose by 35%, which was substantially faster than the contemporaneous increase in the general price level. Wholesale commodity prices in the

**Fig. 8.1** Indexes of New York City residential rents, Northeastern U.S. wholesale prices (ex-housing) and nationwide consumer prices, 1831–1860 (Carter, 2006, pp. Series Cc1–65; Goldin & Margo, 1992, p. 97; Margo, 1996, p. 623)

Northeast, excluding housing, rose by only about 8% over the same period, and the general level of U.S. consumer prices actually declined by about 4%. How much of an impact the rising cost of housing would have had on New Yorkers' standards of living, however, depended on what proportion of their incomes was devoted to shelter. On the plausible assumption that this proportion was about 29%, Margo concluded that his previously published estimates of cumulative real wage growth in New York City between the 1830s and the 1850s, which were based on a price index that excluded housing, may have been too high by about seven percent. Since real wages rose between 25 and 40% over the period, depending on the skill category, Margo concluded that the "degree of overstatement is not too great."

## Affordable Housing: Demand and Supply

Margo did not, however, have enough of the right kind of data to detect differences in prices trends of different qualities of housing.[1] It might have been possible, for example, for rents to have risen by 35% on average at the same time as the annual "owners' equivalent rent" on a newly built modern brownstone near Washington Square rose by only 5% while the monthly rate on a two-room, windowless residence in a Five Points "rookery" nearly doubled and for the differences not to have been detected by Margo's methodology.

There are good reasons to conclude that something along these lines did occur, although precise quantification is impossible. The price of lower-quality housing probably rose faster than that of more comfortable residences, especially after the mid-1840s, because demand for the former was growing more quickly while most new construction added to the supply of the latter.

[1]Margo's specification did not provide for the possibility of time-varying coefficients on rental unit characteristics. Thus, while the general level of rents could vary from year to year, the percentage impact on rent of, for example, the number of rooms in the unit could not. It is unlikely that Margo had enough observations on specific characteristics in a sufficient number of years to estimate time-varying coefficients reliably.

European immigrants, relatively few of whom could, upon arrival, afford more than the cheapest available housing, accounted for a disproportionately large share of the City's population growth through the early 1850s. In 1845, the foreign-born accounted for 36% of City's residents; over the subsequent decade, the increase in the foreign-born population accounted for 72% of the City's population growth (Rosenwaike, 1972, p. 42).

The supply of housing in general must have been tight across the board in New York at the outset of catastrophic agglomeration in the early 1840s. Expansion of the housing stock had been robust during the mid-1830s but slowed abruptly after the panic of 1837. An average of 796 residences were constructed in Manhattan annually between 1834 and 1836, reflecting, in part, the recovery from the great fire of 1835 which destroyed about one-quarter of the City's buildings. The number fell to 502 in 1839 and did not rise above the previous high until 1843. The new homes that were built during this period of boom and bust were heavily weighted toward higher-end, single-family dwellings. Before the late 1840s, real estate developers did not consider purpose-built "affordable" multifamily housing a worthwhile speculation compared to building and selling new single-family houses north of Houston Street or subdividing existing homes in the southern wards (Blackmar, 1989, p. 197). Thereafter tenement construction picked up, but, apparently, not very quickly. In 1864, the Citizens' Association of New York counted a total of 15,309 "tenant houses" in the City, defined as buildings "in which there dwell three or more families who hire their domiciles by a monthly rental." The published report did not distinguish between subdivided former single-family homes and purpose-built tenements. The fact that seven families inhabited the average tenant-house, many fewer than the typical purpose-built tenement, which housed 20 families, suggests that the bulk of the tenant houses in the Citizens' Association sample was in subdivided buildings (Blackmar, 1989, p. 209; Citizens' Association of New York, 1865, p. lxix).

The Citizens' Association *Report* also provided one of the few quantitative comparisons of housing conditions in the two Atlantic metropolises, London and New York. The New York investigators estimated that the 480,368 residents of the enumerated tenant houses occupied approximately two square miles of combined building lots and pro rata share of adjacent street space. On average, therefore, the population density of tenant-house blocks was about 240,000 per square mile. In the City's fourth ward, the per-square-mile density reached 290,000. As a basis of comparison, the Citizens' Association referred to a royal commission report estimate that the population density of East London was 175,816 per square mile.[2]

Most of the tenant houses were apparently converted two- or three-story single-family dwellings. The typical dimensions for the early nineteenth-century New York row houses were 15–20 feet across and 30–40 feet back. Thus, the total floor space for one of these single-family dwellings with three stories would have been around 1,800 square feet. If, as reported by the Citizens' Association, the average number of residents in a tenant house was 30, the average number of square feet available per resident would have been about 60 or a little less than an eight-foot square. Early in the twenty-first century, the U.S. Department of Housing and Urban Development defines "overcrowding" as less than 165 square feet of unit floor space per resident (Citizens' Association of New York, 1865, p. 349; Mason, 2018; U.S. Department of Housing and Urban Development, June, 2018).

Under normal circumstances, this cramped space was just barely affordable for unskilled workers. Historian Elizabeth Blackmar estimated that during the 1850s the rent on one of the twenty units in a newly constructed tenement building would have been about $6 per month or $72 annually. Robert Margo estimates that during that decade common laborers employed by the U.S. War Department in the Northeastern United States were paid an average of about one dollar a day or, for a full-time, all-year worker $312 per year. Rent on some of the better-quality workers' housing available in New York, therefore, would have consumed an affordable 23% of the earnings of a *fully employed* common laborer. The problem, of course, would have been that few urban workers at the time were employed full time in a normal

[2]New York City's most densely population neighborhood in 2013, at 103,000 per square mile was the Upper East Side.

year, and a particularly cold winter could, and frequently did, lead to prolonged periods of unemployment. At such times, fixed rents would have consumed upwards of 30% or more of workers incomes just when food and fuel prices would have been high.

It is hard, therefore, to escape the conclusion that, compared to their peers elsewhere in the United States and to better-off residents of their own City, antebellum New York workers paid a lot and got very little in terms of the quality of shelter. If so, then the estimates that supported Margo's conclusion that, for example, real wages of common laborers in the Northeast increased at an average annual rate of 1.18% between 1820 and 1861 and that the Midwest premium over northeastern wages for these workers declined from 32 to 16% over the same period probably overstates the improvement of relative conditions for this class of workers in New York City. So, to the extent that the decision to stay in or move to New York had been based on the real wages available in the City relative to elsewhere in the United States, it is, indeed, surprising that so many chose to do so.

## Who Stayed in New York City?

In fact, a large majority of immigrants did leave the vicinity of New York within ten years of arrival in the United States. Economic historian Joseph Ferrie estimated that 86.4% of the men who had disembarked in New York during the previous decade were living outside of New York, Kings, and Queens Counties by 1850. By 1860, 89.3% were no longer living in these counties and 86.1% were living more than 25 miles from New York (Ferrie, 1997, p. 43). Because Ferrie also knew each immigrant's year of arrival within the 1840s, he was able to determine that the longer an individual was in the United States the more likely he was to have moved away from New York City.

It does not seem to be the case, therefore, that immigrants in general were "stuck" in New York. They could and usually did move elsewhere in the United States. Few of them chose to move to the southern states, but one-third of those in Ferrie's sample were living in the Midwest by 1850.

This was only marginally less than the 38% of the total non-southern U.S. population living in that region at that time (Ferrie, 1997, p. 59).

Ferrie did find that, although a majority of all immigrant categories did move on from New York fairly quickly after arrival, less-skilled immigrants and the generally poorer Irish were more likely to remain in New York than those with higher occupational status or who were of British or German origin. By 1850, 21.8% of the Irish immigrants in Ferrie's sample were living within 25 miles of New York City compared to only 14.5 and 7.2% of the Germans and British, respectively. Still, a large majority of immigrants from all countries of origin in all occupational categories did leave New York immediately upon or shortly after arrival.

Although most antebellum immigrants left the New York area within a decade of arrival, a disproportionately large minority of European immigrants remained in New York. New York County's 1860 population of 813,669 represented 4.2% of the U.S. total. As New York was the home of 11.2% of the total U.S. foreign-born population, its foreign-born concentration ratio was 2.70 ($=11.2 \div 4.2$). This put New York in the 97th percentile of all 856 counties in the northern states for that year with respect to its concentration of foreign-born residents. Kings County's concentration ratio of 2.24 placed it in the 95th percentile. The only large (population greater than 100,000) jurisdictions with higher foreign-born concentration ratios than New York's were St. Louis City, MO, at 2.90 and Cook County, IL (Chicago), at 2.84. The other large northeastern cities also had high +foreign-born concentrations, but less than New York's; Philadelphia's was 1.77 (90th percentile), Boston's was 2.01 (93rd percentile), and Baltimore's was 1.57 (88th percentile).[3]

Further, the concentration of the foreign born in New York persisted through an after the Civil War. In 1880, a quarter of a century after the first immigration wave crested and before the next wave got underway, New York County's foreign-born concentration ratio of 2.23 placed it

[3]Data in this and the subsequent paragraph were drawn from a Web site, the Historical Census Browser, maintained by the University of Virginia that was subsequently discontinued.

in the 95th percentile of U.S. counties. In that year, only three other counties with populations greater than 100,000—San Francisco (2.50), Cook (2.24), and Milwaukee (2.23)—had higher ratios.

So, at the end of the antebellum period, New York's population was disproportionally foreign born and was destined to remain so. One can also conclude with some justification that the foreign-born population *replaced* either native-born New Yorkers who left the City for elsewhere during the period or native-born Americans who might have migrated there during the years of catastrophic agglomeration. Understanding why this may have been so requires a digression onto the topic of Zipf's Law.

Zipf's Law describes an empirical relationship among the sizes of a country's cities. Surprisingly consistently across countries and over time, the population of a city has been very closely related to its rank order in the regional or national hierarchy of urban places. The population of the second largest city is usually about half that of the largest city, that of the third largest, close to two-thirds of the second largest, and so on. Although statisticians, geographers, and economists have proposed a variety of ingenious reasons for this phenomenon, none of the explanations are entirely satisfying. Nevertheless, the strong consistency of the relationships justifies basing an analysis on what it predicts, especially because Zipf's law precisely describes the relationship between rank order and population for U.S. cities in 1860.[4]

The fact that Zipf's fits the 1860 data so closely overall suggests that cities within the late antebellum U.S. urban hierarchy were probably roughly right-sized for an economy at its state of development. Therefore, given the sizes of the lower-ranked cities and, in particular,

[4]One formulation of Zipf's law, the equation

$$\ln(\text{Rank}) = \alpha + \beta \ln(\text{Population}),$$

where $\alpha$ and $\beta$ are constants, fits the data closely, and $\beta$ is close to 1.00. For the 99 largest U.S. urban areas in 1860, with New York and Kings Counties combined, the estimate,

$$\ln(\text{Rank}) = 13.89 - 1.02 \ln(\text{Population}),$$

has an *r*-squared statistic of 0.99, and the estimate of $\beta$ is very precise (Gabaiz, 1999; U.S. Bureau of the Census, 1998).

second-ranked Philadelphia's population of 565,529, the population of the largest urban area—defined as New York and Kings counties combined—would not have been much larger or smaller than the actual 1,092,791. If so and if New York's foreign-born concentration ratio had been equal to the 1.80 average for counties with populations greater than 100,000, then there would have been 346,655 first-generation immigrants living there in 1860. The actual foreign-born population of the two counties was 492,251. By this reckoning, the character of New York's population at the end of the antebellum period was distinguished by the fact there were about 150,000 more foreign born and, since the total population was *probably* about right at one million, roughly that many fewer native-born residents than one would have expected. Thus, since the urban area's population was approximately evenly divided between the two categories of birthplace, there were roughly 30% more foreign-born residents and 30% fewer native-born than would have occurred by chance. In other words, the large foreign-born population does appear to have displaced some potential native-born Americans who might otherwise have chosen to stay in or move to New York City.

This is a good point at which to reformulate the puzzle explored in Chapter 7 and this chapter. The rental price of affordable housing probably increased substantially in New York over the antebellum period. Therefore, real wages earned by unskilled workers in the City were likely lower than elsewhere in the northeastern states and had remained much lower than what comparably qualified individuals could have earned in the Midwest. It is not surprising, therefore, that a large majority of immigrants, including the least skilled, moved away from New York immediately upon arrival or within a few years thereafter. Nevertheless, New York's population grew very rapidly over the period as the general pace of urbanization increased in the United States and as the City assumed its position at the pinnacle of the North American urban hierarchy. European immigrants accounted for a disproportionately large share of this growth. In other words, native-born Americans were more likely than immigrants locate away from New York City, in places where real wages for unskilled workers were likely substantially higher. Therefore, New York was apparently more attractive as a place to live and work for European immigrants than it was for the native born. Why?

## Why Was New York City More Attractive to Immigrants Than to the Native Born?

The quantity of a standard bundle of consumer goods—food, shelter, clothing, and miscellaneous other items—that could be purchased with the average worker's daily wages was probably smaller in New York than elsewhere. Not all workers, however, wanted to consume the standard bundle of goods used to calculate real wages, and, in particular, many working-class New Yorkers were able to minimize the impact of the high cost of shelter on their well-being. Further, any given family's well-being would have depended, not just by the purchasing power of a single worker's daily wage but also by the number of days multiple family members could find work over the course of a year. Immigrants as a group may have differed from the native-born population with respect to the nature of the goods they wanted to buy and the economic roles of family members in ways that offset New York's real-wage disadvantage.

## Escaping Cramped Quarters

Teenaged or young adult males comprised a much larger proportion of antebellum immigrants than of the American population as a whole. In 1850, for example, about 12% of the total U.S. population were males between the ages of 15 and 30. The same age cohort accounted for 31% of immigrants who entered the country between 1820 and 1860 (Stott, 1990, p. 73; University of Virginia, n.d.). These young men were disproportionately likely to rent only enough space for a bed and minimal storage as a border with a family or in a rooming house (Scherzer, 1992, p. 140), and it is unlikely that they spent many of their non-working waking hours in these residences.

Instead, young men took advantage of the leisure time activities available in antebellum New York City. The City's huge, dense population may have made housing more expensive, but it also provided the critical mass for entertainment venues to suit every taste. The most numerous were the saloons and barrooms, of which there were some 5,550 in

1855, and many denizens of these establishments made a practice of visiting several over the course of an evening. Indeed, many saloons came to offer some of the comforts of home during the 1850s in the form of a "free lunch" with the purchase of beer. Other working-class institutions, such as theaters, volunteer fire companies, political clubhouses, and "disorderly houses" provided places for young adult males to spend their non-working, non-sleeping hours away from their cramped quarters, which mitigated the impact of the high cost of housing on the well-being of this demographic group. The attractions of saloons, theaters, and so on probably appealed to native-born young men as much as to immigrants. But, because young males constituted a much larger proportion of the immigrant than the native population, New York's comparative advantage as a venue for nightlife enhanced the City's relative attractiveness for the foreign born (Stott, 1990, pp. 212–246).

Many young, single working women would also have minimized time spent in cramped living quarters by joining in some of the leisure activities favored by men; the stereotypical street-wise "Bowery b'hoy" was often depicted with a "g'hal" on his arm. Other young women escaped working-class housing conditions by taking jobs as live-in domestic servants. These positions were particularly well-suited for the young, English-speaking Irishwomen arriving alone in the late 1840s and the early 1850s; new skill requirements were minimal, the jobs offered shelter from the dangers of big-city life, and, with room and board paid for, cash wages, such as they were, could be saved and remitted to relatives awaiting funds for passage to New York.[5] By 1855, Irish immigrants accounted for 74% of all domestic servants employed in the City, and, at 29,470, more foreign-born New Yorkers were employed in these positions than any other. By way of comparison, almost 10,000 fewer immigrants were employed in the second most common occupation, laborer (Ernst, 1994, pp. 67, 215, 218).

[5]Christine Stansell points out that domestic servants account for between one-half and two-thirds "of the unskilled workers, male and female, who opened accounts each year at the New York Bank for Savings." (Stansell, 1987, p. 157).

## Employment Opportunities for All

Immigrant households with no choice but to make do with cramped quarters may have found that the potential for gainful employment of all family members in New York compensated for the high cost of low-quality shelter. Immediately prior to or only a few years before departure to America, many immigrant families had been living in rural areas, where all family members except for very young children were expected to do their share of productive work. These households, having incurred the substantial cost of transatlantic migration, were less likely than the native born to own any given stock of material possessions. The latter—clothing in good condition, furniture, or modest jewelry—which could, when illness struck or during periods of seasonal or cyclical unemployment, serve as collateral at a pawn shop, constituted an important form of economic security during the antebellum period. Joseph Ferrie found, for example, that by 1860 the median value of personal wealth (exclusive of real estate) among his sample of immigrants who had arrived in New York during the 1840s and were living in the Middle Atlantic was $75 compared to $250 for native-born Americans in the same region. Thus, immigrant households may have been more highly motivated to "establish" themselves through the gainful employment of all family members than the average native-born household.

The New York City labor market provided opportunities for all family members other the youngest children to generate income in ways that suited immigrant households' situations. Consider a hypothetical two-parent family with two children under six and a pre-teenage boy. The father, if possessed of almost any marketable skill, could find at least some work in the City's industrially diverse economy. An unskilled laborer could migrate to seasonal jobs in railroad construction or agriculture or could seek employment in the rapidly growing City's building industry. The mother would have had to stay at home to care for the youngest children, but could find gainful employment as an outworker in, for example, the men's garment industry.

The list of the top-ten occupations held by the foreign born in New York City in 1855 (Table 8.1) indicates that these descriptions of an

**Table 8.1** Top-10 occupations of foreign-born workers in New York City, 1855 (Ernst, 1994, pp. 214–217)

| Occupation | Foreign-born workers | Predominant national origin | Predominant Nat'l. origin, % of all foreign-born workers |
|---|---|---|---|
| Domestic servants | 29,470 | Ireland | 79 |
| Laborers | 19,783 | Ireland | 88 |
| Tailors | 12,109 | Germany | 55 |
| Dressmakers, seamstresses | 6,606 | Ireland | 69 |
| Shoemakers | 6,491 | Germany | 57 |
| Clerks | 5,921 | Germany | 38 |
| Food dealers | 5,274 | Germany | 58 |
| Carpenters | 4,863 | Ireland | 46 |
| Bakers, confectioners | 3,323 | Germany | 60 |
| Cartmen, draymen, teamsters | 3,185 | Ireland | 79 |

individual female immigrant or of a hypothetical family may be reasonably true to life. Most of these occupations are either in domestic service, open to unskilled male workers (Laborer, cartmen, draymen, and teamsters), involved in the construction industry (carpenters) or offering outwork (tailors, dressmakers, seamstresses, shoemakers). Many of the immigrants engaged in the three remaining occupations—clerks, food dealers, bakers, and confectioners—would have been working in retail enterprises serving immigrant communities.

The pre-teenage boy could generate income as a street scavenger, an occupation that was not enumerated separately in the 1855 census. As Christine Stansell has pointed out, "[s]treet scavenging has probably been a practice of the urban poor for centuries, but this was a specifically nineteenth-century form, which depended on a demand for raw materials from an urban manufacturing system where commercial lines of supply were not fully in place…[C]hildren sold [trash such as shreds of raw cotton, canvas and rags, broken bits of hardware, and bottles and bits of broken glass] to junk dealers, who in turn vended it to manufacturers and artisans to use in industrial processes" (Stansell, 1987, p. 51).

## Social Networks in the Job Market

So there were remunerative occupations in the City that could be performed by all pre-teen and older antebellum household members. None of these occupations was, however, a reliable source of year-round income, with the possible exceptions of domestic service and clerical work. One problem was seasonality. The garment, construction, and street scavenging businesses were seasonal, and all experienced simultaneous slack periods during the winter months, just when household expenses for food and fuel would have been the highest. To make matters worse, few of the firms in these industries provided stable employment, even during the busy seasons. Laborers, cartmen, draymen, and teamsters were usually hired by the day and individual workers could not be sure they would leave the morning shape-up with a job. Construction workers were hired for a specific project with no guarantee that when one job was finished another would be forthcoming immediately. And the garment and footwear industries were highly competitive so that individual jobbers, manufacturers, and subcontractors operated on very thin margins. Employers might suspend operations or close up shop completely as a result of abrupt changes in fashion, fluctuations in demand from the Southern and Midwestern states, or the entry into the market of a new, slightly more efficient, competitor. So, an outworker delivering a batch of completed piecework had no guarantee that they would receive a new bundle of, say, shirts in need of buttonholes. Even a juvenile street scavenger working a lucrative alleyway would have faced the risk that a bigger kid might take over the territory.

For all of these reasons, few antebellum urban households could expect that all of their working-age members would have work 52 weeks a year, and the expected number of aggregate annual days of employment would probably have been at least as important when deciding where to live as the purchasing power of the local wage rate earned when engaged. Further, workers could anticipate that their success in the process of job search and job matching would go a long way to determining their family's standard of living. Households would, therefore, prefer locations where they had ready access to information about, for example, which men's clothing subcontractors were hiring outworkers, which construction projects were scheduled for near-term ground-breaking, or which scavenging territories were in weak hands (Stott, 1990, pp. 108–109).

The instability of job markets imposed costs on employers as well as employees. A clothing sub-contractor who let workers go when demand for a particular product line was slack might have a difficult time finding people to hire if business picked up suddenly. Or a stevedore foreman might find it challenging to assemble a crew after a spell of bad weather broke and a large number of ships arrived in port simultaneously (Montgomery, 1991).

Some worker-job matches were made by formal institutions. "Intelligence offices" specialized in placing domestic servants in New York households and clerks in offices. Help-wanted advertisements began appearing in newspapers during the antebellum period. And in 1850, as part of an effort to prevent gross exploitation of newly arrived immigrants, the State of New York established the Castle Garden Labor Exchange. It is not clear whether this agency functioned as anything more than a publicly owned intelligence office. Most workers, therefore, found their jobs and most employers found workers through connections with family members, friends, and, importantly, acquaintances. Social networks, therefore, were an essential component of nineteenth-century urban labor markets (Rosenbloom, 2002, pp. 70–71).

This is not the first instance in which social networks played an important role in New York City's economic history. Recall that family, ethnic, and religious ties among participants in the Atlantic trading economy made it easier to monitor and enforce honest dealing in a market that depended on credit but lacked formal financial intermediaries. The system worked well enough to support a substantial amount of trading activity because a social network can be an effective mechanism for monitoring and enforcing behavioral norms. Social networks can also facilitate communication within a community, and this function is essential when economically important "information is imperfect, rapidly changing, and not easily codified" (Storper & Venables, 2003) as it was in New York City's antebellum labor market. Economists have shown that reliance on social networks to communicate information about job openings, about individual workers' capabilities, and about employment conditions at different firms *can, under the right circumstances,* enhance labor market outcomes for both workers and employers by reducing unemployment and by improving the match between workers' skills and job requirements (Granovetter, 2005; Storper & Venables, 2003).

Sociologists have demonstrated with considerable empirical detail the importance of social networks or "social capital" in late twentieth-century immigrants' engagement with the labor market (Sanders, Nee, & Scott Sernau, 2002). By comparison, direct, primary evidence—in letters, diaries, or autobiographies—of similar processes in antebellum labor markets is sparse. Even so, it seems reasonable to assume that during the nineteenth century most of the information about job openings, especially for low-skill, occupations and for positions at small firms, would have been conveyed via word of mouth between employed workers and job-seekers who knew each other as relatives, neighbors, friends, or acquaintances. Without more data, however, any reconstruction of the antebellum job-matching process and any assertions about how the operation of social networks may have made New York City relatively more attractive immigrants than for the native born are necessarily based on circumstantial evidence.

One such item of evidence appears in Table 8.1. In our contemporary urban labor markets, network-based job-matching processes tend to lead to what sociologists refer to as "social closure" in which certain industries or occupations become ethnic niches (Sanders et al., 2002, pp. 283–284). It is not hard to imagine how this might happen. Suppose that by chance a disproportionate number of members of an ethnic group happen to wind up working in the same occupation or at the same firm. Suppose, too, that most information about new job openings is communicated by word-of-mouth from current employees, that these workers are more likely to talk to members of their own ethnic group, and that demand for the occupation is growing and/or volatile. Under these circumstances, the initial modest concentration of, say, German employees is likely to increase as more job-seeking Germans hear about new openings. The process will be accelerated if members of a particular ethnic group arrive with skills well-suited to the occupation in question; all the more so if firm ownership in a particular industry is concentrated within a specific national origin and employers prefer hiring co-ethnics.

The two right-hand columns in Table 8.1 confirm that by 1855 certain occupations in New York City had, indeed, become ethnic niches. The predominance of Irish or German immigrants in certain occupations is best understood in relation to the fact that of all the immigrant workers tabulated in the 1855 New York State census 57% had been born in Ireland and 29% in Germany.

In some of these occupations, the process of occupational closure may have been augmented or accelerated by unique characteristics of these immigrant groups. Some concentration of Irish immigrants in domestic service was probably to be expected given that 58% of the Irish immigrants residing in New York City in 1860 were female compared to 48% of those born in other foreign countries. The fact that most Irishwomen spoke English fluently probably also helped. Even so, 79% is a large number. The ethnic concentration in two of the "artisanal" occupations on this list, tailors and bakers, probably reflects the relative preponderance of skilled workers among German immigrants. It is hard, however, to account for the concentration of Irish immigrants in proportions well above their overall share of the labor force in the unskilled occupations in which employment was episodic—laborers, draymen, cartmen, and teamsters—without reference to role of social networks and social closure.

The second type of evidence that social networks played an important role in immigrants' labor market engagement relates to the ways in which the institutions of working-class and immigrant society were particularly well-suited to networking. Time spent in saloons, firehouses, and political clubhouses all facilitated interpersonal engagement and conversation. Richard Stott quotes a contemporary comparison between New York barrooms and English pubs. The latter, by providing a plenitude of chairs at tables, encouraged patrons to drink alone or in small groups. In New York, drinking at a crowded stand-up bar encouraged interpersonal engagement. By contrast, churches, the quintessential antebellum bourgeois institution, where promiscuous one-on-one conversations would have been discouraged, played no more than a modest role in most workers' lives (Stott, 1990, pp. 212–246).

Densely occupied multifamily housing may also have facilitated networking. Close quarters and unlocked doors facilitated intense interaction, at least some of which must have been convivial. Because their residences were so cramped working-class New Yorkers spent a great deal of time out of doors, especially, of course, in the summertime when their tiny, poorly ventilated living quarters would have been stifling. Christine Stansell quotes the report of an English observer: "Numbers of females would be sitting on the 'stoops,' their chins in the hands, their elbows on their knees' conversing." It seems reasonable to assume that at least some of these conversations were on the topic of which garment industry subcontractors were looking for outworkers or which up-town household was looking for a chambermaid.

Finally, several characteristics of New York's antebellum neighborhoods would have facilitated job matching through social networks. At the beginning of the nineteenth century, New York City didn't have really have distinct "neighborhoods;" businesses and all classes of residents clustered together near the tip of Manhattan. As the first half of the century progressed the southernmost wards evolved into a central business district ("CBD"), with few residents, and wealthier New Yorkers began moving northward. The houses situated between the emerging CBD and the new middle- and upper-class neighborhoods, which had previously accommodated single families, were subdivided into the "rookeries" described above. In this way, distinct neighborhoods, each housing a particular class of residents, developed. Residential proximity would have made network formation and communication about job openings easier. As immigration accelerated, some working-class neighborhoods evolved further into ethnic enclaves; information about housing vacancies would likely have circulated within immigrants' social networks along with news about job openings with similar impact on "closure". In these enclaves, locational and cultural proximity could combine to facilitate dense network formation (Scherzer, 1992, pp. 42–120, passim).

Like the Dutch, Huguenot, Jewish, and Quaker social networks that facilitated international trade within the British Empire of goods in the eighteenth century, the dense ethnic neighborhood networks in mid-nineteenth-century New York were not hermetic. Working-class New Yorkers moved frequently, sometimes within and sometimes between neighborhoods. So, residents embedded in one dense neighborhood ethnic network, in which ties were reinforced by frequent encounters on the street or in a local saloon may also have maintained acquaintances and friendships with former neighbors who had moved onto other parts of the city. These now-more-distant friends or acquaintances, in turn, may have become embedded in their new neighborhood's dense social network. In this way, antebellum New York workers, like their eighteenth-century merchant predecessors, operated within a network of networks. And, as pointed out in Chapter 2, such social structures can serve as a particularly effective conduit for information flows in an economic system, an Empire of Goods, or a volatile labor market.

New York's working-class culture may, indeed, have facilitated the development of robust social networks. And the social networks that developed may, indeed, have matched employees with jobs effectively so that unemployment was, at most times, about as low as it could possibly be given the overall incomes of City residents and the demand for the City's products. But the aim of this section is to understand why New York City was relatively more attractive as a place to live and work to immigrants than to native-born Americans. So, we need to ask why the presence of effective social networks would have been particularly important to immigrants. It was not the case, after all, that *only* immigrants participated in social networks. In his history of New York's port, Robert Albion highlights the role family and home-town connections among the first- and second-generation migrants from New England who dominated the City's merchant and shipbuilding industries during the first half of the nineteenth century (Albion, 1939, pp. 242–250).

## Why Were Social Networks Especially Important to Immigrants?

Despite the substantial differences between late twentieth and mid-nineteenth-century job-matching processes, analyses of how recent immigrants engage with the labor market can provide hints as to why social networks may have been particularly important to their antebellum predecessors. A study published by James R. Elliot in 2001 is especially helpful in this regard (Elliot, 2001). Elliot analyzed survey data gathered between 1992 and 1994 from a sample of 2,030 residents of metropolitan Atlanta, Boston, or Los Angeles who had begun working at their current jobs within the previous five years. The sample included both native- and foreign-born respondents, the latter mostly from South America and the Caribbean. Respondents were asked, among many other things, about their personal characteristics and about how they had obtained their current employment. The data showed that, relative to more formal worker recruitment processes, personal referrals by employees of the hiring firm were, indeed, much more important as a job-matching mechanism for recent immigrants than for native-born or earlier-immigrant respondents. The proportion of recent immigrants who had hired through an "insider referral" was 53.2%, compared to 24.6% for native-born whites and 38.7% for native-born Latinos. The "insider-referral" proportion for immigrants who had been in the country more than five years was 42.0% (Elliot, 2001, p. 412).

Additional statistical analysis indicated that recent immigrants relied more than other groups on personal references for job matching for three main reasons; recent immigrants were more likely than other respondents (i) to speak the English language poorly, (ii) to work at relatively small firms, and (iii) to face discrimination in the job market.[6] Lack of fluency in English would make it very hard to conduct a successful job search through formal mechanisms alone. Small firms hire workers relatively

[6]Multivariate analysis indicated that the importance of recent immigrant status as a determinant of how a respondent was matched with his or her job diminished substantially, but remained statistically significant, in specifications that controlled for ability to speak English, firm size, and an interaction term between occupational homogeneity and native-born African-American identity. Elliot cites evidence that, although the overall incidence of insider-referral hiring was not particularly high among African-American respondents, a large proportion of black respondents who were employed in ethnically homogeneous firms did find these jobs through social contacts. Ernst argues that this finding indicates that, because of employer prejudice, it is difficult for African-Americans to dominate employment in a firm, but once such closure does occur, it can be sustained through referral hiring. This analysis seems consistent with the view that job matching through social networks can, in part, reflect the impact of prejudice in the labor market (Elliot, 2001, pp. 413–420).

infrequently, and, so, would be disinclined to incur the up-front cost of setting up a formal recruitment operation. And a personal reference from a current employee with a workplace reputation to maintain can help overcome the effects of a potential employer's prejudices.

Although Elliot analyzed late twentieth-century job-matching processes in Atlanta, Boston, and Los Angeles, the reasons he identified for recent immigrants' disproportionate reliance on social networks to help them find jobs also ring true in the antebellum New York City context.

All British and most Irish immigrants would have been native English speakers, but most Germans were not. Most antebellum firms were very small, but some of publishing houses, newspapers, and shipyards would have been large enough to establish formal employment recruitment practices (Albion, 1939, p. 297; Stott, 1990, p. 50). Immigrant workers were apparently somewhat underrepresented in these industries. Overall the foreign born accounted for 74% of all New York City workers whose occupations were enumerated in the 1855 New York State census. Only 55% of printers and 59% of ships' carpenters, however, were immigrants.[7] This suggests that a relative high proportion of antebellum immigrants would have found jobs in relatively small businesses. Finally, at least some antebellum New York employers were not shy about flaunting their anti-Irish prejudices, even in newspaper advertisements for domestic servants (Ernst, 1994, p. 67).

To summarize: we have some direct evidence based on recent data and considerable circumstantial evidence regarding the 1840s and 1850s that social networks effectively communicated employment-related information in New York City's antebellum labor market. Further, it does not seem like too much of a stretch to conclude, based on analogy from the circumstances of the late twentieth century, that social capital in the form of gainfully employed relatives, neighbors, friends,

[7]These statistics are based on tabulations from manuscripts of the 1855 New York State census. The data set reported by Ernst includes numerous inconsistencies. In nine of the 109 tabulated occupations, for example, the number of foreign-born workers exceeds total employment. The statistics are worth citing, nonetheless, because the differences between percentage of specific country origin in particular occupations and overall immigrant percentage from said country were large (Ernst, 1994, p. 217).

acquaintances, and acquaintances of acquaintances would have been more important relative to formal credentials to immigrants than to the native born during the pre-Civil War period.

## Conclusion

The material presented in this chapter points to a solution to the puzzle initially presented in Chapter 7. Given the sparsity of direct, on point evidence, however, any conclusions must be considered speculative.

The housing available to and affordable by working-class New Yorkers during the two decades immediately preceding the Civil War was, indeed, abominable, both absolutely and, probably, relative to lower-quality residences elsewhere in the United States. It also seems likely that the situation deteriorated through most of the 1840s and 1850s. Because the cost of shelter consumed a substantial proportion of workers' household budgets and because the price per square foot of low-quality residential space was so high, the real wages earned per day by New York workers, while likely still higher than what was being paid in Europe, was also probably much lower than what common laborers could earn in the Midwest. The declining quality and rising price of New York's low-end housing stock probably also suppressed the growth rate of real wages in the City compared with the pace elsewhere in the Northeast. By the criterion of real wages, therefore, the City's relative desirability as a place to live and work probably deteriorated over the antebellum period.

Despite this, the combined population of New York and Kings Counties grew very rapidly during these decades, and, by 1860 was, relative to the populations of lower-ranked places within the U.S. hierarchy of cities, about "right sized" at a few more than 1,000,000. In 1860, too, there were roughly 30% more foreign-born and 30% fewer native-born New Yorkers than would have been expected if the City had been equally attractive to both. Therefore, the solution to puzzle of why New York's population grew as quickly as it did takes the form of an explanation of why immigrants may have been more willing to put up with the wretched quality and high price of New York's working-class housing.

The explanation, in the broadest terms, is that during the pre-Civil War decades, New York's economic and social institutions developed in a way that suited the specific needs of the immigrants who were arriving in large numbers at the time.

First, antebellum immigrants were disproportionately young adults. This demographic found it relatively easy to substitute the consumer goods that New York was able to provide in the greatest variety at the lowest prices—street life, nightlife, varieties of entertainment—for the quality and quantity of residential floor space, which antebellum New York supplied at a comparative disadvantage. Also, many young, single women escaped working-class housing by taking positions as live-in domestic servants in the homes of the City's large and rapidly expanding middle- and upper-classes.

Second, the types of businesses that developed in New York City over the first half of the nineteenth century provided employment opportunities for all but the very youngest first- and second-generation immigrants. So, lower real wages per day's work per family member notwithstanding, striving immigrant households may have been able to earn higher nominal and real aggregate incomes in New York City than they could elsewhere.

Finally, immigrants and their employers may have been able to make the most of the multiple economic opportunities on offer because New York's social institutions—its packed multifamily dwellings, its neighborhood streets, and its entertainment venues—were particularly conducive to the formation of robust social networks. Circumstantial evidence suggests that social capital in the form of numerous and diverse personal connections was in plentiful supply in antebellum New York City. Further, there are good reasons to believe that social connections would have been more important to antebellum immigrant job-seekers than to their native-born contemporaries. In particular, like more recent immigrants, who tend to find jobs through personal introduction, many of their pre-Civil War predecessors would have had limited command of English, would have sought jobs in relatively small firms, and would have faced discrimination in the job market.

It is important to recognize that the chain of causality between New York's social and economic ecosystem and the City's relative attractiveness to European immigrants did not run in only one direction. Immigrants helped create the institutions that immigrants found to be useful or attractive. Immigrants forged the personal connections, the nodes of the social networks that communicated economically relevant information. And as these, mostly ethnically homogeneous, social networks operated in the job market, they created the kind of "socially closed" workplaces that newcomers could readily join.

In a sense, therefore, New York became a "city of immigrants" for the same basic reason that it became the nation's largest city. Economic activity expanded most dramatically in New York in large part because, circa 1840, this City happened to be somewhat larger than its urban competitors, most likely because it had had solidified its position as the nation's busiest port. Once the City began to grow rapidly, a self-reinforcing process of agglomeration set in, assuring that New York would assume its place as and then stay at the pinnacle of the U.S. system of cities.

Similarly, for some reason, perhaps because New York was the port of entry, on the eve of catastrophic agglomeration, the concentration of immigrants in the City was proportionately larger than elsewhere. This concentration gave New York a head start in developing the institutions and economic structure that would make the City particularly attractive to subsequent immigrants as the antebellum decades progressed. Thus, New York's rank in the 97th percentile of foreign-born concentration among northern U.S. counties in 1860, like its status at the top of the urban hierarchy, was the result of a self-reinforcing process that may have had its origin in the City's position as the principal North American port.

## References

Albion, R. G. (1939). *The Rise of New York Port (1815–1860)*. New York: Scribner's.

Blackmar, E. (1989). *Manhattan for Rent, 1785–1850*. Ithaca: Cornell University Press.

Carter, S. B. (2006). *Table Aa22035*. Retrieved from Historical Statistics of the United States Millennial Edition Online http://projects.ilt.columbia.edu/seneca/svcurric/images/byward2_early.html.

Citizens' Association of New York. (1865). *Report of the Council of Hygiene and Public Health Upon the Sanitary Condition of the City*. New York: D. Appleton and Company.

Elliot, J. R. (2001). Referral Hiring and Ethnically Homogeneous Jobs: How Prevalent Is the Connection and for Whom. *Social Science Research, 30,* 401–425.

Ernst, R. (1994). *Immigrant Life in New York City, 1825–1863*. Syracuse, NY: Syracuse University Press.

Ferrie, J. P. (1997). The Entry into the U.S. Labor Market of Antebellum European Immigrants, 1840–1860. *Explorations in Economic History, 34,* 295–330.

Gabaiz, X. (1999). Zipf's Law for Cities: An Explanation. *Quarterly Journal of Economics, 114*(3), 739–767.

Goldin, C., & Margo, R. A. (1992). The Great Compression: The Wage Structure in the United States at Mid-Century. *Quarterly Journal of Economics, 107*(1), 1–34.

Granovetter, M. (2005). The Impact of Social Structure on Economic Outcomes. *Journal of Economic Perspectives, 19*(1), 33–50.

Margo, R. A. (1996). The Rental Price of Housing in New York City, 1830–1860. *Journal of Economic History, 56*(3), 605–625.

Mason, M. K. (2018, June). *Housing: Then, Now, and Future*. Retrieved from http://www.moyak.com/papers/house-sizes.html.

Montgomery, J. D. (1991, December). Social Networks and Labor-Market Outcomes: Toward and Economic Analysis. *American Economic Review, 81*(5), 1408–1418.

Rosenbloom, J. L. (2002). *Looking for Work, Searching for Workers*. Cambridge: Cambridge University Press.

Rosenwaike, I. (1972). *Population History of New York City*. Syracuse, NY: Syracuse University Press.

Sanders, J., Nee, V., & Scott Sernau, S. (2002). Asian Immigrants' Reliance on Social Ties in a Multiethnic Labor Market. *Social Forces, 81*(1), 281–314.

Scherzer, K. A. (1992). *The Unbound Community: Neighborhood Life and Social Structure in New York City, 1830–1875*. Durham, NC: Duke University Press.

Stansell, C. (1987). *City of Women: Sex and Class in New York, 1789–1860*. Champaign: University of Illinois Press.

Storper, M., & Venables, A. J. (2003). Face-to-Face Contact and the Urban Economy. *Journal of Economic Geography, 4*(4), 351–370.

Stott, R. B. (1990). *Workers in the Metropolis: Class, Ethnicity, and Youth in Antebellum New York City*. Ithaca: Cornell University Press.

University of Virginia. (n.d.). Retrieved from Historical Census Browser (Discontinued).

U.S. Bureau of the Census. (1998). Population of the 100 Largest Urban Places: 1860. https://www.census.gov/population/www/documentation/twps0027/tab09.txt.

U.S. Department of Housing and Urban Development. (2018, June). *Measuring Overcrowding in Housing*. Retrieved from https://www.huduser.gov/publications/pdf/measuring_overcrowding_in_hsg.pdf.

# 9

# Money Central

One thing that differentiated New York's economy markedly from that of other large nineteenth-century U.S. cities was its role as the hub of the nation's financial system. The 1870 census provides the earliest detailed urban employment statistics for a wide range of manufacturing, trade, and service occupations. In that year, 0.08% of Americans whose occupations were enumerated were employed "in banking and brokerage of money and stocks." The percentage of enumerated employed residents of Greater New York City working in this industry was 0.7850[1] (U.S. Department of the Interior, Census-Office, 1872, pp. 669–673, 773). Thus New York's employment concentration ratio in banking and financial brokerage was 9.52. This was the highest concentration ratio in Greater New York City among the 74 occupations listed in the published tabulations for the nation's "principal cities." Employment concentration ratios for such renowned New York specialties as book

[1]As occupations were tabulated by residence rather than workplace, the statistics analyzed here for "Greater New York City" include the data for the three immediately adjacent "principal cities" in the region, Brooklyn, Jersey City, and New York City (Manhattan). The only other pair of cities among the other 27 which were equally geographically close were Albany and Troy, NY. These are considered separately. Combining the two would not change any of the conclusions of this section.



A. Gurwitz, *Atlantic Metropolis*, Palgrave Studies in American Economic History,
https://doi.org/10.1007/978-3-030-13352-8_9

**Table 9.1** Occupations with the 20 highest 1870 resident employment concentration ratios in greater New York City (U.S. Department of the Interior, Census-Office, 1872)

| Occupation | Greater NY, number | Greater NY concentration ratio |
|---|---|---|
| All occupations | 516,163 | |
| In banking and brokerage of money and stocks | 4,052 | 9.58 |
| Traders and dealers | 37,852 | 9.13 |
| Bookbinders and finishers | 3,285 | 8.74 |
| Plumbers and gasfitters | 3,442 | 7.48 |
| Officials and employees of street-railroad companies | 1,334 | 6.23 |
| Officials and employees of railroad companies | 3,217 | 5.42 |
| Hat and cap makers | 2,554 | 4.90 |
| Bakers | 5,241 | 4.59 |
| Printers | 7,411 | 4.50 |
| Confectioners | 1,469 | 4.33 |
| Cigarmakers and tobacco workers | 7,109 | 4.28 |
| Clerks, salesman and accountants (in stores) | 43,020 | 3.89 |
| Tailors, tailoresses, and seamstresses | 24,965 | 3.74 |
| Butchers | 6,565 | 3.59 |
| Ship riggers, calkers, carpenters and smiths | 2,967 | 3.52 |
| Officials and employees of express companies | 1,350 | 3.48 |
| Milliners, dress and mantua makers | 13,038 | 3.43 |
| Boarding and lodging house keepers | 1,784 | 3.38 |
| Hucksters, peddlers, and commercial travelers | 5,701 | 3.32 |
| Barbers and hairdressers | 3,280 | 3.32 |

publishing and the needle trades were substantially lower (Table 9.1). Concentrations in banking and brokerage in other large cities were much lower than New York's. By contrast, the urban concentration ratios for "Traders and Dealers," New York's second highest statistic, were as large or even greater in other cities such as regional distribution centers San Francisco and New Orleans (Table 9.2). Table 9.2 also shows that, whatever the reasons for the very high concentration of banking and financial brokerage activity in New York, the same influences did not drive the location of the other major nineteenth-century financial services industry: insurance. Occupations "in insurance" were not concentrated in New York.

**Table 9.2** 1870 occupational employment concentration ratios in large U.S. cities (U.S. Department of the Interior, Census-Office, 1872)

| City* | Total employment | In banking and brokerage of money and stocks | Traders and dealers | In insurance |
|---|---|---|---|---|
| NYC, Brooklyn, Jersey City | 516,163 | 9.58 | 9.13 | 2.58 |
| Philadelphia, PA | 217,685 | 2.58 | 8.32 | 1.25 |
| Boston, MA | 162,740 | 3.01 | 5.77 | 1.34 |
| Chicago, IL | 112,960 | 3.90 | 8.23 | 4.44 |
| Baltimore, MD | 94,737 | 2.67 | 8.54 | 1.81 |
| Cincinnati, OH | 77,923 | 3.40 | 7.09 | 3.29 |
| San Francisco, CA | 68,352 | 7.75 | 9.92 | 3.44 |
| New Orleans, LA | 66,032 | 5.47 | 9.85 | 1.54 |
| Detroit, MI | 51,340 | 2.21 | 3.64 | 2.50 |
| Washington, DC | 41,183 | 2.67 | 5.07 | 0.89 |
| Buffalo, NY | 39,680 | 3.20 | 5.42 | 1.38 |
| Newark, NJ | 37,468 | 7.03 | 6.08 | 3.16 |
| Louisville, KY | 35,800 | 4.94 | 8.28 | 3.13 |
| Cleveland, OH | 30,211 | 3.03 | 6.03 | 3.83 |
| Pittsburgh, PA | 29,854 | 4.78 | 6.55 | 1.71 |
| Providence, RI | 26,266 | 7.01 | 8.85 | 1.54 |
| Allegheny, PA | 25,558 | 3.20 | 5.18 | 2.25 |
| Milwaukee, WI | 23,119 | 3.75 | 8.09 | 4.81 |
| Rochester, NY | 21,927 | 4.56 | 7.49 | 0.98 |
| Albany, NY | 21,376 | 6.16 | 7.85 | 1.43 |
| Charleston, SC | 18,705 | 3.98 | 8.12 | 1.25 |
| Indianapolis, IN | 18,615 | 4.65 | 8.20 | 6.02 |
| Richmond, VA | 18,545 | 3.09 | 8.04 | 2.47 |
| New Haven, CT | 17,962 | 3.94 | 6.59 | 6.04 |
| Worcester, MA | 16,527 | 3.40 | 4.54 | 4.67 |
| Troy, NY | 16,526 | 4.50 | 7.54 | 0.71 |

*Although the title of the table in the Census Office publication encompasses 30 cities, data for only 28 were included in the publication available on line. Two of these 28 cities, Brooklyn and Jersey City, were adjacent to New York in the vicinity of the financial district and accessible by steam ferry service in 1870

The impact of the local economy of the City's role as the nation's financial center extended well beyond the number of New Yorkers working in banks or brokerage houses. The executive offices of large industrial and transportation companies, for which ready access to large-scale financing was an essential element of corporate management, gravitated to the location where the most well-informed and efficient financial services were available. At the turn of the twentieth century, seven of the twelve companies included in the initial version of the Dow Jones Industrial Average had their headquarters in New York City or Jersey City and the other five had representative offices in New York (Moody & Co., 1901; O'Brien, 2014).

A body of research on the economic history of the nineteenth-century U.S. monetary system and financial markets has aimed to determine whether the development of a robust financial sector was a cause or an effect of the country's economic growth. Was the development of the nation's financial systems a necessary precondition for development, as were, for example, advances in transportation technology, or did economic transformation itself—the shift from subsistence to commercial agriculture, the building of the railroad network, urbanization, industrialization, etc.—stimulate the establishment of numerous financial institutions and active financial markets? (Bodenhorn, 2000, pp. 11–15).

This chapter asks a similar question about New York City. Was the concentration of banking and financial market activity in New York just one effect of the City's position at the pinnacle of the North American urban hierarchy? Put differently, was the production of these financial services characterized by such pronounced economies of scale that these activities came to be highly concentrated in the single largest city? Or was the development of the local financial services sector in New York determined by something other than City's sheer size so that the local concentration of this activity served as an independent driver of New York's economic development? Was there, in other words, a plausible alternative chain of causality that would have left New York as the nation's largest city but with a substantially smaller financial services workforce by the end of the nineteenth century, absolutely and relative to other large cities?

The answer to this question emerges from an understanding of the development of the US banking system and capital markets over the course of the nineteenth century. While these two development processes affected each other in numerous ways and while one of these interactions helped drive New York's emergence as the nation's dominant financial center, it will be helpful to analyze the evolutions of the banking system and capital markets separately.

## Money, Credit, and Banking in an Age of Financial *Ad Hockery*

Two circumstances in particular influenced the development of the U.S. money and banking system and securities markets through the displaced nineteenth century and New York City's role in what emerged. First, for most of the period there was little or no centralized national governance or guidance of the system. Second, in part as a result of the first circumstance, the amount of money available to Americans to conduct business—to buy goods, to lend and borrow, and to invest—was powerfully influenced by the flow of funds between the United States and Europe. The financial institutions and instruments that Americans developed between the end of the Napoleonic Wars and the eve of World War I evolved, for the most part, as an assemblage of *ad hoc* means to mitigate the high cost of doing business in a decentralized and often chaotic domestic financial environment that was frequently buffeted by the impact of events taking place abroad.

The role of some of the institutions that emerged was to facilitate transactions within and among all regions of the United States, and, after the Philadelphia-based Second Bank of the United States went out of business in the mid-1830s, most of these *de facto* "national" institutions were located in New York City. And because New York was the nation's busiest port it also became the main channel through which cash flows to and from Europe influenced American financial conditions.

### Three Regimes

Although change was continuous, it is both useful and justifiable to divide the monetary and financial history of the United States over the course of the nineteenth century and of New York City's role therein into three periods.

- **The Two Banks of the United States.** Between about 1791 and about 1836 with a hiatus between 1811 and 1816, American's financial development was influenced in important ways by two federally chartered financial institutions, both called the Bank of the United States (BUS), both modeled in important ways on the Bank of England, both headquartered in Philadelphia, and both operating through extensive branch networks.

- **State Banking**. Between the mid-1830s, when the second BUS's federal charter was not renewed, and 1863 the rules governing the operation of financial institutions and the creation of money was left in the hands of the states. It was during this period that New York rose to its position at the pinnacle of both the hierarchy of cities and of financial centers in the United States.
- **National Banking**. Between 1863, when the nation's system of financial institutions and monetary instruments was fundamentally restructured to help cope with the demands and disruptions of the Civil War, and the passage of the Federal Reserve Act in 1913 the United States had a common, national currency regime. But no central institution managed the quantity of money available in the economy. Nor was there any public body authorized and equipped to act as a "lender of last resort" and, thereby, prevent financial market disruptions from deteriorating into banking crises and economic depressions. Instead, the U.S. money supply was at the mercy of gold prospectors' luck and European central banks' policies. Efforts to nip banking crises in the bud, sometimes successfully, sometimes, less so, were organized by such individual New York-based financiers as John Pierpont Morgan acting through private sector institutions such as the New York Clearing House Association.

During all three of these periods, much of the paper money used for transactions between Americans took the form of notes issued by individual privately held banking corporations operating under state or federal charters.[2] When an individual or a business borrowed money from

[2]The exceptions to this generalization were the "greenbacks" issued by the United State Treasury Department during the Civil War era. These were similar in many respects to the bills of credit—discussed in Chapter 2—issued by colonial governments during the eighteenth century except that greenbacks were, by law, legal tender and had to be accepted at face value for settlement of financial obligations throughout the United States.

one of these institutions, the amount of the loan was often paid to the borrower in the form of banknotes. Or when one withdrew funds from a bank, the teller handed over banknotes. The recipient then used the notes to purchase land, goods, services, or securities. The sellers of the land, goods, services, or securities were willing to accept banknotes in payment because, in principle and at most times in fact, these notes could be redeemed for standardized amounts of gold or silver upon presentation to the issuing bank. To lend credence to the standing offer to redeem notes for specie banks had to maintain some level of reserves that were gold or were widely perceived as being as good as gold. Since it was unlikely that all of a bank's noteholders would demand redemption simultaneously, these reserves could be and were maintained at levels substantially less than the face value of the bank's outstanding notes and deposits. If a bank's noteholders got the impression that its reserves were inadequate, a rush in demand for immediate payment of gold could force the institution to suspend specie redemptions temporarily or to go out of business permanently. How low a reserve ratio could be considered safe was a key question for individual banks' management and for state and federal bank regulators throughout the nineteenth century and beyond.

## Two Central Banks and Their Branches

During the first two of the historical periods, there were many different "brands" of paper currency in circulation within the United States. In 1835, for example, there were 584 chartered banks in the United States, most of which issued their own banknotes (Bodenhorn, 2000, p. 10). Under these circumstances, a $10 note issued by, say, a South Carolina bank would not, in general, be accepted by, say, a merchant in Boston as payment for goods priced at $10 both because of the time and expense involved in shipping the note to Charleston for redemption and because of uncertainty regarding the soundness of the issuing institution (Gorton, 1996, 1999). Whether any given transaction was worthwhile depended on the size of the discount from face value on South Carolina banknotes in Boston, and a South Carolinian who wanted to buy goods cheaply in Boston or a Bostonian who wanted to sell goods profitably to Southerners needed to find ways to reduce the transaction costs associated with monetary diversity.

The differences between the first two periods of U.S. financial history discussed in this chapter relate to the ways in which households, firms, financial institutions, borrowers, lenders, and governments managed to execute a rapidly growing volume of transactions with the wide variety of monetary instruments in circulation.

Legislation adopted by Congress in 1791 granted the First Bank of the United States a 20-year charter, which was allowed to expire in 1811, when Vice President George Clinton cast a tie-breaking vote against renewal in the U.S. Senate. One of the functions of an early nineteenth-century central bank was to lend money to the government in emergencies. Thus, the BUS was sorely missed when the War of 1812 broke out. So, in 1816, shortly after peace was restored, Congress established the second BUS, again with a twenty-year charter. This charter was also allowed to expire when Bank proponents were unable to muster enough votes to override President Andrew Jackson's veto of the charter renewal legislation that had passed both houses of Congress. In both 1811 and 1836, the decision to allow the BUS charter to expire was a very close thing politically.

Another purpose the two central banks served while they were in existence was to help integrate the country's regions into a single national economy. One of the ways they did so, with degrees of effectiveness that varied over time, was by accepting state-chartered banks' notes and other financial instruments in exchange for the BUS's own or BUS branches' paper (Bodenhorn, 2000). In this way, a Boston merchant who had been paid for goods delivered to Charleston with notes issued by a South Carolina bank could exchange this paper at par or at a small, standard discount for BUS notes at the central bank's Boston branch. The Boston branch, in turn, would have been willing to execute the exchange because it was in possession of information provided to the BUS system by its Charlotte branch that the issuing bank's reserves were deemed adequate. Similarly, an Alabama plantation-owner could purchase goods from a Mobile Merchant with a "bill of exchange drawn on New York." The latter was a negotiable commercial instrument committing a particular New York merchant to pay a stated amount upon presentation (or "sight") of the bill on or after a stated future date. The Mobile Merchant would be willing to accept this form of payment because he could receive the stated value of the bill less an acceptable discount from the Mobile branch of the BUS. The Mobile branch would have been willing to "discount" the New York bill of exchange because the southern bank could rightly expect the New York BUS branch either to redeem the bill with the merchant drawee and credit the proceeds to the Mobile branch or to rediscount the paper and credit the Mobile branch an acceptable cash value prior to maturity. The existence of well-functioning markets for out-of-town state-chartered banknotes and depositors' checks and widespread, reasonably priced rediscounting facilities for domestic Bills of Exchange were necessary conditions for the rapid development of interregional trade within the United States that began in the 1820s and accelerated through the antebellum years.[3] Between 1816 and 1836, the Second Bank of the United States actively fostered the development of its branch network to serve this purpose.

## The State Banking Era: Centripetal Forces in a Decentralized System

After 1836, therefore, Americans needed to develop some other way to facilitate interregional transactions absent a single institution the notes of which were accepted in cities across the United States and could be exchanged at modest cost for the obligations of banks located around the country. Fortunately, alternative mechanisms for executing interregional financial transactions had developed even while the BUS system was capturing the lion's share of this type of business. Under the system that evolved individual banks chartered in one state established correspondent relationships with banks in other states.

[3]Between 1839 and 1860, the gross value of trade among the northeastern, mid-western, and southern regions of the United States grew at an annual rate of 6.4% while the wholesale price index *decreased* at a 0.8% annual rate (Census, 1976, p. 201; Fishlow, 1964, p. 360).

The process worked roughly as follows. Suppose a southern Ohio farmer negotiated a loan from a local country banker. The amount of the loan would have been paid to the farmer in notes of the country bank or with funds credited to the borrower's account at the lending institution. Suppose further that the farmer wished to use the loan proceeds to purchase agricultural equipment in Cincinnati. The equipment dealer would be willing to make the sale at a reasonable price if he could be confident that the country banknotes or the farmer's check used to make the purchase were money-good. If the country banker had established an agreement with a Cincinnati bank whereby the former institution agreed to keep funds on deposit in the city bank and the latter agreed to exchange its own banknotes for the rural bank paper or to cash the farmer's check, then the equipment dealer could easily close out the transaction.

Since it would have been impossible for every pair of financial institutions in the United States to reach such agreements bankers had to decide which banks in which locations to choose as correspondents. Country bankers would, of course, want to have at least one correspondent in the nearest central place. More generally, correspondent relationships and interbank deposits would be most useful in the places where a bank's notes, its depositors' checks, or the Bills of Exchange it had discounted would be most likely to be used to make purchases. Thus, banks in the cities that served as distribution centers for goods sold everywhere in the United States would be likely to have the largest number of correspondent relationships and the largest volume of interbank deposits from across all regions. Domestically produced goods were purchased either near the point of production or at regional distribution centers. It is unlikely that interbank correspondent relationships supporting purely domestic transactions would have been much more geographically concentrated than wholesale trade in general. The high concentration of traders and dealers in large cities across the country shown in Table 9.2 is consistent with such multiplicity of distribution hubs. By contrast, a large proportion of goods produced abroad and sold within the United States were distributed nationally through the nation's busiest import port, New York City. Since most banks had at least some clients—regional dry goods distributors or small-town store owners, for example—who purchased foreign-made goods either directly from importers or through jobbers, most banks could also expect that at least some of their paper would find its way to New York City. Some country banks might have served customers who purchased all their imported goods from distributors in regional cities, such as New Orleans or San Francisco, and therefore had little direct need for a New York connection. Payments from country storekeepers would have been forwarded to these regional central places, where rural banks would have maintained interbank deposits. The larger banks located in these regional metropolises would have served the customers who had obligations due in New York and would have had to maintain correspondent relationships backed by interbank deposits at the principal port of entry. In this way, a hierarchy of banking centers evolved with New York at its pinnacle. A larger proportion of state-chartered banks, especially of the largest such institutions, therefore, would have wanted to have at least some funds on deposit in New York.

That, in fact, was the case. Interbank deposits expanded substantially once the national economy began to recover from the depression of 1837–1842. By 1850, close to 600 of the Nation's roughly 700 incorporated banks maintained a total of $17 million on deposit in New York. Aggregate out-of-town funds held in New York and due to banks, other businesses, and individuals located elsewhere may have totaled roughly $35 million, which would have represented about 13% of the estimated $279 million total currency in circulation in the United States at the time (Census U. B., 1976, p. 993; Myers, 1931, p. 115). Further, even before the economic recovery of the 1840s, more than 60% of total interbank deposits held in the five principal East Coast ports were held in New York[4] (Bodenhorn, 2000, p. 196). The volume of out-of-town deposits held in New York diminished substantially only during periods of financial "panic" in 1837 and 1840, when U.S. imports dropped precipitously, self-preservation became more important than facilitating customer transactions in big cities, and country and small-city banks withdrew interbank deposits to shore-up close-at-hand reserves.

[4]The five cities were New York, Philadelphia, Boston, Baltimore, and Charleston.

## New York's Additional Attractions

The dense flow of commercial credit through the nation's principal port in the absence of BUS branch facilities for clearing interregional transactions was probably banks' primary motive for maintaining correspondent relationships and deposits in New York. But that cannot have been the whole story. If finance does, in fact, follow trade, why was banking employment so much more highly concentrated New York than were jobs as "traders and dealers" (see Table 9.2)? In fact, there were additional reasons, which by themselves and in combination with the principal incentive may have boosted the volume of funds on deposit in New York and the aggregate size of the City's banking industry. At the most fundamental level, what drew interbank business and financial capital to New York was a local banking industry that was both highly competitive *and* able to coordinate collective action when necessary.

The growth of interbank deposits in New York might have been slower if the local banking industry had been less competitive than it was. If the number of local banks had been small enough and their individual sizes large enough relative to the flow of funds through the City, New York banks might have been able to exert pricing power to suppress interest rates paid on interbank deposits or to restrict the quantity or quality of the services New York banks provided to out-of-town correspondents. The development of such an oligopolistic market structure might have been possible if entry into the banking industry had been difficult. That might very well have been the outcome had pre-1838 New York State banking laws remained in effect throughout the antebellum period.

Early nineteenth-century policymakers were very wary of chartering too many banks authorized to create currency in the form of banknotes. The concern was that too much money would be created with too little reserve backing, leading to inflation, bank failures, and financial crises. Therefore, before 1838, in New York and in every other state, each individual charter for a note-issuing institution had to be approved by a separate act of the State legislature. As banks were potentially highly profitable in the rapidly expanding, credit- and currency-hungry post-1825 U.S. economy, this system was subject to political manipulation and outright corruption. If the corruption had taken the form of outright per-charter cash payments to legislators, the process might have resulted in a large number of banks being chartered. Instead, however, bribes usually took the form of shares of stock in the new banks gifted to state legislators. Since the value of those shares would be higher to the extent that the newly created banks were able to earn monopoly profits, legislators had an incentive to limit the number of banks that were created. Thus, between 1830 and 1837 the New York State Assembly received 535 petitions requesting bank charters and the State Senate received 199. Over the same period, only 53 chartering acts passed both legislative houses (Bodenhorn, 2006, pp. 231–257).

The chief beneficiaries of this system in New York were a group of upstate Democratic politicians allied with Martin Van Buren. Whig and Anti-Masonic party opposition to this one-at-a-time system of bank chartering coalesced around the concept of "free banking." Under a free-banking regime, the state legislature would enact rules governing the minimum capital requirements and operating standards for newly issued corporate charters. Anyone who could raise the required capital and would conform to the standards could open a bank. To prevent excessive currency creation, free banks were required to post collateral in the form of specie, government bonds, or high-quality mortgages equal in value to their banknotes in circulation. The State of Michigan adopted the first such legislation in 1837 but rescinded that law in 1839. Georgia enacted free banking legislation in 1838, but very few institutions were actually created. When the Whig party gained control of New York State's government in the wake of the 1837 financial panic, the legislature quickly enacted the Free Banking Act of 1838.

New York remained the only state with effective free-banking laws for more than a decade. It was not until the 1850s that seven additional states enacted similar legislation (Rolnick & Weber, 1983, p. 1,082). It is unclear whether the expansion of banking activity in New York was a direct result of the State's pioneering legislation. As Table 9.3 indicates, however, prior to and in the immediate wake of the enactment of free-banking law New York was an "average" state with respect to the volume of bank money (deposits + notes in circulation + other banks'

**Table 9.3** Bank money[a] per capita (Bodenhorn, 2000, p. 63)

| | 1830 | 1840 | 1850 | 1860 |
|---|---|---|---|---|
| New York State | $4.62 | $9.35 | $20.73 | $33.95 |
| 27-state mean | 5.26 | 10.41 | 9.89 | 14.89 |
| 11-Northeastern state mean[b] | 7.69 | 9.25 | 14.25 | 21.44 |

[a]Deposits + bank notes in circulation + other banks' notes
[b]ME, NH, VT, MA, CT, RI, NY, NJ, PA, DE, MD

notes) per capita and was below average for northeastern states. By 1850 and, even more so, by 1860 New York was significantly more densely banked than the average state, nationwide and in the northeast.

As a result of the legislation, barriers to entry into the banking business were relatively low in New York, and the City's banks were apparently unable to exercise oligopolistic pricing policy. Banks apparently competed actively for interbank business by paying the highest possible interest rates on these funds and by providing high-quality correspondent services. Just how banks were able to generate the revenues needed to pay high rates on interbank deposits will be discussed below. At this point, it will suffice to observe that the fact that, through the crucial decade of the 1840s, New York was the only state with an effective free banking system may have attracted more interbank deposits to the City than the concentration of interregional commercial transactions alone would have justified.

Still, the incentive to maintain a large proportion of interbank deposits in New York might have been offset by the risk that a New York-specific problem, a sudden European demand for gold shipments, for example, or one of the City's recurrent episodes of civil disorder, could jeopardize an out-of-town bank's access to their funds on deposit. Concerns about geographic risk concentration would, however, have been assuaged by the New York banking community's track record of acting collectively through its Clearing House Association to enable its members to continuing meeting their obligations when normal sources of funds were blocked.

New York bankers organized the Clearing House Association, which was modeled on a similar London institution, as an operational convenience. Prior to its establishment in 1853, the settlement of interbank obligations involved sending porters carrying bags of cash between each pair of banks every Friday. The process duplicated efforts; if bank A owed bank B $100 and B owed A the same about, both would routinely dispatch porters carrying the same amount of money to no net effect. The result was chaotic and risky and had become untenable by the early 1850s as the volume of interbank transactions grew. Under the new clearinghouse procedures, one member bank was designated as the central clearing bank. All other member banks agreed to maintain specie (gold and silver) deposits at the designated bank in exchange for "clearing house" certificates. Representatives of all member banks would meet once a week to disclose all claims on and obligations to all other member banks. Any interbank debits and credits net of all offsetting obligations would be cleared by an exchange of clearing house certificates, that is by shifting funds on deposit at the central clearing bank from one bank's account to the other's. A bank that, as a result of these transfers, would be left with less than the required minimum amount on deposit at the central clearing bank was required to deliver cash or specie to eliminate the deficit.

When a struck in 1857, banks' specie holdings were severely depleted and many institutions found themselves unable to replenish deficits in their clearinghouse accounts. At that point what had been no more than an operational convenience became a facility for creating what were, in effect, additional reserves. The Clearing House Association began issuing loan certificates secured by such lower-quality assets as out-of-town state banknotes that could not be redeemed immediately. Member banks agreed to accept loan certificates to settle net debits. As the panic subsided and out-of-town banks were again able to redeem their notes, the clearinghouse loan certificates were gradually paid down, and the normal weekly settlement process resumed (Myers, 1931). Clearinghouse loan certificates were issued in New York and other reserve cities nine times between 1860 and 1907. On some of these occasions, clearinghouse action was sufficient to prevent widespread bank failures and/or economic depressions. In 1873, 1893, and 1907, however, the situation deteriorated despite clearinghouse efforts (Timberlake, 1984, pp. 1–15).

By the eve of the Civil War, therefore, a system for clearing large volumes of interregional financial transactions in the absence of a *de jure* central bank branch network had developed in the United States. The system involved a hierarchy of interbank correspondence relationships, and New York banks, acting individually as competitors during normal times and collectively as a community at times of crisis, operated at the pinnacle of that hierarchy.

## National Banking Era: New York Institutions Function as a Quasi-Central Bank

There was, however, one important central bank service that this system could not provide. It could not lend the Federal government large amounts of money on short notice at times of national crisis. As it became obvious that the Civil War was not going to end quickly or cheaply, it also became clear that the decentralized system of State-chartered banks each issuing its own brand of currency and operating under 34 different sets of regulations would be an impediment to successful prosecution of the conflict. The response was the passage of the National Bank Acts of 1863 and 1864. This legislation, as amended from time to time, remained in effect until the Federal Reserve System was created in 1913.

The Acts authorized federally chartered and regulated national banks to issue a uniform brand of currency, national banknotes, which were to be backed by a combination of specie and Federal government bonds. These new banknotes were to be accepted at face value nationwide and, thus, became a national currency.

The '63 and '64 acts also required national banks to hold reserves equal to percentages of their customers' deposits and their banknotes in circulation. The amount and nature of these reserves varied depending on the size and location of the bank. Banks located in the smallest towns were required to maintain reserves equal to 15% of their liabilities. Banks located in 18 (eventually a maximum of 47) "reserve cities" were required to hold 25%. All banks were required to maintain some of their reserves in the form of gold or silver coins or Federal government obligations. Small town, or "country," banks could, however, hold up to three-fifths of their required reserves in the form of deposits at reserve city banks. And the reserve city banks could hold up to half of their required reserves as a deposit in a "central reserve city." Until 1887, when Chicago and St. Louis were added, only New York was designated as a central reserve city (Champ, 2007, pp. 29–33). Since interbank deposits paid interest, while cash in the vault did not, banks had an incentive to maintain the maximum allowable proportion of their reserves in reserve cities or in the central reserve city. In this way, the business practice by which banks around the United States had maintained deposits in New York City was codified under the national banking system. Further, many of these regional banks would still have wanted to maintain relationships with New York institutions over and above these minimum reserve requirements to facilitate their customers' business dealings in the national metropolis.

Thus, the combination of the favored regulatory treatment of central reserve city deposits, the interest paid on interbank deposits, and the reassurance provided by clearinghouse crisis management were evidently sufficient to attract a large proportion of the nation's banking assets to the City. By 1910, New York-based institutions accounted for close to 15% of total national bank capitalization and more than 20% of net national bank earnings (Comptroller of the Currency, 1910, pp. 322–324). At the time, the City accounted for a little more than five percent of the country's population. At 10,838, the number of New Yorkers working as "Bankers and bank officials" in 1910 was also close to 20% of total national employment in this occupation. This was a not inconsiderable contribution to the local economy—the number of bankers was about the same as the number of policemen—but the direct employment in this industry could not have been an important determinant of the aggregate size of the local economy.

This is not to say, of course, that the concentration of bank assets and liabilities in New York had little impact on the size or character of the City's economy. Clearly, that impact was powerful during the national banking era and continues to be so today. The channel through which the banking industry affected the regional economy, however, was not primarily through direct employment of large numbers of people in this industry itself.

Instead, the concentration of banking capital and of funds on deposit in New York City affected the growth of the City's economy through two indirect channels. First, especially during the national banking era New York City's banks charged borrowers somewhat lower interest rates than was the case elsewhere in the country. Between 1870 and 1914, interest rates on loans made by New York City banks were, on average, a bit less than one percentage point lower than what borrowers elsewhere were charged. Cheaper borrowing may have boosted local business activity (Bodenhorn & Rockoff, 1992, p. 185). Second, and probably more importantly, a substantial portion of New York banks' lending took the form of call loans to investors and dealers in financial securities.

## New York's Call on the Securities Markets

Once an out-of-town bank determined how much money to keep on deposit in the central reserve city, the next step would have been to select a particular correspondent from among the New York banks. At least some New York banks must have considered holding interbank deposits a profitable line of business because they evidently competed among themselves to offer the highest interest rates on interbank deposits.

Interbank deposits were, of necessity, demand deposits. Regional institutions might need funds on short notice at any time to cover an unusually large transactional debit balance or to bring reserves back home to meet customers' demand for withdrawals. So, the investments New York banks funded with their interbank liabilities had to be redeemable at any time. It would have been imprudent, for example, to use any large proportion of interbank deposits to make standard three-, six-, or twelve-month loans to commercial borrowers to finance inventories. New York banks were ready, therefore, to supply large volumes of loans to borrowers who were willing and able to repay the money on very short notice. The demand for such funds emerged from New Yorkers who were active in the stock and bond markets as brokers, traders, speculators, or arbitrageurs. Banks would make "call loans" collateralized by securities having a market value somewhat larger than the amount of the loan. If and when the loan was called, the borrower could either sell the position to repay the money or find another bank that was willing to replace the original lender. Financial market participants were willing to pay competitive interest rates on these loans because the securities themselves generated income in the form of stock dividends or bond coupons and because many of the financed holdings were acquired in the expectation of realizing a capital gain.

Thus, the call loan market developed in New York beginning early in the second decade of the nineteenth century in tandem with both the port City's rise to commercial prominence and the growth of bankers' balances in the City. By the early 1840s, the New York financial press was commenting frequently on call loan rates and the state of the call loan market (Myers, 1931, pp. 115, 426–137). The market continued to expand through the national banking era as regulatory reserves augmented commercial transaction balances and as the volume of securities traded on New York's exchanges expanded to meet the needs of railroads and other rapidly growing, capital intensive enterprises. Indeed, the business of short-term lending on financial collateral became so attractive that out-of-town American and even some European banks began dispatching funds with the express purpose of investing in the call loan market via the agency of their New York correspondent.

To at least some extent, the potential supply of bankers' balances to the call loan market probably helped boost the growth of New York's stock and bond markets. Because would-be traders could build securities positions without putting up a large amount of their own funds, more participants were drawn securities markets. And market makers' ready access to cash enhanced the liquidity of securities. Awareness that a stock or bond portfolio could be sold at or near a fair market price if funds were needed quickly attracted investors who might otherwise have deployed their money into, say, real estate or personal loans. No other city's banks had the combination of large, ephemeral volumes of demand deposits seeking the highest available yield with an active local securities market that fostered the growth of call loan market. Further, the ready availability of credit conveyed an advantage to New York's market makers and speculators who were, in turn, able to capture a growing share of the nation's stock and bond transactions. By

1910, New York City's securities markets accounted for 90 and 92% of U.S. stock and bond sales, respectively (Davis & Cull, 1994, p. 73). A growing demand for call loans to support expanding securities market activity further enhanced the attractiveness of keeping funds on deposit in New York. So, the expansions of the securities markets and of New York banks' balance sheets became mutually reinforcing.

New York's dominance in the securities industry and in the closely related investment banking industry was also reflected in the employment statistics. In 1910, when the New York City concentration ratio for "Bankers and bank officials" was 3.41, the equivalent statistic for "stockbrokers" was 4.72.

## Why Weren't American Banks "Universal"?

Call loan facilities, then, helped boost New York's capital market institutions to their pre-eminent position within the U.S. financial system, and this helps explain the high local concentration of securities industry employment in the City. The aim of this chapter, however, is to determine the impact of the financial services industry on the City's economy as a whole. An industry's impact is determined not only by the concentration of industry employment in a city but also, and perhaps more so, by the absolute size and importance of the industry. The U.S. securities industry was, indeed, big and important by the end of the nineteenth century, but it may not necessarily have had to be that way. A "counterfactual" alternative route by which nineteenth-century U.S. companies could have raised the capital they needed is exemplified by the German or "universal banking" path. In Germany, the other rapidly industrializing late nineteenth-century economy, and in several other continental European countries expanding businesses looked to commercial banks as their main source of long-term investment capital. Large "universal" German banks operated essentially as holding companies; they acquired and maintained portfolios of their corporate clients' stocks and bonds, and bank managers took active roles in these companies' governance. The alternative to the "Continental" or "universal banking" model of capital market organization was the system that developed in the UK and the United States, the "Anglo Saxon" model, in which businesses raised a large part of their long-term capital requirements via public offerings of stocks and bonds. The U.S. capital markets that developed during the nineteenth century resembled the latter system, not the former.

The geography of the U.S. financial services industry might have been very different at the end of the nineteenth century and, perhaps, even today, if that development had taken a different path. Specifically, if U.S. companies had looked to commercial banks to meet their long-term funding requirements, the distribution of capital financing activity might have resembled that of commercial banking activity. The latter, was less concentrated in New York in terms of employment than was investment banking as noted above. Therefore, the process by which the U.S. came to resemble the British model of corporate finance is an important episode in New York City's economic history. The evolution of the U.S. and British capital markets through the second half of the nineteenth century are not really two separate stories. The two markets were closely integrated, and in the years after the Civil War New York City became their principle geographic contact point in the Western Hemisphere. The next chapter will explore how this came about in more detail.

## A Counterfactual Trajectory

New York's status as the nation's largest city was unchallenged and probably unchallengeable in the 1850s, and, by the end of the nineteenth-century commercial bank deposits and capital market activity were very highly concentrated there. Did the second of these developments follow inevitably from the first? Or is there a plausible alternative chain of causality at the end of which New York would have been the largest city but financial services employment would have been more broadly dispersed across the country than it actually was?

This chapter highlights one possible alternative pattern of development for the U.S. financial system that might have led to the second outcome. The turning point that sent the country and the City down the path they took was Congress's failure to override President Andrew Jackson's veto of the bill renewing the federal chart of the Second Bank of the United States. This event demoted the Philadelphia-based BUS to a state-chartered institution. That and the bank's eventual failure may have contributed to that city's descent toward the financial minor-league. But that is not the way in which the demise of the BUS led to New York's ascendency. The alternative chain of causality has little to do with the location of the central bank's headquarters. Had the BUS charter been renewed it is reasonable to assume that BUS branches would have continued redeeming inter-regional payments in the form of out-of-town banknotes and checks and rediscounting domestic and international Bills of Exchange. If so, there would have been less reason for banks to maintain large demand balances on deposit with big-city correspondents. Under those circumstances, it is doubtful that such a large proportion of the nation's total bank deposits would have found its way to New York. If so, the chain of forward linkages from the large pool of demand deposits in the City, most notably the call loan market and the liquid stock and bond markets, might never have been forged.

Renewal of the Bank's charter might also have affected New York City's role in long-term capital markets. If U.S. banks had not been induced to focus on managing large volumes of interbank demand deposits, they might have been more willing to hold long-term investments such as mortgages, stocks, and bonds. If American banks had been free to operate as, in effect, investment trusts, U.S. capital markets might, by the end of the century, have come to resemble the German universal banking system. Economic historian Richard Tilly put the analysis this way: "when and where central banks became willing and able to assume responsibility for guiding the country's payments system and to serve as a lender of last resort, universal banks' perceived risks fell and their activities expanded considerably" (Tilly, 1998, p. 17).

Under universal banking system, many of the functions served by the New York-based securities markets would have come under the aegis of commercial banks. U.S. and foreign investors seeking high-yielding, long-term American assets would have bought the stocks and bonds of a small number of large banks, as investors did in Germany, rather than of numerous individual railroads and industrial companies.

No doubt many of the big American banks would have been headquartered in the nation's largest city. In a world with less need for interbank correspondent relationships, for coordination of complex international securities underwriting syndicates, or for pro-active representation of investors on numerous corporate boards, however, location in New York might have been much less compelling. Instead, domestic universal bankers might have done best to locate closer to the geographically dispersed headquarters of their portfolio companies.

Under the BUS-survival scenario, New York, as the nation's largest city, its principal port, and site of its most active public securities markets, might very well have been the locus of a high concentration of financial services employment. But the balance sheets of the City's banks would have accounted for a smaller proportion of the total national capital stock and the volume of activity in the securities markets might have been much smaller than it was. Thus, aggregate size of the City's financial services sector and the magnitude of its impact on the City's economy as a whole would have been smaller.

It seems reasonable to assume that, if the Bank of the United States had continued operating more or less permanently and more or less effectively, the U.S. financial system would have been structured very differently from the way it was. But is BUS survival plausible? It may have been because, as noted above, the failure to renew the federal BUS charters was a close thing politically. Historian Edwin J. Perkins has shown that there was considerable room for compromise between pro- and anti-Bank political interests. The pro-Bank forces' decision to place renewal on Congress's 1832 legislative docket, four years before the charter was scheduled to expire, may have guaranteed that the BUS would become an issue in the presidential election campaign of that year. Perhaps the pro-Bank Whigs thought they had a winning issue, a not unreasonable view given that the charter renewal passed both houses of Congress in 1832 with comfortable, albeit, not veto-proof, majorities. Majorities also defeated amendments offered by Jackson's allies, not all of which would have jeopardized the Bank's ability to perform its functions effectively. Further, despite its vituperative tone, President Jackson's veto message included specific objections that echoed the defeated amendments. Instead of seeking a compromise with the President's anti-Bank allies, however, the pro-Bank forces responded in kind rhetorically, and Jackson's reelection in 1832 sealed the fate of the BUS as a federally chartered institution. We can never know whether Jackson would have accepted a revised act of Congress that allowed a somewhat modified BUS to continue operating effectively or would have stuck to his guns. But Perkins makes a strong case that, given a bit more adept political maneuvering by BUS President Nicholas Biddle, a somewhat modified but still effective institution's survival beyond 1836 was plausible (Perkins, 1987).

By the end of the displaced nineteenth century, New York was established as the Western Hemisphere's predominant financial center. This position may not have been the inevitable result of the City's size and position in the urban hierarchy. If the United States had had a central bank through the entire nineteenth century, then the money and capital markets that evolved might very well have turned out to be much more decentralized and geographically dispersed than the New York-centered structure that did develop. The failure of the U.S. political system to reach a plausible compromise with respect to the renewal of the BUS charter should, therefore, be counted as an important contingency in the City's economy history.

## References

Bodenhorn, H. (2000). *A History of Banking in Antebellum America: Financial Markets and Economic Development in an Era of Nation Building* (pp. 11–15). Cambridge: Cambridge University Press.

Bodenhorn, H. (2006). Bank Chartering and Political Corruption in Antebellum New York: Free Banking as Reform. In E. L. Gleaser & C. Goldin (Eds.), *Corruption and Reform: Lessons from America's Economic History*. Chicago: University of Chicago Press.

Bodenhorn, H., & Rockoff, H. (1992). Regional Interest Rates in Antebellum America. In C. Goldin & H. Rockoff (Eds.), *Strategic Factors in Nineteenth Century American Economic History: A Volume to Honor Robert W. Fogel* (pp. 159–187). Chicago: University of Chicago Press.

Census, U. B. (1976). *The Statistical History of the United States from Colonial Times to the Present*. New York: Basic Books.

Champ, B. (2007, December). *The National Banking System: A Brief History* (pp. 29–33, Working Paper). Cleveland: Federal Reserve Bank of Cleveland.

Comptroller of the Currency. (1910). *Annual Report of the Comptroller of the Currency to the Third Session of the Sixty-First Congress of the United States.* Washington, DC: U.S. Government Printing Office.

Davis, L. E., & Cull, R. J. (1994). *International Capital Markets and American Economic Growth, 1820–1914.* Cambridge: Cambridge University Press.

Gorton, G. (1996). Reputation Formation in Early Bank Note Markets. *Journal of Political Economy, 104*(2), 346–397.

Gorton, G. (1999). Pricing Free Bank Notes. *Journal of Monetary Economics, 44,* 33–64.

J. Moody & Co. (1901). *Moodys Manual of Railroads and Corporation Securities.* New York: J. Moody & Co.

Myers, M. G. (1931). *The New York Money Market, Volume I, Origins and Development.* New York: Columbia University Press.

O'Brien, S. (2014, December 18). *The Complete History of the Original Dow Dozen.* Retrieved from Dividend.com http://www.dividend.com/dividend-education/the-complete-history-of-the-original-dow-dozen/.

Perkins, E. J. (1987). Lost Opportunities for Compromise in the Bank War: A Reassessment of Jackson's Veto Message. *The Business History Review, 61*(4), 531–550.

Rolnick, A. J., & Weber, W. E. (1983). New Evidence on the Free Banking Era. *The American Economic Review, 73*(5), 1080–1091.

Tilly, R. (1998). Universal Banking in Historical Perspective. *Journal of Institutional and Theoretical Economics, 154*(1), 7–32.

Timberlake, R. H. (1984, February). The Central Banking Role of Clearing House Associations. *Journal of Money, Credit, and Banking, 16*(1), 1–15.

U.S. Department of the Interior, Census-Office. (1872). *Ninth Census—Volume I.* Washington, DC: U.S. Government Printing Office.

# 10

# Global City, Mark 1

The conditions that foster the international movement of goods, money, and people, which characterized all of the displaced nineteenth century, became more pronounced in the years between 1870 and 1914 than they had been before or would be again until late in the twentieth century. In particular, the expansion of the flow of commodities, capital, and migrants, especially across and around the Atlantic Ocean, accelerated noticeably over the decades after the American Civil War. While English investors had resumed buying U.S. financial assets shortly after peace was restored in 1815 and while the first wave of mass migration between Northwestern Europe and the United States began in the late 1840s, the movement of people and capital across the Atlantic did not get underway in earnest until the second half of the displaced nineteenth century. By the eve of World War I, foreign investments accounted for between one-quarter and one-third of the wealth of the major European powers. Between 1897 and 1914, the total value of foreign assets held by U.S. residents quintupled, reaching $3.5 billion, the same order of magnitude as the total assets of U.S. life insurance companies at the time. And between 1850 and 1914, some 55 million Europeans migrated to the Western Hemisphere or Australia (Davis &



A. Gurwitz, *Atlantic Metropolis*, Palgrave Studies in American Economic History,
https://doi.org/10.1007/978-3-030-13352-8_10

Cull, 2000; Estevadeordal, Frantz, & Taylor, 2002, p. 2; Frieden, 2006, p. 209; 2006, p. 20; Hatton & Williamson, 1998, p. 3; O'Rourke & Williamson, Globalization and History, MIT Press, 2002, p. 209; U.S. Bureau of the Census, 1976, p. 1,061).

The half century from the 1870s through part of the 1920s was also, in many respects, New York City's economic heyday. This was the period of the City's greatest absolute growth and also a time when, in an echo of the era of catastrophic agglomeration, the City's population grew faster than that of the United States as a whole (Fig. 10.1). This chapter and the next delineate the ways in which these two phenomena—accelerating globalization and the thriving New York economy—were closely connected. This chapter focuses on the local impacts of the flow of goods and capital between Europe and the United States. Chapter 11 will examine the effects of mass immigration from Europe through, and especially, to New York City.

On first consideration, the City's robust growth around the turn of the twentieth century does not necessarily reflect anything unique about New York; much of what happened locally was driven by broad trends in the geographic distribution of the U.S. population.

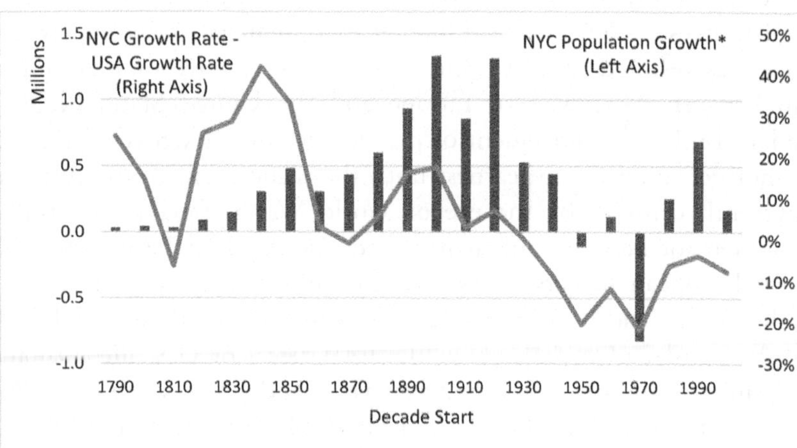


**Fig. 10.1** New York City population growth by decade, absolute and relative to U.S. population growth (Carter, 2006)

The period between 1880 and 1930 was a time of rapid industrialization in the United States and, therefore, by the logic of the new economic geography ("NEG," see Chapter 5), also a period of urbanization. Over this period, the proportion of Americans living in big cities[1] rose by an average of 3.2 percentage points per decade; the equivalent averages for the prior and subsequent half centuries were 1.8 and −1.4 percentage points, respectively. As the U.S. population grew and became more urbanized, the number of big cities increased. In 1880, there were 19 U.S. cities with populations greater than 100,000; by 1930, the number had risen to 80. As the size and number of big cities grew, the U.S. system of cities retained its hierarchical structure with New York at its apex. As anticipated under Zipf's law (see Chapter 8), the population of the second largest U.S. city continued to be roughly half that of New York even as Chicago replaced Philadelphia in the number-two position between 1880 and 1890. In 1880, Philadelphia's population was 44.3% New York's; in 1890, Chicago's population was 43.9% of New York's.[2]

These broad national trends notwithstanding, the City's economic vibrancy during this period does require some New York-specific explanation. For one thing, the City's economic expansion did not simply follow the bare-bones NEG framework in which the geographically footloose industries with the greatest economies of scale agglomerate in the City at the apex of the urban hierarchy. Instead, one particular group of industries that were not characterized by particularly strong economies of scale in production account for the largest proportion of New York's economic growth over the five post-Civil War decades.

One might also wonder why Chicago did not overtake New York as it had Philadelphia. In fact, one particularly well-informed group of contemporary observers raised exactly that question. In 1905, the Board of Trade of the United Kingdom ("BoT") began conducting a series of detailed statistical studies of the "condition of the working classes" in several countries. In 1909, after completing studies of the

[1]Jurisdictions with 1990 populations of 100,000 or more (Carter, 2006).

[2]For both years, New York's population is the sum populations of the five counties that would become Burroughs of New York City in 1898.

UK, Germany, France, and Belgium, the BoT turned its attention to the United States, where the research team collected data from 28 towns and cities, including both New York and Chicago. In their report, published in 1911 the BoT researchers assessed the situation at the apex of the U.S. urban hierarchy as follows.

> The growth of many of the cities of the Middle West is, it is true, considerably more rapid than is that of New York, and the remoteness of the city from the great centres of primary production is probably destined to be a permanent handicap. To some extent this is counteracted by the railway system of which New York is a point of great concentration; by the Erie Canal, which establishes a direct conexion with the Great Lakes and thus with the agricultural States of the Middle West and North; and by the ramifications of the financial, manufacturing and commercial interests which are concerned with the continued prosperity of New York. But the centre of population in the United States has been moving slowly westwards, and the trend of manufacture is towards the centre of production of raw material and of food. Should these two great tendencies become more marked, or should the influx of immigrants be checked either by restrictive legislation or by other causes, it is improbable that the rate at which New York has been expanding will continue and ultimately its position in the States is not unlikely to be challenged. But meanwhile it is supreme and is growing at a pace that if continued will make it in a few years the greatest city in the world. (United Kingdom Board of Trade, 1911, p. 2)

Chicago, in particular, had some clear advantages as a location for business operations of national scope; it was the continental rail transportation hub and was geographically closer to more of the U.S. population than coastal New York. In 1880, Chicago was 327 miles closer to the U.S. population center than New York. Americans continued to move westward so that by 1920 Chicago was 489 miles "more central" than New York. Indeed, New Yorkers of the time were at least somewhat worried about being overtaken; this possibility was apparently a rallying cry for New York's municipal consolidation advocates during the 1890s (Burrows & Wallace, 1999, p. 1252).

Most importantly from an economist's perspective, evidence indicates Chicago workers across a range of skill levels earned noticeably higher real wages than New Yorkers early in the twentieth century. As discussed in Chapter 8, New York's population expanded rapidly during the antebellum period despite what appear to have been relatively low real wages. That newcomers to the country would have chosen to locate in the fastest growing places is not surprising. What is somewhat unexpected is in the context of a NEG model of regional growth is that the fastest growing place was not the one with the highest real wages. And as was probably the case during the antebellum period, the real wages paid to New York workers at the time when the immigrant inflow was at its peak and the City was achieving its fastest absolute population growth were somewhat lower than what many of them could have earned in some other U.S. cities.

The local cost of working-class housing was the culprit that reduced real wages in New York during the antebellum decades. That also seems to have been the case sixty years later. In Chapter 8, the analysis of the impact of housing prices on real wages in New York City relative to elsewhere had to rely on indirect and circumstantial evidence. For the early twentieth century, by contrast, direct evidence on point is available from an unlikely source. The BoT Report[3] (United Kingdom Board of Trade, 1911) on the United States, published in 1911, presented and analyzed data on nominal wages paid to five categories of workers, typical household budgets for a variety of ethnic groups in different regions, and monthly rentals for apartments. Housing price data for the larger cities included typical monthly rentals for apartments ranging from two or three to four or five rooms. In addition to the statistical tabulations, the Report included narrative descriptions of conditions in each city, and, as was to be expected, the greatest level of detail was provided for New York.

[3]Conveniently, data for New York City was used as the benchmark for comparison with other places. Inconveniently, prices were quoted in pounds, shillings, and pence. Exchange rates varied very little under the gold standard of the time, so all conversions into U.S. dollar prices have been based on a constant exchange rate of $4.87 per pound, the average for 1909.

**Table 10.1** Average nominal wage indexes and price indexes for cities with 1910 populations greater than 250,000 (United Kingdom Board of Trade, 1911, p. lxxix)

| City | Average nominal wage[a] | Food price index | Rent index | Real wage index[b] |
|---|---|---|---|---|
| New York | 100 | 100 | 100 | 100 |
| Chicago | 102 | 94 | 70 | 118 |
| Philadelphia | 87 | 96 | 79 | 96 |
| St. Louis | 102 | 97 | 101 | 103 |
| Boston | 88 | 105 | 82 | 90 |
| Cleveland | 89 | 99 | 64 | 101 |
| Baltimore | 84 | 97 | 54 | 100 |
| Pittsburg | 95 | 102 | 94 | 95 |
| Minneapolis-St. Paul | 91 | 95 | 77 | 102 |
| Detroit | 82 | 91 | 57 | 101 |
| Milwaukee | 89 | 93 | 66 | 105 |
| Cincinnati | 90 | 92 | 93 | 98 |
| Newark | 95 | 106 | 78 | 98 |
| New Orleans | 96 | 100 | 72 | 105 |
| 13-city average | 92 | 98 | 78 | 101 |

[a]The numbers in the first column are the unweighted averages of nominal wage index numbers for skilled workers in the building trades (bricklayers, stonemasons, stonecutters, carpenters, plasterers, plumbers, structural iron workers, and painters), unskilled workers in the building trades (hod carriers, and bricklayers, and laborers), skilled workers in the "engineering" (manufacturing) trades (iron-moulders, machinists blacksmiths, and patternmakers), unskilled workers in the engineering trades (laborers), and hand compositors in job print shops
[b]Assumes 30% of earnings is spent on rent and 70% on "food"

Table 10.1 summarizes some of the findings of the BoT study. On average across the 13 cities other than New York with 1910 populations greater than 250,000 nominal wages across five industrial/skill categories averaged about eight percent less than what was paid in New York. In only two large Midwestern cities, Chicago and St. Louis were average wages comparable to what workers earned in New York. Food prices were a bit higher in New York than in the other large cities on average. Rents, on the other hand, were substantially higher on average in New York than anywhere else except St. Louis.[4] In general, the

[4]There was some suggestion in the BoT Report's narrative material on St. Louis that the average quality of housing in that city may have been somewhat better than elsewhere.

higher cost of living in New York was roughly equal to the nominal wage premium local workers received so that cost-of-living-adjusted real wages were approximately equal on average across cities, industries, and skill categories. The comparison with Chicago is, however, noticeable. Nominal wages in the second city were, if anything, a bit higher, food prices somewhat lower, and rents about 30% lower than in New York. If we assume that New Yorkers spent about 30% of their income on rent, these wage and price differences translate into a Chicago real wage premium of about 18%. This was much smaller than the differential between Europe and the overseas destinations of that continent's emigrants; between 1900 and 1913, for example, the average Italian emigrant would have been realistically seeking an opportunity to more than double his real wage (Hatton & Williamson, 1998, p. 35). The Chicago premium relative to New York City reflected in the BoT study was, however, substantially larger than the estimated three percent advantage in median real wages across selected occupations for the East North Central versus the Middle Atlantic regions of the United States in 1890 (Rosenbloom, 2002, p. 124). Further, the cost of moving from the East Coast to the Midwest, in terms of out-of-pocket expenses and travel time, would have been a fraction of trans-Atlantic migration. Finally, for most potential migrants the cultural difference between New York and Chicago would have been smaller than between New York and anywhere in Europe.

Why, then, didn't Chicago overtake New York as it had Philadelphia? The hypothesis examined in this chapter and the next can now be stated more precisely as follows; it was the process of economic globalization that determined the magnitude and industrial composition of New York's economic growth and that enabled the City to maintain its position at the pinnacle of the U.S. urban hierarchy. Put differently, if the global commodities, capital, and labor markets had not been integrating as dramatically as they were during this period, then Chicago might well have overtaken New York as the largest City in North America.

The previous three chapters discussed the direct and indirect impacts of New York's port on the City's antebellum economic trajectory. It was the City's position as the busiest conduit for imports, beginning in the immediate aftermath of War of 1812, that positioned New York as the right place at the right time to benefit most from catastrophic agglomeration in the 1840s. It was also New York's role as the principal distribution point for imported goods that, in the absence of a national bank, attracted a large proportion of the nation's interbank deposits and thereby helped enhance the role of the City's securities markets and established local community of financial institutions as the nation's de facto central bank. And New York's critical masses of resident immigrants created the community institutions and social networks that enabled the City's employers to attract a large industrial workforce while paying nominal wage rates that fell short of offsetting the high local cost of living. For all of the same reasons, at the end of the Civil War New York City was well positioned to benefit from increasing global flows of goods, capital, and people.

## International Flows I: Commodities Through the Port

As discussed in Chapter 5, by the 1820s New York was the premier U.S. port, a position it was to maintain throughout the displaced nineteenth century and for some time thereafter. That said, New York's share of the total volume of U.S. international trade declined gradually over the post-Civil War decades. Table 10.2 and Fig. 10.2 quantify these points.

New York was the premier U.S. port throughout the period in two senses. First, more inward and outward bound cargo by value moved through New York than through any other port. Second, no other port came close to rivaling New York. With only one exception—exports through New Orleans during the cotton boom of the 1830s—New York handled cargo worth more than twice as much as the second busiest port. Indeed, in most years in most categories New York handled more imports and exports by value than the second through tenth busiest ports combined.

Although the City maintained its top-ranked position, New York's share of U.S. imports, exports, and total trade all declined over the post-Civil War decades (Fig. 10.2). A combination of shifts in the nature of

**Table 10.2** Value of exports and imports at U.S. ports during the displaced nineteenth century (Albion, 1939, pp. 390–391; U.S. Department of Commerce and Labor, Bureau of Statistics, 1912, pp. 48–50; U.S. House of Representatives, 1911, pp. 71–138, 193–244, 283–314)

| | | Domestic exports | Re-exports | Imports | Total trade |
|---|---|---|---|---|---|
| 1831 | New York % | 30.9% | | 55.3% | 44.6% |
| | Second busiest port | Louisiana | | Massachusetts | Massachusetts |
| | Second busiest % | 19.8% | | 13.6% | 11.4% |
| | 2–10 Total % | 58.0% | | 38.8% | 47.3% |
| 1871 | New York % | 50.8% | 70.6% | 66.1% | 58.6% |
| | Second busiest port | New Orleans | San Francisco | Boston | New Orleans |
| | Second busiest % | 10.1% | 10.0% | 9.9% | 10.1% |
| | 2–10 Total % | 43.5% | 21.4% | 26.3% | 34.7% |
| 1911 | New York % | 36.7% | 44.9% | 57.7% | 46.2% |
| | Second busiest port | Galveston | Niagara, NY | Boston | New Orleans |
| | Second busiest % | 11.0% | 9.3% | 7.6% | 6.7% |
| | 2–10 Total % | 42.7% | 40.8% | 30.4% | 35.9% |

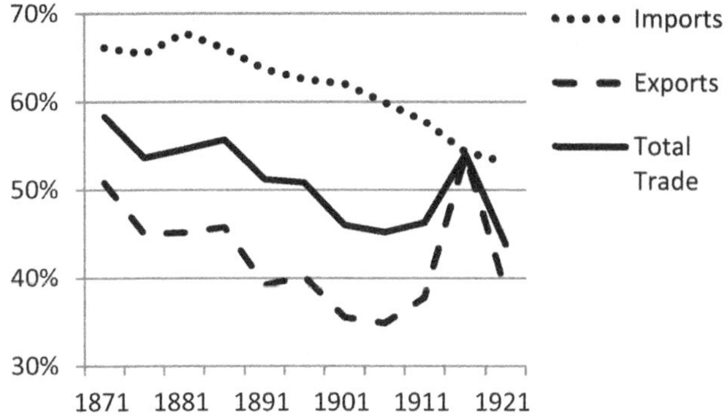


**Fig. 10.2** New York's share of total merchandise trade by value (U.S. Department of the Treasury, 2018)

U.S. international trade, some relatively advantageous to New York, others, somewhat more numerous and collectively more powerful, disadvantageous, explain the downward trend in New York's market share. First, as both Table 10.1 and Fig. 10.2 indicate, New York's share of U.S. imports exceeded its share of exports throughout the period. The latter grew more quickly than the former during the post-Civil War decades; between 1870 and 1913 the nominal value of U.S. exports grew about 15% faster than imports (United States Census Bureau, 1976, p. 865). So even if New York had maintained its shares of exports and imports, the proportion of total trade moving through the City would have diminished.

Second, as Table 10.2 also indicates, New York retained its role as an important Atlantic entrepôt as reflected in the City's large share of the re-export trade. Thus, the decline in re-exports from 4.8% of total exports in 1871 to 0.8% in 1911 probably also reduced the New York's share of total traffic. A near doubling of the proportion of total U.S. trade with the Pacific region—from 5.9% in 1871 to 11.4% in 1911—probably also tended to reduce New York's share of total trade, although the City did a substantial amount of business with South and East Asian destinations. Finally, historians Edwin Burrows and Mike Wallace suggest that the deterioration of New York's port infrastructure may have induced some shippers to direct traffic elsewhere (Burrows & Wallace, 1999, p. 949).

At the same time, a change in the industrial composition of the U.S. export mix probably partially offset the impact of these adverse trends. As Table 10.3 indicates, manufactured goods, as opposed to bulk commodities, accounted for a relatively large share of exports shipped from New York at both the beginning and the end of the

**Table 10.3** Composition of U.S. and New York exports by stage of processing (United States Census Bureau, 1976, p. 889)

| | 1871 | | 1911 | |
|---|---|---|---|---|
| | New York (%) | USA (%) | New York (%) | USA (%) |
| Raw materials | 39.50 | 57.90 | 11.50 | 34.90 |
| Semi-finished goods | 30.00 | 23.90 | 34.60 | 29.80 |
| Finished products | 30.10 | 18.00 | 45.40 | 28.80 |

post-Civil War period while the share of this category of products grew substantially.

Still, increasing trade total trade volumes more than offset the impact of the decreasing market share; the value of goods flowing through New York increased 2.5-fold between 1871 and 1911. The rising value of commodities transshipped through New York's port must surely have generated lots of direct employment, as reflected in the City's 4.82 concentration ratio for "Longshoremen and stevedores" and indirect employment in the general employment category of "Wholesale dealers, importers and exporters" (concentration ratio = 2.75) and, thus, must surely have contributed to local growth over the period. But the increase in local international trade-related employment does not help explain why New York's population was growing so much faster than the United States as a whole over this period (Fig. 10.1). Between 1871 and 1911, while the combined nominal value of exports and imports moving through New York City was growing at an average annual rate of 2.4% total nominal U.S. GNP was increasing at an average 4.0% annual rate (United States Census Bureau, 1976, p. 215).

## International Flows II: Capital Through the Banks

Chapter 9 examined the ways in which New York banks' position as the central reserve depositories for U.S. financial institutions drew the bulk of the Nation's securities market activity to the City via the call loan market. That discussion also noted one of the reasons why American corporations and governments seeking long-term capital raised funds by offering stocks and bonds through public financial markets rather than relying on "universal" banks. This chapter focuses on another reason why the investment banking industry—which facilitated the operations of securities markets—developed as a cornerstone of the U.S. financial system and why that industry became so concentrated in New York. Specifically, the investment banks that emerged in the United States over the last 50 years of the displaced nineteenth century were profoundly international in their origins and operations.

British and other European investors' impact on the development of U.S. capital markets during the nineteenth century is not apparent if we look only at the aggregate magnitude of foreign investments in the country. Economic historians Lance Davis and Robert Cull conclude that net foreign investment in the United States accounted for a little less than five percent of the $60 billion increase in the nation's capital stock between 1799 and 1900 (Davis & Cull, 2000, p. 734). That five percent did, however, exert disproportionately large influence on the structure and functioning of the financial markets that evolved.

Foreigners who invested in the United States did not spread their funds across the broad range of uses of capital in the economy. European capital played relatively little role, for example, in the development of Midwestern farmland, in the construction of housing, or in the building of cities, all of which were financed for the most part by individual household savings or by wealthy U.S. residents. Foreigners purchasing U.S. assets probably anticipated that they would want to repatriate their funds at some point and, therefore, tended to favor investments that could be sold for something close to a fair price in a reasonably liquid market.

Such liquid investments were available as early as the late eighteenth century thanks in large part to the financial program devised by Treasury Secretary Alexander Hamilton and adopted by Congress during the first Washington administration. That set of policies—federal assumption of outstanding state Revolutionary War debts and the establishment of the Bank of the United States (BUS)—created two investment securities: government bonds and BUS stock. The existence of these new, high-quality securities attracted speculators and market makers to the newly organized public financial markets in major U.S. cities. The liquidity of these securities and their convincing credit quality, in turn, attracted both domestic and foreign investors, so that "[b]y 1803, more than half of the government's debt and the stock of the Bank [of the United States], and fully half of all American securities issued to that date were held by European investors" (Rousseau & Sylla, 2005, p. 6).

Subsequent decades saw the introduction of state government securities, beginning with the New York obligations issued to finance construction of the Erie Canal. The latter were being quoted in London in

1817, the year that construction began (Davis & Cull, 2000, p. 745). Other states followed New York's lead with their own public bond offerings to finance internal improvements, and state-chartered banks raised capital by issuing stocks. As the century progressed and at an accelerating rate after the Civil War, stock and bond issues of railroad companies came to dominate U.S. public securities markets and foreign investments in those markets. By 1880, railroad issues, mostly bonds, accounted for 72% of all foreign long-term investments in the United States (Davis & Cull, 2000, p. 742).

Europeans did not necessarily have to execute transactions in U.S. domestic financial markets in order to invest in the United States. Many U.S. stocks and bonds were quoted and traded in Europe and an increasing number were listed on the London Stock Exchange (LSE); by 1890, when 118 stocks were listed on the New York Stock Exchange (NYSE), 108 U.S. companies were listed on the LSE. Further, the US stocks that traded in London were more diversified than those listed on the NYSE. Railroads, the type of company most familiar to stock investors in both countries, accounted for 76% of the issues traded on the NYSE but only 34% of U.S. issues traded in London (Davis & Cull, 2000, p. 789). British investors were apparently more comfortable with investments in industrial and financial companies than were Americans.

## Geographic Consolidation

A large proportion of the U.S. dollar-denominated assets accumulated by Europeans during the nineteenth century were obtained in the first instance when a British manufacturer or a British financial intermediary extended a three-, six-, or twelve-month commercial credit to an American importer. The American importers, in turn, could pay back these commercial loans by purchasing a "sterling bill of exchange" from an American entity to which, say, a British cotton importer owed money.

The bill would then be delivered to England, and the British importer would pay the American's debt. If, as often happened, however, Bills of Exchange were unavailable or were selling at a high premium to face value, the American could ship gold to Europe. Alternatively, the British entity that was owed money by an American importer could to sell that receivable for dollars and use the proceeds to purchase U.S. stocks or bonds (Myers, 1931, pp. 63–65).

By the eve of the Civil War, much of this commercial short-term lending and longer-term investing was intermediated by a small number of merchant banks headquartered in the UK and their agents or affiliates in the United States. The composition of this group changed over time but some of these banks' successor institutions—J.P. Morgan Chase & Co., Edmond de Rothschild Private Merchant Banking LLP, Brown Brothers Harriman & Co.—remain active in the twenty-first century. The close linkage between trade finance and Europeans' accumulation of U.S. government and corporate securities drew both activities to the City that was both the nation's leading import port and the site of its most active financial markets.

Before the Civil War, however, locating their U.S. base of operations in New York was apparently not particularly compelling for these institutions; the agglomeration of trans-Atlantic investment banking activity in the City was not particularly "catastrophic." During most of the antebellum period, trade finance played a larger role in these banks' business mix than investment banking activity. The profits earned on the securities business by George Peabody & Co., the London-based predecessor of the House of Morgan, for example, did not exceed net earnings on the firm's mercantile credit business until 1858 (Carosso, 1987, p. 74). It was to be expected, therefore, that the distribution of international banking activity would have been distributed geographically roughly in proportion to the dollar value of trade.

New York was, to be sure, the busiest port, but late in the antebellum period it accounted for only a little more than half of total U.S. trading activity (imports + exports) (Albion, 1939, pp. 390–391). Accordingly, New York was no more than the first among rough equals as a center for international banking activity before the Civil War. Most of the major merchant banks engaged in trans-Atlantic finance maintained active agency and affiliate relationships in other East and Gulf Coast port cities through the antebellum period. In the early 1850s, well after British investors began to accumulate U.S. government and railroad bonds,

Baring Brothers rejected the suggestion that their New York agent should exercise central control over the Firm's American operations and continued to do business through London-directed, independent agents in Boston, New Orleans, and Mobile (Hidy, 1949, pp. 421–422). Barings was apparently never particularly enamored with New York; as late as 1886, the firm appointed Boston-based Kidder Peabody as its exclusive American Agent (Carosso, 1987, p. 155). The House of Morgan did not establish an independent New York presence until 1861 when John Pierpont Morgan opened his own shop. Before then and only since 1859, Pierpont had been working at Duncan, Sherman & Co., the most active but far from the sole U.S. correspondent of George Peabody & Co., the London firm of which Pierpont's Father, Junius Morgan, was the managing partner.

Two other of the major merchant banking firms engaged in transatlantic business did center their North American operations in New York. The Rothschilds' sole East Coast U.S. agents, until 1837 J. L. and S. I. Joseph & Co and thereafter August Belmont & Co., were located in New York City. Correspondence among Rothschild family members, however, indicates dissatisfaction with this arrangement. Historian Niall Ferguson quotes James Rothschild, head of the French branch of the Family in the 1830s, complaining about Belmont's unwillingness to travel to Philadelphia to collect a debt (Ferguson, 1998, pp. 9,249–9,264/1,4013).

Only one large international banking house intentionally concentrated its U.S. command and control functions in New York before the Civil War. This firm, also the only one of the majors with an unambiguous North American pedigree, had been founded in Baltimore in 1800. A major reorganization in 1839 created a unified partnership that operated through three separate firms: Brown Brothers & Co. in New York, Browns and Bowen in Philadelphia, and Brown, Shipley & Co. in Liverpool. Baltimore operations were handled by an agent in that City, as were transactions in Boston, Charleston, Savannah, Mobile, and New Orleans. The New York branch of the partnership exercised centralized, detailed control over Brown group U.S. operations (Perkins, 1971, pp. 422–426).

After the Civil War, however, the proportions of the trans-Atlantic banks' profits derived from trade finance and capital market activities began to shift; the former diminished in relative contribution and the latter increased (Carosso, 1987, p. 174). One reason was that U.S. domestic products began to replace manufactured imports. During the antebellum decades, for example, financing U.S. imports of British-made steel rails was an important part of the Peabody and Morgan banks' business and was, indeed, the way this group initially got their feet in the door of some of their American railroad investment banking clients. By the 1890s, the New York Life Insurance Company was underwriting bonds to finance Russian railroads' purchase of U.S.-made equipment (Carosso, 1987, pp. 402–403).

At the same time, the capital requirements of the U.S. private and public sectors were increasing rapidly. During the postwar decades, the rapidly expanding North American railroads' appetite for capital became voracious. During the 1850s, U.S. railroad track mileage increased an average of 2,142 miles per year with a peak of 2,465 miles in 1853. During the 1880s, the average was 5,708 miles per years with a peak of 12,876 in 1887 (United States Census Bureau, 1976, p. 731).

Further, the U.S. Federal government executed two huge, complex international financial transactions during the post-Civil War decades. The first and larger of the two aimed to refund the mostly short-maturity Civil War debt with long-term bonds. This operation involved a series of transactions executed between 1871 and 1879 totaling $1.4 billion, an amount that was nearly equal to the total national money supply at the time (Carosso, 1987, pp. 176–200; United States Census Bureau, 1976, p. 993).

The second U.S. Treasury capital markets operation aimed to replenish and stabilize the government's stock of gold during the 1890s. By the latter decades of the nineteenth century, foreign investors had accumulated a substantial volume of U.S. assets mostly in the form of stocks and bonds. To be deemed creditworthy under the gold standard of the time governments, businesses, and individuals had to be prepared to meet their financial obligations by delivering fixed weights of gold per dollar, pound, franc or mark. The assets that met banks' reserve requirements also had to be convertible into gold on demand, and this meant that the amount of gold in a country determined the amount of money available in the country. Under the gold standard, foreigners could exchange their U.S. assets for gold at a fixed dollar price per ounce and ship the proceeds back home, thereby reducing the amount of gold available in the United States, potentially diminishing the nation's money supply, and risking an economic contraction. In most other industrializing countries, the central bank could mitigate the impact of foreign investors' gold sales on the nation's money supply by, for example, raising local interest rates to attract offsetting specie inflows. But the United States did not have a central bank, and unmitigated gold outflows occasionally threatened to jeopardize governments' and the private sector's ability to meet their financial obligations. In the early 1890s, a variety of circumstances had depleted the U.S. government's gold reserves to a dangerously low level and the Treasury contracted with a trans-Atlantic syndicate of banks to underwrite a $60 million bond issue, to deliver the value of the sale proceeds in gold, and to follow-up with open market operations on the government's behalf to keep the gold reserves above $100 million (Carosso, 1987, pp. 311–349).

Bankers soon realized that the way to market large volumes of new securities so as to minimize the risk of winding up with a lot of unsold paper was to offer the stocks or bonds simultaneously on both sides of the Atlantic to as many potential investors as possible. Raising capital for railroads and other industrial enterprises and executing complex financial transactions for the Federal government, therefore, involved marketing identical securities simultaneously in London and the United States through multi-firm syndicates in both markets. Identifying the price at which the market would clear for the volume of the stocks or bonds on offer involved absorbing and processing detailed, rapidly changing information about market conditions in the U.S. and Europe and frequent communication between the U.S. and UK syndicates, among the members of each syndicate, with issuing clients, and with large investors. More and more up-to-date information, more potential syndicate members with London-based affiliates, more large investors, and more representatives of more issuers were present in New York than in any other North American city (Carosso, 1970, pp. 51–78).

The management of the U.S. Treasury's gold holdings illustrates the information-intensivity of nineteenth-century investment banking operations. Replenishing the Treasury's gold inventory with the proceeds of the $60 million bond issue did not solve the government's problem because sporadic gold outflows continued. The Treasury's investment banking team, led by J. P. Morgan, had contracted to assist the government in maintaining the Treasury's holdings above $100 million by undertaking open market operations in currencies and specie. Doing so in a way that did not expose the bankers to excessive risk required detailed day-to-day information on the level of Treasury gold stocks, on likely near-term inflows and outflows, on gold prices in New York and London, and on likely near-term trends in general financial market conditions. Much of the essential information was only available in New York because the local U.S. sub-Treasury office, located across Wall Street from the offices of J. P. Morgan & Co, was the nation's most active gold repository. Further, customs revenue was the Treasury's main source of gold receipts, and the New York was the conduit for 65% of U.S. imports in 1890 (Work Projects Administration for the City of New York, 2004, p. 184).

While access to this dense information nexus eventually drew the bulk of U.S. investment banking activity and the leadership of the international banking business to New York, even after the Civil War the geographical shift was not immediate or complete. The lead bank for the first transaction of the government's refunding program in 1871 was Jay Cooke & Co., the Philadelphia firm that had managed the U.S. government's war-time debt issues, and its London affiliate. And Boston-based Kidder, Peabody continued to leverage its relationships with New England investors and with Baring Brothers to retain a leadership role in some important railroad financings through the late nineteenth century. After Jay Cooke & Co. failed in 1873, however, four trans-Atlantic banks or banking groups competed to lead domestic distribution of the subsequent Treasury refunding tranches: Drexel Morgan & Co., Morton, Bliss & Co., J. & W. Seligman & Co., and August Belmont & Co. All four were based in New York and were led by individuals who had moved permanently to New York from Hartford by way of London, Vermont by way of Boston, Bavaria by way of California, and the German Rhineland, respectively. These firms, along with two other New York-based banks, Kuhn, Loeb & Co. and Speyer & Co., also assumed dominant roles in railroad and later industrial company finance.

European, mostly British, investors provided a large proportion but not all of the capital that fueled U.S. industrialization. This foreign investment was channeled through public financial markets rather than through universal banks because funds from both the U.S. and Europe had to be combined on corporate balance sheets, because British capital financing was also market-based, because foreign investors had confidence in the U.S. judicial system, and because U.S. stock and bond exchanges, like their UK counterparts, provided securities holders seeking to sell positions with ready liquidity most of the time.

Most of the U.S. dollars Europeans accumulated originated in trade credits, most of which was mediated through the main U.S. port. New York securities exchanges, lubricated by the ready availability of call loans, functioned smoothly at most times. For these and other reasons, more of the information trans-Atlantic banks needed to do their business was more readily available in New York than anywhere else in the Western Hemisphere. Further, the fact that the New York banking community acting through its Clearing House Association had cobbled together a reasonably effective, albeit not fool-proof, mechanism for heading-off incipient financial crises may have given foreign (and domestic) investors comfort in allocating money to this market.

In these ways, the flow of foreign capital, the development of U.S. public financial markets, and the agglomeration of activity of those markets in New York City reinforced each other. Thus, by the end of the displaced nineteenth century investment banking had become an important industry highly concentrated in New York City. Thus the New York employment concentration ratios for "bankers and bank officials" and "stockbrokers" were 3.41 and 4.69, respectively, in 1910.

The aim of this chapter, however, was to account for the rapid expansion of New York City's total population and overall economy over the fifty years between 1870 and 1920. As important as it was, the development of the investment banking industry cannot account for more than a small fraction of this growth. The 1870 census enumerated 3,853 residents of New York City and Brooklyn employed "in banking and brokerage of money and stocks." In 1910, 14,489 residents of the five boroughs were working as "bankers and bank officials" or as "stockbrokers." This represents a 276% increase, but over the same period total employment in all occupations increased by 342%. No doubt the bankers and brokers were much better paid than the average New York worker and, therefore, had much more to spend on locally produced goods and services. No doubt, too, some substantial part of the quintupling of the number of lawyers in New York City between 1870 and 1910, from 2,012 to 10,661, can be attributed to the increasing volume of financial transactions. For these and other reasons, the growth of the financial services employment would have had a larger "multiplier" impact on the overall economy than, say, cigar manufacturing.

Still no reasonable multiplier assumption could translate the 10,636 increase in the number of local financiers between 1870 and 1910 into 1.7 million more employed New Yorkers at the end of that period than there had been at the beginning. And even taken together the impact of the rising flow of goods through New York's port and the increasing volume of financial transactions executed by its bankers cannot account for more than a small fraction of the City's rapid population growth around the turn of the twentieth century. What were the masses of the era's new New Yorkers drawn to the City to do?

## References

Albion, R. G. (1939). *The Rise of New York Port (1815–1860)*. New York: Scribner's.

Burrows, E. G., & Wallace, M. (1999). *Gotham: A History of New York City to 1898* (p. 1252). Oxford: Oxford University Press.

Carosso, V. P. (1970). *Investment Banking in America: A History*. Cambridge, MA: Harvard University Press.

Carosso, V. P. (1987). *The Morgans: Private International Bankers, 1854–1913*. Cambridge, MA: Harvard University Press.

Carter, S. B. (2006). *Table Aa22035*. Retrieved from Historical Statistics of the United States Millennial Edition Online http://projects.ilt.columbia.edu/seneca/svcurric/images/byward2_early.html.

Davis, L., & Cull, R. J. (2000). International Capital Movements, Domestic Capital Markets, and American Economic Growth. In S. L. Engerman & R. E. Gallman (Eds.), *The Cambridge Economic History of the United States, Volume II: The Long Nineteenth Century* (pp. 733–812). Cambridge: Cambridge University Press.

Estevadeordal, A., Frantz, B., & Taylor, A. M. (2002, November). *The Rise and Fall of World Trade, 1870–1939* (NBER Working Paper 9318, p. 2).

Ferguson, N. (1998). *The House of Rothschild, Money's Prophets, 1798–1848*. New York: Penguin Books.

Frieden, J. A. (2006). *Global Capitalism: Its Fall and Rise in the Twentieth Century*. New York: W. W. Norton.

Hatton, T. J., & Williamson, J. G. (1998). *The Age of Mass Migration, Causes and Economic Impact*. Oxford: Oxford University Press.

Hidy, R. W. (1949). *The House of Baring in American Trade and Finance: English Merchant Bankers at Work, 1763–1861*. Cambridge, MA: Harvard University Press.

Myers, M. G. (1931). *The New York Money Market, Volume I, Origins and Development*. New York: Columbia University Press.

O'Rourke, K. H., & Williamson, J. G. (2002). *Globalization and History* (2000, p. 209, Frieden, Jeffrey A). Cambridge: MIT Press.

Perkins, E. J. (1971). Financing Antebellum Importers: The Role of Brown Bros. & Co. in Baltimore. *Business History Review, 45*(4), 421–451.

Rosenbloom, J. L. (2002). *Looking for Work, Searching for Workers*. Cambridge: Cambridge University Press.

Rousseau, P. L., & Sylla, R. (2005). Emerging Financial Markets and Early US Growth. *Explorations in Economic History, 42*, 1–26.

U.S. Bureau of the Census. (1976). *The Statistical History of the United States From Colonial Times to the Present* (p. 1061). New York: Basic Books.

U.S. Department of Commerce and Labor, Bureau of Statistics. (1912). *Fhte Foreign Commerce and Navigation of the United States in the Year ending June 30, 1911*. Washington: U.S. Government Printing Office.

U.S. Department of the Treasury, Office of the Comptroller of the Currency. (2018). *The Negotiable CD: National Bank Innovation in the 1960s*. Retrieved from History: 150 Years of the OCC https://www.occ.treas.gov/about/what-we-do/history/150th-negotiable-cd-article.html.

U.S. House of Representatives. (1911). *Annual Report of the Chief of the Bureau of Statistics of on the Commerce and Navigation of the United States*. Washington: U.S. Government Printing Office.

United Kingdom Board of Trade. (1911). *Cost of Living in American Towns, Report of an Enquiry of the Board of Trade into Working Class Rents, Housing and Retail Prices Together with the Rates of Wages in Certain Occupation in the Principal Industrial Towns of the United States of America*. London: His Majesty's Stationery Office.

United States Census Bureau. (1976). *The Statistical History of the United States from Colonial Times to the Present*. New York: Basic Books.

Work Projects Administration for the City of New York. (2004). *A Maritime History of New York*. New York: Going Coastal Inc.

# 11

# Perfectly Matched and Perfectly Timed

## International Flows III: Workers

Migration to the United States from abroad peaked during the decades from the 1880s through the 1910s both absolutely and in terms of percentage contribution to total U.S. population growth (Fig. 11.1). New York had been and remained, more than almost anywhere else in the United States, a city of immigrants. The census found that in 1910 immigrants or their children accounted for 78.6% of New York City's population. That was the second highest such statistic among the 99 U.S. counties with populations of 100,000 or greater in that year.[1] The increase in its foreign-born population accounted for 42.6% of New York's total population growth between 1880 and 1910, a figure exceeded by only two of the country's populous counties[2] (Haines & ISPCR, n.d.).

[1]The "New York City" statistic is for New York, Kings, Queens, and Richmond Counties. The count of the foreign born and their offspring only included white people. The first place County was St. Louis County, Minnesota (Duluth).

[2]This statistic was 50.0 for Hillsborough County, NH. The statistic for Essex County, MA, on Boston's North Shore exceeded the combined statistic for New York, Kings, Queens, and Richmond Counties, NY, in the third decimal place.



A. Gurwitz, *Atlantic Metropolis*, Palgrave Studies in American Economic History,
https://doi.org/10.1007/978-3-030-13352-8_11

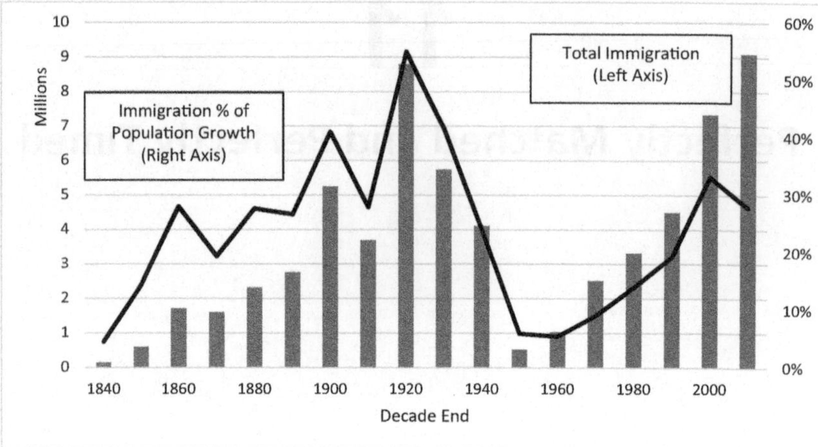


**Fig. 11.1** Immigration to the United States by decade (U.S. Census Bureau, 2018; U.S. Department of Homeland Security, 2018)

In addition to being large New York's immigrant population was distinguished by its ethnic composition. Immigrants from Italy and Russia, the latter mostly Jewish, were overrepresented in New York; Scandinavians and, to a lesser extent, Germans and natives of English-speaking countries were underrepresented (Table 11.1). One path toward an understanding of how and why the absolute growth of New York City's economy around the turn of the nineteenth century differed from and far exceeded that of other large U.S. cities, therefore, runs through the identities, endowments, motivations, and actions of the era's Italian and East European Jewish immigrants. Of particular interest are the ways in which these immigrants differed from those arriving from other countries.

## The Context: Atlantic Migration

The transformations of the Atlantic economies over the course of the nineteenth century—the widespread commercialization of agriculture, industrialization, and urbanization—could not have occurred without

**Table 11.1** 1910 foreign born by places of U.S. residence and birth (U.S. Department of Commerce, Bureau of the Census, 1912, pp. 781, 826)

| Birthplace | USA | New York City | Chicago | Philadelphia |
|---|---|---|---|---|
| Percent foreign born (%) | 14.7 | 40.8 | 35.9 | 24.8 |
| *Birthplace* | *Percent of foreign born by birthplace* | | | |
| Italy (%) | 9.9 | 17.4 | 5.9 | 11.7 |
| Russia and Finland (%) | 12.8 | 25.3 | 15.6 | 23.8 |
| English-speaking[a] (%) | 23.4 | 19.4 | 16.7 | 33.9 |
| Scandinavian (%) | 9.3 | 3.4 | 12.5 | 1.6 |
| Germany (%) | 18.5 | 14.2 | 23.1 | 16.1 |
| Austria (%) | 8.7 | 9.8 | 16.7 | 5.2 |
| Other (%) | 17.4 | 10.5 | 9.5 | 7.7 |

[a]England, Ireland, Scotland, Wales, and English-speaking Canada

the massive relocation of individuals and families. Humans, of course, have always been migratory, but the number of people moving more than a few miles from their birthplace either permanently or temporarily at some point in their lives increased markedly over the course of the displaced nineteenth century. Migrants responded to the obsolescence of traditional ways of earning a living close to home and to awareness of emerging opportunities in distant places.

After 1890, once slavery had been abolished throughout the Atlantic world, each of these relocations was voluntary. They were not, however, idiosyncratic. The vast majority of individual moves followed one of a small number of common patterns.

Many migrations were seasonal or cyclical; the estimated 433,000 workers engaged in the sugar beet harvest east of the Elbe River in Germany in 1914, for example, included temporary migrants from Russian- and Austrian-controlled Poland, Italians, Scandinavians, Ruthenians, and White Russians (Moch, 2003, p. 122). Other relocations were permanent, either intentionally from the outset or as it turned out. Generally, longer-distance migrations, journeys that began before the advent of affordable steam-powered sea transportation, and relocations by entire families were more likely to be permanent (Gould, 1980).

As the pace of urbanization accelerated the well-worn migratory path between a hinterland and its nearby city became much more heavily traveled in both directions. Some farm-to-city moves were temporary, as when a farm family's daughter took a job in a city as a factory worker or household servant for a few years before marrying the boy back home. But some proportion of these moves must have been permanent because natural increase could not have generated the growth rate experienced by nineteenth-century cities, especially where urban birth rates were relatively low, as in France, or urban death rates relatively high, as in Italy (Moch, 2003, p. 131).

Migrations also tended to take place along distinct pathways between specific regions or even between specific villages and specific city blocks. The migration from the New England countryside to the better soils of the Erie Canal counties during the second quarter of the nineteenth century is one example. The migration from the eastern provinces of Germany, where a once vibrant rural textile industry was languishing, to the booming cities of the Ruhr-Rhine region is another (Moch, 2003, pp. 123–124).

Migrations between specific origins to specific destinations also tended to follow similar temporal patterns; they tended to start gradually and almost randomly, accelerate rapidly at some point, and eventually level off or begin to diminish. The necessary conditions for an accelerating migrant flow included

- A large increase in the population growth rate about 20 years earlier,
- A decrease in the proportion of the local population engaged in agriculture,
- The establishment a "pioneering" presence of individuals from the origin at the destination, and
- A growing number of jobs at the destination for workers with skills possessed by potential migrants offering a substantially better level of well-being than what could be earned at home (Hatton & Williamson, 1998, p. 52).

Once these conditions were met and absent any impediments such as wars or legal restrictions migration between the origin and destination tended to accelerate through a process of diffusion and feedback. If, for example, the initial settlers came from one town in a geographic region, the early migrants might all be townsmen of the pioneers. Some of the second-round migrants would have had family members, friends, or acquaintances in neighboring towns who would follow in a third round of relocations. Thus, the process of "feedback" from initial to subsequent settlers would lead to diffusion of migration "fever" from town to town across a geographic region or a country. Immigration from the region or country would then accelerate until one or more of the necessary conditions were eliminated or governments interfered with the process by restricting migration or fighting a war. At that point, the number of net out-migrants from the origin would diminish—very quickly in the last case—eventually reaching zero or less (Gould, 1980).

The point in time at which accelerating migration took hold differed from country to country and from region to region and depended on when the necessary conditions were present. Because birth rates started rising and the industrial revolution took hold sooner in Northwestern Europe, emigration from the British Isles, Scandinavia, and parts of Germany began to accelerate around mid-century, almost 50 years earlier than in Southern and Eastern Europe. By the 1890s conditions for acceleration were demonstrably right in Italy, Spain, and Portugal and were likely so, too, in large parts of Eastern Europe by the 1890s (Gould, 1980).

Economic historians have delved deeply into the reasons for and the effects of international migrants' decisions. Domestic migration within the United States prior to the Great Migration of African-Americans from the rural south to northern cities, which will be discussed in a subsequent chapter, has received less attention. The largest flow of domestic migrants during the period under discussion, from rural America or from an immigrant port of entry, was to cities. The regional distribution of U.S. population changed very little between 1890 and 1920; the proportion of the population living in the Northeast rose from 27.7 to 28.0% and the Midwest's share declined from 35.7 to 32.1%. What did change was the percent of the population living in cities with populations greater than 100,000, which rose from 15.4 to 25.6% (Haines, 2000, p. 189). A disproportionally large percentage of the urban population growth was fueled by immigrants; as Table 11.1 indicates, immigrants were more likely than the native born to be living in large cities in 1910.

## Shovels and Shmattas: How Italian and Jewish Immigrants Made New York's Heyday

Italian and East European Jewish immigrants who arrived around the turn of the twentieth century differed from other immigrant groups and from each other across a number of dimensions that affected the pace and composition of New York's economic development. The distribution of occupations immigrants declared upon arrival highlights some of the most important distinctions among the different immigrant ethnicities (Table 11.2). The concentrations of laborers among the Italians and of craft skills, especially in the needle trades, among the Jews reflect social, economic, and political conditions in their homelands and the opportunities and constraints on offer in other places to which they might have migrated. The latter would have included locations within their home countries, elsewhere in Europe, and, especially for the Italians, in South America.

### Italian Migrations

During the first decade of the twentieth century, Italians were very much on the move around the Atlantic world. Between 1901 and 1910, 107.7 out of every 1,000 Italians emigrated from their homeland; the second highest comparable statistic among 15 Western and Central European countries for this period was Norway's 83.3. Third-ranked Ireland's was 69.8. Italians were relative latecomers to mass migration because the demographic and industrial transformations that tended to induce people to leave their home countries were slower to emerge in Italy than in Northern Europe. Thus, the Italian emigration rate was 50.2 per thousand in the 1890s when Ireland's was 88.5 (Hatton & Williamson, 1998, p. 10).

Migration patterns also differed markedly between Northern and Southern Italy. For one thing, emigration from the northern region began earlier than from the south. In 1882, the average emigration rate in the five northernmost *compartimenti* was 8.2 per thousand

**Table 11.2** Declared Occupational Experience of Immigrants Arriving in the United States, 1899–1910 (Kessner, 1977)

| Occupation | Italian | Jewish | Others |
|---|---|---|---|
| Professionals | 0.3% | 0.8% | 0.9% |
| Merchant/dealer | 0.4% | 3.6% | 1.0% |
| Clerk and accountant | 0.7% | 1.9% | 0.6% |
| Needle trades | 1.4% | 20.9% | 0.8% |
| Building trades | 1.3% | 6.2% | 1.6% |
| Other skilled and semiskilled | 4.7% | 15.7% | 5.3% |
| Laborer | 39.2% | 9.1% | 31.1% |
| Servant | 3.1% | 7.4% | 9.3% |
| Other | 0.9% | 1.1% | 1.9% |

versus 5.88 in the south. In 1912, both figures were higher, but the southern rate of 24.8 was twice the northern rate of 12.6[3] (Hatton & Williamson, 1998, p. 107).

For most of its history, Southern Italy had been much less developed economically than the North, and during the period of mass migration conditions in the south were evidently quite depressed. Angus Maddison estimates that in 1913 real per capita GDP in Italy was about 30% below the European average. In 1914, per capita income in the five southernmost compartimenti was more than 60% lower than in the north. Further, 46.7% of the southern labor force worked as agricultural day laborers compared with 20.0% in the north. And southern Italian agriculture, especially in Sicily, was in trouble at the time. In 1890, citrus products accounted for over 55% of exports from Palermo, and about 80% of the Sicilian orange and lemon exports were headed to the United States. But U.S. orange imports declined by 98% between the early 1890s and the early 1910s as the tariff-protected Florida citrus industry ramped up production (Critz, Olmstead, & Rhode, 1999; Gianni, 1990, p. 122; Hatton & Williamson, 1998, p. 109; Maddison, The World Economy: A Millennial Perspective, 2001, p. 185).

[3]The "northern" compartimenti were Piedmont, Lombardy, Veneto, Friuli-Venezia Giulia, Liguria, and Emilia Romagna. The "southern" are Campania, Puglia, Basilicata, Calabria, and Sicily.

Italians migrated to a particularly wide array of destinations. Between 1876 and 1915, 6.1 million migrated to other countries in Western or Central Europe, 4.3 million to the North America, and 3.0 million to South America. Southern Italians were much more likely than northerners to migrate to the Americas rather than elsewhere in Europe. In 1912 in the southernmost five compartments, the rate of intercontinental emigration exceeded departures for elsewhere in Europe by a factor of 19. This stark difference becomes more explicable in light of the fact that during the period of peak emigration "[a] trip from Sicily to northern Germany on an average cost more than a trip to either New York or Buenos Aires" (Hatton & Williamson, 1998, pp. 100, 107; Rosoli, 1985, p. 98).

Italians were more likely than Northern European emigrants to return home and to make repeated seasonal migrations. Over the period between (fiscal) 1908 and 1914, among immigrants from Italy to the United States the repatriation ratio was 57.9%, which was more than twice the 25.5% average repatriation ratio for 22 European nationalities over the same period (Gould, 1980, p. 57). Much Italian migration was circular, with laborers moving temporarily to agricultural regions at harvest time or to construction sites for the duration of a project. Railroad construction work, in particular and especially for projects crossing the Alps, was highly seasonal, and "Italian men were the mainstay of seasonal construction crews on the continent" (Moch, 2003, p. 121). And by the turn of the twentieth century, ocean travel had become cheap enough and fast enough so that circular migrants could move between Southern Italy and North or South America on a seasonal cycle (Gould, 1980, p. 76). Finally, the vast majority of these cyclical migrants were men.

Any reasonably complete analysis of New York's rapid growth during the last half of the displaced nineteenth century must, therefore, include answers the following two questions. First, what, in particular, attracted Southern Italian men to come to this City, rather than to stay at home or to move elsewhere in Europe or the Americas, as a place to find temporary work or to re-settle permanently? Second, how did these men's willingness to come to New York affect the overall performance of the City's economy during and immediately after the period of mass migration? Put briefly, the answer to the first question is that these migrants were drawn by the ease and speed with which unskilled Southern Italian newcomers could be matched with what were by their standards very high-paying jobs in the City's construction industry. And the answer to the second question is that the City's rapid physical growth around the turn of the twentieth century might have been seriously impeded absent this elastic supply of laborers.

As noted at the beginning of this chapter, the decades around the turn of the twentieth century were the period of New York City's greatest absolute growth. Between 1890 and 1920, the combined population of the five boroughs grew from 2,507,414 to 5,620,048, or by 124%. Since it would have been impossible to cram that many people into lower Manhattan and nearby Brooklyn, population growth necessitated physical expansion, and, accordingly, the 212.9% growth of the four outer boroughs' combined populations accounted for 72.9% of the City's total increase. Accommodating this expansion of both the number of residents and the distances, they had to travel routinely required a massive volume of construction. Even today vintage 1890–1920 buildings account for more than 20% of the total floor space in New York City and around 30% of the residential space in Manhattan and Brooklyn (New York City, Department of City Planning, 2018). These decades were also a boom time for transportation infrastructure construction. About 85% of today's rapid transit track mileage was put in place before 1920 (Hood, 1993). One-third of the City's current 31 miles of bridges and 56% of its 15 miles of tunnels were constructed during this period (Wikipedia, 2018). Against this background, it shouldn't be surprising that in 1910 almost one out of nine employed male New Yorkers was engaged in a construction-related activity and that the local concentration ratio for this geographically ubiquitous category of occupations was 1.18 (Table 11.3).

To be sure, the United States as a whole was growing rapidly at the time and the entire country, especially its burgeoning cities, needed lots of construction workers. Thus, at 1.25, the building-trades concentration ratio for Chicago, with its somewhat higher percentage growth rate, was a bit above New York's. In absolute numbers, of course, New York needed, by far, the most.

Two other statistics in Table 11.3 are noteworthy in the current context. First, the high concentration stonecutters and the low concentration of carpenters reflect New York's greater use of stone and brick construction relative to Chicago and the nation as a whole. The City's concentration ratio for stonecutters would probably have been much higher except for the fact that the category includes both quarrymen and those working close to construction sites. Stonework is a longstanding Italian specialty, and records indicate that Italian stonecutters began migrating cyclically to the United States as early as the 1870s. Between 1899 and 1919, 22,838 immigrants reported stonework to have been their previous occupation. Of these 9,566, or almost 42%, were Italian (Fenton, 1962, p. 191).

Second, the New York construction workforce was more skilled on average than that of the nation as a whole or of Chicago; that is, the New York concentration ratios for the skilled trades listed in Table 11.2 are high for New York and greater than Chicago's while the statistic for laborers is quite low. The high concentration ratios for plasterers and plumbers, etc., may reflect the City's greater urbanity. And the volume of bridge and tunnel construction in a City expanding rapidly across an archipelago probably explains the very high concentration of structural iron (and steel) workers, even relative to post-fire Chicago.

The low concentration of construction laborers, however, suggests that that New York's building contractors, more than their counterparts elsewhere, may have sought to substitute skilled for unskilled labor. And, in fact, some of the findings of the 1909 UK Board of Trade study, discussed the previous chapter, indicate that the City's employers had an incentive to do just that. BoT canvassers found that, with the exception of Chicago, real wages paid on average across all surveyed skill categories and industries were roughly equal across cities; the higher cost of living, especially of housing, more or less completely offset New York's advantage in nominal wages. Unskilled construction workers appear to have been something of an exception to this generalization. The money wages paid to unskilled New York workers in the building trades, the number that was most relevant to local employers, was about 12% higher than the nationwide urban average for that category of employees across the other 12 cities, the New York nominal premium

**Table 11.3** 1910 building trades and employment and occupational concentration ratios (U.S. Department of Commerce, Bureau of the Census, 1913)

| Occupation | Total employment | | | Concentration ratio | |
|---|---|---|---|---|---|
| | NYC | Chicago | USA | NYC | Chicago |
| Apprentices to building and hand trades | 2,179 | 1,024 | 28,031 | 1.37 | 1.36 |
| Brick and stone masons | 15,810 | 7,096 | 169,402 | 1.65 | 1.56 |
| Builders and building contractors | 15,133 | 6,605 | 174,422 | 1.53 | 1.41 |
| Carpenters | 41,444 | 24,051 | 817,120 | 0.90 | 1.10 |
| Laborers, building and hand trades | 41,778 | 23,265 | 934,909 | 0.79 | 0.93 |
| Painters, glaziers, varnishers (building) | 27,219 | 15,475 | 273,411 | 1.76 | 2.11 |
| Paper hangers | 1,293 | 451 | 25,577 | 0.89 | 0.66 |
| Plasterers | 6,388 | 1,913 | 47,682 | 2.36 | 1.50 |
| Plumbers and gas and steam fitters | 19,564 | 6,799 | 148,304 | 2.33 | 1.71 |
| Roofers and slaters | 2,151 | 795 | 14,078 | 2.70 | 2.11 |
| Stonecutters | 3,779 | 1,035 | 35,721 | 1.87 | 0.62 |
| Structural iron workers (building) | 3,355 | 1,166 | 11,427 | 5.18 | 2.20 |
| Total construction | 180,093 | 89,675 | 2,680,084 | 1.18 | 1.25 |

for skilled construction labor was only five percent (United Kingdom Board of Trade, 1911, p. lxxix). This observation suggests that, given the importance of housing stock and infrastructure expansion, unless builders' ability to substitute skilled for unskilled labor was highly elastic, any greater scarcity of unskilled construction workers could have raised construction costs substantially and, thereby, impeded the City's growth.

Assembling a workforce for a particular project involved both attracting a labor force, a pool of potential employees in the vicinity, and turning that labor force into a workforce by matching individual workers with specific jobs. From a potential immigrant's point of view, the decision to travel to New York would have been based on information about prevailing wages in the City relative to what was being paid elsewhere and on the likelihood of landing an acceptable job not too long after arrival. New York builders were clearly willing to pay workers enough to induce Southern Italian craftsmen and laborers to travel from their homes to New York; throughout the period between 1870 and 1910 U.S. wages in general were much higher than the going rate in Southern Italy or Argentina (Hatton & Williamson, 1998, p. 221). And, at least for unskilled construction workers, real wage levels were higher in New York than elsewhere in the United States. Further, it seems likely that Italian men, many traveling alone and intending to return home eventually, would have been less put off by New York's high rents than other contemporary immigrants or potential domestic migrants. But how were these willing workers effectively matched with jobs quickly enough upon arrival and then reasonably steadily for the duration of their stay in the United States?

Many of the challenges involved in matching unskilled workers with jobs around the turn of the twentieth century were the same as they had been during the antebellum years of extensive city-building. A large proportion of job openings for laborers in the City were ephemeral, lasting for the time required to complete one phase of the work on a construction project or to unload a cargo ship. So, any given laborer would be looking for work frequently, and information about openings would have been valuable. Italian immigrant laborers faced an additional challenge. Unlike the unskilled antebellum immigrants, most of whom were Irish, few of the Sicilians and Neapolitans spoke English on arrival. This precluded the employment-seeking tactic of walking from job site to job site and asking about openings and limited the amount and value of information conveyed through laborers' social networks.

Just as the antebellum and turn-of-the-century job-matching problems were similar, so was the general solution. In both periods, institutions emerged within immigrant communities that facilitated the flow of relevant information through social networks. During the antebellum period, saloons, political clubs, firehouses, and ethnic neighborhoods probably served the purpose. Many of these institutions were indigenous to the City before the immigrants arrived. By contrast, Italian workers and their employers surmounted the job-matching challenge by bringing with them institutions and practices that had evolved in their homelands over the previous century. Before beginning the discussion of these Italian institutions, however, it is important to mention one additional similarity between the earlier and later solutions. During both periods many aspects of many of the immigrants' way of life that, among other things, facilitated job matching met with disapproval or contempt from bourgeois native-born Americans.

The institutions Southern Italian immigrants brought with them were themselves adaptations to an earlier wrenching economic transition. In Southern Italy, the shift from a feudal land tenure system to a capitalist structure of large commercialized agricultural estates did not take place gradually as it did elsewhere in Europe. Instead, it was initiated from the top down by the otherwise largely inattentive Spanish dynasty that ruled Southern Italy between 1815 until 1860 and was carried forward thereafter by the northern-dominated post-unification governments. The process abruptly severed the traditional, reasonably-secure link between the region's peasants and the land they worked. Thus, what had been a feudal peasantry became a rural proletariat, which, in the midst of Southern Italy's demographic transition, was growing more rapidly than the local demand for its labor. The rural population lived in a scattering of isolated settlements surrounded by largely uninhabited and dangerous countryside.

What enabled this transformed economy to function was a new class of rural entrepreneurs that took on a range of roles such as recruiting a labor force to work for the mostly absentee landowners, retailing, negotiating the transfer of agricultural products to export markets, and facilitating emigration by acting as agents for shipping companies or foreign employers. Activities were coordinated among the widely scattered rural settlements and between rural areas and the port cities through tightly tied family networks and weaker but functional links among coalitions of families. Most of these networks' activities were government sanctioned or, at least, not illegal, but some engaged in criminal activities. One of the latter became particularly well-known under the name of the mafia. Emigrants from Southern Italy were, therefore, accustomed to engaging with a market economy through intermediaries organized into networks of extended families (Schneider & Schneider, 1976, pp. 41–73; 2005).

Upon arrival in the United States, therefore, even during the earliest years of their mass migration Italian immigrants found a familiar institutional form in operation in their new home. Indeed, some of the intermediaries they encountered were linked through familial or hometown ties with the same networks of entrepreneurs the immigrants and been dealing with at home. The most familiar term used to refer to these entrepreneurial intermediaries is "padrone." Padrones provided a range of services to Italians resident in New York and elsewhere in the United States including retail sales, banking, housing, and protection. The function that was most important in the current context, however, is the padrones' role as labor contractors.

Wage differentials net of travel costs left plenty of room for labor market intermediaries to make money. The wage for a six-day week earned by a laborer around the turn of the century was about $2.22 in Southern Italy and $14.30 in U.S. cities. Steerage steam passage between Naples and New York plus two weeks' foregone Southern Italian wages would have come to about $38. An Italian laborer expecting at least five months of steady work in the U.S. shortly after arrival would have been looking at an income differential net of passage of round $200. In this context, the average $10 fee charged by a padrone for placing a worker in a five-month job would have seemed quite reasonable, even if we assume a very large cost of living differential for a single male laborer between a U.S. city and rural Southern Italy[4] (Baily, 1983; Hatton & Williamson, 1998, p. 109; United Kingdom Board of Trade, 1911, p. xvi).

The smallest scale padrones, probably a majority of the individuals so engaged, served the same function in the same way as a member of social network by introducing a job-seeking acquaintance to an employer with an appropriate opening. The only difference was that the padrone charged a fee for the service usually paid by the worker. At the largest scale, a padrone might contract recruit, house, supervise, and pay the workforce for a factory, a mine, or a large construction project. It was conditions in the work camps overseen by these labor contractors, among other abuses, that gave the "padrone system" an unsavory reputation (Nelli, 1964; Peck, 1998).

Padrones played an important role in the New York market for unskilled labor during a brief but crucial period in the very late nineteenth and very early twentieth centuries. One contemporary analyst reported to the U.S. Department of Labor that in 1897 an estimated half of the Italian adult males in New York City had obtained their jobs through a padrone. Once the Italian immigrant community had established itself in New York City, fee-for-service padrones found themselves unable to compete as intermediaries in the New York labor market against social networks, formal public and private employment agencies, and labor unions. So much so that by the eve of World War I the system had largely disappeared (Baily, 1999, pp. 96–98). During the period immediately around the turn of the twentieth century, however, when construction activity was ramping up rapidly in New York and when the largest number of Southern Italians were seeking a destination for emigration this imported social institution seems to have played a crucial role in making transforming a potential labor force into an actual large workforce.

---

[4]Currency conversions based on .28, 1.51, and 7.32 grams of gold per lira, dollar, and pound, respectively.

Absent the large unskilled Italian immigrant labor force and the job-matching mechanism they brought with them, it isn't clear how New York's construction contractors would have recruited the huge workforce they needed to accommodate the City's growth potential. To be sure, the total number of gentile East European immigrants exceeded the number of Southern Italians; 279 thousand of the former entered the United States as immigrants in 1906, for example, compared to 207 thousand of the latter. But the many East European ethnicities—Poles, Romanians, Ruthenians, Moravians, Hungarians, etc.—shared less in terms of common culture than the Italians. This may be why such evidence as we have indicates that the padrone system of labor market matching was primarily an Italian phenomenon. Registered New York employment agencies placed 14,124 Italians but only 2,476 Slavs and Hungarians in jobs between May 1, 1904 and July 31, 1906. Further, 59% of the Italians but only 10% gentile Eastern Europeans were placed in jobs in New York State. And prior to the disruptions of the World War I, barriers to African-American migration from the rural south were difficult to surmount (Sheridan, 1907, pp. 407, 417). Thus, there was no obvious alternative large migration-ready pool of unskilled laborers who could be efficiently deployed in the New York's construction industry. Higher wages for unskilled construction workers might have drawn native migrants from other regions, but pay rates for this type of labor were already elevated in New York City. A case can be made, therefore, that Chicago might have stood a better chance of overtaking New York had conditions at home not induced mass migration from Southern Italy and had not the immigrants effectively adapted an old-country institution to New World purposes.

An elastic supply of unskilled labor to the construction industry was a necessary condition for New York's growth around the turn of the twentieth century. The sufficient conditions for rapid population growth, however, had to include at least one very large, rapidly growing, and labor-intensive economic "base" industry producing "export" goods and/or services sold to buyers outside City. Port-related and financial services employment was growing rapidly in New York at the time, but the number of workers engaged, directly and indirectly, in these industries was insufficient, even augmented by a large local employment multiplier, to generate the more than four million growth of the five boroughs' population between the 1870 and 1920 censuses. To be sure, New York had been and remained home to a number of large export industries, many of which were growing rapidly in tandem with the expansion of the U.S. economy. Between 1870 and 1910, the number of New Yorkers engaged in the printing publishing industry, for example, more than tripled from 10,696 to 32,088.[5] Similarly, employment in the cigar and tobacco products industry, in which New York's 1870 concentration ratio was 4.28, rose from 7,109 in that year to 18,746 in 1910 (U.S. Department of Commerce, 1913; U.S. Department of Commerce, Census Bureau, 1873). Again, however, neither of these industries was large enough to explain more than a modest proportion of the City's growth over the period.

## Women's Wear: A Burgeoning as Ethnic Niche

One and only one industrial sector was (a) large enough, (b) labor-intensive enough, (c) growing rapidly enough around the turn of the twentieth century, and (d) concentrated enough in New York to account for the kind of employment and population growth the City experienced over this period. That was the women's wear industry or the "*shmatta*" business as it was called using the Yiddish word for "rags". By the beginning of the twentieth century's first decade, the women's clothing industry was certainly very large. In 1909 among the 48 U.S. largest industries—i.e., those producing more than $100 million worth of output—the women's clothing industry ranked 10th by value added by manufacture and 11th in terms of employment. The sector was also growing very quickly; in terms of employment, only two very new industries, automobile and electrical machinery production, had grown faster than women's clothing in percentage terms over the previous ten years. And the women's clothing and related businesses were

[5]Those deemed to have been "engaged in printing and publishing" included "bookbinders and finishers" and "printers" in 1870 and "semiskilled operatives, printing and publishing," and "compositors, linotypers, and typesetters" in 1910.

highly concentrated in New York City. Nationwide in 1909, 154 thousand Americans, or 2.3% of manufacturing wage earners were engaged in producing women's clothing; the equivalent figures for New York City were 93 thousand and 17.0%. The resulting concentration ratio of 7.39 was the highest among important New York goods-producing industries. Local employment in the broader women's fashion industry was further augmented by 5,449 wage earners producing artificial flowers and feathers and plumes, 2,128 in the corset industry, 7,824 in fur goods, 5,381 in hosiery and knit goods, 5,039 in jewelry, and 20,561 in millinery and lace goods, all highly concentrated in New York City. Taken together this means that one-quarter of New York City's manufacturing workforce was engaged directly in one branch or another of the women's clothing or fashion industry. Nor did New York have any close rivals as a center for ladies' garment production. In 1909, 61.3% of nationwide employment in this industry was in New York City; second-ranked Chicago accounted for only 8.7% (Magee, 1930, p. 30; U.S. Department of Commerce, Bureau of the Census, 1913).

Any complete analysis of New York City's rapid expansion around the turn of the twentieth century, must, therefore incorporate an understanding of the size, organization, and geography of the U.S. women's wear industry.

## Prêt à Prêt-à-Porter

Industrial production of clothing was a nineteenth-century innovation. Before then, with very few exceptions, garments had been produced one at a time at home or on order by craftspeople. As discussed in Chapter 6, the transition from bespoke to ready-to-wear clothing production, the "industrialization" of clothing manufacture, began with menswear, initially in the form of cheap "slops" for sailors and slaves and, by mid-century, for better-quality male attire. Although the development of the sewing machine certainly speeded up garment production over the course of the nineteenth century, the impediments to the industrial revolution in the clothing industry were not technological. Instead, they were primarily organizational.

Because capital requirements were minimal and there were few barriers to entry, the market was highly competitive and profit margins were very thin. Demand varied with the season and with the whims of fashion. Successful garment manufacturers needed to be able to ramp production up and down, shift style gears quickly, and keep fixed costs very low. Contracting with a year-round workforce would have made no sense given the frequency of slack periods. Acquiring large factory facilities was also inadvisable for the same reason, especially in cities where floor space was expensive. The system that developed involved the vertical disintegration of the traditional artisanal processes by which an individual tailor or seamstress transformed a bolt of fabric and a collection of findings into a finished garment.

In the antebellum iteration of the disintegrated system, a single "manufacturer" might design the garment, acquire textiles and notions, employ the skilled fabric cutters, and market the final product. Garment assembly, however, was farmed out one batch at a time to one or more contractors who recruited semiskilled workers, frequently women, sometimes working in shops (or in tenement apartments) under the contractor's direct supervision but also frequently working at home, to stitch the pieces together and complete the finishing touches. Manufacturers had no persistent obligations to contractors and contractors had no obligations to the workers they engaged beyond paying for work already completed, so production costs could be cut sharply when demand was slack in general or when a specific product line failed to catch on with consumers. The manufacturer-contractor structure remained important in the garment industries into the twentieth century. More than half of the men's wear manufacturing establishments tabulated in by the Census Bureau in 1909, for example, were categorized as "contract shops."

At that time, however, only 19% of the establishments identified as producing women's clothing were enumerated as contract shops. Census workers may, however, have missed some of these operations because not all contractors had their own shops. Some distributed jobs to homeworkers. Others set up as "Inside" contractors by hiring and paying some assistants of their own and, perhaps, buying or renting a couple of sewing machines but working within the premises of another contractor who brought in the orders. By the early twentieth century, a somewhat different form of vertical disintegration, a division of labor between "jobbers" and "submanufacturers," was emerging in the women's wear industry, especially, apparently, in New York City. Jobbers originated and completed the production and distribution process by selecting or creating a design, acquiring fabric and findings, and selling the finished goods to wholesalers or retailers. The jobber would distribute the pattern and materials to one or more submanufacturers. The latter differed from contractors in three ways. First, submanufacturers employed the skilled workers who cut the fabric as specified by the pattern. Second, submanufacturers operated out of small tenement or loft-building factories that completed all or most of the process of transforming bolts of fabric and trimmings into a finished garment. Third, submanufacturers were able to initiate their own product lines.

This disintegrated market structure could not have functioned unless (a) manufacturers (or jobbers) could easily engage contractors (or submanufacturers) and the latter could assemble an appropriately skilled and reliable workforce quickly when needed and (b) contractors and workers could be confident that they would get enough work to induce them to make themselves available. Manufacturers could be more confident of finding contractors who could deliver and contractors could be more confident of finding jobs to the extent that there were many of both types of businesses in the vicinity. Likewise, workers and contractors would find it easier to achieve their objectives if there were a lot of both. Similarly, jobbers and submanufacturers could expect to do better in places where both types of firms were thick on the ground. In other words, although there were few economies of scale in garment production, the industry as a whole was subject to powerful *economies of agglomeration*; manufacturers, contractors, jobbers, submanufacturers, and workers were able to achieve their objectives more effectively to the extent that many of all of them were located in close proximity to one another. Thus, as soon as the production of garments became industrial with a vertically disintegrated market structure, it also became a quintessentially metropolitan business.

Even if the number of firms of all types and of workers was large enough, a vertically disintegrated market structure could not operate effectively absent a set of institutions that effectively matched contractors with manufacturers, jobbers with submanufacturers, and workers with work. As discussed in Chapter 6, during the antebellum period the men's garment industry was able to function because New York's heritage of social institutions facilitated the communication of fast-changing market information through social networks. A different institutional framework emerged around the turn of the twentieth century that facilitated the transformation of the women's wear industry and its heavy concentration in New York City.

## Women's Wear Decades

The growth of the ready-to-wear women's clothing industry accelerated in the years after about 1890 (Fig. 11.2). Clothing manufacturers had already figured out how to supply ready-to-wear men's garments of acceptable quality in industrial quantities by mid-century. Therefore, the expansion of the women's clothing industry must have been driven by shifts in demand. Increases in working- and lower-middle-class incomes gave some households the wherewithal to buy new, ready-made instead of second-hand clothing that had originally been made

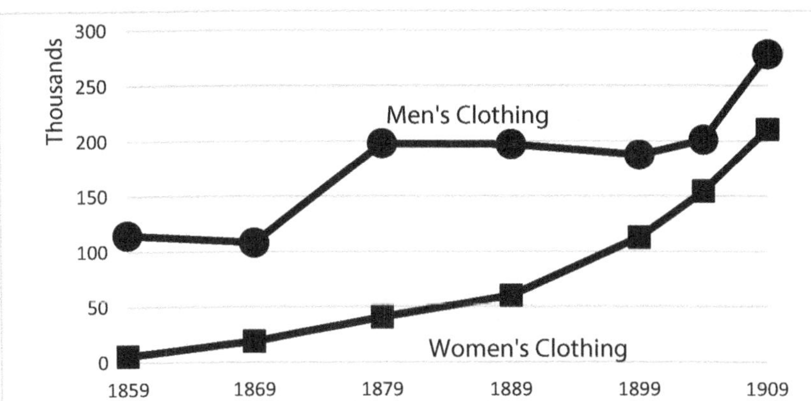


**Fig. 11.2** U.S. clothing industry, wage-earner employment, 1869–1909 (U.S. Department of Commerce, 1913, pp. 398–399)

to order. The accelerating increase in women's labor force participation rate, which rose from 13.1 to 23.4%, from 1870 to 1910 (U.S. Census Bureau, 1976, p. 128), left proportionally fewer hands and less time available to make clothes at home and generated the cash income needed to buy garments. Further, the particularly pronounced increase in the number of women working in the "trade and transportation" sector, which rose from 63,058 in 1880 to 1,202,352 in 1910, would have boosted demand for garments suitable for office or retail store work (U.S. Department of Commerce, Bureau of the Census, 1913, p. 41). Finally, a shift toward simpler styling facilitated the transition from artisanal to industrial production even for more fashionable finery.

The growth of the women's wear industry was particularly dramatic in New York City, which was already home to the nation's greatest concentration of clothing manufacturing and where the clothing industry was, by far, the largest industrial sector. The 1860 census enumerated 30,216 New Yorker's, or about 23% of the metropolitan manufacturing workforce, employed in the men's clothing industry. That was more than 10 times the 2,595 individuals counted as manufacturing women's clothing at the time. Over the subsequent 50 years, the number of New York City men's clothing wage earners a bit more than doubled to 67,142 while employment in the women's clothing industry increased 36-fold to 93,258. And the 1910 women's wear industry was much more concentrated in New York City (concentration ratio = 7.39) than the 1860 men's clothing industry had been in 1860 (concentration ratio = 2.70) or was in 1910 (concentration ratio = 3.34). By way of comparison, U.S. women's clothing manufacturing employment was substantially more highly concentrated in New York than slaughtering and meat packing employment was in Chicago, the "hog butcher for the world," (concentration ratio = 5.53) (U.S. Department of Commerce, 1913, pp. 40–41).

## Query: Why Was the Women's Wear Industry so Heavily Concentrated in New York?

In a 1930 publication, Mabel Magee, a University of Chicago sociologist, puzzled over this question because New York had no clear advantage over other U.S. cities in terms of labor or raw materials costs. Magee noted that the New York garment industry drew its "labor, for the most part, from the same immigrant groups and pays them as high a wage-scale as the other leading centers" and also suggested that a slight New York advantage in the cost of raw materials was too small to account for the observed degree of geographic concentration. Magee identified New York's advantage as a location for garment production as the City's the industry's "marketing and production methods" and specifically to the "jobber-submanufacturing system." Her analysis of the geography of the U.S. women's clothing industry led her to conclude that this market structure was unique to New York and that this gave the City an advantage in terms of flexibility. "New York is more sensitive to style fluctuation and apparently adapts her production more readily to the demands of the moment. Furthermore, the uncertainty of weather conditions and the fear of style piracy causes [sic] a type of buying peculiar to this trade. Few articles of one kind or style are purchased at a time, but orders are sent in repeatedly, sometimes several in a day, from the same buyer, so that the important thing is to be so situated that customers can be readily served" (Magee, 1930, p. 112). Magee did not, however, discuss why the jobber-submanufacturer structure developed in New York's women's wear industry and not in other U.S. cities.

More recently, historian Daniel Soyer has highlighted the simultaneity of the expansion of women's clothing production and Eastern European Jewish immigration into the United States. Both trends accelerated rapidly over the decades straddling the turn of the twentieth century. Correlation does not necessarily imply causality, but Soyer suggests some reasons why the presence of large numbers of Jewish immigrants in New York may have facilitated the growth of the City's garment industry (Soyer, 2005, p. 95).

## Eastern European Jewish Migration vs. Mass Migration in General

At the turn of the twentieth century, more than five million Jews were subjects of the Russian Tsar. Another 850,000 were residents of Galicia, a province of the Austro-Hungarian Empire that had been part of

Poland before 1815. Together Jews may have amounted to about 10% of the total East European population at the time.

Most immigrants to the United States during the displaced nineteenth century were rural peasants or, at most, one generation removed from that status. Jews, however, had played a different role from the peasantry in the social structure of feudal Eastern Europe. As a consequence, around the turn of the century, even in an economy in which roughly 70% of the workforce was engaged in farming and even in the wake of efforts by early nineteenth-century Tsarist governments to encourage Jews to form agricultural settlements only about four percent of Russia's Jews worked the land. Instead, Jews found their niches in handicraft and commercial occupations. The 1897 Russian census (Table 11.4) tabulated a total Jewish workforce of 1.4 million with the greatest concentrations in manufacturing, especially clothing and footwear production, and commercial activities. Further, even at the end of the period under discussion here the bulk of manufacturing activity took place in small shops rather than in large factories (Morawska, 1987, p. 32).

Proportionally even more than the Italians, this population was on the move. Between 1881 and 1914, at least 300,000 East European Jews migrated to Western Europe, South America, Palestine, South Africa, and Australia, more than one million relocated across regions within Russia or Austria-Hungary, and about two million entered the United States (Morawska, 1987, p. 33).

Econometric analysis of the volume, timing, motivations, origins, and destinations of intercontinental migration from Eastern Europe has not been possible because governments in this region collected relatively little data on their populations relatively infrequently. There is no way of knowing, for example, by how much real wages in, say, Chicago exceeded what workers could earn in, say, Pinsk. It does appear, however, that, as in Northwestern and Southern Europe, the late nineteenth-century increase in East European Jewish migration was preceded by accelerating population growth and some degree of economic disruption.

Between the 1861–1870 period and 1911–1913, the death rate in European Russia declined by 28.4% while the birth rate decreased by only 15.0%, and the pattern for the region's Jewish population was apparently similar (Kahan, 1986, p. 4; 1989, p. 3).

**Table 11.4** Occupations of Russian Jews, 1897 (Dijur, 1966, pp. 122–125)

| Sector | # employed | % total employment |
|---|---|---|
| *Crafts and industry* | | |
| Textiles | 34,612 | 2.6 |
| Hides, leather | 21,476 | 1.6 |
| Clothing and footwear | 254,384 | 18.8 |
| Wood, furniture | 42,525 | 3.1 |
| Ceramics | 5,358 | 0.4 |
| Construction and repair | 39,019 | 2.9 |
| Tobacco | 7,856 | 0.6 |
| Food | 46,156 | 3.4 |
| Beverages | 6,582 | 0.5 |
| Metals | 44,867 | 3.3 |
| Printing | 29,436 | 2.2 |
| Total crafts and industry | 532,271 | 39.2 |
| *Trade* | | |
| Agricultural products | 64,880 | 4.8 |
| Including grain | 48,963 | 3.6 |
| Textiles and clothing | 44,183 | 3.3 |
| Hides, furs | 12,551 | 0.9 |
| Construction materials | 27,713 | 2.0 |
| Domestic wares and furniture | 5,853 | 0.4 |
| Food | 145,054 | 10.7 |
| Beverages | 12,136 | 0.9 |
| Metal products | 6,849 | 0.5 |
| Luxury products | 3,065 | 0.2 |
| Commission trade | 15,975 | 1.2 |
| General wholesale and retail | 96,215 | 7.1 |
| Total trade | 483,437 | 35.6 |
| *Services* | | |
| Transportation | 45,618 | 3.4 |
| Domestic service and day labor | 175,732 | 13.0 |
| Central local administration | 2,587 | 0.2 |
| Religious | 20,135 | 1.5 |
| Teaching and education | 35,273 | 2.6 |
| Law and medicine | 10,807 | 0.8 |
| Hygiene | 8,997 | 0.7 |
| Art, literature, sciences | 2,870 | 0.2 |
| Agriculture | 35,261 | 2.6 |
| Forestry | 3,380 | 0.2 |
| Welfare work | 197 | 0.0 |
| Total services | 340,857 | 25.1 |
| Total | 1,356,565 | 100.0 |

It is unlikely, however, that the commercialization of agriculture and large-scale industrialization, which motivated Western and Southern European migrants, were the main drivers of Eastern European Jews' decisions to leave their homes. As noted, hardly any Jews worked the land. If anything, agricultural commercialization would have been good for at least some Jews, the merchants who handled the lion's share of the grain trade in those regions of Russia where Jews were allowed to reside (see below) (Kahan, 1986, p. 15).

Further, prior to World War I relatively few East European craftspeople were apparently displaced by factories. Industrialization came belatedly to Eastern Europe. The institution of serfdom, which tied large proportions of the population to feudal estates and impeded the recruitment of an urban industrial labor force, was not abolished in Austria-Hungary until 1848 and in Russia until 1863. Even after the official abolition of serfdom, some restrictions on rural-to-urban migration remained in place in Russia. To be sure, the transportation network did expand, but large-scale industrialization—adoption of capital-intensive technologies and factory production—did not begin to takeoff in Russia until the 1890s (Kahan, 1989, p. 13). Thus, on the eve of World War I, individual craftspeople working in small shops continued to play the dominant role in the Russian and Austro-Hungarian production of manufactured consumer goods.

So, while the "pull" that drew the bulk of Eastern Europe's Jewish migrants to the United States rather than to Western Europe or the Southern Hemisphere may very well have been largely economic, the disruptions that "pushed" so many Russian Jews to move far from home were somewhat different from what motivated other European emigrants and were probably more political and social than economic. Jews had been subject to a variety of forms of political, social, and economic discrimination across Europe for at least a thousand years before the period under discussion here. While most Western European governments had extended full civil rights to their Jewish residents during the first half of the nineteenth century, Austria-Hungary did not do so until 1867 and the Tsarist government never did. In fact, Russia's rulers and reinforced its anti-Jewish enactments during the last decades of the nineteenth century.

Russian laws restricted geographic mobility of all its subjects until late in the nineteenth century. Thus, when conquest of Polish territory during the reign of Catherine II (1762–1796) brought a large number of Jews under Tsarist rule they were, with very few exceptions, forbidden to establish residence outside of a "Pale of Settlement" in the Empire's Western provinces. Although modified occasionally in ways that sometimes increased and sometimes reduced exceptions, Jews were, for the most part, confined to the Pale throughout the pre-World War I period, even as mobility restrictions were eliminated for the general population.

Restrictive decrees had been relaxed somewhat under the reign of Alexander II (1855–1881), but the reactionary regime that took power after his assassination imposed new discriminatory laws. An 1882 decree forbade Jews, with few exceptions, to live outside of cities and townships within the Pale of Settlement. Most Jews who had obtained permission to live in Moscow were expelled from that city in 1892. Restrictive quotas were imposed on the admission of Jewish students to secondary schools and universities. A law originally promulgated in 1845 governing Jewish trading activity in places where they had been granted permission to reside outside the Pale of Settlement was enforced with increasing stringency in the 25 years preceding World War I. Thus, a kosher butcher, for example, was penalized for having sold meat to gentiles. An 1889 decree imposed the requirement that any application by a Jew to practice law required specific approval by the Minister of Justice; such approvals were granted very sparingly. And employment in civil service jobs was largely out of the question for Jews. Thus, of the roughly 480,000 employees of state railroads at the turn of the century, only about 1,800 were Jews. Finally, the Russian government did little to discourage anti-Jewish violence by the general population. A wave of pogroms followed the assassination of Alexander II, and, most dramatically, two days of violence in the Bessarabian capital of Kishinev in 1903 left some 120 dead and 500 wounded (Kahan, 1986, p. 35).

The legal and social discrimination East European Jews faced surely limited their economic prospects, but also at times, literally, threatened their lives. Most other immigrant ethnicities, for whom the decision to relocate was primarily economic and opportunistic, would have left home with at least an open mind regarding the possibility of returning. More Jews must have left Eastern Europe with the intention of establishing themselves and their families at their immediate destinations or somewhere else away from Eastern Europe. If so, we would expect that relatively few East European Jews would have returned to their homelands and that the proportion of families among Jewish immigrants would have been relatively high. The latter would have been reflected in a smaller proportion of working-age immigrants and of males in the Jewish immigrant cohort.

The data in Table 11.5 confirm these expectations. On the assumption that the average stay for a temporary migrant in the United States during this period was around three to four years, the "repatriation ratio" estimates in the table represent the number of resident aliens of each ethnicity who departed from the United States between fiscal 1908 and fiscal 1913 divided by the number of immigrants of that ethnicity between fiscal 1905 and fiscal 1910. The masculinity and age cohort data are for the fiscal years from 1905 through 1910. With respect to all three immigrant group characteristics, the figure for "Hebrews" is more than a standard deviation below the mean for the 26 ethnic groups.

This is not to say that no Jews returned to Eastern Europe. My own grandmother did so to give birth to my father. Historian Jonathan Sarna has demonstrated that before the Kishinev pogrom return migration was much more common than after that event. Sarna suggests that a reasonable estimate of a pre-1900 return immigration rate for Jews would be in the range of 15–20%. This was within the range of ethnic group repatriation, albeit at the low end, and at least twice as high as the 7.1% figure cited for Hebrews. It is also worth mentioning that a large behavioral shift in the wake of the Kishinev pogrom reinforces the notion that anti-Jewish attitudes were an important emigration incentive (Sarna, 1981).

Thus, many East European Jews arrived during the years of this group's peak immigration rates with the expectation that they would remain in the United States for the rest of their lives and either were accompanied by family members or intended to find a job quickly and save enough money to pay for family member's passage to North America.

**Table 11.5** Repatriant ratio, masculinity, and age group by ethnicity, ~1905–~1913 (see text) (Gould, 1980, p. 60)

| Ethnicity | Repatriation ratio (%) | % male | % ages 14–45 |
|---|---|---|---|
| Turkish | 107.02 | 96.02 | 96.46 |
| Russian | 86.99 | 87.24 | 92.46 |
| Greek | 57.12 | 94.17 | 96.17 |
| Bulgarian, Servian, Montenegrin | 52.86 | 95.37 | 95.58 |
| Magyar | 49.59 | 69.91 | 85.60 |
| English | 47.68 | 60.82 | 74.59 |
| Italian (North) | 47.08 | 76.57 | 87.76 |
| Italian (South) | 42.24 | 77.24 | 83.37 |
| Slovak | 41.53 | 68.56 | 87.35 |
| Croat/Slovene | 40.26 | 81.77 | 92.33 |
| Rumanian | 38.01 | 89.49 | 92.48 |
| Spanish | 35.55 | 80.83 | 83.68 |
| Portuguese | 32.89 | 61.61 | 71.84 |
| Polish | 32.66 | 68.17 | 88.85 |
| French | 27.59 | 56.66 | 72.69 |
| Dutch | 25.47 | 64.94 | 72.73 |
| Scottish | 25.35 | 62.50 | 76.42 |
| Scandinavian | 24.74 | 62.94 | 86.76 |
| Dalmatian, Bosnian, Herzegovinian | 21.37 | 91.66 | 94.76 |
| Lithuanian | 21.19 | 66.86 | 90.27 |
| German | 20.87 | 58.45 | 76.75 |
| Ruthenian | 17.73 | 72.73 | 93.18 |
| Irish | 16.29 | 52.23 | 89.46 |
| Welsh | 12.41 | 66.92 | 76.86 |
| Bohemian/Moravian | 10.77 | 57.40 | 75.14 |
| Hebrew | 7.11 | 53.66 | 68.25 |
| Mean | 36.25 | 72.10 | 84.68 |
| Standard deviation | 22.59 | 13.65 | 8.82 |
| Hebrew rate minus mean in std. deviations | −1.29 | −1.35 | −1.86 |

Prior to arrival, a majority of the adults had acquired either some degree of artisanal skill, most commonly as a tailor, seamstress, or shoemaker, some experience in small-scale commercial operations, or both. The large majority that arrived first in New York found themselves in a booming metropolis in which by far the largest and most rapidly growing economic activity was in the women's clothing and related fashion industries.

## The Right Cohort in the Right Place at the Right Time

It is hard to imagine an industry better suited to the skills and economic objectives of East European Jewish immigrants than that of the garment industry as it had developed in New York City by the end of the nineteenth century. And it is hard to imagine a population group with motives, skills, and communal culture better suited to produce large quantities of marketable women's wear than East European Jews.

For many other contemporary immigrant groups, a principal motive for relocating was to maximize near-term income with a view to returning home within a few years, unless they got particularly lucky in America. For these migrants, economic opportunities on offer would have been evaluated primarily on the basis of the income that could be earned immediately.

For most East European Jews, by contrast, repatriation would have been unattractive and the goal of establishing oneself and one's family permanently and prosperously in America would have informed decisions as to where to live, what skills to learn, and what job to take. Thus, Jewish immigrants would have sought out locations within the United States where all family members, including the relatively numerous women among them, could find remunerative work. And Jews may have been more willing to take a relatively low-paying job in a high-cost location initially upon arrival if the situation offered realistic opportunities for career advancement and higher-than-average earnings in the course of time. The women's wear industry in New York would have scored high in both respects.

Nationwide about 20% of wage earners in manufacturing industries were women or girls; in New York City the equivalent figure was 33%. A large share of this difference was attributable to the concentration of the fashion industries in New York. Women accounted for 58% of wage earners in these businesses, and 46% of women manufacturing wage earners in the City were employed in one of the fashion industries. And there were probably more women manufacturing garments in the City than these statistics indicate because it is not clear whether homeworkers were counted. The availability of homework allowed mothers with young children to contribute to family finances while maintaining their households (U.S. Department of Commerce, 1913, p. 254; U.S. Department of Commerce, Bureau of the Census, 1912, pp. 886, 888).

The availability of paid labor opportunities for women was also attractive to the other large "second wave" immigrant group, Southern Italians, especially those who decided to relocate permanently to America. Although only 23% of this immigrant cohort between 1905 and 1910 was female (Table VIII-7), 35% of Italian-born New Yorkers in 1920 were women, many of whom were engaged as homeworkers in the garment industry (Anbinder, 2016, p. 358; Carnevale, 2005).

The garment industries as they were structured in New York also offered numerous paths toward upward mobility, at least for men. An unskilled stitcher or presser could aspire to a much higher-paying position as a cutter if he could find a willing mentor in the latter occupation. A worker could aim initially to operate as an "inside" contractor in someone else's premises and, if all went well, eventually set up his own shop as an independent contractor, and then as a submanufacturer, and perhaps someday reach the highest levels of the hierarchy. Such aspirations were optimistic but not necessarily unrealistic. Most bosses would have been men. In 1909, there were 41,127 male wage earners in the women's clothing industry in New York. At the same time, 4,332 New Yorkers were enumerated as "proprietors and firm members" in that industry. By itself, of course, the large number of "proprietors and firm members" relative to wage earners does not necessarily measure opportunities for upward mobility. The garment industry, however, was unique in this regard in two ways. First, it was huge and, therefore, offered a large number of entry-level positions so that an immigrant could expect to land a job in a garment shop shortly after disembarkation. Second, the industry's hierarchy included numerous levels so that climbing the career ladder may not have appeared to be too daunting. So, a wage earner looking at the ratio of "bosses" to workers in the context of rapidly expanding industry and assuming that all the "bosses" had started out as workers might have reasonably concluded that the average worker had a little better than a one-in-ten chance of becoming a boss himself someday (U.S. Department of Commerce, Bureau of the Census, 1912, p. 886).

In order to function with its vertically disintegrated structure, the New York garment industry needed a large and elastic supply of appropriately skilled workers and firms and an effective mechanism for matching firms with orders and workers with job openings. The elastic labor supply was provided by the several million adult East European Jews, motivated by developments in their homeland to emigrate whenever to wherever they heard that jobs were available, many with some background in the needle trades. The relatively large proportion of women in this immigrant group suited them particularly well to the garment industry. The low cost of setting up a small contract garment shop—around $50–100 around the turn of the century—and Jewish immigrants' motivation to climb a career ladder in the place they expected would become their new homeland, assured that the industrial organization would remain highly competitive. And the East European communal culture fostered the development of effective mix of dense and weak ties within and between social networks that facilitated the requisite matchmaking.

Bosses—contractors, sub-contractors, and submanufacturers—served many of same the job-worker matching functions in the garment industry that padrones performed among Italian immigrants in the construction sector. Indeed, that may have been one of their principal functions in the market (Carnevale, 2005, p. 144; Soyer, 2005, p. 103). Under its disintegrated structure, however, the women's wear manufacturing required intermediation among employers as well as workers. Here, too, social networks appear to have served the purpose more than, say, professional business brokers, and Jews, like the Italians turned to institutions they brought with them from the old world to facilitate network formation and maintenance. In the Jewish case, however, it was communal organizations rather than individual entrepreneurs that served the purpose.

The imperative to establish communal organizations dates from the earliest centuries of the Jewish Diasporas. Once a critical mass of Jews had settled in a new place, they began the process of establishing synagogues, burial societies, ritual baths, and charities. All of these institutions had stated purposes—providing a prayer quorum, acquiring and maintaining a cemetery, collecting a dowry for an orphan bride, etc.—but they also provided venues and occasions where community members could meet and exchange information. The process of Jewish communal institution formation began in New York City in the seventeenth century, never really ceased, and accelerated markedly with the arrival of large numbers of Central European Jews as part of the mid-nineteenth-century wave of German immigration. The East European Jews augmented the existing institutional array with their own synagogues and mutual aid societies, with memberships usually limited to men who came from the same hometown ("*Landsmanschaften*").

Some of these institutions, such as H.I.A.S. (Hebrew Immigrant Aid Society, originally, perhaps, The Hebrew Sheltering, Relief Society) and the Hebrew Free Loan Society were organized with the express purpose of helping Jewish immigrants establish themselves economically in the United States. H.I.A.S., an organization founded by German Jews, maintained a presence at the Ellis Island immigrant-processing facility and 24-hour walk in offices in lower Manhattan, to provide advice and assistance, in particular, about finding a job. Organizations with other stated purposes, such as synagogues and *Landsmanschaften*, also functioned as places where similarly situated men could gather and, among other things, exchange information about business opportunities and risks. Thus, these communal organizations served the same economic functions in much the same way as saloons, firehouses, ethnic neighborhoods, and athletic clubs did for the Irish and German immigrants two generations earlier. Within each *Landsmanschaft*, interpersonal ties may have been tight, originating, as many did, in the old country, but, like the ethnic trading networks in the British Empire of Goods and like the ethnic neighborhoods of antebellum New York, these organizations were not hermetic. Individuals from different hometowns could and did meet and exchange business-relevant information at work, on the street, or at a wedding. Thus, immigrant workers and bosses lived within the kind of ecosystem of densely and weakly connected social networks that, as discussed in Chapter 3, is particularly effective at communicating economically relevant information.

In these ways, the women's wear industry was particularly suited to meet the needs of East European Jews arriving in the United States. The industry provided a rapidly growing number of jobs at just the time when the immigrants were most motivated and able to leave their homelands. And the garment industry provided visible and plausible paths to upward mobility, a particularly attractive characteristic to immigrants planning to stay in America for the rest of their own lives and those of their offspring. Further, the individual and social characteristics of this immigrant group were particularly well-suited to the needs of a rapidly expanding, vertically disintegrated industry. Large numbers of East European Jews arrived in America having had some experience in the needle trades and as business proprietors and willing to work for, at least initially, at relatively low wages in the hope of starting a career in a growing business. Finally, this community of immigrants brought with them the inclination to create an array of community institutions that could facilitate the economies of agglomeration that made the *shmatta* trade work.

## References

Anbinder, T. (2016). *City of Dreams: The 400-Year Epic History of Immigrant New York*. New York: Houghton Mifflin Harcourt.

Baily, S. L. (1983). The Adjustment of Italian Immigrants in Buenos Aires and New York, 1870–1914. *The American Historical Review, 88*(2), 281–305.

Baily, S. L. (1999). *Immigrants in the Lands of Promise: Italians in Buenos Aires and New York City, 1870 to 1914*. Ithaca: Cornell University Press.

Carnevale, N. C. (2005). Culture of Work: Italian Immigrant Women Homeworkers in the New York City Garment Industry, 1890–1914. In D. Soyer (Ed.), *A Coat of Many Colors: Immigration, Globalization, and Reform in New York City's Garment Industry* (pp. 141–167). New York: Fordham University Press.

Critz, J. M., Olmstead, A. L., & Rhode, A. P. (1999). Horn of Plenty: The Globalization of Mediterranean Horticulture and the Economic Development of Southern Europe, 1880–1930. *The Journal of Economic History, 59*(2), 316–352.

Dijur, I. M. (1966). Jews in the Russian Economy. In J. Frumkin, G. Aronson, & A. Goldenwasser (Eds.), *Russian Jewry, 1860–1917*. New York: Thomas Yosseloff.

Fenton, E. (1962). Italian Immigrants in the Stoneworkers Union. *Labor History, 3*(2), 188–207.

Gianni, T. (1990). *An Economic History of Liberal Italy: 1850–1918*. London: Routledge.

Gould, J. D. (1980). European Inter-Continental Emigration, The Road Home: Return Migration from the U.S.A. *Journal of European Economic History, 9*(1), 41–112.

Haines, M. R. (2000). The Population of the United States, 1790–1920. In S. L. Engerman & R. R. Gallman (Eds.), *The Cambridge Economic History of the United States, Volume II, The Long Nineteenth Century* (pp. 143–206). Cambridge: Cambridge University Press.

Haines, M. R., & ISPCR. (n.d.). *Historical, Demographic, Economic, and Social Data: The United States, 1790–2002*. Retrieved from Inter-university Consortium for Political and Social Research https://doi.org/10.3886/icpsr02896.v3.

Hatton, T. J., & Williamson, J. G. (1998). *The Age of Mass Migration, Causes and Economic Impact*. Oxford: Oxford University Press.

Hood, C. (1993). *722 Miles, The Building of the Subways and How They Transformed New York*. New York: Simon & Schuster.

Kahan, A. (1986). *Essays in Jewish Social and Economic History*. Chicago: University of Chicago Press.

Kahan, A. (1989). *Russian Economic History: The Nineteenth Century*. Chicago: University of Chicago Press.

Kessner, T. (1977). *The Golden Door: Italian and Jewish Immigrant Mobility in New York City, 1880–1915*. Oxford.

Maddison, A. (2001). *The World Economy: A Millennial Perspective*. Paris: Development Studies Center of the Organization for Economic Co-operation and Development.

Magee, M. A. (1930). *Trends in the Location of the Women's Clothing Industry*. Chicago: University of Chicago Press.

Moch, L. P. (2003). *Moving Europeans: Migration in Western Europe Since 1650* (2nd ed.). Bloomington: Indiana University Press.

Morawska, E. (1987). A Replica of the 'Old-Country' Relationship in the Ethnic Niche: East European Jews and Gentiles in Small-Town Western Pennsylvania, 1880s–1930s. *American Jewish History, 77*(1), 27–86.

Nelli, H. S. (1964). The Italian Padrone System in the United States. *Labor History, 5*(2), 153–167.

New York City, Department of City Planning. (2018, August 1). *PLUTO and MapPLUTO*. Retrieved from Data/Maps http://www1.nyc.gov/site/planning/data-maps/open-data/dwn-pluto-mappluto.page.

Peck, G. (1998). Divided Loyalties: Immigrant Padrones and the Evolution of Industrial Paternalism in North America. *International Labor and Working-Class History, 53*, 49–68.

Rosoli, G. (1985). Italian Migration to European Countries from Political Unification to World War I. In D. Hoerder (Ed.), *Labor Migration in the Atlantic Economies: The European and North American Working Classes During the Period of Industrialization*. Santa Barbara: Greenwood Press.

Sarna, J. D. (1981). The Myth of No Return: Jewish Return Migration to Europe, 1881–1914. *American Jewish History, 17*(2), 256–268.

Schneider, J., & Schneider, P. (1976). *Culture and Political Economy in Western Sicily*. Cambridge, MA: Academic Press.

Schneider, J., & Schneider, P. (2005). Mafia, Antimafia, and the Plural Cultures of Sicily. *Current Anthropology, 46*(4), 501–520.

Sheridan, F. J. (1907). Italian, Slavic, and Hungarian Unskilled Immigrant Laborers in the United States. *Bulletin of the Bureau of Labor, 15*, 445–468.

Soyer, D. (2005). Cockroach Capitalists: Jewish Contractors at the Turn of the Twentieth Century. In D. Soyer (Ed.), *A Coat of Many Colors: Immigration, Globalization, and Reform in New York City's Garment Industry* (pp. 91–114). New York: Fordham University Press.

U.S. Census Bureau. (1976). *The Statistical History of the United States from Colonial Times to the Present.* New York: Basic Books.

U.S. Census Bureau. (2018). *Selected Historical Decennial Census Population and Housing Counts.* Retrieved from Census 1990 https://www.census.gov/population/www/censusdata/hiscendata.html.

U.S. Department of Commerce, B. O. (1913). *Thirteenth Census of the United States Taken in the Year 1910, Volume VIII, Manufactures, 1909, General Report and Analysis.* Washington, DC: U.S. Government Printing Office.

U.S. Department of Commerce, Bureau of the Census. (1912). *Thirteenth Census of the United States Taken in the Year 1910, Volume I: Population.* Washington, DC: U.S. Government Printing Office.

U.S. Department of Commerce, Bureau of the Census. (1913). *Thirteenth Census of the United States, Volume 4: Population.* Washington, DC: U.S. Government Printing Office.

U.S. Department of Commerce, Census Bureau. (1873). *Ninth U.S. Census, Volume I, The Statistics of the United States Embracing the Tables of Race, Nationality, Sex, Selected Ages, and Occupations.* Washington, DC: U.S. Government Printing Office.

U.S. Department of Homeland Security. (2018). *Yearbook of Immigration Statistics, 2016.* Retrieved from https://www.dhs.gov/immigration-statistics/yearbook/2016/table1.

United Kingdom Board of Trade. (1911). *Cost of Living in American Towns, Report of an Enquiry of the Board of Trade into Working Class Rents, Housing and Retail Prices Together with the Rates of Wages in Certain Occupation in the Principal Industrial Towns of the United States of America.* London: His Majesty's Stationery Office.

Wikipedia. (2018, August 1). *List of Bridges and Tunnels in New York City.* Retrieved from Wikipedia https://en.wikipedia.org/wiki/List_of_bridges_and_tunnels_in_New_York_City.

# Part III

## Introduction 1924–~1979: The Short Twentieth Century

New York City's population grew faster than that of the United States as a whole over every peacetime decade from the 1780s until the 1920s. Since the 1920s, the number of New Yorkers has either grown at a slower rate than the national population or, as in the 1970s, actually decreased.

From 1815 through 1924, U.S. total international trade—exports plus imports—averaged 13.0% of gross domestic product. Between 1925 and 1972, the average was 7.2%, and the total exceeded 10% in only one year. On average over the eleven decades starting in 1830 and ending in 1930, immigration from abroad accounted for about 28% of total U.S. population growth. The equivalent figure for the period between 1940 and 1970 was nine percent.

Part III of this book explores the coincidence of these temporal patterns and suggests that between 1924 and about 1979, in the absence of the stimulus provided by active engagement between the U.S. economy and that of the rest of the world, the New York City economy languished and then declined.

## Chapters 12 and 13: Interwar Boom and Bust

Chapters 12 and 13 describe the development of New York City's economy over the two decades between World War I and World War II. During this period, the impact of changes in the international flows of goods, money, and people on New York City's aggregate economy was barely perceptible. Instead, in the broadest terms, the City's trajectory was driven almost entirely by purely domestic developments; the local economy expanded robustly during the 1920s boom and collapsed roughly in tandem with the national economy as the Great Depression took hold in the 1930s. There were, however, some differences between developments in New York, on the one hand, and other large northeastern cities, on the other, and many of these distinctions reflected the City's role as the principle nexus of the nation's engagement with the rest of the world.

Chapter 12 describes why and how the United States disengaged with the rest of the world and on the mostly subtle ways in which changes in the magnitude and nature of international trade, finance, and migration affected economic activity in New York. Postwar changes in capital markets exemplify both the existence of local impacts and their barely discernable impact. The effects of the World War, through its duration and thereafter, turned Europeans, who had been important buyers of U.S. assets during the globalization era, into net sellers. U.S. businesses had, therefore, to raise capital to finance their rapid 1920s growth entirely from domestic sources. On the margin, this shift diminished the relative importance of New York's international investment banks as capital market intermediaries. As a consequence, the local concentration of U.S. financial services employment diminished somewhat. But rising stock prices through the 1920s attracted enough "retail" activity to the City's securities markets to more than make up for the effect of domesticization, and the number of stockbrokers working in New York nearly tripled between 1910 and 1930.

The City's 1920s prosperity naturally boosted aggregate local employment, but with restrictive immigration laws coming into effect over the course of the decade, the newly created jobs could no longer be filled, as they had largely been in New York in previous decades, by newcomers from abroad. As was happening in other big cities, African-Americans moving from the rural south to the urban north, the pioneers of the Great Migration, replaced some of the Europeans who were no longer permitted entry. But New York's experience differed in that, at 2.5%, the proportion of African-American interstate migrants in the City's 1930 population was much smaller than 6.5% average for large northeastern cities. The middle sections of Chapter 12 examine several possible explanations for this difference. For one thing, the particular industrial composition of New York's workforce may, given longstanding patterns of discrimination, have offered relatively few employment opportunities to African-Americans. Further, the City's history and political culture may have left New York with a particularly unwelcoming reputation among racial minorities. In addition, the white foreign-born population continued growing faster in the New York City than elsewhere and this population may have left less room for potential migrants from the U.S. South. Finally, migrants from the Caribbean region, who began arriving in New York in large numbers during this period, may have been the first to take those jobs that were open to people of color, thereby crowding out potential interstate migrants.

New York may have been buoyed by urban America's prosperity during the 1920s, but it was also the case that the City's economy lacked an element of dynamism. The expanding production of consumer durables—automobiles and electrical home appliances—drove a large proportion of total U.S. employment growth during this decade, but New York played relatively little role in the manufacture of these products. Instead, with one major exception, the composition of New York City's aggregate product mix remained very much the same as it had been earlier in the twentieth century. Local employment expanded largely because the demand for women's clothing and financial services grew robustly with the rest of the national economy.

Two media industries—publishing and broadcasting—were the exception to the previous paragraph's generalization. It is unlikely that consumer demand for cars and appliances would have grown as quickly as it did without the impetus of advertising. The industries that produce and distribute advertising content—by the advertising agencies themselves, by a growing number of national-circulation magazines, by three national radio broadcasting networks, and by the manufacturers of radio equipment—concentrated in metropolitan New York. Chapter 12 concludes with an analysis of why and how these activities gravitated to this location at that time.

Chapter 13 deals with New York's Great Depression and asks why, somewhat surprisingly, the initial impact of the contraction was less severe in the City than in comparable localities but much worse in New York than elsewhere later in the Depression decade.

The City's early performance was surprising because the collapse of economic activity between 1929 and 1933 was particularly severe in two of the region's economic specialties: financial services and international trade. What likely softened the first blow to New York's economy was the low local concentration of employment in the production of consumer durables, the industries that were hurt the most as demand shrank in the Depression's early years. The immediate effect on the clothing industry was adverse, but not as bad. Relatively proactive ameliorative actions by New York's State and City governments and by local philanthropies may also have helped.

New York failed to benefit as much as many large northeastern cities from the post-1933 recovery, underperformed urban America as a whole through the renewed downturn in 1937 and 1938, and, again, lagged the post-1938 improvement. The reasons for the City's relatively weak performance through the Depression decade's last six years include the tendency for the regions that were hurt the most initially to bounce back most robustly as recovery took hold, the fact that international trade recovered much more slowly than purely domestic activity, the steady westward shift in U.S. population, the relative absence in New York of the period's most technologically dynamic industries, and a sharp turn toward fiscal austerity by New York's State and local governments. Chapter 13 concludes with a consideration of whether the City's highly visible involvement with the Federal government's New Deal programs boosted or impeded the pace of local recovery relative to that of comparable jurisdictions. It probably did neither.

## Chapters 14 and 15: Decentralization and Deindustrialization

Chapters 14 and 15 trace the causes and effects of New York's postwar decline. Between 1950 and 1980, while the total U.S. population grew by about 11%, the New York metropolitan region's increased by only two percent and the City's population *decreased* by about 10%. The metropolitan area's growth was impeded by a process of deindustrialization, which hit the New York region harder and sooner than elsewhere in the country. The shift of regional population out of New York City was, of course, a manifestation of postwar suburbanization.

Chapter 14 focuses on suburbanization and begins with a discussion of why suburbanization, a longstanding tendency of urban areas to expand geographically as populations and incomes increase and as transportation technology improves, had particularly problematic effects the second half of the twentieth century. There is little reason to argue with the common perception that the isolation of low-income, racial minority populations in central cities exacerbated social conditions to the extent that urban civil disorder broke out across the United States, including in New York.

One might have expected, however, that the problems associated with suburbanization would have been less severe in New York than elsewhere, because this region was substantially less suburbanized by any measure than comparable places in the United States. The chapter makes this case by reviewing the range of statistical indicia of suburbanization and showing how New York compared with the 11 other most populous northeastern metropolitan regions by all of these measures.

The discussion then turns to why New York was less suburbanized than other metropolitan areas. The first hypotheses examined derive from the extensive economic and sociological literature on the causes of suburbanization. The conclusions of these analyses are that suburbanization within an urban region ends to be most pronounced to the extent that (a) a metropolitan area's household incomes is high, (b) the limited access highway network is well developed, (c) the central city crime rates is high, and (d) racial minority populations are relatively large.

Consideration of these characteristics in the case of New York would not lead one to conclude that this metropolitan area would be substantially less (or more) suburbanized than its peers.

The next section of Chapter 14 presents an alternative hypothesis that applies to New York City, in particular. That is that government involvement in the local housing market was much more extensive in New York than elsewhere in the United States and that the particular policies adopted and the way they were implemented had the effect of inducing a substantial proportion of the middle-class, white population, many of whom could easily have moved to the suburbs, to live in New York City. These policies included (a) rent control and rent stabilization, (b) the ways in which the City administered federal public-housing projects, (c) State and City government financial support for the construction and maintenance housing projects designed to appeal to middle-class residents, and (d) the prioritization of the provision of such housing among the objectives of urban renewal programs.

The chapter concludes by pointed out that state and local government activity in New York encompassed, not just the housing market, but a broad range of activities including the provision of health care and the City's cultural life. In many respects, therefore, postwar public policy in New York was informed by a social democratic ideology that bore more resemblance to European than U.S. thinking at the time. Viewed in this way, it is not surprising that the residential land use patterns that developed in the New York region—the degree of suburbanization, the proportion of higher income households living in the central city, the likelihood of commuting to work by rail, etc.—was the most "European" of U.S. metropolitan regions.

Chapter 15 presents and analysis of the findings and forecasts of an extensive mid-1950s study of the New York regional economy sponsored by the Regional Plan Association (RPA). The study's goal was to project total 1985 regional employment, its industrial composition, and the proportions of jobs by industry that would be located in the central City, the inner ring of suburbs, and the region's exurban areas. The study team got many forecasts right, but its employment and population projections were, for the most part, much too optimistic. In particular, the team underestimated the extent to which jobs involving the handling and production of physical goods would vanish from New York City and its surroundings.

With respect to the handling of physical goods, during the years between 1955 and 1985 employment in New York's port, which the RPA analysis expected to decline modestly, decreased by about 70% as New York's share of total U.S. port activity dropped sooner and by more than anticipated and as the introduction of containerization technology cut demand for longshoremen and stevedores.

Over the same period, employment in two of the region's largest manufacturing industries, garments, and electronic goods, also contracted unexpectedly sharply. The RPA analysis of these two industries correctly anticipated that New York's share of U.S. employment in these sectors would diminish substantially, but the study team also expected that total national employment would increase by enough so that the total number of regional jobs in these sectors would be stable or rise modestly. In the case of the garment industry, however, total national employment barely increased at all in the face of competition from abroad. And with respect to electronics, the study could not have anticipated Boston's Route 128 and the San Francisco Bay Area's Silicon Valley would displace New York as important national centers of this activity.

Federal government statistical agencies treat "printing and publishing" as a manufacturing sector, although the latter component should be categorized as a part of the media industry. And, indeed, printing jobs diminished substantially in New York between 1955 and 1985 while employment at book and magazine publishers increased substantially. More generally, industries producing intangible products fared much better with respect to employment in New York than the RPA Study anticipated. The financial services sector is, of course, the "intangibles" sector with which New York is most closely identified. Accordingly, Chapter 15 concludes with consideration of how the "financialization" of the U.S. economy contributed to much faster, albeit volatile, job growth in this sector than the RPA anticipated.

# Chapter 16: The Nadir

Between the times, the RPA Study was conducted and its 1985 forecast horizon the increase of employment in finance, media, and other service sectors in New York City roughly balanced the decline in physical goods-related occupations so that total employment in New York City was close to 3.5 million in both 1955 and 1985. This equality, however, conceals a troubled period during the 1970s. Between its peak in 1969 and its nadir in 1977, total employment in New York City declined by 610,000 or by about 16%. Chapter 16 examines this period of sharp decline, its causes, its culmination in the City Government's near bankruptcy, and the irony that what became a robust recovery began very shortly thereafter.

The first part of the chapter makes the case that the City's fiscal crisis was the most visible effect of a "perfect storm" of adverse national and local economic and political trends. Stagflation on the national level—back-to-back national recessions accompanied by rising inflation between 1970 and 1975—was exacerbated locally by an accelerated contraction of the City's manufacturing industries and by a bearish stock market, severe operational challenges, and adverse regulatory changes that combined to shrink financial services employment. As the economy was shrinking, demand for government services, especially for redistributional programs, was rising. Rising unemployment and poverty, constituent and public employee militancy, and the City's social democratic traditions combined to push spending upward at the same time as the local economy's ability to generate revenues was weakening.

For a few years, the New York City was able to deal with the growing mismatch between a shrinking revenue base and increasing demand for public services by using opaque accounting practices to conceal debt-financed operating deficits. When the accumulated debt became too large to hide and the City could no longer borrow the money it needed to meet its obligations, the New York State and the Federal government stepped in to provide funds that allowed the City to meet its immediate needs and to impose a strict regime of fiscal austerity on the City government.

Such limited evidence as has been examined indicates the sharp cutbacks in local government spending did have at least some measurable adverse effects on the well-being of the City's residents. The conclusion of Chapter 16 makes the case that some of the cutbacks, and their ill effects could have been avoided if the City had been permitted to continue borrowing to finance operations for just a few more years. Analysis of the full array of high-frequency local area economic time series statistics that are available for New York City—total and per capita personal income and payroll employment—indicates that absolute and/or relative deterioration ended at some point during the late 1970s or early 1980s.

At first, the post-crisis recovery was barely perceptible. By 1985, total employment had only gotten back to its 1955 level. But as the turn of the twenty-first century approached, the improvement became more robust, more apparent, and more interesting.

# 12

# A Global City in a Less and Less Integrated World

## World Trade: Deceleration, Reversal, Stall

Total world trade, exports plus imports, reached close to 20% of world GDP in 1913 and fell to about 7% by 1938 (A. Estevadeordal, Frantz, & Taylor, 2003). As Fig. 12.1 indicates, the pattern for the United States was similar; as a percentage of GDP, total trade rose from around 10% early in the twentieth century, reached a post-Civil War peak of 16% in 1916 with the wartime surge in exports, and fell to below 5% in 1933. This statistic for the U.S. did not rise above 10% again until 1973 and did not surpass 1916 high until 1980. The post-World War I decline in U.S. trade as a percentage of GDP took place in two phases. After 1920, this statistic returned to and stabilized at levels only slightly lower than before the War. The big drop, which took some forty years to retrace, coincided with the onset of the Great Depression.

Efforts by economic historians to determine what caused the surge and decline of trade have pointed to some fairly clear conclusions. First, the sharp decline in trans-oceanic shipping costs during the last half of the nineteenth century supported rapid trade growth, and the post-armistice stabilization of freight rates facilitated the return to



A. Gurwitz, *Atlantic Metropolis*, Palgrave Studies in American Economic History,
https://doi.org/10.1007/978-3-030-13352-8_12

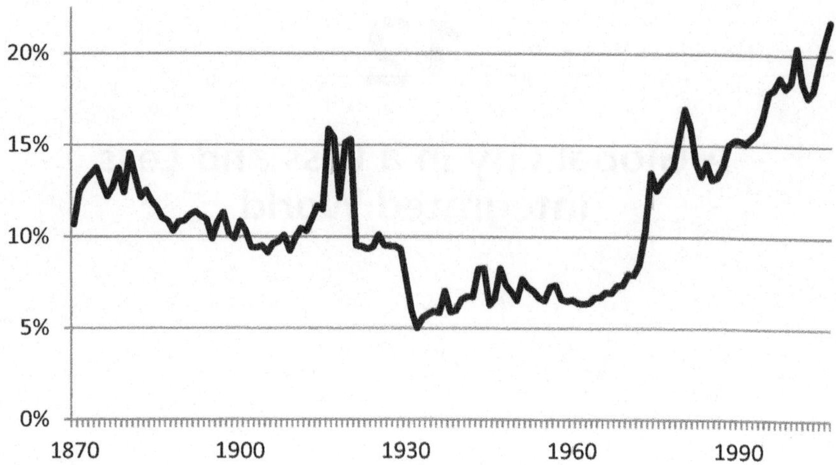


**Fig. 12.1** U.S. trade as a percent of GDP (U.S. Census Bureau, 1976; U.S. Department of Commerce, Bureau of Economic Analysis, n.d.)

pre-war trade levels. Second, countries' widespread adoption of the gold standard between 1897 and 1908, which essentially eliminated currency exchange rate risk as an impediment to international transactions, made an independent contribution to the expansion of trade early in the twentieth century. The re-adoption of a gold standard after wartime suspensions facilitated the return of "normal" trading levels during the 1920s. And the chaos accompanying the abandonment of the standard during the early 1930s clearly worsened the Depression-era collapse. Third, the volume of trade was reduced during the interwar years and, especially, after 1933, by the turn toward economic autarky of Nazi Germany and the Soviet Union, two previously active participants in the international flow of goods. By contrast, the enactment of increasingly protectionist policies beginning in the 1870s by food importers aiming to assist domestic landowners or by manufacturing interests aiming to support "infant industries" does not, by itself, seem to have suppressed trade to any great extent (Estevadeordal et al. 2003).

The magnitude and direction of capital flows between Europe and the United States also shifted dramatically over the period under consideration (Fig. 12.2). Before World War I, foreigners had been buying U.S.

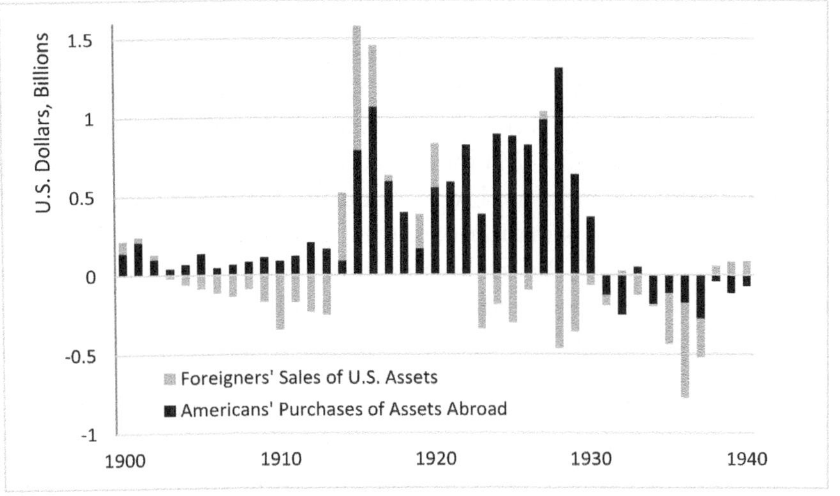


**Fig. 12.2** Eastbound transatlantic flow of long-term capital (U.S. Census Bureau, 1976, p. 869)

assets and Americans had been investing abroad in roughly equal, economically important but, by subsequent standards, modest amounts. The exigencies of war forced the initial belligerents, the British and French, in particular, to forgo producing for export and to buy much larger volumes of goods from America. They had no choice, therefore, but to acquire the U.S. dollars needed for these purchases either by selling U.S. assets they owned or by borrowing money from Americans. Through the 1920s, the United States continued running a trade surplus with the rest of the world, and, as a result, the volume of obligations due from foreigners to Americans continued accumulating at what were then unprecedented rates. During the early 1930s, international capital flows essentially ceased, but later in the decade, when exchange rates reached a new equilibrium with the U.S. dollar re-pegged at $35 per ounce of gold, the major democratic trading countries agreed to act together to stabilize markets and two-way capital flows resumed. As a result of these changes and of the rise and fall of the general price level, the gross nominal value of offshore assets held by U.S. public and private sector entities rose from $3.5 billion in 1914 to $11.5 billion in 1938 (Maddison, 2001, p. 99).

The postwar changes in the pace of emigration from Europe were at least as dramatic as what occurred with respect to goods and money. Between 1870 and 1913, an average of 325,000 Europeans per year emigrated from their home continent. Between 1914 and 1949, the equivalent figure was 105,000 (Maddison, 2001, p. 128). It is doubtful that Europeans were less motivated to leave during the latter period than the earlier. Instead, the destination countries in North and South America and the southwestern Pacific became much less welcoming to immigrants than they had been earlier. Starting in the 1890s, all of the major "new world" receiving countries—Argentina, Australia, Brazil, Canada, and the United States—abandoned neutral or explicitly pro-immigration policies to what were by 1930 highly restrictive regimes. The policy shift was most dramatic in the case of the South American countries and Australia, where governments had previously, directly or in effect, subsidized immigrants. The quantitative impact of the change on international mobility was greatest for the United States, which had been the destination of over 90% of pre-1914 international immigrants to the new world (Maddison, *The World Economy: A Millennial Perspective*, 2001, p. 128; O'Rourke & Williamson, 1999, pp. 188–189).

The disruptions caused by World War I and the Great Depression, especially the abandonment, re-adoption, re-abandonment, and re-adoption at an adjusted basis of the gold standard, go farthest to explaining the demise of early twentieth-century globalization as it affected the international movement of goods and of capital. It is harder to account for the timing of receiving countries nearly simultaneous clamp-down on immigration. A belief that large numbers of unskilled, working-age immigrants suppressed the wages of earlier immigrant and native-born American laborers, a supposition supported by statistical evidence, motivated working-class political support for some form of restriction. What is surprising is that it took twenty years, from 1898, when such legislation was first introduced, until 1917, when Congress overrode President Wilson's veto to impose a literacy requirement for new entrants, for the United States to begin restricting free immigration from Europe. In her analysis of the political economy of immigration restriction in the United States, Claudia Goldin's referred to the entry of some 17 million predominantly illiterate and unskilled immigrants to the United States while this political struggle played-out as a "miracle". A generally benign economic environment after the mid-1890s apparently assuaged concerns enough to keep the issue on the back burner for a couple of decades. What seems to have tipped the political balance in the United States toward restriction were a decrease in the literacy and skill endowment of newly arrived immigrants during the early years of the twentieth century and, possibly, fear of a renewed flood of "low quality" newcomers from a war-torn continent (Anbinder, 2016, p. 446; Goldin, 1994; O'Rourke & Williamson, 1999, pp. 196–206).

## Impact on Port and Financial Services Employment

Despite the fact that New York City was the nation's busiest port, the conduit for about 40% of total trade by value, the fluctuations in trade volumes during the interwar years do not, in and of themselves, appear to have had a particularly large impact on the City's economy as a whole. Only a relatively small number of workers were directly engaged in the port activities. For example, although the real value of goods moving through New York Customs District increased by about 67% between 1910 and the interwar peak in 1929, the number of New York City residents employed as longshoremen and stevedores only increased by about 14% or about 2,500. This was only 0.2% of the total increase in the number of gainfully employed New Yorkers between 1910 and 1930. Indirect impacts of trade fluctuations were larger, but not huge; the number of New Yorkers employed as "wholesale dealers, importers, and exporters" increased by almost 5,000, or 62%, between 1910 and 1930, about the same as the increase in the value of goods moving through the port during that period. Depression decade job losses for port laborers totaled about 4,400 or about 20% of 1930 employment in those occupations. This was about the same percentage decrease as in the real value of goods moving through the port but only 1.2% of the total decrease in the number of gainfully employed New Yorkers between 1930 and 1940[1] (U.S. Census Bureau, 1913; U.S. Census Bureau, 1932; U.S. Census Bureau, 1943; U.S. Department of Commerce, Various).

By contrast, the change in the direction of trans-Atlantic financial flows does seem to have had a noticeable impact on employment in New York's financial services industries. As discussed in Chapter 10, because any given pre-war public offering of securities might have found buyers in both North America and Europe, successful investment banking required the international coordination of underwriting syndicates. But because the distribution of bonds and stocks was limited to only the largest institutional and very wealthiest individual investors, almost all of whom would have had some representation in New York or one of the other northeastern financial centers, it was not necessary for the investment banking industry to penetrate the continent beyond the Middle Atlantic and New England regions.

The war brought two changes in this regard. First, because Europeans were no longer buying U.S. new securities in large volumes, it was no longer necessary for underwriters to coordinate pricing and marketing across the ocean. To be sure, U.S.-based investment banks needed some representation abroad to solicit underwriting assignments and to facilitate Europeans' liquidation of their U.S. dollar assets. The sale of securities to investors, however, would ordinarily take place entirely within the United States.

Second, ownership of financial securities became much more widespread across the U.S. population than before the war. Part of the impetus for this diffusion came from the way the war itself had been financed. The $21.5 billion in bonds issued by the Federal government from 1917 through 1919, for its own needs and to lend to allies, was unprecedented for such a short period of time by orders of magnitude. At year-end 1916, before the U.S. entered the conflict as a combatant, total public and private debt owed by Americans stood at $82.2 billion and that of the Federal government only $1.2 billion. Treasury

[1]Dollar amounts in different years were adjusted based on the wholesale price index for all commodities. Changes in the categorization of occupations between 1930 and 1940 censuses make it impossible to determine the change in the employment of wholesale dealers, importers, and exporters over the course of that period.

officials countered investment bankers' initial pessimism regarding the investors' ability to absorb the required volume of securities by launching an aggressive, nationwide marketing campaign. The target for this sales effort was the mass of relatively affluent Americans who had not previously purchased securities. Much of the appeal was to potential investors' patriotism, but the publicity incorporated an educational element that "emphasized the security, high yield, and probable appreciation of the new Liberty bonds" as well as the exemption of their interest payments from the new federal income tax. The Treasury also made it easy for individuals to buy bonds by introducing small denominations, savings stamps, and installment payments for purchases (Carosso, 1970, p. 224; U.S. Census Bureau, 1976, p. 989).

The marketing campaign met its immediate goal of financing the allied war effort with domestically-raised funds. A by-product of this effort had, for better or worse, a more lasting impact because it expanded the market for direct ownership of financial instruments by "retail" investors. Bankers' initial estimates were that no more than 350,000 individuals were potential bond buyers. In fact, there were over four million purchasers of the initial Liberty Bond offering, and 22.8 million participated in the fourth tranche (Carosso, 1970, p. 226). For many of these 22.8 million, their Liberty Bond purchase would have been their last foray into securities investing. For many others, though, satisfaction with this initial purchase whetted their appetites for financial securities as an alternative to the traditional household investment standbys: bank deposits, real estate, and private businesses. And it is probably safe to assume that the 22.8 million new bond buyers were less concentrated in New York or on the northeast coast than the 350,000 would have been.

In any case, the mass of affluent Americans became much readier buyers of stocks and bonds as the 1920s progressed. Whether the rising volume of aggressively marketed securities offerings over the course of the decade and rising stock prices were effects of or additional stimuli to this new demand, the impacts were the expansion of the securities industry and the dispersion its activities across the country.

As Table 12.1 indicates, an effect of these two postwar trends was to increase overall size of the financial service sector and especially of the

**Table 12.1** Financial services employment and employment concentration, 1910–1930

| | Total employment | Bankers and bank officials | Stockbrokers | Combination |
|---|---|---|---|---|
| United States | | | | |
| 1910 | 38,167,336 | 56,059 | 13,729 | 69,788 |
| 1930 | 48,829,920 | 93,356 | 70,950 | 164,306 |
| % Change | 28 | 67 | 417 | 135 |
| New York City | | | | |
| 1910 | 2,162,433 | 2,683 | 3,651 | 6,334 |
| 1930 | 3,257,459 | 5,092 | 10,686 | 15,778 |
| % Change | 51 | 90 | 193 | 149 |
| NYC concentration ratio | | | | |
| 1910 | | 0.84 | 4.69 | 1.60 |
| 1930 | | 0.82 | 2.26 | 1.44 |

securities industry. This could only benefit the City that was home to the country's most active financial markets. The positive impact of this development on New York's overall economy was offset to some extent by the expansion of broad-based, entirely domestic retail demand for stocks and bonds, which had the effect of reducing the relative concentration of industry employment in the City.

In any case, the roughly 10,000 increase in banking and stock brokerage jobs between 1910 and 1930, even with a very generous assumption regarding these sectors' employment multiplier, cannot account for more than a small percentage of the City's 1.1 million job growth over the period.

## Migrations: Mass, Great, and Caribbean

The demand for unskilled, semiskilled, and entrepreneurial labor in cities, which had been met in large part by immigration from abroad, continued growing even after the previous source of supply had been cut off. In 1910, 46% of the U.S. population was categorized as "urban" by the Census Bureau; by 1940 that percentage had risen to 57. The initial phase of what came to be called the Great Migration, the movement of African-Americans from the rural south to northern cities, accounted for a large share of that increase. Between 1910 and 1940, the percentage of the U.S. African-American population living in urban places rose from 27 to 49%, and the African-American proportion of the U.S. urban population rose from 6.3% of 8.4%. The shift for the 10 largest cities was even more dramatic. In 1910, 3.5% of their combined populations were African-Americans; by 1940 that percentage had more than doubled to 8.2 (U.S. Census Bureau, 1976, p. 12).

The last chapter argued that the New York City economy could not have developed as robustly as it did around the turn of the twentieth century absent the large supply of Italian and Jewish immigrant labor. The demographic, economic, and social characteristics of these migrants were particularly suited to the opportunities on offer for construction laborers, needle trades operatives, and small business entrepreneurs. One would, therefore, have expected that, absent some new source of migrants, the sharp curtailment of immigration from Southern and Eastern Europe would have limited the City's growth potential, both absolutely and relative to other cities that had been less dependent on immigration as a source of labor supply. Yet during most of the interwar period, New York's growth outpaced that of the nation as whole, that of other Northeastern and Midwestern cities, and, despite continuing westward population movement, that of all large U.S. cities (Susan B. Carter, 2006).

As was the case in other urban places, many of the new New Yorkers were people of color, mostly African-American migrants from the U.S. South. The proportion of interstate African-American migrants who chose New York as their destination was, however, disproportionately small. And an unusually large proportion of these newcomers of color began their migrations to the City from outside the United States.

In 1930, African-Americans who had been born in a state other than New York accounted for 2.5% of the City's population. The weighted average of the share of African-American interstate migrants in the populations of nine other large northern cities was 6.5%. Among these cities, only Boston at 1.2% had a lower proportion than New York. On average, the increase in the African-American interstate migrant population accounted for about 18% of the nine cities' total population growth between 1920 and 1930 but only 10% of New York City's growth[2] (U.S. Census Bureau, 1935).

A focus solely on the City's native-born African-American population, however, overstates the difference between New York and other large northern cities with regard to the racial compositions of their population growth. By 1930, the City was home to 56% of the nearly 100,000 foreign-born Blacks living in the United States, most of whom had migrated to New York from the British West Indies (BWI). New York was also home to, perhaps, 75% of the 53 thousand migrants from Puerto Rico living in the United States[3] (U.S. Census Bureau, 1935; Whalen, 2005, p. 3). If we add these to the native-born African-Americans from out of State, the total migrants of color, domestic and international, in New York City's 1930 population rises from 2.5 to 4.5%; still below the 6.5% average for the other nine large northern cities, but closer.

These statistical observations raise two questions. Why did New York attract proportionally fewer migrants of color than other large northern cities? And why did the City's population of these racial minorities include a disproportionately large group of migrants from the Caribbean.

## The Lesser Great Migration

With regard to the first of these questions, one reason may have been that, even as immigration diminished sharply, the foreign-born population of the United States—pre-war arrivals and the smaller number of recent immigrants—continued to gravitate disproportionally to the Atlantic metropolis. Economic historian William J. Collins has shown that between 1870 and 1950, the presence of a large foreign-born population tended to deter African-American migration to a northern state

---

[2]The nine cities are Chicago, Philadelphia, Detroit, Cleveland, St. Louis, Baltimore, Boston, Pittsburgh, and Washington, DC.

[3]Data for New York City's Puerto Rican population in 1930 are not available. The City was, however, home to 62% of Puerto Rican residents of the mainland in 1920 and to 88% in 1940. So, 75% is an approximate linear interpolation of the 1920 and 1940 figures.

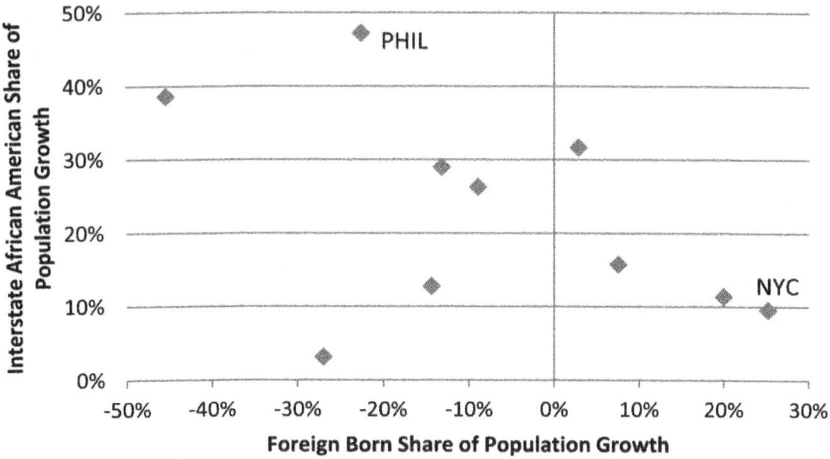


**Fig. 12.3** Interstate African-American migrant and foreign-born contributions to population growth, 1920–1930 (Susan B. Carter, 2006)

or city (Collins, 1997). Figure 12.3 indicates that this tendency was evident among the largest northern cities during the first interwar decade. New York foreign-born population increased by 331,000 between 1920 and 1930, and the City's share of the total foreign-born population of the ten large cities rose from 47% in 1920 to 50% in 1930. The total foreign-born populations of six of these cities—Philadelphia, Cleveland, St. Louis, Baltimore, Boston, and Pittsburgh—decreased between 1920 and 1930.

Another plausible, if heretofore unexamined, reason for African-Americans to steer clear of New York may have been that the City had earned a reputation as being particularly unwelcoming to residents of color. New York and neighboring New Jersey were, by far, the slowest northern states to eliminate slavery entirely. And many African-Americans abandoned the City in the wake of the violence done to individuals and to community institutions during the 1863 draft riots (Anbinder, 2016, p. 249; Wikipedia, 2018). In more concrete and contemporaneous terms, Ira Katznelson has provided evidence that the early twentieth-century political cultures of New York State and City provided African-Americans less access to the spoils of political power than those of Illinois and Chicago. African-Americans accounted for 4.7% of New York City's 1930 population but only 2.7% of the municipal government's 1934 workforce. In Chicago in 1930–1932, by contrast, 6.4% of the City government's workforce and 6.9% of its population was African-American (CD_HISTORYBLOG, 2017; Katznelson, 1973, pp. 83, 99).

A final possibility is that, in comparison with other large northern cities, the industrial composition of the New York economy—as it was before World War I and as it changed during the interwar period—generated fewer jobs for African-Americans. Employment opportunities for racial minorities in the United States were and are limited in two ways: by their lower average level of educational attainment and by a "color line," a web of discriminatory practices that effectively barred large numbers of African-Americans from occupations for which they would otherwise have been qualified.

It is unlikely that differences in educational attainment between the African-American and White populations had much effect on the employment prospects of the former who lived in New York. The illiteracy rate for African-American New Yorkers over 10 years of age in 1930 was 2.1%, less than half the 4.6% rate for the City's white population. That the latter figure was high relative to the total United States urban white population probably reflects the large proportion of the foreign-born whites in New York. What is less obvious is why the 2.1% illiteracy rate among African-American New Yorkers was the second lowest after Boston's 1.9% among large cities and much lower than the average 4.1% rate among urban African-Americans living in the north. One can speculate that, in the context of a low elasticity of substitution between well- and poorly educated labor, the large supply of illiterate foreign-born white workers in New York boosted wages on offer to those who could read making the city relatively attractive to literate job applicants, African-American and White (U.S. Census Bureau, 1935, p. 239).

The effects of racial discrimination, by contrast, probably did affect New York's relative attractiveness for most African-American interstate migrants adversely. Some color lines were explicit and obvious, as when African-Americans were considered unqualified for customer-facing positions in businesses with predominantly white or multi-racial clientele or were barred from supervising white workers.

Other manifestations of the color line were indirect as when geographic or social distance impeded African-American's access to social networks through which information regarding job openings and worker qualifications was communicated. Thus, for example, African-American men accounted for 8.6 of the 1940 U.S. male workforce but only 0.7% of male foremen in manufacturing industries and only 1.1% of "salesmen". And only 3.7% of male carpenters, many of whom would have found work in union halls or through social networks, were African-American. By contrast, 20.5% of the male laborers in manufacturing industries were African-American. Jobs in the garment industry were also filled through social networks. So, it isn't surprising that African-American women, who accounted for 13.8% of the total female workforce, held only 2.5% of the jobs as operatives in the apparel and other fabricated textiles industries (U.S. Census Bureau, 1943, pp. 88–90).

This pattern of occupational color lines and the characteristics of New York's leading specialty industries combined to limit the employment opportunities available to potential migrants of color. Notwithstanding the progressive stance taken with respect to racial discrimination by the Amalgamated Clothing Workers Union and International Ladies Garment Workers Union ("ILGWU"), African-Americans were underrepresented in the fashion industry, by far the City's largest manufacturing sector. Manufacturing industries that did hire large numbers of African-Americans, such as the steel industry, tended not to be concentrated in New York. Color lines also limited employment of African-Americans in New York's huge service sectors. For example, the City's employment 1940 concentration ratio for "other sales agents and brokers" was 2.00, and only 0.1% of African-American New Yorkers versus 2.7% of Whites were employed in these occupations. There were, of course, jobs for domestic servants in New York, and many of these would have been filled by African-American interstate migrants. But affluent New Yorkers did not employ proportionally more domestic servants than residents of other places in the United States; the local concentration ratio for this occupational category was 0.93. Further, the New York's manufacturing industries tended to make less use of unskilled workers than other cities'; the New York employment concentration ratio for manufacturing laborers was 0.23 in 1940.

To be sure, there were some African-American niche occupations that were overrepresented in New York's workforce. New York's 1940 occupational concentration ratio for elevator operators, for example, was 4.99, and the percentage of the City's African-American population holding such jobs was 3.2 times greater than the proportion of whites. By the same measure, African-American men were twice as likely as White men to hold a job as a longshoreman or stevedores, occupations with a 3.87 New York City concentration ratio in 1940. Jobs in these occupations could not offset the quantitative impact of color lines that limited African-Americans' access to jobs in the City's dominant fashion and services specialty industries and steered these workers into occupations that were not in particularly high demand in the local market (U.S. Census Bureau, 1943, pp. 491–492).

## Caribbean Immigration Before World War II

Caribbean migrants were overrepresented among New York City's population of color for four reasons. First, demand for workers of color in New York was limited by the interaction of racism with the City's industrial structure. Thus, whichever group—from a southern state or from a Caribbean island—established themselves and their labor market networks in the City the earliest could "crowd out" potential subsequent migrants. Second, New York's port was the easiest northern destination for Caribbean migrants to reach during the interwar period. Third, by 1920 early migrants had established beachhead Caribbean communities in New York City. Finally, the quotas on immigration enacted during the 1920s did not apply to Puerto Ricans, who were U.S. citizens after 1917, or to residents of politically independent Western Hemisphere countries, including Cuba and the Dominican Republic.

Immigration to the United States from the Caribbean followed the same economic, social, and geographic patterns as the Great Migration and previous waves of immigration from abroad.

Movement from the U.S. South to northern cities tended to follow rail lines. So, for example, African-Americans departing from South Atlantic states tended to follow coastal rail routes and head to cities in the Northeast. Thus, although only about 40% of African-Americans living outside of their birth states in 1930 had been born in a South Atlantic state, about 58% of those living in Philadelphia haled from that region[4] (U.S. Census Bureau, 1935, pp. 26, 32–36).

Migrants from the South Atlantic states could have chosen to get off the train in Baltimore, Philadelphia, Newark, New York City, Providence, Boston, or many other stops along the way. Most Caribbean immigrants, by contrast, had little choice as to where to disembark. Passenger ships and freighters sailed directly between individual Caribbean islands and several U.S. Gulf and East Coast ports, but passenger accommodations on most routes were limited and expensive. By contrast, sailings from San Juan, Puerto Rico, for example, to New York were regular, quick, and cheap. During the interwar decades, fares on the route ranged from $25 to $55 and the fastest ships took only three and a half days to sail between the two cities. So, the first mainland stop for all but a few interwar Caribbean immigrants would have been New York City (Sánchez Korrol, 1985, pp. 44–45).

Of course, if opportunities had beckoned elsewhere, they could have moved on from New York upon or shortly after arrival. After all, as discussed in Chapter 6, even during the antebellum period, when interstate transportation much less well developed, a large majority of immigrants moved on from New York City within a few years of arrival. But Caribbean immigrants did not move on. As noted above, in 1930 more than half of all foreign-born African-Americans and upwards of 80% of migrants from Puerto Rico were living in New York City (Model, 2001, p. 60; Sánchez Korrol, 1985, p. 28; U.S. Census Bureau, 1943, p. 157; Watkins-Owens, 2001, p. 33).

The most likely reason for the concentration of Caribbean immigrants in New York City was the combination of beachhead settlements and social networks. In this respect, the growth of the Caribbean communities followed the same time pattern as other immigrant cohorts. A small number of "pioneers," who arrived at random, established a

[4]The designation "South Atlantic" in this paragraph refers to Virginia, North and South Carolina, Georgia, and Florida.

rudimentary community that provided social support for subsequent newcomers and transmitted information about job openings and about worker qualifications. Then, when economic conditions in the home country and at the U.S. destination were ripe, previous immigrants could subsidize family members' resettlement. At that point, the pace of immigration could accelerate until employment opportunities improved at home or deteriorated at the destination.

Pioneering immigrants from both Puerto Rico and the BWI had established such communities in New York City before 1930. A study undertaken at the time by the Puerto Rican Brotherhood of America found that by 1926 early arrivals had coalesced into seven "*colonias*," neighborhoods that were each home to several thousand Puerto Rican residents. And as early as 1905, the Protestant Episcopal Mission City Society established St. Cyprian's church on West 63rd Street in Manhattan to serve immigrants from the BWI who were living in what was then a largely African-American neighborhood. And by 1920s, social networks, facilitated by residential clustering, had become economically useful as Caribbean immigrants had gravitated into a small number of industries: cigar, garment, and other light manufacturing for Puerto Ricans, transportation services for West Indian men, and domestic service for West Indian women (*New York Times*, September 10, 1956; Sánchez Korrol, 1985, pp. 54, 61; Watkins-Owens, 2001, p. 60).

Thus, by the end of World War I the preconditions were in place, and all that was needed to set off accelerating chain migration was a sufficient combination of economic push from the Caribbean and pull from New York. During the interwar years, the push was probably more powerful than the pull.

From the mid-sixteenth century through the early 1800s, as European and North American consumers' demand for sugar, coffee, and other Caribbean exports continued to grow rapidly, the BWI plantation economies, Jamaica, Barbados, and the smaller islands had experienced a chronic excess demand for labor, which became more acute after the United States and most of Western Europe outlawed the slave trade early in the nineteenth century. During the second half of the nineteenth century, however, the labor market situation began to reverse. Death rates began to decline while birth rates remained roughly constant. Thus, the total Caribbean 10-year population growth rate rose from about 6 to 13% between the first and last decades of the nineteenth century.

Just as the population and the local supply of labor began growing more rapidly, so did the global supply of the close substitutes for the region's main specialty exports. Production of beet sugar in Europe and coffee in Brazil began growing faster than demand and prices began to drop. Further, improvements in transportation technology enabled industrial-scale molasses manufacturers to locate farther away from the cane fields. Greater economies of scale in sugar processing boosted the competitive position of growing regions with larger land areas such as Cuba and the Guyanas, and production shifted away from the smaller islands. Residents of the British and French Caribbean islands responded by migrating away from their birthplaces. From the late nineteenth century and through the interwar years, most of this migration was to the destinations around the Caribbean basin that were faring better in the global economy of the time: to work in Cuba's burgeoning sugar sector or to staff Central American construction projects, for example. Thus by 1930, about 28,000 emigrants from the BWI were living in Cuba and almost 50,000 in Central America. Other British West Indians made their way farther north, to Miami or Tampa in Florida or to join family, friends, and acquaintances already living in New York City (Bulmer-Thomas, 2012, pp. 63–104, 270–273).

The situation in the Spanish colonies in the Caribbean was somewhat different. Neither Cuba nor Puerto Rico had developed initially as plantation economies, perhaps because Spain's imperial focus through the eighteenth century was on its mainland colonies in the Western Hemisphere. Nor did population growth accelerate as early or by as much in the Spanish as in the British colonies, in part, perhaps because slavery was not abolished in Puerto Rico until 1873 or in Cuba until 1886. During the late nineteenth century, therefore, most Puerto Ricans were engaged as proprietors or wage workers in small-scale agriculture. In response to global changes in the market for commodities, the islands' landowners began to shift away from sugar cane to coffee production. Because the latter was less labor intensive than the former, and despite the fact that the population was growing relatively slowly, labor was in excess supply in rural Puerto Rico by the time the United States acquired the Island as a colony in 1898 (Sánchez Korrol, 1985, pp. 17–28).

The imbalance in Puerto Rico's agricultural labor market became more pronounced through the three decades following the Spanish-American War. The U.S. government's policies vis-à-vis its Puerto Rican colony (and its Cuban protectorate) transformed large parts of the Island's agricultural sectors into corporate-owned, efficiently operated plantations. By the end of the first decade of the twentieth century, plantations owned by four U.S. corporations accounted for half of Puerto Rico's total sugar production. The positive impact on production was dramatic, the impact on sectoral employment much less so or in the opposite direction. Between 1910 and 1934, production of sugar in Puerto Rico increased by 220%, employment of sugar workers by only 5.4%. And between 1910 and 1920, tobacco growers increased production by 14% as employment in the sector *declined* by 26%. Some of the emigrants from rural Puerto Rico found jobs in the island's cities, where large-scale cigar production was beginning to take off. Others joined the general movement around the Caribbean basin and toward the North American mainland. Experienced cigar factory workers would have been particularly welcomed in New York City, where that industry was concentrated (Sánchez Korrol, 1985, pp. 25–26).

As similar situations were doing in parts of Europe and North America, high unemployment pushed rural West Indians away from their birthplaces. Young adults from the BWI and Puerto Rico responded in that same way Italians, Greeks, and Russians did, by migrating to nearby cities, to other countries within their home region and to North America. But the restrictions imposed by the United States during the 1920s that reduced immigration from Southern and Eastern Europe sharply did not have as dramatic an effect on the flow from the Caribbean. None of the restrictive legislation affected Puerto Ricans, of course, because Congress had granted them U.S. citizenship by 1917. Entries to the United States from the BWI were governed by the National Origins Act of 1924, but the degree to which the legislation actually affected the volume of migration is uncertain. Immigration from UK colonies was limited by Great Britain's relatively large 34,000 annual quota. Officials in the U.S. embassy in London had the authority to distribute quota slots across the British Empire, and, initially at least, allocations to consulates in the BWI were quite stingy. For example, about 2,000 Jamaicans were planning to emigrate to the United States in 1924, but only 10 immigrant slots were allocated to the U.S. consulate in Kingston for the month of September (Putnam, 2013, pp. 89–90). Still, the constraint could not have been as binding on British West Indians as on other migrant groups. The foreign-born White population of the United States decreased by 16.7% between 1920 and 1940, and the much smaller foreign-born "Negro" population increased by 13.7% over the same period (U.S. Census Bureau, 1943).

New York's population growth continued apace through the interwar years even as the City's previous main source of new residents, migration from Europe, was curtailed sharply by law. The arrival of African-American interstate migrants from the U.S. South replaced some of the Europeans who might have moved to New York, absent the restrictive legislation. In this respect, the City's experience was similar to that of other large northern cities. In other ways, however, changes that took place during the 1920s and 1930s in the geographic origins of New York's population were unique. First, an increasing proportion of the nation's decreasing total foreign-born population chose to locate in New York City. Second, although the Great Migration had a dramatic impact on the racial composition of the local population and although Harlem could justifiably claim to be the cultural capital of Black America, compared with most other northern cities a relatively small proportion of African-American interstate migrants chose New York as their northern destination. Finally, by the end of the interwar period, foreign-born people of color accounted for a much larger proportion of New York's population than that of any other large U.S. city. On the eve of World War II, therefore, New York had reinforced its position as the most "global" U.S. city. That position was, however, less valuable as a wellspring of economic growth than it had been before World War I.

## Manufacturing in the 1920s: More of the Same

Until the onset of the Great Depression, the local demand for and supply of labor grew at roughly similar rates. But, while the growth of the City's economy around the turn of the twentieth century was based on the creation and rapid expansion of a new kind of business, the industrial production of women's clothing, the expansion through the first postwar decade, for the most part, involved "more of the same."

The decade of the 1920s witnessed dramatic changes in the industrial structure of the U.S. economy. One of these developments—the growth and geographic expansion of employment in the securities industry—has already been touched upon in this chapter. More important in terms of the number of jobs created, however, was the production and mass-marketing of consumer durables: automobiles, radios, and household appliances. One of the published reports on the 1929 Census of Manufactures identified 10 industries in which employment had increased by 20,000 jobs or more between 1919 and 1929 and eight industries that had declined by that number. Data for these industries are presented in Table 12.2 (U.S. Census Bureau, 1933, pp. 18, 21–22; U.S. Census Bureau, 1933, pp. 378–380). The decline in total manufacturing employment over the period nationally and in New York probably reflects the facts that postwar industrial demobilization may not have been complete in 1919 and that 1929 reflected the early stages of the Depression.

As the table indicates, New York City was well situated with respect to the changes that were taking place in the U.S. economy. The weighted average concentration ratio for the 10 growing industries (1.47) was much higher than for the eight that were declining (0.28). This was despite the fact that the two fastest growing industries, electrical equipment and motor vehicles, which together accounted for more than 40% of fast-growing industry employment nationwide had minimal presence in New York City[5] (U.S. Census Bureau, 1933).

[5]The electrical equipment industry was highly concentrated in the New York Industrial Area. The published reports of the 1929 census were the first to include tabulations of information about metropolitan economies surrounding large cities. The concentration ratio for electrical machinery, apparatus, and supplies in the New York Industrial Area, which included the City, Westchester County, NY, and Bergen, Essex, Hudson, Middlesex, Passaic, and Union Counties, NJ, was 2.52, and the weighted average concentration for the 10 growing industries was 1.64 (U.S. Census Bureau, 1933, pp. 362–365).

**Table 12.2** Employment in the industries in which wage employment grew or declined by 20,000 or more between 1919 and 1929

| Industry | U.S.A. employment | | | NYC 1929 | |
|---|---|---|---|---|---|
| | 1929 | 1919 | % change | Employment | Conc. ratio |
| All industries | 8,838,743 | 9,000,059 | −2 | 563,249 | |
| *Increase of 20,000 or more* | | | | | |
| 10-industry total | 2,409,113 | 1,882,626 | 28 | 226,304 | 1.47 |
| Electrical machinery, apparatus, and supplies | 328,722 | 212,374 | 55 | 12,470 | 0.60 |
| Motor vehicles; bodies and parts | 447,448 | 343,115 | 30 | 2,049 | 0.07 |
| Bread and other bakery products | 200,841 | 141,592 | 42 | 23,383 | 1.83 |
| Clothing | 464,939 | 410,569 | 13 | 124,907 | 4.22 |
| Furniture, including store and office fixtures | 193,399 | 144,423 | 34 | 10,738 | 0.87 |
| Printing and publishing industries | 281,119 | 244,688 | 15 | 39,107 | 2.18 |
| Knit goods | 208,488 | 172,572 | 21 | 10,874 | 0.82 |
| Chemicals and allied products | 104,695 | 76,918 | 36 | 1,151 | 0.17 |
| Petroleum refining | 80,596 | 58,889 | 37 | n.a. | n.a. |
| Caning and preserving: fruits and vegetables | 98,866 | 77,486 | 28 | 1,625 | 0.26 |
| *Decrease of 20,000 or more* | | | | | |
| Eight-industry total | 1,300,599 | 1,960,601 | −34 | 23,162 | 0.28 |
| Ship and boat building, steel and wooden | 55,089 | 387,446 | −86 | 9,139 | 2.60 |
| Railroad car construction and repair | 368,681 | 484,437 | −24 | 2,341 | 0.10 |
| Lumber and timber products, etc. | 419,084 | 480,945 | −13 | n.a. | n.a. |
| Meat packing, wholesale | 122,505 | 160,996 | −24 | 4,648 | 0.60 |
| Musical instruments, parts, and phonographs | 33,041 | 68,741 | −52 | 483 | 0.23 |
| Cigars and cigarettes | 105,308 | 138,773 | −24 | 6,259 | 0.93 |
| Leather, tanned, curried, and finished | 49,932 | 72,476 | −31 | 292 | 0.09 |
| Woolen goods and worsted goods | 146,959 | 166,787 | −12 | n.a. | n.a. |

The specific fast-growing manufacturing industries that were concentrated in the City should look familiar. Clothing, baking, and printing and publishing had been New York specialties since at least the mid-nineteenth century. New York's prosperity during the 1920s was generated by increasing nationwide demand for products its businesses were already producing. In contrast, the 1920s growth of cities that specialized in the production of consumer durables (Detroit) or of inputs to the production of those goods (e.g., steel in Pittsburgh and rubber in Akron) was driven by the creation and fulfillment of new consumer wants and needs. One can conclude that, although New York was keeping pace with a booming U.S. urban economy during the 1920s, an element of structural dynamism was missing from the City's manufacturing sector.

## Media, Old and New

Viewed from a broader and deeper perspective, however, a pre-Depression snapshot of New York's economy looks somewhat more promising. Expanding the geographic unit of analysis to incorporate the broader metropolitan region and digging a little deeper into the composition of the printing and publishing industry reveals a collection of related businesses that were both highly concentrated in and around New York and growing at a quick and accelerating pace during the 1920s. This was the decade during which a symbiotic relationship between mass-marketed consumer brands and nationwide print and broadcast media empires reinforced the growth of both types of enterprises. And all of the nationwide radio networks and all but one of the decade's ubiquitous magazines' publishers had their headquarters in New York City and sourced large portions of their content there. Further, a concentration of employment in "electrical machinery, apparatus, and supplies" manufacturing, much of it probably involving radio equipment, emerged in northern New Jersey.

The marriage between magazines offering nationwide mass circulation and advertisements for nationally marketed, branded consumer goods had been consummated by the time the United States entered World War I. To exploit the full potential of economies of scale producers of such commodities as Kodak cameras, Campbell's soups, and Ivory soap, needed some way to bring their products to the attention of consumers and retailers across the country. Unlike newspapers, widely circulated magazines, aided by the advent of rural free mail delivery during the last decade of the nineteenth century, could offer advertisers nationwide exposure to well-defined demographic groups. Thus, the *Saturday Evening Post*, the most widely distributed magazine around the turn of the century, reached a circulation of 1,250,000 by the end of 1909 and saw advertising revenues rise from $6,933 in 1897 to $16 million in 1917 (Tebbel & Zuckerman, 1991, pp. 141, 178).

The full combined business potential of mass-marketing and mass-circulation publishing was not realized until consumer spending began to boom after the U.S. economy recovered from the postwar recession of 1920–1921; the average annual growth rate of real U.S. GDP per capita rose from 1.5% between 1890 and 1920 to 4.5% between 1921 and 1929 (U.S. Census Bureau, 1976, p. 224). Advertisers' appetite for cost-effective nationwide product exposure was met in part by new magazines; each designed to reach a well-defined but geographically dispersed socio-economic audience. Many of the publications that held pride of place on newsstands and in subscribers' mailboxes until the advent of the Internet—*Time*, the *Reader's Digest*, *Better Homes and Gardens*, the *New Yorker*, etc.—were founded during the 1920s. The principal editorial and business offices of all but one of these publications and their parent companies were located in the New York metropolitan area and all, except for Westchester-headquartered *Reader's Digest*, were in New York City. The geographic outlier among the group of mass-circulation magazines happened to be the largest of them; the Curtis Company, which published the *Saturday Evening Post* and the *Ladies' Home Journal*, was based in Philadelphia.

The concentration of mass-circulation magazine publishing in New York is not hard to understand. As discussed in Chapter 5, the printing and publishing industry had become highly concentrated in the City by 1860. Given the importance of foreign content in U.S. books and periodicals, it was almost inevitable that the nation's principal port would also be the home to the most publishers. The large number of publishers, in turn, attracted writers, type-setters, printers, printing machine manufacturers, and potential investors in new periodicals, which reduced local start-up costs for the growing number of niche market magazines. By the 1920s, high speed, long-distance communication technology and the increasingly domestic provenance of U.S. cultural trends had reduced New York's advantage as a conduit for foreign intelligence. But New York was still the best place to start a new magazine; the benefit conveyed by the agglomeration of inputs to the publication process, which now included the presence of the nation's leading advertising agencies, more than offset the high cost of office space in the City.

The launch of *Time* magazine by its founders, Henry Luce and Briton Hadden, neatly illustrates the operation of both urban agglomeration economies and social networks in supporting business development and economic growth. The two recent Yale classmates were reunited when both took jobs at the Baltimore *News*. They conceived the idea of a weekly news magazine with a target audience of college graduates. They brought their idea to New York, where both had relatives they could live with, and made the rounds through networks of individuals, mostly but not only Presbyterian Yale alumni, with expertise in the editorial, marketing, and financial aspects of the publishing industry. They organized the advice they received into a prospectus for the new publication, which attracted investments from 70 initial shareholders, mostly New Yorkers, including several J.P. Morgan partners, and mostly Yale alumni or relatives of Yale alumni. When they were close to their start-up funding goal of $100,000, they set up shop in a large room divided into cubicles in the Printing Crafts Building (Tebbel & Zuckerman, 1991, pp. 158–163).

The Printing Crafts Building was what we would today call an "incubator" for the publishing industry. This 1916 vintage, 600,000 square-foot property was the largest of several purpose-built New York structures designed to house various branches of the printing and publishing industry. As the building neared completion, the *New York Times* reported.

> "The Printing Crafts Building is the largest structure in the country devoted to the publishing and printing interests and is the only building in which printing machinery is operated twenty-one stories above the street. The steel framework is reinforced on all sides by heavy plates and brackets in order to prevent vibration or lateral sway.…

> "The floors from the second to the eleventh, inclusive, are given over to printing, binding, lithographing establishments, electrotypers, engravers, ink and paper concerns. All this has been leased. Above the twelfth floor are offices, salesrooms, clubrooms and stockrooms of publishers, advertising agencies and the supply lines catering to the graphic arts....
>
> "The purpose of the building is to concentrate under one roof representatives of all branches of the publishing and printing trades. The new General Post Office Building is in the block below and the Pennsylvania Station is opposite." (*New York Times*, 1956)

*Time* was, of course, a success. The first issue was published on March 3, 1923, a little more than a year after Luce and Hadden had left Baltimore. By the end of 1924, circulation had reached 70,000 and the operation was well on its way to profitability (Tebbel & Zuckerman, 1991, pp. 162–164).

Long-established local networks of residents and existing businesses that could nurture new publishing enterprises like *Time* were present in New York and not in the same density elsewhere in the 1920s. Commercial radio broadcasting, however, did not exist before November 1920, and no supportive ecosystem for these operations existed anywhere. As the 1920s began, the technology of electronic signal transmission had progressed to the degree that it was clear to some astute observers that sound broadcasting would develop into a significant institution of American life. What was not clear is how broadcasting activity would be organized.[6]

The first commercial application of wireless telecommunication technology was to transmit messages among ships at sea and between ships and land stations. In the United States, this service was provided by the Marconi Wireless Communication Company of America, a subsidiary of the British Marconi company. Perhaps because the American Marconi company's principal business involved communication with ships at sea, the headquarters were located in New York City. Availability of labor with relevant expertise may also have helped induce the Marconi Company to locate its manufacturing facility within 10 miles of Thomas Edison's research laboratory in northern New Jersey.

---

[6]Unless otherwise indicated the material in this section on the early days of radio broadcasting is drawn from (Head, 1978, pp. 90–153).

Wireless transmission of voice communication became possible in time to serve the combatants in World War I. After the armistice, the companies that had developed and operated the technology began exploring potentially profitable civilian applications. Several business models were assayed. One approach, government ownership and operation of radio broadcasting in the public interest, which was common in Europe, was apparently not even considered in the United States of the 1920s. The Westinghouse Corporation, a manufacturer of radio receivers, inaugurated the first licensed broadcast station, KDKA, by transmitting reports of the results of the 1920 presidential election interspersed with recorded and live music from the company's Pittsburgh headquarters. Westinghouse apparently viewed its broadcasting function as something of a loss-leader for the principal commercial goal of expanding the market for receivers beyond a small coterie of hobbyists. Radio's potential as a vehicle for using informative and entertaining programming to attract an audience for product advertising, of course, extended beyond the sale of radio receivers themselves. This pioneering model would not, however, have been scalable. Given the narrow band of available broadcast frequencies, if every potential advertiser operated its own local transmission facility, cross-station interference would have precluded clear reception.

About one year after KDKA went on the air AT&T, the manufacturer of radio transmission equipment, began broadcasting from New York City under the call letters WEAF. Not surprisingly, the telephone company's idea was to serve as a "common carrier," producing no content of its own, but charging a toll to transmit programming provided by others with something to sell. Under this model, each locality would be served by a small number of such common carriers that would provide broadcasting facilities to whoever was willing to pay the toll. Thus, WEAF's first revenue-producing broadcast in August 1922 was a 10 minute sales pitch by a Jackson Heights, Queens, apartment developer.

In 1923, AT&T introduced another innovation, the radio network. Using specially adapted long-distance telephone lines, the Company linked WEAF in New York with independently owned transmission stations in the Boston area, allowing simultaneous broadcast of the same content in multiple locations. By 1924, AT&T was able to arrange a coast-to-coast hookup of 22 stations to carry a speech by President Calvin Coolidge.

The consumer- and content-oriented KDKA model was carried forward initially by WJZ, the New York area station of the Radio Corporation of America. RCA was the U.S.-controlled successor to the American Marconi Company and a joint venture of General Electric and Westinghouse, with AT&T holding a smaller share. The RCA broadcasting venture operated at a disadvantage because it was barred from using AT&T's long lines to distribute its quality programming to a network. Meanwhile, the telephone company's hands-off approach to content did not produce a competitive programming. By 1926, therefore, AT&T and RCA, the holders of the key patents, were prepared to agree on a new cross-licensing agreement that facilitated the emergence of the industrial structure—an oligopoly of nationwide networks—that organized the U.S. broadcasting industry until the advent of cable television. So, at the end of the first postwar decade three networks were producing programs for syndication to affiliate stations nationwide. The network's revenues were generated by fees paid for programming by the affiliates and by the sale of advertising time for products distributed to the national market. Affiliates' revenues came from the sale of time to local advertisers and from a share of the network's national advertising fees.

When this structure emerged initially in 1928, two parent companies managed three national networks: the National Broadcasting Company (NBC), a subsidiary and then a spin-off of RCA, which operated "Red" and "Blue" networks, and the Columbia Broadcasting System (CBS). The number of networks eventually increased to four when the Mutual Broadcasting System, essentially a consortium of mostly small independent stations, was organized in 1934. NBC was forced to sell one of its properties in 1943, at which time the Blue network became ABC. From the late 1920s, when the structure emerged, until the advent of cable television, all of the networks that dominated the industry were headquartered and produced a large proportion of their content in New York City.

Further, the New York metropolitan area, although not the City itself, was home to an important concentration of production of radio equipment. The published Census Bureau tabulations of 1929 regional manufacturing employment did not break the "electrical machinery, apparatus, and supplies" industry into its component sectors. Nationally about 18% of the total value of the industry's output consisted of "radio apparatus and tubes." The concentration ratio of the overall electrical machinery industry in the New York Industrial Area was 2.52 in 1929 (U.S. Census Bureau, 1933, p. 1124). Circumstantial evidence indicates that a large proportion of this activity related to radio equipment. The sole manufacturing facility of the American Marconi Company, which had been a monopoly supplier of radio equipment in the United States, was located in northern New Jersey. Further, the early career of Allen B. Dumont, one of the pioneers of the television industry, indicates that there were a number of career opportunities for a young electronic engineer in New Jersey during the 1920s. After graduating from Rensselaer Polytechnic Institute in 1924, Dumont worked for four years developing vacuum tube manufacturing techniques for Westinghouse in Bloomfield, NJ, and for the subsequent three years for the deForest Radio Company in Passaic. In 1931, Dumont founded his own firm with the goal of developing practical television equipment (Brittain, 1997, pp. 2,081–2,082).

No doubt the concentration of technical expertise in the region, which began when the American Marconi Company decided to locate in New York and thus may have had its origin in the City's status as the nation's largest port, helped attract broadcasters to this location. But a similar combination of concentration of expertise and early-adopter status failed to keep the movie industry from leaving metropolitan New York for Los Angeles in the years after World War I. Why didn't the broadcasting industry move elsewhere or disperse more broadly across the country? After all, by its nature radio programming is cheap to transport over long distances, so why locate production in a place where rents are high?

Three differences between the broadcasting and movie industries probably combined to draw the former's production activities, much more than the latter's, to New York. First, the radio programs required much less space to produce than movies, so New York's high rents would have been less relevant for broadcasters. Second, California's weather was very important to the film industry and largely irrelevant for radio production. Third, a location in New York offered privileged access to program content most likely to attract listeners. A large part of radio programming broadcast recorded music, and the 1920s has been characterized as the "golden age of Tin Pan Alley," the period spanning 1910s and 1920s, during which New York-based music publishers exerted dominant influence over the kinds of popular music Americans played and listened to. Finally, and perhaps most importantly, since the broadcasting network business model that evolved during the 1920s was based on the sale of audience "ears" to producers of nationally branded consumer goods, location near the greatest concentration of advertising agencies would have helped generate the highest possible revenues per listener.

## Conclusion

New York's prosperity during the 1920s was based in large part on the growth of industries that were already well established in the City. The characteristics that had boosted New York to its leading position in the women's garment, financial services, and publishing industries remained in place, and as demand for fashionable clothing, stocks and bonds, and advertising platforms continued to expand, employment in those industries continued to grow. Further, during the initial "post-globalization" decade any adverse impact on the City that had benefited the most from the pre-war trend toward greater trans-Atlantic market integration was modest. Once the absolute value of commodities trade returned to previous peacetime levels port activity in New York picked up. Employment in the financial services industry was somewhat more geographically dispersed in 1930 than it had been in 1910, but the nationwide growth of that sector was so rapid that the total number of banking and brokerage jobs in New York increased by almost 150% over those two decades. The radio broadcasting industry, which did not exist in 1920 and had become integral to Americans' lives by 1930, was the one exception to the "more of the same" characterization of New York's economy during the first interwar decade.

Nor, despite the draconian new immigration restrictions, did the bosses of New York's sweatshops, banks, publishing houses, or broadcasting studios find it hard to attract a workforce at wage levels commensurate with continued business success. Greater concentration of the total U.S. foreign-born population in New York City and a large contingent of interstate and international migrants of color generated sufficiently robust laborforce growth.

New York's industrial concentrations and population mix would stand it in good stead during the early phases of the Great Depression of the 1930s, but not thereafter.

## References

Anbinder, T. (2016). *City of Dreams: The 400-Year Epic History of Immigrant New York*. New York: Houghton Mifflin Harcourt.

Brittain, J. (1997). Allen B. Dumont: A Pioneer in Electronic Instruments, Radio, and Television. *Proceedings of the IEEE, 85*(12), 2081–2082.

Bulmer-Thomas, V. (2012). *The Economic History of the Caribbean Since the Napoleonic Wars*. Cambridge: Cambridge University Press.

Carosso, V. P. (1970). *Investment Banking in America: A History*. Cambridge, MA: Harvard University Press.

Carter, S. B. (2006). *Table Aa22035*. Retrieved from Historical Statistics of the United States Millennial Edition Online http://projects.ilt.columbia.edu/seneca/svcurric/images/byward2_early.html.

CD_HISTORYBLOG. (2017, January 9). *When Did Slavery End in the North*. Retrieved from Civil Discourse, A Blog of the Long Civil War Era http://www.civildiscourse-historyblog.com/blog/2017/1/3/when-did-slavery-really-end-in-the-north.

Collins, W. J. (1997). When the Tide Turned: Immigration and the Delay of the Great Black Migration. *The Journal of Economic History, 57*(3), 607–632.

Estevadeordal, A., Frantz, B., & Taylor, A. M. (2003). The Rise and Fall of World Trade, 1870–1939. *The Quarterly Journal of Economics, 118*(2), 359–407.

Goldin, C. (1994). The Political Economy of Immigration Restriction in the United States. In C. A. Goldin (Ed.), *The Regulated Economy* (pp. 223–257).

Chicago: University of Chicago Press. Retrieved from http://www.nber.org/books/gold94-1.

Head, S. W. (1978). *Broadcasting in America: A Survey of Television and Radio* (3rd ed.). New York: Houghton Mifflin.

Katznelson, I. (1973). *Black Men, White Cities: Race, Politics, and Migration in the United States, 1900–1930, and Britain, 1948–1968*. Chicago: University of Chicago Press.

Maddison, A. (2001). *The World Economy: A Millennial Perspective*. Paris: Development Studies Center of the Organization for Economic Co-operation and Development.

Model, S. (2001). Where New York's West. Indians Work. In N. Foner (Ed.), *Islands in the City: West Indian Migration to New York* (pp. 52–80). Berkeley: University of California Press.

*New York Times*. (1956, September 10). *Vicar Asks City to Spare Church, Urges Campaign to Preserve St. Cyprian's in Path of Lincoln Sq. Project.*

O'Rourke, K. H., & Williamson, J. G. (1999). *Globalization and History: The Evolution of a Nineteenth-Century Atlantic Economy*. Cambridge, MA: The MIT Press.

Putnam, L. (2013). *Radical Moves: Caribbean Migrants and the Politics of Race in the Jazz Age*. Chapel Hill: University of North Carolina Press.

Sánchez Korrol, V. E. (1985). *From Colonia to Community: The History of Puerto Ricans in New York City, 1917–1948*. New York City: Greenwood Press.

Tebbel, J., & Zuckerman, M. E. (1991). *The Magazine in America, 1741–1990*. Oxford: Oxford University Press.

U.S. Bureau of the Census. (1976a). *Historical Statistics of the United States, Colonial Times to 1970*. New York: Basic Books.

U.S. Bureau of the Census. (1976b). *The Statistical History of the United States From Colonial Times to the Present* (p. 1061). New York: Basic Books.

U.S. Census Bureau. (1913). *Thirteenth Census of the United States Taken in the Year 1910, Volume IV, Occupation Statistics*. Washington, DC: U.S. Government Printing Office.

U.S. Census Bureau. (1932). *Occupation Statistics, New York*. Retrieved from Fifteenth Census of the United States, 1930 https://babel.hathitrust.org/cgi/pt?id=coo.31924014032860;view=1up;seq=3.

U.S. Census Bureau. (1933). *Fifteenth Census of the United States, Manufactures: 1929, Volume III, Reports by States: Statistics for Industrial Areas, Counties, and Cities*. Washington, DC: U.S. Government Printing Office.

U.S. Census Bureau. (1935). *Negroes in the United States, 1920–1932.* Washington: U.S. Government Printing Office.

U.S. Census Bureau. (1943). *Sixteenth Census of the United States: 1940.* Retrieved from Volume III, Labor Force https://babel.hathitrust.org/cgi/pt?id=coo.31924055066660;view=1up;seq=5.

U.S. Census Bureau. (1976). *The Statistical History of the United States from Colonial Times to the Present.* New York: Basic Books.

U.S. Department of Commerce. (Various). *Annual Reports on the Commerce and Navigation of the United States Accessed Via.* Retrieved from https://catalog.hathitrust.org/Record/001719409.

Watkins-Owens, I. (2001). Early-Twentieth-Century Caribbean Women: Migration and Social Networks in New York City. In N. Foner (Ed.), *Islands in the City: West Indian Immigration to New York* (p. 33). Berkeley: University of California Press.

Whalen, C. T. (2005). Colonialism, Citizenship, and the Making of the Puerto Rican Diaspora: An Introduction. In C. T. Whalen & V. Vázquez-Hernández (Eds.), *The Puerto Rican Diaspora: Historical Perspective.* Philadelphia: Temple University Press.

Wikipedia. (2018). *Timeline of Abolition of Slavery and Serfdom.* Retrieved from Wikipedia https://en.wikipedia.org/wiki/Timeline_of_abolition_of_slavery_and_serfdom#cite_note-54.

# 13

# New York's Great Depression: The Delayed Fade

The U.S. Great Depression had four distinct phases in the: a downward spiral between 1929 and early 1933, a robust recovery from 1933 through early 1937, a second, severe contraction from mid-1937 through 1938, and, finally, a renewed recovery that coincided with a gradual transition to a wartime economy between 1939 and 1941. Somewhat surprisingly, New York City's initial contraction was noticeably less severe than other large cities'. But, as was common among regions that suffered less in the initial downturn, New York's relative performance deteriorated as the decade progressed[1] (Garret & Wheelock, 2006; Wallis, 1989). By the end of the period, conditions in New York were significantly worse than in the average metropolitan region.

Assertions about 1930s relative economic conditions in any geographic region smaller than a state are necessarily based on impressions

[1]The tendency of initially resilient regions to lag the recovery and be hit particularly hard in 1937–1938 was by no means universal. The South Atlantic region, for example, performed better than average across all four Depression phases.



A. Gurwitz, *Atlantic Metropolis*, Palgrave Studies in American Economic History,
https://doi.org/10.1007/978-3-030-13352-8_13

gleaned by analogy and a few irregular direct observations.[2] Nevertheless, the evidence we do have indicates that New York City's experience was as stated, namely initial outperformance followed by prolonged and worsening underperformance. For one thing, New York *State's* trajectory followed the outperformance-underperformance pattern. Total nonfarm employment in New York declined more slowly in the early years of the Depression but then lagged the national recovery and contracted by a bit more than average in 1937 and 1938. What apparently boosted New York State's performance during the initial contraction was the relatively strong performance of the state's non-manufacturing industries. Because New York City accounted for about half of the State's total employment and because an even larger share of the State's nonfarm, non-manufacturing activity took place in New York City, we can take the State's employment trends as a reasonably good indicator of what was going on in the City at the time.

Local area unemployment statistics, available for 1930, 1931, 1937, and 1940, are also consistent with outperformance followed by underperformance.

Table 13.1 lists the unemployment rates for the 19 cities enumerated in the 1931 special census and for 20 large metropolitan labor markets in 1930, 1937, and 1940. These figures provide a reasonably reliable indication of relative conditions across cities or metropolitan areas at each point in time. Because the definitions of some categories of workers changed from one enumeration to another, however, inter-temporal comparisons may not be reliable.

---

[2]Annual statistics on manufacturing and nonfarm, non-manufacturing employment are available for each state. The 1930 and 1940 censuses tabulated a range of relevant information for counties and cities. And Congress authorized two special censuses of unemployment during the Depression years. The 1931 special census gathered information for 19 large cities, including New York City, although the count only covered the Bronx, Brooklyn, and Manhattan. The 1937 enumeration reported county-level information, but since city and county borders don't always coincide, the 1931 and 1937 observations are not always for the same geographic entity. We cannot, therefore, determine the exact trajectory of city or metropolitan area employment or unemployment between 1931 and 1937. Further, the local area data for 1930, 1931, 1937, and 1940 must be used with caution, especially when attempting to make inter-temporal comparisons, because the definition of unemployment changed from survey to survey.

**Table 13.1** Unemployment rates in cities in 1931 and metropolitan areas in 1930, 1937, and 1940 (Haines, n.d.; U.S. Census Bureau, 1933)

| City/Metro. area | 1930 (%) | 1931 (%) | 1937 (%) | 1940 (%) |
|---|---|---|---|---|
| **New York** | **7.6** | **20.0** | **13.4** | **14.0** |
| **Northeast–Midwest** | | | | |
| Baltimore | 4.9 | | 8.0 | 7.9 |
| Boston | 7.6 | 25.0 | 13.4 | 11.2 |
| Birmingham | | 24.6 | | |
| Buffalo | 8.1 | 30.8 | 12.9 | 14.7 |
| Chicago | 9.0 | 28.9 | 10.7 | 10.4 |
| Cincinnati | 7.0 | | 12.2 | 9.9 |
| Cleveland | 9.9 | 31.6 | 12.8 | 10.8 |
| Dayton | | 24.0 | | |
| Detroit | 11.3 | 32.4 | 9.9 | 10.2 |
| Duluth | | 22.0 | | |
| Milwaukee | 7.1 | | 10.8 | 11.1 |
| Minneapolis | 6.6 | 18.3 | 10.3 | 11.3 |
| Philadelphia | 8.0 | 27.7 | 14.4 | 14.2 |
| Pittsburgh | 8.1 | 28.5 | 15.6 | 14.8 |
| **South and West** | | | | |
| Denver | | 17.2 | | |
| Houston | 5.7 | 23.3 | 8.0 | 7.9 |
| St. Louis | 8.0 | 24.0 | 14.1 | 10.3 |
| Washington, DC | 4.0 | | 14.2 | 9.2 |
| Kansas City | 6.5 | | 12.8 | 10.6 |
| Los Angeles | 8.0 | 18.1 | 10.5 | 10.7 |
| Portland, OR | 8.4 | | 13.5 | 10.3 |
| San Francisco | 6.2 | 11.6 | 8.7 | 9.1 |
| Seattle | 7.5 | 20.0 | 12.2 | 10.7 |
| Average | 7.5 | 24.0 | 11.8 | 10.8 |
| Std. Dev. | 1.7 | 5.7 | 2.2 | 1.9 |

At the outset of the Depression in April, 1930, the New York area unemployment rate was very close to the 20-metropolitan area average. This observation, however, obscures New York's relative strength. Unemployment was much higher in all other large northeastern and Midwestern cities.

In January 1931, in the midst of the initial contraction, the unemployment rate among residents of the Bronx, Brooklyn, and Manhattan was below the national big-city average by about two-thirds of a standard deviation and far below levels in other large northeastern and Midwestern cities. The 1937 unemployment counts included both individuals who were without any job and seeking one *and* "emergency workers" employed on work relief projects funded by one or another government program. By this point, metropolitan New York's unemployment rate was two-thirds of a standard deviation *above* the national average. And in 1940, after the United States began to rearm, New York's rate was one-and-a-half standard deviations above the metropolitan mean and above levels in all other metropolitan areas other than Philadelphia, Buffalo, and Pittsburgh.

Why did New York's Depression follow this particular pattern? Why were the City and regional economies relatively resilient during the early phases of the initial contraction but then lag the average city and even many other large northeastern and Midwestern cities as the decade progressed?

From one perspective at least, the early Depression relative resilience is surprising. One would have expected the early 1930s to have been particularly hard on New York because, as the premier U.S. financial center, the nation's most important port, and a City inhabited by a large number of "foreigners," New York was the scene of some of the most dramatic events surrounding the Depression's commencement.

## Financial Crisis "Ground Zero"

Although industrial activity had been decreasing since mid-1929, the series of worsening financial crises that began in October 1929 and continued until 1933 combined with what was in hindsight inept crisis management on the part of policymakers turned what might have been a run-of-the-mill recession into the Great Depression. Histories of the period highlight three precipitating events: the October 1929 stock market crash; the failure of the Bank of United States (BUS), a private New York City institution; and the disorderly global abandonment of the gold standard. One might have expected all three to have affected the local New York City economy particularly adversely.

## The Stock Market Crash

The shorthand assertion that the stock market crash "caused" the Great Depression is not correct. The sharp drop in stock prices was one of a number of international and domestic trends and events and Federal Reserve policies that, together, led to a contraction of credit, defaults by borrowers unable to roll over maturing obligations, consequent failure of large numbers of banks, and the eventual collapse of the national banking system.

Whatever their broader ramifications, however, the stock market bubble of the late 1920s and the subsequent crash led to a buildup and collapse of activity in securities markets. Between 1920 and the 1929 peak, the annual volume of new corporate securities issues more than quadrupled from $2.2 billion to 9.4 billion. By 1934, the volume had fallen to less than $500 million (U.S. Census Bureau, 1975, pp. 1,005–1,006). In an era before the development of computers, processing such transactions was highly labor-intensive, so this expansion and contraction must have been associated with some amount of hiring and firing, much of which would have been concentrated in New York City.

By the time of the stock market crash, New York City had been the Nation's financial center for almost 100 years. The banking industry employment concentration ratio gives us an idea of how this predominance affected the structure of City employment. The concentration ratios for 1931 reflect the industrial composition of the three New York boroughs, Bronx, Brooklyn, and Manhattan relative to the structure of the (weighted) average of all 19 cities surveyed for the special Census of Unemployment in that year. The highest 1931 concentration ratio for New York City was for clothing manufacture (2.00), and the second highest, at 1.39, was for "other" (i.e., non-shoe) leather products. The third highest was 1.38 for the broadly defined "Banking and Brokerage" industry. No doubt, the equivalent ratio for the securities underwriting industry would have been substantially higher. By way of contrast, the concentration ratio for Banking and Brokerage in Chicago was 0.98. Thus, the nation's second largest city, which enjoyed a reputation as something of a financial center in its own right, had about the same proportion of total employment in this industry as the average large U.S. city. Thus, the adverse effects of the stock market crash and continuing financial crisis on securities industry activity should have had a particularly severe impact on New York City employment.

## The Bank of United States Failure

The capital losses associated with the stock market crash would likely have reduced consumer spending somewhat, and the widely publicized panic would have sapped confidence in the economic outlook, but, by themselves, these headwinds would not necessarily have led to a decade-long Depression. Rather, it was a series of commercial bank failures culminating in a complete shutdown of the U.S. banking system that turned the downturn into an economic collapse. The first wave of failures occurred from November, 1930, through January, 1931. Over this three-month period, 806 banks with a total of $628 million in deposits suspended operations nationwide. By far the largest of these failures was that of the Bank of the United States (Bank of U.S.), a private insititution, which had $160 million in deposits when it failed, and which was the third largest bank in New York City by number of branches (*The New York Times*, 1929; Wicker, 1996, p. 29). This was at the time the largest bank failure that had ever taken place in the United States.

Controversies among economists regarding the causes and consequences of the Bank of U.S. failure became embarrassingly vituperative. At issue was the degree to which the fact that most of the bank's owners, managers, and customers were Jewish affected the course of events (Friedman & Schwartz, 1986; Lucia, 1985; O'Brien, 1992; Trescott, 1992). On one side, the view has been that a fundamentally sound institution was allowed to fail at least partly as a result of endemic anti-Semitism among leading New York bankers and that the collapse of the Bank of U.S. had profoundly adverse consequences for the soundness of the U.S. banking system. The other side sees the Bank of U.S. as an imprudently—indeed, criminally—managed institution, the collapse of which was not necessarily any more consequential than would have been the failure of, say, 80 smaller banks each with $2 million in deposits.

All sides of this controversy agree on one point. While the collapse of the BUS is certainly an interesting story and may have served as cautionary tale for bank regulators, the more important aspect of this episode from an economic historian's point of view is the impact this particular failure had or didn't have on subsequent macroeconomic developments in the U.S. economy. There also seems to be some agreement that the failure of the 28th largest U.S. bank under intense media scrutiny must have had some broader economic effect, if only by way of instilling greater fear among depositors and, thereby, making future banking crises more likely. Further, the loss of access to $160 million in funds, even if only temporary, would have had some adverse effect on BUS depositors' spending. The issue on which there is disagreement among parties to the controversy is whether these effects were large or small.

Whatever the effects, psychological or financial, may have been nationwide, however, one would expect them to have been even greater in New York City, and this, indeed, appears to have been the case. Paul B. Trescott, one of the participants in the exchange of journal articles on the Bank of U.S. failure, cited evidence on this point.

One psychological correlate of bank failures is an increased preference for holding cash in the form of currency—"cash under the mattress" —rather than bank deposits. Impacts of local bank failures on inter-regional relative economic confidence can, therefore, be measured by comparing changes in the amount of currency in circulation across the 12 Federal Reserve districts. One would expect the volume of currency to increase the most in districts where the incidence of bank failures was high. On this point, Truscott reported

> ...evidence for individual Federal Reserve districts for 1929–1933 demonstrating that bank suspensions were the major explanation for the currency drain from the banking system. The explanatory power of bank suspension is very high for currency withdrawal for the New York district. In the New York district Federal Reserve note [i.e., currency] circulation had declined by $111 million in the year ending October 1930. In contrast, note circulation at the end of December 1930 was $66 million *above* the preceding year. The New York district was the only one to

> display a large increase compared with the preceding year. By June 1931 note circulation in the New York district was $102 million above the year previous. (Trescott, 1992, p. 385)

We can probably also conclude that the BUS failure was what increased demand for currency in the New York district because the number of bank failures in the Second Federal Reserve District (New York State, northern New Jersey, and Fairfield County, Connecticut) between November 1930 and January 1931 was, in fact, relatively low compared to other districts.

But did the climate of fear engendered by this bank's collapse have an adverse impact on the level of real economic activity in the New York region as opposed to just changing the proportions of currency and bank deposits in New Yorkers' cash portfolios? Apparently it did. Few data that measure high-frequency changes in consumer spending are available for this period. But, as Trescott reports:

> …The New York Fed published monthly data showing the percentage change in [department store] sales from the previous year for the entire second district and also for individual cities…. [A]ctual sales in New York City fell about one percentage point more than would have been predicted based on what happened across the entire second district. And the decline for the entire district was also relatively large. The response is plausible considering that at the time of its closing, the Bank had about $160 million of deposits held by approximately 400,000 depositors…. (Trescott, 1992, p. 386)

It is worth expanding on Trescott's plausibility point. Total U.S. GNP in 1930 was $90.4 billion in current dollars. New York City's population accounted for 5.6% of the U.S. total. So a conservative estimate of New York City's gross municipal product for that year would be about $5 billion. As a result of the failure of BUS, New Yorkers lost access to $160 in deposits, equivalent to roughly 3% of their annual income. A loss of this magnitude might not necessarily have much impact on consumer spending if it were viewed as temporary. In fact, depositors did eventually recover a substantial proportion of their money, and other

New York banks were willing to lend depositors money on the security of their frozen BUS deposits. Under the circumstances, however, depositors could not be confident of getting their money back, and with general economic conditions deteriorating rapidly, a general reduction of spending by an additional one percent does seem plausible or even surprisingly small.

## Global Contraction

The Great Depression was global. And, in the view of some economic historians, most notably Peter Temin, it was primarily events abroad and U.S. policymakers' response to those developments that turned a recession into the Great Depression. Specifically, Temin argued that the maintenance of a fixed dollar price of gold until 1933, long after most other major economies had abandoned the gold standard and allowed their currencies to depreciate, did serious harm to the U.S. economy (Temin, 1994). Whether this line of reasoning is mostly right or mostly wrong, it is true that U.S. total trade declined by more proportionally than real GNP and recovered more slowly. Peak-to-trough U.S. real GNP declined by 30.5%; total trade, by 38.0%. And real GNP returned to its 1929 level by 1939; total trade, not until 1942 (U.S. Census Bureau, 1975, p. 864).

This trend should have affected New York City particularly adversely. By the eve of the Depression, the Port of New York's share of total U.S. trade had begun a long decline; at its peak in 1916, the region moved more than half of all U.S. exports and imports. Even in 1928, the New York port accounted for 35% of U.S. exports and 48% of imports (U.S. Department of Commerce, n.d.). So, presumably, unless the types of goods moved through the New York port were very different in a favorable way from U.S. aggregate trading activity, roughly 40% of whatever decline in total U.S. port employment was associated with the reduction in trade volumes would have been concentrated in the New York region.

Further, New York City's financial service sector had always managed the bulk of U.S. international financial transactions. Financial activity associated with the trade in goods and services would probably have contracted roughly in proportion with the decline in values. In fact, the total volume of private sector international financial flows to and from the United States declined by 44% from its peak in 1928 to its trough in 1936.[3] Processing such transactions in a pre-computer age would have been labor intensive; so the reduction in international flows, as with the decline in purely domestic transactions, must have been accompanied by some substantial reduction in financial services employment.

The three events most often cited as contributing to a transformation of recession into Great Depression over the period from 1929 through 1933 either played out entirely in New York City or may have affected New York more than other places. In each case, there is either clear evidence or good reason to believe that the impact on economic activity in the New York region would have been particularly adverse.

## Accounting for Initial Relative Resilience

### Industrial Specialization and Diversification

Since New York's initial contraction was, in fact, less severe than other cities', some other aspects of the local economy must have offset, if only temporarily, the unique contractionary effects of the stock market crash, the Bank of U.S. failure, and the collapse of world trade. The most likely candidate for this offsetting effect was the industrial composition of employment.

Analyses of geographic differences in the Depression's effects have highlighted the industrial composition of regional employment as an important determinant of relative impact. Industrial composition seems to have affected relative conditions in two ways. First, most obviously

[3]This is the percentage change in the sum of the absolute values of all tabulated private sector capital inflows and outflows. As such it excludes unilateral transfers by the U.S. government, transactions in the U.S. official reserves account, and the "Errors and omissions" residual (U.S. Census Bureau, 1975, p. 867).

and most importantly, the identity of the region's leading industries would have influenced the magnitude of job losses. John J. Wallis, for example, estimated that "the industrial composition of employment … [b]y itself explains about 40% of the variation in state-level employment between 1930 and 1940" (Wallis, 1989, p. 59). Durable goods manufacturing industries, in particular, were hard-hit nationwide, and regions that specialized in those industries had the highest unemployment rates, especially in the Depression's early phases.

Second, diversification of employment across industries may have had an independent influence on regional labor markets. In one of the few studies that examined Depression-era conditions across cities rather than states, economists Curtis Simon and Clark Nardinelli found that, all else held equal, early Depression unemployment was *higher* in places where jobs were spread out across more industries[4] (Simon & Clark Nardinelli, 1992).

But for some statistical luck it would have been impossible to assess New York City's industrial specialization and diversification during the Depression. Fortunately for our purposes, however, the 1931 Census of Unemployment associated both employed workers and most of the unemployed with specific industries.[5] This enables us to calculate both

---

[4]This conclusion was surprising because studies of the effect of industrial diversity on unemployment during the post-World War II period have reached the opposite conclusion, namely that industrial diversity is associated with *lower* average unemployment over the course of a business cycle. Curtis and Nardinelli suggest one possible explanation: When business slows down, employers in industrially diversified cities prefer to lay-off workers rather than reduce wages. Employers fear that, because local jobs are readily available in other industries, any wage reduction will be followed by mass resignations. Under normal circumstances, including run-of-the-mill recessions, jobs in other industries may indeed be available, so that layoffs do not necessarily raise unemployment significantly in industrially diversified regions. When demand reductions are massive and pervasive, however, no industry is doing well and laidoff workers remain unemployed. In industrially concentrated cities during severe downturns, by contrast, employers are not afraid to cut wages and, therefore, are inclined to keep a larger proportion of their workforce on the job.

[5]Because of the frequency of labor mobility across industries, economic statisticians no longer identify unemployed individuals with specific industries. Further, 1931 census distinguished between "Type B" unemployment—workers who had been "laid off" with the possibility of being recalled by their previous employer—or "Type A"—without a job and with no attachment to any employer or industry. This distinction turns out not to have been useful and has been abandoned by labor statisticians. The measure of unemployment used in this section encompasses both types.

industry-specific unemployment rates and concentration ratios for 42 industries in each city relative to all 19 cities. Table 13A.1 in the appendix to this chapter lists New York City's (three-borough) concentration ratios along with the average (unweighted) unemployment rates for those industries across all 19 cities. As indicated, the average urban unemployment rate for these 42 industries was 19%. The average nationwide urban unemployment rate for New York City's "specialty" industries, i.e., those with concentration ratios greater than 1.00, was 16.4%. For industries with New York concentration ratios less than 1.00, the average urban unemployment rate was 21.3%. We can take the difference between these two unemployment rates, 2.3 percentage points, as a measure of how comparatively well-situated New York City was with respect to the industrial specialization of its workforce in 1931 during the initial contraction of the Great Depression. The higher this number, the better. New York's 2.3 was one of the better such statistics among large U.S. cities. Only two other cities, Duluth and Denver, at 2.9 and 3.5 percentage points, respectively, had larger average national unemployment rate differentials between industries with concentration ratios above and below 1.00 than New York City. By contrast, Chicago's statistic was 1.5 percentage points, and Philadelphia's was −2.0, indicating that that City's specialty industries were more severely impacted by the Depression's early stages.

Simon and Nardinelli identified an important, and somewhat counterintuitive, effect of industrial diversification; all else held equal, unemployment was significantly higher in more diversified cities. As it happens, by the statistic Simon and Nardinelli used to measure industrial diversification, the Herfindahl index,[6] New York City's 1931

[6]The Herfindahl index, also referred to as the Herfindahl-Hirschman index, is most often used to measure the degree of market-share concentration across firms in a specific industry. Simon and Nardinelli put this index to a somewhat different use as measure of employment concentration across industries. The index is defined as

$$HERF_i = \sum_j \left(\frac{E_{ij}}{E_i}\right)^2$$

Where $HERF_i$ is the Herfindahl index for city $i$, $E_{ij}$ is employment in industry $j$ in city $i$, and $E_i$ is total employment in City $i$. Simon and Nardinelli's analysis included 25 separate industries, so the range for the Herfindahl index would have been from 0.04, indicating equal employment workforce was neither particularly diversified nor concentrated across industries. The average Herfindahl index for the 19 cities was 0.069. New York City's was 0.067. The most specialized city, as in the Simon-Nardinelli analysis, was, unsurprisingly, Detroit at 0.122, and the most diversified was St. Louis at 0.057.

By the criteria of industrial specialization and diversification, therefore, New York City appears to have been well positioned to weather the early phases of the Depression with less severe damage to the local economy than other large cities. New York's specialty industries were not among the hardest-hit sectors of the national economy, and the City's measured degree of employment diversification across industries was unlikely to have much of a relative effect one way or the other.

Given the importance of industry composition as a determinant of the Depression's relative regional impacts, we can feel comfortable that these characteristics likely offset the severe initial local impact of the stock market crash, the BUS failure, and the collapse of international trade and financial activity. But two additional characteristics of New York City may also have served to offset some of the Depression's initial effects. The first of these was New York's political culture, which, depending on one's ideological orientation was either progressive-activist or free-spending. The second is the access to non-bank credit for small-scale business investment within the City's large Jewish community.

## Alert First Responders

Absent more quantitative information than we have, it is impossible to determine whether the response of state and local governments and civil society to the initial phases of the contraction was more aggressive in New York than elsewhere or, if it was more aggressive, whether the

---

in all industries or perfect diversification, to 1.00, indicating that all employment was concentrated in a single industry. The statistics reported for New York and the other 18 cities surveyed in 1931 encompass 42 industries, so the possible range for the Herfindahl index is 0.0238–1.00. The Herfindahl indexes for the 19 cities appear in Table 13A.2 in the appendix to this chapter.

community's collective actions helped the City avoid the worst impacts of the 1929–1931 contraction. But the historical literature suggests that New York State and City power centers did shift into crisis mode relatively quickly and with substantial resources.

New York City non-governmental organizations had a long history of anti-poverty engagement and of countercyclical philanthropy. Accordingly, the New York Association for Improving the Condition of the Poor (AICP, founded: 1846) and the Charity Organization Society (COS, founded: 1882) quickly joined forces to raise funds for home and work relief. Between November 1930 and September 1931, the committees coordinating this effort had disbursed $8 million for work relief wages. By itself this was not a large amount of money; it amounted to about 0.6% of total New York City manufacturing wages tabulated in the 1930 census. The impact of this private sector effort was more impressive in terms of the number of people provided with work. At its peak in December 1931 wages of over 32,000 individuals were paid by funds raised by the AICP-COS committees. By way of comparison, the number of unemployed persons enumerated by the 1930 census was 338,761. Hence, if the City's NGOs were, in fact, much more active than other cities', privately funded relief work could help explain a substantial part of the difference between New York's 20.0% 1931 unemployment rate and the 19-city average of 23.8% (Millett, 1938, p. 2; Virginia Commonwealth University, 2018).

Deficit spending by the City and State governments in the Depression's early years may also have helped New York suffer less initial damage than some other places. One doesn't ordinarily think of state and local governments engaging in countercyclical fiscal stimulus. The Keynesian economic analysis that argues for the benefits of deficit spending during downturns is based on the assumption of, among other things, a "closed" economy, in which increased demand generated by government deficit spending is filled by goods and services produced within the economy. For a small, open economy, a large part of any additional demand stimulated by local fiscal stimulus might "leak out" and benefit other regions or countries. But the larger an economic region, the more it is like a closed economy, and the larger the potential local multiplier of increased local final demand. Because New York was the largest state in 1930 and the New York City metropolitan area was the largest economic region, deficit spending by the State and City governments might have had some ameliorative effect on the Depression's impact. And there was, indeed, considerable deficit spending by New York City in 1930 and 1931.

Traditionally in the United States providing public home and work relief for unemployed individuals and their families, along with all other "charitable" government activities, had been the province of local, not state or federal, governments. Accordingly, as needs grew and tax revenues diminished in 1930 and 1931, New York City issued long-term revenue bonds and short-term tax revenue anticipation notes to finance relief expenditures. City government efforts added an additional 15,000 relief workers by May 1931. When, however, it became apparent that the crisis was much worse than anything witnessed previously, a special session of the New York State legislature established the Temporary Emergency Relief Administration (TERA). Among other things, this legislation authorized the State government to pay for 40% of total relief expenditures. By January 1932, however, New York City's financial condition had deteriorated to the point where additional borrowing to finance its 60% share was precluded. Through that year the City, with the help of loans from private donors and the Federal Reconstruction Finance Corporation (RFC), was able to maintain its contribution levels (Millett, 1938, pp. 7–8).

By early 1933, though, the City, no longer able to pay off or refinance the short-term loans negotiated to cover early Depression deficits, faced insolvency. An agreement with the major banks allowed the City to avoid default but effectively put an end to additional deficit financing. The City continued spending its own money to help alleviate distress, but after 1933 under the La Guardia administration all local government expenditures were covered by current tax revenue. For a few years, the State government continued providing some degree of aggregate fiscal stimulus by reducing the required local contribution to relief payments from 40 to 33 1/3% and by financing the State's share by borrowing the money. Statewide ballot initiatives authorizing general obligation bond issuance of $40 million and $55 million, largely to finance relief, were passed by large majorities in 1934 and 1935, respectively (Ingalls, 1975, pp. 40, 51, 53).

Although we have no statistical evidence as to whether New York's efforts in this regard was substantially greater than what was done elsewhere or whether local fiscal stimulus was effective in the country's largest city, it is certainly possible that local government borrowing and spending contributed to the City's relative resilience through 1931.

## Ethnicity and Entrepreneurship

The transmission mechanism that turned the recession of 1929–1930 into the Great Depression was an extreme contraction of credit. As loan quality deteriorated, the public became wary of banks' soundness and withdrew deposits. Federal Reserve System lending, which might have staunched the outflow, was, in hindsight, excessively parsimonious, and as a consequence, banks were wary of making loans, even to the soundest of enterprises. So, the businesses that relied on bank lending for expansion or even to smooth out routine cash-flow seasonality were forced to forgo growth, contract, or, in too many cases, default on loans coming due and go out of business.

But not all businesses that needed borrowed funds relied on banks. In particular, individuals who belonged to one of several ethnic communities and needed modest amounts of money to start or maintain small businesses could call upon a variety of non-formal, non-bank lending institutions. Such institutions included revolving credit associations and charities dedicated to making low-interest or interest-free loans to applicants.

Members of revolving credit associations agreed to make periodic payments into a pool of funds. Each period, one member of the group would receive the full amount collected in that period. In some cases, funds were distributed according to a predetermined rotation; in others, members would bid for the use of the period's funds. Free loan societies raised endowments from philanthropists and lent out the funds collected for terms of as little as a few months to as much as a few years. Repayment, which usually began immediately in installments, was secured by a guarantor, usually a family member or friend of the borrower. Thus, the permanent endowment could be rolled over into new loans a few times each decade.

Compliance by association members or loan society borrowers, which was quite high, was enforced by both the structures of these organizations and the behavioral expectations of a close-knit ethnic community. Such institutions were most common in of East Asian, West Indian, and Jewish immigrant communities. The latter two of these were concentrated in New York, and at between 25 and 30% of total City population, the Jewish community was quite large (Light, 1972, p. 51; Tenenbaum, 1993, p. 74).

Historians, sociologists, and anthropologists who have studied these institutions have focused primarily on the community characteristics that fostered their creation and survival, how these organizations operated, and on the impact they may have had on relative economic conditions across ethnic groups. Potential macroeconomic impacts of the availability of non-bank credit has received little or no attention. The implicit assumption seems to be that these institutions were too small to have much aggregate effect on the level of economic activity. That may be a good assumption in general, but, if these institutions ever had any observable effect on the overall level of economic activity in a region it would have been in New York City in the 1930s.

Such evidence as we have suggests that Jewish borrowers' access to non-bank credit may have had some effect on reported unemployment rates in New York City. Unlike revolving credit associations—*aktsiyes* in Yiddish—the free loan societies, including the New York Hebrew Free Loan Society (HFLS) maintained formal records of borrowing and repayment. Data assembled by Historian Shelly Tenenbaum shows that both total HFLS lending and the number of individual loans increased in real terms, after correcting for deflation, in the early years of the Depression (see Appendix Table 13A.1). The data also indicate, however, that the increase in the Society's total lending was quite small relative to the aggregate decline in bank credit. Between 1929 and 1934, total "other[7]"

[7]Exclusive of open market paper, loans, on securities, and real estate loans. Most loans to businesses would have fallen into this "other" category.

loans by New York City Federal Reserve member banks declined by $1.6 billion (Calomris & Barry Wilson, 2004). In this context, the roughly $1 million per year lent by the HFLS during the Depression looks trivial. But this may understate the total impact of non-bank lending. Although the *aktsiyes* did not keep formal records, Tenenbaum cites estimates that lending by these revolving credit societies may have totaled $50 or 60 million nationwide (Tenenbaum, 1993, p. 139). If New York City accounted for roughly the same percentage of total national *aktsiyes* activity as of free loan society lending, about 50%, then total non-formal credit for Jewish borrowers during the depression years may have been stable at around $25–30 million: not huge, but perhaps enough to have made some difference.

The Depression-era performance of the New York City retailing sector provides further evidence of a possible positive effect of these non-bank lenders on regional macroeconomic conditions. A common response to job loss is to go into business for oneself, and this tendency was very much in evidence during the Depression. While nationwide retail sales declined by 22% in nominal and 2.1% in real terms between 1929 and 1935 and the number of retail employees decreased by 9.1% over the same period, the number of retail establishments tabulated by the Census of Business *increased* by 7.5% (Table 13.2). These new small business people would not have been counted as unemployed. The increase in the number of retail establishments was more pronounced in New York City than nationwide or, on average, in the 14 large cities tabulated separately in the censuses. As Tenenbaum reports that the

**Table 13.2** Initial impact of the Great Depression on the retail services industry (U.S. Census Bureau, 1941)

| Percentage change, 1929–1935 | U.S. total (%) | 14 city total[a] (%) | NYC (%) |
|---|---|---|---|
| Retail sales, nominal | −22.0 | −53.8 | −33.1 |
| Total sales, real | −2.1 | −33.9 | −13.2 |
| Total employees | −9.1 | −11.1 | −7.0 |
| Stores | 7.5 | 5.9 | 11.3 |

[a]Baltimore, Boston, Buffalo, Chicago, Cleveland, Detroit, Los Angeles, Milwaukee, New York, Philadelphia, Pittsburgh, St. Louis, San Francisco, Washington, DC

most HFLS loans were used for business purposes, it makes sense to assume that this and other forms of non-bank lending helped boost the number of small new retail establishments in New York. If the number of retail establishments in New York had grown by only the same percentage as the average of the 14 cities and if each new retail establishment kept one person off the unemployment rolls, the City's jobless rate would have been about 0.3 percentage points higher than it was, or by about one-seventh of a (1937) standard deviation. Again, this is not a large difference, but it suggests that the availability of non-bank credit may have softened the blow to New York City's economy, at least in terms of measured unemployment.

The industrial composition of employment in the city was the principal reason New York's economy was more resilient than that of other large northeastern cities in the early years of the Depression. Aggressive first responses by the City and State governments and by local philanthropists probably provided important support. Non-bank, formal, and informal credit providers within New York's large Jewish community may have helped more small business people to stay off the unemployment rolls than in other cities. Absent more detailed data on a cross section of othr citeis, we have no way of knowing how important public and private relief activites were in explaining New York's early-Depression relative performance.

Why didn't these sources of initial resilience carry through the rest of the Depression decade?

## Accounting for the Flaccid Recovery

One possible explanation for New York's late-Depression fade is that the pattern across regions and industries of relatively strong early-cyclical performance followed by relatively poor performance and vice versa is inherent in the nature of business cycles. As economic activity contracts, businesses and households cut back much more on discretionary and big-ticket purchases than on necessities and less expensive goods. During the downturn, therefore, industries that produce the former reduce employment or wages by more, and regions that specialize in those industries are relatively hard hit. As the economy recovers, purchases of goods foregone during the downturn pick up most quickly, so industries and places that were hit the hardest during contraction bounce back the fastest after the business cycle trough. Something like this process of reversion to the mean probably was taking place during the initial period of recovery from 1933 to 1937. Although inter-temporal comparisons using these unemployment data are problematic, it is at least interesting that the correlation between a city's 1931 unemployment rate and the change in its unemployment rate between 1931 and 1937 is −0.93. That is, the hardest-hit regions did tend to experience the most robust recoveries.

But "the farther the fall the bigger the bounce" does not fully explain why the New York metropolitan region performed so poorly after 1937. New York was one of only seven (of 20) metropolitan areas where unemployment actually increased between 1937 and 1940. In other words, there was no "bounce" at all.

## Lagging Trade?

One economic activity that contracted particularly sharply early in the Depression decade and did *not* bounce back particularly quickly was foreign trade. Figure 13.1 tracks the total volume of trade, exports plus imports, from 1924 until 1939. As noted earlier in this chapter, the volume of trade declined more sharply than the economy as a whole between 1929 and 1933. Peak-to-trough real gross national product decreased by about 30%, total trade by 64%. Thereafter, both the economy as a whole and its "international" sectors bounced back, but the trade did not make up for lost ground. Real GDP returned to its pre-Depression level temporarily by 1937 and permanently in 1939. At that point, total trade was still 40% below its 1929 peak. Figure 13.1 also indicates that New York maintained its position as the nation's most active port, with a 40% share of total U.S. trade, through the period. So the relatively weak recovery of exports and imports probably impeded the City's late Depression performance.

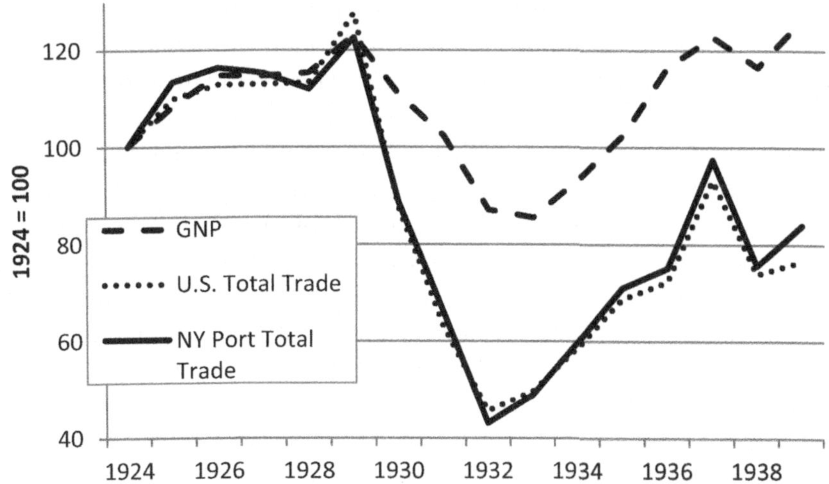


**Fig. 13.1** Trends in real gross national product and total trade (exports+imports), 1924–1939 (U.S. Census Bureau, 1975, p. 224; U.S. Department of Commerce, 2018)

## Unfavorable Long-Term Trends?

The macroeconomic catastrophe notwithstanding, in terms of structural change, the decade from 1930 to 1940 was actually a particularly dynamic period of U.S. economic history. Fundamental shifts in economic activity—south-westward population migration, large, rapid increases in productivity in agriculture and manufacturing, the growth of broadcast media, and so on—that had begun before 1930 and continued during the postwar period were also evident during the Depression years, and some of them actually accelerated during the period. All other determinants of relative performance held equal, agricultural regions performed worse than average and southern and western states, better as the initial recovery got under way. Some of the trends that influenced regional recovery rates may have benefited New York, but more probably worked to the City's relative disadvantage (Garret & Wheelock, 2006; Rosenbloom & Sundstrom, 1999; Wallis, 1989).

First, the movement of U.S. population westward and southward, a trend as old as the Republic, continued through the 1930s. Underlying population growth rates, with their attendant stimulation of economic activity, were faster for western and southern cities. Somewhat higher fundamental population growth rates might have served as a tailwind for the recovery of western and southern cities not enjoyed by northeastern cities like New York. The data in Table 13.1 are consistent with this expectation; all of the cities with 1931 unemployment rates as low as or lower than New York's 20.0% were west of the Mississippi. Metropolitan unemployment rates in 1937 and 1940 also tended to fall with longitude and rise with latitude, although this statistical relationship was generally insignificant at standard levels of confidence.[8]

Second, techological change was particularly rapid during the 1930s. Indeed, Economic historian Alexander J. Field went so far as to title a 2003 article on the 1930s in *The American Economic Review* "The Most Technologically Progressive Decade of the Century." Specifically, Field showed that

> [T]hroughout the Depression, behind the dramatic backdrop of continued high unemployment, technological and organizational innovations were occurring across the American economy, especially but not exclusively in chemical engineering (including petrochemicals and synthetic rubber), aeronautics, electrical machinery and equipment, electric power generation and distribution, transportation, communications, and civil/

---

[8]Metropolitan unemployment rates for 1937 were regressed on the central city's latitude and longitude take from http://www.infoplease.com/ipa/A0001796.html. The results for 1937 were

$$\underset{}{\text{Unemployment}} = \underset{(0.18)}{0.077} + \underset{(0.13)}{0.0019}\,\text{Latitude} - \underset{(0.19)}{0.00039}\,\text{Longitude} \qquad \text{R - square} = 20$$

The 1940 equation was:

$$\text{Unemployment} = \underset{(0.16)}{0.072} + \underset{(0.10)}{0.0019}\,\text{Latitude} - \underset{(0.12)}{0.00026}\,\text{Longitude} \qquad \text{R - square} = 25$$

The numbers in parentheses are p-values.

The actual 1937 unemployment rate for metropolitan New York City was 0.8% above the fitted value, a small residual for that equation. New York unemployment for 1940 was 2.2% above the fitted value, a large residual.

> structural engineering ... and ... the sum total of these changes had, by the onset of World War II, increased the natural or potential output of the U.S. economy far beyond what contemporary observers and economists at the time believed possible. (Field, 2003, p. 1401)

Field points out that some of the 1930s technological innovations were "held in the larder" until wartime or postwar demand expansion brought them into widespread job-creating use. But Michael Bernstein has presented evidence that some industries did, in fact, invest heavily and expand during the Depression years. Bernstein argued that the recovery from initial contraction was slow and halting in large part because the collapse of the U.S. financial system disrupted a process of shifting of investment and employment away from old industries such as textiles, leather goods, and railroad transportation and into petrochemicals, mass-market consumer durables, and broadcast media. His analysis highlights some of the same industries as Field and discusses several additional types of business and products. For example, Bernstein points out that, even as households cut back on the purchase of many consumer durables, the 1930s saw rapid growth in demand for some appliances such as electric refrigerators, annual sales of which nearly tripled between 1930 and 1937. The Depression decade also saw the implementation of distribution and retail marketing innovations. "From 1935... to 1939...the average annual increase in supermarket retailing was almost 1,200 stores" (Bernstein, 1987, pp. 56, 64).

Whether or not 1930s technological innovation or industrial restructuring exerted as important an influence on the national economy's trajectory as Bernstein claims, the observation that some industries were undergoing robust secular growth during the Depression while others were not should have influenced the relative performance of different regions over the course of the decade. Places that specialized in petrochemical production (e.g., Houston) and/or cigarette manufacturing (e.g., North Carolina) would recover relatively quickly. Where pre-Depression economic activity was concentrated in textiles or leather goods (e.g., metropolitan Boston), recovery would have been slower.

Some of the 1930s technological and industrial trends may have benefitted New York City disproportionately. Although there is disagreement on the point, the consensus opinion is that the nation's first supermarket was the King Kullen Market that opened in Jamaica, Queens, in November 1930. While the development of large-scale, self-service grocery stores might have reduced retail sector employment, the build-out of the new industry would have generated local construction activity. The growth of self-service retailing was accompanied by an expansion of food industry advertising, especially through the new medium of radio, which must have benefited two New York-based industries, although neither at the time was likely an especially large employer.

By in large, however, the industries that were expanding most rapidly in the 1930s were not concentrated in New York City. And some of the City's specialty industries lagged badly. Table 13.3 combines information from Bernstein's book with 1931 industry concentration ratios for the combined boroughs of the Bronx, Brooklyn, and Manhattan. Investment levels in 1937 may be taken as typical for the initial recovery period of the Depression decade. Although the second contraction began in the middle of that year, the severe pullback came as a surprise to most policymakers and businesspeople and was unlikely to have affected immediate capital spending. As the juxtaposition of the two data items indicates, in general, the industries that were expanding the most were not concentrated in New York.

The data Table 13.3 may be somewhat deceptive with respect to two industries: chemical and allied products and tobacco products. New York City was a center of some elements of the U.S. chemical and pharmaceutical industry since the middle of the nineteenth century, and the petroleum refining, chemical, and drug industries are still quite visible in the region today. In fact, in 1958, the earliest year for which such data are readily available, chemical and allied industries concentration ratio for the combined New York City and Jersey City primary metropolitan statistical areas was 1.05, which is about one-third higher than the figure in Table 13.3. Thus, 1931 employment in this industry of Bronx, Brooklyn, and Manhattan residents may not accurately represent the importance of the sector to the region during the 1930s. This industry, however, is not particularly labor-intensive. Nor were the non-labor inputs to the production process produced locally. So, although

**Table 13.3** Depression-era investment and New York City concentration ratios (Bernstein, 1987; U.S. Census Bureau, 1933)

| Industry | 1937 net investment, equipment, % of 1929 level | 1931 three-borough Conc. ratio |
|---|---|---|
| Chemicals and allied products | 369.9 | 0.75 |
| Sone, clay, and glass products | 850.3 | 0.60 |
| Petroleum and coal products | 131.9 | |
| Tobacco products | 130.2 | 1.05 |
| Food and kindred products | 178.2 | 0.67[a] |
| Nonelectrical machinery | 96.9 | 0.56 |
| Apparel & other textile products | 32.6 | 2.00 |
| Rubber and plastic products | 22.2 | 0.00 |
| Transportation equipment | 34.7 | 0.07 |
| primary metal industries | 38.6 | 0.37[b] |
| Fabricated metal products | 18.7 | 0.91[c] |
| Printing and publishing | Negative | 1.1[d] |
| Paper and allied products | 27.4 | |
| Leather and leather products | 19.0 | 1.24[e], 1.39[f] |
| Lumber and wood products | Negative | 0.77 |
| Textile mill products | Negative | 1.06 |

[a]Other food and allied industries, ex. Bakeries and slaughter and packing houses
[b]Iron and steel industries
[c]Metal industries, except iron and steel
[d]Paper, printing, and allied industries
[e]Shoe factories
[f]Other leather industries

the New York metropolitan area may have derived some benefit from the investment in the chemical industries that took place in the 1930s, it is unlikely that this activity would have generated a large enough local multiplier effect to boost the region's general recovery.

Investment in the tobacco products was relatively heavy, and this labor-intensive industry was concentrated in New York in 1931. But the net investment in the tobacco industry that took place in the 1930s did not benefit New York. Bernstein points out that Depression-era investment in this industry financed a transition in the product mix from cigars and pipe tobacco to cigarettes. New York's specialty within the tobacco products industry was cigar manufacture, and during the 1930s, this sub-subsector was in the midst of a long-term decline (Bernstein, 1987, p. 71).

The effects on New York City of Sunbelt migration and industrial restructuring will be more obvious when we examine what happened in the first three post-World War II decades. But many of the forces behind the secular contraction of the City's economy through the third-quarter of the twentieth century were already in evidence during the second-quarter and probably impeded—or at least didn't accelerate—the region's recovery from the Depression.

## State and Local Fiscal Austerity

So many of New York's Depression-era Governor Herbert Lehman's policies and programs mirrored those his immediate predecessor, President Franklin Roosevelt, was advocating in Washington that this period in New York State's political history has been referred to as the "Little New Deal." As with their federal equivalents, many of Lehman's initiatives involved structural reforms affecting, for example, the dairy industry, electric utilities, and housing markets. These policies, whether well- or ill-advised, probably had minimal near-term impact on the State or City's macroeconomy and any marginal effect may have been negative in the short run. But the way New York State decided to finance late Depression relief payments also reflected the same thinking that informed Federal fiscal policy. By the mid-1930s, as job growth lagged the general pace of GDP expansion, policymakers came to the conclusion that a substantial proportion of the population would likely remain on the dole more or less permanently. If so, this line of thinking continued, relief payments should no longer be financed as extraordinary "emergency" measures, but like other routine government expenditures should be paid for out of current tax revenues. Since the cost of relief payments was not shrinking, the conclusion had to be that taxes should be raised (Ingalls, 1975, p. 51).

The State's last large "relief" bond issue was enacted in 1935 for the subsequent fiscal year. Thereafter, relief payments became routine operating expenses, and, as such, generally financed by current tax revenues, the State's budget was either balanced or in surplus in all but one fiscal year after 1936. The abrupt shift in State fiscal policy after 1936 may have done the regional economy serious harm, coming, as it did, at a time when the La Guardia administration in the City was tightening its fiscal belt to eliminate recurring operating deficits and just before premature Federal fiscal and monetary tightening exacerbated a renewed economic contraction.

## Was New York's New Deal No Big Deal?

Bernstein and Field had to dig deep into the data to make the case that the Depression period was a time of technological and structural dynamism. Evidence of the decade's tectonic political shifts is, by contrast, obvious at first glance. In 1929, the Federal government's purchases of goods and services amounted to 1.7% of gross national product; by 1939, the last pre-war year, the percentage had risen to 6.0%. In 1929, state and local governments' purchases were 5.3 times the Federal Government's. In 1939, the ratio was 1.8 to one (U.S. Census Bureau, 1975, pp. 224, 1005, 1127).

Much of this increase in Federal government activity was associated with New Deal programs. The goals of the New Deal were, in President Roosevelt's words, relief, recovery, and reform. The consensus among economic historians is that the New Deal did achieve the first and third of these goals. Although some of the "relief" money coming from Washington may have displaced state and local government or private charitable funds; no institution other than the Federal government had resources commensurate with the magnitude of the nationwide need. And the "reforms" put in place under the New Deal—social security, securities industry regulation, agricultural price supports, rural electrification, etc.—represented radical departures from previous government uninvolvement in the economy and have become integral to the fabric of American life.

With regard to "recovery," there is also widespread agreement that New Deal policies did not achieve this goal but no consensus as to why it failed to do so. Opinions range from the view that the magnitude of pre-war fiscal stimulus was insufficient to boost growth to the belief that many of the New Deal policies, far from boosting, actually impeded recovery (Cole & Ohanian, 2004; Romer, 1992). To shed light on the controversy as to whether more aggressive fiscal policy might have accelerated the recovery economic historians have devoted considerable attention to the effects of differences in New Deal spending on regional economies' relative post-1933 recovery rates. If, *all else held equal*, geographic regions where per capita New Deal spending was higher recovered faster, then, perhaps, the whole country would have recovered faster if total *gross*[9] spending had been higher.

Economic historians' efforts to shed light on this issue have produced a series of journal articles that aim to determine why some census divisions, states, or counties received more Federal government aid than others. Their specific question has been: Which set of regional characteristics most influenced the amount of aid a region received per capita? To what degree was it the relative severity of the Depression in the region, as measured by the unemployment rate or the percentage decline in income? Put differently, to what degree was it a jurisdiction's political influence in Washington, rather than objectively measured need, that directed the New Deal dollars? There certainly were ways in which power and politics could have influenced the geographic distribution of dollars. Even where funds were distributed by formula, as with the Federal highway program, powerful Congressional committee chairmen could design the allocation parameters so as to favor their home states or districts. And legislation establishing agencies such as the Public Works Administration (PWA) and the Works Progress Administration (WPA) granted program administrators a great deal of discretion with regard to which projects would go forward. Efforts to determine whether local economic conditions or political influence was most important remain entangled in methodological disagreements and the question remains unresolved. But it does seem clear that a politically influential jurisdiction was likely to benefit from a disproportionate share of New Deal spending independent of the severity of the local

[9]Unfortunately, none of the studies I have identified analyzed the effects of *net* spending, gross outlays in a region *minus* the Federal tax payments by residents, which would have been a more relevant measure of relative net fiscal stimulus.

downturn and independent of other regional characteristics that might have influenced the pace of recovery. Further, places that got more money for these political reasons did, all else held equal, tend to recover faster on average than otherwise similar regions where the New Deal was less generous.

The debate on the fundamental question of the potential effectiveness of greater fiscal stimulus continues. But the insights generated by these studies can be put to the purpose of understanding the degree to which New York City and its metropolitan area benefitted from New Deal spending during the 1930s. Did the City get more than its "fair share" of New Deal dollars? If it did, why didn't the regional economy recover faster? At the same time, the extensive literature on the political history of 1930s fiscal federalism in New York City can help evaluate the econometric studies of the Depression decade's political economy. Do the statistical findings "ring true" in light of the experience of one, highly visible jurisdiction?

As it happens, the econometric literature on the geographic distribution of New Deal funds and the general historical literature on the Depression decade nationwide and in New York create somewhat different impressions.

The general literature conveys the sense, sometimes explicitly sometimes implicitly, that New York City was particularly well positioned to benefit from the New Deal. It would be difficult to conclude otherwise, given the cast of characters. Four commanding personalities dominate many of the accounts of the City's Depression years: Franklin Roosevelt, Fiorello La Guardia, Robert Moses, and Harry Hopkins. President Roosevelt, a New Yorker, entered office in 1933, steeped in the State's tradition of progressivism and with a mind to reproduce some of the emergency relief and reform measures he had introduced as its Governor. Almost to a man the small group of Presidential advisors, dubbed the "brains trust" and instrumental in designing much of the New Deal legislation, lived, worked, and cut their political and public policy teeth in New York City prior to joining Roosevelt in Washington (Kennedy, 1999, p. 119).

Also, in contrast to some other big cities, the political climate in New York State was particularly New Deal-friendly. Mayor La Guardia, a progressive Republican, was an enthusiastic supporter of administration policies and a key Roosevelt interlocutor on urban issues (Gelfand, 1975, pp. 46–47; Kessner, 1989, p. 341). Further, although it would have been easy for La Guardia and Governor Herbert Lehman to come into conflict given that they belonged to different parties and held traditionally antagonistic offices, they did not. The contrast with two other large cities is instructive. Through most of the 1930s, Illinois and Chicago were bedeviled by a counterproductive intra-party blood feud between Governor Henry Horner and Mayor Edward Kelly (Masters, 2007). And the Republican machine that ran Philadelphia was uncooperative with the Democrats' New Deal (Williams, 2013).

New York was also particularly well positioned to benefit quickly when New Deal money became available. Historian Mason Williams puts it this way: "[M]ost American cities possessed relatively great capacity to plan new public construction projects. New York stood out in this respect....Organizations such as the Regional Plan Association and the Mayor's Committee on Plan and Survey...had assembled inventories of desirable public works projects such that, when the PWA [Public Works Administration] arrived, New York could draw upon a great number of already-developed plans (some of which had already been started, only to be halted by the depression)" (Williams, 2013, p. 179). Williams also noted the role played by New York's public authorities, government chartered public benefit entities that were able to act more quickly to initiate projects than government bureaucracies and could circumvent general obligation borrowing limitations by issuing revenue bonds. That New York City had so many "shovel-ready" projects also reflected the influence of Robert Moses who, during the 1920s, had honed the aggressive political, public relations, and managerial skills necessary to get large infrastructure projects underway and completed.

Harry Hopkins, a social worker by training, who wielded considerable discretion regarding the allocation of relief funds as administrator of the Civil Works Administration (CWA) and theWPA, also had an urban orientation and a New York connection. From 1922 until, he left for Washington to join the Roosevelt administration Hopkins held a variety of leadership positions in public and private social welfare agencies in New York. This period of his career culminated with his service as President of New York State's TERA, which became the model for many of the early New Deal agencies.

Finally, New York City and its environs commanded Washington's political attention. The City and State's leverage with respect to traditional, Republican-vs.-Democrat electoral and pork-barrel politics will be discussed below. But Roosevelt and the New Dealers were also aware of potential opposition from the political left (Kessner, 1989, p. 297), and New York City, home to one-third of U.S. "card-carrying" Communists and to that party's national headquarters, was a notorious hotbed of radicalism. Referring to the Louisiana Senator and "share the wealth" advocate Huey Long historian David Kennedy points out that "...[A] poll indicated that [he, Long,] would command upward of 100,000 votes in New York State, a pivotal state in any national election; and a vote of that size could easily mean the difference between victory or defeat" (Kennedy, 1999, p. 240). To the extent, therefore, that New Deal money was allocated to "tame the beast," New York City was a likely target.

Not all historical writing concludes or implies that New York City was in some way special with respect to the attention of New Deal policymakers or the distribution of Federal government funds. For one thing, in designing New Deal programs policymakers placed no special emphasis on conditions in large cities. Contemporaries tended to trace the root cause of the Depression to the low price of farm products in the 1920s and the consequent financial failure of highly leveraged farmers (Kennedy, 1999, p. 123). The solution of choice for this problem was to reduce the supply and raise the price of food paid by urban consumers. Further, to the extent that senior policymakers, very much including the President, thought about specifically "urban" policy at all, their premise was that biggest cities were too big and that Federal policy should encourage movement to new satellite cities away from the urban core. On this point, Mason Williams reports: "The president still saw massive unemployment as a symptom of social imbalance, and the old talk of decentralization picked up again as Roosevelt and Hopkins began discussing plans for meeting the unemployment crisis. 'There are a million people too many [in New York],' FDR remarked at a press conference. 'Suppose we could come back to the 1929 level of industry? Wouldn't we still have a million people on relief in the City of New York?'" (Williams, 2013, pp. 164–165).

Some of this anti-urban predisposition was based on New Dealers' previous experience with big-city political machines. Roosevelt had, as Governor of New York, to maintain his distance from his own party's Tammany Hall organization in New York City, which in 1931 and 1932 was under intense, widely publicized scrutiny by a State legislative committee investigating corruption. Harold Ickes, Roosevelt's secretary of the Interior and in charge of the PWA, also had a history of confrontation with urban political machines. Regarding Ickes urban historian Mark Gelfand observed that "He ignored their [the mayors'] most crucial piece of advice: to decentralize his office and place more confidence in municipal officials. 'Honest Harold,' a lifelong foe of corruption in Chicago government, was unwilling to let even a hint of scandal attach itself to his agency; thus, the bottleneck in the administrator's office continued…" (Gelfand, 1975, p. 12).

Although none of the econometric analyses of the New Deal's geographic dimension address the distribution of aid to New York City in particular or to metropolitan areas in general, the implications of their findings are quite clear. In the aggregate, the New Deal had, in effect, an anti-urban and, perhaps, a specifically anti-New York bias. In part, this finding probably reflects real elements of U.S. politics in the 1930s, and in part, the results may be an artifact of the limitations of broad-based statistical analysis when dealing with such "outliers" as the nation's largest city. The studies generally identified a list of political and economic characteristics that, individually and taken together, explain a substantial proportion of the variance in per capita New Deal spending across states.[10] None of these statistical results would have led one to expect a high level of per capita spending in New York City.

First, the formula governing the distribution of highway funds, for example, included land area, so the higher the land area per capita—or

[10] Much of this literature is summarized in (Fishback, Kantor, & Wallis). The subsequent discussion was informed by (Fishback, Horrace, & Kantor, 2005; Fleck, 2001; Fleck, 1999; Wallis, 1998, 2002; Wright, 1977).

the lower its inverse, population density—the greater the per capita spending, all else held equal. In 1930, New York ranked 44th among the 48 states in land area per capita. Second, residents of low population states are overrepresented in the Senate and the Presidential election process. From the point of view of a program administrator distributing discretionary federal aid, therefore, senate and electoral votes are "cheaper" in terms of per capita grants in lower-population states. As the country's most populous State, New York ranked lowest by this criterion. Third, unsurprisingly, New Deal money tended to go to states and counties whose votes were considered "up for grabs." So "swing" districts got more money and reliably Republican *or* Democratic places got less, all else held equal. In presidential elections prior to 1932, New York had been almost as reliably Republican as Alabama was Democratic. Fourth, power in the U.S. Congress during the 1930s was disproportionally wielded by committee chairmen, and chairmanships were allocated among members of the majority party on the basis of seniority of service. None of the New York Democrats in the 73rd Congress had enough seniority to chair any of the House of Representatives committees that influenced New Deal authorizations or appropriations. Finally, most studies conclude that, while political influence was important, the magnitude of the local economic contraction also influenced how much New Deal money was directed to a state or congressional district. The bulk of the New Deal legislation was enacted in two phases in 1933 and in 1935. Based on economic indicators that were available at those points in time, it would have appeared that the impact of the Depression on New York was less severe than for the average State or average large city (Table 13.1). And so, again, the econometric studies of the distribution of New Deal program funds would not lead one to expect that New York would have received a disproportionately large share of this money.

## What Was New York's Share?

Table 13.4 summarizes the information on New Deal spending across large metropolitan areas detailed in Appendix Table 13A.4. Compared

**Table 13.4** New Deal spending on "urban[a]" programs across 30 large metropolitan areas, 1932–1939 (U.S. Office of Government Reports, 1940a, b)

| Region | Per registered unemployed person | Per capita |
|---|---|---|
| Metropolitan New York-Northern New Jersey | 3,327 | 273 |
| New York City, NY | 3,182 | 289 |
| 30-metropolitan area average | 3,432 | 243 |
| 30-area standard deviation | 1,446 | 88 |
| Northeast[b] average | 2,829 | 201 |
| Midwest[c] average | 4,224 | 271 |
| South[d] average | 3,138 | 230 |
| West[e] average | 3,531 | 271 |

[a]See Table 14.5 for a list of "urban" programs
[b]Albany, Baltimore, Boston, Buffalo, New York, Philadelphia, Pittsburgh, Providence, Washington, DC
[c]Chicago, Cincinnati, Columbus, Detroit, Indianapolis, Milwaukee, Minneapolis, St. Louis, Youngstown
[d]Birmingham, Dallas, Fort Worth, Houston, New Orleans, San Antonio
[e]Denver, Kansas City, Los Angeles, Portland, OR, San Francisco, Seattle
Comparisons across "cities" are based on metropolitan areas to account for the fact that, while data are reported for counties, city, county, and labor market boundaries are seldom contiguous. "Metropolitan areas" incorporated counties included in the Census Bureau's definition of SMSAs in 1950, the first year such regions were defined. The population figures for computing per capita amounts were the average of 1930 and 1940 levels. The definition of unemployed persons for the 1937 special census included labor force participants who were completely without work and "Emergency Workers," those employed under one of the New Deal work relief programs. The per capita and per-unemployed person figures for each of the 30 metropolitan areas are listed in Appendix Table 13A.4. The specific programs included in the total spending figure are listed in Table 13.5

to the nationwide sample, whether as measured per capita or per unemployed person, and whether based on the City's or the metropolitan area's allocation, New York did not fare especially well or especially poorly. If the distribution of aid was intentionally tilted in any direction—and, statistically, we cannot reject the hypothesis that the allocation across broad regions was random—it was away from the northeastern cities and toward the Midwest. If there was such a bias, New York appears to have "beat" it by receiving as much support as the average metropolitan area. The fact that Albany and especially hard-hit

Buffalo got proportionally less than New York City suggests that a "state" effect does not explain why New York got more than the average northeastern city.

Not all New Deal programs were equally effective or ineffective. In particular, programs created and funded earlier in the decade rather than later might have provided greater local stimulus as any lagging multiplier effects worked through the economy. These early Federal programs include the short-lived CWA, the Federal Emergency Relief Administration (FERA) and some of the first projects of the PWA. Further, some programs in some regions required substantial matching funds from state or local governments. Where Federal money was used to leverage greater state and local spending and especially where, as in New York, at least part of this spending was financed by borrowing, a given Federal contribution could, in principle, have had a greater aggregate stimulative effect than the same amount of money allocated without a matching requirement. The programs that required State or local contributions were the Reconstruction Finance Corporation[11] (RFC) loans, FERA grants, and programs to aid impoverished elderly, blind, and dependent children managed by the Social Security Administration. Some PWA projects—those designated "Non-federal Projects"—were jointly funded. Public Buildings Administration, Public Roads Administration, and the Works Projects Administration (WPA) projects were entirely federally funded activities, and Mortgage lending programs administered by the Homeowners Loan Corporation and the Federal Housing Administration would have provided some debt relief during the Depression and may have induced more home construction activity in the 1930s than would have occurred otherwise, but it's unlikely that these programs would have accelerated local recoveries significantly.

For these reasons, it is important to test the assertion that New York City was particularly well positioned to take advantage of Federal

[11]The RFC, created under the Hoover Administration, was not strictly speaking a "New Deal" program. It was, however, an anti-Depression program, it distributed a great deal of money, and its loans were tabulated in the "New Deal" databases.

**Table 13.5** Distribution of total New Deal spending on "Urban" programs (U.S. Office of Government Reports, 1940a, b)

| Program | Metro NYC | NYC | 30 large metro areas | Chicago | LA | Phil. |
|---|---|---|---|---|---|---|
| RFC (%) | 18.8 | 16.6 | 20.0 | 21.4 | 14.0 | 16.9 |
| Home Owners' Loan Corporation | 15.3 | 11.3 | 15.2 | 19.1 | 11.7 | 11.3 |
| PWA—Non-Federal Projects | 4.6 | 5.6 | 4.4 | 6.5 | 4.9 | 3.1 |
| PWA—Federal Projects | 2.1 | 2.2 | 3.5 | 0.6 | 1.3 | 16.7 |
| Public Roads Admin. | 0.7 | 0.5 | 1.7 | 1.5 | 1.6 | 1.6 |
| Public Buildings Admin. | 1.0 | 1.4 | 1.2 | 0.6 | 1.2 | 2.4 |
| WPA | 30.0 | 36.4 | 23.5 | 23.5 | 16.3 | 10.8 |
| Other Works Projects | 0.6 | 0.6 | 1.0 | 0.3 | 4.2 | 0.0 |
| Social Security Board | 1.1 | 1.3 | 1.6 | 1.1 | 3.8 | 1.9 |
| F.E.R.A. | 12.1 | 12.7 | 11.7 | 13.4 | 10.4 | 21.4 |
| CWA | 2.3 | 2.1 | 2.6 | 2.9 | 2.1 | 1.2 |
| PWA—Housing | 0.6 | 0.9 | 0.8 | 1.3 | 0.0 | 1.1 |
| FHA—Insured Improvement Loans | 5.3 | 5.1 | 3.6 | 0.5 | 6.7 | 1.9 |
| FHA—Insured Mortgages | 5.3 | 3.4 | 9.3 | 7.4 | 22.0 | 9.6 |
| Other | 18.6 | 16.4 | 19.8 | 21.2 | 13.8 | 16.8 |
| 1937 Emergency Workers, % of Registered Unemployed | 27.8 | 26.8 | 34.1 | 28.4 | 31.9 | 23.0 |

spending during the crucial early years of the New Deal. For one thing, the activities of the Regional Plan Association and of the various entities overseen by Robert Moses may have endowed the region with a uniquely well-stocked inventory of "shovel ready" projects. Further, as a wealthy state with an investment banker as Governor and an electorate willing to approve large general obligation bond issues, New York was able to finance its contribution to FERA, PWA, and CWA funding with debt. The implication of this line of thinking is that, even though New York did not receive a greater total amount of New Deal funding than the average big city, the City's mix of Federal program funds may have been more effective in that the money was spent sooner and was more highly leveraged than elsewhere.

Such does not appear to have been the case. Table 13.5 reports the distribution of total "urban" program spending across all 30 large metropolitan areas and the specific distributions for the New York metropolitan area, New York City, Chicago, Los Angeles, and Philadelphia. New York does not appear to have captured a much larger share of the earlier programs such as the CWA and FERA or of the leveraged funds provided by the RFC or the PWA. The only "outlier" allocation for New York was the WPA, which was created in 1935, imposed no fixed matching requirement, and may, to some extent, have displaced state and local government relief employment (Williams, 2013, p. 196). To some extent, New York's success in capturing a disproportionate share of spending under this largest and most "urban" of the New Deal programs may reflect the fact that the City's WPA programs got up and running relatively quickly (Williams, 2013, p. 205). It may, however, also reflect the decision by WPA Administrator Harry Hopkins' decision to use his discretion over the local matching requirement to alleviate New York of some of this burden in recognition of the substantial funding the State and City provided to other public works and relief programs (Williams, 2013, p. 257). If so, the proportionally large WPA expenditures may have been offset by smaller proportionate Federal shares of other programs. Further, because the WPA (and CWA) wage rates were regionally adjusted, each job created by the WPA would have cost about 33% more in the Northeast than in the Midwest and 50% more than in the South (Kennedy, 1999, p. 176). In this respect, the most remarkable item in Table 14.5 may be the low level of spending on these programs in Philadelphia. Finally, it is important to remember that not all WPA expenditures provided net new spending. Many of the workers hired by the WPA were simply moved from the rolls of State- or City-funded work programs. Finally, total WPA employment in New York City peaked early in the life of agency and over the latter half of the 1930s, including the crucial period when the 1937–1938 recession took hold, the number of workers engaged in the agency's projects was declining steadily and substantially. WPA employment in New York City peaked at 248,474 on February 19, 1936. By the end of May, 1937, the number had declined by more than a quarer, to 179,644. According to John D. Millett, the author of a 1938 report on the WPA's activities in New York City, "More than anything else, the story of the New York City WPA from 1936 on was a story of the difficulties encountered in attempting to cut the work-relief rolls" (Millett, 1938).

Whatever the reasons for the magnified role of the WPA in New York City, it is not apparent that this type of spending was particularly effective in creating local jobs or in stimulating local economic activity. The proportion of unemployed New Yorkers who were able to land relief jobs as "Emergency Workers" was, in fact, smaller than in other large cities. Data from the 1937 Census of Unemployment show that on average in 20 large metropolitan areas, the number of emergency workers was 34.0% of the total number of persons registered as unemployed (standard deviation = 10.8%). The figure for the New York metropolitan area was 27.8% (Haines, 2018).

## The Delayed Fade

Although the initial blow was not a knockout, over the course of the subsequent decade the Great Depression did more serious damage to the New York economy than to that of other large U.S. metropolitan regions. Initially, New York's specialty sectors suffered less damage as demand collapsed than did the durable goods and consumer discretionary industries that dominated the economies of some other large, northeastern and Midwestern cities. The rapid, leveraged responses of New York's governments and established private sector charities may also have cushioned the initial blow. And the continuing availability of non-bank credit may have helped some New Yorkers stay off the unemployment rolls by starting their own, small retail businesses.

As the decade progressed, however, some of New York's early relative strengths evolved into relative weaknesses. New York's main industries, which didn't contract as quickly as some other sectors, also failed to bounce back as quickly as aggregate demand in the economy expanded rapidly between 1933 and 1937. And one New York-centered economic activity, international trade, that contracted particularly sharply early in the recession, remained depressed through the entire decade. Around mid-decade, New York governments' fiscal policies shifted abruptly from net borrowing to budget balancing. Long-term demographic and industrial trends, many of which began before the 1930s and would accelerate through most of the second half of the twentieth century, acted, on balance, as headwinds for New York's recovery. While concentrated spending on New Deal programs did tend on average to accelerate regional recoveries, New York did not get any more than its proportionate share of Federal largess. Indeed, as the nation's wealthiest state and, therefore, a disproportionately large Federal taxpayer, New York may well have been a net loser under the New Deal fiscal policies.

## Post-Trauma

The period from 1945 through some time in the 1960s is often referred to as the "post-war" era, but in many respects "post-depression" might be a more accurate characterization. The experiences of the 1930s may have altered an entire generation's tolerance for career, business, and investment risk. And the activist public sector responses to the traumas of the Depression altered Americans' presuppositions as to what they could and should expect from their Federal, state, and local governments. New Yorkers' experiences with respect to unemployment, economic distress, and relief were not very different from what other Americans lived through. Nor did New York receive much more or less than its fair share of New Deal spending in general or of any particular urban program's resources. Nevertheless, New Yorkers may have reached somewhat different conclusions from other Americans about the proper role of government in the economy. For one thing, New York State, because of its wealth and because of its progressive political tradition, spent more proportionally on relief programs (Ingalls, 1975, p. 41). And, although total New Deal spending in the City was not disproportionately large, the charismatic and occasionally histrionic leadership of New York's CWA, PWA, and WPA projects may have fostered a particularly profound psychological or ideological impression. Likewise, the fact that New York City was treated as the 49th state for WPA administrative purposes may have magnified the local government's perceived role in the operation of that highly visible program. So

New Yorkers may have emerged from the Depression decade with more optimistic expectations as to how effectively governments in general and State and local governments in particular could solve problems.

The first postwar decades were also the post-Depression era because many of the Federal reform, relief, and recovery policies put in place during the 1930s had their greatest impact on the national and local economy after the Depression and subsequent war had ended. For better or worse, the mortgage insurance agencies created during the 1930s and after the World War helped pave the way for the suburban housing boom that started in the late '40s. For better or worse, after the Depression and the war the Federal and State public housing programs initiated during the Depression, became the only providers of new, affordable rental housing in central cities and changed the face of low-income central city neighborhoods. And, for better or worse, decisions regarding which infrastructure projects would be undertaken with Depression-era funds influenced the ways and places suburbanization would take place. Thus, one can view the contents of the next several chapters as, in part, an excursus on the aftereffects of the Great Depression.

# Appendix

**Table 13A.1** Urban avg. industry unemp. and New York City conc. ratio (U.S. Census Bureau, 1933)

| Industry | Average city unemp. rate (%) | 3-borough concentration ratio |
|---|---|---|
| Agriculture | 25.9 | 0.29 |
| Forestry and fishing | 30.1 | 0.00 |
| Extraction of Minerals | 22.3 | 0.17 |
| Building industry | 35.4 | 1.02 |
| **Durables Manufacturing** | **37.0** | **0.39** |
| Automobile factories | 24.4 | 0.08 |
| Iron and steel industries | 23.3 | 0.37 |
| Metal industries, except iron and steel | 21.8 | 0.91 |
| Lumber and furniture industries | 24.5 | 0.77 |

Table 13A.1 (continued)

| Industry | Average city unemp. rate (%) | 3-borough concentration ratio |
|---|---|---|
| Electrical machinery and supply factories | 20.9 | 0.56 |
| **Non-durables Manufacturing** | **26.4** | **1.20** |
| Clothing industries | 20.1 | 2.00 |
| Shoe factories | 28.6 | 1.24 |
| Rubber factories | 28.0 | 0.00 |
| Chemical and allied industries | 13.2 | 0.75 |
| Cigar and tobacco factories | 23.4 | 1.05 |
| Clay, glass, and stone industries | 22.3 | 0.60 |
| Bakeries | 15.0 | 0.98 |
| Slaughter and packing houses | 14.3 | 0.21 |
| Other food and allied industries | 19.1 | 0.67 |
| Other leather industries | 24.8 | 1.39 |
| Paper, printing, and allied industries | 13.4 | 1.10 |
| Textile Mills | 25.9 | 1.06 |
| Independent hand trades | 11.0 | 1.23 |
| Other manufacturing industries | 19.7 | 1.15 |
| **Transportation and Communications** | **20.6** | **0.98** |
| Construction and maintenance of streets and sewers | 32.0 | 0.87 |
| Garages, greasing stations, etc. | 20.7 | 0.80 |
| Steam railroads | 16.1 | 0.45 |
| Street railroads | 8.6 | 1.01 |
| Telegraph and telephone | 9.4 | 1.13 |
| Other transportation, including postal service | 18.7 | 1.33 |
| **Trade** | **14.5** | **1.06** |
| Banking and brokerage | 6.3 | 1.38 |
| Insurance and real estate | 7.5 | 1.10 |
| Automobile agencies and filling stations | 11.2 | 0.49 |

(continued)

**Table 13A.1** (continued)

| Industry | Average city unemp. rate (%) | 3-borough concentration ratio |
|---|---|---|
| Wholesale and retail trade, except automobiles | 13.8 | 1.06 |
| Other trade industries | 12.9 | 0.91 |
| **Public service (n.e.c.)** | **9.3** | **0.79** |
| **Professional Services** | **7.7** | **1.08** |
| Recreation and amusement | 15.0 | 1.18 |
| Other professional service | 4.6 | 1.06 |
| Personal Services | 22.0 | 1.12 |
| Hotels, restaurants, boarding houses, etc. | 17.0 | 1.08 |
| Laundries and cleaning, dyeing and pressing shops | 16.1 | 0.99 |
| Other domestic and personal services | 18.9 | 1.17 |
| Automobile repair shops | 19.5 | 0.81 |
| **Industry not specified** | **33.0** | **1.32** |
| Average Industry Unemployment Rate | 19.3 | |

**Table 13A.2** Herfindahl indexes of industrial diversification in employment for cities surveyed in the 1931 Census of Unemployment (U.S. Census Bureau, 1933)

| City | Herfindahl index |
|---|---|
| St. Louis | 0.057 |
| Philadelphia | 0.058 |
| Buffalo | 0.058 |
| Chicago | 0.059 |
| Boston | 0.062 |
| Los Angeles | 0.062 |
| Seattle | 0.063 |
| San Francisco | 0.064 |
| Houston | 0.064 |
| Denver | 0.066 |
| New York City (three boroughs) | 0.067 |
| Cleveland | 0.067 |
| Minneapolis | 0.068 |

(continued)

Table 13A.2 (continued)

| City | Herfindahl index |
|---|---|
| Duluth | 0.069 |
| New Orleans | 0.070 |
| Pittsburgh | 0.072 |
| Birmingham | 0.083 |
| Dayton | 0.087 |
| Detroit | 0.122 |
| Average | 0.069 |
| Standard deviation | 0.015 |

**Table 13A.3** Total and per-borrower loans made by the New York Hebrew Free Loan Society, 1925–1937 (Tenenbaum, 1993; U.S. Census Bureau, 1975, p. 197)

| Indicator | 1925 | 1932 | 1935 | 1937 |
|---|---|---|---|---|
| HFLS total nominal lending ($1000) | $1,185 | $910 | $1,056 | $1,001 |
| Normalized GDP deflator | 100 | 63 | 77 | 83 |
| HFLS real lending (1925 $1000) | $1,185 | $1,444 | $1,363 | $1,199 |
| Average loan, nominal | $92.31 | $68.46 | $52.07 | $57.90 |
| Average loan, real | $92.31 | $108.60 | $67.20 | $69.35 |

**Table 13A.4** Total New Deal spending on "Urban[a]" programs, 1933–1939, in 30 large metropolitan[b] areas (U.S. Office of Government Reports, 1940a, b)

| Metropolitan area | Per-unemployed[c] population, 1937 | Per capita[d] |
|---|---|---|
| Albany, NY | 2,949 | 157 |
| Atlanta, GA | 2,463 | 203 |
| Baltimore, MD | 5,855 | 253 |
| Birmingham, AL | 2,225 | 199 |
| Boston, MA | 2,817 | 220 |
| Buffalo, NY | 2,834 | 201 |
| Chicago, IL-IN | 4,034 | 258 |
| Cincinnati, OH-KY | 3,866 | 217 |
| Columbus, OH | 4,366 | 358 |
| Dallas, TX | 3,353 | 250 |
| Denver, CO | 1,210 | 135 |
| Detroit, MI | 7,107 | 375 |
| Fort Worth, TX | 2,880 | 191 |

(continued)

Table 13A.4 (continued)

| Metropolitan area | Per-unemployed[c] population, 1937 | Per capita[d] |
|---|---|---|
| Houston, TX | 3,999 | 192 |
| Indianapolis, IN | 3,596 | 257 |
| Kansas City, MO-KS | 2,960 | 223 |
| Los Angeles, CA | 4,381 | 279 |
| Milwaukee, WI | 4,648 | 320 |
| Minneapolis, MN | 2,374 | 159 |
| New Orleans, LA | 3,510 | 335 |
| **New York, NY-NJ** | **3,327** | **273** |
| **New York City, NY** | **3,182** | **289** |
| Philadelphia, PA | 1,992 | 162 |
| Pittsburgh, PA | 2,369 | 200 |
| Portland, OR-WA | 1,781 | 148 |
| Providence, RI-MA | 854 | 98 |
| San Antonio, TX | 3,536 | 238 |
| San Francisco, CA | 7,583 | 593 |
| Seattle, WA | 3,272 | 246 |
| St. Louis, MO | 3,034 | 245 |
| Washington, DC-VA-MD | 2,461 | 241 |
| Youngstown, OH-PA | 4,995 | 253 |
| Weighted metropolitan average | 3,376 | 253 |
| Unweighted average | 3,432 | 243 |
| Standard deviation | 1,446 | 88 |

[a]See Table 13.5 for a list of these programs
[b]Metropolitan areas include all the counties in each SMSA as defined in the 1950 census. Cleveland has been omitted because data for Cuyahoga and Lake Counties, OH, were missing from the National Archives Files
[c]Unemployed as defined in the 1937 census of unemployment. This includes both members of the labor force who are completely without jobs and "Emergency Workers" employed on one of the New Deal Work Relief programs such as the Civil Works Administration (CWA) or the Works Projects Administration (WPA)
[d]Based on the average of the populations reported in the 1930 and 1940 censuses

## References

Bernstein, M. (1987). *The Great Depression: Delayed Recovery and Economic Change in America, 1929–1939, 1987*. Cambridge: Cambridge University Press.

Calomris, C., & Barry Wilson, B. (2004). Bank Capital and Portfolio Management: The 1930s "Capital Crunch" and the Scramble to Shed Risk. *The Journal of Business, 77*(3), 421–455.

Cole, H. L., & Ohanian, L. E. (2004). New Deal Policies and the Persistence of the Great Depression: A General Equilibrium Analysis. *Journal of Political Economy, 112*(41), 779–816.

Field, A. J. (2003). The Most Technologically Progressive Decade of the Century. *American Economic Review, 93*(4), 1399–1413.

Friedman, M., & Schwartz, A. (1986). The Failure of the Bank of the United States: A Reappraisal: A Reply. *Exploration in Economic History, 23,* 199–204.

Garret, T. A., & Wheelock, D. C. (2006). *Why Did Income Growth Vary Across States During the Great Depression* (Working Paper 2005-01-013B). St. Louis: Federal Reserve Bank of St. Louis, Research Division.

Gelfand, M. I. (1975). *A Nation of Cities: The Federal Government and Urban America, 1933–1965*. Oxford: Oxford University Press.

Haines, M. R. (2018). *Historical, Demographic, Economic, and Social Data: The United States, 1790–2002 [Computer File]. ICPSR02896-v3*. Ann Arbor, MI: Inter-university Consortium for Politica. Retrieved from Inter-university Consortium for Political and Social Research https://www.icpsr.umich.edu/icpsrweb/.

Ingalls, R. P. (1975). *Herbert H. Lehman and New York's Little New Deal*. New York: New York University Press.

Kennedy, D. M. (1999). *Freedom from Fear: The American People in Depression and War, 1929–1945*. Oxford: Oxford University Press.

Kessner, T. (1989). *Fiorello H. La Guardia and the Making of Modern New York*. New York: Penguin Books.

Light, I. H. (1972). *Business and Welfare Among Chinese, Japanese, and Blacks*. Berkeley: University of California Press.

Lucia, J. (1985). The Failure of the Bank of United States: A Reappraisal. *Explorations in Economic History, 22,* 402–416.

Masters, C. J. (2007). *Governor Henry Horner, Chicago Politics, and the Great Depression*. Carbondale: Southern Illinois Press.

Millett, J. D. (1938). *The Works Progress Administration in New York City*. Chicago: Public Administration Service.

O'Brien, P. (1992, August). The Failure of the Bank of United States: A Defense of Joseph Lucia. *Journal of Money, Credit and Banking, 24,* 374–384.

Romer, C. D. (1992, December). What Ended the Great Depression? *The Journal of Economic History, 52*(4), 757–784.

Rosenbloom, J. L., & Sundstrom, W. A. (1999). The Sources of Regional Variation in the Severity of the Great Depression: Evidence from U.S. Manufacturing, 1919–1937. *The Journal of Economic History, 59*(3), 714–747.

Simon, C. J., & Clark Nardinelli, C. (1992). Does Industrial Diversity Always Reduce Unemployment? Evidence from the Great Depression and After. *Economic Inquiry, 30*, 384–397.

Temin, P. (1994). *The Great Depression, NBER Working Paper Series on Historical Factors in Long Run Growth*. National Bureau of Economic Research.

Tenenbaum, S. (1993). *A Credit to Their Community: Jewish Loan Societies in the United States, 1880–1945*. Detroit: Wayne State University Press.

*The New York Times*. (1929, May 10). $300,000,000 Merger of Banks Approved.

Trescott, P. (1992). The Failure of the Bank of United States, 1930. *Journal of Money, Credit and Banking, 24*, 384–399.

U.S. Census Bureau. (1933). *Fifteenth Census of the United States: 1930, Unemployment, Volume II, General Report: Unemployment by Occupation, April 1930 with Returns from the Special Census of Unemployment January 1931*. Washington, DC: U.S. Government Printing Office.

U.S. Census Bureau. (1941). *Sixteenth Census of the United States, 1940: Census of Business, Retail Trade: 1939*. Washington: U.S. Government Printing Office.

U.S. Census Bureau. (1975). *Historical Statistics of the United States, Colonial Times to 1970, Volume 2*. Washington: U.S. Government Printing Office.

U.S. Department of Commerce. (2018). *Annual Reports on the Commerce and Navigation of the United States*. Retrieved from Hathi Trust https://catalog.hathitrust.org/Record/001719409.

U.S. Department of Commerce. (n.d.). *Annual Reports on the Commerce and Navigation of the United States*. Retrieved from Hathi Trust https://catalog.hathitrust.org/Record/001719409.

U.S. Office of Government Reports. (1940a). *County Reports of Estimated Federal Government Expenditures March 4 1933–June 30, 1939* (Report No. 10, Vol. 1).

U.S. Office of Government Reports. (1940b). *Direct and Cooperative Loans and Expenditures of the Federal Government for Fiscal Years 1933 through 1939* (Report No. 9, Vol. 1).

Virginia Commonwealth University. (2018). *Social Welfare History Project*. Retrieved from VCU Libraries https://socialwelfare.library.vcu.edu.

Wallis, J. J. (1989). Employment in the Great Depression: New Data and Hypotheses. *Explorations in Economic History, 26*, 45–72.

Wicker, E. (1996). *The Banking Panics of the Great Depression*. Cambridge: Cambridge University Press.

Williams, M. B. (2013). *City of Ambition: FDR, La Guardia, and the Making of Modern New York*. New York: W. W. Norton.

# 14

# Social Democracy and Suburbanization

Between 1950 and 1980, New York City's population decreased by about 820,000 or about 10%; that of the surrounding suburban counties increased by about 1,082,000.[1] As Fig. 14.1 indicates, however, the three decades can be usefully divided into two distinct periods. For the first two decades, the New York region as a whole lagged the national population growth rate by a narrow margin while the City's population stagnated. During the 1970s, however, while the U.S. population grew by 11.5%, the New York region's grew by only two percent and the City's population declined by about 10%. Analysis of the New York economy during this period, therefore, must focus on two developments: (i) suburbanization through the entire post-World War II period and its effects and (ii) the weakness of the broader regional economy, especially during the 1970s.

This chapter deals with the first of these topics. The next chapter will focus on the local, national, and global economic developments that

[1]At the time, the New York Standard Metropolitan Statistical Area included the City, Putnam, Rockland, and Westchester Counties, NY, and Bergen County, NJ. Depending on the context and the time period, this and the subsequent chapters will refer to different definitions of the New York region. Definitions will be provided for each such reference.



A. Gurwitz, *Atlantic Metropolis*, Palgrave Studies in American Economic History,
https://doi.org/10.1007/978-3-030-13352-8_14

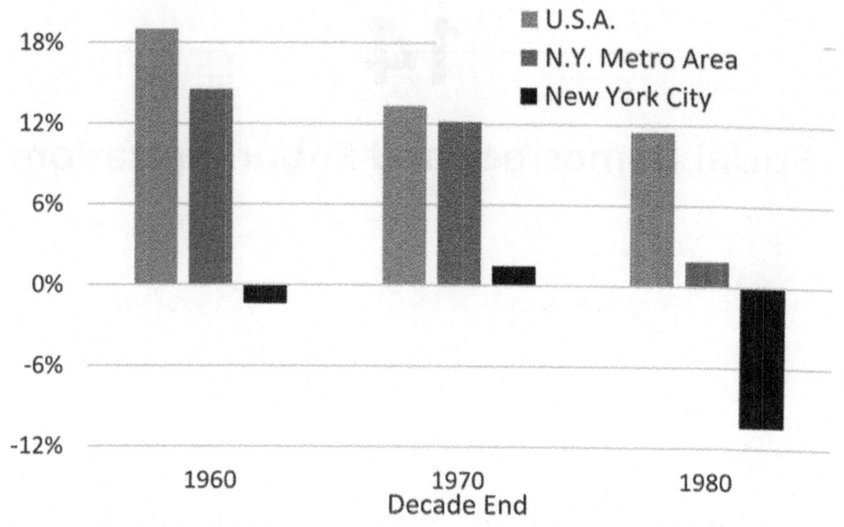


**Fig. 14.1** Population growth rates by decade (U.S. Census Bureau, 1982, p. 902)

placed the New York metropolitan region as a whole at a competitive disadvantage during this period.

## The Problematics of Postwar Suburbanization

Suburbanization is not solely a post-World War II phenomenon. The substantial growth of any city's population is necessarily accompanied by an expansion of its land area, especially so before high-rise construction became feasible. And after an urban area's radius extends beyond the limit of reasonable walking distance, further growth depends on the development of cost-effective intra-urban transportation technology. New York City's urban land area reached the limit of routine walking distance by the second quarter of the nineteenth century. During the antebellum decades, the City's increasingly rapid expansion involved the construction of single-family row houses farther and farther north on Manhattan Island with commutation facilitated in the first instance by multi-passenger carriages ("omnibuses") and rail cars, both drawn by horses. During the late nineteenth and early twentieth centuries, after the construction of bridges spanning the East River and the installation of electric-powered trolley lines, settlement extended into the "street car suburbs" of northern Manhattan, the Bronx, Queens, and especially Brooklyn. During the same period upper-middle-class New Yorkers began moving to villages clustered around the stations of rail lines extending northward into Westchester County, eastward on Long Island, and in westward into northern New Jersey.

As higher-income families, who could afford commutation costs and the larger, newly constructed single-family dwellings, moved north-, east-, and westward, poorer households became increasingly concentrated in the areas of earliest settlement in the southern parts of Manhattan, either in older single-family dwellings that had been subdivided or, starting in the 1860s, in purpose-built, cramped, stuffy, and often poorly maintained but affordable tenements. Observers at the time may have decried living conditions in the densely settled "slums," but were not apparently troubled by the general process of urban expansion through the growth of what might have been but generally were not at the time called "suburbs." Indeed, as urban historian Kenneth Jackson has shown, the most influential mid- and late nineteenth-century architects and journalists established the single-family dwelling in the midst of a surrounding garden as a North American ideal (Jackson, 1985).

After World War II, however, the shift of metropolitan populations to the suburbs came to be viewed as problematic in ways that it had not been before. What was different?

There was little difference between pre-war and postwar suburbanization with respect to some of the fundamental drivers of the process: regional population growth, an expanding and increasingly prosperous middle class, faster and more extensive transportation infrastructure, and deteriorating living conditions close to the central business district (CBD). The urbanized land area expanded rapidly as the baby boom boosted metropolitan populations and as widespread automobile ownership and limited-access highway construction enabled a prospering middle class to act on their preference for larger and more widely spaced living quarters.

But the postwar process differed from what had gone before in three ways that led critics to adopt the terms "suburban sprawl" and "urban crisis" to characterize the emerging metropolitan land use patterns.

First, previous stages of urban spatial expansion in the United States had been accompanied by the annexation of newly developed neighborhoods into central city political jurisdictions. The most dramatic and, for our purposes, most relevant such instance, although it wasn't strictly speaking an annexation, was the incorporation of Kings, Richmond, western Queens, and southern Westchester counties into the City of New York in 1898. By the middle of the interwar years, however, most residents of towns and counties surrounding northeastern and Midwestern central cities came to view the costs of annexation as greater than its benefits and, when given the choice, opted to remain politically separate. Thus, over the twenty years between 1910 and 1930, the total land area of 12 large northeastern and Midwestern cities increased by 24%; over the subsequent 60 years, the increase was only five percent[2] (Gibson, 1998) Because suburbanites tended to have higher incomes than central city residents, impediments to annexation had the effect of dividing metropolitan areas into "rich" suburban jurisdictions and "poor" central cities. The social and fiscal ramifications of these developments came home to roost in cities nationwide during the 1960s and 1970s.

Second, rapid postwar suburbanization and the concentration of lower-income populations in politically circumscribed central cities coincided with an acceleration of the Great Migration of mostly poor African-Americans from the rural south to northern and western cities. So, trends in metropolitan spatial structure became entwined with America's "original sin" of racial injustice.

Third, although city governments had always influenced the pace and patterns of urban expansion, state and Federal policies did not have important effects on metropolitan land use patterns before World War II. Post-Depression governments—Federal, state, and municipal—were

[2] Throughout this section, the following will be used to represent "large Northeastern and Midwestern" cities, the municipalities, and regions that were and are most comparable to New York City: Baltimore, Boston, Chicago, Cincinnati, Cleveland, Detroit, Minneapolis, New York, Philadelphia, Pittsburgh, St. Louis, and Washington, DC.

much more activist than they had been. Many of the policies governments adopted or failed to adopt, individually and in combination, had the effect of magnifying and accelerating the expansion of suburbs beyond what rising incomes, population growth, and affordable cars alone would have generated. Critics of sprawl and diagnosticians of the urban crisis could, therefore, argue that a policy bias had generated too much suburbanization.

By the 1960s suburbanization, the concentration of poor populations in central cities and the accelerating Great Migration along with racial discrimination in the labor and housing markets combined to create large concentrations of low-income African-Americans in particular neighborhoods of northern central cities. The most powerful motive for postwar interstate African-American migration was not the "pull" of rising demand for labor in northern cities but, rather, the "push" of declining demand for agricultural workers in the south. This was especially the case during the 1960s, when mechanical harvesters replaced human cotton pickers. Further, as a result of the color lines discussed in Chapter 9 and of some of the industrial changes that will be the subject of the next chapter, northern urban labor markets did not absorb the new arrivals quickly.

As the decade of the 1960s progressed, the large, isolated concentrations of poor and/or unemployed people became tinderboxes for riots in northern cities. During the first nine months of 1967, at least 161 incidences of civil disorder occurred in U.S. towns and cities. About one-quarter of these were characterized as either "major" or "serious," and National Guard or regular military forces were called out to control eight of them (The National Advisory Commission on Civil Disorders, 1988, pp. 112–114). The epidemic of riots, unprecedented in scale and geographic scope, drew national attention to conditions in central cities and to suburbanization, which had left so many low-income African-Americans socially and politically isolated in economically troubled municipalities. The National Advisory Commission on Civil Disorders (the "Kerner Commission"), established by President Lyndon Johnson in 1967 to examine the causes and consequences of these incidents, warned that the trends the commissioners observed "would lead to the permanent establishment of two societies: one predominantly white and located in the suburbs… and one largely Negro located in central cities" (The National Advisory Commission on Civil Disorders, 1988, p. 398).

## Suburbanization Outlier

To the extent that suburbanization created economic, political, social, and, indeed, military problems in cities and metropolitan areas, New York should have been less vulnerable to those challenges than comparable regions. As measured by a range of criteria, New York was, by a wide margin, the least suburbanized populous metropolitan region in the northeastern quadrant of the United States.

Economists have deployed several statistical measures of metropolitan areas' relative rates and degrees of suburbanization. Many of these focus on the populations and population densities of the central city and its surrounding counties; the greater the population of the surrounding counties relative to that of the central city, the greater the degree of suburbanization. Other measures reflect the effects of suburbanization as the process has played out in the United States during the postwar period. Because central city residents have tended to be poorer on average than those living in surrounding counties, the relative median household incomes of the two geographic segments have been taken as an indicator of suburbanization. And, since a relatively large proportion of U.S. suburbanites lived in owner-occupied single-family dwellings, homeownership rates and the proportion of metropolitan area residents living in single-family homes can also be taken as correlates of suburbanization.

By the simplest indicator, the central city's share of the metropolitan area's population, New York was less suburbanized than other large northeastern and Midwestern cities. In 1980, the City accounted for 60.7% of the New York Standard Metropolitan Statistical Area (SMSA)'s population. This was, by far, the largest and twice the average statistic among 12 comparable metropolitan regions. Chicago ranked second in this regard, but Cook County accounted for only 42.3% of its metropolitan area's population. This comparison is somewhat misleading, however, because New York City's land area is large relative to its metropolitan region by the standards of big northeastern and Midwestern cities, some of which are very small. St. Louis's land area, for example, accounts for less than 0.5% of its metropolitan area's while New York City accounts 5.6% of its SMSA's land area, the second largest such statistic among 12 large northeastern and Midwestern metropolitan regions (Chicago, at 5.7%, was number one)[3] (Carter, Gartner, & Haines, 2006).

A proper comparison of relative degrees of suburbanization requires a statistic that reflects both relative populations and relative land areas of the central city and the metropolitan region. One such statistic, the Greek letter θ (theta) in the following equation, was initially proposed by David F. Bradford and Harry H. Kelejian (Bradford & Kelejian, 1973).

(A Central City's Share of Metropolitan Population) = (That City's Share of its Metropolitan Land Area)$^{\theta}$

Theta takes on values between zero and one and reflects the degree to which central city population density exceeds that of the metropolitan region as a whole in a way that corrects for differences in relative land areas. Larger values of theta reflect greater degrees of suburbanization.

Theta statistics for 12 large northeastern and Midwestern cities for the years 1940 and 1980 are depicted in Fig. 14.2. Prior to World War II, New York's degree of suburbanization was about the same as that of most other comparable cities. At the end of the period of the most rapid suburbanization, metropolitan New York's population was decidedly more concentrated in the central city than that of other metropolitan areas, even after taking into account the City's relatively large geographic size.[4]

The effect of suburbanization troubled many observers, including a majority of members of the Kerner Commission, the most was the

[3]"Large cities" are those that had populations greater than 100,000 in 1990. The New York metropolitan area refers to New York City, Nassau, Putnam, Rockland, Suffolk, and Westchester Counties, NY, and Bergen, Essex, Hudson, Morris, Somerset, and Union Counties, NJ.

[4]Note that the conclusions regarding the relatively dense concentration of metropolitan area population in New York City do not change if the basis of geographic comparison is changed from Metropolitan Statistical Area (MSA) to the larger Consolidated Statistical Area (CSA).

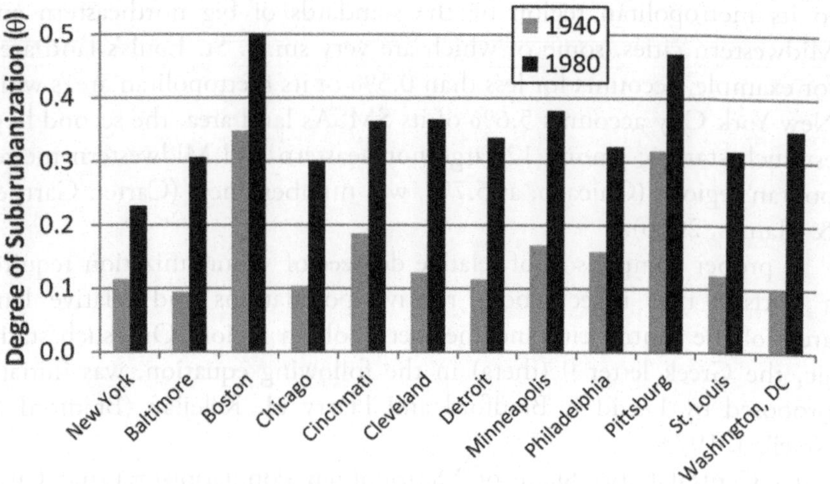


**Fig. 14.2** Relative degrees of suburbanization as measured by θ among 12 northeastern and Midwestern metropolitan regions, 1940 and 1980 (Gibson, 1998)

emerging pattern of income segregation across central city-suburban jurisdictional boundaries. By this criterion, too, New York stood out as much less affected than comparable regions. In 1979, for example, on average across 12 large northeastern and Midwestern primary metropolitan statistical areas (PMSAs), the median income of central city residents was 72.6% of PMSA median income. The figure for the New York region was 94.8%, which was, by far, the highest among these metropolitan areas. The figure for second-place Pittsburgh was 75.9%.

This straightforward comparison could be subject to the same criticism applied to raw population or density comparisons; it might be influenced by the land area of the central city relative to the region as a whole. A geographically large central city might include outlying neighborhoods that would be suburbs in any other region and that would boost the city's median income. As Fig. 14.3 indicates, this does not appear to have been the case with respect to New York relative to its comparable PMSAs. This figure illustrates the degree to which New York was an outlier among comparable regions with respect to both the

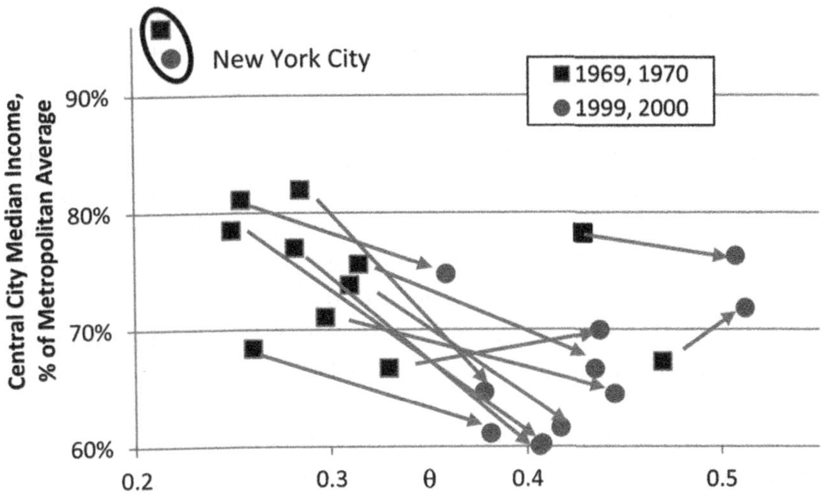


**Fig. 14.3** Relative degrees of suburbanization and central city median income as a percentage of metropolitan median income in 12 northeastern and Midwestern metropolitan regions, 1969–1970 and 1999–2000 (U.S. Department of Housing and Urban Development, Office of Policy Development and Research, 2018)

amount of suburbanization that took place between 1970 and 2000 and the relative median incomes of the City and its suburbs. The City's relatively large geographic size may have had some impact on the median income-suburbanization relationship, but probably not such a large effect.[5]

Other correlates of postwar suburbanization also highlight how different New York was in this regard. In 1986, across the 75 largest MSA, an average of 61.2% of housing units were owner-occupied. At 60.8%, the average for large northeastern and Midwestern metropolitan areas was about the same. The figure for New York was 32.1%. The second lowest figure nationwide was for the Miami, FL, metropolitan area at 47.9% (U.S. Census Bureau, 2018).

[5] 1969 was the first year for which these data were available.

As one would expect in the most populous, less suburbanized metropolitan area, a relatively small proportion of New York's population lived in single-family dwellings. In 1980 on average across the 12 comparable metropolitan regions, 61.4% of the homes were single-family dwellings. In New York, the figure was 20.7%. Chicago at 50.4% ranked second lowest in this regard. New York also differed from comparable regions in the extent to which units in multifamily dwellings were owner-occupied as condominiums or as apartments in cooperative buildings. On average across the 12 comparable metropolitan areas, 11.3% of the residences in buildings with two or more units were owner-occupied. In New York, it was 38.1%, about twice second-place Chicago's level (U.S. Census Bureau, 1983).

Why was New York so different across all of these indicia of suburbanization? Two types of explanation need to be explored. One set of possibilities is that although the fundamental drivers of suburbanization, such as population and income growth or changes in transportation costs, were the same across all metropolitan areas, *the specific New York values of the relevant variables* were such that this region's outcomes were as described in the previous paragraphs. The alternative type of explanation would be that the suburbanization process worked out very differently in New York from otherwise comparable metropolitan areas because of some combination of the region's unique economic, political, or social characteristics. Subsequent sections of this chapter will work through both approaches.

## The Causes of Suburbanization: An Econometric Score Card

The developing urban crisis of the 1960 also captured the attention of the economics profession, and it probably isn't a coincidence that between 1964 and 1969, just when the incidence of civil disorder was peaking, three researchers, William Alonso, Edwin Mills, and Richard Muth, working separately, developed and elaborated what became a standard model of urban residential land use (Alonso, 1964; Mills, 1970; Muth, 1969).

The Muth, Alonso, Mills (MAM) models demonstrate how a free-market equilibrium could be characterized by (a) residential density and (estimated constant-quality) housing prices that decreased with distance from a city's CBD and (b) with the lowest-income households choosing to live close to the CBD while higher-income households chose to live in less densely inhabited areas relatively distant from their workplaces. The models were also consistent with the observation that overall urban residential density tended to decrease as transportation costs declined and as residents' average income rose. Thus, the theoretical work of these economists proved that, through the actions of utility-maximizing households in free markets alone, at least some amount of suburbanization was to be expected during the postwar decades.

The key phrase in the previous sentence was "at least some amount." The initial MAM models were highly abstract and completely ahistorical. In the assumed world of these models, individual households, all of whom worked in the single CBD of city situated on a "flat featureless plane extending indefinitely in all directions," would, as their incomes rose and as they acquired automobiles, demand larger homes in bigger yards at greater distances from their workplaces. Demand for smaller, more densely packed residences closer to the CBD would decrease. And the supplies of the right-sized homes would adjust quickly to the demand changes. Nationalities, geographic peculiarities, durable housing stocks, government or multiple governments, racial discrimination, and numerous other complexities were absent from the initial model formulations.

These path-breaking urban economists, of course, recognized that any, all, or any combination of these initially un-modeled considerations could influence the equilibrium spatial structure. National differences must have some impact on urban spatial structure because metropolitan regions in other highly developed countries tend to be less suburbanized than in the United States. And in many European and Latin American cities, higher-income households are more likely to live near the CBD with poorer families gravitating to densely populated suburban *favelas* or *banlieues*. Further, the geographic characteristics of a city's region will, of course, influence its spatial structure. There is a good reason to expect, for example, that transportation costs will be higher and decline more slowly over time in a city, like New York, scattered across an archipelago than in a place like Dallas, which is, indeed, situated in the midst of an extensive, flat, and nearly featureless plane. Also, because houses are durable capital goods, supply cannot adjust downward quickly as soon as rising incomes or lower transportation costs reduce demand for residences close to the CBD. Instead, central city housing may be offered at very low prices for years or decades while (quality-adjusted) supply declines slowly and painfully as owners allow properties to deteriorate.

Finally, although the development of the MAM models may have been motivated in part by the goal of counteracting the view that government policies were *the* principal drivers of postwar suburbanization in the United States, there is little doubt that local, state, and Federal governments played an important role in the process. For one thing, State and local governments set the rules that determine how easy or hard it is for central city municipalities to annex neighboring jurisdictions. Forestalling annexation after some point opens the way for metropolitan areas to be divided up into numerous separate local governments: suburban counties, towns and villages, school districts, fire districts, sanitation districts, and so on.

The operation of such multi-jurisdictional regions is described and analyzed in a family of economic models of metropolitan spatial structure that focus explicitly on households' residential choices across multiple political jurisdictions. These models, elaborations of initial work by Charles Tiebout, posit that multiple communities in a metropolitan area differ in the nature, quantity, and quality of local governmental services, such as public schools and recreational facilities, and in the taxes they levy to pay for those services. Households choose residential locations, in part, on the basis of which municipality offers their subjectively most desirable package of services and taxes. Subsequent applications of the model's basic structure explore the impacts of other ways in which municipalities may differ such as with respect to their degree of socioeconomic, racial, or ethnic homogeneity. Explorations of the phenomenon of "white flight" from central cities are, in effect, extensions of the Tiebout model (Tiebout, 1961).

State and local governments had also always influenced the timing and location of road and bridge construction. During the postwar period, however, the Federal government also began to influence the planning of the national highway system and, then, under 1956 legislation, the dominant role in the financing of limited-access roadway construction. The federally inspired and financed interstate highway system primarily aimed to facilitate transportation *between* the nation's metropolitan areas, but many of the roads constructed under this legislation passed through central cities and, thereby, reduced local residents' commutation costs.

Federal housing and housing finance programs—some initiated during the Great Depression and others adopted after World War II—facilitated consumers' purchase of single-family detached homes much more effectively than buying multifamily owner-occupied units, such as coops or condominiums. Further, some Federal public housing, urban renewal, and "slum-clearance" programs may have, in effect, encouraged the concentration of low-income households in general and African-Americans, in particular, in segregated neighborhoods.

What the MAM and Tiebout models did was to set the theoretical and empirical research agenda for urban economists over the subsequent decades. One general goal has been to estimate the relative impact of each of the potential causes of suburbanization—income and transportation costs, geographic differences, crime rates, the number of limited-access highways within the central city, etc.—by comparing the residential locations of individual households and measures of spatial structure for U.S. metropolitan areas, cross-sectionally and over time. That project is still underway, but one general conclusion is quite clear: All of the hypothesized drivers of suburbanization discussed above appear to have played at least some role.

As predicted by the MAM models, income growth and reduced transportation costs were quite important. Economic historian Robert A. Margo has reported that a statistical comparison of the changes between 1950 and 1980 in the likelihood that any given household in any given U.S. metropolitan area lived in a suburb indicated that "slightly less than half of population suburbanization between 1950 and 1980 can be attributed to rising household incomes" (Margo, 1992, p. 301).

And Nathaniel Baum-Snow estimated that U.S. central city populations, which declined by 17% between 1950 and 1990, would have grown by 8% over that period had the interstate highway system not been built (Baum-Snow, 2007).

The jurisdictional characteristics, the focus of Tiebout-type models, were also important. Most obviously, the geographic size of the central political jurisdiction relative to that of the metropolitan area as a whole will go a long way to determine what percentage of the region's population and how much of its middle class lives in the central city.

As suburbanization has progressed, central cities, whatever their geographic size, have become increasingly seen as places where poor people, many of them African-American, live and where crime rates are relatively high. These characterizations were generally true during the period of peak suburbanization. In particular, during the 1960s and 1970s, the incidence of crime increased sharply in "ghetto" neighborhoods. It stands to reason that such central city "disamenities" would become additional reasons for middle-class households to move to now much safer suburbs. It is somewhat surprising, therefore, that empirical economists have had a hard time detecting a significant impact of crime rates on the pace and degree of metropolitan suburbanization. The statistical challenge is to separate cause and effect. Suppose suburbanization was particularly pronounced in a metropolitan area because, for example, regional middle-class incomes have been increasing rapidly or new highways have opened. If so, that region's central city may now be poorer and its residents more prone to criminal activity that would be the case in metropolitan areas that were slower to suburbanize. In this case, suburbanization caused rising crime rather than the other way around. There are ways of overcoming this empirical challenge, and in 1999, economists Julie Berry Cullen and Steven D. Levitt concluded that across metropolitan areas "a 10% increase in crime corresponds to a 1% decline in city population." They also found that better educated city residents, both African-American and white, were more likely to move in response to higher crime rates than were those with lower levels of schooling. Finally, their statistical results indicated that central city residents who "fled" a central city where crime rates were high were more likely to move to that city's suburbs than to move away from the metropolitan region (Cullen & Levitt, 1999).

Subsequent empirical work produced more ambiguous results. Ray Burnham, Robert M Feinberg, and Thomas A. Husted found that higher violent crime rates did tend to slow total and per capita income growth in central cities and nearby suburbs and to boost growth slightly in more distant suburbs. But the effects they detected were small, and they found no impact of higher property crime rates. They concluded: "The results are not as robust as anticipated. An obvious explanation is simply that households decide where to locate based primarily on factors other than crime like the quality of school districts and the ease of transportation to work…" (Burnham, Feinberg, & Husted, 2004).

Attempts to estimate the effect, if any, of "white flight" from central cities are subject to the same cause and effect challenge as efforts to identify the impact of crime. Central city residents of metropolitan regions suburbanized relatively quickly and markedly tended to be poorer and, in the context of the Great Migration, disproportionately African-American. So suburbanization could result in racial segregation across jurisdictions even if (higher-income) whites were in no way averse to living near blacks. Economic historian Leah Platt Boustan was, however, able to overcome this statistical challenge and to identify clear evidence of "white flight." She estimated that the arrival of one additional African-American resident in a city between 1940 and 1970 was associated on average with a decrease of 2.7 white residents so that, in the aggregate, the change in the racial composition of their populations led to a 17% decline in central city populations (Boustan, 2010).

In a survey of the literature on the causes of suburbanization, Peter Mieszkowski and Edwin S. Mills noted that, although suburbanization occurred across all of North America during the postwar years, in 1975 metropolitan populations were more highly concentrated in central cities in Canada than in the U.S. Citing work by Michael Goldberg and John Mercer, they suggested that these national differences reflected both MAM and Tiebout-type influences. Commutation costs probably differed across the border because Canada had built fewer limited-access highways per capita and made more use of public transportation. And Canadians had fewer jurisdictional choices than U.S. residents; the

Dominion's metropolitan areas were divided into fewer fiscal entities than in the United States (Mieszkowski & Mills, 1993, p. 142).

Mieszkowski and Mills also cited studies of urban spatial structure in Japan, Germany, and Britain. Metropolitan populations in Japan and Germany were much more highly concentrated in central cities and much slower to suburbanize than in the United States. Population density patterns in the UK, however, were similar to those in the United States. As these comparisons suggest, international variations can shed light on the determinants of suburbanization and the degree to which universal economic variables such as income and commutation costs influence outcomes relative to such "non-economic" influences as cultural predilections, political structure, racial heterogeneity, and government policies. Unfortunately, problems of data availability and comparability have impeded such empirical analysis and we can rely on little more than the nearly universal impressions that metropolitan populations outside of the United States are more densely concentrated in central cities, that they rely more on public transportation and less on automobiles than Americans do, that they are more likely to rent than to own their residences, and that in many countries higher-income households live relatively close to the CBD with lower-income people living in the suburbs.

So postwar suburbanization was a nationwide phenomenon, which, at least in its rapidity, its magnitude, and the degree to which lower-income and racial minority populations became concentrated in central cities, may have been peculiar to the United States. By 1980, suburbanization was more pronounced in U.S. metropolitan areas with relatively high incomes, relatively low automotive commutation costs as reflected in the density of limited-access highways, higher crime rates, larger African-American populations in their central cities, and where central city land area was small relative to the metropolitan area as a whole. To what extent do the values these variables for New York explain the region's remarkably low degree of suburbanization?

## New York in the National Context

The empirical literature has identified six characteristics of metropolitan regions that are conducive to the process of suburbanization.

**Relatively large proportions of the regional population as a whole and of the region's higher-income households will live in suburban jurisdictions where the central city is geographically large relative to its metropolitan area.** New York City's land area is large, both absolutely and relative to its metropolitan region. The assertions in the following paragraphs, therefore, share the common presupposition that drivers of suburbanization have their effects on *central city geographic size held constant.*

**The larger the metropolitan area's population, the smaller the proportion of the region's population that lives within any given distance from the central city.** Although neither the MAM nor the Tiebout-type models necessarily predict this, it is, in fact, an empirical regularity. The New York metropolitan region is, of course, the nation's most populous (Anas, Arnott, & Small, 1998, p. 1438).

**Higher household incomes are associated with more suburbanization.** Robert A. Margo's study, cited above, did not directly compare degrees of suburbanization across metropolitan areas but focused on the location of individual households. Nevertheless, it seems reasonable to conclude on the basis of his findings that suburbanization is likely to be more rapid and extensive in regions where real family incomes are relatively high and/or growing relatively quickly. In this regard, "real" income refers to nominal money income adjusted to take into account both the U.S. inflation rate and interregional differences in the cost of living. Table 14.1 compares real median family incomes relative to the contemporaneous level in New York across 12 large northeastern and Midwestern metropolitan regions during the decades of most rapid suburbanization.

New York's ranking among these metropolitan regions in this regard deteriorated between 1959 and 1979 and then improved toward the end of the period. This time pattern will be examined in much greater detail in subsequent chapters. At this point, it will suffice to observe that during the 1960s, a period of particularly rapid suburbanization nationwide, median household income around New York was very close to the average across comparable metropolitan areas. If this information suggests anything, it might be that the process of suburbanization in New York might have slowed slightly relative what was going

**Table 14.1** Regional median family income relative to the New York metropolitan area (U.S. Census Bureau, 2018)

| Metropolitan region | 1959 | 1969 | 1979 | 1989 |
|---|---|---|---|---|
| New York | 100 | 100 | 100 | 100 |
| Baltimore | 92.2 | 97.6 | 102.7 | 99.2 |
| Boston | 95.3 | 98.7 | 100.0 | 100.8 |
| Chicago | 107.9 | 111.1 | 117.0 | 99.2 |
| Cincinnati | 99.3 | 98.6 | 111.1 | 92.3 |
| Cleveland | 106.0 | 110.7 | 109.5 | 90.8 |
| Detroit | 100.8 | 110.0 | 114.2 | 96.5 |
| Minneapolis | 105.8 | 113.5 | 121.1 | 105.0 |
| Philadelphia | 94.5 | 97.0 | 99.6 | 96.3 |
| Pittsburgh | 90.8 | 93.1 | 104.9 | 83.1 |
| St. Louis | 93.6 | 97.1 | 103.9 | 92.3 |
| Washington, DC | 108.5 | 117.0 | 129.2 | 124.5 |
| 11-region average | 99.5 | 104.0 | 110.3 | 98.2 |

on in other northeastern (U.S. Federal Highway Administration, 2018) metropolitan regions during the period around 1979.

**Regions that were well endowed with limited-access roadways tend to be more suburbanized**. Through the first half of the short twentieth century, before the Federal government became actively involved in the financing of highways, New York State was in the forefront of highway development. Until some point during the 1920s, automobile use was thought of primarily as a recreational activity. Thus, the nation's first limited-access highway to open for traffic, the Vanderbilt Motorway on Long Island, was a private undertaking intended initially to serve as a race track. The second such project to start construction, a public enterprise that ran through Westchester County's leafy suburbs parallel to the New York Central Railroad's Harlem Line, was designed for scenic "automobiling" and dubbed the Bronx River Parkway. Even after automobile ownership became more widespread during the 1920s, driving was still seen as a leisure time activity. Thus, Robert Moses, New York's mid-twentieth-century master builder of transportation infrastructure and everything else, cut his road-building teeth when, as Chairman of the Long Island State Parks Commission, he oversaw the construction of the access roads to Jones Beach on Long Island.

The New York region also pioneered the large-scale use of an important innovation in highway finance. The interstate compact that created the Port of New York Authority (now the Port Authority of New York and New Jersey) in 1920 authorized that agency to issue debt instruments secured by its own revenues. The ability to issue such revenue bonds and, thereby, to pledge contractually through bond indentures to charge high enough user fees to meet its obligations enabled the Port Authority and its imitators to withstand political pressure regarding rate setting. This financing mechanism also freed agencies charged with building and operating public facilities and authorized to charge user fees from statutory and constitutional limitations on the issuance of full-faith-and-credit general obligation bonds. One of the Port Authority's most avid early imitators was Robert Moses, who used the revenue bond mechanism during the Depression decade—the money it raised and the political independence of its granted issuers—to initiate, finance, and push through to completion construction of the Henry Hudson Memorial Bridge, the Bronx-Whitestone Bridge, the Triborough Bridge, and the Saw Mill and Hutchinson River Parkways. Finally, early in the first postwar decade, two new public benefit corporations, the New York Thruway Authority and the New Jersey Turnpike Authority, issued revenue bonds to build multi-lane toll highways spanning their respective states.

Thus, New York had an extensive and well-articulated regional bridge and highway system in place earlier in the postwar period than other large cities. Critics of suburbanization and its attendant ills such as the fiscal and social isolation of low-income and African-American households, sprawl, traffic congestion, etc., charge Robert Moses and other highway promoters with creating an excessively automobile-oriented transportation system. And, in light of Nathaniel Baum-Snow's finding regarding the impact on highways on urban spatial structure, one might, indeed, expect that, all else held equal, suburbanization would have been more rapid and more extensive in the New York region than elsewhere.

In fact, however, despite the region's early start on highway building, the Greater New York remained and remains one of the least automobile-dependent metropolitan areas in the United States. In 1999, for example, the average U.S. urbanized area with population greater than one million was endowed with 0.613 freeway-equivalent lane miles per 1,000 of the population. New York's figure was 0.401. By itself, this relative lack of freeway mileage would lead one to expect that, all else held equal, New York would have been less "suburbanized" than metropolitan areas where limited access highways were thicker on the ground (Wendell Cox Consultancy, 2019; Wikipedia, 2017).

Any assessment of the impact of this relative paucity of highways per capita on the region's rate and degree of suburbanization must, however, consider the fact that in 1945 the New York, northern New Jersey, and southwestern Connecticut metropolitan regions was also endowed with an extensive and heavily used network of subways and commuter rail lines. In fact, in 2017, the New York metropolitan area accounted for three-quarters of total U.S. heavy-rail public transportation ridership (American Public Transportation Association, 2018).

No doubt Robert Moses and other regional leaders could have set a better example for transportation planners nationwide by making better provision for public transit. He could, for example, have ordered bridge and highway designs that accommodated rail lines as well as automobiles. Nevertheless, New York was and is the least automobile- and most commuter rail-oriented major U.S. metropolitan area. And, given the heavy usage of commuter railroads, it is not clear, Professor Baum-Snow's findings notwithstanding, whether the nature of the region's transportation infrastructure would have led to more or less suburbanization, income segregation, racial isolation, etc., than in other metropolitan areas.

**Relatively high central city crime rates *may* have led to more and more rapid suburbanization.** Between 1960, when uniform data on the subject were first compiled by the Federal Bureau of Investigation, and 1991, when the statistic peaked, the U.S. violent crime rate per 100,000 of the population rose from 160.9 to 758.1, a 371% increase. We know that New York State also experienced a sharp rise in the incidence of crime, although the increase over the same period at 258% was somewhat lower, albeit from the higher 1960 base (325.4 per 100,000) one would expect in a highly urbanized state. Thus, the State of New York suffered a crime wave during the 1960s, 1970s, and 1980s, but the local trend was certainly no worse than what was happening nationwide. Unfortunately, we can't pin down precisely how New York City fared with respect to its crime rate, absolutely or relative to other cities, for the period of peak postwar suburbanization. The New York State figures may be taken as somewhat indicative given that between 1985, the first year for which uniform crime reporting (UCR) statistics are available for cities, and 1991, a bit more than 80% crimes reported in the State of New York took place in the City (U.S. Federal Bureau of Investigation, 2018).

Even for years after 1985, the UCR data must be used warily when making inter-city comparisons because crime reporting definitions, practices, and data quality controls vary from jurisdiction to jurisdiction. That said, unless New York City Police Department was doing a much worse job than authorities in other large northeastern and Midwestern cities in maintaining and reporting crime incidence statistics, which is unlikely, it does *not* seem that the City stood out as relatively crime-ridden or relatively safe (Fig. 14.4). A reasonable characterization might be that during the early 1980s New York was the safest of the high crime cities.

**A central city's population tended to decrease by greater percentages, the larger the proportion of African-Americans among its residents.**

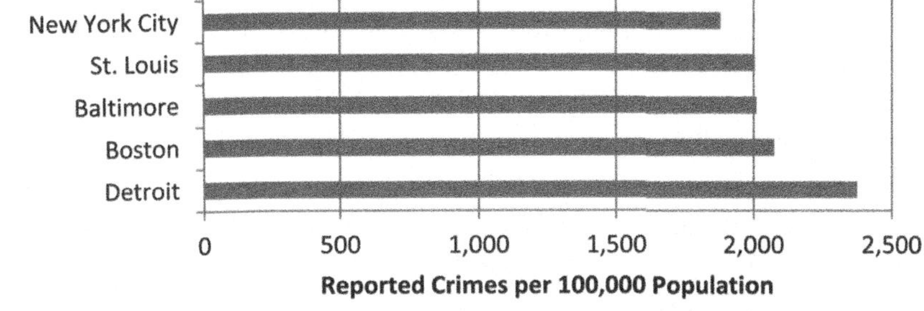


**Fig. 14.4** 1985 reported violent crimes per 100,000 of population in 10 northeastern and Midwestern cities (U.S. Federal Bureau of Investigation, 2018) (*Note* The FBI did not report statistics for Chicago during this period because of differences regarding the definition of some crimes)

As was the case for all northern and western cities, New York's population of native-born African-Americans continued to grow rapidly as the Great Migration accelerated in the 1940s and, especially, the 1960s. The proportion of this population group remained somewhat smaller, however, in New York than in most other northeastern and Midwestern cities. And, as during the interwar period but even more markedly, New York's population of color was augmented by arrivals from the Caribbean. In contrast to the earlier decades of the twentieth century, when a majority of this population came from the British West Indies, between the 1940s and the 1970s a large majority of Caribbean migrants to the U.S. mainland originated from Puerto Rico. And a large majority of the newly arrived Puerto Ricans settled initially in New York. Arrivals from that Island began to increase during World War II and accelerated rapidly thereafter. Especially during the early years of this accelerating inflow, most Puerto Rican migrants' initial destination was New York City. In 1980, toward the end of the peak period of postwar suburbanization, New York's communities of color made up a slightly larger percentage of the total population than the average of the comparison group of cities. But New York's minority population was proportionally much more Hispanic than in any other comparable city (Tables 14.2 and 14.3) (Whalen, 2005).

The econometric literature analyzing differences in suburbanization across metropolitan areas sheds little light on what overall impact the unique composition of New York's racial minority communities might have had on the region's relative degree of suburbanization. Was the New York metropolitan area less suburbanized in some way because it's relatively small African-American population induced relatively little white flight or did "Anglo flight" have a similar impact? As for most of the period New York was the only northeastern city with such a large Latino population, a straightforward statistical estimate of the combined impact of different communities of color would be impossible.

There is, however, evidence that, with respect to residential opportunities and outcomes, conditions for the City's Puerto Ricans and African-Americans were similar and that both differed from the situation of Anglo and non-Puerto Rican Latino New Yorkers.

New York's Puerto Rican population was particularly impoverished. In a study of minority housing choices in New York City, sociologist

**Table 14.2** African-American and Hispanic populations of 12 large northeastern and Midwestern cities, 1940 and 1980 (Gibson & Jung, 2005)

| City | 1940 | | | 1980 | | |
|---|---|---|---|---|---|---|
| | % Black | % Hispanic | Total | % Black | % Hispanic | Total |
| New York | 6.1 | 1.6 | *7.8* | 25.2 | 19.9 | 45.1 |
| Baltimore | 19.3 | 0.1 | *19.4* | 43.9 | 1.0 | 44.8 |
| Boston | 5.0 | 0.1 | *5.1* | 22.4 | 6.4 | 28.8 |
| Chicago | 8.2 | 0.5 | *8.7* | 39.8 | 14.0 | 53.9 |
| Cincinnati | 12.2 | | *12.2* | 33.8 | 0.8 | 34.6 |
| Cleveland | 9.6 | 0.1 | *9.7* | 43.8 | 3.1 | 46.9 |
| Detroit | 9.2 | 0.3 | *9.5* | 63.1 | 2.4 | 65.5 |
| Minneapolis | 0.9 | | *0.9* | 7.7 | 1.3 | 8.9 |
| Philadelphia | 13.0 | 0.1 | *13.1* | 37.8 | 3.8 | 41.6 |
| Pittsburgh | 9.3 | 0.1 | *9.4* | 24.0 | 0.8 | 24.8 |
| St. Louis | 13.3 | 0.3 | *13.6* | 45.6 | 1.2 | 46.8 |
| Washington, DC | 28.2 | 0.1 | *28.3* | 70.3 | 2.8 | 73.1 |
| Mean | 11.2 | 0.3 | 11.5 | 38.1 | 4.8 | 42.9 |
| 11-city Std. Dev. | 7.2 | 0.5 | 7.2 | 17.8 | 3.9 | 18.2 |

**Table 14.3** Puerto Rican population of the United States and the City of New York (Whalen, 2005, p. 3)

| Year | In U.S. | % in NYC | In NYC | % in NYC |
|---|---|---|---|---|
| 1910 | 1,513 | 37 | 554 | 37 |
| 1920 | 11,811 | 62 | 7,364 | 62 |
| 1930 | 52,774 | – | – | – |
| 1940 | 69,967 | 88 | 61,463 | 88 |
| 1950 | 226,110 | 83 | 187,420 | 83 |
| 1960 | 892,613 | 69 | 612,574 | 69 |
| 1970 | 1,391,463 | 59 | 817,712 | 59 |
| 1980 | 2,014,000 | 43 | 860,552 | 43 |
| 1990 | 2,728,000 | 33 | 896,763 | 33 |
| 2000 | 3,406,178 | 23 | 789,174 | 23 |

Emily Rosenbaum found that, among a sample of 5,056 New Yorkers who had moved into their residences at some point between 1978 and 1987, the median income of the 970 Puerto Rican households was $9,431 1986 dollars. Those of the whites, African-Americans, and non-Puerto Rican Hispanics were $23,034, $13,098, and $13,678, respectively. Prof. Rosenbaum's analysis identified a strong tendency for New Yorkers to move into residences in neighborhoods that were already home to a large proportion of members of their own racial or ethnic group. But she also found "spatial proximity between blacks and Puerto Ricans, but distance between these groups and other Hispanics" and whites (Rosenbaum, 1993).

It also seems to be the case that New York differed from comparable metropolitan areas in the degree to which its Hispanic population was segregated from the white Anglo community. Demographers Douglas Massey and Nancy Denton calculated five distinct measures of African-American and Hispanic residential segregation in 60 U.S. metropolitan areas. These statistics represented:

A. Evenness: The proportion of the minority group that would have to move to achieve a uniform distribution of that population across census tracts in the region.
B. Isolation: The likelihood that two members of a minority group live in the same census tract.
C. Clustering: The extent to which census tracts inhabited by minority group members adjoin one another.
D. Centralization: The extent to which a minority population lives closer to the central business district than the majority population.
E. Concentration: The land area per capita in areas inhabited by the minority group as compared to the majority population.

In all cases, the closer each measure is to zero, the *less* segregated the minority group is within the metropolitan area. Table 14.4 shows these five measures of metropolitan segregation for African-Americans and Hispanics for New York and the 11 large northeastern and Midwestern metropolitan areas. African-Americans were, for the most part, about as segregated in their residences in New York as in comparable metropolitan areas.[6] By contrast, New York's Hispanics were significantly more segregated by all measures in New York than in other metropolitan

[6]The only exception was with respect to centralization. Massey and Denton found that, even after controlling for metropolitan areas' geographic size, African-American neighborhoods were significantly less "centralized," that is more distant from the central business district, in New York than in other northeastern cities.

**Table 14.4** Measures of metropolitan residential segregation, 1980 (Massey & Denton, 1989, pp. 381, 385)

| City | African-American | | | | | Hispanic | | | | |
|---|---|---|---|---|---|---|---|---|---|---|
| | A | B | C | D | E | A | B | C | D | E |
| New York | 0.82 | 0.63 | 0.47 | 0.80 | 0.89 | 0.66 | 0.40 | 0.26 | 0.84 | 0.88 |
| Baltimore | 0.75 | 0.72 | 0.62 | 0.86 | 0.76 | 0.38 | 0.02 | 0.01 | 0.66 | 0.31 |
| Boston | 0.77 | 0.55 | 0.49 | 0.87 | 0.80 | 0.58 | 0.13 | 0.08 | 0.79 | 0.71 |
| Chicago | 0.88 | 0.83 | 0.79 | 0.87 | 0.89 | 0.64 | 0.38 | 0.32 | 0.81 | 0.75 |
| Cincinnati | 0.72 | 0.54 | 0.16 | 0.88 | 0.67 | 0.30 | 0.01 | 0.00 | 0.70 | 0.24 |
| Cleveland | 0.88 | 0.80 | 0.74 | 0.90 | 0.93 | 0.55 | 0.08 | 0.05 | 0.84 | 0.70 |
| Detroit | 0.87 | 0.77 | 0.85 | 0.92 | 0.84 | 0.45 | 0.07 | 0.06 | 0.75 | 0.37 |
| Minneapolis | 0.69 | 0.31 | 0.10 | 0.94 | 0.89 | 0.42 | 0.05 | 0.01 | 0.86 | 0.50 |
| Philadelphia | 0.79 | 0.70 | 0.67 | 0.86 | 0.76 | 0.63 | 0.22 | 0.19 | 0.78 | 0.55 |
| Pittsburgh | 0.73 | 0.54 | 0.27 | 0.81 | 0.82 | 0.42 | 0.01 | 0.00 | 0.64 | 0.21 |
| St. Louis | 0.81 | 0.73 | 0.26 | 0.93 | 0.89 | 0.34 | 0.02 | 0.00 | 0.75 | 0.47 |
| Washington, DC | 0.69 | 0.67 | 0.45 | 0.85 | 0.44 | 0.31 | 0.05 | 0.02 | 0.76 | 0.52 |
| 12-city average | 0.78 | 0.65 | 0.49 | 0.87 | 0.80 | 0.47 | 0.12 | 0.08 | 0.77 | 0.52 |
| Standard deviation | 0.07 | 0.15 | 0.25 | 0.05 | 0.13 | 0.13 | 0.14 | 0.11 | 0.07 | 0.21 |
| NYC off Average, standard deviations | 0.53 | −0.15 | −0.09 | −1.75 | 0.69 | 1.40 | 2.01 | 1.61 | 1.07 | 1.71 |

A = Evenness; B = Isolation; C = Clustering; D = Centralization; E = Concentration (See Text) areas. And while one could say that in most places Hispanics were consistently less segregated from the non-Hispanic white population than were African-Americans, the same cannot be said about New York.

Although there is no direct evidence of a nationwide "Anglo flight" phenomenon, the evidence suggests that those New Yorkers whose residential choices were relatively unconstrained, both whites and non-Puerto Rican Hispanics, behaved in a way that was consistent with an equal aversion to living in proximity to African-Americans and Puerto Ricans. This apparently somewhat unique dual aversion may not have had much impact on the pace and degree of suburbanization in the New York metropolitan area because at 45.1%, the proportion of African-Americans plus Hispanics in the region's population was very close to the average for comparable cities. One can assert with some degree of confidence, however, that any expectation that suburbanization around New York would have been particularly retarded because whites had fewer African-Americans to flee would be mistaken.

In sum, none of the measurable characteristics of metropolitan areas that have been determined to drive differences in the pace and degree of suburbanization would have led one to expect that New York's trajectory in this regard would have been very different from what occurred elsewhere. Nevertheless, as we have seen, New York was substantially less suburbanized by a range of measures than other large northeastern and Midwestern metropolitan areas. Why?

## The Uniqueness of New York's Postwar Housing Market

Suburbanization is, essentially, a process affecting metropolitan housing markets, and New York's housing market differed from that of *all* comparable localities in United States in four ways. For this reason, it is impossible to assess the impact of these differences on the regions' pace of suburbanization using statistical techniques. Three of these differences reflect direct state and local government interventions in the housing market. The governments of the State and City of New York adopted policies that affected the supply and price of housing much more directly and more powerfully than was the case anywhere else in the United States.

Three aspects of New York housing policy in particular may have affected residents' collective inclination to locate in the central city or the suburbs. First, apartment rentals in New York City have been subject to outright government control since World War II. Second, the proportion of New York's housing stock that was built, owned, and operated by government agencies or was publically subsidized in other ways was much greater than any other large city's. Third, State and City policies subsidized the development of landlord- or tenant-owned apartment buildings that provided below-market, central city housing for middle-income households. Governments' role in the fourth unique characteristic of New York's postwar housing market, the prevalence of owner-occupied units in multifamily buildings—condominiums and, especially, cooperatives—was indirect.

## Rent Control and Rent Stabilization

Federal wartime rent controls were lifted across the United States in stages between 1947 and 1953. New York City, unlike almost every other jurisdiction in the United States but like many war-ravaged European countries, continued regulating rents under State laws and local ordinances into the twenty-first century. Initially, New York's controls involved, with very few exceptions, a freeze on rents for apartments in buildings that had been occupied in 1947. Rapidly rising inflation starting in the late 1960s wreaked financial havoc for the landlords of controlled apartments and with tenants living on fixed incomes in newer buildings. The response, in both Europe and New York, was not to deregulate rents entirely but to adopt new, more flexible systems of rent regulation. New York's new laws, enacted in 1969 and 1971 and modified periodically thereafter, (a) brought post-1947 buildings under a new regulatory system termed "rent stabilization," (b) allowed formula-based rent increases in the remaining controlled pre-1947 buildings, (c) initially allowed for full decontrol upon the voluntary departure of a tenant from a rent-controlled apartment, and (d) established new governmental entities to administer the more complex regulations and to adjudicate disputes regarding their application. Subsequent modifications to the law

(e) limited decontrol on vacancy and (f) allowed for full deregulation of very high-rent apartments and for units occupied by very high-income tenants.

The impact of regulation is so extensive that, even without considering the large supply of publically owned and government-subsidized apartment projects, New York City's rental housing sector could not and cannot be deemed a free market. In 1981, 62.7% of the City's rental units fell under either rent control or rent stabilization. That figure has been decreasing gradually; by 2011, the controlled sector had decreased to a still-large 47.2% of rental housing. Such percentages of privately owned non-market-rate rentals are not that different from those of many European countries. The broad coverage and 70 + year duration of New York City's rent controls and regulations are, however, unique in the United States (The Furman Center for Real Estate and Urban Policy, 2012).

Because economists tend to be fascinated by the impact of price controls and because government agencies collect a great deal of data on housing, the City's system of rent regulation has been the subject of a large volume of theoretical and empirical analysis. Much of this research has aimed to determine the effects of regulation on the efficiency and equity of New York's rental housing market. Analysis of efficiency aims to answer questions like: Is the occupant of any given rent-regulated apartment the type of household who would be willing, if they could afford it, to pay the highest uncontrolled rent for that residence? Thus, one example of inefficiency is the proverbial elderly widow living alone in a rent-controlled six-room apartment and unwilling to move because a smaller, more easily maintained residence would be more expensive. Surely a family with two or three children would be willing to pay more for that space. Another source of inefficiency is the chance that landlords under rent control will, to the extent that regulators let them get away with it, spend less on routine maintenance than they would have otherwise because they cannot recapture the cost. Tenants might be willing to pay a bit more in exchange for a more frequent new coat of paint than regulators require, but there's no easy way for such an agreement to be effectuated.

Analysts distinguish between two types of equity with respect to government policies. The effects of a policy are horizontally equitable if equally deserving households capture roughly equal benefits. A regulation enhances vertical equity if the greatest (absolute or proportional) benefits of the policy accrue to households that were the worst-off *ex ante*.

Most studies conclude that outright rent control fails numerous equity and efficiency tests. Richard Arnott summarized the general conclusions of this literature as follows: "There is widespread agreement that New York City's rent controls have caused tenant mobility in the controlled sector to fall, have driven a wedge between rents in the controlled and uncontrolled sectors, and have had capricious redistributional effects apart from favoring long-term residents at the expense of in-migrants. There is no consensus, however, on the effects of New York City's controls on maintenance" (Arnott, 1995, p. 111).

The allocation of the benefits and costs of rent control across households and household types—the "redistributional effects"—may have been "capricious" with respect to the criteria of vertical and horizontal equity, but they may also have had an impact on the size, demographics, and income of the City's residents over time. Specifically, the institution of rent control may have slowed the rate at which certain central city residents moved to the suburbs. One of the most consistent findings of studies of rent control, especially after the institution of full or partial decontrol upon vacancy, is that the system favored long-term residents of individual apartments. The longer the resident household's tenure in a unit, the greater the benefit of control to the tenant. And we know that this incentive structure affected who lived in controlled apartments. Economists Joseph Gyourko and Peter Linneman found that in 1968 in a sample of 14,668 New York City households the average length of tenancy in their current residence was 8.7 years. The average for the 5,144 sample households living in rent-controlled units was 10.4 years, which was close to the 10.9-year tenure for the 5,095 owner-occupiers. For the 4,429 residents in uncontrolled (post-1947 vintage) rental units, the average was 4.1 years (Gyourko & Linneman, 1989, p. 59).

Gyourko and Linneman also devised a method for estimating the benefit of each resident household in a controlled unit derived from the difference between the controlled and estimated market-rate rents. They found that the magnitude of the benefit tended to be higher for residents of Manhattan than for those living in the outer boroughs. The estimated benefit of rent control also tended to rise with the tenant's age and with the size of the household. Perhaps, in part, because, during the peak years of migration from the U.S. South and the Caribbean, the longer the renter's tenure in an apartment, the less likely it was that the household was Black or Puerto Rican, the benefits of rent control tended to be higher and for whites than for racial minorities. Finally, although occupants of regulated apartments had significantly lower incomes on average than market-rate renters or owner-occupants, among residents of controlled units there was no statistically significant relationship between household income and the realized benefit of a below-market rent (Gyourko & Linneman, 1989).

It seems reasonable to conclude that rent regulation created an incentive for New Yorkers to remain in their City apartments longer than they might have otherwise. This would have diminished residential mobility within the metropolitan area, including movement from the central city to the suburbs. Further, because of the way in which the benefits of rent control were distributed across racial and ethnic groups, at any given time through the postwar period, New York City's population would have been whiter and more Anglo than might otherwise have been the case. Finally, although the beneficiaries of rent control tended to have lower income than the average City resident, because they tended to be older, longer-term residents, and were more likely to be white, rent control may have had the effect of keeping more people in general and more upper-working-class and lower-middle-class households, in particular, in New York than was the case in comparable metropolitan regions.

## Social Housing

Government policies aimed at making residences of acceptable quality affordable for impoverished and working-class households did not begin to affect the New York housing market in any quantitatively substantial way until after World War II. The policy instruments deployed to serve this purpose, however, had a long pre-war history. As urban population growth accelerated in the mid-nineteenth century, concerned observers on both sides of the North Atlantic began expressing dissatisfaction with prevailing housing market conditions as they affected poor people in large cities. Incomes of these households were insufficient to purchase life's absolute necessities *and* to pay the rent on residences of what middle-class writers deemed to be the minimal acceptable quality for the maintenance of public health and morals.

As early as the mid-nineteenth century, this climate of opinion induced philanthropic individuals and institutions in both Northern Europe and the United States to explore ways of providing "social housing," dwellings deemed to be of adequate quality let at below-market rentals. And as befitted the first great age of globalization ideas about how to deal with the problem flowed across the ocean, mediated by a combination of Americans' graduate studies abroad, organized "sociological grand tours" of Europe for leaders of what are now called non-governmental organizations (NGOs), and a series of international conferences on workers' housing. Nineteenth-century European initiatives aimed at providing adequate affordable housing for workers and the poor included (i) the enactment of minimal quality standards for newly constructed multifamily dwellings, (ii) construction of model tenements and suburban housing estates by charitable organizations, (iii) formation of "reduced dividend" private housing companies that attracted "socially conscious" investments, (iv) encouragement of "cooperative" resident-owned enterprises, many organized by trade unions, (v) subsidization of private developers and landlords of "affordable" housing through tax abatements or direct government financing, and (vi) outright construction and management of "public" housing by governments. Some of these initiatives added to the overall supply of urban housing; others aimed to clear and replace slums. Collectively, these initiatives did produce a noticeable quantity of affordable housing of acceptable quality in European cities in the years before World War I. In England, for example, local government activity accounted for almost five percent of all residences built between 1890 and 1914. In Frankfurt, site of one of the most extensive programs, on the eve of

World War I, 7.2% of the total housing stock had been constructed by government-supported limited-dividend associations (Rodgers, 1998, pp. 62–64, 192). After the armistice social housing development activity accelerated sharply as the continent recovered from World War I, unsubsidized private market activity accounted for only about half of the housing units built in Europe between 1919 and 1933 (Bloom, 2008, p. 19).

U.S. NGO leaders were well aware of developments in Europe and adopted some of them, and a number of philanthropical below-market rental apartment buildings were constructed in American cities. American housing reformers, however, devoted their greatest efforts to inducing governments to legislate minimum quality standards for tenement dwellings and then to demand enforcement of those regulations once they had been adopted. Increasingly stringent and increasingly actively enforced tenement laws adopted periodically in New York State beginning in 1867 imposed maximum resident density and lot coverage limitations on newly constructed multifamily dwellings, outlawed back-building and basement apartments, and eventually required running water and indoor toilets. Thus, even in New York, where the leading philanthropists were apparently most enthusiastic about the direct provision of social housing, the number of "model tenement" units never reached more than a small fraction of what was available in many European cities. In 1916, New York City's Tenement House Department reported that some 18,000 New Yorkers were living in "model tenements." This figure probably represents an underestimate of the availability of "philanthropic housing" in the City at the time, but adding any undercount would be unlikely to bring the total anywhere near the 123,000 Londoners living in housing developed by limited-dividend companies in 1905 (Plunz, 1990, p. 106; Rodgers, 1998, p. 188). At the time, New York City's population was about 70% of London's.

Despite the trivial impact of philanthropic activity on New York's aggregate housing supply and despite the fact that a robust pace of new housing construction during the mostly prosperous early decades of the twentieth century, which allowed many slum dwellers to upgrade their accommodations, agitation for urban housing reform continued through the 1920s. Over the course of that decade New York State enacted a series of laws directly affecting the City's housing market, initially aimed at alleviating a postwar housing shortage and including a short-lived "emergency" rent control law, property tax abatement for new construction, and an authorization for State-regulated life insurance companies to invest in housing projects. In 1926, however, after the postwar "emergency" had passed, the legislature and Gov. Al Smith aimed specifically to encourage the development of social housing by authorizing local governments to exercise eminent domain powers to acquire land for construction of affordable housing by limited-dividend corporations. The law also designated the debt obligations of these corporations as exempt from taxation. And local governments were authorized to grant property tax exemption to the buildings constructed under the law. The encouragement provided by this legislation did apparently stimulate a reasonable volume of activity, especially with respect to the development of tenant-owned cooperative apartment complexes, many organized by a range of center-left and left-wing, predominantly Jewish labor organizations including the Amalgamated Clothing Workers, the Workmen's Circle, and the Jewish National Workers Alliance. These cooperative corporations, like many other enterprises initiated during the boom years of the late 1920s, faced serious financial problems as the Great Depression took hold (Columbia Law Review, 1926; Plunz, 1990, pp. 153–161).

## Public Housing in New York: Intergovernmental and Multi-Governmental

A revival of housing construction activity, either to add net new supply or to replace slums, was widely viewed as one of the best ways to stimulate economic activity during the 1930s. The Federal government's involvement in this sector of the economy expanded and became much more direct as the Depression decade progressed. Initially, the Reconstruction Finance Corporation (RFC), the Hoover administration's principle Depression-fighting instrument, channeled low-interest loans through state and local agencies to limited-dividend housing companies. Early New Deal legislation transferred the RFC loan program to the new Public Works Administration (PWA) and expanded the housing construction mandate to include direct payments to local authorities for up to 30% of development project costs. Then, in 1934, the PWA Housing Division began initiating and managing housing construction entirely on its own. This early program never amounted to much; the PWA only managed to produce about 25,000 units nationwide in the four and half years that the agency served as the principal Federal conduit for urban housing investment (The Eleanor Roosevelt Papers Project, 2018). A potentially much larger program was launched in 1937 when Congress passed the Wagner–Steagall Act. The legislation, which was conceived of as an intergovernmental enterprise, authorized the newly created United States Housing Authority (USHA) to issue bonds to finance its activities, to enter into contracts with local government agencies to plan and construct the projects, and to provide ongoing operations and maintenance (O&M) support after the buildings were occupied. The USHA didn't get up and running until the Depression was almost over, so little additional public housing was built before World War II halted most non-defense-related construction. But the ideological battle over whether governments were responsible for assuring adequate urban housing supply had been won. Early in the postwar period, therefore, the Wagner–Steagall legislation was modified and the USHA's activities were expanded, most dramatically by the American Housing Act of 1949. By 1967, when the program ended, some 633,000 units of federally financed public housing were in operation (McDonald, 2011, p. 4).

Although the U.S. Senate's principal Depression-era advocate for social housing was Robert Wagner (D-NY) and even though the State acted quickly to establish the proactive New York City Housing Authority (NYCHA), the local government agency designated to work with the USHA, New York did not get any more than its proportionate share of total federally financed public housing. In 1967, in the 46 largest cities participating in the USHA program, the number of public housing units per 1000 of the population ranged from 0.8 in Rochester, NY, to

26.9 in Newark, NJ. The average figure was 8.96 and New York City had 8.3 (McDonald, 2011, p. 5).

The fact that the City received no more than its proportionate per capita share of federally funded public housing, however, belies the importance of social housing in New York region's economy.

For one thing, much more than anywhere else, State and local government-funded public housing programs augmented what was supplied by the Federal government. New York's left-leaning political leaders, most notably Governor Herbert Lehman and Mayor Fiorello LaGuardia, were dissatisfied with the PWA's slow building pace and with the limitations on New York's share of Wagner–Steagall money. Their frustration was expressed in a provision of a revised constitution that authorized the State of New York to issue up to $300 million in bonds to finance the construction and ongoing support of social housing. The new constitution, which was approved by the State's electorate in 1938 by a wide margin, also authorized the City of New York to initiate the only local government public housing program in the country. As with the Federal legislation, the State and local programs authorized ongoing financial support for O&M. Subsequent City-financed "unsubsidized" public housing programs provided support only for the construction of new projects, which were expected to charge rents that were high enough to cover O&M costs.

Together New York's State and City public housing construction programs produced a combined 88,555 rental units, 50% more than the number of Federal public housing apartments in the City. Thus, it was the combination of Federal, State, and City programs that left New York with substantially more public housing than other large U.S. cities. In 2008, public projects accounted for 5.3% of New York City's housing stock; the figures for the rest of the nation's five largest cities, Los Angeles, Chicago, Houston, and Philadelphia, were 0.5, 1.8, 0.4, and 2.2%, respectively. Timing differences across the programs were also important. As Table 14.5 indicates, the State and City programs were very active and the Federal program quiescent during the first postwar years, a period that set the stage for subsequent patterns of

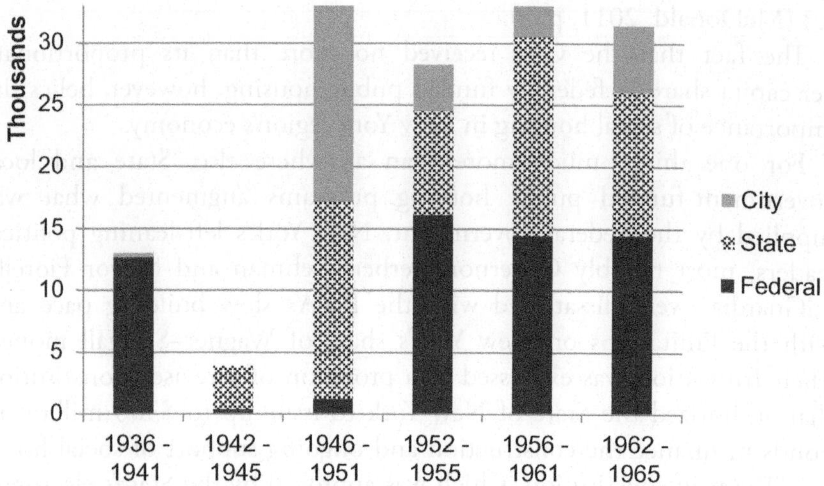


**Fig. 14.5** Public housing units in New York City by construction sponsor and year of initial occupancy (Bloom, 2008, pp. 270–276)

suburbanization (Bloom, 2008, pp. 270–276; The Furman Center for Real Estate and Urban Policy, 2011).

By itself the provision of relatively large quantities of public housing would not necessarily have slowed the pace of suburbanization. If the newly constructed projects did no more than replace slum housing that was being cleared and if the public projects became subject to the same social and economic challenges that were plaguing other poor neighborhoods, then the incentives for middle-class families to leave the city would be largely unaffected. Indeed, the impact of public housing on metropolitan Chicago has been roughly characterized in just that way. And the same thing could have happened in New York because the local urban renewa l/slum-clearance activity did remove large numbers of older affordable housing from the market and because through the 1970s and 1980s conditions in many of the City's largest high-rise projects did deteriorate badly.

Through the 1950s and 1960s, however, many of New York's social housing offerings continued to attract residents for whom moving to the suburbs was a viable alternative. Why?

## Public Housing for Whom?

A fundamental disagreement regarding the role of government-owned apartment buildings divided social housing advocates during the Depression and thereafter. One side viewed public projects as the functional equivalent of almshouses, residences of last resort for the most impoverished segment of the population. Advocates of this view were wary of government enterprises that competed directly with the private sector. Whether public housing made policy sense in this context, therefore, depended on whether it was substantially cheaper for the government to provide households receiving welfare with rental units directly or to grant them enough money to pay private landlords. In an era when slum clearance was intentionally reducing the supply of the cheapest housing, the private market would have been hard pressed to meet the needs of this population.

There were several arguments in favor of the alternative view that public housing should also serve the working poor and lower-middle-income households. First, it was likely that the free market would be unable to provide enough affordable housing quickly enough to meet the needs of, not just the poorest of the poor but also of households slightly higher up the income distribution. During the early postwar years, when population was growing rapidly while slums were being cleared and following a 15-year period during which residential construction virtually ceased, housing of all qualities was in very short supply. Also, the residents of the "slums" that were being demolished were not all impoverished; they included significant numbers of working poor and middle-income households. To be sure, a great deal of residential construction activity was taking place, but, as had been the case during earlier periods of rapid urban population growth, private, unsubsidized developers were finding that building suburban homes for higher-income households was more profitable than adding more tenements. A second argument posited that high residential concentrations of the most disadvantage populations were associated with social problems. An urban neighborhood or public housing project that was home to a mix of welfare families, the working poor, and the lower-middle-class was more likely to develop as a socially healthy environment. Finally, advocates of public housing for middle-income households argued that the rents that these tenants could afford to pay could help support the ongoing maintenance of the projects that also served households living on the margin, thereby reducing the level of ongoing taxpayer support. No doubt, too, middle-income working families would likely be more effective political advocates for ongoing support of public housing than the welfare population, especially in New York during the early postwar decades, when the City's manufacturing workforce was still large, well organized, and politically conscious.

Federal public housing policy and its implementation in most large cities were largely driven by advocates of the view that public housing was a form of welfare. The second, more expansive view of the proper role of public housing won the day in most of Europe and in New York. The differences in policy orientation were reflected in the percentages of welfare recipients and racial minorities among the residents of public housing in different cities. The Chicago Housing Authority (CHA) followed the Federal policy lead and specifically aimed to serve impoverished residents, so that in 1940 36% of public housing tenants in that City had been or were then on relief. In projects managed by the NYCHA, which established a system for evaluating potential tenants that intentionally favored the working poor and lower-middle class, the percentage of tenants on welfare never rose above 15% through the mid-1960s. Even after the NYCHA succumbed to USHA pressure to accept more very low-income tenants in Federal projects and to evict families whose rising incomes had made them ineligible, State and, especially, City projects continued to recruit relatively large proportions of tenants who could afford market-rate housing. As the condition of the New York economy and living conditions in many of the City's neighborhoods deteriorated through the late 1960s and 1970s, the welfare share of the NYCHA's residents rose sharply. But even at its peak of 34% in 1973, the NYCHA's figure was still well below the CHA's 49% at that time. And, although the racial and ethnic composition of individual projects' tenantry tended to mirror that of the surrounding neighborhood, the aggregate population of New York's public housing was more diverse than that of many other large cities. Thus, in 1954, for example, about 75% of Chicago's public housing residents were non-white while 41% of NYCHA project residents were Black or Puerto Rican (Bloom, 2008, pp. 170, 211).

The NYCHA's approach to project management and maintenance may also have helped attract and retain more tenants who might have moved to the suburbs. No detailed studies comparing management policies and their effects across urban housing authorities have been published. But Nicholas Dagen Bloom presents a great deal of evidence that New York's projects were "public housing that worked." The NYCHA explicitly aimed to assure that the social environment of their projects was reasonably benign: that individual apartments and public spaces were well maintained, that crime was kept under control, and that community institutions developed and thrived. No doubt, some aspects of New York's approach to public housing worked against these objectives. In particular, the design of many high-rise projects, isolated from commercial blocks, militated against the kind of active street life that had played an important social role in New York's working-class neighborhoods for a hundred years. But the NYCHA did provide protection; it was the only U.S. housing authority to establish its own police force that patrolled stairwells and corridors as well as project grounds. During the pre-war years, specially trained rent collectors, who kept the NYCHA delinquency rate at about half the national average, were also qualified to provide homemaking advice and rudimentary social services. Project design included community centers housing club rooms, recreational facilities, and childcare centers. Maintenance was intensive; by the 1970s, when high-rise buildings were pervasive in the system, the NYCHA employed "350 mechanics solely devoted to the maintenance of its approximately 3000 elevators" (Bloom, 2008, pp. 92–106, 220).

## Subsidized Middle-Class Multifamily Housing

The legislation that created in the NYCHA was not the only New York State policy that provided social housing to middle-class households, most of whom earned incomes that were too high to qualify for public housing. Another facet of New York State's social housing policy, however, was explicitly aimed at this population segment. Under the 1955 Limited Profit Housing Companies Law (the Mitchell-Lama Law), New York State continued and augmented the policy adopted in 1926 of indirectly subsidizing the development of below-market rental units for middle-income households by providing incentives to developers. The Mitchell-Lama program authorized the use of State and City revenue bond proceeds to provide low-interest mortgage loans for construction and granted long-term property tax exemption. Although private developers were eligible to sponsor Mitchell-Lama projects, the bulk of the activity under this law was organized as cooperatives, mostly sponsored by unions or other not-for-profit institutions. Residents ("cooperators") paid a "monthly carrying charge" in lieu of rent to cover debt service and building O&M. A new tenant's income could not exceed six or seven times the monthly carrying charge. Unlike the policy enforced in Federal public housing projects, however, a household would not be required to leave their apartment if their income subsequently rose above that multiple. Instead, a surcharge of up to 50% was added to the monthly payment for higher-income families[7] (DeSalvo, 1975, p. 792; Sazama, 1996, p. 3).

As of 1995, there were about 376,000 residential units in affordable coop buildings in cities nationwide; about 120,000 of them were in New York City (Sazama, 1996). If we assume that each affordable coop was home to the city average of 2.5 individuals, then the resident population of this type of housing might have totaled about 300,000 or about four percent of the City's population at the time and, presumably, a somewhat larger proportion of New York's middle-income households. This, however, may understate the impact of affordable cooperatives on the City's income distribution because the presence of middle-class housing in a neighborhood apparently had positive

[7]When referring to cooperatives in New York City, it is important to distinguish between "affordable cooperatives," mostly developed under the Mitchell-Lama program, and "market-rate cooperatives." The latter receive no development or tax abatement subsidies, are much more expensive to buy into, and serve an upper-middle- and higher-income group of residents. The role of market rate coops in the New York City housing market will be discussed in a separate section below.

spillover effects on its surroundings. Joseph DeSalvo found that the development of a new Mitchell-Lama project tended to accelerate the increase in property values in the surrounding neighborhood. He also found that this positive effect was confined to neighborhoods that were already home to a middle-income population. The "spillover" effect was much smaller or entirely absent in very low- and very high-income neighborhoods, but this finding does suggest that the presence of Mitchell-Lama and middle-income public housing projects may have helped attract middle-class households to the City, even those who wound up living in market-rate apartments (De Salvo, 1974).

Even households higher up the incomes scale than Mitchell-Lama residents were able to benefit from some aspects of government policy. Under Title I of the U.S. Housing Act of 1949, the Federal government was authorized to pay a substantial share of the cost incurred by cities that acquired slum property through condemnation and then resold the area to private-sector developers. Qualifying redevelopment plans could include either social housing, market-rate residences, both or neither. The Chairman of Mayor's Slum Clearance Committee, which oversaw New York's Title I program, was Robert Moses, who, true to form, had begun planning projects even before the 1949 legislation was enacted. As was the case with public housing, however, despite the City's early start, New York does not appear to have received more than its proportionate share of Title I money. Of the $10 billion in urban renewal grants issued by the Federal government between 1950 and 1974, cities in New York State received $1.2 billion, or about 12%. In 1960, New York State accounted for 11.4% of the nation's urban population. Pennsylvania, home to 6.4% of the U.S. urban population and recipient of 11.6% of urban renewal grants, did better than New York. Illinois, by contrast, was much less active in this regard. That State accounted for 6.5% of the urban population but was granted only 2.5% of the grants (U.S. Department of Housing and Urban Development, 1974, p. 18).

Although New York did not receive more than its proportional share of Federal urban renewal funding, it may have been the case that Moses's strategy for the use of this money differed from what other cities were doing. Historian Hilary Ballon concluded that "other cities ... used Title I to lure banks and department stores and office buildings back into ailing downtowns. New York under Moses avoided commercial land uses" (Ballon, 2007, pp. 106, 242). Ballon argues that retention of the City's middle-class population was a clear objective of Moses's slum-clearance/urban renewa l strategy, and, in fact, most of the housing that was constructed under the Title I program was sold or rented at market rates. Indeed, many of the critics of slum clearance as an urban renewal strategy in New York, as opposed to, for example, subsidized renovation of existing dwellings, cited the demolition of poor and working people's homes and their replacement with "luxury" apartments.

## New York's Market-Rate Coops

Unsubsidized or "market-rate" cooperative apartment buildings provided a way for middle- and upper-middle-income New Yorkers to live in economically and racially homogeneous surroundings, one of the motives for suburbanization, within the City. Under this form of residential tenure, residents own shares of a not-for-profit business, usually organized as a corporation or a limited liability company, which either financed the building's construction or purchased it from a previous owner with the proceeds of mortgage loan. Residents lease their individual apartments from that company. Residents may transfer their shares in the cooperative company that owns the building together with the right to lease their particular dwellings to third parties; in effect, they can "sell" their apartments. Since all residents share the coop's collective liabilities, however, default by one shareholder could jeopardize the neighbors' financial situation. Therefore, transfers to new purchasers are subject to approval of the transaction by the coop's board of directors.

Cooperative tenure is one of two ways residents may combine the benefits of apartment living and homeownership. The alternative is the condominium structure, under which each resident household owns its particular apartment. Condominium residents incur no collective liabilities except for the cost of building maintenance, and there are fewer restrictions on transfer than in a co-op. As noted previously, at 31.8%, the proportion of New York City households living in multifamily buildings as owner-occupants was much higher than the 11.3% average across 12 large northeastern and Midwestern cities.

The local popularity of multifamily owner-occupancy is one of the effects of rent regulation. Conversion of multifamily properties subject to rent control or rent stabilization into condominiums or coops for sale to residents or to speculators offered landlords a way to realize something close to what their buildings would be worth in an unregulated market. But, although condominiums are common both in New York and nationwide, in 1980 about 95% of the nation's coops were located in the City (Kane, 1999, pp. 121–124; Maldonado & Rose, 1995).

The purchase, financing, and sale of a condominium unit are much more straightforward than similar transactions with respect to coop ownership shares and apartment leases. Therefore, it is hard to escape the conclusion that the preference for conversion to coops rather than condominiums reflects, at least in part, the ability to exercise greater control over who could move into the building. Although they are required to comply with Federal, State, and City antidiscrimination statutes, unless they are challenged in court, coop boards are not required to provide their reasons for rejecting applicants. When rejected applicants have sued, courts have not generally ruled in favor of plaintiffs absent explicit evidence of racial prejudice on the part of board members. The effects of subjective screening based on economic status and the difficulty of proving racial discrimination are pretty clear. Potential cooperators who anticipate rejection do not apply to purchase coops and real estate agents steer minority group members, even those who could meet objective income requirements, away from coops. Thus, although rejection rates are low, close to 80% of New York's coop, residents were white in 1993, at a time when more than half of the City's population was African-American or Hispanic (Maldonado & Rose, 1995, p. 1249; The Furman Center for Real Estate and Urban Policy, 2011).

## A North American Social Democracy

By the end of the short twentieth century, metropolitan New York was demonstrably less suburbanized than comparable U.S. regions. Much larger proportions of the metropolitan population lived in the central city in multifamily rental housing and commuted to work using public transportation that was the case elsewhere in the United States. And the difference between the incomes of central city and suburban residents was much less pronounced in New York.

These differences reflected unique characteristics of New York City's housing market, most of which were the result of State and City policies that were not implemented to the same degree or not adopted at all elsewhere in the United States. These included rent control, construction and management of "social" housing for residents with a broad range of incomes, and subsidization of below-market housing for middle-income households.

The differences between New York and other U.S. metropolitan regions with respect to their degrees of suburbanization and the role of government in their housing markets are the same as what distinguished the metropolitan economic geographies of the United States and Northwestern Europe. Population density gradients were generally steeper in Europe than in America; European urbanites were more likely to live in multifamily rental units and to use public transit than Americans; and middle- and upper-income households were more likely to live close to the city center in Europe than in the United States. With respect to housing market policy, rent control was widespread across Europe and the provision of social housing for both low- and middle-income households was seen as very much a core governmental responsibility.

New York, in short, was the most European of American cities with respect to the policies that influenced the region's economic geography during the postwar years. This similarity did not emerge by happenstance. While World War I and the Depression may have constricted the movement of goods and capital from Europe to America, ideas continued to flow freely across the Atlantic. The ideas, like the goods and the money, tended to arrive soonest and have their greatest impact in New York.

This transatlantic influence is reflected in the biographies of the three individuals who arguably had the greatest impact on New York City's political culture and physical structure during the short twentieth century: Robert Moses, Robert Wagner, Sr., and Fiorello LaGuardia. Moses attended Oxford University between 1909 and 1911 and, upon his return, submitted an admiring study of the British civil service system to the Columbia University political science department as his

PhD thesis (Caro, 1975, pp. 48–55). Robert Wagner, Sr., the architect of and political force behind most Federal housing legislation who also influenced State and local policy in New York, was born in Germany, maintained ties with his extended family in Europe, and undertook a fact-finding tour of the continent's public housing projects in 1936 (Rodgers, 1998, p. 446). And New York City's polyglot Mayor lived part of his childhood in Europe and worked for a time as a translator in U.S. consulates around the Austro-Hungarian Empire (Kessner, 1989, pp. 18–21).

The general outlook and specific ideas these leaders and others brought with them were those espoused by Europe's social democratic political parties. In his history of postwar Europe, Tony Judt characterized this worldview as the belief that an "interventionary state" could and should be expected to provide its citizenry with social services including "education, housing, and medical care, as well as urban recreation areas, subsidized public transport, publically funded art and culture and other indirect benefits…" (Judt, 2005, p. 73). The social democrats' skepticism regarding market solutions and faith in state intervention found a particularly receptive audience in early postwar New York among City's blue-collar workforce, about two-thirds of whom were either foreign-born themselves or the children of immigrants. In 1947, New York's garment workers, longshoremen, construction tradespeople, retail employees, dental technicians, and so on belonged to 1,107 union locals, many of which wielded considerable power over the operation of their industries and the City's politics. The unions' political influence was reflected in the ballot box. In the 1945 City Council elections, a candidate of the American Labor Party (ALP), Transit Workers Union leader Michael Quill, received the highest citywide vote total, and Communist Party candidates garnered the second and fourth largest vote counts. And under the City's proportional representation electoral system of the time, members of social democratic parties, the ALP and the Liberal Party, another labor movement creation, won five of the total 23 City Council seats (Freeman, 2000, pp. 40, 56–57).

High vote counts for explicitly social democratic political parties is emblematic, but during the early postwar years leaders of all of the City's political parties enthusiastically supported government intervention in the City's economy. LaGuardia and Moses were, after all, Republicans. Through the postwar period, the City government provided or arranged to have provided the full checklist of social services enumerated by Tony Judt: education, housing, health care, urban recreation, public transit, and culture. The State and City had been providing free public elementary, secondary, *and* higher education since the mid-nineteenth century. Social housing was discussed previously. Public provision of indigent hospital care in New York City traced its ancestry to 1736. When efforts by Wagner and others to establish a universal, national health insurance program failed in Congress in 1944, LaGuardia used City funds to help jump-start a local, voluntary prepaid medical insurance system, the Health Insurance Plan (HIP) (Freeman, 2000, p. 127). Robert Moses began and ended his career creating the New York region's extensive parks and recreation facilities. When New York's privately owned subway companies ran into severe financial difficulties during the Great Depression, LaGuardia oversaw the public takeover of the newly unified system, preserving the politically sacrosanct five-cent fare, and, in fact, in 1946, two years before it doubled, the real cost of a New York subway ride fell to 52 (2013) cents, its lowest level ever (Hood, 1993, pp. 231–239; Mashable, 2018). LaGuardia also engineered the conversion of the huge Shriners Temple on West 55th Street, which had come into the City's possession, into the nonprofit City Center for Music and Drama to serve as a venue for high-quality, low-cost symphony, theater, opera, and ballet performances (Freeman, 2000, p. 67). In the same vein, one of the largest and most controversial Title I projects overseen by Robert Moses centered on the development of the Lincoln Center for the Performing Arts. Joshua Freeman was not exaggerating when he characterized early postwar New York City as a European-style "social democratic polity." And it seems reasonable to conclude that State and local governmental intervention in the City's housing market, more than anything else, led to a spatial arrangement of metropolitan residences that was substantially less suburbanized than that of comparable U.S. cities.

New York's government was more inclined to provide the City's people with a broad array of European-style social services than other populous U.S. municipalities. And social democracy as it influenced the City's housing market probably helped New York to retain a relatively large share of its metropolitan area's total population and of the region's middle-income households. But this combination of policies and outcomes did not immunize New York from US urban crises of the 1960s, 1970s, and 1980s. New York had its share of serious riots, suffered through devastating crime waves and, for a few hours on October 17, 1975, defaulted on financial obligations to its lenders. Perhaps the combination of less suburbanization and a full array of social services *along with* a robust regional economy could have headed off or at least ameliorated these crises. During the later 1960s and 1970s, however, the New York metropolitan economy was far from robust; powerful technological and geographic trends left it deeply troubled.

## References


Alonso, W. (1964). *Location and Land Use: Toward a General Theory of Land Rent*. Cambridge: Harvard University Press.

American Public Transportation Association. (2018, March 13). *Public Transportation Ridership Report* (Fourth Quarter 2017). Retrieved from https://www.apta.com/resources/statistics/Documents/Ridership/2017-Q4-Ridership-APTA.pdf.

Anas, A., Arnott, R., & Small, K. A. (1998). Urban Spatial Structure. *Journal of Economic Literature, 36*(3), 1426–1464.

Arnott, R. (1995). Time for Revisionism on Rent Control. *Journal of Economic Perspectives, 9*(1), 99–120.

Ballon, H. (2007). Robert Moses and Urban Renewal: The Title I Program. In H. Ballon & K. T. Jackson (Eds.), *Robert Moses and the Modern City: The Transformation of New York*. New York: W. W. Norton.

Baum-Snow, N. (2007). Did Highways Cause Suburbanization? *The Quarterly Journal of Economics, 122*(2), 755–805.

Bloom, N. D. (2008). *Public Housing That Worked: New York in the Twentieth Century*. Philadelphia: University of Pennsylvania Press.

Boustan, L. P. (2010). Was Postwar Suburbanization 'White Flight'? *Evidence from the Black Migration, 125*(1), 417–443.

Bradford, D. F., & Kelejian, H. H. (1973). An Econometric Model of the Flight to the Suburbs. *Journal of Political Economy, 81*(3), 566–589.

Burnham, R., Feinberg, R. M., & Husted, T. A. (2004). Central City Crime and Suburban Economic Growth. *Applied Economics, 36*(9), 917–922.

Caro, R. (1975). *The Power Broker: Robert Moses and the Fall of New York*. New York: Vintage Books.

Carter, S. B., Gartner, S. S., & Haines, M. R. (2006). *Historical Statistics of the United States Millennial Edition Online*. New York: Cambridge University Press.

Columbia Law Review. (1926). Legislative Housing Relief in New York: The State Housing Law and the Extension of the Emergency Rent Laws. *Columbia Law Review, 26*(8), 1015–1016.

Cullen, J. B., & Levitt, S. D. (1999). Crime, Urban Flight, and the Consequences for Cities. *The Review of Economics and Statistics, 81*(2), 159–169.

DeSalvo, J. S. (1974). Neighborhood Upgrading Effects of Middle-Income Housing Projects in New York City. *Journal of Urban Economics, 1*, 269–277.

DeSalvo, J. S. (1975). Benefits and Costs of New York City's Middle-Income Housing Program. *Journal of Political Economy, 83*(4), 791–806.

Freeman, J. B. (2000). *Working Class New York: Life and Labor Since World War II*. New York: The New Press.

Gibson, C. (1998, June). *Population of the 100 Largest Cities and Other Urban Places in the United States: 1790–1990*. Retrieved from U.S. Census Bureau https://www.census.gov/population/www/documentation/twps0027/twps0027.html.

Gibson, C., & Jung, K. (2005, February). *Historical Census Statistics on Population Totals by Race, 1790 to 1990, and by Hispanic Origin, 1970 to 1990, for Large Cities and Other Urban Places*. Retrieved from U.S. Census Bureau https://www.census.gov/population/www/documentation/twps0076/twps0076.html.

Gyourko, J., & Linneman, P. (1989). Equity and Efficiency Aspects of Rent Control: An Empirical Study of New York City. *Journal of Urban Economics, 26*, 54–74.

Hood, C. (1993). *722 Miles, The Building of the Subways and How They Transformed New York*. New York: Simon & Schuster.

Jackson, K. T. (1985). *Crabgrass Frontier: The Suburbanization of the United States*. Oxford: Oxford University Press.

Judt, T. (2005). *Postwar: A History of Europe Since 1945*. New York: Penguin Books.

Kane, R. J. (1999). The Financing of Cooperatives and Condominiums: A Retrospective. *St. John's Law Review, 73*(1), 101–134.

Kessner, T. (1989). *Fiorello H. La Guardia and the Making of Modern New York*. New York: Penguin Books.

Maldonado, R., & Rose, R. D. (1995). The Application of Civil Rights Law to Housing Cooperatives: Are Co-ops Bastions of Discriminatory Exclusion or Self-Selecting Models of Community Based Living. *Fordham Urban Law Review, 23*(4), 1245–1282.

Margo, R. A. (1992). Explaining the Postwar Suburbanization of Population in the United States: The Role of Income. *Journal of Urban Economics, 31*(3), 301–310.

Mashable. (2018). *1904 to Today: See How New York City Subway Fare Has Climbed Over 111 Years*. Retrieved from https://mashable.com/2015/03/22/new-york-city-subway-fare/#lGmkm2R8RPqK.

Massey, D. A., Denton, N. A. (1989). Hypersegregation in U.S. Metropolitan Areas: Black and Hispanic Segregation along Five Dimensions. *Demography, 26*(3), 373–391.

McDonald, J. F. (2011). Public Housing Construction and the Cities, 1937–1967. *Urban Studies Research*, 1–12.

Mieszkowski, P., & Mills, E. S. (1993). The Causes of Metropolitan Suburbanization. *Journal of Economic Perspectives, 7*(3), 135–147.

Mills, E. (1970). Urban Density Function. *Urban Studies, 7*(1), 5–20.

Muth, R. F. (1969). *Cities and Housing; The Spatial Pattern of Urban Residential Land Use*. Chicago: University of Chicago Press.

Plunz, R. (1990). *A History of Housing in New York City: Dwelling Type and Social Change in the American Metropolis*. New York: Columbia University Press.

Rodgers, D. T. (1998). *Atlantic Crossings: Social Politics in the Progressive Age*. Cambridge: The Belknap Press of Harvard University Press.

Rosenbaum, E. (1993). The Constraints on Minority Housing Choices, New York City, 1978–1987. *Social Forces, 72*(3), 736, 743.

Sazama, G. (1996). *A Brief History of Affordable Housing Cooperatives in the United States* (Working Paper Number 1996–09). Department of Economics, University of Connecticut.

The Eleanor Roosevelt Papers Project. (2018). *Teaching Eleanor Roosevelt Glossary: Public Works Administration.* Retrieved from The George Washington University https://www2.gwu.edu/~erpapers/teachinger/glossary/pwa.cfm.

The Furman Center for Real Estate and Urban Policy. (2011). *Subsidized Housing: A Cross-City Comparison.* New York: New York University School of Law, The Wagner School.

The Furman Center for Real Estate and Urban Policy. (2012). *Rent Stabilization in New York City.* New York: Fact Brief, New York University, School of Law The Wagner School of Public Service.

The National Advisory Commission on Civil Disorders. (1988). *The Kerner Report: The 1968 Report of the National Advisory Commission on Civil Disorders.* New York: Pantheon Books.

Tiebout, C. M. (1961). An Economic Theory of Fiscal Decentralization. In U.-N. Research (Ed.), *Public Finances: Needs, Sources, and Utilization* (pp. 79–96). Princeton: Princeton University Press.

U.S. Census Bureau. (1982). *Statistical Abstract of the United States, 1982–83.* Washington: U.S. Government Printing Office.

U.S. Census Bureau. (1983). *1980 Census of Housing, Volume 2, Metropolitan Housing Characteristics.* Washington: U.S. Government Printing Office.

U.S. Census Bureau. (2018). *Selected Historical Decennial Census Population and Housing Counts.* Retrieved from Census 1990 https://www.census.gov/population/www/censusdata/hiscendata.html.

U.S. Department of Housing and Urban Development. (1974). *1974 Statistical Yearbook.* Washington: U.S. Government Printing Office.

U.S. Department of Housing and Urban Development. (2018, June). *Measuring Overcrowding in Housing.* Retrieved from https://www.huduser.gov/publications/pdf/measuring_overcrowding_in_hsg.pdf.

U.S. Federal Bureau of Investigation. (2018). *Reported Crime by Locality (City, County), State, and Nation.* Retrieved from Uniform Crime Reports https://www.ucrdatatool.gov/Search/Crime/Crime.cfm.

U.S. Federal Highway Administration. (2018). *State and Urbanized Area Statistics.* Retrieved from Office of Highway Policy Information https://www.fhwa.dot.gov/ohim/onh00/onh2p11.htm.

Wendell Cox Consultancy. (2019). *Lane Miles Per Capita 1999: US Urbanized Areas over 1,000,000.* Retrieved from The Public Purpose http://www.publicpurpose.com/hwy-tti99ratio.htm.

Whalen, C. T. (2005). Colonialism, Citizenship, and the Making of the Puerto Rican Diaspora: An Introduction. In C. T. Whalen & V. Vázquez-Hernández (Eds.), *The Puerto Rican Diaspora: Historical Perspective*. Philadelphia: Temple University Press.

Wikipedia. (2017). *List of United States Commuter Rail Systems by Ridership*. Retrieved from Wikipedia: The Free Encyclopedia https://en.wikipedia.org/wiki/List_of_United_States_commuter_rail_systems_by_ridership.

# 15

# All That Is Solid Melts into Air

In 1956, the Regional Plan Association (RPA), a local civic organization founded in 1922, engaged Harvard University's Graduate School of Public Administration to undertake an analysis of the economic and demographic characteristics of the 22-county region in and around the City of New York. The ultimate aim of the study was to produce projections for the years 1965, 1975, and 1985 of the total regional population, total employment by industry, and the geographic distributions of jobs and people. Harvard recruited a team of geographers and regional economists headed by Raymond Vernon to produce a series of detailed, studies, the titles of which reflect the breadth and depth of the analysis that supported the forecasts. These include, for example,

- *Freight and the Metropolis: The Impact of America's Transport Revolutions on the New York Region,*
- *The Newcomers: Negroes and Puerto Ricans in a Changing Metropolis,*
- *1400 Governments: The Political Economy of the New York Metropolitan Region,*
- *Money Metropolis: A Locational Study of Financial Activities in the New York Region,*



A. Gurwitz, *Atlantic Metropolis*, Palgrave Studies in American Economic History,
https://doi.org/10.1007/978-3-030-13352-8_15

- *One-tenth of a Nation: National Forces in the Economic Growth of the New York Region,*
- An edited compilation entitled *Made in New York: Case Studies in Metropolitan Manufacturing*, which included analyses of the garment, printing and publishing, and electronics industries nationwide and in the New York region.

Prof. Vernon also prepared a summary volume entitled *Metropolis 1985: An Interpretation of the Findings of the New York Metropolitan Region Study*.

One must be in awe of the boldness required to predict so many variables so far into the future and by the fact that many of the long-term forecasts were astonishingly accurate. The study's projections of New York City's population, for example, were very close to the actual outcomes, and the small discrepancy was pretty much entirely attributable to the Federal Census Bureau's overestimate of U.S. population growth between 1955 and 1985. The RPA Study team projected that the City's population would be 2.7% of the U.S. total in 1985; in fact, the actual figure was closer to 3.0% (Vernon, 1960, pp. 197, 232, 239).

It should not be surprising, however, that many of the projections turned out to be very far from the mark. For the most part, the study team's expectations were overly optimistic. With respect to populations, the Study anticipated much more rapid growth in the region's suburban and exurban counties than actually occurred. In the most extreme case, the Study's projection of the 1985 population of the region's "outer ring" exceeded the combined actual population of those counties by 63%. In essence, RPA Study team concluded in light of the evidence that was available to them that the region's population growth rate would lag the national rate by less than it actually did and that the process of suburbanization would play out around New York City in much the same way as elsewhere.

Notwithstanding the forecast errors, the Metropolitan Region Study is worthy of careful consideration. Its conclusions were based on as thorough and insightful analysis of the regional economy and its geographic and industrial components as was possible at the time. For an economic historian, the information assembled and organized by the

RPA team is valuable in and of itself. What is more, consideration of what we know now but the Study failed to recognize directs one's attention to the post-1950s developments and trends that explain why the predicted outcomes were generally so much better than what actually occurred.

## The Metropolitan Study Approach

One fundamental premise of the Study was that the development of a region is driven primarily by the size, especially with respect to employment, of the area's "base," or export, industries.[1] The authors recognized, of course, that developments in the "multiplier" industries that primarily served local needs—retail sales, construction, intra-urban transportation, etc.—especially trends in these sectors' labor intensivity, would affect the size of the region's 1985 population and income. Presumably, however, trends affecting these local industries would impact all metropolitan areas in similar ways. Absent the emergence of a new local industrial base, what would have distinguished Greater New York's trajectory from the others' were developments in the region's long-standing economic mainstays: freight handling, the garment industry, electronic goods manufacturing, media, and financial services.

The approach to forecasting taken by the individual monographs and by Raymond Vernon in his compendium was to focus on these sectors. Analyses of individual industries aimed to develop projections of their aggregate size nationwide, the proportion of total U.S. industry activity likely to take place in the New York region, and the proportions of local industry employment in the metropolitan area's core, inner ring, and outer ring. The next sections of this chapter will review and, with perfect hindsight, critique the RPA Study's analyses of New York's principal export industries.

---

[1]This concept was introduced in Chapter 1 in the discussion of the role of beaver pelt exports in the economy of New Netherland.

More than anything else, it was the failure to anticipate the sharp contraction of the region's involvement with the production and handling of physical goods that led to the Study team's overly optimistic expectations regarding New York's economic performance over the subsequent three decades. Between 1956 and 1986, employment in four physical goods-related base industries increased by 6.2 nationwide but declined by 16% in the 22-county RPA region. And between 1958 and 1982, total manufacturing employment increased by about 24% nationwide but decreased by 18% in the New York Metropolitan Area (U.S. Census Bureau, 2018; U.S. Department of Commerce; U.S. Department of Health Education and Welfare, 1958).

Since port activity was the first cause of so much of the region's economic history, beginning the consideration of the RPA projections with Benjamin Chinitz's analysis of the region's goods-handling industry seems appropriate (Chinitz, 1960).

## Freight and the Metropolis

Chinitz correctly identified the national and global developments that would influence the volume of goods moving through the New York region and the number of workers required to handle that flow. He anticipated an increase in international trade. He recognized that New York's share of total U.S. port activity would decline as the nation's population center continued moving southwestward and as trade with Asia grew faster than Atlantic-basin traffic. He also realized that containerization would reduce the number of freight-handling jobs per ton of goods shipped. What he failed to anticipate, however, was the magnitude of these changes.

One development Chinitz, all the other scholars who contributed to the RPA Study, and pretty much everyone else did not foresee was the magnitude of the subsequent three decades' increase in international trade. In 1955 to volume U.S. general cargo foreign trade, imports plus exports, totaled 46 million long tons. On the assumption that imports would grow at about the same rate as GDP while exports would increase somewhat more slowly, Chinitz based his projections of

New York port activity on the assumption that total U.S. trade would increase to 73 million long tons by 1985. The actual figure was closer to 129 million.

The rise in total U.S. trade did not lead to a commensurate increase in general cargo tonnage moving through the Port of New York because another of the trends Chinitz correctly foresaw was also more powerful than he expected it to be. The RPA forecast projected a substantial decrease in the Port of New York's share of the nation's ocean borne cargo from 30% in 1955 to 20% in 1985. As it turned out, in its 1985 annual report the Port Authority of New York and New Jersey (PANYNJ) boasted that its share of total U.S. general cargo traffic, a narrower category than "ocean borne cargo" and a category in which New York specialized, had risen to 10.7% from 10.5% the previous year. The combined effects of rapid trade growth and loss of market share were that the volume of general cargo moving through the Port of New York grew by only about seven percent, from 12.8 million long tons in 1955 only to 13.7 million tons in 1985, while the total volume of the nation's international trade nearly tripled[2] (Chinitz, 1960, pp. 57, 79–81; Port Authority of New York and New Jersey, 1986, p. 12).

This modestly larger 1985 volume of goods was handled by a much smaller workforce than in 1955. Chinitz was absolutely right in his expectation that containerization would be important. Well, he might have because the maiden voyage of the world's first commercially successful containership departed from Newark with some fanfare bound for Houston in April 1956, while the RPA Study was getting underway. Chinitz's estimate that the labor cost of loading a container ship would be as low as 10% or 20% of conventional longshore operations was roughly correct. The Study failed, however, to anticipate the speed with which the shipping companies and the port authorities that served them would adopt containerization. In fact, the PANYNJ was a pioneer in the process, not just with the first voyage but with the construction of facilities in Newark and, especially at the huge Sea-Land terminal at

[2]"General cargo" is freight that, unlike "bulk cargo," does not require specialized containers for shipment.

Port Elizabeth, which opened in 1962, specifically designed to load and unload container ships. By the late 1960s, the collapse of union efforts to stem waterfront job losses by requiring unloading and reloading of container contents had opened the way for more widespread adoption of the new technology and for the shift of almost all regional port operations from New York City's now-obsolete docks to the new facilities in New Jersey. By the mid-1960s, the Port Authority had considerable justification when it advertised itself as "America's container capital." And by the mid-1980s at about 20% the Port's proportion of total U.S. container trade tonnage was roughly twice its share of all general cargo (Levinson, 2006; U.S. Department of Transportation, Maritime Administration, 1984, p. 16).

The RPA Study anticipated only a moderate decrease in regional waterfront employment over its forecast period, but between 1956 and 1986 regional employment in the water transportation industry declined by 70%. Not surprisingly, given the decrease in the region's overall market share and its rapid adoption of containerization, that was twice the rate at which total U.S. employment in this sector fell over that period.

The same developments that reduced water transportation employment also affected other goods-handling industries (Table 15.1) to similar effect. Employment in these sectors in New York City contracted substantially across the board so that at the end of the RPA forecast horizon about the same proportion of the region's population was working in the goods-handling sectors as in the nation as a whole. Thus, by

**Table 15.1** Goods-handling industries, changes in employment and employment concentration ratios, 1956–1986 (U.S. Census Bureau, 2018; U.S. Department of Commerce; U.S. Department of Health Education and Welfare, 1958)

| Industry/location | | New York City | RPA region | USA |
|---|---|---|---|---|
| Trucking & warehousing | | −13.2% | 51.8% | 90.0% |
| Water transportation | | −80.1% | −69.1% | −34.8% |
| Wholesale trade | | −76.5% | −31.6% | 6.2% |
| Total goods handling | | −70.9% | −23.6% | 19.2% |
| Goods handling concentration ratio | 1956 | 1.41 | 1.16 | n.a. |
| | 1986 | 0.83 | 1.09 | n.a. |

the end of the short twentieth century, New York City was no longer a national hub for the distribution of physical goods. It certainly was no longer *the* national center for this activity as it had been for much of the previous 150 years.

Much the same could be said with respect to the *production* of physical commodities.

## Women's and Children's Apparel (Helfgott, 1959)

Roy B. Helfgott, who prepared the Study's monograph on the women's and children's apparel industry, undertook his projection of employment in this sector on what would at the time have been a reasonable presupposition that "[n]ational employment … [in this industry] … will depend, first of all, on aggregate demand, and secondly on any technological changes which might affect the amount of labor required to satisfy this demand" (Helfgott, 1959, p. 116). With the benefit of hindsight, it is obvious that this presupposition misses the potential impact of imports on the demand for US-made garments. Although Helfgott did note that the value of wool sweaters imported from Japan had increased from $336,000 in 1954 to $7,058,000 in 1957, he could not have foreseen that the percentage of clothing and shoes sold in the United States that had been manufactured abroad would rise from around five percent during the 1960s to 26% in 1988. Helfgott projected about a 50% increase in the number of people employed in the women's and children's apparel industry nationwide, from 607,000 to 919,000 between 1955 and 1985. As it happened, total industry employment increased by a little more than four percent between 1958 and 1982 (Helfgott, 1959, p. 92; Murray, 1995, p. 66; Wee, 2013).

Helfgott's understanding of New York's attraction to the women's wear industry will be familiar to readers of previous chapters of this book. The volatility of business conditions facing firms and workers in this industry—its seasonality and its sensitivity to ephemeral fashions—placed a high premium on flexibility with respect to production levels and on access to information about demand-side developments. The garment manufacturers, jobbers, and contractors that were fittest to survive in this environment tended to be relatively small and to rely on other, independent businesses to provide specialized inputs. Entrepreneurs and workers did best if they could access information about fashion trends, skilled worker availability, and job openings through formal institutions (e.g., the International Ladies' Garment Workers' Union, the "ILGWU," *Women's Wear Daily* on the doorstep each weekday morning), and established social networks. New York's dense array of these "external economies," to use the Study team's term, was what fostered the concentration of this industry's employment in the City.

There was by the mid-1950s considerable evidence that the power of external economies to attract garment manufacturing activity to New York and, therefore, the region's share of total industry employment was waning. Accordingly, Helfgott expected that decrease in the region's share of total nationwide industry employment from 48.7% in 1947 to 43.5% in 1954 would continue or accelerate.

Helfgott identified three broad reasons for the diminution of the City and region's role. First, a shift in consumer taste toward more casual garments that were less subject to rapid style changes reduced the advantage of proximity to the center of fashion "buzz." Second, labor market conditions in New York disadvantaged local producers. Nominal wages were higher in New York, work rules more restrictive, and some skills were becoming scarcer. Helfgott reported that New York's production workers in the women's and children's apparel industries were paid 28% more than the national average per week. Some or all of this regional wage premium did no more for workers than make up for the region's higher cost of living, but from the point of view of manufacturers selling into the national market, it was the nominal wage that entered into the cost of production. Part of the New York wage premium may also have reflected a higher average skill level among New York City garment workers, but the shift to simpler garments helped accelerate the general deskilling of production work in the industry. Further, the ILGWU used some of its power in the New York labor market to slow the deskilling process locally. And, in any case, skilled garment labor was becoming scarcer in New York as the turn-of-the-century Jewish and Italian immigrants left the labor force and because tailoring skills were less prevalent among the Puerto Ricans and African-Americans who might have replaced them. Finally, reductions in transportation costs were making it easier to shift the components of the production process that were less reliant on external economies to locations away from New York City and away from the metropolitan region. In particular, truck transport and the development of interurban highway networks enabled New York-based jobbers to assign large parts of their work, with minimal loss of flexibility, to contractors and affiliates located within overnight trucking distance of Manhattan's garment district. One destination for some of this work during the 1950s was the economically declining coal mining regions around Wilkes-Barre, Pennsylvania. Helfgott estimated that in the mid-1950s, the contracting cost of producing a $6.75 retail-priced dress would have been $2.50 in Manhattan and $2.06 in Wilkes-Barre. More routine garment production, which involved little contact with New York's external economies, could also relocate to non-unionized locations in the U.S. southeast, to Puerto Rico, or, as Helfgott mentions in passing, to Japan or Hong Kong (Helfgott, 1959, pp. 67–112).

For these reasons, the RPA Study team anticipated that the trends that had reduced the New York region's share U.S. women's and children's apparel manufacturing employment early in the postwar period would strengthen and accelerate over the subsequent decades. Their projection was that the region's share of this industry's jobs would fall to 24.5% by 1985. That would still amount to a high concentration of garment industry employment in New York, and the forecast reflected the expectation that large parts of the industry would continue to rely on external economies to support their profitable operations. The team's anticipation that total national employment would continue to expand reasonably robustly led them to conclude that, after declining gradually total employment in the women's and children's apparel industry in the New York metropolitan region would stabilize at around 225,000 by 1985. That would have been about 35,000 fewer workers than in 1954.[3]

[3]Ibid., pp. 69, 128–129; Vernon, op. cit., p. 233.

As it happened the team turned out to have been overly optimistic about both New York City's share of total U.S. industry employment and about the total number of industry jobs in the region, but much closer to actual outcome with respect to the former than the latter. By 1982, the region's share of total U.S. employment in these sectors had fallen to 21.0. But total 1982 industry employment in the region was only about 134,000 or 40% below the forecast and 48% below the 1954 employment level. A large proportion of that decline was attributable to inability of U.S. garment industry as a whole, its bosses and its workers, whether in Wilkes-Barre or South Carolina or New York, to compete successfully with producers abroad.

In 1982, the garment industry was still one of the region's largest manufacturing industries and New York remained one of the world's fashion capitals. But the sector was much less important as a source of local working-class jobs in the 1980s than it had been at the beginning of the postwar period. The magnitude of the decline in regional employment in this sector had less to do with New York City's attractiveness to the industry relative to other locations in the United States than with one of the earliest manifestations of the second great era of economic globalization.

## Electronics

During the first two interwar decades, the rapidly expanding electronics industry—at the time primarily the production of parts for and the assembly of radio transmitters and receivers—gravitated disproportionally to the New York metropolitan area. As detailed in Chapter 12, the concentration of this industry's employment in the region was probably a manifestation of early adopter's advantage combined with network externalities. The earliest use of wireless technology in the United States was to communicate with ships at sea, an activity which naturally gravitated to the nation's busiest port. And the presence of Thomas Edison's workshop and its industrial spin-offs in northern New Jersey along with AT&T's Western Electric/Bell Labs affiliate, which was located in New York City until the 1940s and thereafter in northern New Jersey, boosted the supply of technicians and managers familiar with all things electrical and electronic.

At the time of the RPA Study, the industry was still to some degree concentrated in and around New York City. In 1958, about 15% of the nation's employment in the electronics industry but only about 10% of total manufacturing employment was located in the region (U.S. Census Bureau, 2018). James M. Hurd, the author of the RPA's monograph on the electronics industry, demonstrated that New York offered few advantages to mass producers of consumer electronics: at the time, mostly radios, televisions, and their standard components. Midwestern locations that were closer to the nation's population center offered lower unit labor and shipping costs. Hurd argued, however, the New York retained an advantage in the production of "custom and nonstandard items" items such as specially designed vacuum tubes, early semiconductors, and military and industrial electronics. Given how quickly electronic technology and its applications were evolving at the time, specialized product runs tended to be very short and individual firms could not rely on internal resources alone to stay up-to-date on market developments. Thus, the industrial organization that emerged in these branches of the electronics industry was similar in some ways to that of the garment industry in that the business was populated by relatively small firms that relied on outside resources, or "external economies," for assistance with product and production-process development. New York's ecosystem of specialty subcontractors, the presence in New York State at the time of one-third of the nation's electrical engineering graduate students, and the location on Long Island of the Grumman Aircraft Engineering Corporation and the Fairchild Camera and Instrument Corporation, two of the nation's largest buyers of military electronics, combined to draw a disproportionate share of the "custom and nonstandard" segment of the industry to the region. Data from the 1958 Census of Manufacturing confirm the region's attractiveness to this industrial sector. At that time 38% of the nation's total employment in the Engineering and Scientific Instruments industry, the closest Standard Industrial Classification (SIC) to the specialty electronics sector, was located in the New York metropolitan region (Gustafson, 1959; Hurd, 1959).

Hurd and his colleagues on the Study team were cautiously optimistic about the region's ability to retain its position as an important center of the U.S. electronics industry. They correctly anticipated that national employment in the sector would grow rapidly, that its pace of technological change would remain very high, and that the individual firms closest to the cutting edge would continue to rely on external economies to remain competitive in a rapidly evolving technological and business environment. They were wrong, however, in their conclusion that the New York region would lag the national growth rate by a narrow enough margin so that local employment in this industry would continue to expand. Specifically, they anticipated that nationwide electronics employment would increase by 177% between 1954 and 1985 and that regional employment in the sector would rise by 87%. Their projection was remarkably close to what happened on the national level; combined employment in SICs 357, 366, and 3881 increased by 159% between 1958 and 1982, and the difference between this outcome and the RPA projection could easily reflect no more than slight year-span and industry categorization differences. But they were very wrong about what would occur in the region. In fact, electronics industry employment in the New York region *decreased* by 18% between 1958 and 1982. What did they miss?

The development they, quite understandably, missed, of course, was the rapid advance of semiconductor technology and the powerful attraction two other U.S. regions—metropolitan Boston, Massachusetts, and, especially, metropolitan San Jose, California, or "Route 128" and "Silicon Valley"—would have for the most innovative, most successful, and largest firms in the industry spawned by this developing technology. The New York region's "niche" in the electronics industry circa the mid-1950s was in the production of "custom and nonstandard" products, which, at the time mostly involved vacuum tube technology or the use of transistors to replace vacuum tubes in a few applications. By the 1970s, however, essentially all the "custom and nonstandard" electronic goods under development or in production involved applications of semiconductor technologies—integrated circuitry and its applications such as hard disk drives, local area networks, minicomputers—and a huge proportion of this activity was taking place in two locations, neither of which was New York.

This development raises two questions. Why did the semiconductor industry agglomerate so dramatically in a small number of locations? And why wasn't metropolitan New York one of those places?

The most common answers to the first of these questions make the second one even more perplexing. Economic geographers have devoted considerable attention to the development of agglomerations of activity involving advanced and advancing technologies. The necessary conditions identified for the emergence of a Silicon Valley include the presence of research universities and/or corporate R&D centers, networks of suppliers with the requisite capabilities, discerning venturesome capitalists, and an entrepreneurial cultural milieu (Kenney & von Burg, 1999, p. 70). The perplexing fact of the matter is that the New York area was endowed with all of these necessary conditions in the early 1960s when the digital revolution was getting under way. As noted previously, New York State, very much including New York City, was at the time an important center of graduate education in electronic engineering. The region was also home to Bell Labs, where the transistor had been invented. As the RPA Study team observed, the region was endowed with a rich array of suppliers of nonstandard electronic equipment. Nor was there any noticeable local shortage of capitalists willing to engage in speculative ventures. And New Yorkers' entrepreneurial inclinations had nurtured the region's fashion and media industries. In other words, if by the mid-1980s people were referring to, say, the banks of New Jersey's Raritan River as "Silicon Valley," it would not have been particularly surprising.

Clearly, the necessary conditions for the development of innovative industry clusters identified in the literature are not, even collectively, sufficient for the development of a technology agglomeration. One likely sufficiency condition was identified by Steven Klepper in a 2010 article in the *Journal of Urban Economics* that analyzed the development of two industrial agglomerations involving advanced technologies. The two examples were the automobile industry in the Detroit area during the first decades of the twentieth century and Silicon Valley between 1960 and 1990. Klepper hypothesized that the process of agglomeration begins with some modest number of firms entering a cutting-edge manufacturing industry in a variety of places. One of these firms, which is destined to become an industry leader, happens to be established in a region that offers the necessary agglomeration conditions listed above. From time to time thereafter managers and employees of this "parent" firm leave to found "spinoffs" producing a similar product line or its components or its applications. These spin-offs tend to locate near the parent presumably, in part, because the regional business environment is conducive to their growth. Offspring firms inherit some of the traits that contributed to the parent's success and generate some of their own descendants. The founding firm, its immediate offspring, and the subsequent generations form an industrial agglomeration. Statistical analysis of the development, growth, and demise of individual firms in the early automobile and semiconductor industries indicate that spin-offs from the top firms have a pronounced tendency to be more successful and to survive longer than de novo start-ups or the offspring of less successful parents. As a result, the industry becomes highly concentrated in the region where the progenitor firm was initially established, and other potential agglomeration sites wither on the vine (Klepper, 2010).

The ancestor firm of Detroit's automobile industry, Olds Motor Works, founded in Lansing, Michigan in 1901, spawned the most spin-offs of any firm in the industry. By 1910, Detroit area automobile manufacturers' combined market share was 65% and rose further thereafter (Klepper, 2010, p. 17).

Olds's Silicon Valley counterpart was Fairchild Semiconductor. By 1975, three of the Valley's top four firms were Fairchild spin-offs and the fourth was a second generation Fairchild descendant. The identity of Silicon Valley's progenitor is especially ironic from a New York perspective because the California Firm was a subsidiary of Long Island-based Fairchild Camera and Instrument. The 1957 establishment of Fairchild Semiconductor in Palo Alto must count as one of the "contingencies" of economic history that set the trajectory of New York's regional development.

Although there had been a few electronics firms in the Bay Area before 1955, the local development of the semiconductor industry effectively began in that year when William Shockley, one of the transistor's inventors, after failing to raise capital to develop commercial applications of the new device on acceptable terms around New York or Boston, found an "angel" investor on the West Coast and established his company in Palo Alto. Shockley's enterprise was not a success, but Fairchild Camera and Instrument Company provided the capital that enabled eight of the founder's top science and engineering subordinates to launch Fairchild Semiconductor. The founding team was able to foster advances in transistor production and, then, some of the first functional integrated circuits with commercial applications. Further, the eight defectors from Shockley's initial enterprise negotiated a particularly favorable deal from their point of view with the Fairchild parent, and by the early 1960s they were all quite wealthy. The quality of the cutting-edge work undertaken and Fairchild Semiconductor, the expertise its employees developed, and the demonstration that this new industry could create fortunes ignited the self-reinforcing wave of multigenerational spin-offs that created Silicon Valley and drew technology-oriented enterprises that might have located elsewhere to Northern California.

The idea that the explosive growth of the semiconductor industry in Silicon Valley and, to a lesser extent, around Boston essentially "sucked the air out" of the post-1950s specialty electronics sector in the rest of the country provides a plausible explanation for the decline of New York as a center of this industry between 1958 and 1982.

One other, complementary but even more tentative explanation is worth mentioning. It begins with the observation that early in the postwar period the New York region specialized in the telecommunications applications of electronic technology. In 1958, more than half of the region's total employment in the "non-standard and custom" electronics industry as defined by Hund was in the communication equipment sector (SIC 366). This should not be surprising given AT&T's presence in the region. But this apparent advantage may not have served New York particularly well as the postwar period progressed for two reasons. First, the specialization in telecommunications may have blinded New Yorkers to the other potential applications of semiconductor technology such as Shockley may have been proposing. Second, as of the end of World War II AT&T was a monopoly that controlled much of the nation's local and long-distance telephone system *and* all of the manufacturing of equipment used on that system. Thus, any potential that Western Electric/Bell Labs might have had to evolve into metropolitan New York's equivalent of Fairchild Semiconductor could have been impeded in the first instance by a monopoly's lack of incentive to innovate (Olley & Pakes, 1996).

## Printing and Publishing

The RPA Study team was remarkably prescient with respect to its projection of 1985 nationwide employment in the printing and publishing industry. W. Eric Gustafson, who prepared the monograph on that topic, forecasted that industry employment would be 1,178,000 in 1985, up from 804,382 in 1954. In fact, the 1982 Census of Manufactures counted 1,291,800 employees in this industry. As was the case with the other goods-related sectors, however, Gustafson's forecast for New York City employment in this industry was overly optimistic. He anticipated that the region's share of total U.S. industry employment would contract only modestly, from 22.8% in 1954 to 19.7% in 1985. In fact, Census of Manufactures statistics indicate that the region's employment share decreased from 19.8% in 1958 to 13.3% in 1982. Still, Gustafson's optimism regarding the future of the region's printing and publishing industry turns out to have been more justified that the RPA team's similarly benign expectations with respect to the women's and children's apparel and specialty electronics industries. All three projected that the region's share of national employment in the industries they analyzed would decrease substantially between 1954 and 1985 but that U.S. total employment in these sectors would increase by enough so that absolute level of New York employment would rise over the projection period. Instead total regional employment in women's and children's apparel and specialty electronics sectors *declined* by 39.5 and 18.1%, respectively between 1958 and 1982. By contrast, the number of printing and publishing jobs in the New York area remained essentially unchanged over the same period (Gustafson, 1959).

Any assessment of what the RPA Study got right and what it got wrong must begin with Gustafson's correct observation that printing and publishing are two very distinct activities, especially with respect to their economic geographies. Publishers deliver content, in the form of manuscripts, pictures, or graphics, to printers who transform what they received into newspapers, books, magazines, engravings, etc. Some publishing activities rely heavily on external economies. Chapter 5, for example, highlighted competitive edge New York's antebellum book and periodical publishers gained by their location in the nation's busiest port city. More recently it has been advantageous for publishers of magazines with national circulation to locate near where freelance writers and illustrators can be recruited quickly and close to the headquarters of advertising agencies.

For some printed products—local daily newspapers or securities prospectuses for hot deals, for example—it has been important for content producers and printers to operate in close proximity. But for books and for weekly or monthly periodicals there is no particular need for publishers or printers to operate in the same town or region, especially as technological changes reduce the cost of moving content over relatively long distances. Transportation costs for printed matter are determined by the complex rate schedules of the U.S. postal system, which do not appear to have particularly advantaged or disadvantaged New York relative to other locations. Unit labor costs, however, boosted by the relatively high cost of living in the metropolitan area and, possibly, by the power of local unions, were higher in New York than in most other potential U.S. locations for printing activities (Gustafson, 1959, p. 208). And by the early postwar period, technological advances had made it easier to locate related content-development and physical-production activities quite far away from each other. Gustafson, who was particularly impressed by the impact of teletypsetting machines on the production of periodicals, noted that "[n]ot a single large national periodical is printed in New York City at the present time, whereas in 1920 almost all were" (Gustafson, 1959, p. 190).

Where Gustafson went wrong was in his belief that the migration of footloose printing activities away from the New York metropolitan region was largely complete by the mid-1950s. He did anticipate that then-emerging technologies such as facsimile transmission might make it easier for publishers to review page proofs that had been printed far away, but he did not expect that this would induce much more shifting of printing activities away from New York than had already taken place. He also noted that printing-trades wage differentials between New York and other regions were diminishing and expected that this would stem regional job losses. As it happened, combined regional employment in the book and commercial printing sectors decreased by about 10,000 jobs or about 19% between 1958 and 1982. The loss of printing jobs was, however, more than offset by the increase in positions in the combination of periodicals, book, and miscellaneous publishing, which increased by 19,000 jobs, or by 39%, between 1958 and 1982. As a result, the printing and publishing industry was able to avoid the fate of the other two regional manufacturing sectors, both of which contracted sharply in total employment as the postwar period progressed.

A focus on the printing and publishing industry, however, obscures a broader trend in the economic role of the New York region in the U.S. economy. The combination of printing and publishing as a single *manufacturing* industry probably reflects the fact that these two activities were closely connected, frequently within a single business enterprise and almost always operating in close physical proximity, at the time when the Federal government first began collecting economic statistics. But the production of content for newspapers, magazines, and books is now better understood as a sector of the broader "media" industry, other branches of which, such as broadcasting and advertising, are categorized as part of the service sector.

The Census Bureau's County Business Patterns (CBP) program, which publishes data on both goods- and service-producing activities, does not distinguish between the two distinct components of the printing and publishing industry. A comparison of CBP statistics for 1958 and 1986 indicates that over this period printing and publishing employment in the 22-county RPA region grew by 11%, while employment in the advertising and broadcasting industries increased by 76 and 66%, respectively. These seem like appropriate statistics to mark a shift in focus from the businesses that made and moved physical goods, employment in which was "melting away" in the New York region during the postwar period, to the industries that trafficked in intangibles and were performing noticeably better.

## Money Metropolis

Sidney M. Robbins and Nestor E. Terleckyj's monograph examining the commercial banking, insurance, real estate, and securities industries was drafted about two decades before a twenty-year period of what has been characterized as "revolutionary" financial innovation (Miller, 1986). Circa the mid-1950s, the financial service sectors that loomed largest in New York's business landscape were the commercial banking and life and health insurance industries. The former was pretty much solely engaged in serving as a safe and convenient repository for U.S. domestic households' and businesses' "retail" deposits, in making commercial loans to U.S. businesses, and in accumulating portfolios of federal, state, and local government bonds. The RPA Study relegated consideration of the securities and investment banking industry, along with property insurance companies, savings banks, and finance companies, into a catchall chapter on "the rest of the financial community" (Robbins & Terleckyj, 1960, pp. 148–176).

Robbins and Terleckyj based their projections of future total U.S. financial services employment and of the New York region's share on the explicit assumption that the growth rate of these industries would be determined on the most fundamental level on expansion of the overall national and regional economies. Whether employment in the finance, insurance, and real estate ("FIRE") industries grew faster or more slowly than the national workforce as a whole would depend on the balance within each sector of productivity enhancements, mostly associated with the diffusion of computer technology, and the expansion of the range of services these businesses provided to their customers. For example, the authors anticipated, correctly as it turned out, that the advent of machine-readable routing and account numbers of the face of checks would, all else held equal, reduce commercial banks' labor requirement. At the same time, however, they expected that banks would expand the types of credit and debit functions they provided their clients (e.g., credit cards, bill paying, etc.). They also foresaw a substantial expansion of health insurance coverage as this became an increasingly commonplace fringe benefit of employment but also anticipated substantial productivity improvements in the life insurance industry. The authors also correctly, albeit somewhat prematurely, predicted the mechanization of transaction entry, execution, and settlement in the securities industry and expected that this would lead to a substantial reduction in employment in this sector.

Taken together the authors' judgment regarding the cumulative impacts of overall economic growth, productivity enhancements, and service expansions would lead to about a doubling of finance sector employment between 1956 and 1985 and an increase in these industries' share of total U.S. employment from 3.0 to 3.9%. It is not possible to compare the RPA forecasts finance employment with published data for years after 1956 because of differences in the way industries were defined. However it is clear that these sectors grew substantially faster, both absolutely and relative to the entire U.S. workforce, than Robbins and Terleckyj anticipated. Bureau of Labor Statistics tabulations of FIRE sector employment increased by close to 150% over that period, and the percentage of total nonfarm employment engaged in these sectors rose from 4.6 to 6.1%. The Department of Commerce's CBP series indicated even faster growth; by that measure finance sector employment increased by 235% over the period and rose from 1.4 to 2.2% of the total "industry and commerce" workforce[4] (Robbins & Terleckyj, 1960, p. 179; U.S. Bureau of Labor Statistics, 2018; U.S. Department of Commerce; U.S. Department of Health Education and Welfare, 1958).

The RPA Study recognized that New York's financial services industries served two functions: providing "retail" services to local households and businesses and serving as the locus of what were by far the nation's most active money and capital markets. Any business that could benefit

[4]The County Business Patterns industrial classifications included in these calculations are: Depository Institutions, Nondepository Credit Institutions, Security & Commodity Brokers, Dealers, Exchanges & Services, Insurance Carriers, Insurance Agents, Brokers and Service, Real Estate, and Holding and Other Investment Offices.

from the most up-to-date information about financial market conditions had to establish either its headquarters or at the very least some significant presence in or near Manhattan's financial district. Robbins and Terleckyj anticipated that employment in both types of activity would grow more slowly in the New York region than nationwide over the subsequent thirty years. Retail financial services would grow relatively slowly around New York because the region's overall population and aggregate personal income growth rates were expected to lag their national equivalents. Improvements in communication technology and, possibly, the emergence of new "wholesale" financial centers in other Cities, would reduce the advantage of proximity to financial exchanges. Accordingly, they projected that the region's share of total U.S. financial employment, by their definition, would decline from 15.6% in 1956 to 13.8% in 1985. This forecast was closer to the actual outcome than these authors' expectation regarding nationwide financial industry employment growth. CBP data indicate that the RPA region's share of total U.S. financial services employment decreased from 18.9 to 14.9% between 1956 and 1986, and Bureau of Labor Statistics data show New York City's share of total U.S. FIRE employment declined from 15.3 to 8.5% over the same period (Robbins & Terleckyj, 1960, p. 179; U.S. Census Bureau, 2018; U.S. Department of Commerce; U.S. Department of Health Education and Welfare, 1958). The effect of extremely rapid growth nationwide in combination with a moderate decrease in the region's share of total industry employment was that the finance sector was a notable relative bright spot in New York's late-postwar economic history. Between 1956 and 1986, while total regional employment increased by 52%, the number of finance sector jobs rose by 165%. In contrast to the insufficiently pessimistic forecasts for freight-handling and manufacturing, therefore, Robbins and Terleckyj's projection of 1985 regional finance industry employment was insufficiently optimistic. Their expectation of about a 70% increase was less than half the actual pace.

It is worth noting at this point, although the relevance will only be apparent in the context of the next chapter, that the growth of New York's financial services industry did not follow a stable trajectory between 1956 and 1986. Between the late-1960s and mid-1970s, the

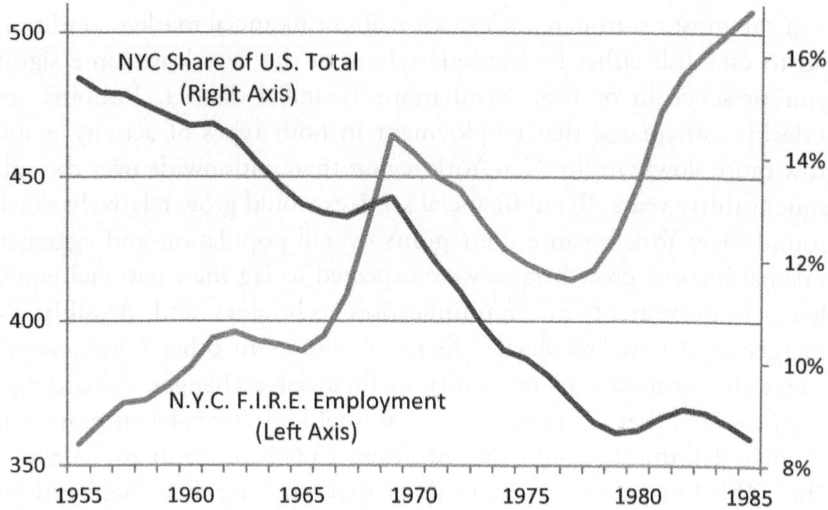


**Fig. 15.1** Finance, insurance, and real estate employment in New York City (U.S. Bureau of Labor Statistics, 2018)

securities industry, nationwide and, especially, locally, experienced a boom in total employment, followed by a dramatic bust, followed by a recovery (Fig. 15.1). Between 1965 and 1968, as more and more investors began seeking protection from rising inflation and as a nearly 50-year, nearly uninterrupted stock market rally reached its peak, activity on all stock exchanges began rising rapidly. Daily New York Stock Exchange volumes doubled between 1964 and 1968. This caught securities firms, which had barely begun exploring potential computer applications for transaction processing, by surprise. Hiring large numbers of inexperienced clerks did not prevent backlogs of uncleared trades and delayed payments from accumulating, and the resulting paperwork crisis forced several well-established firms into liquidation. After 1968, as the stock market entered a 14-year decline, trading volumes stabilized, cost-effective computer technology became available, securities industry profitability came under pressure as fixed commissions on stock trades were eliminated, and, in response, Wall Street firms reduced staffing levels substantially. It was not until the stock market had begun to recover in the early 1980s that financial services employment began to increase.

Figure 15.1 illustrates the boom-bust-recovery pattern, but it also indicates that the employment gains and losses associated with these fluctuations were concentrated in New York; the City's share of national FIRE employment has been declining on a trend basis, as one would expect given the region's decreasing share of U.S. population. But note also that the City's share tends to stabilize when employment in the sector is growing rapidly. This stands to reason in the case of the paperwork crisis and its aftermath because most transactions cleared in New York City. The next section of this chapter will discuss some of the reasons, other than the late '60s spike in stock trading volume, for the growth of FIRE employment during the first two decades following the RPA Study. Subsequent chapters will return to this topic.

What the authors of *Money Metropolis*, quite understandably, failed to anticipate was the *financialization* of the U.S. and global economies. The RPA Study's explicit assumption that nationwide growth in financial services employment would be no more than a little faster or a little slower than overall workforce expansion was based on the *implicit* assumption that the basic functions of banks, insurance companies, and securities houses would remain unchanged over the forecast horizon. Commercial banks would continue to gather local retail deposits, lend money to domestic companies, and buy government bonds. Commissions paid by individual and institutional investors on stock and bond transactions would remain securities firms' principle source of revenues. Instead, by 1985 the functions of financial services business, especially in the banking and securities sectors, had begun to change fundamentally in ways that made them much more prominent among the full range of activities in the economy and also much more lucrative.

Economic sociologist Greta Krippner defines "financialization as a pattern of accumulation in which profits accrue primarily through financial channels rather than through trade and commodity production …'Financial' here refers to activities relating to the provision (or transfer) of liquid capital in expectation of future interest, dividends, or capital gains" (Krippner, 2005, p. 174). It is clear at this point that something along the lines of what Krippner describes has been occurring. This can be seen most clearly in the increased percentage of total national income accruing in the form of interest, dividends, and rents as

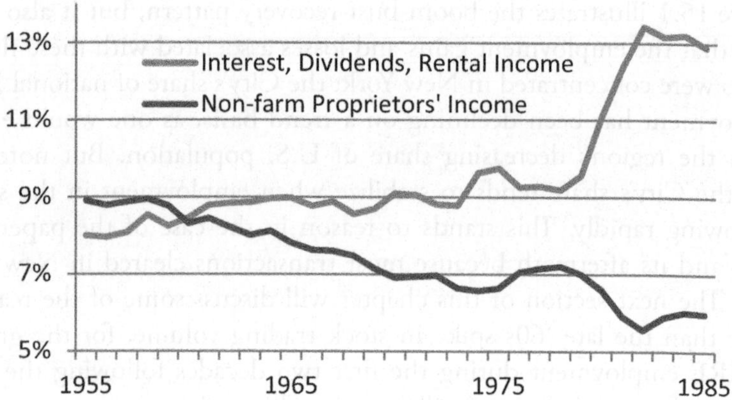


**Fig. 15.2** Shares of national income (U.S. Department of Commerce, Bureau of Economic Analysis, 2018)

returns on financial investments and the decreased share earned directly by hands-on business-owners (Fig. 15.2). It can also be seen in the growing percentage of the U.S. workforce engaged in financial services activity and, even more dramatically, in the share of total wage and salary income accruing to those employed in these industries (Fig. 15.3). The share of total corporate profits generated by financial activities has also risen substantially, both for companies that are primarily engaged in FIRE activities and for nonfinancial businesses in the form of interest and dividend revenues (Krippner, 2005, pp. 181–188).

The process of financialization began relatively recently and the concept has yet to gain much traction among mainstream economic historians. Those who have studied the phenomenon have devoted the bulk of their efforts to establishing that something of this nature is happening and to analyzing its effects, especially on the distribution of income. Less attention has been paid to understanding the causes of what has been occurring or to considering the broad range of its impacts. At least some of the changes in the financial services industry that had occurred by 1985 do, however, help explain why this sector generated more jobs in the New York region by the mid 1980s than the RPA Study authors anticipated.

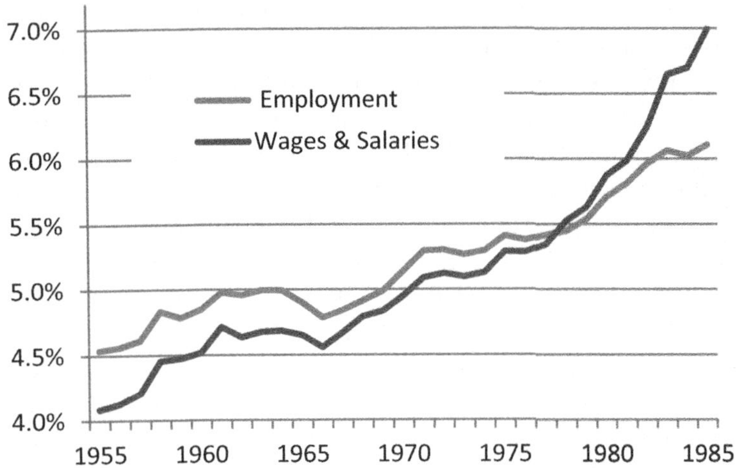


**Fig. 15.3** FIRE shares of national totals (U.S. Department of Commerce, Bureau of Economic Analysis, 2018)

For example, one of Robbins and Terleckyj's concerns about the future of New York's financial service sector was that the region's declining share of total U.S. population and personal income would limit local banks' future access to retail deposits, and therefore, their ability, relative to competitors in other regions, to provide loans to blue-chip borrowers. This might, indeed, have been a problem if commercial banks had continued to rely on retail deposits as essentially their sole routine source of funding. In August 1960, however, First National City Bank of New York began offering large corporations a new cash-management vehicle: the negotiable certificate of deposit (CD). From large depositors' point of view negotiable CDs combined the advantages of time and demand deposits, the former because they paid interest and the latter because they could be liquidated at any time via sale to a third party. As such the new instrument brought funds back into banks that corporate treasurers might otherwise have invested in commercial paper or Treasury Bills. From the issuing banks' point of view negotiable CDs provided a source of funds that could be dialed up and down to accommodate fluctuations in loan demand more easily than retail deposits through adjustments in the interest rates on offer. Although these new instruments were negotiable in principle, initially there was no ready secondary market. In early 1961, however, the Discount Corporation of New York, a major government bond dealer, began facilitating such transactions, and, thereafter, volume of this kind of paper began expanding rapidly. By year-end 1966 the roughly the $15 billion negotiable CDs outstanding accounted for about 20% of total national bank time-deposit liabilities and probably a substantially higher percentage of the large New York banks' (Board of Governors of the Federal Reserve System, 1968; Summers, 1980, p. 9; U.S. Department of the Treasury, Office of the Comptroller of the Currency, 2018).

Although it probably wasn't one of the bankers' intentions at the time, the development of this instrument also had the effect of loosening the previously tight linkage between the size of a money-center bank's balance sheet and the condition of the regional economy in which it was located. Thus the development of negotiable CDs, a manifestation of financialization, may have been one the developments than enabled employment at New York area depository institutions to grow almost three times faster than the total regional workforce (145% vs. 52%).

Not all of the early aspects of financialization were necessarily beneficial to institutions employing New Yorkers in New York. For example, the emergence of the Eurodollar money and bond markets drew a substantial volume of financial market activity to London that would, most likely, otherwise have taken place in New York. "Eurodollars" are U.S. currency invested in European assets: deposits at European banks, deposits at European branches of American banks, or US dollar denominated debt securities issued in Europe (for example, "Eurobonds").

European banks had been accepting U.S. dollar deposits during the interwar years, but the Depression, the War, and strict early postwar controls on the international capital flows had put an end to the practice. By the mid-1950s, however, and increasingly so thereafter conditions had evolved to the point where foreigners again had the means and the motive to hold U.S. dollar deposits outside the United States. They had the means because the Bretton Woods system, the collection of international agreements and institutions that governed international economic relations for the first 27 postwar years, facilitated the rapid recovery of the European and Japanese economies. U.S. businesses responded by purchasing business assets abroad, mostly to establish and expand multinational operations. Bretton Woods also established the U.S. dollar as the world's only reliably stable currency. Europeans, therefore, had an incentive to retain at least some dollar balances. Thus, Europeans were accumulating dollars.

Now they might have chosen to deposit their dollar holdings in U.S. banks, but by and large they did not because U.S. financial regulations provided a motive for keeping these funds "offshore." Most notably the Federal Reserve Board's Regulation Q, which capped the interest rate U.S. banks could pay on deposits, created an opportunity for European banks to compete for these funds successfully by offering slightly higher yields. For example, Britain's Midland Bank paid $1^7/_8$% on the first postwar Eurodollar deposit, which was $^7/_8$% above the then-current Regulation Q cap. UK regulators, who, all else held equal, would probably have preferred that local bank deposits be denominated in sterling, could have impeded the emergence of Eurodollar facilities. For the most part, they chose not to do so, in part to support London's role as an international financial center (Frieden, 2006, pp. 278–300; Schenk, 1998).

U.S. government policy also unintentionally fostered the development of the Eurobond market. Chapters 10 and 12 described how foreign bond issues sold in the U.S. market had become an increasingly important component of international capital flows during the twentieth century's first three decades and also an important line of business for New York's investment banks. This activity resumed during the early postwar decades. By the mid-1960s, however, the U.S. government had become concerned that foreigners were holding too many dollars. Under the Bretton Woods agreements, the U.S. Treasury had the obligation to buy gold from foreigners in exchange for dollars at $35 per ounce. If too many Europeans decided to avail themselves of this opportunity, the U.S. might risk running out of gold. Under such circumstances, the Federal Reserve might feel forced to induce foreign investors to retain their U.S. currency by raising U.S. interest rates at cyclically inopportune times. To head off this eventuality, the Kennedy and Johnson administrations adopted a series of policies aimed at curtailing the outflow of capital. One of these was an Interest Equalization Tax ("IET"), a levy on U.S. residents' purchases of securities issued by foreign entities. The IET, which was first imposed under President Kennedy in 1963, had the effect of increasing the effective interest cost to foreign issuers of bonds underwritten in the United States (Hayes & Hubbard, 1990, pp. 32–33).

By the early 1960s, however, European investors, who had been important buyers of foreign issues underwritten in New York, had accumulated enough U.S. currency offshore so that borrowers whose obligations would have been subject to the tax could meet their dollar financing needs by issuing bonds in London that would be exempt from the IET. Despite warnings that the IET and other such policies policy would do little more than shift financial activity that might otherwise have taken place in New York to London, the IET was raised and extended repeatedly. It was not finally abolished until 1974; three years after President Nixon eliminated the problem the IET was intended to address by abandoning the country's Bretton Woods commitments. By that point, however, the Eurobond market was well established and able to flourish without the extra incentive provided by the IET. By 1985 Eurobond issuance, mostly executed in London, totaled $136 billion, a significant volume in the context of that year's $761 billion total increase in debt securities outstanding in the U.S. (Board of Governors of the Federal Reserve System, 2018; Hayes & Hubbard, 1990, p. 36).

Most of the work involved in underwriting and trading Eurobonds took place in London, at first mostly at European banks. As the market expanded, however, New York-headquartered Banks began capturing a large share of this business through their London branch offices or affiliates. In 1963 and 1964, for example, only two US-based firms, Kuhn Loeb & Co. and White Weld & Co., appeared on the list of the top-ten lead managers of Eurobond offerings. Together these two accounted for 11% of that biennium's $551 million Eurobond offerings. By 1968, six U.S. firms (Morgan Stanley, Lehman Brothers, White Weld, Kuhn Loeb, Goldman Sachs, and First Boston) accounted for 59% of that single year's $2.2 billion total offerings. It is likely, therefore, that at least some of the work associated with Eurobond market activity took place in New York. It is also likely that New York's share of this activity has increased over time. Once the repeal of the IET eliminated the economic disincentive for U.S. residents to buy these securities, domestic institutional investors could and did begin buying Eurobonds when doing so was advantageous. So it is unclear how much the shift in the underwriting of non-U.S. entities' dollar bond issues to London impeded the growth of finance industry employment in New York. That said, the development of the Eurodollar and Eurobond markets highlights a recurrent theme in the recent history of New York's financial services industry: a Wall Street vs. City of London rivalry. The story of how the Eurodollar and Eurobond markets developed also highlights British regulators' support for London's role as an international financial center in contrast to U.S. policymakers' apparent indifference to New York's (Hayes & Hubbard, 1990, pp. 37, 39; Schenk, 1998, p. 234).

## Any New Regional Specialties?

The RPA Study's forecasting methodology involved careful consideration of the outlook for the New York region's major mid-1950s export or "base" industries: freight handling, women's apparel manufacturing, specialty electronic equipment, printing and publishing, and financial services. This approach was based on an additional assumption, namely, that no additional important base industries would emerge in the region over the subsequent three decades. This assumption was unstated. It turns out to have been correct.

The U.S. Census Bureau's CBP data support comparisons of 1956 and 1986 regional employment totals for 62 individual industries. Employment in only two of these industries grew at a faster rate in the RPA region than in the United States as a whole over this 30-year period. They were (a) Local and Suburban Transit and Interurban Highway Passenger Transport and (b) Museums, Art Galleries and Botanical and Zoological Gardens. The former is not a base or export industry. The latter is emblematic of an important regional strength which has

**Table 15.2** Industries in which 22-county employment grew by more than 100,000 between 1956 and 1986 (U.S. Census Bureau, 2018; U.S. Department of Commerce; U.S. Department of Health Education and Welfare, 1958)

| Industry | Employment growth, 1956–1986 |
|---|---|
| Health services | 550,963 |
| Miscellaneous business services | 465,042 |
| Educational services | 178,519 |
| Depository institutions | 145,352 |
| Eating and drinking places | 144,950 |
| Security & commodity brokers, dealers, exchanges & services | 138,433 |

become increasingly important during the current phase of the region's economic history. With total 1986 local employment of less than 8,000, however, this sector cannot have had a much impact on the overall regional economy.[5]

A list of the industries that added the most regional jobs over the period reinforces the conclusion that no new large industrial base industry emerged over the period, but also highlights the difficulty of distinguishing precisely between "export" and "local service" industries. Table 15.2 lists the six industries that added more than 100,000 jobs in the 22-county over the RPA Study's three-decade forecast horizon. The continuing absolute and relative strength of the two financial services sectors has already been discussed. In a major metropolitan center like New York, the other four industries include some activities that primarily meet the needs of the local population and some that serve clients nation- or worldwide. The clientele of New York's miscellaneous business services sector, which includes accounting and advertising firms, are not confined to the region. And even local clients of these service firms may, themselves, be regional export industries that choose to locate in New York, in part, because of the ready availability of world-class business services in the City. Patients from around the country

[5]These are all the two-digit Standard Industrial Classifications for which sufficient information is available for both 1956 and 1986 (U.S. Census Bureau, 2018; U.S. Department of Commerce; U.S. Department of Health Education and Welfare, 1958).

and the world travel to New York for treatment at the City's tertiary care teaching hospitals, and students from around the country and the world attend the region's colleges and universities. And, in the City with five of North America's 13 Michelin three-star restaurants, the region's economic "export" base may even include a segment of the retail food services industry. These industries did grow robustly over the period and some component of their growth may have expanded the local production of services that were sold to customers outside the New York region, but none of them can be could be considered "new" during the postwar decades.

## Conclusion

One aim of this chapter was to explain why the population of the New York region grew only about one-fifth as fast as the nation as a whole between 1950 and 1980. It is tempting to dismiss this question with the answer that, given the rapid southwestward shift of the U.S. population during this period, it should not be surprising that any given northeastern metropolitan region's growth was relatively slow. To be sure, the population center of the United States moved an additional 182 miles toward the Sunbelt between 1950 and 1980, the fastest pace since the official closing of the western frontier in 1890 (U.S. Census Bureau, 2018).

No doubt the growing attractiveness of the Sunbelt, particularly after the advent of affordable home air-conditioning technology, slowed the New York area's growth as it did that of other metropolitan regions in the northeastern quadrant of the United States. But, by itself, this explanation cannot be complete for two reasons. First, population growth rates varied over a wide range across northeastern metropolitan areas, and New York's performance was below average within this group. There are 33 metropolitan areas in the United States that had reached a population of one million or more by 1990. The populations of the 12 northeastern metropolitan areas in this group grew by 35% on average between 1950 and 1980. The average growth rate for the other 21 was 208%. Among the northeastern group, however, the three-decade growth rate ranged from a low of 12.0% (Buffalo) to a high of 81.2% (Minneapolis—St. Paul). The New York metropolitan area's population grew by 26.8 over the period. So, while the sunbelt/rust-belt dichotomy accounts for a great deal, there is still a substantial amount of variation among the laggards left to be explained.

Second, and more importantly, the analyses presented in this chapter indicate the New York region's particularly sluggish employment growth during this period can be traced to specific changes in the situations of New York's principal early postwar base industries: freight handling, apparel manufacturing, electronics, printing and publishing, and financial services. Few of these specific changes involved a shift in the locus of activity to the sunbelt. The exception to this generalization might be the freight-handling industries, as West Coast and Gulf ports became more efficient points of entry. Even in this case, however, the mechanization of freight handling associated with containerization, a development in which the Port of New York led the way, may account for more of the dramatic job losses than the decline in the region's market share.

Initially, some of the relatively low skill apparel industry work that would have taken place in New York during earlier decades moved to the South Atlantic states or to Los Angeles. Increasingly by the mid-1980s, however, the destination of footloose garment manufacturing was not in the Southern or Western states, but outside the United States. Nor did the physical-production components of the printing and publishing industry show any particular tendency to move closer to Arizona or Texas. Even after the 182-mile southwestward shift of the nation's population center, the Midwest remained the optimal region from which to ship goods nationwide. To be sure, Silicon Valley is very much in the sun-belt, and it is easy to understand why Fairchild Semiconductor's founders would have been reluctant to leave their new homes near Palo Alto. But during the period under discussion the other hotbed of integrated circuitry's applications was in metropolitan Boston.

The authors of *Money Metropolis* expressed some concern that the population shifts within the United States in combination with improved communication technology and the emergence of electronic trading might lead to the development of new geographic agglomeration of tertiary financial services and attendant business services activity, presumably somewhere in the West, that could rival New York. That had not happened by 1985. It still hasn't; quite the contrary, in fact. Before we can focus on what happened beyond the RPA Study's forecast horizon, however, we must relate the sorry tale of the economic, political, social, and biomedical crisis that closed New York's short twentieth century.

## References


Board of Governors of the Federal Reserve System. (1968). *Fifty-Fourth Annual Report Covering Operations for the Year 1967.* Washington.

Board of Governors of the Federal Reserve System. (2018). *All Sectors; Total Debt Securities; Liability [ASTDSL].* Retrieved from FRED, Federal Reserve Bank of St. Louis https://fred.stlouisfed.org/series/ASTDSL.

Chinitz, B. (1960). *Freight and the Metropolis: The Impact of America's Transportation Revolutions on the New York Region.* Cambridge: Harvard University Press.

Frieden, J. A. (2006). *Global Capitalism: Its Fall and Rise in the Twentieth Century.* New York: W. W. Norton.

Gustafson, W. E. (1959). Printing and Publishing. In M. Hall (Ed.), *Made in New York: Case Studies in Metropolitan Manufacturing* (pp. 135–240). Cambridge, MA: Harvard University Press.

Hayes, S. L., & Hubbard, P. M. (1990). *Investment Banking: A Tale of Three Cities.* Cambridge, MA: Harvard Business School Press.

Helfgott, R. B. (1959). Women's and Children's Apparel. In M. Hall (Ed.), *Made in New York: Case Studies in Metropolitan Manufacturing* (pp. 19–134). Cambridge, MA: Harvard University Press.

Hurd. (1959). M. Hall, *Made in New York: Case Studies in Metropolitan Manufacturing.* Cambridge, MA: Harvard University Press.

Kenney, M., & von Burg, U. (1999). Technology, Entrepreneurship and Path Dependence: Industrial Clustering and Silicon Valley and Route 128. *Industrial and Corporate Change, 8*(1), 67–103.

Klepper, S. (2010). The Origin and Growth of Industry Clusters: The Making of Silicon Valley and Detroit. *Journal of Urban Economics, 67,* 15–32.

Krippner, G. R. (2005). The Financialization of the American Economy. *Socio-Economic Review, 3*(2), 173–208.
Levinson, M. (2006). Container Shipping and the Decline of New York, 1955–1975. *The Business History Review, 80*(1), 49–80.
Miller, M. H. (1986). Financial Innovation: The Last Twenty Years and the Next. *Journal of Financial and Quantitative Analysis, 21*(4), 148–176.
Murray, L. A. (1995). Unravelling Employment Trends in Textiles and Apparel. *Monthly Labor Review, 118*(8), 62–72.
Olley, G. S., & Pakes, A. (1996). The Dynamics of Productivity in the Telecommunications Equipment Industry. *Econometrica, 64*(6), 1263–1297.
Port Authority of New York and New Jersey. (1986). *Comprehensive Annual Financial Report for the Year Ended December 31, 1985*. New York: PANYNJ.
Robbins, S. M., & Terleckyj, N. E. (1960). *Money Metropolis: A Locational Study of Financial Activities in the New York Region*. Cambridge, MA: Harvard University Press.
Schenk, C. R. (1998). The Origins of the Eurodollar Market in London: 1955–1963. *Explorations in Economic History, 35*, 221–238.
Summers, B. J. (1980, August). Negotiable Certificates of Deposit. *Economic Review, Federal Reserve Bank of Richmond*.
U.S. Bureau of Labor Statistics. (2018). *Employment, Hours, and Earnings from the Current Employment Statistics Survey (National) SIC*. Retrieved from https://data.bls.gov/cgi-bin/dsrv; https://www.census.gov/data/datasets/1986/econ/cbp/1986-cpb.html.
U.S. Census Bureau. (2018). *County Business Patterns, 1956*. Retrieved from https://www.census.gov/data/datasets/1986/econ/cbp/1986-cpb.html.
U.S. Department of Commerce, Bureau of Economic Analysis. (2018). *Table 6.1B National Income Without Capital Cunsumption Adjustment by Industry, Interactive Data, GDP and Personal Income Data*. https://www.bea.gov/iTable/iTable.cfm?reqid=19&step=2#reqid=19&step=3.
U.S. Department of Commerce; U.S. Department of Health Education and Welfare. (1958). *County Business Patterns, First Quarter 1956, Parts 1, 2, and 3*. Washington: U.S. Government Printing Office.
U.S. Department of Transportation, Maritime Administration. (1984). *Containerized Cargo Characteristics, Calendar Year 1983*. Washington: U.S. Government Printing Office.
U.S. Department of the Treasury, Office of the Comptroller of the Currency. (2018). *The Negotiable CD: National Bank Innovation in the 1960s*.

Retrieved from History: 150 Years of the OCC https://www.occ.treas.gov/about/what-we-do/history/150th-negotiable-cd-article.html.

Vernon, R. (1960). *Metropolis 1985: An Interpretation of the Findings of the New York Metropolitan Region Study*. Cambridge, MA: Harvard University Press.

Wee, H. (2013, September 23). *'Made in USA' Fuels New Manufacturing Hubs in Apparel*. Retrieved from CNBC https://www.cnbc.com/2013/09/23/inside-made-in-the-usa-showcasing-skilled-garment-workers.html.

# 16

# The Perfect Storm and the Turning Point

The economic history of New York City to date does not have a plot line, but if it did, the mid-1970s would mark its climax. By the evening of October 16, 1975, it had become clear that the plans initiated the previous spring to enable the essentially insolvent City of New York to continue providing essential services while meeting its obligations to its lenders was not working. Accordingly, Mayor Abraham Beame ordered preparation of a statement to be released the next morning, which began as follows: "I have been advised by the Comptroller that the City of New York has insufficient cash on hand to meet debt obligations due today" (Nussbaum, 2015). The statement went on to announce that, in order to continue providing essential services, the City would ask a State Supreme Court judge for protection from creditors' immediate demands, that is, for a declaration of bankruptcy. As it turned out, the statement was never released because the City, saved by a cash infusion from the United Federation of Teachers (UFT) pension fund, was able to make the required payment. But there was a high price for New York's residents, taxpayers, and employees to pay as the City gradually and painfully recovered from its 1975 fiscal crisis.



A. Gurwitz, *Atlantic Metropolis*, Palgrave Studies in American Economic History,
https://doi.org/10.1007/978-3-030-13352-8_16

A perfect storm is defined as "detrimental or calamitous situation or event arising from the powerful combined effect of a unique set of circumstances" (Collins English Dictionary, 2018). It was, indeed, a unique set of macroeconomic, industrial, demographic, and political circumstances, many of them tracing their origins to the early in the short twentieth century, that had brought the City to this exigency. The years immediately following 1975, however, also marked the nadir of the City's postwar economic contraction. Total nonfarm payroll employment in New York City had peaked in 1968 at 3.8 million and fell to a postwar low of 3.2 million in 1977. The subsequent recovery began almost imperceptibly; total local employment did not surpass its old high until 2010, and the City's economy continued to underperform the nation as a whole. A recovery did, nevertheless, begin by the end of the 1970s.

This chapter tallies the circumstances that combined to precipitate the 1975 crisis and presents evidence that at least some of those conditions had changed in important ways by 1980.

## The Circumstances

The events surrounding New York's near bankruptcy were fraught with high political drama, and most of the published accounts of the episode focus on the interactions among senior elected and appointed government officials, public employee union leaders, bankers, and political activists. No doubt different public policies adopted over the years prior to 1975 would have led to a different fiscal outcome, and, accordingly, the political context will come under scrutiny below. But both the policies that were implemented in the years leading up to the crisis and the effect they had on the City's fiscal situation were driven in large part by demographic, political, and macroeconomic developments on the national level and by the sharp contraction of the City's economic base through the second and third postwar decades. No combination of local public policies could have altered these trends, and it is safe to say that for New York City by the mid-1970s some form of severe fiscal difficulty was inevitable.

## Climatic Conditions

Providing public services to members of the baby-boom generation through early childhood to young adulthood was the principal demographic challenge facing U.S. state and local governments during the postwar decades because these are the jurisdictions that bear responsibility for elementary and secondary education and for public safety. Starting in the early 1950s, school districts had to expand their physical plants and recruit personnel. State colleges and universities and, in the case of New York, city-financed institutions of higher education had to expand capacity by the late 1960s. And during the 1970s, law enforcement services had to cope with the largest cohort ever of the most crime-prone age group.

State and municipal governments were also influenced and affected by the same ideological mind-set that inspired and bedeviled the Johnson administration in Washington: rising expectations regarding the public sector's ability to solve social and economic problems combined increasing distrust of and willingness to confront government institutions and officials (Heclo, 2005).

Developments in the bond market in general and the municipal bond market in particular must also be numbered among the unique set of circumstances that led to the City's fiscal crisis. As inflation rose through the late 1960s and early 1970s, bond buyers demanded higher interest rates to compensate for the expected diminution of their principal's purchasing power. Accordingly, yields on long-term U.S. government bonds rose from about 5.75% in January 1969 to 6.68% in January 1975. Yields on municipal bonds were initially lower than U.S. Treasuries' because the former were tax-exempt, but they increased by more. Between 1969 and 1975, yields on generic 20-year tax-exempt bonds rose from about 4.85 to 7.08% (Federal Reserve Bank of St. Louis, 2018). No doubt some proportion of this increase reflected investor concerns arising from New York City's fiscal problems, but it is also the case that the volume of municipal bonds on offer was increasing quickly. Between 1967 and 1974, the annual supply of new tax-exempt bond issues increased by 140% while over the same period nominal U.S. GDP rose by only 80%. At the same time, rising inflation and weak loan demand reduced commercial banks' profitability and reduced these institutions' appetite for tax-exempt investments (Shalala & Bellamy, 1976, pp. 1126–1127). To make matters much worse, in February 1975 the Urban Development Corporation, a New York State agency, announced that it had insufficient funds to redeem notes that were coming due at that time and no source of additional money. Default by an important issuer left investors wary of debt obligations with "New York" in the entity's name (Phillips-Fein, 2017, pp. 82–83).

## Stagflation

The macroeconomic setting in which New York's fiscal drama played out—slowing real GDP growth and rising inflation—was at least unhelpful and, in some respects, may have made matters much worse. After almost nine years of uninterrupted growth, the U.S. economy contracted through most of 1970. Then in late 1973, another recession began. This one went on for 16 months and was the longest such postwar episode up to that time (National Bureau of Economic Research, 2018). Thus, New York's fiscal crisis played out in the wake of back-to-back prolonged recessions. New York had severe economic problems of its own during the early 1970s independent of the national economic cycle, but stagnant or shrinking demand for the goods and services the City's businesses sold to buyers outside the region would have made matters at least somewhat worse. Further, given widespread economic weakness, the Gerald Ford administration may have been especially wary of providing fiscal assistance to City than they would have been during better times (Phillips-Fein, 2017, p. 93).

A second aspect of the early-1970s macroeconomic environment, rising inflation, also affected New York's fiscal situation, although in this case measuring the magnitude or even determining the direction of the impact would require additional research. In contrast to previous and subsequent experience, the 1970 and 1973–1975 recessions were accompanied by rising inflation. From the end of the Korean War in 1953 until 1965, U.S. consumer price index rose on average 1.4% at an annual rate. After 1965 inflation rose sharply, as the Federal Reserve policy sought to maintain healthy private sector economic growth despite rising Vietnam War and Great Society expenditures. From 1966 through 1970, the average inflation rate was 4.3% and over the five-year period that ended with New York's fiscal crisis the annual rate of inflation averaged 6.8% (Federal Reserve Bank of St. Louis, 2018).

Inflation increases government expenditures by raising the nominal cost of providing services. This was certainly the case in New York in the years leading up to the financial crisis. David Greytak, Richard Gustely, and Robert J. Dinkelmeyer found that rising prices accounted for about 30% of the total increase in New York City's government expenditures between 1965 and 1972 (Greytak, Gustely, & Dinkelmeyer, 1974). Inflation, however, also augments government revenues by boosting a jurisdiction's nominal tax base. Whether the combined impact of the two effects creates net fiscal gains or stringencies depends on which category of budget items rises more rapidly as the price level increases. The general conclusion of studies of the subject is that tax revenues are more elastic with respect to the general price level than are government expenditures and that, therefore, all else held equal, rising inflation tends to improve governments' fiscal situation. Most of these analyses, however, have dealt with the central governments of developed countries, and there are reasons to expect that the effects of inflation on local government tax revenues might be different.

Specifically, if there is a long lag between the time when a tax liability is created and the time when tax payments show up as cash in government accounts, the prices of the goods and services governments buy may have risen substantially by the time the money to pay for those goods and services becomes available. For example, when income tax is withheld from a worker's wages, the lag between the time when the liability is incurred and the time the government receives the revenues is minimal. By contrast, property taxes may be due only once a year and may be based on the previous year's assessed value of the property, which itself may reflect the prices of real estate transactions that took place several years in the past. Further, if statutory interest charges levied on delinquent taxes are below market rates, a likely occurrence during a period of rising inflation, property owners will find it advantageous to delay payments beyond their due date. And especially hard-pressed landlords facing higher tax bills but stagnant rents may abandon properties, in which case revenues may not arrive until several years after the initial tax liability was created. Thus, inflation might be detrimental to the fiscal condition of a government that relies heavily on property taxes, especially so if the jurisdiction's taxpayers are prone to delinquencies (Tanzi, 1977).

It seems likely that rising inflation would have done more harm than good to New York's fiscal condition. Property taxes accounted for 62% of the City's local tax revenues during the 1970–1971 fiscal year. And as the City's economy shrank and as inflation reduced the return on rent-controlled properties, the annual volume of tax delinquencies rose from $115 million in 1964–1965 to $502 million in 1974–1975. To make matters worse, until procedures were revised in 1976, it took four years for the City to foreclose on an abandoned property (Morris, 1980, pp. 132, 143).

## Local Conditions

By themselves, early-1970s recessions would not necessarily have precipitated a fiscal crisis. After all, New York had, with some help from the State and Federal governments, managed its way through much worse national economic downturns in the past and would do so in the future. And on this occasion, other large, northeastern and Midwestern cities managed to cope with fiscal challenges without coming as close to insolvency. Why did these developments lead to a crisis in New York City and not, until Cleveland's 1978 brush with bankruptcy, elsewhere?

For one thing, the recessions of 1970 and 1973–1975 hit New York's economy especially hard. A disproportionate share of the contraction of employment New York's goods-related base industries, the reasons for which were detailed in the previous chapter, took place during the early 1970s. Total manufacturing employment in the City decreased by 611,000 over the 30 years between 1955 and 1985. The single five-year period between 1970 and 1975, or 17% of the three decades, accounted for 37% of the job losses in this sector.

New York's especially poor performance in manufacturing during this period may reflect another manifestation of the nation's contemporaneous economic challenges, an overvalued dollar. Through the 1950s and 1960s, Western Europe and Japan recovered from wartime devastation and their economies caught up with the United States in productivity and production. And by the late 1960s, the Asian tiger economies, South Korea,

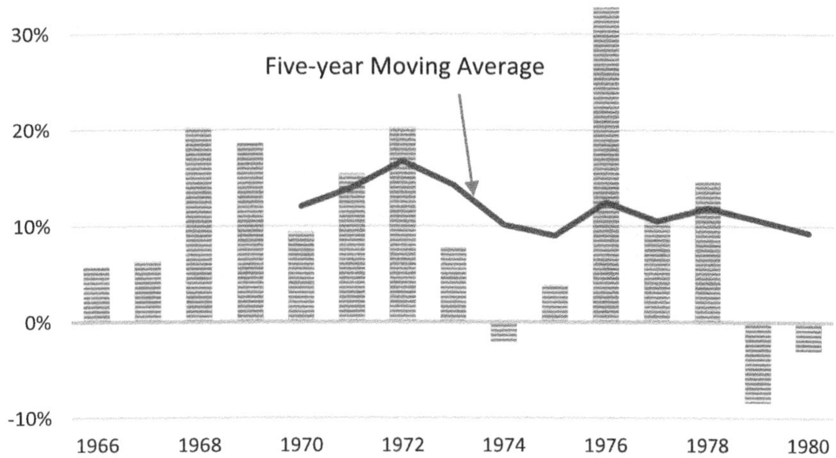


**Fig. 16.1** Year-on-year growth rate of the U.S. dollar real value of U.S. imports of apparel for consumption, market value in country of origin (National Academy of Engineering; Commission on Engineering and Technical Systems, 1983, p. 41)

Taiwan, Hong Kong, and Singapore, had initiated their export-driven development programs. Under such circumstances, all these countries' currencies would have appreciated against the U.S. dollar, if they had been allowed to. Under the Bretton Woods agreement, however, the value of the dollar was fixed, and the U.S. currency became increasingly overvalued. As a result, imports surged and exports faltered, until President Nixon abandoned Bretton Woods in August 1971 setting off a series of dollar devaluations that continued until 1973. The garment industry, New York City's largest manufacturing sector, would have been hit particularly hard by a sharp increase in imports; U.S. apparel imports increased by an average of 16% per year between 1968 and 1972 (Fig. 16.1). And competition from low-cost producers abroad evidently had a particularly adverse effect on the City's garmet manufacturers. Between 1970 and 1975, while total U.S. apparel industry employment decreased by 8.8%, the number of New Yorkers engaged in the sector fell by 27.2%, the largest five-year percentage decrease on record until the half decade ending in 2001 (U.S. Bureau of Labor Statisitcs, 2018a, b).

To make local matters worse, the bulk of the employment bust that followed Wall Street's late-1960s paperwork crisis, as detailed in the

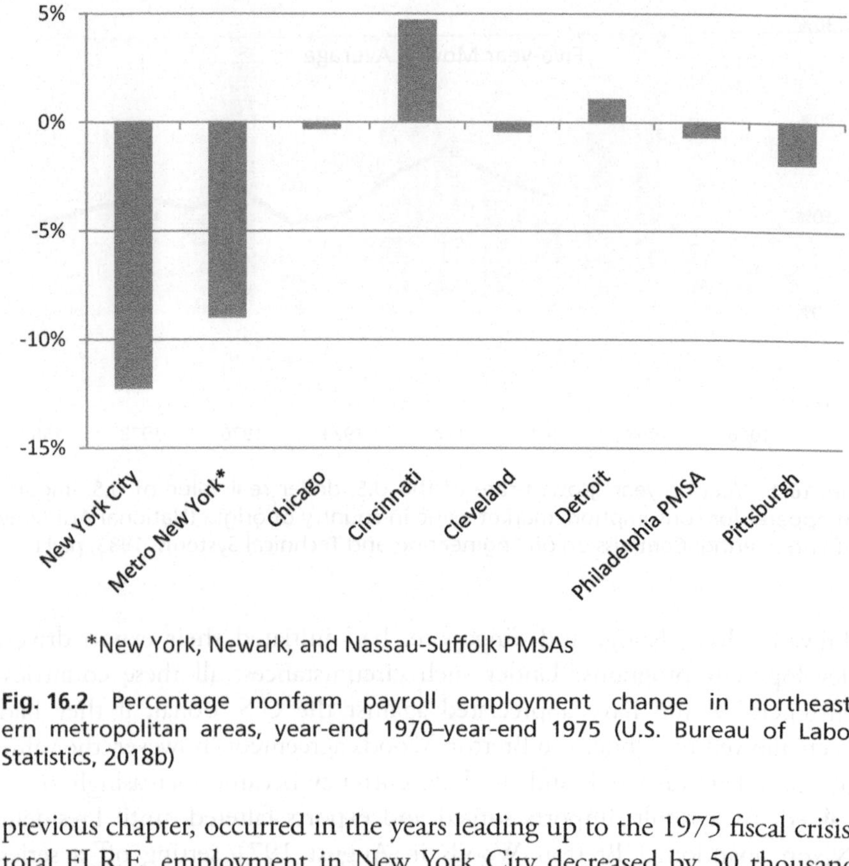


**Fig. 16.2** Percentage nonfarm payroll employment change in northeastern metropolitan areas, year-end 1970–year-end 1975 (U.S. Bureau of Labor Statistics, 2018b)

previous chapter, occurred in the years leading up to the 1975 fiscal crisis; total FI.R.E. employment in New York City decreased by 50 thousand between 1969 and 1975 (U.S. Bureau of Labor Statistics, 2018b).

Finally, as Fig. 16.2 indicates, although one cannot say that other large northeastern and Midwestern metropolitan areas were thriving during the period, New York was doing much worse than the others.[1]

[1]The difference between New York and the other metropolitan regions is real and substantial, but the chart may overstate the case somewhat. The Bureau of Labor Statistics publishes monthly employment statistics for all metropolitan areas and for a few large central cities, one of which is New York. Because, in comparison with other cities, New York is large relative to its metropolitan area in terms of land area, population, and employment the metropolitan area statistics for this region may reflect the impact of the central city urban crisis of the 1960s and 1970s more than, say, the data for metropolitan Philadelphia or Chicago.

## Social Democracy Augmented, Then Confounded

The social democratic political culture that developed in New York through the first half of the twentieth century influenced the City government's response to the changing economic circumstances of the years leading up to the financial crisis. By 1960, New York was already endowed with a uniquely extensive and expensive array of City-owned, operated, and funded institutions that served functions not provided to the same extent or at all by most other municipal governments in the United States. These included 28 City hospitals, four senior and three community colleges, and 106 thousand units of public housing (Bloom, 2008, pp. 270–276; Morris, 1980, p. 44; Sayre & Kaufman, 1960, p. 777).

Further, New York's political traditions left the administrations of Governor Nelson Rockefeller (1959–1973) and Mayors Robert Wagner (1954–1965) and John Lindsay (1966–1973) ill-equipped and disinclined to resist increasingly militant and often mutually incompatible demands from public employee unions for higher pay and lighter workloads, from communities of color for more responsive, more effective, and more generous programs, and from middle-class households for high-quality public services and low taxes.

To make matters even more challenging for the political leadership, the Charter under which the City operated as an instrumentality of the State of New York assigned more responsibilities to the local general government than was generally the case in other large urban areas. The budget of the City's public elementary, secondary, and post-secondary schools, for example, which was governed by a separate school board in many other large cities, fell under the fiscal purview of the Mayor and City Council in New York. Likewise, the management and financing of welfare programs, an increasingly expensive and politically charged field of government activity during the 1960s and 1970s, falls under the purview of separate county governments elsewhere in New York State and nationwide but not in New York City. In their 1974 analysis of New York City economy and tax base Roy W. Bahl, Alan K. Campbell, and David Greytak distinguished between common functions that are performed by almost all City governments and variable functions that are assigned to some but not all large urban municipalities. The common functions include street maintenance, parks and recreation, libraries, water supply, police, fire, and sanitation services. Education, welfare, health and hospitals, and housing belong to the variable functions category. Among the 10 largest U.S. cities in 1970, only New York, Baltimore, and Washington, DC, fulfilled all of the listed variable functions. The variable functions accounted for the bulk of the City's expenditures and were growing more rapidly than the common municipal responsibilities. In 1966, education, welfare, health, hospitals, and housing accounted for 76% of total New York City expenditures, and in 1972 that figure had risen to 82% (Bahl, Campbell, & Greytak, 1974, pp. 169–173).

At the same time as it assigned the City government a very broad range of responsibilities, the municipal Charter tightly constrained the City's fiscal flexibility. Even the most modest increases in tax rates or modifications of tax structures and, of course, any changes in State aid formulas had to be authorized by the Legislature and Governor in Albany.

Thus, through the 1960s rising needs and demands for City government services and money arrived on the doorstep of Gracie Mansion, the Mayor's official residence, where, in general, they were not unwelcome. There is an interesting story behind each broad category of City government spending. These individual sagas have been recounted in dramatic detail in numerous publications.[2] Some broad quantitative generalizations regarding trends with respect to expenditures and revenues will suffice here to highlight the path to the 1975 crisis.

Total real (i.e., inflation-adjusted) City government spending, aggregate and per capita, rose massively (Fig. 16.3) and across the board (Table 16.1) between 1961 and 1975. By 1966, the growth had brought per capita spending by New York on common functions performed by all large municipalities, roughly one-quarter of the City's total spending, to about one standard deviation above the average for

[2]These include Morris (1980), Roberts (2010), Brecher, Horton, Cropf, and Dean (1993), and Shefter (1992).

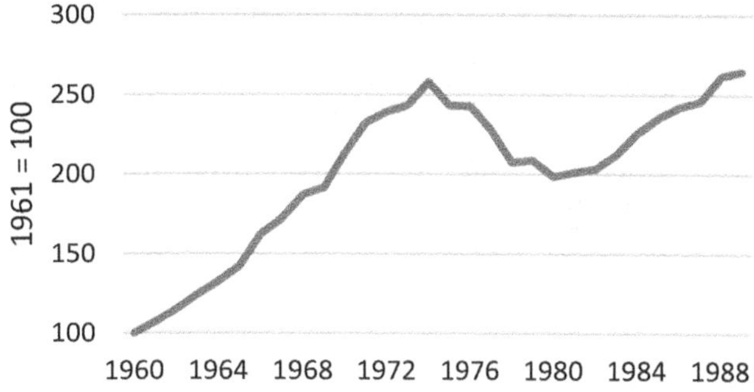


**Fig. 16.3** Trend in real per capita New York City government spending, 1961–1989 (Brecher et al., 1993, p. 20)

Chicago, Los Angeles, Philadelphia, Detroit, Houston, Baltimore, Dallas, and Cleveland. And although in subsequent years, the growth in common-function spending may have been more rapid elsewhere than in New York, in 1972 New York was still spending about one-half of a standard deviation more than the eight-city average. And in 1972, the City was spending 50% more than Baltimore, which had the same broad range of responsibilities as New York and a bit more even than Washington, DC, which performed the functions of both a state and a municipal government (Bahl et al., 1974).

Table 16.1 indicates that real spending on every City government function increased between 1961 and 1975, some more than others and some more during some time periods than others, but all quite substantially. The only marked absolute decrease from one of the years listed in Table 16.1 to the next was for transportation between 1961 and 1969. This probably reflects the incorporation between those two years of the City's Transit Authority into the Metropolitan Transportation Authority (MTA), a State agency. This reorganization reduced, but did not eliminate, the City government's contribution to the operating budgets of the subway and bus systems. Total spending growth was a bit slower during the 1969–1975 period than it had been during the 1960s, but it remained quite high compared with other measures of economic activity; the U.S. economy, for example, grew at an average annual real rate of only 1.2% between 1969 and 1975.

**Table 16.1** City of New York real total spending by function, 1961, 1969, 1975 (Brecher et al., 1993, p. 21)

| Function | Percent of FY1975 expenditures (%) | Annualized rate of change (%) | | | |
|---|---|---|---|---|---|
| | | 1961–1969 | 1969–1975 | 1975–1983 | 1983–1989 |
| **Primarily redistributive functions** | **33** | **13** | **3** | **−3** | **3** |
| Public assistance | 12 | 17 | −1 | −6 | −1 |
| Health | 10 | 9 | 1 | −3 | 5 |
| Social services | 10 | 13 | 10 | −1 | 3 |
| Housing | 2 | 6 | 20 | 1 | 12 |
| **Primarily development functions** | **11** | **0** | **18** | **−7** | **7** |
| Infrastructure | 9 | 7 | 15 | −11 | 6 |
| Transportation | 3 | −17 | 31 | 2 | 7 |
| **Education** | **29** | **9** | **5** | **−4** | **4** |
| Elementary and secondary | 24 | 9 | 4 | −3 | 4 |
| Higher | 5 | 12 | 10 | −18 | 6 |
| **Criminal justice** | **13** | **6** | **7** | **−4** | **8** |
| Police | 10 | 6 | 6 | −4 | 6 |
| Other | 3 | 4 | 9 | −4 | 14 |
| **Other allocative functions*** | 15 | 6 | 1 | −1 | 5 |
| Total | 100 | 8 | 5 | −4 | 5 |

*Brecher and Horton, et al., define "allocative functions" as expenditures that "are not viewed as having differential impacts among income groups or classes but as serving residents generally. Examples include refuse collection and fire protection" (Brecher et al., 1993, p. 19)

A breakdown with respect to who received the increased payments paints a similar picture (Table 16.2). The mid- to late 1960s were marked by a series of dramatic and disruptive disputes between the City government and one or another public employee union. At midnight on January 1, 1966, the moment John Lindsay began his first term as New York's 103rd mayor, for example, the members of the City's Transit Workers Union, who operated the subways and buses, left

**Table 16.2** New York City government real labor costs, 1961, 1969, 1975 (Brecher et al., 1993, p. 36)

| | 1961 | 1969 | 1975 | Average annualized % increase 1961–1969 | 1969–1975 |
|---|---|---|---|---|---|
| | Spending, 1982$, billions | | | | |
| Total spending | 8,572 | 16,216 | 21,139 | 8 | 5 |
| Total labor costs[a] | 4,559 | 7,841 | 10,198 | 7 | 4 |
| Salaries and wages | 3,706 | 6,330 | 6,804 | 7 | 1 |
| Pensions and other benefits | 853 | 1,512 | 2,403 | 7 | 8 |
| Number of employees[a] | 200,706 | 278,161 | 294,522 | 4 | 1 |
| Labor cost per employee (1982 dollars) | 22,715 | 28,190 | 34,626 | 3 | 3 |
| Labor cost, % of total spending | 53 | 48 | 48 | | |

[a]Includes Health and Hospitals Corporation employees

work on what would be a massively disruptive 12-day strike demanding larger pay increases and more flexible work rules than either the outgoing Wagner administration or the new Lindsay team were willing to offer. The workers were led, part of the time from a jail cell since the strike was, in fact, illegal, by Irish immigrant Michael Quill, a one-time American Labor Party member of the City Council and the personification of worker militancy. Then in 1968, Sanitation Department employees went on strike for seven days, also demanding higher pay and easier work schedules than the City was offering. During the seven-day strike, 10,000 tons of garbage per day piled up on the City's streets. Also in 1968, members of the UFT were on strike nearly continuously from the beginning of the school year until mid-November. The issue in this case was the degree of control mostly

**Table 16.3** City of New York, real total revenues by source, 1961, 1969, 1975 (Brecher et al., 1993, pp. 23, 24)

| Year | Borrowing | | Intergov. Aid | | Local | Total |
|---|---|---|---|---|---|---|
| | Capital | Operating | Capital | Operating | taxes | |
| Percent of total revenues | | | | | | |
| 1961 | 11 | 0 | 1 | 18 | 71 | 100 |
| 1969 | 8 | 2 | 1 | 32 | 59 | 100 |
| 1975 | 9 | 7 | 3 | 27 | 54 | 100 |
| 1983 | 5 | 0 | 2 | 34 | 59 | 100 |
| 1989 | 9 | 0 | 1 | 30 | 61 | 100 |
| Average annualized rate of change (%) | | | | | | |
| 1961–1969 | 3.3 | N.A. | 7.6 | 16.7 | 5.5 | 8.2 |
| 1969–1975 | 7.4 | 32.2 | 40.4 | 1.7 | 3.1 | 4.5 |
| 1975–1983 | −9.5 | N.A. | −7.9 | −0.6 | −2.3 | −3.4 |
| 1983–1989 | 13.8 | N.A. | −9.4 | 2.0 | 5.0 | 4.4 |

African-American community school boards would exercise over the continuing employment of mostly white UFT members.

The high drama surrounding these and other contract negotiations may have created the impression that a disproportionately large share of the growth in City government spending during this period was attributable to higher labor costs. Table 16.2 indicates, however, that, on the contrary, even as real total compensation per employee and the number of City workers increased substantially over the period, labor costs' share of total spending actually decreased somewhat between 1961 and 1969 and then held steady during the years leading up to the fiscal crisis. Higher disbursements to other vendors and to program beneficiaries accounted for a somewhat larger share of spending increases than did labor costs.

The City government's revenues also increased rapidly between 1961 and 1975 (Table 16.3). The 1961–1969 period included the most active years of the Great Society programs, and this was reflected financially in the rapid growth of intergovernmental grants as a proportion of City revenues. Taken together local taxes and federal and State subventions rose on average at roughly the same rate as spending. This is reflected in the fact that borrowing did not constitute an important source of operating revenues until the late 1960s.

Before 1969 with few and small exceptions, the City sold two types of debt instruments for two and only two purposes: (i) long-term bonds to finance the construction of long-lived infrastructure and (ii) tax and revenue anticipation notes (TRANs) with maturities of 12 months or less to redress mismatches between the timing of revenue receipts and outlays for operations *within a single fiscal year*. The latter were not a source of revenue to the City because by the end of the fiscal year, they would not have added to the total amount of money that could be spent. In fact, the interest paid on notes issued to facilitate cash-flow management raised operating expenses slightly.

Between 1970 and 1975, however, as the national economy endured two recessions, as Federal and State government revenue sharing programs became less generous, and as the City's economy contracted sharply, the growth of local tax revenues and intergovernmental grants failed to keep pace even with the somewhat slower expenditure increases. As a result, the City began accumulating operating deficits and resorted to borrowing funds to meet recurring expenses, although the mismatch between revenues and expenditures never appeared as such in the City's financial statements. By 1975, borrowing to cover cumulative tax and grant revenue shortfalls had reached $1.6 billion or 7.2% of total City disbursements for that fiscal year.

The way the City dealt with the situation when revenues were insufficient to cover spending was to stop paying bills that came due near the end of the fiscal year. Under the accounting standards in effect at the time, these past-due liabilities didn't show up on the City's year-end financial statement. Shortly after the new fiscal year began, the City would issue notes with maturities of less than one year and use the proceeds to pay the accumulated bills. Before those new notes came due near the end of the second fiscal year, the City would again begin to postpone paying bills that were due to accommodate another year's shortfall and to accumulate enough cash to pay off the borrowing. Thus the process would start again with two years of operating deficits not appearing in the City's fiscal year-end financial statements.

Except for the inherent lack of transparency, such practices would not necessarily represent bad fiscal practice, if revenue shortfalls were occasional and cyclical. If a temporary economic downturn reduced revenues and boosted expenditure requirements, then it would make sense to avoid making matters worse in the short term by raising taxes and cutting expenditures during a recession. It might make more sense to borrow enough money to balance the income statement at year-end in the expectation of being able to bring costs under control and/or to raise taxes a bit once the economic recovery began. That would enable the City to pay off the notes that had been rolled over from the recession and get back on a pay-as-you-go basis for subsequent fiscal years. One hopes that this quick-recovery scenario was what political leaders and fiscal watchdogs had in mind when they acquiesced in allowing the volume of what was, in effect, recurrent, accumulating deficit financing to increase year after year through the early 1970s. The problem, of course, was that the national economy failed to recover quickly or sustainably while the City economy contracted sharply and steadily over a period of years.

Even during the early- and mid-1960s, the growth of local tax revenues was not entirely a consequence of the relatively benign local economic conditions; the City, with the State government's permission, also raised a range of tax rates and imposed entirely new taxes over the course of that decade (Table 16.4). In 1963, the City sales tax was increased from two to three percent, the first such increase in 12 years and also the last increase in that levy until 1974, when the rate was raised by an additional percentage point to help cope with the emerging the fiscal crisis (N.Y.S. Department of Taxation and Finance, n.d.; Shefter, 1992, p. 61). Then in 1966, the State Legislature and Governor authorized the City to collect taxes on residents' personal income and on commuters' wage, salary, and proprietorship income (Brecher et al., 1993, p. 204). In addition, the City added, adjusted, and augmented a variety of business income taxes.

Taken together all of these changes in the City's finances reflect a clear augmentation of the City government's primarily redistributive functions. These were the programs that grew the most in absolute terms and at among the highest rates over the course of the 1961–1975 period (Table 16.1). Nor were the functions listed as primarily redistributive in Table 16.1 the only ones that aimed to aid low-income households. The rapid growth of education expenditures also had a substantial redistributive character. The bulk of Federal government's aid authorized by Title

**Table 16.4** Percentages of New York City tax revenues by source (Brecher et al., 1993, p. 25)

| Year | Real estate (%) | Sales (%) | Personal income (%) | Business income (%) | Commercial rent (%) | Other (%) | Total (%) |
|---|---|---|---|---|---|---|---|
| 1961 | 63.6 | 19.1 | | 11.3 | 0.1 | 5.9 | 100 |
| 1969 | 54.1 | 14.3 | 6.4 | 11.2 | 2.6 | 11.3 | 100 |
| 1975 | 53.6 | 16.0 | 9.4 | 10.8 | 3.9 | 6.3 | 100 |
| 1983 | 43.3 | 17.3 | 15.2 | 14.0 | 3.8 | 6.4 | 100 |
| 1989 | 41.3 | 16.2 | 17.1 | 14.4 | 4.5 | 6.5 | 100 |

I of the Elementary and Secondary Education Act of 1965 was allocated to school districts serving high concentrations of children living in poverty. And the higher education spending increase prior to 1975 reflects, in part, the 1969 adoption of open enrollment at the then tuition-free City University system. This was, in large part, a response to demonstrations demanding increases in the enrollment of African-American and Puerto Rican students (Phillips-Fein, 2017, p. 243).

The redistributive impact of the changes that took place in the composition of local tax revenues between 1961 and 1975 is somewhat ambiguous. The general view among analysts of tax incidence is that real estate (property) and sales taxes are relatively regressive; that is, they tend to produce a distribution of after-tax income that is more unequal than the distribution of pre-tax income. Personal and business income taxes, by contrast, can be more progressive. The problem with applying this generalization to New York City is that landlords whose buildings are subject to rent control or rent stabilization may not be able to pass the full burden of the property tax on to tenants. The consensus among those who have analyzed New York City's tax structure, however, is that the decrease in the combined share of real estate and sales taxes from 82.7% in 1961 to 69.6% in 1985 along with the increase in the resident and commuter income taxes' share from 11.3 to 20.2% did produce a very mildly progressive system. Charles Brecher and Raymond Horton, for example, reported estimates that in 1975 a household earning $10,000 a year would have paid about 18.1% of their income in local taxes while one earning $40,000 would pay about 20.1% (Brecher et al., 1993, p. 199). Given these estimates, it seems unlikely that the system would have been at all progressive prior to the adoption of the local personal income tax and the commuter earnings tax in 1966. That said, the increase in New York City local taxes over the course of the decade-and-a-half leading up to the fiscal crisis probably affected all income classes of residents about equally.

About equally and quite substantially. Real local tax revenues increased at an average annualized rate of 3.1% between 1969 and 1975. Over the same period of time, the average real per capita personal income across the five boroughs increased by an average annual rate of only 0.5. Thus in the years leading up to the financial crisis, local taxes were increasing six times faster than local incomes.

## All Hands on Deck

The practice of carrying cumulative operating deficits forward from one fiscal year to the next worked well until it didn't work anymore. As late as the spring of 1975, Moody's Investors Service and Standard & Poor's maintained solidly investment-grade ratings on the City's long- and short-term obligations. By April of that year, however, "due diligence" investigations undertaken by the City's underwriters and their lawyers no longer provided confidence that the City would be able to redeem its notes when due or, given legal limits on total municipal indebtedness, whether these issues were even valid. There was, in short, no market for the notes the City needed to issue in order to pay its bills (U.S. Securities and Exchange Commission, 1977).

To get the required cash into the City's hands, the State of New York adopted a package of expedients. These included a one-time advance of State aid, tax increases, and the creation the Municipal Assistance Corporation ("MAC"). The latter was authorized to issue long-term bonds and transfer the proceeds to the City for the purpose of retiring outstanding short-term debt. Debt service on the MAC bonds was secured a first call on certain specified tax revenue streams and by the "moral obligation" of the State of New York. It is unlikely that investors would have viewed the State's moral obligation as much of an enhancement just two months after the default of the Urban Development Corporation.

The October brush with bankruptcy described at the beginning of this chapter demonstrated that the expedients adopted in the spring were insufficient to stabilize the City's finances. The package of provisions enacted in the wake of that second episode imposed some costs on the City's creditors and State and federal taxpayers. The bulk of the burden of eliminating operating deficits, however, would be borne by the City's taxpayers and by its residents who depended on or availed themselves of municipal services. The rescue plan, which was put in place during the fourth quarter of 1975 in a series State Legislative and U.S. Congressional enactments included direct aid/or loans from the State and Federal governments, investment in City and MAC bonds by City public employee pension funds, commitments by banks to underwrite and/or purchase MAC bonds, and a suspension of investors' rights with respect to outstanding short-term City obligations. More specifically, the enabling legislation

- Turned authority over the City's budgeting, borrowing, and financial planning to an Emergency Financial Control Board (EFCB), which was dominated by State officials,
- Authorized the U.S. Treasury to lend money to the City of New York to meet seasonal financing needs, and
- Suspended payments on outstanding short-term City obligations when held by investors who had been offered but rejected an opportunity to exchange these notes for long-term MAC bonds (Shalala & Bellamy, 1976, pp. 1128–1131).

The rescue package did succeed in its stated goals. In the short run, it secured City access to the funds it needed to meet its ongoing operational and most of its debt service obligations. Over the medium term, the EFCB was also able and in devise and implement policies and procedures that insured that future fiscal year revenues and expenditures would, in fact, be equal.

Although some new taxes were imposed, the bulk of the adjustment took place on the expenditure side. As Table 16.3 indicates, both real intergovernmental grants for operational purposes and real local tax revenues declined between 1975 and 1983, and borrowing to finance operation was, of course, eliminated.

The impact, as illustrated in Fig. 16.1, was a sharp contraction of the City's government. Total real per capita spending decreased by more than 20% between the 1975 high point and the early 1980s, when the City and the nation began to recover from another episode of back-to-back recessions. The cutbacks affected almost all municipal functions. Real spending on all but two of the specific functions listed in Table 16.1 decreased over the 1975–1983 period, and growth in the two exceptions was very small. Some of the larger negative numbers in the table probably do overstate the impact of the changes in City spending on the quality and quantity of municipal services. The decrease in expenditures on higher education, for example, reflects some very real and substantial cutbacks in enrollment and staffing and the imposition of tuition in 1976, but the decrease in City spending also reflects the shift in responsibility for financing the system's four-year colleges to the State.

Given the visibility of New York City's fiscal crisis, the draconian nature of the response, and social scientists' affinity for "natural experiments," it is somewhat surprising that relatively little research has been published on the effects of the spending and service reductions on residents' lives.

One study, however, did present evidence that the spending reductions were associated with a measurable deterioration of the quality, and, indeed, the quantity of life for many of the City's residents. Public health researchers Nicholas Freudenberg, Marianne Fahs, Sandro Galea, and Andrew Greenberg reported that the incidence of tuberculosis in New York City began to rise in 1978 following the closure of seven of the 20 Department of Health (DOH) district health centers and six of its 14 chest clinics and after staffing reductions at City hospitals hampered efforts to follow up on discharged patients. Thereafter, TB rates in New York City increased every year until 1992, a period during which the nationwide incidence of this disease decreased in most years and never returned to the 1978 level. Post-crisis spending reductions may not have been the sole cause of the estimated 52,000 excess TB cases by 1992, but it was almost certainly one of the causes.

The same study pointed out that 41% of AIDS cases in New York City were related to intravenous drug use compared to 25% nationwide. So it is hard to escape the conclusion that the 20% reduction in the size of the Police Department (NYPD), the dismantling of that Department's narcotics squad, the closure DOH health centers, and the elimination of the City's Addiction Services Agency, all around the onset of the HIV/AIDS epidemic, certainly didn't help and may have made matters worse (Centers for Disease Control and Prevention, 2018; Freudenberg, Fahs, Galea, & Greenberg, 2006).

The City also cut funds for elementary and secondary education in the years after the fiscal crisis. Between 1975 and 1977, expenditures on City schools decreased by 1.8% in nominal terms and about 13% in purchasing power. This reduction in spending must have had some impact on the quantity and quality of services provided to the City's school children in the years immediately following the financial crisis. That might not have been terribly problematic if before 1975 greater resources had been devoted to the City's school children, correcting for needs differentials, than in other school districts or if spending and resources had been restored to pre-crisis levels quickly after accumulated operational deficits had been paid off and the local economy began to recover. Robert Berne and Leanna Stiefel have shown, however, that neither of these was the case. In a 1993 publication, they reported that in 1975 per pupil spending in the City was not inordinately high relative to other school districts in New York State once one adjusts to account for the high local concentration of handicapped and non-English speaking students. The adjusted figure was 103% of the Statewide (ex-City) average. In 1977, the need-adjusted figure had fallen to 89%. And far from bouncing back after the end of the crisis and after the City's economy had begun to recover, per pupil school spending in New York City continued to decline relative to the rest of the State. In 1989, the figure stood at 78% (Berne & Stiefel, 1993).

By 1975, therefore, it had become clear that, absent more assistance than the State or Federal governments were willing to provide and even with a tax burden growing six-times faster than local incomes, the shrinking local economy could not generate sufficient resources to sustain the full array of policies the City had put in place over the postwar decades. Draconian spending and service reductions were required to bring the City's budget into line with the revenues that were expected to be available while servicing the debt that had been accumulated over a series of fiscal years. The cutbacks reduced the quantity and quality of municipal services and may have cost some New Yorkers their lives, both in the immediate aftermath of the crisis and for many years thereafter. It is, therefore, sadly ironic that at the same time that class sizes in the schools were increasing, health centers were closing, and the municipal infrastructure was deteriorating, the City was experiencing the first stirrings of what would eventually become a robust economic recovery. If the storm had been a bit less perfect and if New York could have staved off the crisis with just a few more years of gradually diminishing cumulative deficit financing and smaller and more systematic spending reductions, some of the most damaging impacts might have been avoided or ameliorated.

## Pinpointing the Turning

All of the measures of local economic conditions that are published by the U.S. government show that New York City's economic condition had begun to improve by 1980.

The City's population was lower in 1980 than in both 1970 and 1990, and the Census Bureau estimates that the turning point between contraction and growth occurred around the end of the crisis decade (Fig. 16.4).

In 1969, the Commerce Department's Bureau of Economic Analysis began publishing annual estimates of aggregate personal income (P.I.) for local areas. New York City's share of total national P.I. declined through the 1970s and stabilized thereafter (Fig. 16.5).

The contraction in the aggregate was not simply a reflection of the City's declining population share. Per capita personal (PCPI) income of City residents decreased as a percentage of the national average through the 1970s and then recovered rapidly (Fig. 16.6). The fact that PCPI in New York City is higher than the national average should not be taken as an indication that the average New Yorker lives better than the average American; the difference reflects the higher cost of living in the

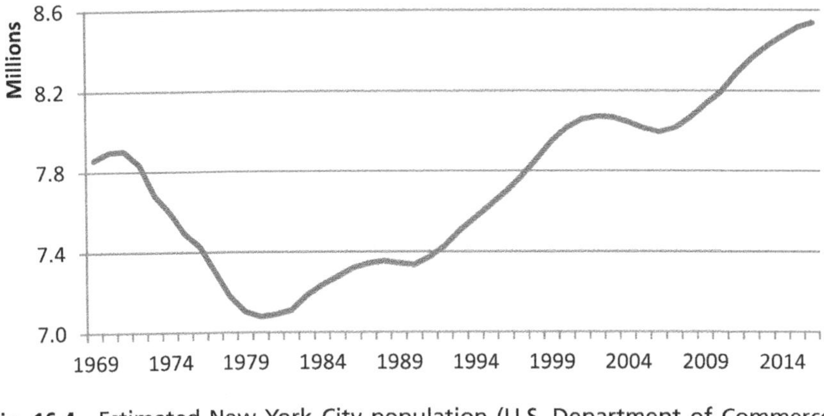


**Fig. 16.4** Estimated New York City population (U.S. Department of Commerce, Bureau of Economic Analysis, 2018)

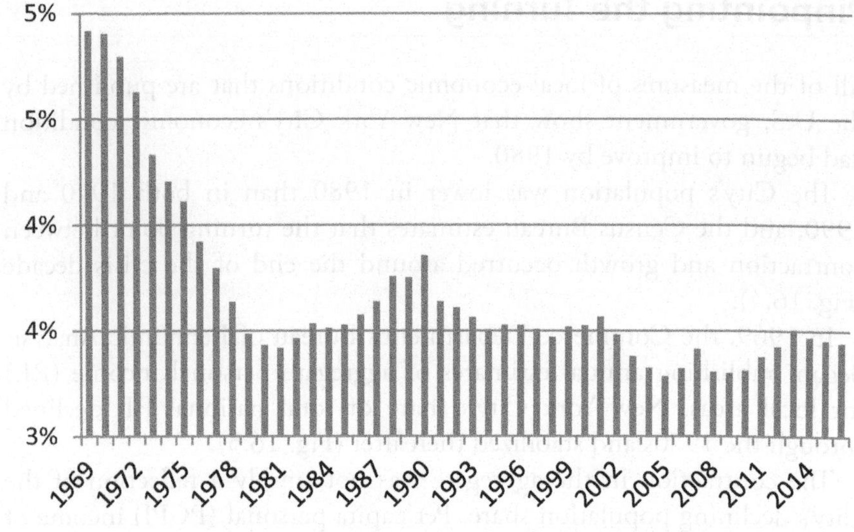


**Fig. 16.5** New York City personal income, percent of U.S. total (U.S. Department of Commerce, Bureau of Economic Analysis, 2018)

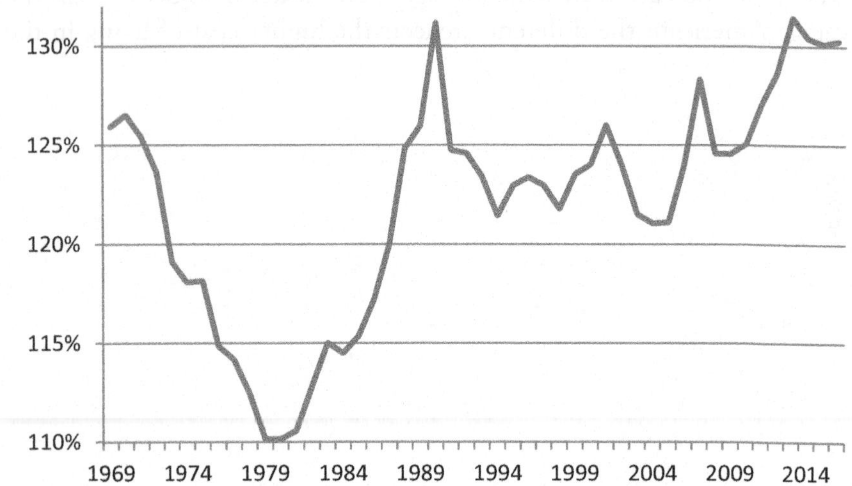


**Fig. 16.6** New York City per capita personal income, percent of U.S. average (U.S. Department of Commerce, Bureau of Economic Analysis, 2018)

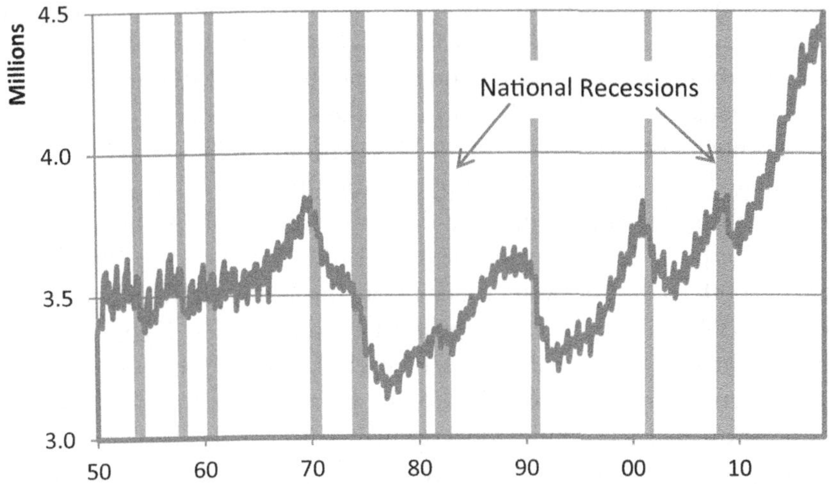


**Fig. 16.7** Total nonfarm payroll employment in New York City, not seasonally adjusted (U.S. Bureau of Labor Statistics, 2018b)

City and also, probably, the presence in New York of a small number of extremely high-income residents who bring up the average.

The Bureau of Labor Statistics has been reporting total monthly nonfarm payroll employment statistics for New York City since 1950. Figure 16.7, which tracks the total number of jobs in the City, illustrates several of the changes in New York's economy that have been discussed in this and previous chapters and will be the subjects of the rest of this book. Note first the jaggedness of the line. The underlying data series is not seasonally adjusted, and so the short-term ups and downs reflect the month-to-month variability of business activity in the City. The line is most jagged in the 1950s and early 1960s, when a large proportion of the City's workforce was engaged in the seasonal garment industry. The relative smoothing of the line probably reflects, at least in part, the near disappearance of that sector as an employer in the City. Second, while the New York economy was less seasonal after the 1960s than it had been before, it was also much more cyclical. The recessions of the 1950s and early 1960s barely registered in the City's employment statistics. Again this may reflect the importance of the garment industry and other consumer non-durables manufacturing sectors, which were seasonal but not particularly cyclical. As noted earlier in this chapter, the back-to-back recessions extending from the fourth quarter of 1969 until the first quarter of 1975, which coincided with sharp, permanent declines in manufacturing employment, were particularly devastating for New York City and culminated in the fiscal crisis. None of the subsequent recessions had as severe an impact, but the ups and downs in total local employment concurrent with the downturns in the early 1980s, 1990–1991, 2000–2001, 2007–2009 recessions were much more pronounced than what happened locally during the earlier postwar business cycles. Figure 16.7 also shows that the second half of 1976 marked absolute the low point for postwar employment in New York City. Finally, the figure illustrates the acceleration of local employment growth through the last years of the twentieth century and the early decades of the twenty-first century. The subsequent chapters will deal with this upswing.

Absolute job growth is one criterion for evaluating the performance of a local economy. Another is whether local job growth is slow or fast relative to elsewhere. Nonfarm payroll employment in New York was

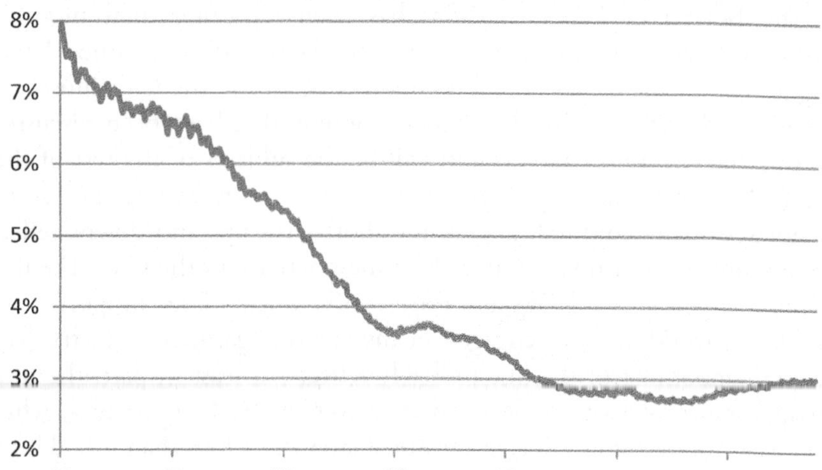


**Fig. 16.8** Total nonfarm payroll employment in New York City, not seasonally adjusted, percentage of U.S. total (U.S. Bureau of Labor Statistics, 2018b)

stable on average over the 1950s and early 1960s. The City's share of total U.S. employment, however, was decreasing steadily through the early postwar decades (Fig. 16.8), indicating that the City's economy growing more slowly than that of the country as a whole. During the 1980s and thereafter, this relationship changed. The City continued to grow more slowly than the nation, but during the 1980s and 1990s, the difference was much smaller than it had been. Thereafter, in the most recent period it appears that percentage employment increases in New York City have begun to outpace the national rate of job growth by a small margin.

The New York City economy passed a turning point at some point during the late 1970s or early 1980s. The global, national, and local circumstances that had led to City's underperformance and then absolute contraction gave way to developments that at first stabilized the City's economic condition and then stimulated robust growth. Thus, the years after the financial crisis of 1975 mark the end of one epoch of New York economic history, the short twentieth century, and the beginning of the next, the post-crisis recovery.

## References

Bahl, R. W., Campbell, A. K., & Greytak, D. (1974). *Taxes, Expenditures, and the Economic Base: Case Study of New York City*. New York: Praeger.

Berne, R., & Stiefel, L. (1993). Cutback Budgeting: The Long-Term Consequences. *Journal of Policy Analysis and Management, 12*(4), 664–684.

Bloom, N. D. (2008). *Public Housing That Worked: New York in the Twentieth Century*. Philadelphia: University of Pennsylvania Press.

Brecher, C., Horton, R., Cropf, R. A., & Dean, M. M. (1993). *Power Failure: New York City Politics and Policy Since 1960*. Oxford: Oxford University Press.

Centers for Disease Control and Prevention. (2018). *TB Incidence in the United States, 1953–2016*. Retrieved from Tuberculosis (TB) https://www.cdc.gov/tb/statistics/tbcases.htm.

Collins English Dictionary. (2018). *Perfect Storm*. Retrieved from Dictionary.com https://www.dictionary.com/browse/perfect-storm.

Federal Reserve Bank of St. Louis. (2018). *Download, Graph, and Track 527,000 US and International Time Series from 87 Sources.* Retrieved from FRED Economic Data https://fred.stlouisfed.org.

Freudenberg, N., Fahs, M., Galea, S., & Greenberg, A. (2006). The Impact of New York City's 1975 Crisis on the Tuberculosis, HIV, and Homicide Syndemic. *American Journal of Public Health, 96*(3), 424–434.

Greytak, D., Gustely, R., & Dinkelmeyer, R. (1974). The Effects of Inflation on Local Government Expenditures. *National Tax Journal, 27*(4), 583–598.

Heclo, H. (2005). Sixties Civics. In S. M. Milkis & J. M. Mileur (Eds.), *The Great Society and the High Tide of Liberalism* (pp. 53–82). Amherst: University of Massachusetts Press.

Morris, C. R. (1980). *The Cost of Good Intentions: New York City and the Liberal Experiment, 1960–1975.* New York: W. W. Norton.

National Academy of Engineering; Commission on Engineering and Technical Systems. (1983). *The Competitive Status of the U.S. Fibers, Textiles, and Apparel Complex: A Study of the Influences of Technology in Detrmining International Industrial Comparative Advantage.* Washington: National Academy Press.

National Bureau of Economic Research. (2018). *U.S. Business Cycle Expansions and Contractions.* Retrieved from http://www.nber.org/cycles.html.

N.Y.S. Department of Taxation and Finance. (n.d.). *Enactment and Effective Dates of Sales and Use Tax Rates, Publication 718-A.* Albany: State of New York.

Nussbaum, J. (2015, October 18). The Night New York Saved Itself from Bankruptcy. *The New Yorker.*

Phillips-Fein, K. (2017). *Fear City: New York's Fiscal Crisis and the Rise of Austerity Politics.* New York: Henry Holt.

Sayre, W. S., & Kaufman, H. (1960). *Governing New York City: Politics in the Metropolis* (p. 777). New York: Russell Sage Foundation.

Shalala, D. E., & Bellamy, C. (1976). A State Saves a City: The New York Case. *Duke Law Journal, 6*, 1119–1132.

Shefter, M. (1992). *Political Crisis, Fiscal Crisis: The Collapse and Revival of New York City.* New York: Columbia University Press.

Tanzi, V. (1977). Inflation, Lags in Collection, and the Real Value of Tax Revenue. *Staff Papers (International Monetary Fund), 24*(1), 154–167.

U.S. Bureau of Labor Statistics. (2018a, July 25). *Create Customized Tables: State and Area Employment, Hours, and Earnings—Seasonal.* Retrieved from Data Tools: Create Customized Tables https://data.bls.gov/cgi-bin/dsrv?sm.

U.S. Bureau of Labor Statistics. (2018b). *State and Area Employment, Hours, and Earnings*. Retrieved from Create Customized Tables https://data.bls.gov/cgi-bin/dsrv?sm.

U.S. Department of Commerce, Bureau of Economic Analysis. (2018). *Interactive Data*. Retrieved from https://www.bea.gov/itable/iTable.cfm?ReqID=70&step=1#reqid=70&step=31&isuri=1&7022=20&7023=7&7024=non-industry&7025=4&7001=720&7029=20&7090=70.

U.S. Securities and Exchange Commission. (1977). *Staff Report on Transactions in the Securities of the City of New York*. Washington: U.S. Government Printing Office.

# Part IV

## ~1979–~2008: The Post Crisis Recovery

In 1960, there were 26 cities in the United States with populations of 500,000 or more. By 1980, the populations of 15 of these cities had decreased. Over the subsequent 20 years, six of these 15—New York, Boston, Kansas City, San Francisco, Seattle, and Denver—began growing again. The "resurgence" of these cities attracted considerable attention from urban studies specialists seeking reasons why these places in particular experienced turnarounds. New York was on this list, but its resurgence was particularly notable. For one thing, it was the only large northeastern city that (a) was more populous in 2000 than it had been in 1960 but (b) did not annex neighboring suburban communities during this period. Further, the notion that New York could achieve a robust economic revival would have been greeted with considerable skepticism from the vantage point of 1980, only five years after the City's brush with bankruptcy. Accordingly, the final part of this book aims to explain New York's resurgence through the decades around the turn of the twenty-first century.

The first two of these three chapters view New York's turnaround through the lens of four general models of urban resurgence. Chapter 17 considers three bodies of scholarly literature—tests of the "consumer," "skilled," and "creative" cities hypotheses—that marshal statistical analysis to identify purely domestic explanations of late twentieth-century interurban growth differentials.

The "consumer cities" hypothesis begins with the observation that post-industrial businesses are less tied to locations near the sources of raw materials or close to large numbers of consumers than are companies that produce physical commodities. Such firms, therefore, have an incentive to locate in places offering attractive residential amenities—good weather, good restaurants, a range of entertainment options, etc.—in the expectation that workers there might be satisfied with somewhat lower wages than they would demand in colder, cloudier, less interesting metropolitan areas. Analysis of the second, "skilled cities," model finds that regions historically well endowed with higher education institutions do, in fact, have better-educated populations and that it has, all else held equal, been easier for such places to make a successful transition from a manufacturing-based local economy to one more reliant on post-industrial activities. The third group of models, the "creative cities" hypotheses, builds on the finding that raw years of schooling are not the best measure of the skills that are most conducive to regional economic growth in the late twentieth century. This line of research goes on to identify the specific occupational categories and associated "creative" skills that have been most closely associated with rapid regional economic growth. An extension of the analysis goes on to identify "tolerance" or "openness to diversity," as characteristics of cities that are most attractive to "talent," individuals possessed of these "creative" skills, and are, therefore, likely to have grown faster in recent decades.

The second half of Chapter 17 considers whether a 1980 observer possessed in advance of the conclusions of the consumer city, skilled city, and creative city literatures would have identified New York as the late twentieth-century "winner" it, in fact, was. The conclusion is that such an observer could not have made that prediction with confidence. While New York benefits from accessible nearby beaches, plenty of good restaurants, and a lively performing arts scene, it does not score at all well on what is an immutable and, arguably, the most important "consumer city" characteristic, namely warm sunny weather year-round. Nor is New York a particularly skilled city. True, the percentage of the metropolitan area's population who are college graduates is a bit above the big-city average. But it is also the case that the proportion of the central City's population who do not possess a high school diploma is well above the national average. Finally, New York's scores on measures of tolerance and openness to diversity are on the high side, but probably not enough so to explain the City's very robust post-crisis performance. Overall, the fact that New York City began growing again after 1980 does not contradict the general conclusions of the consumer, skilled, and creative cities literature, but it is hard to explain the robustness of New York's recovery relative to that of other northeastern cities as a function solely of some combination of its residential amenities, the educational attainments of its populace, or its attractiveness to creative talent. Further, none of the three models identify the reasons for the timing of the shift from population contraction to expansion at some point around 1980.

An upsurge in international flows of goods, capital, and people earned the decades around the turn of the twenty-first century designation as the second great age of globalization. Sociologist Saskia Sassen's analysis of how this powerful trend has affected the international hierarchy of cities, her "Global Cities" hypothesis, sheds considerable light on how New York City's economy has changed over the past 40 years. This is the subject of Chapter 18.

Sassen's analysis begins with the observation that a large proportion of the international flows of goods no longer involve the simple sale of finished goods produced in one country from start to finish to purchasers in another country. Instead, the "supply chain" of any given product—its conceptualization, design, parts manufacture, assembly, packaging, advertising, shipping, delivery, final sale, after-service, etc.—may extend through multiple countries and be undertaken by many different firms. And large proportions of international flows of capital no longer involve just the direct purchase of individual companies' bonds and stocks denominated in the issuer's home currency by individual investors seeking assets in that currency. To be sure, the volume and variety of such portfolio investment transactions have expanded rapidly. But direct international investments—the purchase of physical assets or entire businesses in one country by residents of another country—have increased even more rapidly. Put differently, during this second age of globalization flows of goods and money have increased not only in magnitude but in organizational complexity. Sassen posits that this global order could not operate without the direct and detailed involvement of a range of business service professionals—lawyers, accountants, investment bankers, management consultants, and advertising agencies—advising producer company managements, sometimes independently but often as part of multidisciplinary teams. She goes on to argue that these services cannot be provided with sufficient quality and variety except in places where the highest order of *all* of the requisite professional specialties is present in a single location. The Global Cities hypothesis, then, is that there are only a very few cities around the world where the best-qualified business service professionals in all areas of expertise can be assembled on short notice and brought to bear to design and facilitate the most complex international business initiatives.

A detailed empirical effort by a team headed by Peter Taylor to map the hierarchies and international connections of business service professionals found that, indeed, there are very few cities where one can assemble all of the requisite broad expertise that might be needed for any given high-level business decision. There are, in fact, only two such cities in the world, London and New York.

Chapter 18 concludes with evidence that, somewhat surprisingly, New York's function as one of the only two global cities in a rapidly globalizing world has not had much direct impact on total employment levels in the City. To be sure, the number of local jobs in business services and investment banking increased very substantially around the turn of the twenty-first century. In the aggregate, however, the expansion of these industries just about made up for job losses in declining local base industries. Thus, for example, investment bankers replaced commercial bank loan officers. And management consultants replaced garment factory bosses. Of course, wages in the growing businesses were, on average, much higher than in the contracting sectors. But this upgrading does not seem to have boosted either per capita personal income or the degree of local income inequality in New York by more than what was occurring in other large northeastern urban centers.

After contracting from 1969 until 1977, total employment in New York began growing again on a trend basis. It surpassed its old high temporarily in 2008 and then shrank somewhat during the subsequent recession. But City employment began setting new records in 2011 and in each year thereafter. It was not New York's base industries themselves—the local "export" sectors that sell their products elsewhere in the United States or around the world—in which total job growth was most dramatic. No doubt New York benefited from the fact that, as the composition of its base industries changed at the end of the twentieth century; aggregate employment in the City's "export" sectors did not decline. In this regard, it was doing much better than most other northeastern cities. But it was the local "multiplier" industries, those that primarily serve local residents, that collectively generated all of the net new jobs.

Chapter 19 aims to make the case that, just as during previous globalization era, immigration from abroad provided the impetus for New York City's robust growth around the turn of the twenty-first century. It was rapidly growing local immigrant communities that created the demand for new, locally supplied goods and services. And it was rapidly growing immigrant communities that provided the elastic supply of labor that facilitated broader local economic growth.

After being suppressed by the 1920s-era restrictions through the early postwar decades, aggregate immigration to the United States began increasing after adoption of the Hart-Celler Act in 1965 and accelerated rapidly in the early 1990s when that legislation was amended to raise aggregate caps on permanent residency visas. Immigrants from the Americas and East and South Asia were overrepresented nationwide and in New York. As in previous generations, this new cohort tended to settle in a few large cities, including New York. Indeed, the increase in the number of foreign-born New Yorkers accounts for more than 100% of the City's total population growth since 1960.

In many respects, the analysis presented in Chapter 19 echoes that of Chapter 11, which dealt with the ways in which the large cohorts of Southern Italian and Eastern European Jewish immigrants had facilitated the rapid expansion of the New York City's physical infrastructure and its garment industry early in the twentieth century. The contemporary story, however, is much more complex because it involves many more immigrant origins and many more individual industries. The bulk of Chapter 19 reviews case studies of these industry-ethnicity niches: Chinese and Dominicans in the garment industry, West Indian women in the healthcare sector, Dominicans working in hotels, and South Asian taxi drivers. The individual case studies provide evidence that the elastic supply of immigrant workers and the role of immigrant social networks in enhancing the efficiency of these industries' labor markets have, at the very least, removed potential impediments to New York's recent economic growth.

The chapter also examines the role of ethnic enclave economies in New York's recent economic development. These are parts of the City—Chinatown in Flushing or Little Odessa in Brooklyn's Brighton Beach, for example—where many of the individual local businesses and most of those firms' customers are members of the same ethnic community. In a sense, these are new towns within the City. They add to the aggregate local economy but are as distinct from the rest of the City as, say, a distant suburb.

In sum, Chapter 19 aims to make the case that the combination of these niches and enclaves produced an urban economy in which the local "multiplier" sector was much larger relative to the "base" or export industries than had been the case in the past.

# 17

# Resurgent Cities

In 1960, there were 26 cities in the United States with more than 500,000 residents. Table 17.1 indicates what happened to the populations of those cities over the last four decades of the twentieth century. The organization of the table highlights the most obvious pattern; most of the cities in the nation's northeastern quadrant were much smaller in 2000 than they had been in 1960 while most cities located elsewhere had grown substantially.[1] This outcome stood in contrast with previous historical periods when the rising tide of urbanization tended to boost the populations of *all* North American cities. Observe, too, that, with the exception of Columbus, OH, and Indianapolis, IN, the populations of all big northeastern cities decreased between 1960 and 1980. Most of the western and southern cities grew during all four decades, but the populations of San Francisco, Seattle, Denver, and New Orleans also decreased during the earlier period. Finally, note that the populations of six of the cities—New York, Boston, Kansas City (slightly), San Francisco, Seattle, and Denver—that had contracted between 1960

[1] The 14 "northeastern" cities were all located east of the Mississippi River and north of the Ohio River or in the State of Missouri.



A. Gurwitz, *Atlantic Metropolis*, Palgrave Studies in American Economic History,
https://doi.org/10.1007/978-3-030-13352-8_17

**Table 17.1** Population change in cities with 1970 population 500,000 or greater (U.S. Department of Housing and Urban Development, 2018)

| City | Population change | | Percent population change | |
|---|---|---|---|---|
| | 1960–1980 | 1980–2000 | 1960–1980 | 1980–2000 |
| Northeastern quadrant | | | | |
| New York, NY | (710,345) | 1,202,888 | −9.1 | 17.0 |
| Chicago, IL | (545,332) | (168,414) | −15.4 | −5.6 |
| Philadelphia, PA | (314,302) | (238,576) | −15.7 | −14.1 |
| Detroit, MI | (466,776) | (286,416) | −27.9 | −23.8 |
| Baltimore, MD | (152,283) | (179,828) | −16.2 | −22.9 |
| Cleveland, OH | (302,228) | (135,780) | −34.5 | −23.7 |
| Washington, DC | (125,524) | (50,140) | −16.4 | −7.9 |
| St. Louis, MO | (297,225) | (104,612) | −39.6 | −23.1 |
| Milwaukee, WI | (105,027) | (34,106) | −14.2 | −5.4 |
| Boston, MA | (134,203) | 36,357 | −19.2 | 6.5 |
| Pittsburgh, PA | (180,373) | (89,396) | −29.8 | −21.1 |
| Indianapolois, IN | 235,281 | 83,919 | 49.4% | 11.8 |
| Kansas City, MO | (27,511) | 2,347 | −5.8 | 0.5 |
| Columbus, OH | 93,705 | 182,734 | 19.9 | 32.3 |
| Rest of the country | | | | |
| Los Angeles, CA | 489,513 | 865,812 | 19.7 | 29.2 |
| Houston, TX | 656,919 | 613,042 | 70.0 | 38.4 |
| San Francisco, CA | (61,342) | 86,002 | −8.3 | 12.7 |
| Dallas, TX | 224,915 | 335,900 | 33.1 | 37.1 |
| New Orleans, LA | (69,598) | (73,253) | −11.1 | −13.1 |
| San Antonio, TX | 198,222 | 543,044 | 33.7 | 69.1 |
| San Diego, CA | 302,314 | 391,193 | 52.7 | 44.7 |
| Seattle, WA | (63,241) | 100,364 | −11.4 | 20.3 |
| Memphis, TN | 148,650 | 27,854 | 29.9 | 4.3 |
| Denver, CO | (1,201) | 95,663 | −0.2 | 19.4 |
| Phoenix, AZ | 350,534 | 762,555 | 79.8 | 96.6 |
| Jacksonville, FL | 339,890 | 194,697 | 169.1 | 36.0 |

and 1980 subsequently began growing again. The upturns these cities' growth trajectories have been referred to, perhaps a bit overdramatically in some cases, as urban "resurgence."

The statistics presented in Table 17.1 set the agenda for analysis of late twentieth-century U.S. urban economies. Three questions need to be answered. First, why did most northeastern cities decline in population between 1960 and 2000 while most western and southern cities grew? Second, why did some cities that declined during the first two decades recover subsequently while others did not? Finally, what changed around 1980 that explains the timing of urban resurgence in those places where it occurred?

This and the next two chapters also aim to answer another question. Were the causes and consequences of New York's resurgence similar to or, in important ways, different from those that affected other resurgent municipalities?

One part of the explanation of why southern and, especially, western cities grew faster on average than those in the northeastern quadrant is straightforward and more political than economic. The statistics depicted in Fig. 17.1 do not represent constant geographies; the land areas of many of western municipalities and also of Columbus, OH, grew substantially over this period through annexation, that of others did not. Further, relatively large land area as of 1970, even without additional annexation, helps explain the growth of Indianapolis and Jacksonville. These two had been consolidated politically with the counties in which they were located not long before 1970 and, consequently, much of the population growth that would have been categorized as "suburban" in geographically smaller municipalities was attributed to these two central cities.

Central cities' land areas, initially or after post-1970 annexation, are, of course, far from the whole story behind Table 17.1. There were also large differences in the growth rates in the metropolitan regions encompassing the 26 cities. The total population of the 14 northeastern metropolitan areas grew by 13.7% from 1970 to 2000. The comparative figure for the twelve western and southern regions was 82.6%. Individual regional 1970–2000 growth rates across the 26 metropolitan areas ranged from −12.1% (Pittsburgh) to +214.1% (Phoenix) (U.S. Census Bureau, 2018; U.S. Department of Housing and Urban Development, 2018).[2]

[2]Throughout this chapter for regions divided by the Census Bureau into several primary metropolitan statistical areas (PMSAs), the term "metropolitan area" will refer to the sum or a weighted average of the statistics for the underlying PMSAs. In the case of New York, metropolitan region consists of the Bergen-Passaic, NJ, Bridgeport, CT, Danbury, CT, Dutchess Co., NY, Jersey City,

Unsurprisingly, this wide dispersion in outcomes across cities and metropolitan areas along with the wealth of data that can be used to analyze the differences has attracted the attention of economists and other social scientists engaged in urban and regional studies. These scholars, most prominently Edward Glaeser of Harvard University and Richard Florida of the University of Toronto, have identified the municipal and regional characteristics that have been the most reliable predictors of recent trends in economic geography. Their findings can be conveniently categorized into three groups of hypotheses; the U.S. municipalities and metropolitan areas that have grown the fastest since 1980 could be characterized as "consumer cities" and/or "skilled cities" and/or "creative cities." This chapter will examine these hypotheses and consider the extent to which they shed light on the particulars of New York City's post-1980 resurgence.

## Consumer Cities

The analysis underlying the consumer cities hypotheses begins with the observation that the cost of transporting the goods and services produced by the average U.S. worker declined sharply during the latter years of the twentieth century. This cost decreased for two reasons. First, with the completion of the interstate highway network transportation within the U.S. became more efficient. Second, and, probably even more importantly, the industrial composition of the U.S. workforce shifted markedly. In 1960, for example, 38% of the U.S. workforce was engaged in goods production; by 2000 that figure had declined by half to 19%. Equivalent figures for the production of, presumably more transport-cost intensive, durable manufactured goods were

---

NJ, Middlesex-Somerset-Hunterdon, NJ, Monmouth-Ocean, NJ, Nassau-Suffolk, NY, New Haven-Meridien, CT, New York, NY, Newark, NJ, Newburgh, NY-PA, and Stamford-Norwalk, CT, PMSAs.

17% in 1970 and 8% in 2000 (U.S. Bureau of Labor Statistics, 2018). Services are either essentially impossible to transport—a haircut, for example, must be "produced" in the immediate vicinity of wherever the consumer happens to reside—or can be moved very cheaply over very long distances.

When a large proportion of workers was engaged in transforming heavy inputs into heavy products, location in the northeastern quadrant, near raw materials and final consumers, was advantageous to firms. As transportation costs faded in relative importance for more and more U.S. employers—that is, as firms became more "footloose"—other regional differences in the cost of doing business assumed increasing influence over firms' location decisions. In particular, if workers have strong preferences with respect to the characteristics of places they would like to live and if, therefore, the minimum wage rates they would be willing to accept differ markedly across locations, firms seeking relatively low labor costs would be drawn to the places potential employees find most attractive. And producers of personal services would follow their consumers. Empirical tests of the consumer city hypothesis have, therefore, focused on the relationship among geographical population growth rates, regional "amenities," and local wage differentials. So, for example, evidence that cities with relatively benign year-round weather have been growing faster than other places *and* that this relatively rapid growth has *not* been accompanied by rising relative wages would support the consumer city hypothesis.

The "consumer city" literature has generated clear answers to the question about why some cities grew and others contracted during the late twentieth century. The role of good climate—warm temperatures and low precipitation—as an attractive regional amenity has, of course, been the clearest example of how consumer preferences have influenced cities' trajectories. The growth of the Sunbelt has been, by far, the most salient trend in North American economic geography of the past forty years (Glaeser, Edward, Kolko, & Saiz, 2001). The fact that the mean daily low temperature in January was 18 Fahrenheit degrees lower on average across the 14 northeastern cities than in the other 12, together with the annexation differences discussed above, probably account for most of the interregional growth rate differential (Current Results, 2018). This is why it will make sense in many contexts to compare New York's economic performance with that of other large urban places in the northeastern quadrant rather than with all 26 cities.

Glaeser and his co-authors also identified a range of other amenities, in addition to climate, that were associated with higher population growth between 1977 and 1995. These included proximity to an ocean coast, live performance venues per capita, and restaurants per capita. Art museums per capita have had little effect on local economic growth, and places with large numbers of movie theaters and, especially, bowling alleys per capita have tended to grow more slowly or contract faster (Glaeser et al., 2001, pp. 35–38).

There can be little doubt that the consumer city hypothesis is valid and explains a large part of the variation in big-city growth rates around the end of the twentieth century, especially the marked dichotomy between the northeastern quadrant and the rest of the country. But residential amenities alone cannot account for why the populations of some northeastern cities rebounded after about 1980 while others did not.

Of the residential amenities identified in the consumer city literature as conducive to population growth and housing price increases, only weather and proximity to an ocean are, as it were, inelastically supplied. If population is increasing in a locality and if a disproportionate number of the new residents enjoy nights out on the town, the number of restaurants per capita can increase relatively quickly, and popular performers can add the growing cities to their tours. And if population is decreasing but the remaining residents are the ones who most enjoy convivial indoor sporting events, the number of bowling alleys per capita will rise. So, we still need an explanation of why, among cities with similar climates, some grow rapidly (and have lots of restaurants) and some shrink (but still have plenty of bowling alleys). For example, the mean January low temperature in about the same in Pittsburgh and Kansas City, but the population for the former metropolitan area decreased by 12% between 1970 and 2000, while that of the latter grew by 45%. It is implausible that more and better restaurants and entertainment venues in Pittsburgh might have reversed these outcomes.

## The Skilled City

Statistical tests of the skilled city hypothesis, undertaken by Prof. Glaeser with a different group of collaborators, point toward an explanation of the difference in these two relatively cold regions' population growth rates. One of the study's findings is not surprising; the average educational attainment of a region's or city's population and its subsequent population growth rate are positively correlated. One more interesting finding is that the impact of education on growth is greater among cold cities than among places that would likely be growing quickly in any case (Glaeser, Saiz, Burtless, & Strange, 2004). The difference between Pittsburgh's and Kansas City's metropolitan population growth rates is consistent with this broader finding. Among Pittsburgh's 1970 residents, 27.0% were high school dropouts and 5.3% had college degrees; the comparable figures for Kansas City were 22.2% and 6.2%, respectively (U.S. Department of Housing and Urban Development, 2018).

By itself, this finding does not tell us that a relatively well-educated local populace *causes* population growth. Again, the causality might run in the opposite direction. Well-educated people may be more aware than their less-schooled contemporaries of different regions' relative prosperity. If so, more educated people may be more likely to move to places that are growing relatively rapidly or are expected to do so. That may well be the case, but additional statistical analysis by Glaeser, et al. indicated that at least some of the causality runs from local education levels to subsequent population growth. Specifically, it turns out that the greater the number of colleges in a city or metropolitan area *as of 1940*, the higher the average level of educational attainment of the population as of 1970 *and* the faster the local rate of population growth late in the twentieth century.

Does education exert its effect on regional population growth by enhancing workforce productivity, or is a well-schooled local populace is just one of the "consumer" amenities that attract residents? One can imagine a number of reasons why one would prefer a well-educated neighbor to a high school dropout. It is possible to distinguish between the amenity and productivity effects of schooling by analyzing the relationship among education, wages, housing prices, and population growth. To the extent that higher education levels are associated with wages that are increasing faster than the local cost of housing—that is, to the extent that local *real* wages are rising relatively quickly—we can be confident that some proportion of causality runs from enhanced worker skills through increased productivity and higher local wages to faster local population growth. Conversely, evidence that housing prices tend to be rising faster than nominal wages in cities with well-schooled populations would suggest that educated neighbors are an attractive amenity.

The analysis of these relationships by Glaeser, et al. indicated that the productivity impact of an educated workforce was more powerful than the amenity value of well-schooled neighbors as a determinant of *metropolitan area* growth. That is a higher educational attainment of the regional populace apparently raised local wages—of both those with and without college degrees—proportionally more than housing prices. Further, the effect was greatest for regions with relatively insalubrious climates. That is, the impact of education on wage and population growth was greatest in those regions that would, absent the schooling effect, probably be declining.

*Within central cities*, by contrast, a relatively well-educated workforce appears to have boosted local housing prices more than local wages relative to levels of both variables across the surrounding metropolitan area as a whole. This suggests that an educated workforce enhances the productivity potential of a broad metropolitan area, making that region's firms willing to pay relatively high wages. But workers' decisions as to where to live *within* the metropolitan area seem to be more influenced by local-area amenities, including the average educational attainment of the neighborhood. The statistics on educational attainment and measures of regional prosperity also indicate that the characteristic most conducive to strong economic performance on the metropolitan level is the proportion of college graduates. Within central cities, however, the negative effect of large numbers of high school dropouts is apparently stronger than the positive effect of higher education.

The skilled city analysis also sheds light on how an educated workforce helps a region that would otherwise likely be losing population avoid that fate. It turns out that it is not only the technical skills and knowledge that trained workers bring to their jobs that boosts regional productivity. It also seems to be the case that an educated workforce can help a region with an obsolete industrial base "reinvent" itself economically. We have already observed that the decline of most northeastern cities, very much including New York, was associated with the concurrent decrease in the proportion of the workforce engaged in manufacturing. Statistical analysis indicates that the impact of education on population growth was greater not only in colder regions but also to the extent that a metropolitan area began the postwar period with a higher proportion of its workforce engaged in manufacturing. This association can be taken to indicate that a relatively educated workforce may facilitate the transition of a regional economy from an old, declining economic base to a more promising new one.

Like the consumer city framework, the skilled cities model helps explain why some cities recovered after 1980 while others did not. In the same way that durable-goods manufacturers were drawn to locations that minimized the combined costs of transporting their raw materials and products, "post-industrial" firms are attracted to the places where their key input, a skilled workforce, is readily found. Most such places are in regions offering consumer amenities, especially the amenity of good weather. There are, however, some cold, wet regions that had once been centers of manufacturing activity but had also been endowed with an educated populace, and that have continued to attract a relatively well-schooled labor force. These are the northeastern cities that began growing again after about 1980.

Even taken together, however, the consumer city and skilled city frameworks leave some of this chapter's questions unanswered. Neither model accounts adequately for the timing of the post-1980 turnaround. Nor, even taken together, can they explain why so many well-educated workers elected to remain in and contribute to the resurgence of one or another of the cities "back east" when they could, like so many of their peers, have moved to one of the rapidly growing western or southern metropolises. After all, college graduates tend to be geographically mobile and there are few obvious reasons why the consumer amenities on offer in northeastern cities, such as they are, could not be made available in Los Angeles or Phoenix.

Further, one of the findings of the skilled city studies raises an additional question. The linkage between a region's average educational achievement and a region's ability to reinvent itself economically suggests that, by itself, years of schooling may be too crude a measure of a region's human capital endowment. Colleges don't, after all, offer courses in "economic reinvention." What is it about schooling that is conducive to revitalization of metropolitan regions that would be declining if their populations included fewer college graduates and/or more high school dropouts? Is a plentiful supply of other skills or population characteristics that aren't reliably measured by years in the classroom a necessary condition for urban resurgence?

## Creative Cities

Among other things, the creative cities literature aims to answer two questions posed at the end of the previous section. What combination of human resources enables an urban economy that might otherwise be contracting to reinvent itself and start growing again? And what attracts those resources to some cities and not others?

This line of thought originated in the early 1960s writings of Jane Jacobs (Jacobs, 1961, 1969). Her principle concern at the time was to defend the vibrant street life of neighborhoods like her own West Greenwich Village against plans to turn large swaths of the City into express highways or into what she saw as lifeless and dangerous high-rise "renewal" projects. To buttress her case, she articulated an understanding of healthy cities as incubators of economic and cultural innovation and identified haphazard interaction among a wide range of diverse individuals, communities, and activities as the source of this creativity.

About 20 years ago, after it became apparent that some large cities in the northeastern United States and in Northwestern Europe had begun growing again, some of them quite robustly, a number of regional economists and other social scientists began formalizing and testing Jacobs's ideas to see what light they might shed on this urban resurgence. Professor Richard Florida of the University of Toronto participated as a co-author in many of the statistical analyses that supported this way of thinking and also popularized the conceptual framework.

Florida identified a "creative class" of occupations whose proportion in a local labor force goes a long way to explaining a city or region's late twentieth-century economic trajectory. These occupations were:

> "Super-creative Core
> Computer and mathematical occupations
> Architecture and engineering occupations
> Life, physical, and social science occupations
> Education, training, and library occupations
> Arts, design, entertainment, sports, and media occupations
>
> "Creative Professionals
> Management occupations
> Business and financial operations occupations
> Legal occupations
> Health-care practitioners and technical operations
> High-end sales and sales management." (Florida, 2012)

A focus on the incidence of certain occupational titles in a region is justified by the finding of several studies that more of the variation in wages and population growth rates across cities and metropolitan areas can be accounted for if one introduces multidimensional measures of worker skills, beyond years of schooling, into the analysis. These studies make use of a Bureau of Labor Statistics (BLS) database identifying the specific aptitudes and skills required for each of 1,122 occupations (U.S. Bureau of Labor Statistics, 2018).

The BLS's list of skills can be conveniently sorted into three categories:

- Analytical or cognitive skills such as "[t]he ability to quickly make sense of, combine and organize information into meaningful patterns,"

- Social intelligence such as "[s]electing and using training/instructional methods and procedures appropriate for the situation when learning or teaching new things," and
- Physical or manual skills such as "[t]he ability to time your movements or the movement of a piece of equipment in anticipation of changes in the speed and/or direction of a moving object or scene" (Florida, Mellander, Stolarick, & Ross, 2012, pp. 373–377).

Statistical analysis of the relationship between indexes of cities' occupational/skills distributions, and average wage rates undertaken by Prof. Florida and his co-authors supported the following conclusions. First, all other observable differences across cities, including the average educational attainment of the population, held equal, the larger the city, the higher the average levels of cognitive skills and social intelligence. The incidence of physical skills tended to be higher in smaller cities. Second, high average levels of cognitive skills and social intelligence but not of physical skills were associated with higher average wages. Third, the wage premium associated with higher cognitive and social skills increased between 1999 and 2008, but the premium associated with higher levels of schooling did not (Florida et al., 2012, pp. 368, 369).

Finally, Florida and his co-authors also found that "certain occupations affect regional development to a much greater degree than others. Education and healthcare employment have little effect on regional development, while occupations like computer science, engineering, management, and business and financial operations have a relatively large effect…., [and a]rtistic and entertainment occupations exert considerable influence on regional development" (Florida et al., 2012, p. 645).

None of the studies relating skills/occupations to indicia of metropolitan prosperity looked specifically into the ways in which the presence of the creative class enhanced the likelihood that a cold metropolitan area that had historically specialized in manufacturing would be able to reinvent itself by developing new economic concentrations. There are several clear hints, however, that "creativity" and "reinvention" might go hand in hand.

First, studies of the geography of economic innovation have identified the communication of "tacit knowledge" as essential to the process of new product creation. Geographer Meric Gertler distinguishes "between knowledge that could be effectively expressed using symbolic forms of representation – explicit or codified [knowledge] – and other forms of knowledge which defied such representation – tacit knowledge" (Gertler, 2003, p. 76). Communicating explicit knowledge, or "information," has, of course, become easier and cheaper as telecommunications technology has advanced. By contrast, it is very hard to convey tacit knowledge other than by frequent, direct, face-to-face contact. The essential role of personal contact in the creative process is probably one of the reasons why invention and new product introductions tend to cluster geographically (Audretsch & Feldman, 2004).

Second, among the individual skills categorized under social intelligence, one—"adaptability to dealing with people beyond giving and receiving instructions"—seems particularly relevant to the communication of tacit knowledge and, therefore, to the ability of a metropolitan economy innovate. In a 2009 study, Marigee Bacolod, et al., focused on, among other things, the impact of the incidence of occupations requiring this skill, in particular, on metropolitan prosperity. They found that, at any given level of educational attainment, possession of this form of social intelligence does tend to enhance an individual's earning power and that the wage premium associated with this skill increases with city size (Bacolod, Blum, & Strange, 2009).

Finally, while none of the studies of innovation in urban areas cited here has focused explicitly on the role of social networks in facilitating communication most have either mentioned or alluded to their importance. For example, although network interactions are not a primary focus of the article, geographer Allen Scott of UCLA asserts "than neither cultural homogeneity nor exaggerated forms of heterogeneity appear to be conducive to high levels of learning and innovation … but that a mix of strong and weak ties and/or interpersonal signals is more likely to maximize overall synergies" (Scott, 2006, p. 8).

Taken together, the creative cities literature suggests that the presence of three T's—technology, talent, and tolerance—are the sufficient conditions for metropolitan economic success, even absent attractive physical attributes, around the turn of the twenty-first century.

Since technology-related industries—designers and producers of information processing hardware and software, developers and users of software applications, and businesses engaged in biotechnology—are among the fastest growing industries nation- and worldwide, a regional concentration in these activities conveys distinct advantages. To measure a region's technology endowment, Florida and his co-authors adopt an index of regional concentrations across a range of these industries developed by Ross C. DeVol and co-authors for Milken Institute (DeVol, 1999).

A large, dense population of well-educated people, who collectively possess high-level cognitive skills and social intelligence and who can integrate into at least one of many local tightly linked social networks of similar individuals while maintaining loose ties with members of other groups appears to be an essential ingredient for economic revitalization. Richard Florida refers to individuals with this combination of characteristics as "talent," and he uses the proportion of the workforce engaged in creative class occupations to measure this attribute of cities. What, other than good weather, which can't be changed, or good restaurants and live entertainment, which will show up if and only if reinvention is successful, might attract talent to a city that has begun to decline and might otherwise continue to do so?

Florida identified "tolerance" or "openness to diversity" or "low barriers to entry for individuals" as a city characteristic likely to attract talent. Tolerance applies to races, religions, nationalities, and sexual orientations. Florida and his co-authors measure metropolitan tolerance with an index combining information on the foreign-born population, the degree of racial and ethnic residential segregation, and indicators of the size of local gay and bohemian populations. The gay population was measured by census tabulations of the number of adult males living together. Area residents engaged in occupations in the arts were categorized as bohemians.

Statistical analysis indicates that a metropolitan area's degree of tolerance makes a statistically significant and quantitatively important contribution to the growth of the local talent pool, well-educated people with the skills required for creative class occupations. And, by helping to attract talent, tolerance supports regions' overall prosperity. There is also some evidence that a region's degree of tolerance is also associated with high metropolitan technology scores, thereby contributing to resurgence along a somewhat different path (Florida & Gates, 2001).

## The Case of New York

The consumer cities, skilled cities, and creative cities lines of thought all shed light on the reasons why some cities that had contracted during the 1970s began growing thereafter. Looked at individually and taken together, do the insights generated by this research account for New York City's post-crisis recovery? In other words, to what extent is New York a typical resurgent North American city and to what extent is it a special case? The answer, of course, is: "To some extent, both" (Glaeser et al., 2001; Glaeser & Gottlieb, Urban Resurgence and the Consumer City, 2006).

### Fairly Cold, Very Wet, Very Well Fed, and Highly Entertained

Is New York a "consumer city?" If we base the answer to this question on the amenities analyzed in Edward Glaeser and his co-authors' 2001 study, the answer would be a qualified "yes."

In terms of climate, New York is not a winner. Its mean January low temperature of 27 degrees Fahrenheit is five degrees higher than the 14 northeastern city average, but still 13 degrees below the other 12 cities' mean. And New York is very rainy; its annual average annual precipitation of 49.9 inches is higher than that of any other northeastern city (Current Results, Weather and Science Facts, 2018). With respect to its physical amenities, the region does get credit for its proximity to an ocean coast and, in particular, to beautiful, accessible, and well-maintained public beaches.

New York ranks reasonably well with respect to the other attractive consumer amenities identified in the literature: restaurants and access to live entertainment. The region and the City have plenty of restaurants. In 2001, among the metropolitan areas referenced throughout this chapter, the New York region ranked fifth in the number of full-service restaurants per capita, after San Francisco, Seattle, Boston, and New Orleans, in that order. In terms of *haute cuisine*, the City ranked better. Of the 39 Michelin Guide two- and three-star restaurants in the United

States, 16 were located in New York City, and only three other large cities (San Francisco, Chicago, and Washington, DC) had any at all. In per capita terms, however, the San Francisco Bay Area, with 11 (or 14 if you count the Napa Valley), did better in this regard, too. The New York region ranks very high with respect to the number of performing arts companies per capita. In 2002 metropolitan New York, with 7.7 such organizations per 100,000 of population, ranked second in this regard among the 26 regions, after Los Angeles (9.5). The average for the 26 regions was 3.0. Finally, it may be worth noting that metropolitan New York ranked 17th among the 26 metropolitan regions with respect to the number of bowling alleys per capita, a correlate of economic decline[3] (U.S. Bureau of Labor Statistics, 2018; U.S. Census Bureau, 2018; Viamichelin, 2018).

## Semi-Skilled City

By the measure of average educational attainment, however, New York cannot be considered a particularly skilled region. True, New York scored a bit above average on the educational attainment measure most closely associated with wage, housing price, and employment increases on the metropolitan level, the proportion of college graduates in the regional population. Greater New York's 7.3% in 1970 was above the 6.3% average for the 26 metropolitan areas, but by less than a half of a standard deviation.

Recall, however, that a relatively low percentage of dropouts is an independent predictor of central city resurgence as reflected in housing price increases. In this case, where a lower statistic is better, New York City scored higher than the average; the proportion of New Yorkers without a high school diploma was 32.1% in 1970, which was close to one standard deviation above the 27.2% average for the 26 central

[3]For most cities, the statistics in this paragraph pertain to 2001 or 2002. But the BLS did not publish data for some of the industries mentioned for some of the cities for those years. In these cases, the data were from 2003 or 2004. The specific statistics mentioned in the paragraph are all for 2001 or 2002.

cities.[4] Based on significant statistical associations across metropolitan areas and central cities, the proportions of college graduates in the New York metropolitan area and of residents without high school diplomas in the central city would have led us to expect that, all else held equal, regional economic growth would have been about average and that housing price increases in the central city would have been relatively subdued.

In fact, however, the general economic growth in both New York City and its metropolitan area, as measured, for example, by the percentage increase in median household income, was well above average. Nominal median family income in the New York metropolitan area increased by upwards of 180% between 1980 and 2000, and that was more than one standard deviation above the 26-region average of 154%. And housing prices also rose rapidly in New York City, in both absolute terms and relative to the increase in median income. The latter point is illustrated in Fig. 17.1.

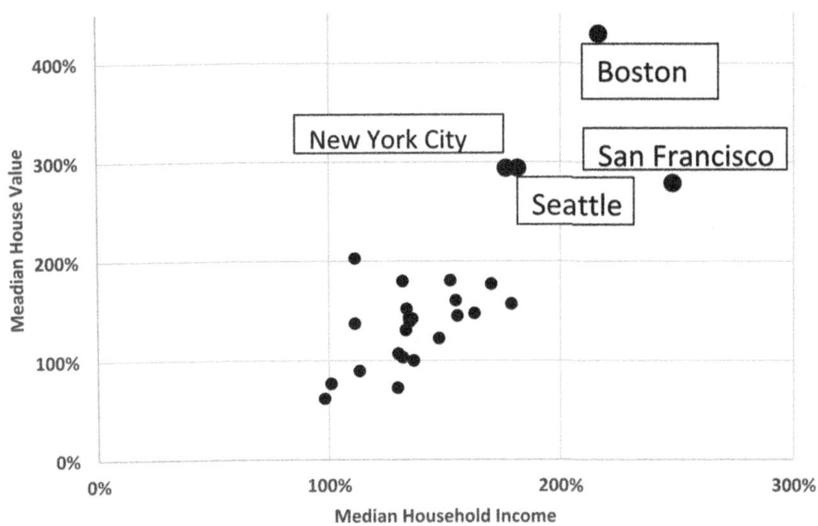


**Fig. 17.1** Percentage increases in central city median household income and median home values, 1980–2000 (U.S. Department of Housing and Urban Development, 2018)

[4]The standard deviation of the percent of metropolitan population who were college graduates was 1.5 percentage points. The equivalent figure for the percentage of high school dropouts in the central city was 5.3 percentage points.

This chart demonstrates that, by these measures, New York is clearly one of the resurgent cities identified in Fig. 17.1. But Boston, San Francisco, and Seattle, the three other cities where income growth was high but housing price increases even faster, were all "skilled central cities" as measured by the proportion of the population with at least a high school diploma; the proportion of high school dropouts was below the 26-city average in all three places. New York was the only "resurgent" central city with an above average proportion of its population lacking a high school diploma.

## Was New York's Economy Reinvented?

The skilled city literature also noted the particular importance of relatively well-schooled workforces in cities that had been manufacturing centers. Glaeser and his co-authors suggested that education enhances workers' collective ability to "reinvent" a city or region's economic base. By the end of the 1970s, New York certainly looked like it needed reinventing. It had declined as a goods-producing hub; much more so, by that point, than any of the other large northeastern regions. Figure 17.2 tracks the percentage of total U.S. manufacturing employment in six northeastern metropolitan areas and for New York City, starting with the earliest year available. Clearly, the process of "de-industrialization" started sooner and was greater in magnitude in New York than elsewhere.

But what constitutes "reinvention?" That term is not defined precisely in the skilled cities literature. A local economic base is apparently deemed to have been reinvented if the city or region had been an important manufacturing hub early in the postwar period, had subsequently lost a large proportion of its goods-producing jobs but had begun growing again after 1980. In that sense, New York City did undergo reinvention between 1970 and 2000. But the term can also be taken to imply that the city or region had developed one or more new economic base industries.

That did not happen in New York. To be sure, the sizes of various industries in the City changed substantially, some growing rapidly and

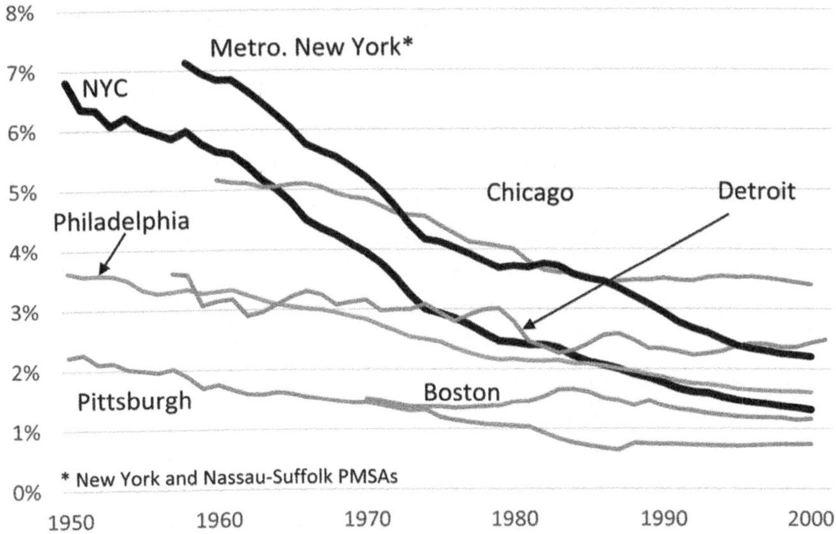


**Fig. 17.2** Selected northeastern metropolitan areas' and New York City's percentages of total U.S. manufacturing employment (U.S. Bureau of Labor Statistics, 2018)

others contracting almost as quickly. But New York's economic specializations within the U.S. economy, as measured by industrial concentration ratios, barely changed at all between 1970 and 2000.[5]

The BLS data Web site provides data on total employment data for 80 industries for these two years for both New York City and the national as a whole. Some of these industries are broadly defined (e.g., "manufacturing" or "wholesale and retail trade") and some are quite narrowly focused (e.g., "handbags and personal leather goods manufacturing"). The detailed list of New York City concentration ratios for each of these industries in 1970 and 2000 along with information on the sizes of these industries can be found in the appendix to this

[5]As defined in several previous chapters, a concentration ratio is the proportion of a city's workforce employed in a given industry divided by the percentage of the total national workforce employed in that same industry. A concentration ratio for an industry in a city greater than 1.0 indicates that the city specializes in that industry, and the higher the ratio the more unique the city is as a center for that industry.

chapter. The "reinvention" implications of these data, such as they are, can be summarized succinctly. Of the 43 industries for which the 1970 New York City concentration ratio was below 1.00, only one (men's and boys' clothing accessories) had a 2000 concentration ratio greater than 1.00. So, it does not appear that New York developed any new industrial specialties over this period. Nor did the relinquish many business lines. Of the 37 industries with 1970 concentration ratios greater than 1.00, only six fell below that specialization level in 2000.[6] In 2000 as in 1970, New York was the national center for financial market activities, for periodical and book publishing, for business services, including law, and for the fashion industry. New Yorkers had been and remained almost entirely unengaged in goods production, with the exception of the remnants of the garment industry and the catchall category of "miscellaneous manufacturing,[7]" which employed about 20,000 people in the City as of 2000 (U.S. Bureau of Labor Statistics, 2018).

New York City, where a huge early postwar manufacturing sector had contracted precipitously, managed to start growing again after 1980, and that relatively robustly, despite not having a particularly well-educated populace and without shifting to a new mix of industrial specialties. Further, New York's objectively measurable consumer city amenities might be characterized as reasonably competitive vis-à-vis other northeastern metropolises, but not necessarily compelling. Might it, then, have been the case that New York's workforce was especially creative?

## On the Creative Side

Prof. Florida calculated and published the creativity indexes and technology, talent, and tolerance rankings for 361 U.S. metropolitan areas based on data from the first decade of the twenty-first century. By these

[6] These lost specialty industries were newspaper publishing and printing, electrical lighting and wiring equipment manufacturing, commercial printing, partitions and fixtures manufacturing, toys and sporting goods manufacturing, miscellaneous fabricated textile products.

[7] This category includes jewelry, musical instrument, toy, sporting goods, and office supply manufacturing.

**Table 17.2** Metropolitan area rankings with respect indicia of creativity potential (U.S. Bureau of Labor Statistics, 2018)

| Metro. area | Among 26 large Metro. areas | | |
|---|---|---|---|
| | Technology | Talent | Tolerance |
| New York | 14 | 7 | 10 |
| Boston | 4 | 2 | 3 |
| Among 14 large northeastern Metro. areas | | | |
| New York | 6 | 4 | 3 |
| Boston | 1 | 2 | 1 |

criteria, New York scored as very much on the creative side, but not dramatically so. New York's overall creativity score was 0.871, which was about half a standard deviation above the mean for the 26 largest U.S. cities. Boston, with its 0.968 creativity index, much more than New York, should be considered the northeastern paradigm of creativity-driven resurgence. Table 17.2 presents New York's and Boston's ranks among metropolitan areas with respect to the indicators that Florida and his co-authors found to be associated with high creativity scores and with late twentieth-century economic performance (Florida, 2012, pp. Loc. 6024–6032).

It should be noted, however, that by a somewhat different, perhaps more traditional, understanding of "creativity" New York ranks much higher than any other U.S. city. Professor Elizabeth Currid, who has written extensively on the role of the arts and of artists—painters, sculptors, musicians, dancers, designers, the actors, theatrical and cinematic technicians, teachers of all of the above, etc.—in the New York's economy, found that individuals primarily employed in this field were much more highly concentrated in this metropolitan area than anywhere else in the United States. Currid went beyond the statistical analysis to argue that the concentration of so many diversely creative professionals in a few neighborhoods of a single City nurtured a cultural milieu that influenced consumer tastes worldwide and, therefore, generated lucrative commercial opportunities across a range of industries (Currid, 2006, 2007).

## The Timing Question

Except for Elizabeth Currid's suggestion that cheap housing available in New York during the mid-1970s may have helped attract "bohemians" to the City, the three broad "resurgence" hypotheses do not shed much light on the third question raised at the beginning of this chapter, namely, what accounts for the shift in some cities' economic growth trajectories around 1980. One possible explanation for a post-1980 shift can be dismissed pretty quickly; the average U.S. employer's business did not suddenly become more footloose after 1980 than it had been before. Consumers' geographic preferences became more important over time as a determinant of employment growth because interregional transportation costs became less important in determining firm location. One of the developments that reduced domestic transportation costs, the interstate highway system, was 74% complete by 1970 (Wendell Cox Consultancy, 2018). And the shift of employment out of goods production was a steady process; there was no noticeable acceleration of the trend around 1980.

One might have expected that the sharp rise in urban crime during the 1960s and 1970s and equally sharp decline after 1980 would initially have made some cities more repellant and then more attractive, with a turning point around 1980. Somewhat surprisingly, however, this appears to have had had no more than a modest quantitative impact on interurban population growth rates. That is, during the 1960s and 1970s the populations of cities with relatively high crime rates did tend to contract faster or grow more slowly than in less dangerous places, but not by a lot. The rise and subsequent decline in big-city crime rates do, however, appear to have suppressed and then boosted urban housing prices in quantitatively important ways (Glaeser & Gottlieb, 2006).

## Conclusion

Figure 17.3 highlights the difference between New York's population change between 1960 and 2000 and that of the 11 other large northeastern cities that were also unable to annex adjacent previously suburban territory either during or shortly before this period. What accounts for the fact that New York City managed to grow during this period while its peers all contracted, most quite dramatically? The three explanatory "urban resurgence" frameworks that have been developed and empirically tested would not, circa 1970, have picked New York as likeliest northeastern winner. Given the revealed preference for good weather and the fact that the local climate is about as cold and substantially rainier than the northeastern average, it is hard to describe New York as a "consumer city." Nor, given the high percentage of high school dropouts among its residents and the importance of this variable in explaining central city prosperity, can New York be considered a "skilled city." To be sure, New York's creative class is proportionally larger than average, but the City does not stand out dramatically in this respect relative to its northeastern peers. Finally, in general, none of the three theories shed much light on the timing of the turning point around 1980, which as the previous chapter argued was particularly dramatic in New York.

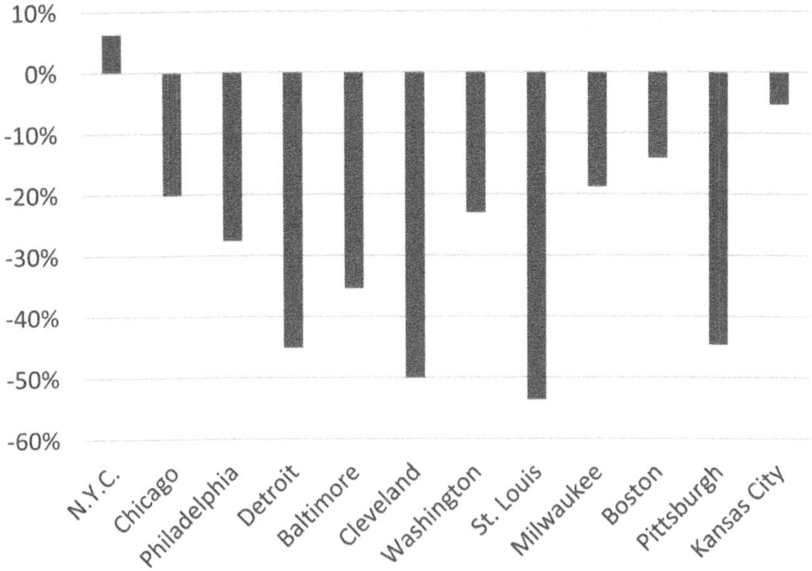


**Fig. 17.3** Percentage population change, large northeastern cities, 1960–2000 (U.S. Department of Housing and Urban Development, 2018)

The clarity of the underlying analysis and the robustness of the statistical results make it hard to argue that taken separately or together the consumer, skilled, and creative cities frameworks are invalid. It is much more likely that the three models account well for conditions in cities below the pinnacle of the urban hierarchy, but that New York represents a special case. That is a congenial conclusion for a historian, and, in any case, it motivates the contents of the next two chapters.

# Appendix

**Table 17A.1** Employment, employment growth, and employment concentration by industry: 1970, 2000

| Industry | Conc. ratio 1975 | Conc. ratio 2000 | NYC employment, 2000, Thousands | U.S. empl. change 1975–2000 (%) |
|---|---|---|---|---|
| Security and commodity brokers | 9.20 | 8.64 | 183.6 | 344 |
| Miscellaneous manufacturing industries | 7.65 | 4.10 | 20.4 | 31 |
| Periodicals | 6.67 | 7.72 | 32.4 | 118 |
| Handbags and personal leather goods | 5.59 | 6.63 | 1.2 | −79 |
| Women's and misses' outerwear | 4.07 | 8.34 | 43.4 | −54 |
| Printing trade services | 3.63 | 1.55 | 2.1 | 16 |
| Books | 3.45 | 3.87 | 13.8 | 29 |
| Misc. fabricated textile products | 2.86 | 0.79 | 4.8 | 37 |
| Women's and children's undergarments | 2.81 | 2.35 | 1.4 | −78 |
| Apparel and other textile products | 2.79 | 3.33 | 59.6 | −49 |
| Business services | 2.57 | 1.23 | 341.8 | 481 |

(continued)

Table 17A.1 (continued)

| Industry | Conc. ratio 1975 | Conc. ratio 2000 | NYC employment, 2000, Thousands | U.S. empl. change 1975–2000 (%) |
|---|---|---|---|---|
| Men and boys' suits and coats | 2.51 | 1.38 | 0.8 | −77 |
| Legal services | 2.42 | 2.75 | 78.6 | 196 |
| Finance, insurance and real estate | 2.36 | 2.29 | 491.1 | 82 |
| Blankbooks and bookbinding | 2.35 | 1.24 | 2.1 | 9 |
| Local and interurban passenger transit | 2.32 | 1.89 | 25.5 | 76 |
| Soap, cleaners, and toilet goods | 2.00 | 1.68 | 7.4 | 28 |
| Printing and publishing | 1.98 | 1.75 | 76.6 | 43 |
| Knitting mills | 1.87 | 1.34 | 4.8 | -45 |
| Social services | 1.77 | 2.18 | 178.9 | 320 |
| Insurance carriers | 1.76 | 1.04 | 47.0 | 47 |
| Toys and sporting goods | 1.70 | 0.35 | 1.0 | −12 |
| Partitions and fixtures | 1.69 | 0.50 | 1.3 | 79 |
| Communications | 1.64 | 1.43 | 67.2 | 41 |
| U.S. postal service | 1.55 | 1.26 | 30.7 | 23 |
| Commercial printing | 1.54 | 0.68 | 10.9 | 64 |
| Insurance agents, brokers, and service | 1.53 | 1.14 | 24.4 | 113 |
| Educational services | 1.49 | 1.84 | 121.1 | 133 |
| Leather and leather products | 1.41 | 1.01 | 2.0 | −72 |
| Transportation and public utilities | 1.39 | 1.07 | 213.3 | 55 |

(continued)

Table 17A.1 (continued)

| Industry | Conc. ratio 1975 | Conc. ratio 2000 | NYC employment, 2000, Thousands | U.S. empl. change 1975–2000 (%) |
|---|---|---|---|---|
| Apparel and accessory stores | 1.35 | 1.64 | 54.8 | 47 |
| Services | 1.30 | 1.27 | 1457.2 | 191 |
| Hospitals | 1.24 | 1.37 | 154.1 | 75 |
| Local government | 1.16 | 1.22 | 451.8 | 50 |
| Electrical lighting and wiring Equipment | 1.10 | 0.75 | 3.9 | 1 |
| Newspapers | 1.07 | 0.93 | 11.5 | 17 |
| Health services | 1.04 | 1.13 | 321.8 | 144 |
| Bakery products | 0.99 | 0.83 | 4.8 | −13 |
| Membership organizations | 0.98 | 1.00 | 69.4 | 70 |
| Total government | 0.91 | 0.97 | 569.5 | 41 |
| Department stores | 0.89 | 0.34 | 23.9 | 53 |
| Trade | 0.87 | 0.73 | 627.1 | 78 |
| Electric, gas, and sanitary services | 0.85 | 0.68 | 16.3 | 17 |
| General merchandise stores | 0.82 | 0.41 | 33.0 | 36 |
| Furniture, Homefurn. and Equip. stores | 0.79 | 0.75 | 24.0 | 120 |
| Total federal government | 0.78 | 0.87 | 68.2 | 1 |
| Drugs | 0.77 | 0.69 | 6.1 | 87 |
| Miscellaneous retail | 0.75 | 0.89 | 77.5 | 91 |
| Food stores | 0.74 | 0.63 | 62.1 | 74 |
| Special trade contractors | 0.73 | 0.72 | 86.3 | 139 |
| Eating and drinking places | 0.71 | 0.70 | 160.8 | 141 |

(continued)

Table 17A.1 (continued)

| Industry | Conc. ratio 1975 | Conc. ratio 2000 | NYC employment, 2000, Thousands | U.S. empl. change 1975–2000 (%) |
|---|---|---|---|---|
| Textile mill products | 0.71 | 0.41 | 6.2 | −39 |
| Paperboard containers and boxes | 0.70 | 0.31 | 1.9 | 12 |
| Men's and boys' furnishings | 0.69 | 1.24 | 4.6 | −63 |
| Manufacturing | 0.69 | 0.47 | 242.8 | 1 |
| Hotels and other lodging places | 0.66 | 0.75 | 40.5 | 111 |
| Chemicals and allied products | 0.63 | 0.52 | 15.2 | 2 |
| Furniture and fixtures | 0.61 | 0.28 | 4.4 | 33 |
| Paper and allied products | 0.61 | 0.28 | 5.2 | 4 |
| Construction | 0.53 | 0.65 | 121.9 | 89 |
| Food and kindred products | 0.51 | 0.27 | 13.0 | 2 |
| Electronic and other electrical products | 0.49 | 0.25 | 12.4 | 20 |
| Fabricated structural metal products | 0.39 | 0.34 | 4.8 | 12 |
| Instruments and related products | 0.38 | 0.11 | 2.7 | 5 |
| Fabricated metal products | 0.38 | 0.22 | 9.7 | 6 |
| Heavy construction | 0.37 | 0.30 | 7.7 | 23 |
| Total state government | 0.35 | 0.37 | 49.6 | 51 |
| General building contractors | 0.29 | 0.66 | 28.0 | 48 |
| Building materials and garden supplies | 0.28 | 0.34 | 9.9 | 97 |
| Metal forgings and stampings | 0.28 | 0.15 | 1.1 | 3 |

(continued)

Table 17A.1 (continued)

| Industry | Conc. ratio 1975 | Conc. ratio 2000 | NYC employment, 2000, Thousands | U.S. empl. change 1975–2000 (%) |
|---|---|---|---|---|
| Rubber and Misc. plastic products | 0.28 | 0.10 | 3.0 | 57 |
| Railroad transportation | 0.26 | 0.33 | 2.2 | −57 |
| Automotive dealers and service stations | 0.25 | 0.22 | 14.7 | 44 |
| Stone, clay, and glass products | 0.20 | 0.14 | 2.3 | −3 |
| Industrial machinery and equipment | 0.18 | 0.07 | 4.1 | 2 |
| Primary metal products | 0.17 | 0.05 | 0.9 | −39 |
| Lumber and wood products | 0.14 | 0.11 | 2.5 | 32 |
| Transportation equipment | 0.07 | 0.04 | 1.9 | 9 |
| State government education | 0.06 | 0.07 | 4.1 | 54 |
| Mining | 0.05 | 0.01 | 0.2 | −28 |

## References

Audretsch, D. B., & Feldman, M. P. (2004). Knowledge Spillovers and the Geography of Innovation. In J. V. Henderson & T. J. F. Bounen (Eds.), *Handbook of Regional and Urban Economics* (pp. 2713–2739). New York: Elsevier.

Bacolod, M., Blum, B. S., & Strange, W. C. (2009). Skills in the City. *Journal of Urban Economics, 65*(2), 136–153.

Current Results. (2018, April 24). *Average Temperatures for Large US Cities in January*. Retrieved from Current Results: Weather and Science Facts https://www.currentresults.com/Weather/US/average-city-temperatures-in-january.php.

Current Results, Weather and Science Facts. (2018, May 8). *Average Annual Precipitation by City in the United States*. Retrieved from https://www.currentresults.com/Weather/US/average-annual-precipitation-by-city.php.

Currid, E. (2006). New York as a Global Creative Hub: A Competitive Analysis of Four Theories on World Cities. *Economic Development Quarterly, 30*(4), 330–350.

Currid, E. (2007). *The Warhol Economy: How Fashion, Art, and Music Drive New York City*. Princeton: Princeton University Press.

DeVol, R. C. (1999). *America's High-Tech Economy: Growth, Development, and Risks for Metropolitan Areas*. Santa Monica, CA: The Milken Institute.

Florida, R. (2012). *The Rise of the Creative Class, Revisited*. New York: Basic Books.

Florida, R., & Gates, G. (2001). *Technology and Tolerance: The Importance of Diversity to High-Technology Growth*. Washington, DC: The Brookings Institution, Center on Urban & Metropolitan Policy.

Florida, R., Mellander, C., Stolarick, K., & Ross, A. (2012). Cities, Skills and Wages. *Journal of Economic Geography, 12*, 355–377.

Gertler, M. S. (2003). Tacit Knowledge and the Economic Geography of Context, or The Undefinable Tacitness of Being (There). *Journal of Economic Geography, 3*, 75–99.

Glaeser, E. L., & Gottlieb, J. D. (2006). Urban Resurgence and the Consumer City. *Urban Studies, 43*(8), 1288.

Glaeser, E. L., Edward, Kolko, J., & Saiz, A. (2001). Consumer City. *Journal of Economic Geography, 1*, 28.

Glaeser, E. L., Saiz, A., Burtless, G., & Strange, W. C. (2004). The Rise of the Skilled City. In W. G. Gale & J. R. Pack (Eds.), *Brookings-Wharton Papers on Urban Affairs* (pp. 47–105). Washington: Brookings Institution Press.

Jacobs, J. (1961). *The Death and Life of Great American Cities*. New York: Vintage Books.

Jacobs, J. (1969). *The Economy of Cities*. New York: Random House.

Scott, A. J. (2006). Creative Cities: Conceptual Issues and Policy Questions. *Journal of Urban Affairs, 26*(1), 1–17.

U.S. Bureau of Labor Statistics. (2018, July 25). *Create Customized Tables: State and Area Employment, Hours, and Earnings—Seasonal*. Retrieved from Data Tools: Create Customized Tables https://data.bls.gov/cgi-bin/dsrv?sm.

U.S. Census Bureau. (2018). *Annual Statistics: 2015 (Including Historical Data by State and MSA)*. Retrieved from Housing Vacancies and Homeownership (CPS/HVS) https://www.census.gov/housing/hvs/data/ann15ind.html.

U.S. Department of Housing and Urban Development. (2018, April 19). *SOCDS Census and American Community Survey Data*. Retrieved from https://socds.huduser.gov/Census/Census_Home.html?.

Viamichelin. (2018, May 11). *United States Michelin Restaurants*. Retrieved from https://www.viamichelin.com/web/Restaurants/Restaurants-United_States.

Wendell Cox Consultancy. (2018, April 25). *Urban Transport Fact Book*. Retrieved from USA Interstate Highway System: Miles/Kilometers Opened by Year http://www.publicpurpose.com/hwy-intmiles.htm.

# 18

# America's "Global" City

The consumer city, skilled city, and creative city frameworks all seek the causes of urban resurgence primarily in U.S. domestic developments. And, of course, the nationwide decrease in manufacturing employment, the build-out of the interstate highway system, the changing skill requirements demanded by urban occupations, the rising value of creativity in a rapidly evolving economy, and so on all influenced New York City. As had been the case throughout its history, however, more than for any other U.S. urban region, a complete understanding of New York's economic trajectory around the turn of the twenty-first century must incorporate consideration of developments elsewhere in the world and of the manner in which the United States engaged with the global economy. During the decades following 1970, shifts in the global geographic distribution of people and economic activity and in America's economic relationship with the rest of the world were profound and powerful.

The two phases of globalization that bracketed the twentieth century were similar in their fundamental manifestations. Both involved rapid expansions in global trade, in cross-border flows of capital, and in international migration of individuals and families. During the first phase of globalization New York City, as the nation's busiest port and most



A. Gurwitz, *Atlantic Metropolis*, Palgrave Studies in American Economic History,
https://doi.org/10.1007/978-3-030-13352-8_18

active financial center and as the locational choice of a disproportionate share of the nation's immigrant population, benefited from all three burgeoning flows. More recently, the growth of the trade in goods was a headwind for the City's economy as foreign-made apparel replaced New York's principal manufactured product on retailers' racks. Other differences between Globalizations Mark I and Mark II will come to the fore as this chapter progresses.

The international influences on some cities' recent histories are the subject of a fourth body of urban resurgence analysis: the global cities hypothesis. This line of thinking and the related "world cities" literature examine the impact of the increase in international goods and services trade and of international financial flows during the late twentieth century on cities and on the emerging global system of cities. World cities are loci of the international border-spanning command and control functions. Such activities have become increasingly important for the operation of a globalized economy in which "product chains"—the conceptualization, design, manufacturing, marketing, and distribution of individual tangible and intangible products—routinely run through many widely dispersed locations. In some cases, these activities are undertaken within a single multinational firm. Other products are designed, made, and sold by different enterprises under short- or long-term contractual arrangements.

As has been the case with national systems of cities, contemporary world cities form a hierarchy. Production coordination activities undertaken with successively greater economies of scale or greater economies of agglomeration take place higher in the global metropolitan ranking. At the pinnacle of this hierarchy are a very small number of places where the highest-order command and control functions can be executed with maximum achievable efficiency. It appears that these functions can *only* be performed effectively in places where the most highly qualified managerial, financial, legal, accounting, and marketing resources are all present and can engage with each other face-to-face (Friedmann, 1995; Sassen, 2001, p. 5). Scholars have developed a variety of ways of identifying world cities, of ordering them by rank, and, thereby, determining which are the global cities. These efforts will be discussed below. At this point, it will suffice to say that two

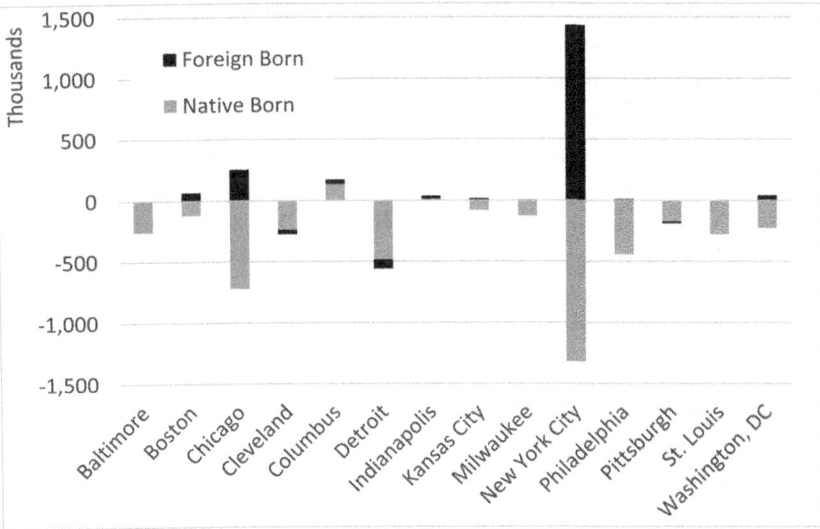


**Fig. 18.1** Change in northeastern cities' native and foreign-born populations, 1970–2000 (U.S. Census Bureau, 2018)

cities, London and New York, invariably find their places near, if not at, the top of these hierarchies.

The global cities hypotheses do not account for all of the international sources of New York City's resurgence. This literature focuses primarily on the implications of rapidly rising international flows of goods, services, capital, and ideas. Although some of the urban resurgence analyses note in passing that U.S. cities that have attracted the greatest number of immigrants have tended to perform relatively well economically, the effects of international human migration on cities' economic fates have received relatively little detailed attention. International migration has been particularly important to New York City. Recall that the previous chapter closed with the question of why New York City's population was larger in 2000 than it had been in 1960 while that of all other large northeastern cities, other than Columbus and Indianapolis, had declined. Figure 18.1 points toward one of the answers to that question. All of the cities represented in the chart, except, again, for the two annexation beneficiaries, lost native-born population between 1970 and 2000. In 2000, New York's native-born population was 1.32

million or 20% smaller than it had been in 1970. Foreign-born populations increased in most cities over this period. But only in New York did the settlement of immigrants from abroad more than make up for the loss of native-born population. Between 1970 and 2000, the City's foreign-born population increased by 1.43 million, a near doubling.

The task of this chapter is to examine the causes, manifestations, and effects of New York's position as a global city. The next and final chapter will focus on the most powerful impetus boosting the City's resurgence, namely its large, diverse, and rapidly growing foreign-born population.

## Globalization, Global Cities, Global City

### Globalization

World trade expanded faster than the global economy as a whole over the course of the decades after 1970 and especially so between 1993 and 2008 (Fig. 18.2).

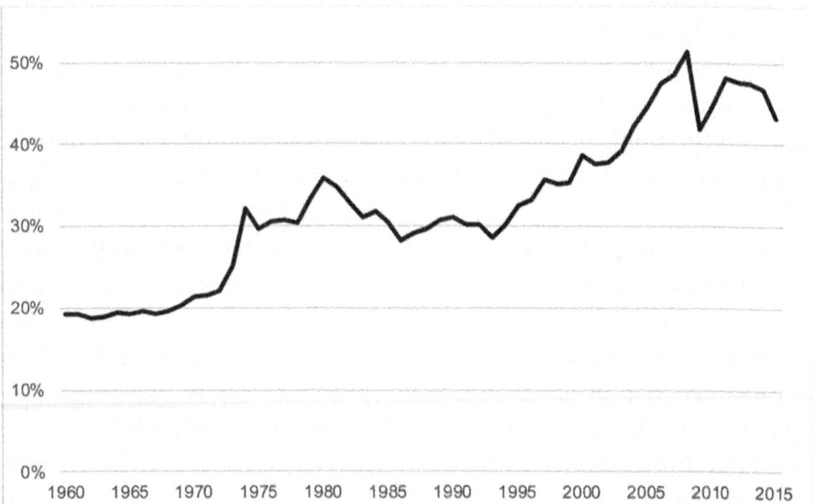


**Fig. 18.2** Total world trade (exports + imports), percent of global GDP (The World Bank, 2018)

International investment flows also grew rapidly, roughly in tandem with trade. Figure 18.3, which represents this expansion from a U.S. perspective, indicates that U.S. investments abroad ("Assets") and foreigners' investments in the United States ("Liabilities") both grew much more rapidly than GDP, the latter somewhat faster than the former. The chart also divides international investments into two categories. Direct investments are purchases of physical or operational assets, such as real estate or whole companies. Portfolio investments are stocks, bonds, and other financial instruments purchased on securities exchanges or in over-the-counter transactions. For example, Apple's 2002 acquisition of the German software company EMagic would have been recorded as an increase in U.S.-owned direct assets, while the People's Bank of China's purchase of U.S. Treasury Notes would have increased U.S. portfolio liabilities. The distinction will become important because the two categories of investments affect New York City's economy in somewhat different ways.

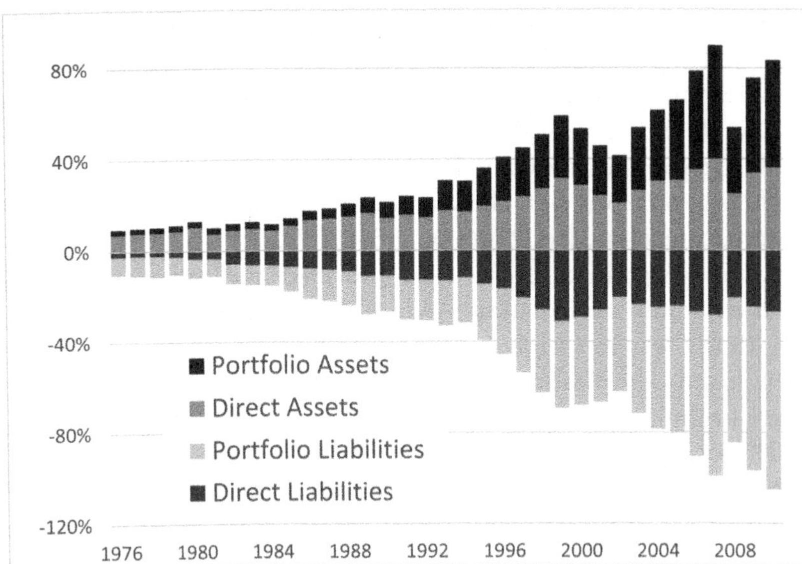


**Fig. 18.3** The United States international investment position: assets and liabilities, percent of GDP (Federal Reserve Bank of St. Louis, 2018; International Monetary Fund, 2018)

The developments leading to the late twentieth-century expansion of trade and financial flows included a decrease in intercontinental freight transport costs, "neoliberal" political shifts in country after country around the world, and the ramifications of rapidly rising oil prices.

Decreases in maritime shipping costs were modest and varied over time. The very real benefits of containerization technology, for example, were offset during the 1970s and 1980s by rising fuel costs and by the sluggish expansion of port facilities. Despite rising fuel prices, by contrast, the cost of delivering goods by air decreased rapidly as jet propulsion and jumbo-jet technology came into their own. Between 1972 and 2003, average air carrier revenue per cargo-ton kilometer declined by two-thirds. The impact of cheaper air freight costs on the value of goods shipped was particularly dramatic. Between 1970 and 2000, the proportion by value of U.S. intercontinental imports arriving by air rose from 12.0 to 36.0%. For exports, the equivalent figures were 19.5% in 1970 and 57.6% in 2000 (Hummels, 2007, pp. 133, 152).

Of the national political changes that facilitated the expansion of world trade, arguably, the most profound and far-reaching was China's ideological shift, under Deng Xiaoping's direction, from autarkic perpetual revolution to a market- and export-oriented development strategy. No doubt, too, Margaret Thatcher's 1979 election in the UK, Ronald Reagan's in the United States the next year, and similar shifts elsewhere also helped clear the way for the growth of international market transactions (Frieden, 2006, pp. 364–377).

Specific geopolitical events also provided the impetus for widespread economic reorientation. Arab oil exporters' response to the third Arab–Israeli War in October 1973, the overthrow of the Iranian Shah in 1979, and Organization of Petroleum Exporting Countries's (OPEC) success in limiting production led to oil price increases of more than a 1000% between 1970 and 1980. Jeffry Frieden encapsulated the impact of these developments on international economic relations succinctly. "The oil price explosion gave OPEC members far more money than they could spend, and they deposited much of it … into the world's financial markets. International bankers were eager to lend OPEC's 'petrodollars,' and among the principal users of these funds were the nonoil developing countries … which needed to pay for more expensive oil"

(Frieden, 2006, p. 370). To service the debt they were incurring to buy oil, countries, both advanced and emerging, were pressed by creditors to boost foreign exchange earnings by increasing exports. The investments required to produce goods for export necessitated further fund-raising in international capital markets.

The ramifications of one characteristic of late twentieth-century globalization, in particular, conditioned the impact of these developments on the economies of some of the world's largest cities. A very large proportion of late twentieth-century international trade and financial transactions has been taking place between, within, or on behalf of large multinational (or "transnational") enterprises ("MNEs"). These are companies that, under single ownership, operate in two or more countries. Such businesses engaged in and, in some cases, dominated a few capital-intensive industries, such as petroleum extraction and refining, through most of the twentieth century. But MNEs have come to play a much larger—even dominant—role in a broad range of industries during the era of Globalization Mark II.

The reduction in transportation costs and the lowering of trade barriers, along with rapid advances in telecommunications and information processing technology, which facilitated more geographically extensive and intricate logistical arrangements, combined to encourage MNEs to "decentralize" their operations. That is, the developments that encouraged the growth of world trade and international finance also encouraged MNEs to position each separate phase of their production processes—product conceptualization, development, parts fabrication, final assembly, marketing, and final sales—in its most cost-advantageous location around the world.

As a result, by 2010 about 80% of the $19 trillion in total world exports involved MNEs on one or both sides of the transaction. International transfer of goods or services between two divisions or subsidiaries of a single MNE located in different countries accounted for one-third of all global exports. Another third involved "arm's length" transactions between an MNE and another entity, which might itself also be an MNE. Transactions between an MNE and a joint venture partner, contractor, franchisee, licensee, or other related but not wholly owned affiliate ("non-equity mode," or "NEM" affiliate) accounted for about 13% (United Nations Conference on Trade and Development (UNCTAD), 2013, p. 16).

The $2.5 trillion of 2010 international transactions with or between such NEM affiliates draws attention to another manifestation of global economic decentralization. In the past, all phases of the production, marketing, and distribution process would ordinarily have been executed through departments or wholly owned subsidiaries within a single company, often at a single centralized location. More recently many firms, especially those in industries subject to rapid technological change, to the vagaries of consumers' tastes, or to complex governmental regulation have increasingly opted for more flexible modes of affiliation. A joint venture between Sony Corporation and the Shanghai Oriental Pearl Company to make and market PlayStation game consoles in China can be taken as a paradigm of such international inter-firm relationships. Computer hardware technology tends to change quickly and fashions in electronic gaming even more rapidly. Further, segments of the Chinese consumer economy are tightly regulated by the government; imports of game consoles were, in fact, banned from 2000 until January 2014 (Reuters, 2014). In international trade statistics payments from the Chinese partner to Sony may have been recorded as purchases of parts for assembly and/or as royalties for intellectual property between NEM affiliates.

Interactions between MNEs and their non-equity affiliates are not limited to direct product manufacturing or sales. Firms also routinely "outsource" essential management and control functions through long-term, stable, contractual relationships to such service providers as investment banks, law firms, accountants, and advertising and public relations agencies. This was a long-standing practice well before 1970. What has changed more recently is that the role of these external business service providers has expanded and become increasingly complicated and mutually interdependent in a world of decentralized and international production processes. Any given management decision of an MNE that manufactures and sells its products all around the world might require expert advice in some combination of labor and environmental regulations, trade and tax law, tax accounting, macroeconomic conditions, media market practices, consumer preferences, and so on in some combination of countries. The next decision might require a somewhat or very different combination of expertise with respect to a somewhat or very different combination of countries. And the information received from an expert in one specialty might necessitate getting additional input from some other authority.

It was and is unlikely, of course, that all of the requisite expertise on all relevant topics for all countries would have been available in any single location. It is not surprising, therefore, that international trade in business services expanded in tandem with goods trade. In fact, commercial services trade grew faster than goods trade. Total world goods exports grew at an average annual rate of 5.4% between 1988 and 2010 while total commercial services exports increased at 6.2 annually on average. And financial services exports rose at a 10.8% average annual rate (World Bank, 2018).

Indeed, the necessity of multidimensional, international service capabilities became particularly acute in the field of finance. The collapse of the postwar Bretton Woods regime of fixed exchange rates in 1971 complicated MNE's decision making with respect to where to borrow money. For example, suppose a German automobile manufacturer is considering introducing a redesigned car to be manufactured in a new plant in the United States. In addition to all of the legal, accounting, and marketing issues that need to be considered, the question would arise as to whether to finance the project in Euros in the Frankfurt or London markets, in dollars in New York or London, or in some other currency in some other city. Dollars will be spent to build the plant, but the car company presumably reports its profits in Euros, while issuing in some third market might produce a lower all-in cost of funds even after taking into account the cost of hedging some or all of the resulting currency risk. All of these options would have to be evaluated, and only an investment bank active in financial markets around the world through the years after 1971 would possess the expertise needed to provide something close to the right answer.

Further, the market volatility and general financial turmoil engendered by the demise of Bretton Woods and the oil price increases posed new problems for borrowers and investors and demand for solutions. Meanwhile, the deregulation following on rightward political shifts permitted a wave of innovative product development in the financial services industry to supply solutions (or purported solutions) to these problems. The new products designed often involved transactions in multiple national financial markets as investment bankers and investors sought to register new securities in the venues—the Cayman Islands, the State of Delaware, Luxembourg, etc.—offering the friendliest combination of market conditions, tax treatment, and financial regulation. The team of experts needed to identify the optimal booking center for any given transaction and then to get the deal done may have been as large and diverse as a group recruited to analyze and execute a German automaker's direct investment in a U.S. plant.

These conditions—the expansion of world trade and of international investment flows, the dominance of multinational enterprises in the execution of these activities, the critical role of high-level business service providers in the operation of the global economy, and the opportunities and challenges associated with the increased volume and complexity of financial transactions—combined to set the stage for the emergence of global cities.

## Global Cities

The fundamental premises of the global cities hypothesis are that

1. The territorial and organizational "dispersal of current economic activity creates a need for expanded central control and management" (Sassen, 2001, p. 4),
2. These central functions are performed within dense geographic agglomerations of high-level business service providers with multinational expertise (Sassen, 2001, p. 127), and
3. Such agglomerations are only found in a very few, very large cities around the world (Sassen, 2001, p. 5).

It is only natural that the phrase "central control and management" is associated with the activities of corporate headquarters. After all, major business decisions are still made by top executives and boards of directors within companies' head offices. And before the second era of globalization, most of the analytical work in support of senior executive decision making would have been undertaken in-house or, if this activity is "farmed out," very close physically to the CEO's office suite. It is apparently now less often the case, however, that the information corporate governors need is necessarily gathered and processed in close proximity to where their decisions are finalized. Over the past 30 or 40 years, global corporations have moved their official headquarters away from large cities, but the formulation of the expert advice MNE executives require takes place in dense geographic concentrations of diverse business service providers in a very small number of the world's largest metropolitan areas.

The official headquarters of the world's largest MNEs are much less concentrated in the world's largest cities now than was the case early in the second globalization era. In 1984, the headquarters of 211 of the world's largest companies were located in one or another of the world's 17 largest cities. By 1999, the number of such big-city company headquarters had fallen to 56 (Sassen, 2001, p. 109).

By contrast, the activities of firms providing internationally oriented business services are highly concentrated in a few very large cities. In 2011, a large, international team of geographers, under the leadership of Peter Taylor, produced a thorough and detailed mapping of the multiple business locations across 525 cities of the world's 75 leading financial services firms and 25 each of the leading law, advertising, accounting, and management consulting firms. The goal of the effort was to identify the principal nodes of these firms' national, regional, and global networks. The presence of, say, the office of a global accounting firm in a city, weighted by the importance of the local office, and the number of other cities in which that firm has offices, adds to that place's score as a network node. The "importance" weights range from zero (no presence) to five (global headquarters). Raw connectivity scores, the sums of weighted intra-firm interurban connections, are converted into index numbers. For each service sector and for all business service industries combined, the most connected of the 525 cities is assigned a score of 100 and other cities lower index numbers in proportion to their aggregate weighted connections (Taylor, Ni, Derudder, Huang, & Witlox, 2011).

Table 18.1 presents the results of this analysis for the 25 highest-ranked cities with the greatest number of intra-firm, interurban connections in each of the five business services sectors and overall.

The results are consistent with the global cities premises. First, business service firms operate in agglomerations characterized by dense networks of interurban connections. The subset of the 175 global business service firms examined with at least a representative office in 25th-ranked Jakarta, Indonesia, for example, had among them a total of nearly 53,000 weighted connections.

Second, in all sectors but one connectivity scores drop sharply below the second-ranked city. The third-ranked city overall and in each sector except financial services is consistently more than 25% less connected than the top-ranked place.

Finally, dense, full-service agglomerations of globally connected firms are found only in London and New York. One or the other of these two ranks either first or second across all sectors, and and no other city consistently appears in the top five across all sectoral rankings.

Peter Taylor's team also examined global networks of media companies. Although a wave of mergers and acquisitions has produced a small number of huge media conglomerates—Comcast and British Sky Broadcasting, for example—these businesses tend not to open branch offices around the world and remain geographically anchored in their initial home market. Global connections among media companies tend to take the form of international acquisitions, joint ventures, and partnerships. To identify the nodes of these networks, the researchers tabulated international ownership relationships and revenue sources of the 25 largest global media conglomerates.

The results of this analysis confirmed New York City's status as a global city *par excellence*. New York was the top-ranked city in terms of global media network connectivity and, therefore, had an index score of 1.00. Second-ranked London's score was 0.72. Washington, DC, (index = 0.53) ranked fifth, and Los Angeles (index = 0.39), which has a reputation as a global media center, ranked 16th worldwide.

Careful empirical work confirms that the global cities framework identifies a true characteristic of current world economic geography.

**Table 18.1** Global network connectivity indexes for the 25 highest-ranked cities in each business services sector and overall (Taylor et al., 2011, pp. 50–60)

| Rank | Service sector | | | | | | | | | | Overall | | |
|---|---|---|---|---|---|---|---|---|---|---|---|---|---|
| | Finance | | Law | | Advertising | | Accounting | | Management consulting | | | | |
| | City | Index | City | Index | City | Index | City | Index | City | Index | City | Score | Index |
| 1 | London | 1.00 | London | 1.00 | New York | 1.00 | London | 1.00 | New York | 1.00 | London | 96,267 | 1.00 |
| 2 | New York | 0.96 | New York | 0.89 | London | 0.75 | New York | 0.79 | London | 0.67 | New York | 95,838 | 1.00 |
| 3 | Hong Kong | 0.93 | Paris | 0.70 | Paris | 0.75 | Hong Kong | 0.74 | Paris | 0.65 | Hong Kong | 80,330 | 0.83 |
| 4 | Tokyo | 0.82 | Frankfurt | 0.59 | Hong Kong | 0.73 | Sydney | 0.69 | Chicago | 0.62 | Paris | 75,322 | 0.78 |
| 5 | Singapore | 0.82 | Washington | 0.58 | Tokyo | 0.71 | Singapore | 0.67 | Hong Kong | 0.61 | Singapore | 72,594 | 0.75 |
| 6 | Paris | 0.79 | Brussels | 0.54 | Singapore | 0.70 | Milan | 0.67 | Singapore | 0.56 | Tokyo | 70,773 | 0.74 |
| 7 | Shanghai | 0.77 | Hong Kong | 0.53 | Moscow | 0.65 | Paris | 0.66 | Tokyo | 0.56 | Sydney | 68,263 | 0.71 |
| 8 | Sydney | 0.77 | Moscow | 0.50 | Shanghai | 0.64 | Beijing | 0.64 | Zurich | 0.55 | Milan | 65,988 | 0.69 |
| 9 | Seoul | 0.70 | Tokyo | 0.48 | Warsaw | 0.63 | Buenos Aires | 0.63 | Madrid | 0.55 | Shanghai | 65,950 | 0.69 |
| 10 | Madrid | 0.70 | Beijing | 0.45 | Sydney | 0.63 | Kuala Lumpur | 0.62 | Beijing | 0.53 | Beijing | 65,939 | 0.68 |
| 11 | Milan | 0.70 | Shanghai | 0.42 | Brussels | 0.62 | Toronto | 0.61 | Mumbai | 0.50 | Madrid | 62,599 | 0.65 |
| 12 | Beijing | 0.69 | Amsterdam | 0.40 | Buenos Aires | 0.62 | Tel Aviv | 0.61 | Atlanta | 0.50 | Moscow | 61,387 | 0.64 |
| 13 | Taipei | 0.64 | Munich | 0.40 | Taipe | 0.61 | Tokyo | 0.60 | Washington | 0.49 | Seoul | 60,597 | 0.63 |
| 14 | Toronto | 0.64 | Milan | 0.39 | Mumbai | 0.61 | Shanghai | 0.60 | Rome | 0.48 | Toronto | 60,454 | 0.63 |
| 15 | Moscow | 0.61 | Chicago | 0.38 | Toronto | 0.61 | Jakarta | 0.60 | Mexico City | 0.48 | Brussels | 60,253 | 0.63 |
| 16 | Frankfurt | 0.61 | Madrid | 0.37 | Athens | 0.60 | Moscow | 0.60 | Amsterdam | 0.47 | Buenos Aires | 58,091 | 0.60 |
| 17 | Zurich | 0.60 | Singapore | 0.35 | Stockholm | 0.60 | Brussels | 0.59 | Dublin | 0.47 | Mumbai | 57,902 | 0.60 |
| 18 | Mumbai | 0.59 | Warsaw | 0.34 | Beijing | 0.60 | Aukland | 0.59 | Boston | 0.47 | Kuala Lumpur | 57,532 | 0.60 |
| 19 | Brussels | 0.57 | Düsseldorf | 0.32 | Bangkok | 0.60 | Seoul | 0.59 | Frankfurt | 0.47 | Chicago | 55,324 | 0.57 |
| 20 | Kuala Lumpur | 0.57 | Prague | 0.31 | Madrid | 0.60 | Lisbon | 0.57 | Milan | 0.46 | Warsaw | 53,880 | 0.56 |

(continued)

**Table 18.1** (continued)

| Rank | Service sector | | | | | | | | | | Overall | | |
|---|---|---|---|---|---|---|---|---|---|---|---|---|---|
| | Finance | | Law | | Advertising | | Accounting | | Management consulting | | | | |
| | City | Index | City | Index | City | Index | City | Index | City | Index | City | Score | Index |
| 21 | Chicago | 0.56 | Budapest | 0.31 | Milan | 0.60 | Rome | 0.57 | Seoul | 0.45 | São Paulo | 53,319 | 0.55 |
| 22 | Amsterdam | 0.56 | Rome | 0.30 | Seoul | 0.59 | Mumbai | 0.57 | Stockholm | 0.44 | Zurich | 53,197 | 0.55 |
| 23 | Dublin | 0.56 | Palo Alto | 0.28 | Budapest | 0.57 | Mexico City | 0.57 | Shanghai | 0.44 | Amsterdam | 53,105 | 0.55 |
| 24 | Jakarta | 0.54 | Los Angeles | 0.27 | Vienna | 0.56 | São Paulo | 0.56 | Kuala Lumpur | 0.43 | Mexico City | 52,903 | 0.55 |
| 25 | São Paulo | 0.54 | San Francisco | 0.25 | Istanbul | 0.56 | Berlin | 0.56 | Munich | 0.43 | Jakarta | 52,645 | 0.55 |

Agglomerations of multinational business service and media enterprises with tight, world-spanning connections exist in big cities worldwide. Service and media enterprises in two cities, in particular, have, by far, more such international connections than anywhere else. Those two cities are London and New York.

How has its status as one of two truly global cities affected the size and structure of New York City's economy?

## Global City

Between 1990 and 2008, prior to the onset of a severe recession, the total number of employed New York City residents, the local workforce, increased by 604,142 or by 19.5%.[1] This was considerably better than the job growth performance of most other large northeastern cities (Table 18.2).

It is tempting to attribute this relatively strong performance to these years' accelerated growth of international trade and financial flows in the context of New York's stature as one of the world's two unambiguously global cities. If, however, there is such a causal connection, it is neither direct nor obvious. For one thing, the broad economic sectors associated with global cities—finance, business services, media—did not make a disproportionate contribution to New York's economic expansion.

[1]The source for this figure is the Local Area Unemployment Series (LAUS) data assembled by the U.S. Bureau of Labor Statistics (BLS) and based on the Current Population Survey (CPS), a monthly sample survey of households. Annual average data from the LAUS are available for all U.S. and Puerto Rican counties or the local jurisdictional equivalents of counties. Another BLS data source, the Current Employment Statistics (CES), is based on a monthly survey of employers. The CPS-derived information provides a great deal of geographic detail but little industrial breakdown. The CES data are detailed on the industrial level but are for only a small number of cities. Unfortunately, the two sources are not readily comparable, and the two series differ substantially in some cases. The CES data, for example, indicate that total nonfarm payroll employment in New York City rose by 6.6% between 1990 and 2008, far below the 18.1% figure reported by the LAUS series. Some of the difference between the two figures may reflect definitional differences. Other possible sources of the discrepancy will be discussed below. The general conclusions of this chapter do not depend on which source is used. Both the LAUS and CES series indicate that total employment in New York grew faster than in other large northeastern cities (Bureau of Labor Statistics, 2018).

**Table 18.2** Percentage change in total employed persons and aggregate and per capita nominal disposable income for the central counties of large north-eastern metropolitan areas, 1990–2008 (Bureau of Labor Statistics, 2018)

| Location | Employed population (%) | Nominal personal income | |
|---|---|---|---|
| | | Total (%) | Per capita (%) |
| United States total | 26.3 | 155 | 110 |
| New York City | 19.5 | 119 | 99 |
| District of Columbia | 0.3 | 131 | 141 |
| Cook County, IL (Chicago) | 0.6 | 114 | 112 |
| Marion County, IN (Indianapolis) | 7.0 | 107 | 86 |
| Baltimore City, MD | −16.4 | 69 | 100 |
| Suffolk County, MA (Boston) | 7.6 | 138 | 125 |
| Wayne County, MI (Detroit) | −8.6 | 56 | 77 |
| Jackson County, MO (Kansas City) | −2.7 | 102 | 93 |
| St. Louis City, MO | −12.9 | 63 | 104 |
| Cuyahoga County, OH (Cleveland) | −5.9 | 71 | 87 |
| Franklin County, OH (Columbus) | 13.9 | 128 | 93 |
| Hamilton County, OH (Cincinnati) | −2.2 | 84 | 99 |
| Allegheny County, PA (Pittsburgh) | −0.7 | 93 | 111 |
| Philadelphia County/City, PA | −10.6 | 121 | 133 |
| Milwaukee County, WI | −2.4 | 89 | 95 |
| 15-city average | 0.8 | 102.6 | 104.0 |

Combined total payroll employment in the three "globalization" sectors grew by 6.9% between 1990 and 2008, only slightly faster than the 6.6% rate at which total nonfarm payroll employment rose over this period. The only one of the three broadly defined sectors that grew substantially was business services, in which the number of jobs increased by 136,000 or by 29.2%. Aggregate employment in the media or Information sectors was basically unchanged between 1990 and 2008, and the total number of jobs in financial activities actually decreased by 56,700 (10.9%) over the period.

The impact of the decrease in total financial service jobs on the overall economy was offset to some extent by changes in the composition employment within that sector from traditional commercial banking activities and into the creation, maintenance, and manipulation of financial instruments. Over the period under examination combined total local employment in "credit intermediation and related" industries, which consist for the most part of traditional commercial and savings banks, and in "insurance carriers and related" businesses decreased from 250,600 to 152,200. The contemporaneous 28,000 job increase in "financial investments and related activities including financial vehicles" from 160,000 to 188,000 did not make up in sheer numbers for the employment decrease in traditional banking and insurance. Jobs in the growing sector, however, were much higher paid than in the former. In 2001, average annual pay in the securities, commodities contracts, and investments industry in New York County was $250,502, more than twice as high as in traditional banking and 25% above what the average employee of insurance carriers earned (Bureau of Labor Statistics, 2018).

The shift to high-paying finance jobs seems, however, to have had little effect on broad measures of regional income or its distribution. Nominal per capita personal income received by New York City residents increased by about 99% between 1990 and 2008, which was a bit below the average for 15 large northeastern cities (Table 18.2).

Nor was the increase in the number of New Yorkers receiving extremely high incomes associated with an atypical increase local income inequality. Table 18.3 lists the Gini coefficients for the average U.S. county, New York City's five Burroughs, an estimate of that statistic for the City as a whole, and for the central counties of 14 other large northeastern metropolitan areas. The Gini coefficient is a standard measure of inequality. It would have a value of 0.00 for a population in which everyone has exactly the same income and a value of 1.00 if one person has all the income and everyone else has none. By this measure, the distribution of income in New York City was somewhat more unequal than that of the nation as a whole or of most other large northeastern cities. Indeed, Manhattan's Gini coefficient was the second highest among the 3100+ U.S. counties in both 1990 and 2000. But the change in New York's Gini coefficient over this decade of pronounced globalization reflected about the same increase in inequality experienced pretty much across the board in the United States and in the 15 northeastern cities.

**Table 18.3** Gini coefficients of household income in the central counties of large northeastern metropolitan areas, 1990–2010 (Bureau of Labor Statistics, 2018)

| Location | Gini coefficient | | |
|---|---|---|---|
| | 1990 | 2000 | Change '90–'00 |
| U.S.A. County weighted[a] average | 0.429 | 0.434 | 0.005 |
| U.S.A. County standard deviation | 0.039 | 0.039 | – |
| Bronx County | 0.487 | 0.515 | 0.028 |
| Kings County (Brooklyn) | 0.484 | 0.516 | 0.032 |
| New York County (Manhattan) | 0.587 | 0.604 | 0.017 |
| Queens County | 0.417 | 0.444 | 0.027 |
| Richmond County (Staten Island) | 0.404 | 0.431 | 0.027 |
| New York City weighted[b] average | 0.490 | 0.514 | 0.024 |
| District of Columbia | 0.502 | 0.549 | 0.047 |
| Cook County, IL (Chicago) | 0.456 | 0.475 | 0.019 |
| Marion County, IN (Indianapolis) | 0.423 | 0.439 | 0.016 |
| Baltimore City, MD | 0.475 | 0.504 | 0.029 |
| Suffolk County, MA (Boston) | 0.469 | 0.506 | 0.037 |
| Wayne County, MI (Detroit) | 0.457 | 0.460 | 0.003 |
| Jackson County, MO (Kansas City) | 0.374 | 0.401 | 0.027 |
| St. Louis City, MO | 0.464 | 0.488 | 0.024 |
| Cuyahoga County, OH (Cleveland) | 0.462 | 0.477 | 0.015 |
| Franklin County, OH (Columbus) | 0.423 | 0.442 | 0.019 |
| Hamilton County, OH (Cincinnati) | 0.468 | 0.488 | 0.020 |
| Allegheny County, PA (Pittsburgh) | 0.461 | 0.474 | 0.013 |
| Philadelphia County/City, PA | 0.459 | 0.487 | 0.029 |
| Milwaukee County, WI | 0.420 | 0.440 | 0.020 |
| 15-county average | 0.454 | 0.476 | 0.023 |

[a]Individual county Gini coefficients are weighted by the number of households in the county to compute the average. The result of this calculation may differ from the Gini Coefficient calculated based on direct observations of household in New York City or nationwide

[b]Individual county statistics are weighted by county populations

What effect, then, did accelerated globalization have on the overall economy of a paradigmatic global city? A broader perspective on changes in the industrial composition of employment in New York City points to an answer to this question. That answer, of course, raises some additional questions.

## Base Multiplier Analysis Revisited

The first chapter of this book introduced the distinction between a city or region's base, or export, industries, which produce goods and services sold mostly to nonresidents, and more purely local activities that serve the resident population. New Amsterdam's most important base industry, by far, involved beaver pelts. Locally oriented activities included the production of consumer goods that were costly to transport over long distances. Through all of the twentieth and into the twenty-first centuries, the City's base industries were commercial and financial services, media, and apparel.

Expansion of the base industries' employment, and the associated population increase, will lead to more activity and employment in local industries, and the proportion between these two growth rates is referred to as the base multiplier. A city's economy can expand either because its existing base industries grow, because a new local export industry emerges, or because its multiplier increases. It does not appear that any new export specialties emerged in New York City between 1990 and 2008. Specifically, all but one of the industries with local concentration ratios below 1.00 in 1990 and above that level in 2000 were in the areas of personal or health-care services. The exception was "Management of Companies and Enterprises," which, as a separate industry, has been treated as an export sector for both years.

Between 1990 and 2008, the peak years of Globalization Mark II, total base industry employment remained roughly constant. Employment in the apparel industry continued to decline rapidly while the growth of some sectors of the commercial and financial service and media industries just about made up for the contraction of other service-export sectors. Table 18.4 presents the data that support these assertions.

The list of industries in Table 18.4 requires some justification because there is no definitive way of determining whether or not a particular activity in a particular place serves a market extending beyond its immediate region. Further, all businesses sell goods and/or services to both local residents and out-of-towners. Even a corner bodega will have sold

**Table 18.4** Employment, employment growth, and employment concentration for New York City base (or "export") industries in 1990 and 2008 (Bureau of Labor Statistics, 2018)

| Sector | Employment, 1000s | | | Conc. Ratios | |
|---|---|---|---|---|---|
| | 1990 | 2008 | Change | 1990 | 2008 |
| Total non-farm | 3,563.0 | 3,849.7 | 286.7 | 1.00 | 1.00 |
| Manufacturing | 250.5 | 91.5 | (159.0) | 0.44 | 0.25 |
| Publishing industries (except Internet) | 59.5 | 53.0 | (6.5) | 2.09 | 2.18 |
| Motion picture and sound recording industries | 34.8 | 44.3 | 9.5 | 4.09 | 4.39 |
| Broadcasting (except Internet) | 22.9 | 24.0 | 1.1 | 2.49 | 2.67 |
| Credit intermediation and related | 166.1 | 92.6 | (73.5) | 2.14 | 1.22 |
| Financial investments and related | 156.6 | 182.8 | 26.2 | 9.98 | 7.10 |
| Insurance carriers and related activities | 84.5 | 59.6 | (24.9) | 1.90 | 1.43 |
| Legal services | 79.8 | 84.6 | 4.8 | 2.61 | 2.58 |
| Accounting, tax preparation, bookkeeping, and payroll services | 29.1 | 51.0 | 21.9 | 1.40 | 1.89 |
| Architectural, engineering, and related services | 21.3 | 29.5 | 8.2 | 0.71 | 0.74 |
| Computer systems design and related services | 15.6 | 46.5 | 30.9 | 1.17 | 1.13 |
| Management, scientific, and technical consulting services | 17.0 | 32.5 | 15.5 | 1.69 | 1.13 |
| Scientific research and development services | 15.6 | 15.9 | 0.3 | 0.97 | 0.90 |
| Advertising, public relations, and related services | 48.2 | 56.2 | 8.0 | 3.89 | 4.39 |
| Management of companies and enterprises | 46.4 | 63.7 | 17.3 | 0.86 | 1.18 |
| Administrative and support services | 161.8 | 189.0 | 27.2 | 1.15 | 0.91 |
| Investigation and security services | 35.0 | 48.7 | 13.7 | 2.11 | 2.12 |
| Arts, entertainment, and recreation | 44.3 | 70.5 | 26.2 | 1.29 | 1.38 |
| Traveler accommodation | 35.7 | 42.1 | 6.4 | 0.72 | 0.86 |
| Base industry total | 1,324.7 | 1,278.0 | (46.7) | | |
| Local industry total | 2,238.3 | 2,571.7 | 333.4 | | |
| Multiplier | 1.69 | 2.01 | | | |

something to an out-of-town visitor to the neighborhood, and even the most global investment bank will likely have more than a few customers who live in New York City. So, the list of sectors in Table 18.4 reflects some observation of statistics, some common sense, and some judgment calls. The statistics are the industrial concentration ratios. These are generally well above 1.00, indicating a high local concentration of activity and suggestive that the demand does not all come from the local market. A high concentration ratio is not, however, an unambiguous indicator of export industry status. The New York City concentration ratio for home health-care services was 1.66 in 1990 and 2.28 in 2008. The high concentration in this business may reflect public policy peculiarities of New York State health-care system or the agglomeration economies associated with naturally occurring retirement communities, but the statistics certainly do not reflect any large proportion of that service's consumers living outside the New York City vicinity. A more ambiguous situation involves colleges, universities, and professional schools. The New York City concentration ratio for this growing sector was 2.3 in 1990 and 2.6 in 2008, and schools like Columbia and New York University attract students from around the nation and the world. Clearly, the output of New York's higher education sector includes a substantial "export" component. Still, if we take into account the City University students, almost all of whom are New York area residents and who may account for as much as one-third of total local higher education enrollment, it is also clear that a very substantial proportion of the sector's output serves local demand.

Alternative calculations based on versions of Table 18.4 with more inclusive lists of export sectors did not, however, change the fundamental nature of the conclusion. Aggregate base industry employment in New York City did not grow between 1990 and 2008. If anything, the total number of workers engaged in producing goods and services sold to nonresidents, including those services associated with New York's role as a global city, decreased somewhat during the heyday of Globalization Mark II. Instead, the growth that did occur must have been induced by the increase in the base employment multiplier. Why and how did that happen?

## References


Bureau of Labor Statistics. (2018, July 22). *Quarterly Census of Employment and Wages*. Retrieved from Data Tools https://data.bls.gov/cgi-bin/dsrv?en.

Federal Reserve Bank of St. Louis. (2018). *Download, Graph, and Track 527,000 US and International Time Series from 87 Sources*. Retrieved from FRED Economic Data https://fred.stlouisfed.org.

Frieden, J. A. (2006). *Global Capitalism: Its Fall and Rise in the Twentieth Century*. New York: W. W. Norton.

Friedmann, J. (1995). Where We Stand: A Decade of World City Research. In P. L. Knox & P. J. Taylor (Eds.), *World Cities in a World-System* (pp. 21–47). Cambridge: Cambridge University Press.

Hummels, D. (2007). Transportation Costs and International Trade in the Second Era of Globalization. *Journal of Economic Perspectives, 21*(3), 131–154.

International Monetary Fund. (2018, June). *International Finanacial Statistics: External Sector Selected Indicators*. http://data.imf.org/regular.aspx?key=61545863.

Reuters. (2014, May 26). Sony Forms Joint Ventures in China for PlayStation. *New York Times*.

Sassen, S. (2001). *The Global City; New York, London, Tokyo* (2nd ed.). Princeton, NJ: Princeton University Press.

Taylor, P. J., Ni, P., Derudder, B. H., Huang, J., & Witlox, F. (eds.). (2011). *Global Urban Analysis: A Survey of Cities in Globalization*. New York: Earthscan.

The World Bank. (2018). *Dominican Republic*. Retrieved from Data https://data.worldbank.org/country/dominican-republic.

U.S. Census Bureau. (2018, August). *American Fact Finder: Place of Birth for the Foreign-Born Population*. https://factfinder.census.gov/faces/tableservices/jsf/pages/productview.xhtml?pid=DEC_00_SF3_PCT019&prodType=table.

United Nations Conference on Trade and Development (UNCTAD). (2013). *Global Value Chains and Development: Investment and Value Added in the Global Economy*. New York: United Nations.

# 19

# A City of Niches and Enclaves

Recall that around the turn of the twentieth century, the period of New York's most rapid expansion, the City's growth was fueled in important ways by how two groups of immigrants engaged in the local economy. The build-out of the City's essential infrastructure, a necessary condition for robust growth, would at least have been much costlier than it was absent the Italian immigrant workforce organized and deployed by Italian immigrant padrones. And New York's largest base industry at the time and for decades thereafter, women's apparel manufacturing, developed as a largely Jewish and Italian immigrant workforce employed by largely Jewish immigrant bosses.

In broad outline, the account of the City' employment resurgence around the turn of the twenty-first century parallels the earlier experience. As pointed out at the beginning of the previous chapter, the increase in the number of New York's foreign-born residents accounted for more than 100% of the City's population growth between 1960 and 2000. In other words, as important as the expanding international movement of goods and money during the two episodes of rapid globalization were to New York's development, on both occasions, it was immigration from abroad and what the newcomers did when they got there that had the greatest impact on the City's size.



A. Gurwitz, *Atlantic Metropolis*, Palgrave Studies in American Economic History,
https://doi.org/10.1007/978-3-030-13352-8_19

The parallels between the causes of economic growth at the end of the displaced nineteenth century and during the City's late twentieth-century economic recovery only extend so far, of course. In broad outline, the earlier episode involved only two immigrant ethnicities, Southern Italians and Eastern European Jews, working in two industries, infrastructure construction and women's wear manufacturing. The more recent developments involve many more ethnicities and many more individual industries. Nevertheless, a complete account of New York's resurgence must at least include and may primarily be based on an understanding of why immigration increased around the turn of the twenty-first century, who the newcomers were, why so many of them decided to settle in New York, and what they did after they arrived.

## Immigration Resurgence

Through the first two postwar decades immigration to the United States was governed by a series of laws enacted between 1921 and 1927. Collectively, these laws set maximum limits (quotas) on the number of immigrants, other than immediate family members of U.S. citizens or permanent residents, from each European country who could be admitted to the United States each year. Admissions from Western Hemisphere countries were not subject to quotas, while immigration from Asia and Africa was, in effect, barred. Within Europe country, quota allocations were biased against from Southern and Eastern Europe, and most family unifications also involved admissions from Northwestern Europe (Hatton & Williamson, 2005, pp. 183–187). Through the war years and early postwar period Congress responded occasionally to pro- and anti-immigration pressures, sometimes by temporarily increasing admissions in response to humanitarian or geopolitical crises and sometimes by tightening restrictions with the ostensible intention of barring the entry of political subversives. Until 1965, however, advocates of a less discriminatory regime were stymied by resistance from powerful nativist Congressional committee chairmen of both parties.

By the mid-1960s, the political climate had shifted sufficiently so that a major revision of U.S. immigration policy could take its place as one of President Johnson's initiatives. The Immigration and Nationality Act of 1965, also referred to as the Hart-Celler Act, eliminated the quota system's most obvious manifestations of bias. Individual country quotas were eliminated. The initial Hart-Celler caps on total admissions were 170,000 from the Eastern Hemisphere, now including Asian and African countries, and 120,000 from the Americas. No more than 20,000 entry visas could be issued for residents of any individual country in any year.

Pro-immigration advocates did, however, make some important concessions to gather the votes needed for passage. The imposition of the first cap on Western Hemisphere admissions was one such. The '65 Act assigned a high priority to family unification. Since, at the time, most U.S. citizens and permanent residents were of European descent, congressional supporters of the existing system of quotas may have taken comfort from the expectation that most of the individuals admitted under the new law would also be Caucasian. Admissions of parents, spouses, and minor children of U.S. citizens were exempt from the hemispheric caps, and preference was assigned to the immediate families of permanent residents and extended families of citizens in the allocation of permanent entry visas under the new quotas. Professionals, workers with skills that were in high demand in the United States, and refugees were also assigned preferred positions in the visa queue, but behind citizens' and permanent residents' family members (Tichenor, 2002, Loc. 4392–4416/7788).

The number of individuals granted permanent resident status did begin to increase, albeit gradually, after passage of the Hart-Celler legislation and with the admission of 175,000 Indochinese refugees after the U.S. withdrew from Vietnam. The pace of immigration did not begin to accelerate rapidly, however, until after the passage of the Immigration Act of 1990, which raised the annual cap on admissions from 290,000 to 675,000 (see Fig. 19.1).

The family-unification provisions of the '65 Act did not have the effect of bringing in large numbers of European immigrants. In fact, the proportion of Europeans among the foreign-born residents of the United States and, indeed, the total number of such individuals continued to decline in the years after the elimination of national quotas. By the mid-1960s

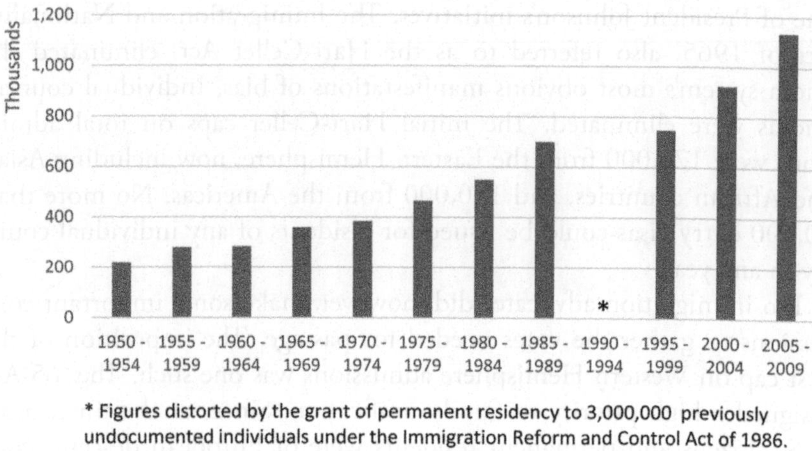


**Fig. 19.1** Average annual number of persons obtaining lawful permanent resident status, 1950–2009 (U.S. Department of Homeland Security, 2018)

Western Europe had recovered from the war and trans-Atlantic real wage differentials had diminished substantially, eliminating the economic incentive to migrate. And at that point, residents of the East European communist bloc countries were, by-and-large, barred from emigrating. So, the relatively small number of European newcomers did not offset deaths among the turn-of-the-century immigrants (Migration Policy Institute, 2018; U.S. Census Bureau, 2018).

Instead, the bulk of the new immigrants hailed from countries in the Western Hemisphere and East and South Asia, where real wages were substantially lower than in the U.S. but where people were not so impoverished that the cost of migration would have been prohibitive.

The pro-family unification bias of U.S. immigration law did have two important effects. First, it tended to boost average annual immigration rates gradually as new arrivals became citizens, allowing unlimited numbers of immediate family members to join them. Thus, even before 1990 annual immigration rates exceeded the initial 270,000 global cap. Together, the successive increases in aggregate quotas and the immediate-family exemptions increased the demographic importance of immigration in the United States. First-generation immigrants rose from an all-time census-year low of 5.4% of total U.S. population in 1960 to

11.1% in 2000. And because immigration was rising while the nation's birth rate was falling, the increase in the number of foreign-born Americans accounted for an all-time high of 37.8% of total U.S. population growth between 1990 and 2000.

Second, preferences granted extended family members of citizens and permanent residents combined with the relatively large per-country caps on total visas facilitated the formation of immigrant social networks within rapidly growing ethnic communities. Consider, for example, a pioneer immigrant who managed to establish herself in a good job in a growing industry. Suppose, that she then returned home to marry her fiancé, who, as the husband of a permanent resident, would take a place near the front of the home country's visa queue. If the original immigrant, her husband, or both became U.S. citizens, their parents could skip the queue and apply for permanent residency. Once the parents were in the United States as permanent residents their other children would qualify for family preference under their home country's quota and the pioneer couple's siblings might then encourage their own spouses and offspring to join them. Thus, the system of visa preferences could result in the growth of social networks of immigrants with increasingly distant familial connections. The incentive for additional family members to join the growing community would be especially strong if the industry that employed the pioneers continued to prosper and even more so if it had become an immigrant employment niche. And the presence of a culturally cohesive immigrant community, or enclave would ease newcomers' transition to life in the United States, further encouraging additional immigration of individuals not even distantly related to the pioneers.

Thus, over time the increase in immigration along with the preferences granted to family members fostered the creation of large close-knit immigrant communities. Further, those communities tended to be concentrated geographically in the places where pioneer immigrants had established ethnic employment niches and/or economic enclaves.

New York was one of those places. At 35.7% the foreign-born share of New York's total 2014 population ranked third among the 20 largest U.S. cities, behind Los Angeles (39.7%) and San Jose (38.1%) and ahead of San Francisco (34.1%) and Houston (28.5%) (Governing the States and Localities, 2018).

## Why Again a City of Immigrants?

Around the turn of the twenty-first century, more native-born Americans have been leaving than moving into most northeastern and midwestern cities. Immigrants have been moving into those cities, but not in sufficient numbers to make up for the decline of the local native-born population. In New York, by contrast, the increase in the immigrant population has more than made up for the loss of the native-born. Again, as in the mid-nineteenth century, New York City has characteristics that make it much more attractive as a place to live and work for immigrants than it is to native-born Americans. What are those characteristics?

## Probably Not High Real Wages

As was the case during previous immigration waves, after 1965 it was the opportunity to earn higher real incomes that drew immigrants from their home countries to the United States (Hatton & Williamson, 2005, pp. 236–241). As during those previous episodes, too, real wage differentials do not seem to have played as important a role in determining where in the United States immigrants settled. The evidence we have indicates that real wages were substantially lower in New York City than in the Midwest during the 1850s (see Chapter 7). And in 1910, at the crest of the greatest migration wave, real wages in New York were close to the large-city average but may have been around 20% lower than in Chicago (see Chapter 10).

With respect to relative real wages across urban areas, the contemporary situation mirrors that of the early twentieth century except that there does not appear to be any large city that has a dramatic advantage over New York.

Table 19.1 presents an illustrative calculation of inter-metropolitan real wage differentials for 2008 by combining data on regional price indexes from the Bureau of Economic Analysis with nominal wage data from the Bureau of Labor Statistics (BLS). Price levels, especially housing costs (not shown), were higher in New York, but so were the

**Table 19.1** 2008 price indexes and retail service workers' nominal and real average wages relative to New York City (U.S. Bureau of Economic Analysis, 2018; U.S. Bureau of Labor Statistics, 2018)

| Metropolitan area | All items price index relative to New York | Average weekly wage relative to New York | |
|---|---|---|---|
| | | Nominal | Real |
| *Northeast and Midwest* | | | |
| Baltimore | 0.89 | 0.85 | 0.95 |
| Boston | 0.93 | 0.87 | 0.94 |
| Chicago | 0.88 | 0.84 | 0.95 |
| Cleveland | 0.75 | 0.75 | 1.00 |
| Columbus | 0.78 | 0.81 | 1.04 |
| Detroit | 0.83 | 0.83 | 1.01 |
| Kansas City | 0.77 | 0.79 | 1.02 |
| Milwaukee | 0.79 | 0.73 | 0.92 |
| Philadelphia | 0.90 | 0.86 | 0.95 |
| Pittsburgh | 0.76 | 0.75 | 0.99 |
| St. Louis | 0.73 | 0.79 | 1.08 |
| Washington | 0.99 | 1.11 | n.a. |
| Regional average | 0.83 | 0.83 | 0.98 |
| *South and West* | | | |
| Dallas-Ft. Worth | 0.85 | 0.92 | 1.09 |
| Denver | 0.84 | 0.86 | 1.03 |
| Houston | 0.83 | 0.87 | 1.04 |
| Los Angeles | 0.96 | 0.97 | 1.01 |
| Miami | 0.88 | 0.88 | 1.00 |
| Phoenix | 0.86 | 0.92 | 1.07 |
| San Antonio | 0.78 | 0.81 | 1.04 |
| San Diego | 0.96 | 0.91 | 0.95 |
| San Francisco | 1.02 | 1.11 | 1.08 |
| San Jose | 1.02 | 1.22 | 1.19 |
| Regional average | 0.9 | 0.95 | 1.05 |
| All city average | 0.86 | 0.88 | 1.02 |

nominal wages paid to retail workers, a sector in which large numbers of immigrants are employed, and to about the same degree across other northeastern and Midwestern areas. Southern and Western metropolitan areas may have, on average, offered retail workers some modest advantage relative to New York with respect to real wages. Metropolitan

**Table 19.2** Average 2008 weekly real wages relative to New York City (U.S. Bureau of Economic Analysis, 2018; U.S. Bureau of Labor Statistics, 2018)

| Industry | Northeast and midwest | | West and south | |
|---|---|---|---|---|
| | Average | # | Average | # |
| Retail trade | 0.98 | 11 | 1.05 | 10 |
| Grocery stores | 1.06 | 10 | 1.17 | 9 |
| Convenience stores | 1.01 | 10 | 1.03 | 8 |
| Urban transit systems | 0.72 | 4 | 0.73 | 4 |
| Taxi & limousine service | 0.96 | 10 | 0.98 | 8 |
| Security guards and patrol services | 1.27 | 9 | 1.11 | 8 |
| Janitorial services | 0.77 | 11 | 0.77 | 10 |
| Continuing care, assisted living facilities | 1.03 | 7 | 0.99 | 9 |
| Child day care services | 0.96 | 11 | 1.02 | 7 |
| Traveller accommodation | 0.71 | 9 | 0.75 | 9 |
| Full service restaurants | 0.81 | 11 | 0.87 | 6 |
| Limited-service eating places | 0.97 | 10 | 1.03 | 9 |
| General automotive repair | 1.13 | 8 | 1.08 | 9 |
| Personal care services | 1.08 | 12 | 1.09 | 10 |
| Average | 0.96 | | 0.98 | |

San Jose's 19% real wage premium relative to New York, which boosts the South and West average substantially, is, however, quite surprising, indeed somewhat suspect, given the anecdotal evidence regarding the high cost of housing in and around Silicon Valley.

Table 19.2 presents average 2008 inter-metropolitan wage statistics for a range of industries that, as will be shown below, (a) grew in New York during the post-1975 period, (b) had become employment niches for one or more immigrant ethnicities, and (c) for which nominal wage data are available. The underlying calculations are the same as those used to derive the information in Table 19.1. The number of metropolitan areas for which data on each industry's wage rate was available is included because the statistical reliability of the averages differs.

These data indicate that the situation in most industries mirrors the conclusion with respect to retail services; in general, real wages in New York do not differ markedly from the average of other metropolitan areas. But six notable exceptions stand out. New York real wages were higher than the large metropolitan area average in urban transit, janitorial services, full-service restaurant, and traveler accommodation industries while security guards and automotive mechanics are apparently paid substantially less in cost-of-living adjusted terms in the New York region than elsewhere.

The statistic for urban transit systems may not be reliable because data were available for only four cities other than New York. We can speculate that because New York's highest-end restaurants may be more expensive than elsewhere workers at these establishments earn a premium wage, which may include tips. The relatively low wages earned by security personnel and automotive repair workers in the New York area is something of a mystery.

The high wages earned by traveler accommodation industry employees do highlight a unique aspect of the New York City labor market. This industry is much more highly unionized in New York than elsewhere. Nationwide 7.4% of the employees of the hotel and accommodation industry are union members; the equivalent figure for New York City is 36%. This reflects the fact that New York is more of a union town than most places; while 10.7% of all U.S. workers are union members, in New York City, 24.3% are. It is hard, however, to generalize about the impact of unionization on relative wage rates. In New York, 56.5% of employees of nursing care facilities are union members compared to only 7.0% nationwide. But the average real wage paid to employees of continuing care and assisted living facilities locally was almost exactly the same as the average across large metropolitan areas. And the unionization rate for building and security services was 8% in New York and 4.7% on average across the country. But this industrial category includes both janitorial services, an industry in which New Yorkers were paid much more than elsewhere, and security services in which local real wages were much lower than average across large metropolitan areas (Milkman & Luce, 2017).

These intriguing exceptions notwithstanding, the general conclusion that employment in New York does not appear to offer any distinct across-the-board advantage or disadvantage relative to other populous metropolitan areas with respect to average real wage rates in the industries that employ large numbers of immigrants. We must, therefore, look elsewhere for an answer to the question of what New York's attraction for post-1965 immigrants has been.

A good place to start is to find out which immigrants were most attracted to New York.

## Who Has Been Coming to New York?

With respect to its national origins and the timing of its growth New York City's foreign-born population was, in many but not all ways, a microcosm of the national phenomenon. In terms of broad geographic origins New York's 2000 foreign-born population was very similar to that of the nation as a whole, except that the City was home to proportionally more East Asians and Caribbeans and proportionally fewer Vietnamese and Mexicans than the rest of the country (Migration Policy Institute, 2018; U.S. Census Bureau, 2018).

These broad regional categories are insufficiently fine-grained, however, to serve as the basis for analysis of the varying roles of immigrant ethnic communities in the City's economy. Caribbean-New Yorkers, for example, include large numbers of Dominicans, Jamaicans, and Haitians, whose respective native languages are Spanish, English, and Kreyòl.

Table 19.3 provides a breakdown of the national origins of New York City's foreign-born population as reported in the 2000 census and highlights one reason why an account of the role of immigrants in New York's economy around the turn-of-the-twenty-first century must be much more complicated than what occurred 100 years earlier. In 1920, more than half of New York City's population of first-generation immigrants had been born in Italy, Russia, or Poland (NYC Department of City Planning, 2018). The preponderance of the Italians came from a

**Table 19.3** Birth countries of foreign-born residents of New York City, 2000 (U.S. Census Bureau, 2018)

| Country | Population | % of total foreign-born |
|---|---|---|
| Dominican Republic | 369,186 | 12.9 |
| China[a] | 261,551 | 9.1 |
| Jamaica | 178,922 | 6.2 |
| Guyana | 130,647 | 4.6 |
| Mexico | 122,550 | 4.3 |
| Ecuador | 114,944 | 4.0 |
| Haiti | 95,580 | 3.3 |
| Trinidad and Tobago | 88,794 | 3.1 |
| Colombia | 84,404 | 2.9 |
| Russia | 81,408 | 2.8 |
| Italy | 72,481 | 2.5 |
| Korea | 70,990 | 2.5 |
| Ukraine | 69,727 | 2.4 |
| India | 68,263 | 2.4 |
| Poland | 65,999 | 2.3 |
| Philippines | 49,644 | 1.7 |
| Bangladesh | 42,865 | 1.5 |
| Pakistan | 39,165 | 1.4 |
| Honduras | 32,358 | 1.1 |
| Greece | 29,805 | 1.0 |
| Other | 801,749 | 27.9 |

[a]Including immigrants from Hong Kong and Taiwan

small number of southern *compartimenti*, and most of the Russians and Poles were Yiddish-speaking Jews. Thus, the economic role of immigrants at the earlier period could be reasonably encompassed in an analysis of two immigrant ethnicities in two industries.

In the late twentieth century, by contrast, the national origins and cultural affinities of the foreign-born population were much more diverse than in 1920; it took nine national origins to get to 50% of the total number of foreign-born residents in 2000. Further, the Chinese population was divided among speakers of Cantonese and Mandarin, mutually unintelligible as spoken languages. And the Guyanese and Trinidadian communities each included two distinct ethnic groups, those of African and those of South Asian origin.

## What Employment Opportunities Have Been on Offer?

The diverse cohorts of post-1965 immigrants took large numbers of jobs and created ethnic employment niches in many more than two growing industries in New York City. Not surprisingly, given the broad trends in the national and local economies, almost all of these industries were in the service sector. As will be discussed below, the garment industry was a sole, temporary, but important exception to this generalization. Table 19.4 lists all of the industries in which (a) employment was growing rapidly between 1990 and 2008 and (b) unlike, for example, elementary and secondary education, jobs were accessible to recent immigrants.

**Table 19.4** New York City employment and employment growth, total and in key[a] service sectors, 1990–2008 (Bureau of Labor Statistics, 2018)

| Sector | Total employment change, 1000s | Percent |
|---|---|---|
| Total non-farm employment | 237.1 | 7 |
| Goods producing | −151.3 | −40 |
| Service producing | 388.5 | 12 |
| *Representative service sectors* | | |
| Retail trade | 36.6 | 14 |
| Transit and other ground transportation | 9.8 | 54 |
| Colleges, universities, professional schools | 36.4 | 50 |
| Ambulatory health care services | 86.8 | 117 |
| Home health care services | 45.2 | 290 |
| Nursing & residential care facilities | 19.8 | 36 |
| Accommodation and food services | 65.8 | 38 |
| Representative sectors total | 300.4 | 70 |
| Percent of total service producing | 77% | |

[a]See text

Each of these sectors either became important employment niches for one or more of New York's immigrant communities, played an important role in the development of ethnic enclave economies, or influenced the ethnic composition of New York's population in some other way.

Sociologist Roger Waldinger, who has written extensively on the subject of immigrant communities' engagement in New York City's economy, defines an ethnic employment niche as "an industry, employing at least one thousand people, in which a group's representation is at least 150% of its share of total employment" (R. Waldinger, 1996, p. 95). Recent immigrants are not the only New Yorkers who are likely to work in ethnic niches. The information in Table 19.5 indicates that large proportions of second- and third-generation European immigrants or the descendants African-American migrants to New York tend to gravitate to industries in which their co-ethnics are overrepresented. Nor is it the case that all ethnic employment niches are in the private sector.

The development and persistence of ethnic employment niches are yet another manifestation of the importance of social networks in the operation of an urban economy, in this instance as a means of conveying information about job openings to job seekers or about potential employees' qualifications to bosses or to human resources departments.

Philip Kasinitz and Milton Vickerman describe an ethnic enclave as a compact area within a city "characterized by a high degree of coethnicity among owners and employees of firms, the spatial concentration of

**Table 19.5** Percentage of employed populations working in ethnic niches[a] (R. Waldinger, 1996, pp. 96, 104, 110, 120, 126, 130)

| Ethnicity | 1970 (%) | 1980 (%) | 1990 (%) |
|---|---|---|---|
| *Largely native-born populations* | | | |
| African-Americans | 43 | 34 | 37 |
| Jews | 49 | 41 | 49 |
| Italians | 32 | 14 | 17 |
| *Largely immigrant populations* | | | |
| West Indians | 50 | 40 | 34 |
| Chinese | 79 | 61 | 50 |
| Dominicans | 65 | 65 | 55 |

[a]See text for definition

ethnic businesses … and sectoral specializations among immigrant businesses" (Kasinitz & Vickerman, 2001, p. 193). This concept lacks a precise quantitative formulation, but its paradigm in the United States is the local centered on *Calle Ocho* in Miami, the heart of South Florida's Cuban-American enclave.

The identification of the largest immigrant communities in late twentieth-century New York and of the City's fastest-growing industries provides the context for the hypothesis that will be explored in the remainder of this chapter. The contention is that population and employment growth in New York was relatively robust around the turn of the twenty-first century because of the collective success specific immigrant communities achieved in establishing employment niches in specific industries and prosperous ethnic business enclaves. This assertion will be supported by a review of the published studies of the individual industries, individual immigrant ethnicities, or combinations of the two.

## Niches and Their Denizens

### Garments Again?!

Garment manufacturing was not, of course, one of fastest-growing industries in New York in the years after 1990; it was, in fact, shrinking rapidly. In 1965, the year that President Johnson signed the Hart-Celler legislation, however, 241,300 New Yorkers or 6.7% of the City's total workforce were still employed in the "apparel and other textile products industry." As the third wave of mass migration began arriving in the United States from the Americas and from Asia, therefore, the garment industry was still an employer of considerable consequence in New York City. Further, the 1960s and 1970s were the decades during which my Grandmother's generation, who, as young immigrants, had taken jobs in the garment industry early in the twentieth century, was leaving the workforce while their descendants were disinclined to follow the same career path. The retirees, both the workers and the bosses, were, in large part, replaced by new New Yorkers. For a period of time early in the postwar period, many of the factory-floor positions that had previously been occupied by immigrant Jews or Italians and had not yet vanished by attrition were filled by African-Americans or native-born Hispanics. The latter, at that time and place, would mostly have been Puerto Rican (Fig. 19.2). By 1990, however, foreign-born Asians and Hispanics had become the most common ethnicities among garment industry workers.

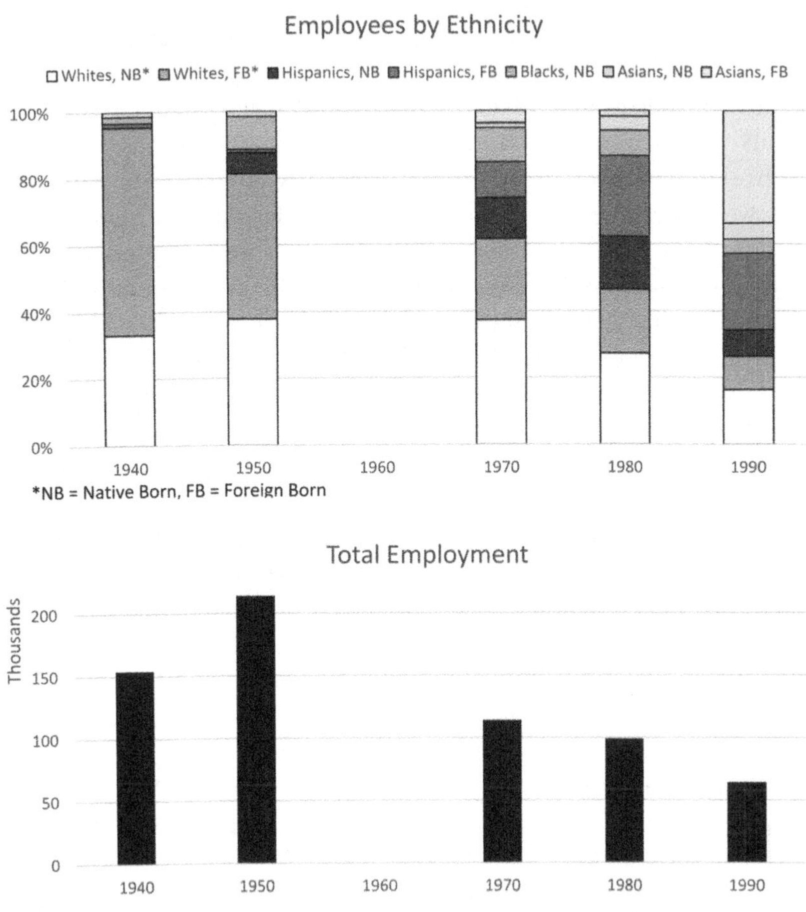


**Fig. 19.2** Apparel industry employment in New York City, number of workers and distribution by ethnicity and nativity, 1940–1990 (R. Waldinger, 1996, p. 144)

And these groups were also increasingly engaged as firm owners in this industry.

This generational and ethnic succession attracted considerable general and scholarly attention as it was taking place, but the new immigrant employment niche was far from robust or long-lived. By 1990, local employment in the apparel sector had fallen to 90,300 or 1.1% of the City's workforce and in 2008 the 21,900 local garment workers were only 0.6% of employed New Yorkers. Nevertheless, for a period of time during the City's resurgence New York's garment industry was, once again, an important venue in which the City's two largest immigrant ethnicities engaged in the local economy.

Both the persistence of garment manufacturing in New York City and its eventual near disappearance were manifestations of globalization. Purveyors of standardized garments for sale to Americans, underwear, for example, or persistently popular fashion items such as, say, tight-fitting blue-jeans, had shifted a great deal of production offshore by the early 1980s. And, even if bulk apparel manufacturing had remained in the United States, it is unlikely that much such production would have taken place in high-nominal wage and high-rent New York City. But, given how rapidly consumer tastes change, it often took too long to gear production up in, say, South Korea, to meet demand for the new, possibly ephemeral styles. So, the fashion industry still needed a cadre of flexible manufacturers who could, on short-notice, reliably produce modest quantities of goods for quick delivery to North American stores. New York, where fashion-trends were conceived, where chain-store buyers congregated, and where a product manager could find an agglomeration of small, diversified, flexible, highly competitive subcontractors, was still a good location to place such orders. By the early years of the twenty-first century, however, communication technology had advanced, air-freight costs had fallen, and globe-spanning business networks had developed to the point that New York's suppliers no longer had much advantage when it came to just-in-time delivery of ephemeral product lines.

What effects, then, did the garment industry's temporary ethnic transitions have on the economies of New York's Chinese and Dominican communities and of the City as a whole? In the aggregate, the impacts on the two communities were different. To be sure, there were both Dominican and Chinese shop-owners and workers, and the money earned while New York's garment industry was still viable did support the development of ethnic enclave economies for both national origins. But entrepreneurship was much more common in the Chinese community than among Dominicans. Roger Waldinger found, for example, that while the proportions of the two ethnic groups in New York's 1980 garment industry workforce were roughly equal, Chinese accounted for 7.8% of the self-employed in the garment industry and Dominicans for only 2.1%. Waldinger also found that Chinese-owned firms were larger and longer-lived than Dominican enterprises (R. D. Waldinger, 1986, p. 167).

Waldinger explored several explanations for this difference, three of which seemed most likely. First, a larger proportion of Chinese than Dominican had pre-migration occupational backgrounds that may have prepared them better to establish and sustain a business. Only a minority of immigrants arriving in the United States declared an occupation upon arrival. Of those that did, however, half of the Chinese but only 11% of the Dominicans had been employed in either professional, technical, and kindred occupations or as managers and administrators in their home countries. Second, Waldinger suggests that Dominican immigrants may be less committed than the Chinese to live the rest of their lives in the United States. The evidence for this is circumstantial. A larger proportion of foreign-born Chinese than Dominicans have become U.S. citizens, and many more Dominicans arrive in the United States with tourist and other short-term visas than as bona fide permanent residents. Immigrants who intend to return to their home country may be less willing to forego immediate accumulation of cash in favor of tying up capital in a risky business enterprise. And those who remain longer than their entry visas allow and become undocumented aliens are probably averse to the visibility associated with going into business on one's own. Further, any small initial advantage could have been magnified as members of the Chinese community may have been more aware business opportunities that could be communicated through social networks to compatriot would-be entrepreneurs (R. D. Waldinger, 1986, pp. 167–187).

The Chinese garment industry's demand for labor, along with that of restaurants, fostered the growth of this ethnic community in New York City. The availability of jobs in Chinese-speaking workplaces for both men and women with minimal skills would have helped attract immigrant families to New York. In fact, it seems unlikely that, absent the temporary but timely engagement with the garment industry, New York would have become home to the nation's largest concentration of Chinese immigrants by the turn of the twenty-first century (R. Waldinger, 1996, pp. 124–128).

Whatever the reasons, by the early twenty-first century, after the City's garment industry had essentially vanished as an important local employer of working-class immigrants, New York's Chinese community was considerably better off than the Dominican. In 2005, the New York metropolitan area unemployment rate for Asians was 4.2%, well below the 6.4 and 7.0% rates for all Latinos and African-Americans, respectively, and only slightly above the 3.7% rate for Whites. At the same time, at 7.4%, Dominicans had the highest unemployment rate among Hispanic ethnicities. Puerto Ricans ranked second highest in this regard at 6.8% (Limonic, 2005, pp. 3, 6).

We will revisit the economic trajectories of these two immigrant ethnicities below.

## Health Services: A Gendered Jamaican Niche

By any measure, the health services industry became a much more important employer, both nationwide and, especially, in New York City over the turn of the twenty-first century. As Table 19.6 indicates, health services employment accounted for a much larger share of total job growth in the City than nationwide.

**Table 19.6** Percentage employment growth, 1990–2008 (U.S. Bureau of Labor Statistics, 2018)

| | Total jobs (%) | Health services (%) | Ratio |
|---|---|---|---|
| U.S.A. | 25.3 | 61.9 | 2.4 |
| NYC | 6.6 | 44.7 | 6.8 |

It also is the case that the medical labor market has become international. In 2002, the Organization for Economic Cooperation and Development (OECD) reported that "foreign-educated health professionals represent more than a quarter of the medical and nursing workforces of Australia, Canada, the United Kingdom, and the United States" (Kingma, 2006, p. 13).

Although globalization has affected all of the jobs in the health-care hierarchy, scholarly attention has been focused most intently on the market for registered nurses (RNs). And it won't be surprising that analysis of the domestic economic geography of the phenomenon finds that the proportion of immigrants in New York's health-care workforce is among the highest in the nation. In the year 2000, for example, at 50%, New York ranked second after Miami (58%) among the nation's largest metropolitan areas with respect to the share of the foreign-born in the region's workforce of RNs. By way of comparison, the equivalent figure for Boston was 13% (Cortes & Pan, 2014, p. 32).

Where New York differs from most other metropolitan areas, again, except for Miami, was in the proportion of Jamaican nurses. To be sure, the region's hospitals employ a substantial number of Philippines-born nurses, the most common foreign-born ethnicity among immigrant RNs both nationwide (30%) and in New York City (20%). On average between 1980 and 2010, 15% of the metropolitan area's foreign-born RNs or seven percent of all the region's RNs had been born in Jamaica (Cortes & Pan, 2014, p. 40). And the Jamaican presence in the local health-care sector extended well beyond this single occupational category. In 1990, 7.5% of Jamaica-born women working in New York City were employed as RNs, but 21.4% of that population were working as "nurses' aides, orderlies, and attendants" in health-care facilities.

One would not ordinarily think that information transmitted through ethnic social networks would play an important role in recruiting the workforce in an industry, like big-city hospitals, dominated by large institutions served by bureaucratic, process-oriented human resources departments. Nevertheless, such industries have become important ethnic niches for minority populations. For example, New York City's African-American population had established an employment niche in state and local governments, a bureaucratic sector *par excellence*. In 1990, when 16.8% of the City's total workforce was employed in the public sector, 27.8% of African-Americans worked in government jobs. It is, therefore, reasonable to speculate that a combination of the preference granted to nurses in post-1965 immigrant visa queues along with Jamaican immigrants' relatively high average level of educational attainment, served as the community's initial entrée into the health services field. Thereafter, the operation of social networks within a tight-knit immigrant community—90% of the Jamaicans who entered the country legally as immigrants between 1983 and 1991 were admitted under the family-unification provisions of the Hart-Celler legislation—could have fostered the development of a reliable ethnic employment niche (Kasinitz & Vickerman, 2001, pp. 195, 199; U.S. Bureau of Labor Statistics, 2018; R. Waldinger, 1996, p. 110).

More precisely, employment in the health-care sector was an ethnic niche for Jamaican women.

In 1970, 50% of employed (foreign- and native-born) West Indian[1] New Yorkers were working in ethnic niche industries. By 1990 that percentage had declined to 34%, which was lower than the equivalent figure for any of New York's other populous ethnic minorities (see Table 19.6). This figure for the degree of niche employment, however, conceals a large difference between the ways in which West Indian women and men engage in the New York City economy. West Indian women's jobs were highly concentrated in ethnic niches: mostly in the health-care and hospitality industries. In 1990, 73% of the West Indian employees in niches were women. By the end of the twentieth century, West Indian men, by contrast, were employed in a wide range of non-niche activities.

[1]Some of the literature summarized in this section focuses specifically on immigrants from Jamaica. Roger Waldinger, however, discusses "West Indian" New Yorkers, a group that includes English-speaking immigrants from Trinidad and Tobago, Barbados, and, in some instances, French- or Kreyol-speaking Haitians. About 60% of New Yorkers who hail from the formerly British West Indies are Jamaican.

## Accommodators

Although it did not expand as much as the health care, the hotel industry did grow robustly on average during the post-crisis period. As Fig. 19.3 indicates, however, this expansion was interrupted for one-year periods during the 1990–1991 recession and in the wake of the September 11, 2001, terrorist attack. The growth of New York's hotel industry through the period of resurgence is, in substantial part, another manifestation of globalization. One analysis concluded, for example, that in 2015 international travelers accounted for 45.8% of the total demand for hotel accommodations in New York City. The only U.S. city with a higher such statistic was Miami at 57.5%. The figure for third-ranked, Oahu, HI, was 37.5% (Corgel & Sellers, 2017).

The jaggedness of the line in Fig. 19.3 reflects the seasonality of hotel employment. Employers in seasonally variable industries need efficient ways of recruiting an adequate workforce when business picks up. Workers in such sectors, who expect to be laid off occasionally, need efficient ways of finding replacement jobs. For this reason, along with the fact that housekeeping and kitchen jobs at hotels are not particularly

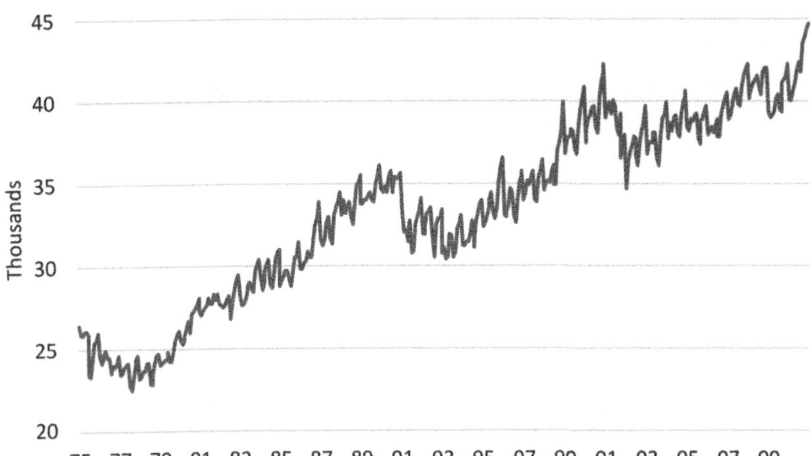


**Fig. 19.3** Hotel employment in New York City, 1975–2010 (U.S. Bureau of Labor Statistics, 2018)

attractive occupations, staffing hotels can quite difficult in most of the United States. Roger Waldinger quotes an industry consultant who reported that in 1987 a "labor shortage" facing this industry was bad and getting worse but also cited New York as an exception to this generalization. At the turn of the twentieth-first century, New York recent immigrants are still willing to take these jobs, while social networks can help human resource managers identify willing workers when the need arises. It isn't surprising, therefore that, as in the garment industry, the hotel industry workforce has undergone a process of ethnic succession in the decades after 1965. By 1990, Dominican and West Indian immigrants had replaced many of the African-Americans and Puerto Ricans who had held the "back of the house" positions in hotels earlier in the post-War period (R. Waldinger, 1996, pp. 155–163).

## Taxi Wallahs

Both the importance of taxis to New York's post-industrial economy and the fact that this industry has become an ethnic niche would be obvious to anyone running late to an uptown client event around sundown during the month of Ramadan. In fact, large proportions of the City's yellow-cab drivers and owners were born in Pakistan, Bangladesh, or India. Collectively, these three communities constitute the New York's fourth largest immigrant ethnicity after Dominicans, Chinese, and Jamaicans (see Table 19.3).

New York's yellow-cab industry is governed by access to taxi "medallions." Since 1930s the City government has limited the number of cabs on the street by issuing a fixed number of taxi licenses, evidenced by numbered medallions affixed to the cab body, and made it illegal for any unlicensed vehicle to pick up customers. Some medallions were issued to individual owner-drivers, others to corporate operators of taxi fleets. Beginning in the 1950s, sales of medallions to other qualified operators were permitted and even facilitated by the City government. Because the number of medallions was essentially fixed even as the City's population grew and became more prosperous, the right to operate a yellow cab became a very valuable capital asset. The prices of a medallion peaked at above $1 million in 2014, possibly boosted by a credit-fueled bubble, and then began declining as ride-sharing services such as Uber and Lyft, which operate under a different regulatory regime, began becoming popular (Mathew, 2005, pp. 49–55; Perry, 2014).

As the capital cost of medallions rose beyond the means of individuals likely to find a taxi-drivers' job worthwhile a system evolved whereby drivers would lease a medallion or a medallion with a vehicle for periods of time as short one day's working hours or as long as several months. The separation of medallion (or combined medallion and vehicle) ownership from the cab operator created what economists refer to as a "moral hazard." Medallion-owners, not drivers, are subject to penalties imposed for violation of some of the Taxi and Limousine Commission's (TLC's) many rules and regulations. And when the driver leases both the medallion and the vehicle, the cost of repairs and replacement is borne by the vehicle's owner, the lessor.

The structure of this problem led economists C. Kirabo Jackson and Henry S. Schneider to examine whether social network connections between co-ethnics might help taxi- and medallion-owners enforce behavioral norms that would induce drivers to play by the TLC rules and to drive carefully. In other words, they were seeking evidence that the same social mechanisms that helped facilitate credit availability in the eighteenth-century Atlantic economy might also aid the operation twenty-first-century yellow-cab industry (Jackson & Schneider, 2010).

To test their hypotheses Jackson and Schneider, with the assistance of the TLC, assembled data on a sample of individuals engaged in the taxi industry whose birth-country was known. Most of the individuals in the sample were either (i) "owners" who held single medallions outright or under long-term lessees and drove their cabs themselves during one of two daily work-shifts or (ii) "drivers" who leased the cab for only the duration of the other daily shift. The data also included parties' birth-countries, along with information on the number and type of violations cited while the "driver" was operating the cab. Although it was not their principal focus, the data Jackson and Schneider assembled also demonstrate the extent to which the taxi industry an employment niche for immigrants from South Asia. Table 19.7 lists the number of

**Table 19.7** Yellow-cab "owners" and "drivers" by birth-country (See Text) (Jackson & Schneider, 2010, p. 47)

| Country | Drivers | Owners |
|---|---|---|
| Afghanistan | 15 | |
| Bangladesh[a] | 272 | 138 |
| China | 17 | 44 |
| Columbia | 50 | 62 |
| Dominican Republic | 38 | |
| Ecuador | 33 | |
| Egypt | 64 | 43 |
| Ghana | 53 | |
| Greece | 10 | 50 |
| Haiti | 151 | 235 |
| Hong Kong | 10 | |
| India[a] | 392 | 359 |
| Morocco | 24 | |
| Nigeria | 14 | |
| Pakistan[a] | 285 | 136 |
| Peru | 10 | |
| Puerto Rico | 18 | |
| Romania | 16 | |
| Russia | 51 | 149 |
| Senegal | 16 | |
| Turkey | 7 | |
| U.S. | 35 | 127 |
| Ukraine | 18 | 40 |
| Vietnam | 15 | |
| Other | 210 | 441 |
| Total | 1,824 | 1,824 |
| Total South Asian | 949 | 633 |
| Percent South Asian | 52.0% | 34.7% |

[a]South Asian

"owners" and "drivers" by country of birth and indicates that more than half of the drivers and more than one-third of the owners are South Asians.

Jackson and Schneider's analysis of the data led to several conclusions that help understand how the involvement of ethnic networks enhanced the operation of the taxi industry, in particular. The authors found, first of all, that intra-ethnicity leasing contracts were much more common than what would have been generated by chance matching of owners and drivers. Upwards of 40% of these leasing relationships were between individuals who were born in the same country. Analysis of the data also showed that drivers who worked for co-ethnic owners did, in fact, incur fewer-than-average citations.

By itself, this finding would not have allowed Jackson and Schneider to conclude that the network connection did, in fact, counteract the moral hazard involved in leasing. One might have hypothesized, for example, that social network connections served mainly to convey information to owners about potential drivers' reliability. After testing several other alternative explanations for the finding that co-ethnic drivers had fewer violations, however, Jackson and Schneider were able to conclude that it was, in fact, the sanctions and rewards conveyed through social networks that counteracted the moral hazard implicit in these contractual relationships.

More broadly, these findings illustrate one way in which social networks can facilitate the effective operation of markets. If moral hazard is mitigated owners may, all else held equal, be willing to pay more on the margin to lease taxi medallions and to offer more attractive lease terms to potential drivers. It is not surprising, therefore, that an industry structured in this way would become an ethnic niche.

The attraction of the taxi industry to South Asian men, in particular, mirrors, in some respects, what drew Italian male immigrants to the construction industry early in the twentieth century. Both groups were engaged in seasonal or circular migration, looking for opportunities to earn money reasonably quickly with the aim of accumulating a "nest egg" to bring home. The life stories of individual taxi drivers reported by Biju Mathew involved multiple migrations between their homelands and workplaces in Europe and North America (Mathew, 2005, p. 147). The sex ratio of New York's South Asian population may also reflect a disinclination to settle families permanently in the United States. In 2000, for example, there were 161 men who had been born in Pakistan living in New York City for every 100 women, the highest such statistic among the City's 20 most common birth countries (New York City Department of City Planning, Population Division, 2004, p. 150). Further, the skill requirements of work as an early twentieth-century construction laborer and as a taxi driver 100 years later were roughly commensurate. The latter requires the ability to drive a car and enough

English language fluency to pass the TLC licensing examination and to deal with riders. Many South Asian immigrants possess the latter on arrival. Finally, fleet-owners and medallion lease brokers may be playing a similar role in assembling and deploying a workforce to what *padrones* did some one-hundred years earlier.

This is not to say that driving a cab in New York City is an easy way to make money. Because lease payments are fixed the driver bears the risk that cold weather may keep potential rides at home or that a no-tip round-trip to from midtown Manhattan to John F. Kennedy Airport through rush-hour traffic might take up a third of a shift. And the lessor-lessee business relationship leaves drivers without many of the benefits and legal protections enjoyed by employees. Finally, many "owners" who went into debt to buy medallions at peak prices were driven into bankruptcy when the market for these assets collapsed. Nevertheless, given the regulatory framework as it stands today and the condition of the City's labor market, a taxi industry organized as an ethnic niche seems to meet New Yorkers' needs for just-in-time surface transportation more effectively than any feasible alternative (New York Times, 2019).

## Colleges and Universities

Employment at New York City's post-secondary schools increased by 50% between 1990 and 2008. Although the City's colleges and universities employ more than a few foreign-born faculty members, the sector cannot be characterized as an ethnic employment niche. It is worth noting, though, that the number of F-1 student visas issued by the U.S. State Department also increased by about 50% over the same period of time (U.S. Department of State, Bureau of Consular Affairs, 2018).

In any case, local universities are an economically significant point of contact between the New York economy and the rest of the world. Columbia University, New York University, and the City University of New York ranked second, fourth, and sixth, respectively, among institutions nationwide in terms of the number of F-1 visa-holders enrolled between 2008 and 2012. And the New York ranked 15th nationwide and third among the largest metropolitan areas in the proportion of foreign students in total local post-secondary enrollment. To this extent and to the degree that a large proportion of the City's post-secondary students come from elsewhere in the United States, higher education should be counted as one of New York's base or export industries (Ruiz, 2018, pp. 11, 13, 15).

The foreign students who attend New York's local colleges, universities, and professional schools are not, however, only consumers of the "educational services" produced locally. Many of them also become suppliers of labor after they finish their degrees. F-1 visa holders are permitted to extend their residency for up to 36 months for Optional Practical Training (OPT) as employees of U.S. firms. Between 2004 and 2016, 144,400 students who had received degrees from New York institutions spent at least some of their immediate post-graduate years working in the New York metropolitan area. At 85% New York's retention rate for graduates of local institutions was the highest in the country. Further, "temporary" employment at a New York firm for between 12 and 29 months may give OPT program participants who wish stay longer a leg up with respect to applying for more permanent residency (Ruiz & Budiman, 2018).

## Shopkeepers

Between 1990 and 2008, the number of workers in New York's retail establishments grew by 16%, about the same rate as national employment in this sector and twice as fast as the overall expansion of the City's workforce.

There are good reasons to believe that growth of the City's immigrant population fueled the expansion of this sector on both the demand and the supply sides of the market for retail services.

With respect to demand, foreign-born New Yorkers accounted for more than 100% of the post-crisis increase in the City's population of retail customers. Further, in contrast to earlier eras' less culturally heterogenous cohorts, the ethnically and linguistically diverse post-1965 immigrants generate demand for a greater variety of consumer goods and, therefore, a larger number of different specialty retailers.

On the supply side, as a large and growing body of research demonstrates, self-employment, very much including ownership of retail shops, is, as it has been for generations, integral to many immigrant communities' engagement with the American economy. In fact, as Ivan Light and Carolyn Rosenstein have pointed out, "in every decennial census between 1880 and 1980, the foreign-born evidenced persistently higher rates of self-employment than did the native born (Light & Rosenstein, 1995, p. 181). This tendency is still quite evident in more recent data. In 2015, 6.1% of native-born Americans and 7.6% of the foreign born were self-employed in (generally small) unincorporated businesses (Hipple & Hammond, 2016).

One would have expected that, since New York's foreign-born population is so large, the proportion of self-employed in the local workforce would be relatively high. Data for 2007 (Table 19.8), however, indicates that this does not appear to be the case. With 9.6 of its workforce self-employed New York is right in the middle of the pack of the 16 most populous metropolitan areas. These data also demonstrate that big-city self-employment rates tend to be higher in Southern and Western metropolitan areas than in the northeast and that New York has the highest self-employment rate of any large northeastern metropolitan area.

The same data source demonstrates that the tradition of immigrant ownership of retail businesses is very much alive in New York. In 2007, 24% of the City's retail businesses were owned by Asians. Another

**Table 19.8** Self-employment rates in the 16 largest U.S. metropolitan areas (U.S. Census Bureau, 2018)

| Metropolitan area | Percent self employed |
|---|---|
| Miami | 14.3 |
| Los Angeles | 12.3 |
| San Francisco | 11.8 |
| San Diego | 11.4 |
| Atlanta | 10.2 |
| Houston | 9.9 |
| Seattle | 9.8 |
| New York | 9.6 |
| Boston | 9.3 |
| Dallas | 8.8 |

11% had an owner who was categorized as "Other Hispanic,[2]" most of whom, in the context of this time and place, would have been either Dominican or of Dominican descent (U.S. Census Bureau, 2018).

So, a disproportionate number of New York's immigrants are retail business owners and a disproportionate share of the City's shops are owned and operated by immigrants. But was the retail services industry an immigrant ethnic niche like those discussed above? Not exactly. The clientele of the other niche industries—garment manufacturing, health care, hotels, and taxis—were drawn from the general population, not predominantly from the employees' ethnic group. To be sure, many immigrant-owned retailers serve a diverse clientele; Korean-owned nail-salons and newsstands operated by South Asians can be found all over the City. But the offerings of other immigrant-owned businesses—herbalists in Chinatown, Russian nightclubs in Brighton Beach, or Dominican-owned bodegas in Washington Heights—will appeal almost exclusively to co-ethnics. And the impact of immigrant-owned businesses on the City's economy may differ depending on whether these establishments constitute an employment niche or are integral to an ethnic enclave economy.

## Enclaves, Ghettos, and Urban Economies

Most of the research on spatial concentrations of racial or ethnic group residences or businesses has focused on the impact of such geographic segmentation on the economic condition of members of particular minority groups. Taken together the conclusions of these studies have been ambiguous. Under some circumstances, at some times, and for some groups, the impact of living in segregated neighborhoods has been adverse. That is, members of the particular minority who live outside the "ghetto" tend, personal characteristics held equal, to be better off than those in it. Residents are not attracted to such "ghettos" by the

[2] "Other Hispanic" refers to individuals who were born in or descended from someone born in a Spanish-speaking country other than Mexico, Puerto Rico, or Cuba.

opportunities such locations offer. Rather they are excluded from places where they would be better off by racial or ethnic prejudice.

By contrast, the research on enclaves presupposes that their residents could, if they wished to, live elsewhere. Their locational choice and reflects some combination a preference for living in proximity to others who share their cultural heritage or the economic benefits associated with living in an enclave. Evidence that residents of an "enclave" earn higher incomes on average than similarly qualified co-ethnics supports the economic choice hypothesis.

The only clear generalization that has emerged from the studies of these relationships is that living and/or working in an enclave is more likely to be beneficial to the extent that one's co-ethnics are relatively highly educated (Cutler, Glaeser, & Vigdor, 2008).

By contrast, little or no analytical attention has been paid to the impact immigrant enclaves on the economies of the cities and metropolitan areas in which they are located. This is unfortunate for two reasons. First, the concurrence of the most recent increase in immigration and the era of urban resurgence highlight the importance of understanding whether and how large and growing immigrant communities affect metropolitan economies. Second, it seems likely that the application of models of urban economies—especially the new economic geography with its emphasis on the benefits of diverse local offerings of consumer goods—could shed light on the operation of businesses in ethnic enclaves. The following sections examine the development and operation of several such neighborhoods with the aim of shedding light on whether and how New York's "enclaves" or "ghettos" have affected the City's post-crisis recovery for better, for worse, or not much at all.

Chinatown is New York's closest equivalent to Miami's *Calle Ocho*, in terms of size, range of businesses, and geographic off-shoots.

## Chinese New York: Towns Within a City

Although intense Chinese involvement as workers in garment manufactures may have been temporary the impact of this industry-ethnicity pairing on the City's Chinese community has been substantial and long-lasting. Job opportunities for workers with limited English-speaking ability—for women workers within in Chinese-owned garment factories for men in the expanding restaurant industry—helped attract Chinese families to the City (Chin, 2005, pp. 200–202). And the fact that the annual cap on immigrant visas from any one country was applied separately to Mainland China, Macau, Hong Kong, and Taiwan also accelerated the growth of this community (Zhang & Associates, P.C., 2007).

The expansion of distinct Chinese neighborhoods was further boosted by the newcomers' preference for in neighborhoods where English-speaking ability was not required for life's routines (Portes & Zhou, 1992, p. 507). In 1990, 48.4% of Metropolitan New York's Chinese population lived in ethnic neighborhoods[3] (Logan, Zhang, & Alba, 2001, p. 309). Among New York's populous immigrant nationalities only Dominicans were more likely to live in proximity to co-ethnics. By the 1990s, therefore, New York City's Chinese population had reached the critical mass and possessed the necessary resources to sustain full-service enclave economies centered in three City neighborhoods, the original Chinatown in lower Manhattan, Flushing in Queens, and Sunset Park in Brooklyn.

Table 19.9, which lists the number of Chinese-owned firms in New York City in the most common activities as of 1988. Of course, not all of these businesses catered primarily to Chinese clientele nor were they all located in one of New York's Chinatowns. Chinese restaurants, in particular, are scattered throughout the City. A 2010 analysis of a random sample of 111 of the City's Chinese restaurants found that only about 8% of them were located in Chinatown, Flushing, or Sunset Park (Minn, 2009). That said, most of the clients of many, if not most, of these businesses are probably Chinese.

The Table illustrates the broad range of businesses in which members of New York's Chinese community were engaged in 1988.

[3]In computing this statistic Logan, Zhang, and Alba defined an ethnic neighborhood as "a set of contiguous [census] tracts, which must contain at least one tract where a group is represented as 40% or more of the residents and whose other tracts each have a level of ethnic concentration among residents of at least 35%" (Logan et al., 2001, p. 304).

**Table 19.9** Chinese-owned businesses in the New York metropolitan area in 1988 (Portes & Zhou, 1992, p. 510)

| Sector | Number of businesses |
|---|---|
| Restaurants | 781 |
| Garment factories | 437 |
| Insurance, real estate agencies and stockbrokers | 320 |
| Medical doctors | 300 |
| Grocery shops | 187 |
| Lawyers | 186 |
| Import & export firms | 164 |
| Travel agencies | 115 |
| Barber shops & beuty salons | 111 |
| Accountants | 107 |
| Herbalists | 101 |
| Dentists | 98 |
| Jewellery shops | 97 |
| Restaurant equipment | 92 |
| Gift shops | 65 |
| Herbal stores | 53 |
| Fish markets | 53 |
| Bakeries | 46 |
| Meat & poultry stores | 45 |
| Video rentals and related firms | 41 |
| Banks | 39 |
| Bookstores | 32 |
| Newspapers & periodicals | 24 |
| Drugstores | 22 |
| Laundries | 20 |
| Photo labs & studios | 19 |
| Noodle manufacturers | 18 |
| Florists | 17 |
| Television & radio stations | 12 |
| Language training centers | 8 |
| Theaters & cinemas | 7 |

Unsurprisingly, the stereotypical Chinese enterprises of the time—restaurants and garment factories—top the list. The numerous grocers, travel agents, beauticians, and other retail establishments that cater to the tastes and needs a Chinese clientele is also to be expected. Concentrations of such businesses are found in any ethnic neighborhood. What may be more noteworthy about the Chinatowns is the number of financial and professional service providers and media companies. It is probably safe to assume that a large proportion of these professionals' clients and the media's readers, listeners, and watchers were also Chinese. The ability of the Chinese community to source professional services from within its own ranks reflects in large part the high educational attainment of this group of immigrants. As of 1980 37% of U.S. residents who had been born in China, Hong Kong, or Taiwan had completed four years of college that was more than twice as high as the 16.2% of the total U.S. population who were college graduates (Portes & Zhou, 1992, p. 508).

Another impression conveyed by the list of businesses is that pretty much everything a Chinese household might need in their ordinary course of their lives was available within the ethnic economy. In this sense, the Chinatowns function like suburban towns, economically, if not physically distant from the central city in which they are embedded. Fiscally, of course, these communities are part of the municipality; their residents pay City income taxes and their children attend the City's public schools. And many of these neighborhoods' residents "commute" to jobs elsewhere in the City. But the economic activity taking place in these locations may not generate very much demand for the local goods and services produced outside of the ethnic economy.

A final impression conveyed by Table 19.9 is that this is a business community focused on serving its local clientele; very little of what it produces is "exported" from the New York metropolitan area. A comparison of the Chinese ethnic economies of metropolitan New York and Los Angeles published in Yu Zhou in 1998 shows that this local orientation is not an essential characteristic of an ethnic enclave economy. In 1990, at about 250,000, the two communities were almost exactly the same size, but Chinese residents of metropolitan Los Angeles were noticeably more successful in economic terms (Table 19.10). Although both communities were relatively well educated—at least some post-secondary education was the common norm—the average Chinese Angelino earned a higher income than the average Chinese New Yorker and was more likely to own his or her own businesses and/or to be employed in a relatively prestigious occupation.

Prof. Zhou also found that the Los Angeles community was more directly engaged with the dynamic economies of China, Hong Kong, and Taiwan. He summarized the range of transnational linkages as

**Table 19.10** Economic characteristics of the Chinese populations of metropolitan New York and Los Angeles (Zhou, 1998)

| Statistic | New York | Los Angeles |
|---|---|---|
| 1990 population | 248,980 | 248,415 |
| *Chinese-owned businesses* | | |
| Number | 19,837 | 26,279 |
| Annual sales ($, millions) | 2,633 | 8,077 |
| Paid employees | 17,037 | 48,480 |
| *Birthplace (%)* | | |
| USA | 21.9 | 23.1 |
| Mainland China | 47.5 | 27.0 |
| Taiwan | 7.9 | 19.9 |
| Hong-Kong | 11.4 | 8.0 |
| Other | 11.3 | 22.0 |
| Self-employed (%) | 8.7 | 13.0 |
| *Industry (% of local Chinese workforce)* | | |
| Manufacturing | 26.1 | 20.7 |
| Wholesale trade | 5.0 | 8.6 |
| Retail trade | 26.8 | 21.4 |
| Finance, insurance, and real estate | 9.0 | 11.0 |
| Professional and related services | 13.9 | 17.8 |
| Other | 19.2 | 20.5 |
| *Occupation (% of local Chinese workforce)* | | |
| Managerial and professional specialties | 20.6 | 31.0 |
| Technical, sales, and administrative support | 28.0 | 37.2 |
| Service occupations | 20.5 | 13.0 |
| Operators, fabricators, and laborers | 24.1 | 11.4 |
| Other | 6.8 | 7.4 |
| *Income and education* | | |
| Median Chinese household income | $30,610 | $37,900 |
| Median foreign-born Chinese household income | $26,667 | $36,224 |
| Average years of schooling | 13.5 | 15.3 |

follows. "In short, the international dimension and the local ethnic economy are inseparable in Los Angeles. Overseas capital fuels the ethnic economy, while the ethnic economy anchors the overseas flow to the local community. Monetery Park in Los Angeles, a Chinese dominated suburban business center, has established itself as a hub for cross-cultural and transnational business services, with many legal, accounting, trade, traveling, advertising, and real estate service firms. It has become a necessary stop for most business visitors from mainland China, Hong Kong, and Taiwan" (Zhou, 1998, p. 549).

Another of Prof. Zhou's publications focused on the role of Chinese social networks in the Los Angeles wholesale computer industry during the late 1980s and early 1990s. At the time, he was able to identify 493 Chinese-owned computer firms in the Los Angeles area and found that, among the owners of the 96 companies that responded to a mail survey, 45% also owned businesses outside the U.S. and that 62% of the firms had closely related overseas associates. Zhou also traced the development of the geographic concentration of these firms in the City of Industry back to the 1987 decision by a Taiwanese computer manufacturer to locate its Southern California branch in that part of Los Angeles County (Zhou, 1996, p. 282).

Businesses and investors based in Mainland China, Taiwan and elsewhere in the Asian Chinese diaspora have also invested in New York and availed themselves of the global city's financial and advanced business services. But Prof. Zhou argues that New York's resident Chinese community is not nearly as engaged in these transnational interactions as is the case in Los Angeles. New York's Chinatown is, much more than Los Angeles's, a working-class enclave and its enclave economy is geared toward serving that community. There are several plausible reasons that account for the different trajectories of these two ethnic enclaves. West Coast U.S. cities serve as gateways for interactions between the East Asian and North American economies. This may be why a relatively well-educated and prosperous cadre of immigrants from Taiwan was attracted to Southern California during the 1970s and 1980s. The early development of New York's post-1965 Chinatown, by contrast, was boosted most powerfully by the ethnic transition of the garment industry, which attracted working-class immigrants from Mainland China.

By the turn of the twenty-first century, New York's Chinese population had found jobs in a broad range of local economic activities, including, but not limited to the robust restaurant and the waning garment manufacturing niches. The local Chinese population had become large enough and geographically concentrated enough to support the development of several full-service local economies that provide pretty much everything local residents need. The contrast with the same-sized community in Los Angeles suggests that New York's Chinese community is not generating the kind of broader benefit to the regional economy that can come from transnational engagement with East Asia.

Chinese newcomers constitute New York's second largest immigrant nationality. The economic life of the largest community, the Dominicans, is decidedly more transnational.

## Transnational Dominicans

The topic headings for a discussion of the role in the local economy of New York City's two largest immigrant nationalities, the Chinese and the Dominicans, are the identical. Both communities were extensively engaged in the garment industry, and both developed enclave economies. But these two communities' roles in the City's economy through the decades of New York's employment resurgence around the turn of the twenty-first century are very different in two ways. First, the Dominican enclave's economy was likely less diverse than the Chinatowns'. Second, members of the Dominican community operated in a "transnational" economy in ways Chinese New Yorkers did not.

Linguistic, cultural, and educational similarities enabled post-1965 immigrants from the Dominican Republic fit easily into Puerto Rican employment niches in the garment, other light manufacturing, and hospitality industries. Jobs in these sectors did not need to be particularly plentiful or lucrative to offer a distinct improvement in expectations for this relatively impoverished group of newcomers. In 1990, U.S. residents of Dominican ancestry included proportionally fewer high school and college graduates and had lower labor force participation rates, and higher unemployment rates than Puerto Ricans, Cubans, Haitians, or Jamaicans. For example, only 5.3% of Dominican-Americans were professionals. The next lowest such statistic among the five Caribbean ethnicities was 9.1% for Puerto Ricans (Grasmuck & Grosfoguel, 1997, p. 341). Low average education levels left the Dominican community less able to cope with the post-1990 rapid decline in the City's manufacturing sector, and it is, therefore, unsurprising that in 2005 the unemployment rate among Dominicans in the New York Metropolitan area was the highest among eight Latino national origins (Limonic, 2005).

True, Roger Waldinger cites rising self-employment rates in Dominican niches in retail and wholesale groceries and automotive repair located in ethnic enclaves "jam-packed with retail and service businesses." Given the low average educational level of this population, however, it is unlikely that the service businesses in Dominican enclaves include anywhere near the proportions of professionals in New York's Chinese communities (R. Waldinger, 1996, p. 132).

New York's Dominicans remained much more closely engaged with their home country and its economy than was the case with the City's Chinese residents. As noted previously, Dominicans gave less evidence of an intention to remain in the United States permanently than other immigrant groups. And the Dominican government encouraged continued engagement of their expatriates with the political economy of their home country by legalizing dual nationality, encouraging overseas Dominicans to vote in national elections, and by including expatriate representatives on governmental policymaking bodies (Graham, 2001, p. 87).

Most of Dominican New Yorkers' engagement with their home country takes the form of remittances, which totaled $3.8 billion in 2010 or about seven percent of the Dominican Republic's GDP at the time (Ratha, Mohapatra, & Silwal, 2011; The World Bank, 2018). Most of this money would have come from metropolitan New York, home to about 70% of Dominicans living in the United States. No doubt much of this money supplemented the incomes of emigrants' families. To this extent, these funds were money earned by New Yorkers but spent elsewhere and, as such, a net drain on the local economy. Some portion of remittances, however, took the form of personal investments by Dominican-Americans in home country businesses. Sociologists Alejandro Portes and Min Zhou describe a sample of 113 businesses in operation in either Santo Domingo or Santiago, DR, in 1989. Owners of 90% of these firms either were living in New York at the time or had lived there, 89% of the businesses were founded with capital accumulated abroad, and 72% of the employees of these firms were returnees to the Dominican Republic.

Portes and Zhou suggest that some of the capital goods and raw materials used in these factories would have been purchased in New York City. In 1989 and for the subsequent decade a large proportion of these funds would probably have been invested in garment factories, an economic sector in which Dominican New Yorkers had established some level of expertise. The Dominican apparel industry grew rapidly until 2000, supported by the Multi Fiber Agreement (MFA), the international system of garment import quotas in effect at the time that favored exports from the Western Hemisphere countries. In that year Dominican garment industry employment peaked at 145,000. Thereafter, as the MFA was phased out, the Dominican industry shrank rapidly so that by 2009 employment in the sector had declined to 41,000. Despite this setback, Dominican economic growth has remained reasonably robust in recent decades, as has Dominican New Yorkers' involvement in that economy (Arthur, 2011; Portes & Zhou, 1992, pp. 501–503).

No doubt economic growth in the Dominican Republic does generate some demand for goods and services procured in New York. Any such positive local impact of this variety of transnationalism is probably more than offset by the drain on local demand associated with remittances flowing in the opposite direction. And even if the net impact on the New York economy were positive, it would likely be very small. The Dominican Republic is not China.

## African-Caribbeans: Enclaves Within Ghettos?

With a total City population in 2000 close to 500,000, non-Hispanic West Indians of all national origins combined—Jamaica, Guyana,[4] Haiti, Trinidad and Tobago, etc.—constitute the most populous group

[4]Categorizing Guyana with this group is a little problematic for two reasons. First, the country is situated on the South American mainland. Second, like Trinidad and Tobago, a large proportion

of immigrants in New York (NYC Department of City Planning, 2018, p. 17).

Like other newcomers, African-Caribbeans evidently prefer living near their co-ethnics, but in the United States racial prejudice limits the places in the City where these immigrants can reside. The combined effect of these two influences is that West Indians tend to live in residential enclaves either surrounded by or adjacent to African-American neighborhoods. As a result, with respect to residence, African-American and African-Caribbean New Yorkers are much less isolated from each other than either group is from either non-Hispanic Whites or from other immigrant communities (Crowder & Tedrow, 2001, p. 90).

African-Caribbean neighborhoods differed from other immigrant enclaves in another way. The latter are concentrations of both immigrant residents and immigrant-owned businesses. To be sure, there are West Indian-owned businesses in central Brooklyn—Flatbush, East Flatbush, and Crown Heights—where African-Caribbeans constituted one-third of the population in 2000. But immigrants from these countries of origin, like native-born African-Americans, are much less likely to be self-employed than newcomers from Asia or the Dominican Republic (NYC Department of City Planning, 2018, pp. 160, 165; Razin & Light, 1998, p. 340). So ethnic retail businesses are not as thick on the ground in West Indian neighborhoods as they are in Chinatown or the Dominican enclaves.

With respect to their impact on economic outcomes, West Indian neighborhoods function more like enclaves, which support residents' advancement, than like ghettos, which have the opposite impact. African-Caribbean New Yorkers who live in West Indian enclaves, in fact, earn higher incomes and are more likely to have attended college and to own their own homes than their more isolated co-ethnics (Bereton, 2018; Richardson & Menke, 2018).

of its population—40% in 2012 in Guyana and 35% in Trinidad and Tobago—is of South Asian origin. The Indo-Guyanese enclave will be discussed briefly below. African-Guyanese tend to gravitate to diverse African-Caribbean neighborhoods.

## An Archipelago of Enclaves

The Dominican, Chinese, and West Indian communities and their economic enclaves are, by far the largest in the New York area, but there are many others.

In 2000, 22,804 individuals who had been born in the former Soviet Union, most of whom came to the United States as refugees, lived in the Sheepshead Bay—Brighton Beach section of Brooklyn, where they constituted 29% of the population. This community's integration into the U.S. economy was facilitated by government and private philanthropic grant programs dedicated to assisting political refugees adjust to life in America. These programs included the Microenterprise Development Initiative of the Federal Government's Office of Refugee Resettlement, which provided loans to start businesses.

In a 1998 publication geographer, Ines M. Miyares describes the 165 businesses identified along the seven-block stretch of Brighton Beach Avenue that is the commercial heart of "Little Odessa." While most of the business signs were in English, Prof. Miyares reported the following. "Twenty-nine have signs entirely in Russian, and 30 have a portion in Russian. Three have signs partially in Hebrew and 5 in Spanish" (Miyares, 1998, p. 524).

In New York City, Little Guyana lies 13 miles northeast of Little Odessa. About 32% of Guyanese New Yorkers, and probably a much higher percentage of the City's Guyanese who are of South Asian descent, live in nine contiguous south Queens zip codes centered on the Richmond Hill neighborhood, the enclave's business and cultural center. A 2014 article in the *Washington Post*'s travel section reported, regarding Liberty Avenue, Richmond Hill's main commercial thoroughfare, that "within three minutes of people-watching, I'd spotted Hindus, Sikhs, Muslims and cross-wearing Christians passing by the same street corner. In a five block radius you'll find a Pentecostal church, a Jehovah's Witness kingdom hall, a Shri Lakshmi Narayan Mandir Hindu temple and an Islamic clothing store" (Cananaugh, 2014; New York City Department of City Planning, Population Division, 2004, p. 79).

Not all of these ethnic enclaves are residential. More than a few Korean restaurants, herbal apothecaries, and import shops have gravitated to West 32nd Street between fifth and sixth avenues in Manhattan. And the largest Korean commercial banks and chain restaurants have chosen to locate branches on the adjacent avenues. Geographer Jinwon Kim coined the term "transclave," or "transnational enclave" to describe this kind of economic and cultural, but not residential, outpost of a home country (Kim, 2018). The original attraction of this block may have been its proximity to the garment district, but Manhattan's Koreatown remained viable well into the twenty-first century even though there are twice as many Korean-born New Yorkers living in Flushing's two zip codes than in all of Manhattan.

Likewise, a cluster of South Asian restaurants, grocery stores, and ethnic clothing shops line Lexington Avenue between 25th and 30th streets despite the fact that few Indians, Pakistanis, Bangladeshis, or Sri Lankans live in the vicinity. Some of these businesses may be supported by taxi drivers who spend large parts of their shifts in Manhattan.

## The "Old Ways" Redux Redux

When describing the role of ethnic niches in Chinese New Yorkers' engagement with the City economy, Roger Waldinger concluded that "the old ways of making it in New York have not disappeared, the advent of the postindustrial economy and its skill-intensive employers notwithstanding" (R. Waldinger, 1996, p. 127). The context of this assertion was the discussion, referred to above, of the availability at the time of plentiful jobs for both men and women with limited English-speaking ability in the restaurant and garment industries. The "old ways" referred to niche industry jobs for all adult family members providing the first step upward toward more remunerative employment for first- or second-generation immigrants within an ethnic enclave or in the broader regional economy.

The "old ways" analogy could be applied to the sources of the New York's economic dynamism during its periods of particularly robust growth: the nineteenth century's antebellum decades and the turns of the twentieth and twenty-first centuries. In all three eras, one or more broad global or national trends boosted demand for one or more of the City's exports: banknote brokerage, *prêt-à-porter* women's wear, tertiary global business services, etc. Either the export industries themselves (e.g., typesetting, garment manufacturing) or some essential ancillary activity (e.g., infrastructure construction, traveler accommodation) was labor intensive. Nominal wage premiums paid to local workers, at best, barely made up of the high cost of living in the nation's most densely populated place. Competing for workers in the domestic labor market would likely have raised nominal local labor costs substantially relative to what was being paid in Philadelphia or Chicago or San Francisco and that might have stymied New York's expansion. But an elastic supply of labor from abroad allowed New York employers to recruit the labor force they needed without paying too much more in nominal terms than similarly qualified workers were getting elsewhere in the United States. Immigrant workers were more willing to live in New York than native-born Americans, even absent a real wage incentive, because sufficient numbers of their compatriots were established in the City to support economically effective social networks and efficiently provided ethnic goods.

How did the "old ways" play out through New York's late twentieth-century resurgence?

As demonstrated in the previous chapter, while globalization did boost demand for New York's sophisticated financial and business services and media content, aggregate base industry employment in the City did not grow over the course of the post-1975 decades. Nevertheless, globalization conveyed an advantage to the New York economy compared with most other northeastern and midwestern metropolitan areas, where base industry employment contracted sharply. Because Americans' demand for health care has been increasing, sustaining constant "base industry" employment and population in any U.S. metropolitan region during this period required increasing the number of people employed in health services. For that reason alone, one would have expected the ratio of local to export industry employment to have increased in recent decades. The growth of New York's global tertiary services industry, however, also generated rapidly increasing demand for locally supplied ground transportation, restaurants, and traveler accommodations, all labor-intensive activities. If the supply of labor had been less elastic than it was, then, New York employers in the health care and other local "multiplier" sectors would have had to pay higher wages relative to other cities than they did. Apparently, the 14% nominal wage premium required to make up for the high local cost of living was enough because the supply of immigrant labor was sufficiently elastic. Post-1965 immigrants preferred settling in New York to other places where on average real wages were roughly the same because it was easier to find first jobs and because goods and services suited to newcomers' tastes were more readily available.

As in the past, social networks that facilitated job placement increased immigrants' expected earnings by shortening the time it took to find jobs initially and periodically thereafter. Chinese and Dominican social networks facilitated the operation both the demand and the supply sides of the garment industry's labor markets through its waning days. The fact that a large proportion of Jamaican immigrants were related to earlier arrivers suggests that networks forged by family connections among Jamaican women served as de facto recruitment offices of hospitals, nursing homes, and in-home health-care agencies. The predominance of Caribbean immigrants in the hospitality industry looks to have facilitated the smooth back-of-the-house hotel operations through seasonal cycles. And networks facilitated the operation of New York's taxi industry and offered enough of an opportunity so that South Asian men include New York City as a stop on their global search for opportunities to accumulate a nest egg. And all of these groups could find at least a taste of home and, in some cases, the full range of exactly the goods and services they most preferred offered in their native tongue.

The details of the interactions between immigrants with the New York City economy are more varied in recent years than they were during the antebellum period or the early 1900s—there are more different ethnicities working more different industries—but the essential elements of the stories are the same.

In the context of globalization, as the phenomenon was manifest in the late twentieth century, New York's consumer amenities, especially its cornucopia of entertainment venues and the creative potential of its diversely skilled workforce were necessary conditions for the City's economic recovery in the decades after 1980. But the post-crisis recovery might have faced powerful headwinds if the thousands of Dominicans, Chinese, Jamaicans, Pakistanis, Russians, and others who moved to New York from other countries were barred, as they had been for decades, from taking up residence in the United States. More than for other U.S. city, high, non-discriminatory immigration quotas were a necessary condition for New York's resurgence. So, the passage of the Hart-Celler Act in 1965 should be counted as one of the critical junctures in New York City's economic history.

## References

Arthur, C. (2011, March 30). *Coming Undone: The Dominican Republic's Garment Assembly Sector*. Retrieved from MakingItMagazine.net http://www.makingitmagazine.net/?p=3293.

Bereton, B. E. (2018, October 14). *Trinidad and Tobago*. Retrieved from Encyclopaedia Britannica https://www.britannica.com/place/Trinidad-and-Tobago.

Bureau of Labor Statistics. (2018, July 22). *Quarterly Census of Employment and Wages*. Retrieved from Data Tools https://data.bls.gov/cgi-bin/dsrv?en.

Cananaugh, R. (2014, October 9). Little Guyana, and Indo-Guanese Enclave in Queens. Retrieved from *The Washington Post* https://www.washingtonpost.com/lifestyle/travel/2014/10/02/38ec1260-4998-11e4-a046-120a8a855cca_story.html?noredirect=on&utm_term=.5ed5a933e4d8.

Chin, M. M. (2005). Expanding Spheres: Men and Women in the Late Twentieth-Century Garment Industry. In D. Soyer (Ed.), *A Coat of Many Colors: Immigration, Globalization, and Reform in New York City's Garment Industry*. New York: Fordham University Press.

Corgel, J., & Sellers, K. (2017, September 25). *A Look at US Hotels' Dependence on International Guests*. Retrieved from Hotel News Now http://www.hotelnewsnow.com/Articles/240035/A-look-at-US-hotels-dependence-on-international-guests.

Cortes, P., & Pan, J. (2014). *Foreign Nurse Importation to the United States and the Supply of Native Registered Nurses* (Working Paper No. 14-7). Boston: Federal Reserve Bank of Boston.

Crowder, K. D., & Tedrow, L. M. (2001). West Indians and the Residential Landscape of New York. In N. Foner (Ed.), *Islands in the City: West Indian Migration to New York* (pp. 81–114). Berkeley: University of California Press.

Cutler, D., Glaeser, E. L., & Vigdor, J. L. (2008). When Are Ghettos Bad? Lessons from Immigrant Segregation in the United States. *Journal of Urban Economics, 63*(3), 759–774.

Governing the States and Localities. (2018). *Foreign Born City Population Data*. Retrieved from Data http://www.governing.com/gov-data/census/foreign-born-city-population-changes-data.html.

Graham, P. M. (2001). Political Incorporation and Re-incorporation: Simultaneity in the Dominican Migrant Experience. In H. R. Cordero-Guzman, R. C. Smith, & R. Grosfoguel (Eds.), *Migration, Transnationalization, and Race in a Changing New York* (pp. 87–108). Philadelphia: Temple University Press.

Grasmuck, S., & Grosfoguel, R. (1997). Geopolitics, Economic Niches, and Gendered Social Capital Among Recent Caribbean Immigrants in New York City. *Sociological Perspectives, 40*(3), 339–363.

Hatton, T. J., & Williamson, J. G. (2005). *Global Migration and the World Economy: Two Centuries of Policy and Performance*. Cambridge, MA: MIT Press.

Hipple, S. F., & Hammond, L. A. (2016, March). *Self-Employment in the United States*. Retrieved from U.S. Bureau of Labor Statistics https://www.bls.gov/spotlight/2016/self-employment-in-the-united-states/pdf/self-employment-in-the-united-states.pdf.

Jackson, C. K., & Schneider, H. S. (2010). *Do Social Connections Reduce Moral Hazard? Evidence from the New York Taxi Industry*. National Bureau of Economic Research.

Kasinitz, P., & Vickerman, M. (2001). Ethnic Niches and Racial Traps: Jamaicans in the New York Regional Economy. In H. R. Cordero-Guzman, R. C. Smith, & R. Grosfoguel (Eds.), *Migration, Transnationalization, and Race in a Changing New York* (pp. 190–211). Philadelphia: Temple University Press.

Kim, J. (2018). Manhattan's Koreatown as a Transclave: The Emergence of a New Ethnic Enclave in a Global City. *City & Community, 17*(1), 276–295.

Kingma, M. (2006). *Nurses on the Move: Migration and the Global Health Care Economy*. Ithaca: ILR Press.

Light, I., & Rosenstein, C. (1995). *Race, Ethnicity, and Entrepreneurship in Urban America*. New York: Aldine De Gruyter.

Limonic, L. (2005). *Unemployment and Labor Force Participation Rates Among Racial/Ethnic Groups and Latino Nationalities in the New York Metro Area and the Five Boroughs.* New York: Center for Latin American, Caribbean, and Latino Studies, The Graduate Center, The City University of New York.

Logan, J. R., Zhang, W., & Alba, R. D. (2001). Immigrant Enclaves and Ethnic Communities in New York and Los Angeles. *American Sociological Review, 67*(2), 299–322.

Mathew, B. (2005). *Taxi! Cabs and Capitalism in New York City.* Ithaca: ILR Press.

Migration Policy Institute. (2018). *State Immigration Data Profiles—United States.* Retrieved from Data Hub https://www.migrationpolicy.org/data/state-profiles/state/demographics/US.

Milkman, R., & Luce, S. (2017). *The State of the Unions 2017: A Profile of Organized Labor in New York City, New York State, and the United States.* New York: The City University of New York, The Joseph S. Murphy Institute for Worker Education and Labor Studies.

Minn, M. (2009). *The Geography of Chinese Restaurants in New York City.* Retrieved from http://michaelminn.net/newyork/food/chinese-restaurants/index.html.

Miyares, I. M. (1998). "Little Odessa"—Bright Beach, Brooklyn: An Examination of the Former Soviet Refugee Economy in New York City. *Urban Geography, 16*(6), 518–530.

New York City Department of City Planning, Population Division. (2004). *The Newest New Yorkers.* New York.

New York Times. (2019, May 19). *'They Were Conned': How Reckless Loans Devastated a Generation of Taxi Drivers.* https://www.nytimes.com/2019/05/19/nyregion/nyc-taxis-medallions-suicides.html? action=click&module=Top%20Stories&pgtype=Homepage.

NYC Department of City Planning. (2018, August 10). *Historical Population Information: Decennial Census.* Retrieved from Data/Maps https://www1.nyc.gov/site/planning/data-maps/nyc-population/historical-population.page.

Perry, M. J. (2014, May 3). *Chart of the Day: NYC Taxi Medallion Prices* Retrieved from American Enterprise Institute, AEI Ideas http://www.aei.org/publication/chart-of-the-day-nyc-taxi-medallion-prices/.

Portes, A., & Zhou, M. (1992). Gaining the Upper Hand: Economic Mobility Among Immigrant and Domestic Minorities. *Ethnic and Racial Studies, 15*(4), 491–522.

Ratha, D., Mohapatra, S., & Silwal, A. (2011). *The Migration and Remittances Factbook 2011*. Retrieved from http://siteresources.worldbank.org/INTPROSPECTS/Resources/334934-1199807908806/Top10.pdf.

Razin, E., & Light, I. (1998). Ethnic Entrepreneurs in America's Largest Metropolitan Areas. *Urban Affairs Review, 33*(3), 332–360.

Richardson, B. C., & Menke, J. K. (2018, October 12). *People*. Retrieved from Guyana https://www.britannica.com/place/Guyana/People.

Ruiz, N. (2018). *The Geography of Foreign Students in U.S. Higher Education: Origins and Destinations*. Washington, DC: Global Cities Initiative: A Joint Project of Brookings and JPMorgan Chase.

Ruiz, N. G., & Budiman, A. (2018, May 10). *Where Do Foreign Graduates Work in the United States*. Retrieved from Pew Research Center: Global Attitudes & Trends http://www.pewglobal.org/interactives/where-do-foreign-student-graduates-work-in-the-united-states/?msa=san-jose.

The World Bank. (2018). *Dominican Republic*. Retrieved from Data https://data.worldbank.org/country/dominican-republic.

Tichenor, D. J. (2002). *Dividing Lines: The Politics of Immigration Control in America*. Princeton: Princeton University Press.

U.S. Bureau of Labor Statistics. (2018, July 25). *Create Customized Tables: State and Area Employment, Hours, and Earnings—Seasonal*. Retrieved from Data Tools: Create Customized Tables https://data.bls.gov/cgi-bin/dsrv?sm.

U.S. Census Bureau. (2018). *Selected Historical Decennial Census Population and Housing Counts*. Retrieved from Census 1990 https://www.census.gov/population/www/censusdata/hiscendata.html.

U.S. Department of Commerce, Bureau of Economic Analysis. (2018). *Regional Data, GDP & Personal Income*. Retrieved from https://apps.bea.gov/iTable/iTable.cfm? reqid=70&step=1&isuri=1&acrdn=8#reqid=70&step=1&isuri=1.

U.S. Department of Homeland Security. (2018). *2017 Yearbook of Immigration Statistics*. Table 1. Persons Obtaining Lawful Permanent Resident Status: Fiscal Years 1820 to 2017. Retrieved from https://www.dhs.gov/immigration-statistics/yearbook/2017/table1.

U.S. Department of State, Bureau of Consular Affairs. (2018). *Nonimmigrant Visa Statistics*. Retrieved from U.S. Visa Law & Policy https://travel.state.gov/content/travel/en/legal/visa-law0/visa-statistics/nonimmigrant-visa-statistics.html.

Waldinger, R. D. (1986). *Through the Eye of the Needle: Immigrants and Enterprise in New York's Garment Trades*. New York: New York University Press.

Waldinger, R. (1996). *Still the Promised City? African-American and New Immigrants in Postindustrial New York*. Cambridge, MA: Harvard University Press.

Zhang & Associates, P. C. (2007, May 17). *HK, Macau, Taiwan Born Aliens Not Subject to Visa Number of China*. Retrieved from https://hooyou.com/news/news051707visa.html.

Zhou, Y. (1996). Inter-firm Linkages, Ethnic Networks, and Territorial Agglomeration: Chinese Computer Firms in Los Angles. *Papers in Regional Science, 75*(3), 265–391.

Zhou, Y. (1998). How Do Places Matter? A Comparative Study of Chinese Ethnic Economies in Los Angeles and New York City. *Urban Geography, 19*(6), 531–553.

# Epilogue

As work on this book is completed, New York's post-crisis recovery is still very much under way. At 4.5 million in December 2017, total non-farm payroll employment in the City was at an all-time high and 17% above where it had been at the previous cyclical peak 10-years earlier. Over that same decade, total U.S. employment increased by only seven percent.

Can this robust performance continue? No one can say for sure, of course, but what we know about the drivers of New York's economic history does help identify which potential global and national economic and political developments would be most supportive of the City's continuing prosperity and which would be most adverse. We can be reasonably confident, for example, that if the trend toward increasing globalization of production continues—that is, if more and more goods and services are produced and delivered via lengthier and more articulated multinational supply chains—New York's agglomeration of advanced business services will remain in high demand. Rising protectionist sentiment in the U.S. and elsewhere would, by contrast, be a strong headwind for the City's economy.

Even in the absence of increased protectionism, however, the shift in global economic activity toward East and South Asia, mentioned



A. Gurwitz, *Atlantic Metropolis*, Palgrave Studies in American Economic History,
https://doi.org/10.1007/978-3-030-13352-8

previously only in passing, could make it difficult for New York to maintain its position, along with only London, at the pinnacle of the international urban hierarchy. East and South Asia's combined share of global GDP increased at an accelerating pace from 23% in 1990 to 34% in 2017, and this trend seems almost certain to continue. As reflected in this book's title, however, the "world" that made New York what it became—an important entrepot in the British Empire of Goods, a vertex of the cotton triangle, North America's money center, a city of immigrants, and one of only two global cities—was very much an Atlantic world.

The increasing importance of Asia may very well disadvantage New York as a global center relative to London or other European cities. The problem is that the time in New York is behind that in Shanghai, Tokyo, and New Delhi by 13, 14, and 10.5 hours, respectively. This means that there is no overlap between "normal" business hours in the Eastern United States and East and South Asia. This time difference also disadvantages Asian cities as potential global centers; they are equally far away from the concentration of economic activity in North America. By contrast, London (only five hours later than New York) is behind these three Asian cities by only 8, 9, and 5.5 hours.

A personal anecdote may bring this issue into focus. In my last job in investment banking, I split my time between New York and London and managed an international team of economists and investment strategists located in those two cities, Mumbai and Tokyo. When I was in London, it was possible to interact with everyone on the team directly in real time, by video, voice, or text-message, during normal (investment banking) business hours. Of course, New York-based professionals can serve clients in East Asia, but any personal interaction between service provider and client or between a manager and a team requires either extensive travel or working in the middle of the night. So, at least to the extent that time compatibility matters, Asia's inexorable economic rise will likely generate more work for Europe's business services industry than New York's.

As discussed in Chapter 18, however, the number of local jobs in the business services activities associated with globalization has not been particularly large. Instead, the bulk of the new jobs in post-crisis New York have been in a wide array of primarily local service businesses, most of them immigrant employment niches, integral to an immigrant enclave economy, or both. Further, New York's large and well-educated Chinese and South Asian immigrant communities may, one hopes, be able to establish lucrative business connections with their homelands and, thereby offset, to some extent, New York's time zone disadvantage vis-à-vis those regions.

Policies that restrict or attitudes that discourage continued immigration are, arguably, the most serious threat to New York's continued economic growth in the twenty-first century. The positions taken by the region's congressional delegation on these issues are evidence that New Yorkers are well aware that their hometown was, is, and, if allowed to, will be a City of immigrants.

# Bibliography


Acemoglu, D. S. (2005). The Rise of Europe: Atlantic Trade, Institutional Change, and Economic Growth. *The American Economic Review, 95*(3), 546–579.

Adams, D. R. (1982). The Standard of Living During American Industrialization: Evidence from the Brandywine Region, 1800–1860. *The Journal of Economic History, 42*(4), 903–917.

Akerlof, G. A. (1970). The Market for 'Lemons': Quality Uncertainty and the Market Mechanism. *The Quarterly Journal of Economics, 84*(3), 488–500.

Albion, R. G. (1938). *Square-Riggers on Schedule: The New York Sailing Packets to England, France, and the Cotton Ports*. Princeton: Princeton University Press.

Albion, R. G. (1939). *The Rise of New York Port (1815–1860)*. New York: Scribner's.

Allen, R. C. (2001). The Great Divergence in European Wages and Prices from the Middle Ages to the First World War. *Explorations in Economic History, 38*, 426.

Alonso, W. (1964). *Location and Land Use: Toward a General Theory of Land Rent*. Cambridge: Harvard University Press.

Ambinder, T. (2001). *Five Points: The 19th-Century New York City Neighborhood that Invented Tap Dance, Stole Elections, and Became the World's Most Notorious Slum*. New York: Free Press.




A. Gurwitz, *Atlantic Metropolis*, Palgrave Studies in American Economic History,
https://doi.org/10.1007/978-3-030-13352-8

American Public Transportation Association. (2018, March 13). *Public Transportation Ridership Report* (Fourth Quarter 2017). Retrieved from https://www.apta.com/resources/statistics/Documents/Ridership/2017-Q4-Ridership-APTA.pdf.

Anas, A., Arnott, R., & Small, K. A. (1998). Urban Spatial Structure. *Journal of Economic Literature, 36*(3), 1426–1464.

Anbinder, T. (2016). *City of Dreams: The 400-Year Epic History of Immigrant New York*. New York: Houghton Mifflin Harcourt.

Anonymous. (1828, Reprint 2017). *Remarks Upon the Auction Systems, as Practised in New-York: To Which Are Added Numerous Facts in Illustration.* New Delhi: Reink Books.

Arnott, R. (1995). Time for Revisionism on Rent Control. *Journal of Economic Perspectives, 9*(1), 99–120.

Arthur, C. (2011, March 30). *Coming Undone: The Dominican Republic's Garment Assembly Sector*. Retrieved from MakingItMagazine.net http://www.makingitmagazine.net/?p=3293.

Audretsch, D. B., & Feldman, M. P. (2004). Knowledge Spillovers and the Geography of Innovation. In J. V. Henderson & T. J. F. Bounen (Eds.), *Handbook of Regional and Urban Economics* (pp. 2713–2739). New York: Elsevier.

Bachman, V. C. (1969). *Peltries or Plantations: The Economic Policies of the Dutch West India Company in New Netherland, 1623–1639.* Baltimore: The Johns Hopkins Press.

Bacolod, M., Blum, B. S., & Strange, W. C. (2009). Skills in the City. *Journal of Urban Economics, 65*(2), 136–153.

Baer, W. N. (1933). *The Economic Development of the Cigar Industry in the United States.* Lancaster, PA: The Art Printing Company.

Baer, W. N. (2008). *The Economic Development of the Cigar Industry in the United States.* Mansfield Center, CT: Martino Publishing.

Bahl, R. W., Campbell, A. K., & Greytak, D. (1974). *Taxes, Expenditures, and the Economic Base: Case Study of New York City.* New York: Praeger.

Baily, S. L. (1983). The Adjustment of Italian Immigrants in Buenos Aires and New York, 1870–1914. *The American Historical Review, 88*(2), 281–305.

Baily, S. L. (1999). *Immigrants in the Lands of Promise: Italians in Buenos Aires and New York City, 1870 to 1914.* Ithaca: Cornell University Press.

Bailyn, B. (1988). *Voyagers to the West: A Passage in the Peopling of America on the Eve of the Revolution.* New York: Vintage Books.

Bailyn, B. (2012). *The Barbarous Years: The Conflict of Civilizations: 1600–1675.* New York: Alfred A. Knopf.

Ballon, H. (2007). Robert Moses and Urban Renewal: The Title I Program. In H. Ballon & K. T. Jackson (Eds.), *Robert Moses and the Modern City: The Transformation of New York*. New York: W. W. Norton.

Baptist, E. E. (2014). *The Half Has Never Been Told: Slavery and the Making of American Capitalism*. New York: Basic Books.

Baron, S. (1962). *Brewed in America: A History of Beer and Ale in the United States*. Boston: Little Brown.

Baum-Snow, N. (2007). Did Highways Cause Suburbanization? *The Quarterly Journal of Economics, 122*(2), 755–805.

Ben-Atar, D. (1995). Alexander Hamilton's Alternative: Technology Piracy and the Report on Manufactures. *The William and Mary Quarterly, Third Series, 52*(3), 390–391.

Bennett, C. A. (1962). Cotton Ginning Systems in the United States and Auxilliary Developments. *Cotton Ginners Journal and the Cotton Gin and Oil Mill Press*. Mimeo.

Bereton, B. E. (2018, October 14). *Trinidad and Tobago*. Retrieved from Encyclopaedia Britannica https://www.britannica.com/place/Trinidad-and-Tobago.

Berne, R., & Stiefel, L. (1993). Cutback Budgeting: The Long-Term Consequences. *Journal of Policy Analysis and Management, 12*(4), 664–684.

Bernstein, M. (1987). *The Great Depression: Delayed Recovery and Economic Change in America, 1929–1939, 1987*. Cambridge: Cambridge University Press.

Bernstein, P. L. (2005). *Wedding of the Waters: The Erie Canal and the Making of a Great Nation*. New York: W. W. Norton.

Blackmar, E. (1989). *Manhattan for Rent, 1785–1850*. Ithaca: Cornell University Press.

Bloom, N. D. (2008). *Public Housing That Worked: New York in the Twentieth Century*. Philadelphia: University of Pennsylvania Press.

Blue M. M. (2007, January 6). *Excel Formula to Calculate Distance Between 2 Latitude, Longitude Points*. Retrieved from http://bluemm.blogspot.com/2007/01/excel-formula-to-calculate-distance.html.

Board of Governors of the Federal Reserve System. (1968). *Fifty-Fourth Annual Report Covering Operations for the Year 1967*. Washington.

Board of Governors of the Federal Reserve System. (2018). *All Sectors; Total Debt Securities; Liability [ASTDSL]*. Retrieved from FRED, Federal Reserve Bank of St. Louis https://fred.stlouisfed.org/series/ASTDSL.

Bodenhorn, H. (2000). *A History of Banking in Antebellum America: Financial Markets and Economic Development in an Era of Nation Building* (pp. 11–15). Cambridge: Cambridge University Press.

Bodenhorn, H. (2006). Bank Chartering and Political Corruption in Antebellum New York: Free Banking as Reform. In E. L. Gleaser & C. Goldin (Eds.), *Corruption and Reform: Lessons from America's Economic History*. Chicago: University of Chicago Press.

Bodenhorn, H., & Rockoff, H. (1992). Regional Interest Rates in Antebellum America. In C. Goldin & H. Rockoff (Eds.), *Strategic Factors in Nineteenth Century American Economic History: A Volume to Honor Robert W. Fogel* (pp. 159–187). Chicago: University of Chicago Press.

Boustan, L. P. (2010). Was Postwar Suburbanization 'White Flight'? *Evidence from the Black Migration, 125*(1), 417–443.

Bradford, D. F., & Kelejian, H. H. (1973). An Econometric Model of the Flight to the Suburbs. *Journal of Political Economy, 81*(3), 566–589.

Brecher, C., Horton, R., Cropf, R. A., & Dean, M. M. (1993). *Power Failure: New York City Politics and Policy Since 1960*. Oxford: Oxford University Press.

Bridenbaugh, C. (1955). *Cities in Revolt: Urban Life in America, 1743–1776*. New York: Knopf.

Bridenbaugh, C. (1971). *Cities in the Wilderness: The First Century of Urban Life in America, 1625–1742*. Reddich, England: Read Books, Ltd. (Reprint)

Britannica Encyclopedia on Line. (2018). *Catastrophe Theory*. Retrieved from http://www.britannica.com/EBchecked/topic/99235/catastrophe-theory.

Brittain, J. (1997). Allen B. Dumont: A Pioneer in Electronic Instruments, Radio, and Television. *Proceedings of the IEEE, 85*(12), 2081–2082.

Brock, L. V. (1975). *The Currency of the American Colonies, 1700–1764: A Study in Colonial Finance and Imperial Relations, Arno Press, 1975, 74 (N)*. New York: Arno Press.

Bruegel, M. (2002). *Farm, Shop, Landing: The Rise of a Market Society in the Hudson Valley, 1780–1860*. Durham, NC: Duke University Press.

Bulmer-Thomas, V. (2012). *The Economic History of the Caribbean Since the Napoleonic Wars*. Cambridge: Cambridge University Press.

Bureau of Labor Statistics. (2018, July 22). *Quarterly Census of Employment and Wages*. Retrieved from Data Tools https://data.bls.gov/cgi-bin/dsrv?en.

Burnham, R., Feinberg, R. M., & Husted, T. A. (2004). Central City Crime and Suburban Economic Growth. *Applied Economics, 36*(9), 917–922.

Burrows, E. G. (1999). *Gotham: A History of New York City to 1898*. New York: Oxford University Press.

Burrows, E. G., & Wallace, M. (1999). *Gotham: A History of New York City to 1898* (p. 1252). Oxford: Oxford University Press.

Butler, J. (1983). *The Huguenots in America: A Refugee People in New World Society*. Cambridge: Harvard University Press.

Calomris, C., & Barry Wilson, B. (2004). Bank Capital and Portfolio Management: The 1930s "Capital Crunch" and the Scramble to Shed Risk. *The Journal of Business, 77*(3), 421–455.

Cananaugh, R. (2014, October 9). Little Guyana, and Indo-Guanese Enclave in Queens. Retrieved from *The Washington Post* https://www.washingtonpost.com/lifestyle/travel/2014/10/02/38ec1260-4998-11e4-a046-120a8a855cca_story.html?noredirect=on&utm_term=.5ed5a933e4d8.

Carnevale, N. C. (2005). Culture of Work: Italian Immigrant Women Homeworkers in the New York City Garment Industry, 1890–1914. In D. Soyer (Ed.), *A Coat of Many Colors: Immigration, Globalization, and Reform in New York City's Garment Industry* (pp. 141–167). New York: Fordham University Press.

Caro, R. (1975). *The Power Broker: Robert Moses and the Fall of New York*. New York: Vintage Books.

Carosso, V. P. (1970). *Investment Banking in America: A History*. Cambridge, MA: Harvard University Press.

Carosso, V. P. (1987). *The Morgans: Private International Bankers, 1854–1913*. Cambridge, MA: Harvard University Press.

Carter, S. B. (1976). *Historical Statistics of the United States Millennial Edition Online*. Cambridge: Cambridge University Press.

Carter, S. B. (2006a). *Table Aa22035*. Retrieved from Historical Statistics of the United States Millennial Edition Online http://projects.ilt.columbia.edu/seneca/svcurric/images/byward2_early.html.

Carter, S. B. (2006b). *Table Eg1-59: Population, by Race and by Colony or Locality: 1610–1780*. Retrieved from Historical Statistics of the United States Millennial Edition Online http://hsus.cambridge.org/SeriesEg1-193.

Carter, S. B., Gartner, S. S., & Haines, M. R. (2006). *Historical Statistics of the United States Millennial Edition Online*. New York: Cambridge University Press.

CD_HISTORYBLOG. (2017, January 9). *When Did Slavery End in the North*. Retrieved from Civil Discourse, A Blog of the Long Civil War Era http://www.civildiscourse-historyblog.com/blog/2017/1/3/when-did-slavery-really-end-in-the-north.

Ceci, L. (1980a). The First Fiscal Crisis in New York. *Economic Development and Cultural Change, 28*(4), 839–847.

Ceci, L. (1980b). *Locational Analysis of Historic Algonquin Sites in Coastal New York: A Preliminary Study* (Research Report 19). Proceedings of the Conference on Northeastern Archaeology, Anthropology Research Report Series. Retrieved from https://scholarworks.umass.edu/cgi/viewcontent.cgi?article=1006&context=anthro_res_rpt19nce.

Ceci, L. (1982). The Value of Wampum Among the New York Iroquois: A Case Study in Artifact Analysis. *Journal of Anthropological Research, 38*(1), 97–107.

Census, U. B. (1976). *The Statistical History of the United States from Colonial Times to the Present*. New York: Basic Books.

Centers for Disease Control and Prevention. (2018). *TB Incidence in the United States, 1953–2016*. Retrieved from Tuberculosis (TB) https://www.cdc.gov/tb/statistics/tbcases.htm.

Cernog, E. (1996). *The Birth of Empire: DeWitt Clinton and the American Experience*. Oxford: Oxford University Press.

Champ, B. (2007, December). *The National Banking System: A Brief History* (pp. 29–33, Working Paper). Cleveland: Federal Reserve Bank of Cleveland.

Chin, M. M. (2005). Expanding Spheres: Men and Women in the Late Twentieth-Century Garment Industry. In D. Soyer (Ed.), *A Coat of Many Colors: Immigration, Globalization, and Reform in New York City's Garment Industry*. New York: Fordham University Press.

Chinitz, B. (1960). *Freight and the Metropolis: The Impact of America's Transportation Revolutions on the New York Region*. Cambridge: Harvard University Press.

Citizens' Association of New York. (1865). *Report of the Council of Hygiene and Public Health Upon the Sanitary Condition of the City*. New York: D. Appleton and Company.

CNW Research. (2013). *Will Surge in Private Party Used Vehicle Sales Affect Fleets*. Retrieved from Automotive Digest http://automotivedigest.com/2013/06/will-surge-in-private-party-used-vehicle-sales-affect-fleets/.

Cohen, D. S. (1981). How Dutch Were the Dutch of New Netherland. *New York History, 62*(1), 47.

Cohen, I. (1971). The Auction System in the Port of New York, 1817–1837. *The Business History Review, 45*(4), 491–492.

Cohen, R. L. (2009). *Mass Migration Under Sail: European Immigration to the Antebellum United States*. Cambridge: Cambridge University Press.

Cole, A. H., & Williamson, H. F. (1941). *The American Carpet Manufacture: A History and Analysis*. Cambridge, MA: Harvard University Press.

Cole, H. L., & Ohanian, L. E. (2004). New Deal Policies and the Persistence of the Great Depression: A General Equilibrium Analysis. *Journal of Political Economy, 112*(41), 779–816.

Collins English Dictionary. (2018). *Perfect Storm*. Retrieved from Dictionary.com https://www.dictionary.com/browse/perfect-storm.

Collins, W. J. (1997). When the Tide Turned: Immigration and the Delay of the Great Black Migration. *The Journal of Economic History, 57*(3), 607–632.

Columbia Law Review. (1926). Legislative Housing Relief in New York: The State Housing Law and the Extension of the Emergency Rent Laws. *Columbia Law Review, 26*(8), 1015–1016.

Committee to Review the New York City Watershed Management Strategy. (2000). *Watershed Management for Potable Water Supply: Assessing the New York City Strategy.* Washington, DC: National Academy Press.

Comptroller of the Currency. (1910). *Annual Report of the Comptroller of the Currency to the Third Session of the Sixty-First Congress of the United States*. Washington, DC: U.S. Government Printing Office.

Corgel, J., & Sellers, K. (2017, September 25). *A Look at US Hotels' Dependence on International Guests*. Retrieved from Hotel News Now http://www.hotelnewsnow.com/Articles/240035/A-look-at-US-hotels-dependence-on-international-guests.

Cortes, P., & Pan, J. (2014). *Foreign Nurse Importation to the United States and the Supply of Native Registered Nurses* (Working Paper No. 14-7). Boston: Federal Reserve Bank of Boston.

Crawford, G. W. (1996). Migration in Prehistory: Princess Point and the Northern Iroquoian Case: Comments. *American Antiquity, 61*(4), 782–790.

Crean, J. F. (1962). Hats and the Fur Trade. *The Canadian Journal of Economics and Political Science, 28*(3), 376.

Critz, J. M., Olmstead, A. L., & Rhode, A. P. (1999). Horn of Plenty: The Globalization of Mediterranean Horticulture and the Economic Development of Southern Europe, 1880–1930. *The Journal of Economic History, 59*(2), 316–352.

Cronon, W. (1991). *Nature's Metropolis: Chicago and the Great West*. New York: W. W. Norton.

Cronon, W. (1994). *Nature's Metropolis: Chicago and the Great West*. New York: W. W. Norton.

Crowder, K. D., & Tedrow, L. M. (2001). West Indians and the Residential Landscape of New York. In N. Foner (Ed.), *Islands in the City: West Indian Migration to New York* (pp. 81–114). Berkeley: University of California Press.

Cullen, J. B., & Levitt, S. D. (1999). Crime, Urban Flight, and the Consequences for Cities. *The Review of Economics and Statistics, 81*(2), 159–169.

Current Results. (2018, April 24). *Average Temperatures for Large US Cities in January*. Retrieved from Current Results: Weather and Science Facts https://www.currentresults.com/Weather/US/average-city-temperatures-in-january.php.

Current Results, Weather and Science Facts. (2018, May 8). *Average Annual Precipitation by City in the United States*. Retrieved from https://www.currentresults.com/Weather/US/average-annual-precipitation-by-city.php.

Currid, E. (2006). New York as a Global Creative Hub: A Competitive Analysis of Four Theories on World Cities. *Economic Development Quarterly, 30*(4), 330–350.

Currid, E. (2007). *The Warhol Economy: How Fashion, Art, and Music Drive New York City*. Princeton: Princeton University Press.

Cutler, D., Glaeser, E. L., & Vigdor, J. L. (2008). When Are Ghettos Bad? Lessons from Immigrant Segregation in the United States. *Journal of Urban Economics, 63*(3), 759–774.

David, P. A. (2007). Path Dependence—A Foundational Concept for Historical Social Science. *Cliometrica—The Journal of Historical Economics and Econometric History, 1*(2), 3.

Davis, J. H. (2004). An Annual Index of U.S. Industrial Production, 1790–1915. *The Quarterly Journal of Economics, 119*(4), 1177–1215.

Davis, K. G. (1974). *The North Atlantic World in the Seventeenth Century*. St. Paul: University of Minnesota Press.

Davis, L. E., & Cull, R. J. (1994). *International Capital Markets and American Economic Growth, 1820–1914*. Cambridge: Cambridge University Press.

Davis, L., & Cull, R. J. (2000). International Capital Movements, Domestic Capital Markets, and American Economic Growth. In S. L. Engerman & R. E. Gallman (Eds.), *The Cambridge Economic History of the United States, Volume II: The Long Nineteenth Century* (pp. 733–812). Cambridge: Cambridge University Press.

Davis, P. (1949). *The Development of the American Glass Industry* (pp. 42, 73). Cambridge: Harvard University Press.

Davis, D. R. (1998). The Home Market, Trade and Industrial Structure. *American Economic Review, 88*(5), 1264–1276.

Davis, D. R., & Weinstein, D. E. (1998, November). *Market Access, Economic Geography and Comparative Advantage: An Empirical Assessment* (National Bureau of Economic Research Working Paper No. 6787).

DeSalvo, J. S. (1974). Neighborhood Upgrading Effects of Middle-Income Housing Projects in New York City. *Journal of Urban Economics, 1,* 269–277.

DeSalvo, J. S. (1975). Benefits and Costs of New York City's Middle-Income Housing Program. *Journal of Political Economy, 83*(4), 791–806.

DeVol, R. C. (1999). *America's High-Tech Economy: Growth, Development, and Risks for Metropolitan Areas*. Santa Monica, CA: The Milken Institute.

de Vries, J., & van der Woude, A. (1997). *The First Modern Economy: Success, Failure, and Perseverance of the Dutch Economy, 1500–1815*. Cambridge: Cambridge University Press.

Dijur, I. M. (1966). Jews in the Russian Economy. In J. Frumkin, G. Aronson, & A. Goldenwasser (Eds.), *Russian Jewry, 1860–1917*. New York: Thomas Yosseloff.

Dubin, L. (2006). Introduction: Port Jews in the Atlantic World Jewish History. *Jewish History, 20,* 119–120.

Duranton, G., & Puga, D. (2003). *Micro-foundations of Urban Agglomeration Economies* (NBER Working Paper 9931).

Elliot, J. R. (2001). Referral Hiring and Ethnically Homogeneous Jobs: How Prevalent Is the Connection and for Whom. *Social Science Research, 30,* 401–425.

Eltis, D. (2001). The Volume and Structure of the Transatlantic Slave Trade: A Reassessment. *William and Mary Quarterly, Second Series, LVIII*(1), 17–46.

Emsley, C., Hitchcock, T., & Shoemaker, R. (2018). *London History—Currency Coinage and the Cost of Living*. Retrieved from Old Bailey Proceedings Online https://www.oldbaileyonline.org/static/Coinage.jsp#costofliving.

Engelbrecht-Wiggans, R., & Nonnenmacher, T. (1999). The Theoretical Baiss for 19th-Century Changes to the Port of New York Imported Goods Auction. *Explorations in Economic History, 36,* 232–245.

Engerman, S., & Goldin, C. (1991). *Seasonality in Nineteenth Century Labor Markets* (Working Paper No. 20: NBER Working Papers Series on Historical Factors in Long Run Growth).

Ernst, R. (1994). *Immigrant Life in New York City, 1825–1863*. Syracuse, NY: Syracuse University Press.

Estevadeordal, A., Frantz, B., & Taylor, A. M. (2002, November). *The Rise and Fall of World Trade, 1870–1939* (NBER Working Paper 9318, p. 2).

Estevadeordal, A., Frantz, B., & Taylor, A. M. (2003). The Rise and Fall of World Trade, 1870–1939. *The Quarterly Journal of Economics, 118*(2), 359–407.

Federal Reserve Bank of St. Louis. (2018). *Download, Graph, and Track 527,000 US and International Time Series from 87 Sources*. Retrieved from FRED Economic Data https://fred.stlouisfed.org.

Fenton, E. (1962). Italian Immigrants in the Stoneworkers Union. *Labor History, 3*(2), 188–207.

Ferguson, N. (1998). *The House of Rothschild, Money's Prophets, 1798–1848*. New York: Penguin Books.

Ferrie, J. P. (1997). The Entry into the U.S. Labor Market of Antebellum European Immigrants, 1840–1860. *Explorations in Economic History, 34*, 295–330.

Fichter, J. R. (2010). *So Great a Profit: How the East Indies Trade Transformed Anglo-American Capitalism*. Cambridge: Harvard University Press.

Field, A. J. (2003). The Most Technologically Progressive Decade of the Century. *American Economic Review, 93*(4), 1399–1413.

Fishlow, A. (2000). Internal Transportation in the Nineteenth and Early Twentieth Centuries. In S. Engerman & R. E. Gallman (Eds.), *The Cambridge Economic History of the United States, Volume II, The Long Nineteenth Century* (pp. 543–642). Cambridge: Cambridge University Press.

Florida, R. (2012). *The Rise of the Creative Class, Revisited*. New York: Basic Books.

Florida, R., & Gates, G. (2001). *Technology and Tolerance: The Importance of Diversity to High-Technology Growth*. Washington, DC: The Brookings Institution, Center on Urban & Metropolitan Policy.

Florida, R., Mellander, C., Stolarick, K., & Ross, A. (2012). Cities, Skills and Wages. *Journal of Economic Geography, 12*, 355–377.

Fogel, R. W. (1989). *Without Consent or Contract: The Rise and Fall of American Slavery*. New York: W. W. Norton.

Freedley, E. T. (1859). *Philadelphia and Its Manufactures: A Hand-Book Exhibiting the Development, Variety, and Statistics of the Manufacturing Industry of Philadelphia in 1857*. Philadelphia: Edward Young.

Freeman, J. B. (2000). *Working Class New York: Life and Labor Since World War II*. New York: The New Press.

Freudenberg, N., Fahs, M., Galea, S., & Greenberg, A. (2006). The Impact of New York City's 1975 Crisis on the Tuberculosis, HIV, and Homicide Syndemic. *American Journal of Public Health, 96*(3), 424–434.

Frieden, J. A. (2006). *Global Capitalism: Its Fall and Rise in the Twentieth Century*. New York: W. W. Norton.

Friedman, M., & Schwartz, A. (1986). The Failure of the Bank of the United States: A Reappraisal: A Reply. *Exploration in Economic History, 23,* 199–204.

Friedmann, J. (1995). Where We Stand: A Decade of World City Research. In P. L. Knox & P. J. Taylor (Eds.), *World Cities in a World-System* (pp. 21–47). Cambridge: Cambridge University Press.

Fujita, M., Krugman, P., & Venables, A. (1999). *The Spatial Economy: Cities, Regions, and International Trade*. Cambridge: MIT Press.

Gabaiz, X. (1999). Zipf's Law for Cities: An Explanation. *Quarterly Journal of Economics, 114*(3), 739–767.

Garret, T. A., & Wheelock, D. C. (2006). *Why Did Income Growth Vary Across States During the Great Depression* (Working Paper 2005-01-013B). St. Louis: Federal Reserve Bank of St. Louis, Research Division.

Gehring, C. T. (1992). Dutch and Indians in the Hudson Valley: The Early Period. *Hudson River Valley Review, 9,* 9–25. http://www.hudsonrivervalley.org/review/pdfs/hvrr_9pt2_gehringandstarna.pdf.

Gelfand, M. I. (1975). *A Nation of Cities: The Federal Government and Urban America, 1933–1965*. Oxford: Oxford University Press.

Gertler, M. S. (2003). Tacit Knowledge and the Economic Geography of Context, or The Undefinable Tacitness of Being (There). *Journal of Economic Geography, 3,* 75–99.

Gianni, T. (1990). *An Economic History of Liberal Italy: 1850–1918*. London: Routledge.

Gibson, C. (1998, June). *Population of the 100 Largest Cities and Other Urban Places in the United States: 1790–1990*. Retrieved from U.S. Census Bureau https://www.census.gov/population/www/documentation/twps0027/twps0027.html.

Gibson, C., & Jung, K. (2005, February). *Historical Census Statistics on Population Totals by Race, 1790 to 1990, and by Hispanic Origin, 1970 to 1990, For Large Cities and Other Urban Places*. Retrieved from U.S. Census Bureau https://www.census.gov/population/www/documentation/twps0076/twps0076.html.

Gilmore, R. G. (2013). St. Eustatius: The Nexus for Colonial Caribbean Capitalism. In D. Comer (Ed.), *The Archaeology of Interdependence: European Involvement in the Development of a Sovereign United States* (p. 44). Berlin: Springer.

Glaeser, E. L., Edward, Kolko, J., & Saiz, A. (2001). Consumer City. *Journal of Economic Geography, 1*, 28.

Glaeser, E. L., & Gottlieb, J. D. (2006). Urban Resurgence and the Consumer City. *Urban Studies, 43*(8), 1288.

Glaeser, E. L., Saiz, A., Burtless, G., & Strange, W. (2003, December). *The Rise of the Skilled City* (National Bureau of Economic Research Working Paper 10191).

Glaeser, E. L., Saiz, A., Burtless, G., & Strange, W. C. (2004). The Rise of the Skilled City. In W. G. Gale & J. R. Pack (Eds.), *Brookings-Wharton Papers on Urban Affairs* (pp. 47–105). Washington: Brookings Institution Press.

Goldin, C. (1994). The Political Economy of Immigration Restriction in the United States. In C. A. Goldin (Ed.), *The Regulated Economy* (pp. 223–257). Chicago: University of Chicago Press. Retrieved from http://www.nber.org/books/gold94-1

Goldin, C., & Margo, R. A. (1992). The Great Compression: The Wage Structure in the United States at Mid-Century. *Quarterly Journal of Economics, 107*(1), 1–34.

Goodfriend, J. D. (1992). *Before the Melting Pot: Society and Culture in Colonial New York City, 1664–1730*. Princeton: Princeton University Press.

Gorton, G. (1996). Reputation Formation in Early Bank Note Markets. *Journal of Political Economy, 104*(2), 346–397.

Gorton, G. (1999). Pricing Free Bank Notes. *Journal of Monetary Economics, 44*, 33–64.

Gould, J. D. (1980). European Inter-Continental Emigration, The Road Home: Return Migration from the U.S.A. *Journal of European Economic History, 9*(1), 41–112.

Governing the States and Localities. (2018). *Foreign Born City Population Data*. Retrieved from Data http://www.governing.com/gov-data/census/foreign-born-city-population-changes-data.html.

Goyal, S. (2007). *Connections: An Introduction to the Economics of Networks*. Princeton: Princeton University Press.

Graham, P. M. (2001). Political Incorporation and Re-incorporation: Simultaneity in the Dominican Migrant Experience. In H. R. Cordero-Guzman, R. C. Smith, & R. Grosfoguel (Eds.), *Migration, Transnationalization, and Race in a Changing New York* (pp. 87–108). Philadelphia: Temple University Press.

Granoveter, M. S. (1973). The Strength of Weak Ties. *American Journal of Sociology, 78*(6), 1360–1380.

Granovetter, M. (2005). The Impact of Social Structure on Economic Outcomes. *Journal of Economic Perspectives, 19*(1), 33–50.

Grasmuck, S., & Grosfoguel, R. (1997). Geopolitics, Economic Niches, and Gendered Social Capital Among Recent Caribbean Immigrants in New York City. *Sociological Perspectives, 40*(3), 339–363.

Greeley, H. E. (1872). *The Great Industries of the United States—Being an Historical Summary of the Origin, Growth, and Perfection of the Chief Industrial Arts of This Country—Quarries.* Retrieved from Stone Quarries and Beyond http://quarriesandbeyond.org/articles_and_books/great_industries.html.

Green, J. P., & Morgan, P. D. (2009). *Atlantic History: A Critical Appraisal.* Oxford: Oxford University Press.

Greytak, D., Gustely, R., & Dinkelmeyer, R. (1974). The Effects of Inflation on Local Government Expenditures. *National Tax Journal, 27*(4), 583–598.

Grumet, R. S. (2011). *First Manhattans: A Brief History of the Indians of Greater New York* (63rd ed.). Norman: University of Oklahoma Press.

Gustafson, W. E. (1959). Printing and Publishing. In M. Hall (Ed.), *Made in New York: Case Studies in Metropolitan Manufacturing* (pp. 135–240). Cambridge, MA: Harvard University Press.

Gyourko, J., & Linneman, P. (1989). Equity and Efficiency Aspects of Rent Control: An Empirical Study of New York City. *Journal of Urban Economics, 26,* 54–74.

Haggerty, S. (2006a). *The British Atlantic Trading Community, 1760–1781: Men, Women, and the Distribution of Goods.* Leiden: Brill.

Haggerty, S. (2006b). *The British-Atlantic Trading Community, 1760–1810: Men, Women, and the Distribution of Goods* (pp. 151, 204, 206). Leiden: Brill.

Haines, M. R. (2000). The Population of the United States, 1790–1920. In S. L. Engerman & R. R. Gallman (Eds.), *The Cambridge Economic History of the United States, Volume II, The Long Nineteenth Century* (pp. 143–206). Cambridge: Cambridge University Press.

Haines, M. R. (2018). *Historical, Demographic, Economic, and Social Data: The United States, 1790–2002 [Computer File]. ICPSR02896-v3.* Ann Arbor, MI: Inter-university Consortium for Politica. Retrieved from Inter-university Consortium for Political and Social Research https://www.icpsr.umich.edu/icpsrweb/.

Haines, M. R., & ISPCR. (n.d.). *Historical, Demographic, Economic, and Social Data: The United States, 1790–2002*. Retrieved from Inter-university Consortium for Political and Social Research https://doi.org/10.3886/icpsr02896.v3.

Harrington, V. D. (1935). *The New York Merchant on the Eve of the Revolution*. New York: Columbia University Press.

Hart, J. P. (2008). Evolving the Three Sisters: The Changing Histories of Maize, Bean, and Squash in New York and the Greater Northeast. *Current Northeast Paleoethnobotany, II*, 87–88.

Hatton, T. J., & Williamson, J. G. (1998). *The Age of Mass Migration, Causes and Economic Impact*. Oxford: Oxford University Press.

Hatton, T. J., & Williamson, J. G. (2005). *Global Migration and the World Economy: Two Centuries of Policy and Performance*. Cambridge, MA: MIT Press.

Hayes, S. L., & Hubbard, P. M. (1990). *Investment Banking: A Tale of Three Cities*. Cambridge, MA: Harvard Business School Press.

Heaton, H. (1941). Non-importation, 1806–1812. *Journal of Economic History, 12*, 178–198.

Head, S. W. (1978). *Broadcasting in America: A Survey of Television and Radio* (3rd ed.). New York: Houghton Mifflin.

Heclo, H. (2005). Sixties Civics. In S. M. Milkis & J. M. Mileur (Eds.), *The Great Society and the High Tide of Liberalism* (pp. 53–82). Amherst: University of Massachusetts Press.

Helfgott, R. B. (1959). Women's and Children's Apparel. In M. Hall (Ed.), *Made in New York: Case Studies in Metropolitan Manufacturing* (pp. 19–134). Cambridge, MA: Harvard University Press.

Henretta, J. A. (1978). Families and Farms: Mentalité in Pre-industrial America. *William and Mary Quarterly, 35*(1), 7–8.

Hickey, D. (1981). American Trade Restrictions During the War of 1812. *The Journal of American History, 68*(3), 528–529.

Hickey, D. R. (2012). *The War of 1812: A Forgotten Conflict*. Champagne: University of Illinois Press.

Hidy, R. W. (1949). *The House of Baring in American Trade and Finance: English Merchant Bankers at Work, 1763–1861*. Cambridge, MA: Harvard University Press.

Hipple, S. F., & Hammond, L. A. (2016, March). *Self-Employment in the United States*. Retrieved from U.S. Bureau of Labor Statistics https://www.bls.gov/spotlight/2016/self-employment-in-the-united-states/pdf/self-employment-in-the-united-states.pdf.

Hood, C. (1993). *722 Miles, The Building of the Subways and How They Transformed New York*. New York: Simon & Schuster.

Hoover, E. M. (1937). *Location Theory and the Shoe and Leather Industries*. Cambridge, MA: Harvard University Press.

Hummels, D. (2007). Transportation Costs and International Trade in the Second Era of Globalization. *Journal of Economic Perspectives, 21*(3), 131–154.

Hurd. (1959). M. Hall, *Made in New York: Case Studies in Metropolitan Manufacturing*. Cambridge, MA: Harvard University Press.

Ingalls, R. P. (1975). *Herbert H. Lehman and New York's Little New Deal*. New York: New York University Press.

International Monetary Fund. (2018, June). *International Finanacial Statistics: External Sector Selected Indicators*. http://data.imf.org/regular.aspx?key=61545863.

International Telecommunications Union. (2018, June 5). *Statistics*. Retrieved from Committed to Connecting the World: International Telegraphic Union (ITU) http://www.itu.int/en/ITU-D/Statistics/Pages/stat/default.aspx.

Irwin, D. A. (2003). The Optimal Tax on Antebellum US Cotton Exports. *Journal of International Economics, 60*, 277.

J. Moody & Co. (1901). *Moodys Manual of Railroads and Corporation Securities*. New York: J. Moody & Co.

Jacks, D. S. (2005). Intra- and International Commodity Market Integration in the Atlantic Economy, 1800–1913. *Explorations in Economic History, 42*, 381–413.

Jackson, C. K., & Schneider, H. S. (2010). *Do Social Connections Reduce Moral Hazard? Evidence from the New York Taxi Industry*. National Bureau of Economic Research.

Jackson, K. T. (1985). *Crabgrass Frontier: The Suburbanization of the United States*. Oxford: Oxford University Press.

Jacobs, J. (1961). *The Death and Life of Great American Cities*. New York: Vintage Books.

Jacobs, J. (1969). *The Economy of Cities*. New York: Random House.

Jacobs, J. (1998). Between Repression and Approval: Connivance and Tolerance in the Dutch Republic and in New Netherland. *de Halve Maen, 71*(3), 57.

Jacobs, J. (2009). *The Colony of New Netherland: A Dutch Settlement in Seventeenth-Century America*. Ithaca: Cornell University Press.

Johnston, L., & Williamson, S. H. (2018). *What Was the U.S. GDP Then?* Retrieved from MeasuringWorth.com https://www.measuringworth.com/datasets.html.

Jones, J. H. (2007, January). *Falmouth Packets*. Retrieved from TPO & Seapost Society http://www.tpo-seapost.org.uk/tpo2/spfalmouthpkt.html.

Judt, T. (2005). *Postwar: A History of Europe Since 1945*. New York: Penguin Books.

Juet, R. (1909). The Third Voyage of Master Henry Hudson. In J. Franklin (Ed.), *Narratives of New Netherland, 1609–1664* (p. 14). New York: Scribner, Electronic Reproduction by General Books, 2009.

Kahan, A. (1986). *Essays in Jewish Social and Economic History*. Chicago: University of Chicago Press.

Kahan, A. (1989). *Russian Economic History: The Nineteenth Century*. Chicago: University of Chicago Press.

Kammen, M. (1975). *Colonial New York: A History*. Oxford: Oxford University Press.

Kane, R. J. (1999). The Financing of Cooperatives and Condominiums: A Retrospective. *St. John's Law Review, 73*(1), 101–134.

Kasinitz, P., & Vickerman, M. (2001). Ethnic Niches and Racial Traps: Jamaicans in the New York Regional Economy. In H. R. Cordero-Guzman, R. C. Smith, & R. Grosfoguel (Eds.), *Migration, Transnationalization, and Race in a Changing New York* (pp. 190–211). Philadelphia: Temple University Press.

Katznelson, I. (1973). *Black Men, White Cities: Race, Politics, and Migration in the United States, 1900–1930, and Britain, 1948–1968*. Chicago: University of Chicago Press.

Kemp, S. (1998). Perceiving Luxury and Necessity. *Journal of Economic Psychology, 19*(6), 591–606.

Kennedy, D. M. (1999). *Freedom from Fear: The American People in Depression and War, 1929–1945*. Oxford: Oxford University Press.

Kenney, M., & von Burg, U. (1999). Technology, Entrepreneurship and Path Dependence: Industrial Clustering and Silicon Valley and Route 128. *Industrial and Corporate Change, 8*(1), 67–103.

Kessner, T. (1977). *The Golden Door: Italian and Jewish Immigrant Mobility in New York City, 1880–1915*. Oxford.

Kessner, T. (1989). *Fiorello H. La Guardia and the Making of Modern New York*. New York: Penguin Books.

Kim, J. (2018). Manhattan's Koreatown as a Transclave: The Emergence of a New Ethnic Enclave in a Global City. *City & Community, 17*(1), 276–295.

Kim, S. B. (1978). *Landlord and Tenant in Colonial New York: Manorial Society, 1664–1775*. Raleigh: University of North Carolina Press.

Kingma, M. (2006). *Nurses on the Move: Migration and the Global Health Care Economy*. Ithaca: ILR Press.

Klepper, S. (2010). The Origin and Growth of Industry Clusters: The Making of Silicon Valley and Detroit. *Journal of Urban Economics, 67*, 15–32.

Krippner, G. R. (2005). The Financialization of the American Economy. *Socio-Economic Review, 3*(2), 173–208.

Kugler, P. (2013). *The Changing Regime of the Pound/Guilder Exchange Rate 1600–1912*. Mimeo. Basel: University of Basel.

Lee, A. M. (1937). *The Daily Newspaper in America: The Evolution of a Social Instrument*. New York: Macmillan.

Lemon, J. T. (1967). Urbanization and the Development of Eighteenth Century Southeastern Pennsylvania and Adjacent Delaware. *The William and Mary Quarterly, Third Series, 24*(4), 501–542.

Levinson, M. (2006). Container Shipping and the Decline of New York, 1955–1975. *The Business History Review, 80*(1), 49–80.

Liebowitz, S. (2015, August). *Paradise Lost: The Payment of British Authors in 19th Century America*. Retrieved from http://papers.ssrn.com/sol3/papers.cfm?abstract_id=2676048.

Light, I. H. (1972). *Business and Welfare Among Chinese, Japanese, and Blacks*. Berkeley: University of California Press.

Light, I., & Rosenstein, C. (1995). *Race, Ethnicity, and Entrepreneurship in Urban America*. New York: Aldine De Gruyter.

Limonic, L. (2005). *Unemployment and Labor Force Participation Rates Among Racial/Ethnic Groups and Latino Nationalities in the New York Metro Area and the Five Boroughs*. New York: Center for Latin American, Caribbean, and Latino Studies, The Graduate Center, The City University of New York.

Logan, J. R., Zhang, W., & Alba, R. D. (2001). Immigrant Enclaves and Ethnic Communities in New York and Los Angeles. *American Sociological Review, 67*(2), 299–322.

Lucia, J. (1985). The Failure of the Bank of United States: A Reappraisal. *Explorations in Economic History, 22*, 402–416.

Maddison, A. (2001). *The World Economy: A Millennial Perspective*. Paris: Development Studies Center of the Organization for Economic Co-operation and Development.

Magee, M. A. (1930). *Trends in the Location of the Women's Clothing Industry*. Chicago: University of Chicago Press.

Malanima, P. (2009). *Pre-modern European Economy: One Thousand Years (10th–19th Centuries)*. Leiden: Brill.

Maldonado, R., & Rose, R. D. (1995). The Application of Civil Rights Law to Housing Cooperatives: Are Co-ops Bastions of Discriminatory Exclusion or Self-Selecting Models of Community Based Living. *Fordham Urban Law Review, 23*(4), 1245–1282.

Margo, R. A. (1992). Explaining the Postwar Suburbanization of Population in the United States: The Role of Income. *Journal of Urban Economics, 31*(3), 301–310.

Margo, R. A. (1996). The Rental Price of Housing in New York City, 1830–1860. *Journal of Economic History, 56*(3), 605–625.

Margo, R. A. (2000). New Estimates of Nominal and Real Wages for the Antebellum Period. In R. A. Margo (Ed.), *Wages and Labor Markets in the United States, 1820–1860*. Chicago: University of Chicago Press.

Marshall, A. (1895). *Principles of Economics* (Vol. 1, 3rd ed.). New York: Macmillan.

Mashable. (2018). *1904 to Today: See How New York City Subway Fare Has Climbed Over 111 Years*. Retrieved from https://mashable.com/2015/03/22/new-york-city-subway-fare/#lGmkm2R8RPqK.

Mason, M. K. (2018, June). *Housing: Then, Now, and Future*. Retrieved from http://www.moyak.com/papers/house-sizes.html.

Massey, D. A., Denton, N. A. (1989). Hypersegregation in U.S. Metropolitan Areas: Black and Hispanic Segregation along Five Dimensions. *Demography, 26*(3), 373–391.

Masters, C. J. (2007). *Governor Henry Horner, Chicago Politics, and the Great Depression*. Carbondale: Southern Illinois Press.

Mathew, B. (2005). *Taxi! Cabs and Capitalism in New York City*. Ithaca: ILR Press.

Mathias, P. (2000). Risk, Credit and Kinship in Early Modern Enterprise, Camb. In J. J. McCusker & K. Morgan (Eds.), *The Early Modern Atlantic Economy* (pp. 15–62). Cambridge: Cambridge University Press.

Matson, C. (2002). *Merchants and Empire: Trading in Colonial New York*. Baltimore: Johns Hopkins University Press.

McCusker, J. J., & Menard, R. R. (1985). *The Economy of British America, 1607–1789*. Raleigh: The University of North Carolina Press.

McDonald, J. F. (2011). Public Housing Construction and the Cities, 1937–1967. *Urban Studies Research*, 1–12.

McManus, J. C. (1972). An Economic Analysis of Indian Behavior in the North American Fur Trade. *The Journal of Economic History, 32*(1), 36–53.

Mendeslsohn, A. D. (2015). *The Rag Race: How Jews Sewed Their Way to Success in America and the British Empire*. New York: New York University Press.

Mieszkowski, P., & Mills, E. S. (1993). The Causes of Metropolitan Suburbanization. *Journal of Economic Perspectives, 7*(3), 135–147.

Migration Policy Institute. (2018). *State Immigration Data Profiles—United States*. Retrieved from Data Hub https://www.migrationpolicy.org/data/state-profiles/state/demographics/US.

Milkman, R., & Luce, S. (2017). *The State of the Unions 2017: A Profile of Organized Labor in New York City, New York State, and the United States*. New York: The City University of New York, The Joseph S. Murphy Institute for Worker Education and Labor Studies.

Miller, M. H. (1986). Financial Innovation: The Last Twenty Years and the Next. *Journal of Financial and Quantitative Analysis, 21*(4), 148–176.

Millett, J. D. (1938). *The Works Progress Administration in New York City*. Chicago: Public Administration Service.

Mills, E. (1970). Urban Density Function. *Urban Studies, 7*(1), 5–20.

Minn, M. (2009). *The Geography of Chinese Restaurants in New York City*. Retrieved from http://michaelminn.net/newyork/food/chinese-restaurants/index.html.

Mintz, S. W. (1985). *Sweetness and Power: The Place of Sugar in Modern History*. New York: Penguin.

Miyares, I. M. (1998). "Little Odessa"—Bright Beach, Brooklyn: An Examination of the Former Soviet Refugee Economy in New York City. *Urban Geography, 16*(6), 518–530.

Moch, L. P. (2003). *Moving Europeans: Migration in Western Europe Since 1650* (2nd ed.). Bloomington: Indiana University Press.

Model, S. (2001). Where New York's West. Indians Work. In N. Foner (Ed.), *Islands in the City: West Indian Migration to New York* (pp. 52–80). Berkeley: University of California Press.

Mokyr, J. (1977). Demand vs. Supply in the Industrial Revolution. *Journal of Economic History, 37*(4), 981–1008.

Montgomery, J. D. (1991, December). Social Networks and Labor-Market Outcomes: Toward and Economic Analysis. *American Economic Review, 81*(5), 1408–1418.

Morawska, E. (1987). A Replica of the 'Old-Country' Relationship in the Ethnic Niche: East European Jews and Gentiles in Small-Town Western Pennsylvania, 1880s–1930s. *American Jewish History, 77*(1), 27–86.

Morgan, K. (2000). Business Networks in the British Export Trade to North America, 1750–1800. In J. J. McCusker & K. Morgan (Eds.), *The Early Modern Atlantic Economy* (pp. 16–62). Cambridge: Cambridge University Press.

Morris, C. R. (1980). *The Cost of Good Intentions: New York City and the Liberal Experiment, 1960–1975*. New York: W. W. Norton.

Morrison, K. M. (1984). *The Embattled Northeast: The Elusive Ideal of Alliance in Abenaki-Euramerican Relations*. Berkeley: University of California Press.

Mullilgan, G. E., & Fik, T. J. (1994). Úsing Dummy Variables to Estimate Economic Base Multipliers. *Land Economics, 46*(3), 368–377.

Murray, L. A. (1995). Unravelling Employment Trends in Textiles and Apparel. *Monthly Labor Review, 118*(8), 62–72.

Muth, R. F. (1969). *Cities and Housing; The Spatial Pattern of Urban Residential Land Use*. Chicago: University of Chicago Press.

Myers, M. G. (1931). *The New York Money Market, Volume I, Origins and Development*. New York: Columbia University Press.

N.Y.S. Department of Taxation and Finance. (n.d.). *Enactment and Effective Dates of Sales and Use Tax Rates, Publication 718-A*. Albany: State of New York.

Nash, G. B. (1986). *The Urban Crucible: The Northern Seaports and the Origins of the American Revolution* (pp. 40–42). Cambridge: Harvard University Press.

National Academy of Engineering; Commission on Engineering and Technical Systems. (1983). *The Competitive Status of the U.S. Fibers, Textiles, and Apparel Complex: A Study of the Influences of Technology in Detrmining International Industrial Comparative Advantage*. Washington: National Academy Press.

National Bureau of Economic Research. (2018). *U.S. Business Cycle Expansions and Contractions*. Retrieved from http://www.nber.org/cycles.html.

Neary, J. P. (2001). Of Hype and Hyperbolas: Introducing the New Economic Geography. *Journal of Economic Literature*, 536–561.

Nelli, H. S. (1964). The Italian Padrone System in the United States. *Labor History, 5*(2), 153–167.

New York City, Department of City Planning. (2018, August 1). *PLUTO and MapPLUTO*. Retrieved from Data/Maps http://www1.nyc.gov/site/planning/data-maps/open-data/dwn-pluto-mappluto.page.

New York City Department of City Planning, Population Division. (2004). *The Newest New Yorkers.* New York.

New York State, Department of Economic Development, State Data Center. (2018). *Population of New York State by County: 1790 to 1990.* Retrieved from http://ocgov.net/sites/default/files/planning/PlanPages/censustables/nyshist17902000.pdf.

*New York Times.* (1956, September 10). *Vicar Asks City to Spare Church, Urges Campaign to Preserve St. Cyprian's in Path of Lincoln Sq. Project.*

*New York Times.* (2019, May 19). *'They Were Conned': How Reckless Loans Devastated a Generation of Taxi Drivers.* https://www.nytimes.com/2019/05/19/nyregion/nyc-taxis-medallions-suicides.html?action=click&module=Top%20Stories&pgtype=Homepage.

North, D. C. (1966). *The Economic Growth of the United States, 1790–1860.* New York: W. W. Norton.

North, D. C. (1968). Sources of Productivity Change in Ocean Shipping, 1600–1850. *Journal of Political Economy, 76*(5), 953–970.

Norton, T. E. (1974). *The Fur Trade in Colonial New York, 1686–1776.* Madison: University of Wisconsin Press.

Nussbaum, J. (2015, October 18). The Night New York Saved Itself from Bankruptcy. *The New Yorker.*

NYC Department of City Planning. (2018, August 10). *Historical Population Information: Decennial Census.* Retrieved from Data/Maps https://www1.nyc.gov/site/planning/data-maps/nyc-population/historical-population.page.

O'Brien, P. (1992, August). The Failure of the Bank of United States: A Defense of Joseph Lucia. *Journal of Money, Credit and Banking, 24,* 374–384.

O'Brien, S. (2014, December 18). *The Complete History of the Original Dow Dozen.* Retrieved from Dividend.com http://www.dividend.com/dividend-education/the-complete-history-of-the-original-dow-dozen/.

Ó Gráda, C. (1916, May 14). *The New York Times.*

Ó Gráda, C. (1989). *The Great Irish Famine.* Cambridge: Cambridge University Press.

Olley, G. S., & Pakes, A. (1996). The Dynamics of Productivity in the Telecommunications Equipment Industry. *Econometrica, 64*(6), 1263–1297.

Ormrod, D. (1993). The Atlantic Economy and the 'Protestant Capitalist International', 1651–1775. *Historical Research, 66*(160), 201.

O'Rourke, K. H., & Williamson, J. G. (1999). *Globalization and History: The Evolution of a Nineteenth-Century Atlantic Economy.* Cambridge, MA: The MIT Press.

O'Rourke, K. H., & Williamson, J. G. (2002a). After Columbus: Explaining Europe's Overseas Trade Boom, 1500–1800. *The Journal of Economic History, 62*(2), 452–453.

O'Rourke, K. H., & Williamson, J. G. (2002b). *Globalization and History* (2000, p. 209, Frieden, Jeffrey A). Cambridge: MIT Press.

O'Rourke, K. H. (2006). The Worldwide Economic Impact of the French Revolution and Napoleonic Wars, 1793–1815. *Journal of Global History, 1*, 123–149.

Paullin, C. O., & Wright, J. K. (1932). *Rates of Travel from New York City, 1857*. Retrieved from Atlas of the Historical Geography of the United States http://dsl.richmond.edu/historicalatlas/138/c/.

Peck, G. (1998). Divided Loyalties: Immigrant Padrones and the Evolution of Industrial Paternalism in North America. *International Labor and Working-Class History, 53*, 49–68.

Peña, E. S. (2001). The Role of Wampum Production at the Albany Almshouse. *International Journal of Historical Archaeology, 5*(2), 155–174.

Perkins, E. J. (1971). Financing Antebellum Importers: The Role of Brown Bros. & Co. in Baltimore. *Business History Review, 45*(4), 421–451.

Perkins, E. J. (1987). Lost Opportunities for Compromise in the Bank War: A Reassessment of Jackson's Veto Message. *The Business History Review, 61*(4), 531–550.

Perry, M. J. (2014, May 3). *Chart of the Day: NYC Taxi Medallion Prices*. Retrieved from American Enterprise Institute, AEI Ideas http://www.aei.org/publication/chart-of-the-day-nyc-taxi-medallion-prices/.

Pettegree, A. (1996). The Politics of Toleration in the Free Netherlands, 1572–1620. In O. P. Grell & B. Scribner (Eds.), *Tolerance and Intolerance in the European Reformation* (pp. 182–198). Cambridge: Cambridge University Press.

Phillips-Fein, K. (2017). *Fear City: New York's Fiscal Crisis and the Rise of Austerity Politics*. New York: Henry Holt.

Pierenkemper, T., & Tilly, R. (2004). *The German Economy During the Nineteenth Century*. New York: Berghahn Books.

Plunz, R. (1990). *A History of Housing in New York City: Dwelling Type and Social Change in the American Metropolis*. New York: Columbia University Press.

Port Authority of New York and New Jersey. (1986). *Comprehensive Annual Financial Report for the Year Ended December 31, 1985*. New York: PANYNJ.

Portes, A., & Zhou, M. (1992). Gaining the Upper Hand: Economic Mobility Among Immigrant and Domestic Minorities. *Ethnic and Racial Studies, 15*(4), 491–522.

Prados de la Escosura, L. (2000). International Comparisons of Real Product, 1830–1990: An Alternative Data Set. *Explorations in Economic History, 37*, 1–41.

Proper, E. E. (1900). *Colonial Immigration Laws, A Study of the Regulation of Immigration by the English Colonies in America* (p. 37). Dissertation, Columbia University, New York.

Prus, M. J. (1990). Mechanisation and the Gender-Based Division of Labour in the US Cigar Industry. *Cambridge Journal of Economics, 14*, 63–79.

Putnam, L. (2013). *Radical Moves: Caribbean Migrants and the Politics of Race in the Jazz Age*. Chapel Hill: University of North Carolina Press.

Putnam, T. R. (2015). Joseph Long's Slops: Ready-Made Clothing in Early America. *Winterthur Portfolio, 49*(2 and 3), 63–91.

Rapp, R. T. (1975). The Unmaking of the Mediterranean Trade Hegemony: International Trade Rivalry and the Commercial Revolution. *The Journal of Economic History, 35*(3), 499–525.

Ratha, D., Mohapatra, S., & Silwal, A. (2011). *The Migration and Remittances Factbook 2011*. Retrieved from http://siteresources.worldbank.org/INTPROSPECTS/Resources/334934-1199807908806/Top10.pdf.

Razin, E., & Light, I. (1998). Ethnic Entrepreneurs in America's Largest Metropolitan Areas. *Urban Affairs Review, 33*(3), 332–360.

Reuters. (2014, May 26). Sony Forms Joint Ventures in China for PlayStation. *New York Times*.

Rich, E. (1960, February). Trade Habits and Economic Motivation Among the Indians of North America. *The Canadian Journal of Economics and Political Science, 26*(1), 50.

Rich, E., & Wilson, C. (2008). *The Cambridge Economic History of Europe, Vol 5, The Economic Organization of Early Modern Europe* (Vol. 5). Cambridge: Cambridge University Press.

Richardson, B. C., & Menke, J. K. (2018, October 12). *People*. Retrieved from Guyana https://www.britannica.com/place/Guyana/People.

Richter, D. K. (1992). *The Ordeal of the Longhouse*. Chapel Hill: University of North Carolina Press.

Rink, O. (1981). The People of New Netherland: Notes on Non-English Immigration to New York in the Seventeenth Century. *New York History, 62*(1), 15, 18.

Rink, O. A. (1986). *Holland on the Hudson: An Economic and Social History of Dutch New York*. Ithaca: Cornell University Press.

Rink, O. A. (2009). Seafarers and Businessmen: The Growth of Dutch Commerce in the Lower Hudson River Valley. In R. Panetta (Ed.), *Dutch New York: The Roots of Hudson Valley Culture* (p. 21). New York: Fordham University Press.

Robbins, S. M., & Terleckyj, N. E. (1960). *Money Metropolis: A Locational Study of Financial Activities in the New York Region.* Cambridge, MA: Harvard University Press.

Rodgers, D. T. (1998). *Atlantic Crossings: Social Politics in the Progressive Age.* Cambridge: The Belknap Press of Harvard University Press.

Rolnick, A. J., & Weber, W. E. (1983). New Evidence on the Free Banking Era. *The American Economic Review, 73*(5), 1080–1091.

Romer, C. D. (1992, December). What Ended the Great Depression? *The Journal of Economic History, 52*(4), 757–784.

Romney, S. S. (2014). *New Netherland Connections: Intimate Networks and Atlantic Ties in Seventeenth-Century America.* Chapel Hill: University of North Carolina Press.

Rosenbaum, E. (1993). The Constraints on Minority Housing Choices, New York City, 1978–1987. *Social Forces, 72*(3), 736, 743.

Rosenbloom, J. L. (2002). *Looking for Work, Searching for Workers.* Cambridge: Cambridge University Press.

Rosenbloom, J. L., & Sundstrom, W. A. (1999). The Sources of Regional Variation in the Severity of the Great Depression: Evidence from U.S. Manufacturing, 1919–1937. *The Journal of Economic History, 59*(3), 714–747.

Rosenwaike, I. (1972). *Population History of New York City.* Syracuse, NY: Syracuse University Press.

Rosoli, G. (1985). Italian Migration to European Countries from Political Unification to World War I. In D. Hoerder (Ed.), *Labor Migration in the Atlantic Economies: The European and North American Working Classes During the Period of Industrialization.* Santa Barbara: Greenwood Press.

Rostow, W. W. (1956). The Take-Off into Self-Sustained Growth. *The Economic Journal, 66*(261), 29.

Rousseau, P. L., & Sylla, R. (2005). Emerging Financial Markets and Early US Growth. *Explorations in Economic History, 42*, 1–26.

Rubin, J. (1961). Canal or Railroad? Imitation and Innovation in the Response to the Erie Canal in Philadelphia, Baltimore, and Boston. *Transactions of the American Philosophical Society, New Series, 51*(7), 48–57.

Ruiz, N. (2018). *The Geography of Foreign Students in U.S. Higher Education: Origins and Destinations*. Washington, DC: Global Cities Initiative: A Joint Project of Brookings and JPMorgan Chase.

Ruiz, N. G., & Budiman, A. (2018, May 10). *Where Do Foreign Graduates Work in the United States*. Retrieved from Pew Research Center: GlobalAttitudes. & Trends http://www.pewglobal.org/interactives/where-do-foreign-student-graduates-work-in-the-united-states/?msa=san-jose.

Rumsey, D. (2018, June 6). *Pennsylvania, Nova Jersey et Nova York*. Retrieved from David Rumsey Map Collection, Cartography Associates https://www.davidrumsey.com/luna/servlet/detail/RUMSEY~8~1~283018~90055432:45--Pensylvania,-Nova-Jersey-et-Nov?sort=Pub_List_No_InitialSort%2CPub_Date%2CPub_List_No%2CSeries_No&qvq=w4s:/where%2FNew%2BYork%2Fwhen%2F1748;sort:Pub_List_No_InitialSort%2CPub_D.

Sánchez Korrol, V. E. (1985). *From Colonia to Community: The History of Puerto Ricans in New York City, 1917–1948*. New York City: Greenwood Press.

Sanders, J., Nee, V., & Scott Sernau, S. (2002). Asian Immigrants' Reliance on Social Ties in a Multiethnic Labor Market. *Social Forces, 81*(1), 281–314.

Sarna, J. D. (1981). The Myth of No Return: Jewish Return Migration to Europe, 1881–1914. *American Jewish History, 17*(2), 256–268.

Sassen, S. (2001). *The Global City; New York, London, Tokyo* (2nd ed.). Princeton, NJ: Princeton University Press.

Sayre, W. S., & Kaufman, H. (1960). *Governing New York City: Politics in the Metropolis* (p. 777). New York: Russell Sage Foundation.

Sazama, G. (1996). *A Brief History of Affordable Housing Cooperatives in the United States* (Working Paper Number 1996-09). Department of Economics, University of Connecticut.

Schenk, C. R. (1998). The Origins of the Eurodollar Market in London: 1955–1963. *Explorations in Economic History, 35*, 221–238.

Scherzer, K. A. (1992). *The Unbound Community: Neighborhood Life and Social Structure in New York City, 1830–1875*. Durham, NC: Duke University Press.

Schneider, J., & Schneider, P. (1976). *Culture and Political Economy in Western Sicily*. Cambridge, MA: Academic Press.

Schneider, J., & Schneider, P. (2005). Mafia, Antimafia, and the Plural Cultures of Sicily. *Current Anthropology, 46*(4), 501–520.

Schofield, R. (1994). British Population Change, 1700–1871. In R. Roderick Floud & D. N. McCloskey (Eds.), *The Economic History of Britain Since 1700: 1700–1860* (p. 88). Cambridge: Cambridge University Press.

Scott, A. J. (2006). Creative Cities: Conceptual Issues and Policy Questions. *Journal of Urban Affairs, 26*(1), 1–17.

Segal, H. H. (1972). Cycles of Canal Construction. In C. Goodrich (Ed.), *Canals in American Economic Development* (pp. 211–213). Port Washington, NY: Kennikat Press.

Sellers, C. (1991). *The Market Revolution: Jacksonian America, 1815–1846* (pp. 137 ff.). Oxford: Oxford University Press.

Shalala, D. E., & Bellamy, C. (1976). A State Saves a City: The New York Case. *Duke Law Journal, 6*, 1119–1132.

Shefter, M. (1992). *Political Crisis, Fiscal Crisis: The Collapse and Revival of New York City*. New York: Columbia University Press.

Shepherd, W. R. (1917). *The Story of New Amsterdam*. New York: The Holland Society of New York.

Sheridan, F. J. (1907). Italian, Slavic, and Hungarian Unskilled Immigrant Laborers in the United States. *Bulletin of the Bureau of Labor, 15*, 445–468.

Shorto, R. (2004). *The Island at the Center of the World: The Epic Story of Dutch Manhattan and the Forgotten Colony That Shaped America*. New York: Doubleday.

Simon, C. J., & Clark Nardinelli, C. (1992). Does Industrial Diversity Always Reduce Unemployment? Evidence from the Great Depression and After. *Economic Inquiry, 30*, 384–397.

Smith, W. E. (2001). Anthony Trollope in America: A Brief Survey of His Publishing History. *The Princeton University Library Chronicle, 62*(3), 479–500. Retrieved from Princeton. https://www.jstor.org/stable/pdf/10.25290/prinunivlibrchro.62.3.0479.pdf?refreqid=excelsior%3A427686083492f762e3f5ca9676e15555.

Snow, D. R. (1995). Migration in Prehistory: The Northern Iroquoian Case. *American Antiquity, 60*(1), 59–79.

Sokoloff, K. L. (1988). *Inventive Activity in Early Industrial America: Evidence from Patent Records, 1790–1846* (NBER Working Paper #2707). National Bureau of Economic Research.

Sokoloff, K. L., & Villaflor, G. C. (1982). The Early Achievement of Modern Stature in America. *Social Science History, 6*(4), 453–481.

Soyer, D. (2005). Cockroach Capitalists: Jewish Contractors at the Turn of the Twentieth Century. In D. Soyer (Ed.), *A Coat of Many Colors: Immigration, Globalization, and Reform in New York City's Garment Industry* (pp. 91–114). New York: Fordham University Press.

Stansell, C. (1987). *City of Women: Sex and Class in New York, 1789–1860*. Champaign: University of Illinois Press.

Starna, W. A. (2009). American Indian Villages to Dutch Farms: The Settling of Settled Lands in the Hudson Valley. In R. Panetta, *Dutch New York: The Roots of Hudson Valley Culture* (p. 74). New York: Fordham University Press.

Stewart, R. M. (1989). Trade and Exchange in Middle Atlantic Region Prehistory. *Archaeology of Eastern North America, 17*(Fall), 47–78.

Stokey, N. L. (2001). A Quantitative Model of the British Industrial Revolution, 1780–1850. *Carnegie-Rochester Conference Series on Public Policy, 55*(1), 55–109.

Storper, M., & Venables, A. J. (2003). Face-to-Face Contact and the Urban Economy. *Journal of Economic Geography, 4*(4), 351–370.

Stott, R. (1989). Hinterland Development and Differences in Work Setting: The New York Region, 1820–1870. In W. Pencak &υ C. Wright (Eds.), *New York and the Rise of Capitalism: Economic Development and Social and Political History of an American State, 1780–1870*. New York: The New York Historical Society.

Stott, R. B. (1990). *Workers in the Metropolis: Class, Ethnicity, and Youth in Antebellum New York City*. Ithaca: Cornell University Press.

Stotz, L. (1938). *History of the Gas Industry*. New York: Stettiner Brothers.

Stover, J. F. (1961). *American Railroads*. Chicago: University of Chicago Press.

Stover, J. F. (1995). *History of the Baltimore and Ohio Railroad*. Lafayette, IN: Purdue University Press.

Stuart, R. C. (1984). Special Interests and National Authority in Foreign Policy: American-British Provincial Links During the Embargo and the War of 1812. *Diplomatic History, 8*(4), 311–328.

Summers, B. J. (1980, August). Negotiable Certificates of Deposit. *Economic Review, Federal Reserve Bank of Richmond*.

Susan B., & Carter, E. A. (2006). *Historical Statistics of the United States Millennial Edition Online*. Cambridge: Cambridge University Press.

Swanson, C. E. (1985, July). American Privateering and Imperial Warfare, 1739–1748. *The William and Mary Quarterly, Third Series, 42*(3), 357–382.

Tanzi, V. (1977). Inflation, Lags in Collection, and the Real Value of Tax Revenue. *Staff Papers (International Monetary Fund), 24*(1), 154–167.

Taylor, A. (2006). *The Divided Ground: Indians, Settlers, and the Northern Borderland of the American Revolution*. New York: Alfred A. Knopf.

Taylor, G. R. (1951). *The Transportation Revolution: 1815–1860*. New York: Rinehart & Co., Inc.

Taylor, P. J., Ni, P., Derudder, B. H., Huang, J., & Witlox, F. (eds.). (2011). *Global Urban Analysis: A Survey of Cities in Globalization*. New York: Earthscan.

Tebbel, J. (1963). *The Compact History of the American Newspaper*. Portland, OR: Hawthorn Books.

Tebbel, J. (1972). *A History of Book Publishing in the United States, Volume I: The Creation of an Industry, 1630–1865*. Ann Arbor: R. R. Bowker.

Tebbel, J., & Zuckerman, M. E. (1991). *The Magazine in America, 1741–1990*. Oxford: Oxford University Press.

Temin, P. (1994). *The Great Depression, NBER Working Paper Series on Historical Factors in Long Run Growth*. National Bureau of Economic Research.

Tenenbaum, S. (1993). *A Credit to Their Community: Jewish Loan Societies in the United States, 1880–1945*. Detroit: Wayne State University Press.

The Eleanor Roosevelt Papers Project. (2018). *Teaching Eleanor Roosevelt Glossary: Public Works Administration*. Retrieved from The George Washington University https://www2.gwu.edu/~erpapers/teachinger/glossary/pwa.cfm.

The Furman Center for Real Estate and Urban Policy. (2011a). *Subsidized Housing: A Cross-City Comparison*. New York: New York University School of Law, The Wagner School.

The Furman Center for Real Estate and Urban Policy. (2011b). *The Changing Racial and Ethnic Make-Up of New York City Neighborhoods*. New York: New York University, School of Law, The Wagner School.

The Furman Center for Real Estate and Urban Policy. (2012). *Rent Stabilization in New York City*. New York: Fact Brief, New York University, School of Law The Wagner School of Public Service.

The National Advisory Commission on Civil Disorders. (1988). *The Kerner Report: The 1968 Report of the National Advisory Commission on Civil Disorders*. New York: Pantheon Books.

*The New York Times*. (1929, May 10). $300,000,000 Merger of Banks Approved.

The World Bank. (2018). *Dominican Republic*. Retrieved from Data https://data.worldbank.org/country/dominican-republic.

The World Bank. (2019). *World Development Indicators*. Retrieved from DataBank https://databank.worldbank.org/data/reports.aspx?source=2&series=NY.GDP.MKTP.CD&country=#.

Thomas, R. P. (1965). A Quantitative Approach to the Study of the Effects of British Imperial Policy upon Colonia Welfare: Some Preliminary Findings. *The Journal of Economic History, 25*(4), 615–638.

Tichenor, D. J. (2002). *Dividing Lines: The Politics of Immigration Control in America*. Princeton: Princeton University Press.

Tiebout, C. M. (1961). An Economic Theory of Fiscal Decentralization. In U.-N. Research (Ed.), *Public Finances: Needs, Sources, and Utilization* (pp. 79–96). Princeton: Princeton University Press.

Tilly, R. (1998). Universal Banking in Historical Perspective. *Journal of Institutional and Theoretical Economics, 154*(1), 7–32.

Timberlake, R. H. (1984, February). The Central Banking Role of Clearing House Associations. *Journal of Money, Credit, and Banking, 16*(1), 1–15.

Tolles, F. B. (1948). *Meeting House and Counting House: The Quaker Merchants of Colonial Philadelphia, 1682–1763*. Chapel Hill: University of North Carolina Press.

Trescott, P. (1992). The Failure of the Bank of United States, 1930. *Journal of Money, Credit and Banking, 24*, 384–399.

Truxes, T. M. (2008). *Defying Empire: Trading with the Enemy in Colonial New York*. New Haven: Yale University Press.

Turner, F. J. (1920). *The Frontier in American History* (pp. 82–83). New York: Henry Holt.

U.S. Bureau of the Census. (1998). Population of the 100 Largest Urban Places: 1860. https://www.census.gov/population/www/documentation/twps0027/tab09.txt.

U.S. Bureau of Labor Statistics. (2018a, July 25). *Create Customized Tables: State and Area Employment, Hours, and Earnings—Seasonal*. Retrieved from Data Tools: Create Customized Tables https://data.bls.gov/cgi-bin/dsrv?sm.

U.S. Bureau of Labor Statistics. (2018b). *Employment, Hours, and Earnings from the Current Employment Statistics Survey (National) SIC*. Retrieved from https://data.bls.gov/cgi-bin/dsrv; https://www.census.gov/data/data-sets/1986/econ/cbp/1986-cpb.html.

U.S. Bureau of Labor Statistics. (2018c, April 22). *Employment, Hours, and Earnings from the Current Employment Statistics Survey (National)*. Retrieved from Create Customized Tables https://data.bls.gov/cgi-bin/dsrv?ce.

U.S. Bureau of Labor Statistics. (2018d, May 7). *O*NET, The Occupational Information Network*. Retrieved from https://www.bls.gov/careeroutlook/1999/Spring/art01.pdf.

U.S. Bureau of Labor Statistics. (2018e, May 11). *Quarterly Census of Employment and Wages—Industry*. Retrieved from https://data.bls.gov/cgi-bin/dsrv?en.

U.S. Bureau of Labor Statistics. (2018f). *State and Area Employment, Hours, and Earnings*. Retrieved from Create Customized Tables https://data.bls.gov/cgi-bin/dsrv?sm.

U.S. Bureau of the Census. (1976a). *Historical Statistics of the United States, Colonial Times to 1970*. New York: Basic Books.

U.S. Bureau of the Census. (1976b). *The Statistical History of the United States From Colonial Times to the Present* (p. 1061). New York: Basic Books.

U.S. Census Bureau. (1913). *Thirteenth Census of the United States Taken in the Year 1910, Volume IV, Occupation Statistics*. Washington, DC: U.S. Government Printing Office.

U.S. Census Bureau. (1932). *Occupation Statistics, New York*. Retrieved from Fifteenth Census of the United States, 1930 https://babel.hathitrust.org/cgi/pt?id=coo.31924014032860;view=1up;seq=3.

U.S. Census Bureau. (1933a). *Fifteenth Census of the United States, Manufactures: 1929, Volume III, Reports by States: Statistics for Industrial Areas, Counties, and Cities*. Washington, DC: U.S. Government Printing Office.

U.S. Census Bureau. (1933b). *Fifteenth Census of the United States: 1930, Unemployment, Volume II, General Report: Unemployment by Occupation, April 1930 with Returns from the Special Census of Unemployment January 1931*. Washington, DC: U.S. Government Printing Office.

U.S. Census Bureau. (1933c). *Location of Manufactures, 1899–1929: A Study of the Tendencies Toward Concentration and Toward Dispersion of Manufactures in the United States*. Washington: U.S. Government Printing Office.

U.S. Census Bureau. (1935). *Negroes in the United States, 1920–1932*. Washington: U.S. Government Printing Office.

U.S. Census Bureau. (1941). *Sixteenth Census of the United States, 1940: Census of Business, Retail Trade: 1939*. Washington: U.S. Government Printing Office.

U.S. Census Bureau. (1943a). *Sixteenth Census of the United States, 1940, Volume II, Characteristics of the Population, U.S. Government Printing Office, 1943*. Washington, DC: U.S. Government Printing Office.

U.S. Census Bureau. (1943b). *Sixteenth Census of the United States: 1940*. Retrieved from Volume III, Labor Force https://babel.hathitrust.org/cgi/pt?id=coo.31924055066660;view=1up;seq=5.

U.S. Census Bureau. (1975). *Historical Statistics of the United States, Colonial Times to 1970, Volume 2*. Washington: U.S. Government Printing Office.

U.S. Census Bureau. (1976). *The Statistical History of the United States from Colonial Times to the Present.* New York: Basic Books.

U.S. Census Bureau. (1982). *Statistical Abstract of the United States, 1982–83.* Washington: U.S. Government Printing Office.

U.S. Census Bureau. (1983). *1980 Census of Housing, Volume 2, Metropolitan Housing Characteristics.* Washington: U.S. Government Printing Office.

U.S. Census Bureau. (2018a, April 24). *Annual Estimates of the Resident Population: April 1, 2010 to July 1, 2016—United States—Metropolitan and Micropolitan Statistical Area; and for Puerto Rico More Information 2016 Population Estimates.* Retrieved from American FactFinder https://factfinder.census.gov/faces/tableservices/jsf/pages/productview.xhtml?src=bkmk.

U.S. Census Bureau. (2018b). *Annual Statistics: 2015 (Including Historical Data by State and MSA).* Retrieved from Housing Vacancies and Homeownership (CPS/HVS) https://www.census.gov/housing/hvs/data/ann15ind.html

U.S. Census Bureau. (2018c). *County Business Patterns.* Retrieved from https://www.census.gov/programs-surveys/cbp/data.html.

U.S. Census Bureau. (2018d). *County Business Patterns, 1956.* Retrieved from https://www.census.gov/data/datasets/1986/econ/cbp/1986-cpb.html.

U.S. Census Bureau. (2018e). *National Centers of Population, 1790–2010.* Retrieved from Geography https://www.census.gov/geo/reference/centersofpop/natcentersofpop.html.

U.S. Census Bureau. (2018f). *Population in the Colonial and Continental Periods.* Retrieved from https://www2.census.gov/prod2/decennial/documents/00165897ch01.pdf.

U.S. Census Bureau. (2018g, May 10). *Section 1: Population* (pp. 29–31). Retrieved from Statistical Abstract of the United States: 2003 https://www.census.gov/library/publications/2003/compendia/statab/123ed.html.

U.S. Census Bureau. (2018h). *Selected Historical Decennial Census Population and Housing Counts.* Retrieved from Census 1990 https://www.census.gov/population/www/censusdata/hiscendata.html.

U.S. Census Bureau. (2018i). *State Area Measurements and Internal Point Coordinates.* Retrieved from Geography https://www.census.gov/geo/reference/state-area.html.

U.S. Census Bureau. (2018j, August). *American Fact Finder: Place of Birth for the Foreign-Born Population.* https://factfinder.census.gov/faces/tableservices/jsf/pages/productview.xhtml?pid=DEC_00_SF3_PCT019&prodType=table.

U.S. Department of Commerce, B. O. (1913). *Thirteenth Census of the United States Taken in the Year 1910, Volume VIII, Manufactures, 1909, General Report and Analysis.* Washington, DC: U.S. Government Printing Office.

U.S. Department of Commerce, Bureau of Economic Analysis. (2018a). *Interactive Data.* Retrieved from https://www.bea.gov/itable/iTable.cfm?ReqID=70&step=1#reqid=70&step=31&isuri=1&7022=20&7023=7&7024=non-industry&7025=4&7001=720&7029=20&7090=70.

U.S. Department of Commerce, Bureau of Economic Analysis. (2018b). *Regional Data, GDP & Personal Income.* Retrieved from https://apps.bea.gov/iTable/iTable.cfm?reqid=70&step=1&isuri=1&acrdn=8#reqid=70&step=1&isuri=1.

U.S. Department of Commerce, Bureau of Economic Analysis. (2018c). *Table 6.1B National Income Without Capital Cunsumption Adjustment by Industry, Interactive Data, GDP and Personal Income Data.* Retrieved from https://www.bea.gov/iTable/iTable.cfm?reqid=19&step=2#reqid=19&step=3.

U.S. Department of Commerce. (n.d.). *Annual Reports on the Commerce and Navigation of the United States.* Retrieved from Hathi Trust https://catalog.hathitrust.org/Record/001719409.

U.S. Department of Commerce. (2018). *Annual Reports on the Commerce and Navigation of the United States.* Retrieved from Hathi Trust https://catalog.hathitrust.org/Record/001719409.

U.S. Department of Commerce, Bureau of the Census. (1912). *Thirteenth Census of the United States Taken in the Year 1910, Volume I: Population.* Washington, DC: U.S. Government Printing Office.

U.S. Department of Commerce, B. O. (1913). *Thirteenth Census of the United States, 1910* (Vol. 4). Washington, DC: U.S. Government Printing Office.

U.S. Department of Commerce, Bureau of the Census. (1913). *Thirteenth Census of the United States, Volume 4: Population.* Washington, DC: U.S. Government Printing Office.

U.S. Department of Commerce, Census Bureau. (1873). *Ninth U.S. Census, Volume I, The Statistics of the United States Embracing the Tables of Race, Nationality, Sex, Selected Ages, and Occupations.* Washington, DC: U.S. Government Printing Office.

U.S. Department of Commerce and Labor, Bureau of Statistics. (1912). *Fhte Foreign Commerce and Navigation of the United States in the Year ending June 30, 1911.* Washington: U.S. Government Printing Office.

U.S. Department of Commerce; U.S. Department of Health Education and Welfare. (1958). *County Business Patterns, First Quarter 1956, Parts 1, 2, and 3.* Washington: U.S. Government Printing Office.

U.S. Department of Commerce. (Various). *Annual Reports on the Commerce and Navigation of the United States Accessed Via*. Retrieved from https://catalog.hathitrust.org/Record/001719409.

U.S. Department of Homeland Security. (2018a). *Yearbook of Immigration Statistics, 2016*. Retrieved from https://www.dhs.gov/immigration-statistics/yearbook/2016/table1.

U.S. Department of Homeland Security. (2018b). *2017 Yearbook of Immigration Statistics*. Table 1. Persons Obtaining Lawful Permanent Resident Status: Fiscal Years 1820 to 2017. https://www.dhs.gov/immigration-statistics/yearbook/2017/table1.

U.S. Department of Housing and Urban Development. (1974). *1974 Statistical Yearbook*. Washington: U.S. Government Printing Office.

U.S. Department of Housing and Urban Development. (2018, June). *Measuring Overcrowding in Housing*. Retrieved from https://www.huduser.gov/publications/pdf/measuring_overcrowding_in_hsg.pdf.

U.S. Department of Housing and Urban Development. (2018, April 19). *SOCDS Census and American Community Survey Data*. Retrieved from https://socds.huduser.gov/Census/Census_Home.html?.

U.S. Department of State, Bureau of Consular Affairs. (2018). *Nonimmigrant Visa Statistics*. Retrieved from U.S. Visa Law & Policy https://travel.state.gov/content/travel/en/legal/visa-law0/visa-statistics/nonimmigrant-visa-statistics.html.

U.S. Department of the Interior. (1865). *Manufactures of the United States in 1860; Compiled from the Original Returns of the Eighth Census*. Washington, DC: Government Printing Office.

U.S. Department of the Interior, Census-Office. (1872). *Ninth Census—Volume I*. Washington, DC: U.S. Government Printing Office.

U.S. Department of the Interior. (1990). *Abstract of the Statistics of Manufactures according to the Returns of the Seventh Census*. New York: Norman Ross Publishing.

U.S. Department of the Treasury, Office of the Comptroller of the Currency. (2018). *The Negotiable CD: National Bank Innovation in the 1960s*. Retrieved from History: 150 Years of the OCC https://www.occ.treas.gov/about/what-we-do/history/150th-negotiable-cd-article.html.

U.S. Department of Transportation, Maritime Administration. (1984). *Containerized Cargo Characteristics, Calendar Year 1983*. Washington: U.S. Government Printing Office.

U.S. Federal Bureau of Investigation. (2018). *Reported Crime by Locality (City, County), State, and Nation*. Retrieved from Uniform Crime Reports https://www.ucrdatatool.gov/Search/Crime/Crime.cfm.

U.S. Federal Highway Administration. (2018). *State and Urbanized Area Statistics*. Retrieved from Office of Highway Policy Information https://www.fhwa.dot.gov/ohim/onh00/onh2p11.htm.

U.S. House of Representatives. (1911). *Annual Report of the Chief of the Bureau of Statistics of on the Commerce and Navigation of the United States*. Washington: U.S. Government Printing Office.

U.S. Office of Government Reports. (1940a). *County Reports of Estimated Federal Government Expenditures March 4 1933–June 30, 19 39* (Report No. 10, Vol. 1).

U.S. Office of Government Reports. (1940b). *Direct and Cooperative Loans and Expenditures of the Federal Government for Fiscal Years 1933 through 1939* (Report No. 9, Vol. 1).

U.S. Securities and Exchange Commission. (1977). *Staff Report on Transactions in the Securities of the City of New York*. Washington: U.S. Government Printing Office.

U.S. Treasury, Bureau of Statistics. (1889). *Tables Showing the Arrivals of Alien Passengers and Immigrants in the United States from 1820–1888*. Washington, DC: U.S. Government Printing Office.

United Kingdom Board of Trade. (1911). *Cost of Living in American Towns, Report of an Enquiry of the Board of Trade into Working Class Rents, Housing and Retail Prices Together with the Rates of Wages in Certain Occupation in the Principal Industrial Towns of the United States of America*. London: His Majesty's Stationery Office.

United Nations Conference on Trade and Development (UNCTAD). (2013). *Global Value Chains and Development: Investment and Value Added in the Global Economy*. New York: United Nations.

United States Census Bureau. (1976). *The Statistical History of the United States from Colonial Times to the Present*. New York: Basic Books.

University of Virginia. (n.d.). Retrieved from Historical Census Browser (Discontinued).

Van der Donck, A. (1993). *A Dialogue Between a Netherland Patriot and a New Netherlander, on the Advantages of the County* (J. Johnson, Trans.). Ithaca, NY: Cornell University Library Digital Edition.

Van Zanden, J. L. (1995). Tracing the Beginning of the Kuznets Curve: Western Europe During the Early Modern Period. *The Economic History Review, New Series, 48*(4), 643–664.

Vernon, R. (1960). *Metropolis 1985: An Interpretation of the Findings of the New York Metropolitan Region Study*. Cambridge, MA: Harvard University Press.

Viamichelin. (2018, May 11). *United States Michelin Restaurants*. Retrieved from https://www.viamichelin.com/web/Restaurants/Restaurants-United_States.

Virginia Commonwealth University. (2018). *Social Welfare History Project*. Retrieved from VCU Libraries https://socialwelfare.library.vcu.edu.

Waldinger, R. (1996). *Still the Promised City? African-American and New Immigrants in Postindustrial New York*. Cambridge, MA: Harvard University Press.

Waldinger, R. D. (1986). *Through the Eye of the Needle: Immigrants and Enterprise in New York's Garment Trades*. New York: New York University Press.

Wallis, J. J. (1989). Employment in the Great Depression: New Data and Hypotheses. *Explorations in Economic History, 26*, 45–72.

Watkins-Owens, I. (2001). Early-Twentieth-Century Caribbean Women: Migration and Social Networks in New York City. In N. Foner (Ed.), *Islands in the City: West Indian Immigration to New York* (p. 33). Berkeley: University of California Press.

Wee, H. (2013, September 23). *'Made in USA' Fuels New Manufacturing Hubs in Apparel*. Retrieved from CNBC https://www.cnbc.com/2013/09/23/inside-made-in-the-usa-showcasing-skilled-garment-workers.html.

Wendell Cox Consultancy. (2018, April 25). *Urban Transport Fact Book*. Retrieved from USA Interstate Highway System: Miles/Kilometers Opened by Year http://www.publicpurpose.com/hwy-intmiles.htm.

Wendell Cox Consultancy. (2019). *Lane Miles Per Capita 1999: US Urbanized Areas over 1,000,000*. Retrieved from The Public Purpose http://www.publicpurpose.com/hwy-tti99ratio.htm.

Whalen, C. T. (2005). Colonialism, Citizenship, and the Making of the Puerto Rican Diaspora: An Introduction. In C. T. Whalen & V. Vázquez-Hernández (Eds.), *The Puerto Rican Diaspora: Historical Perspective*. Philadelphia: Temple University Press.

White, P. L. (1956). *The Beekman Mercantile Papers, 1746–1799* (Vol. II). New York: The New York Historical Society.

Wicker, E. (1996). *The Banking Panics of the Great Depression*. Cambridge: Cambridge Univefrsity Press.

Wikipedia. (2017). *List of United States Commuter Rail Systems by Ridership*. Retrieved from Wikipedia: The Free Encyclopedia https://en.wikipedia.org/wiki/List_of_United_States_commuter_rail_systems_by_ridership.

Wikipedia. (2018a, August 1). *List of Bridges and Tunnels in New York City*. Retrieved from Wikipedia https://en.wikipedia.org/wiki/List_of_bridges_and_tunnels_in_New_York_City.

Wikipedia. (2018b). *Timeline of Abolition of Slavery and Serfdom*. Retrieved from Wikipedia https://en.wikipedia.org/wiki/Timeline_of_abolition_of_slavery_and_serfdom#cite_note-54.

Wilentz, S. (2004). *Chants Democratic: New York City and the Rise of the American Working Class, 1788–1850*. Oxford: Oxford University Press.

Williams, M. B. (2013). *City of Ambition: FDR, La Guardia, and the Making of Modern New York*. New York: W. W. Norton.

Williamson, J. G. (1995). The Evolution of Global Labor Markets Since 1830: Background Evidence and Hypotheses. *Explorations in Economic History, 32*, 141–196.

Woodman, H. D. (1968). *King Cotton and His Retainers: Financing and Marketing the Cotton Crop of the South, 1800–1925*. Lexington: University of Kentucky Press.

Work Projects Administration for the City of New York. (2004). *A Maritime History of New York*. New York: Going Coastal Inc.

World Bank. (2018, July 10). *World Integrated Trade Solution*. Retrieved from Trade Stats https://wits.worldbank.org/country-indicator.aspx?lang=en.

Zabin, S. R. (2009). *Dangerous Economies: Status and Commerce in Imperial New York*. Philadelphia: University of Pennsylvania Press.

Zakin, M. (2003). *Ready-Made Democracy: A History of Men's Dress in the American Republic, 1760–1860*. Chicago: University of Chicago Press.

Zhang & Associates, P. C. (2007, May 17). *HK, Macau, Taiwan Born Aliens Not Subject to Visa Number of China*. Retrieved from https://hooyou.com/news/news051707visa.html.

Zhou, Y. (1996). Inter-firm Linkages, Ethnic Networks, and Territorial Agglomeration: Chinese Computer Firms in Los Angles. *Papers in Regional Science, 75*(3), 265–391.

Zhou, Y. (1998). How Do Places Matter? A Comparative Study of Chinese Ethnic Economies in Los Angeles and New York City. *Urban Geography, 19*(6), 531–553.

# Index




A. Gurwitz, *Atlantic Metropolis*, Palgrave Studies in American Economic History,
https://doi.org/10.1007/978-3-030-13352-8

The manufacturer's authorised representative in the EU is Springer Nature Customer Service Centre GmbH, Europaplatz 3, 69115 Heidelberg, Germany. If you have any concerns regarding our products, please contact ProductSafety@springernature.com

Printed and bound by CPI Group (UK) Ltd, Croydon, CR0 4YY
22/09/2026
02221051-0001